The Free Press
A Division of Macmillan Publishing Co., Inc.
866 Third Avenue, New York, N.Y. 10022

Collier Macmillan Canada, Ltd.

Library of Congress Catalog Card Number: 74-25601

Printed in the United States of America

printing number
1   2   3   4   5   6   7   8   9   10

Library of Congress Cataloging in Publication Data

Paige, Jeffery M
   Agrarian revolution.

   Bibliography: p.
   Includes index.
   1. Underdeveloped areas--Agriculture. 2. Underdeveloped areas--Peasantry. 3. Revolutions. I. Title.
HD1417.P34   338.1'09172'4   74-25601
ISBN 0-02-923580-4

Agrarian Revolution

Social Movements and Export Agriculture
in the Underdeveloped World

JEFFERY M. PAIGE

University of California, Berkeley

 THE FREE PRESS
A Division of Macmillan Publishing Co., Inc.
NEW YORK

Collier Macmillan Publishers
LONDON

Contents

List of Tables

List of Figures

List of Maps

Preface

THIS IS A BOOK about the politics of people who draw their living from the land, both those who perform the physical labor of cultivation in the fields and plantations of the underdeveloped world and those who share the proceeds of this labor in the form of rent, profits, interest, and taxes. It is also necessarily a book about conflict over the wealth produced by the land, the control of the land itself, the political power that makes that control possible, and, in many cases, the survival of one class or another. This conflict is frequently a matter of small bargains and local compromises, but from time to time it explodes into revolutionary movements which engulf whole societies, and it is these agrarian revolutions in the export economies of the underdeveloped world in general and in the cases of Peru, Angola, and Vietnam in particular which are the principal concern of this book. Although these rural social movements involve extraordinary rather than ordinary political happenings, the politics of revolutionary change, like the politics of everyday life, is shaped by the relationship between upper and lower classes in rural areas. The nature of this conflict and political choices open to both classes are limited by the irreducible role of land in agriculture and by the compelling force of the international market in agricultural commodities. If conflicts between cultivators and noncultivators so often lead to hard choices between repression and revolution, it is because the control of landed property and the exigencies of efficient production leave them with few other alternatives. Both upper and lower agrarian classes use force in economic conflicts not because they have not carefully considered all possible alternatives, but because they have. There is a calculus of force just as orderly and rational in its way as the principles of economics, and despite the passions which surround the use of violence, it is important to realize that men risk their lives only with the greatest reluctance; when, in Peru, Angola, or Vietnam, they do so, it is usually because their opponents have left them with no other choice.

No book about revolution in the contemporary underdeveloped world can, nor probably should, avoid wider political implications, although in both the dry language of statistics and in the descriptive accounts of the three major revolutions I have tried to report as objectively as possible the behavior of both the agricultural upper and lower classes. Nevertheless, it is important to note at the outset that this book grows out of the fundamental questions raised by United States involvement in revolutionary movements in the underdeveloped world in general and Vietnam in particular. In Peru, Angola, Vietnam, and many other areas of the underdeveloped world the United States has chosen to side with the landlords and plantation owners against the peasants, sharecroppers, and agricultural laborers who took up arms against them. American military alliances, American trained officers, American military aid and equipment, and, finally, American armed forces have been used either singly or in combination against the peasants of the Peruvian sierra, the contract laborers of northern Angola, and the tenant farmers of the Mekong delta of Vietnam. This book cannot and does not attempt to explain why we chose to help the landlords rather than the cultivators, although it does attempt to explain the landlords' desperate need for outside military aid. Even though agrarian revolution has occupied much of American political life for the past decade, the lives and aspirations of the men who made these revolutions are far from the American understanding or even consciousness. At minimum, then, this book attempts to raise the question of whether most of us, had we been in the *selva* of Peru, the jungles of Angola, or the rice paddies of Vietnam, would have supported the landlords or the laborers. Most Americans will find that we have chosen strange allies indeed.

This book contains both a cross-sectional statistical study of 135 agricultural export sectors in 70 independent states and colonies in the underdeveloped world and three case studies of export economy reform, revolt, and revolution in Peru, Angola, and Vietnam. The reader who finds that statistical reasoning causes his eyes to glaze over would be well advised to pass quickly over Chapter 2, the world analysis, and proceed directly from the introductory chapter to the analytical case studies. In any such broadly comparative endeavor the researcher is invariably dependent on the work of others, and my debts in particular are many. The statistical agencies of the United Nations, Peru, Angola, and Vietnam and the newspaper reporters and editors in both the United States and the underdeveloped world provided the raw data for this study, and the findings are ultimately dependent on their efforts, even though the information has been put to uses other than those for which it was originally intended. In the case studies in particular, I received much good advice and was saved from many egregious errors through conversations with researchers with extensive field experience in each of the three countries. Patrick O'Shea, my collaborator on the Peru study, provided the detailed information on rural conditions which can only be obtained by a skilled ethnographer. His ready charm and Irish wit opened many doors that otherwise would have remained closed to us. We are both particularly grateful for the kind assistance of Dr. José Ignacio de Olazábal, Chief of the Archives of the Lima, Peru, daily newspaper *El Comercio*, for making these facilities available for our use. The Angolan case study owes a great deal to Eduardo Cruz de Carvalho, Jorge Vieira da Silva, and Jerry Bender of the African Studies Center, University of California, Los Angeles. Jorge and Eduardo kindly devoted hours of their time to explaining the meaning of agricultural statistics in terms of their own experiences as directors of the Angolan Department of Agriculture and Agricultural Census, respectively. Sam Popkin's encouragement, criticism, advice, and enthusiasm did much both to save me from errors too embarrassing to relate and to convince me to continue my study of Vietnam. Needless to say, all this good advice cannot save me from my own mistakes, and none of these scholars bears any responsibility for the inevitable errors and omissions which are the burden of comparativists and the delight of area specialists.

Many of the ideas which found their way into this book at various points derive directly or indirectly from my experience in the sugar plantation country of southern Louisiana in the winter of 1970. H. L. Mitchell, who, then as now, was attempting to convert an organizing committee into a labor union among the tractor drivers of the sugar plantations, shared with me his experiences in organizing both plantation workers and sharecroppers. In the 1930s Mitchell had been one of the founders of the interracial Southern Tenant Farm Workers Union, and he is therefore one of the few men to have successfully organized sharecroppers under centralized estate management. His account of both the successes and failures of this movement did much to shape my thinking about the political contrast between the relatively quiescent cotton sharecroppers of the American South and the revolutionary sharecroppers of Vietnam, and this difference became crucial in the theory of agrarian revolution described in Chapter 1.

I would also like to thank the tractor drivers of the plantations of Terrebone and St. Mary's parishes who kindly invited me into their homes and, at some personal risk given the labor environment of Louisiana plantations, provided me with an insider's view of plantation political economy. The concept of structural linkages between worker and management discussed in Chapter 1 owes much to their accounts of plantation life. In southern Louisiana sugar plantations "structural linkages" mean that the manager can threaten the eviction of union members from company housing, and ensure that the sermons preached at the plantation-owned church praise the humility of labor and deplore profligacy rather than penury as the cause of worker poverty. At this writing plantation laborers in Louisiana have not reached the standards of union organization of any number of plantation systems in the underdeveloped world, including those of Costa Rica, Ceylon, and even prerevolutionary Cuba.

This book has also benefited from the criticisms and advice of colleagues both at Berkeley and elsewhere. Arthur Stinchcombe has been a constant source of theoretical inspiration, meticulous criticism, and moral support as well as being a good friend, although an indifferent San Francisco Bay sailor. Mark Traugott provided many helpful suggestions in the initial design stages of the project. Guy E. Swanson and Harold Wilensky read the entire manuscript and provided helpful general suggestions and criticisms. Charles Tilly and William Gamson also provided detailed reviews of an earlier version of the manuscript. I am grateful to the members of the South East Asia Development Advisory Group seminar on peasants and revolution, especially to Juan Linz and Henry Landsberger for their sometimes trenchant but always constructive criticisms of an earlier draft of Chapter 1. All this help is gratefully acknowledged, but I, of course, bear full responsibility for suggestions that I have stubbornly resisted and for all data and conclusions contained in the work.

Financial support for the project was generously provided by grants from the National Science Foundation and from the Institute of International Studies and the Survey Research Center, University of California, Berkeley. I am also grateful to the Survey Research Center for providing grant administration and computing services. The cross-national data collection was assisted by a number of talented research assistants. Robert Stam assisted in research on Portuguese language materials and translated selections from Portuguese quoted in the text. Jacques Brissey, Ronald Royce, Fernando Uricoechea, Lea Ybarra, Elinor Ratner, and Will Tate assisted in collecting data on agricultural organization or rural events and in compiling the cross-national bibliography in Appendix 4. I am grateful for the visual imagination and technical skill of Adrienne Morgan who drafted the maps of Peru, Angola, and Vietnam. A word of thanks should also go to the librarians of the documents division of the Berkeley Library, whose unfailing courtesy and helpfulness to both myself and my assistants greatly accelerated our access to often obscure government publications. The arduous task of editing and checking references and foreign terms fell to Linda Fuller, who carried it out with patience and precision.

Finally, I would like to thank Karen Paige for her good humor and grace during the usual emotional traumas associated with the final stages of a writing project. In this case her task was made even more difficult by the fact that she was also in the midst of writing a book on which I was simultaneously attempting to collaborate. Our modest suggestion to other professional couples and to ourselves in the future is that collaboration is fine, but be sure to stagger your book writing.

JEFFERY M. PAIGE

Berkeley, California

CHAPTER 1

A Theory of Rural Class Conflict

IN THE NINETEENTH and early twentieth centuries the social and political life of large areas of Latin America, Asia, and Africa was transformed by the world market in agricultural commodities which developed in response to the demands of the industrial economies of Europe and North America. The agrarian states of what is now called the underdeveloped world participated largely as the economically dependent suppliers of primary agricultural products. The demands of the industrial economies led to specialized forms of agricultural organization adapted to production for world markets and created profound changes in traditional patterns of land tenure and rural class relations. These new forms of agricultural organization and new systems of land ownership and social classes were based on the productive requirements of a relatively small number of export crops. In the eighteenth century these crops were largely tobacco and sugar, and their production was confined to the Caribbean and the southern United States. By the end of the nineteenth century the number of crops had expanded to include other beverages and foodstuffs such as coffee, tea, cocoa, rice, and bananas and such industrial raw materials as rubber, cotton, sisal, and palm oil, and the agricultural export economy had established enclaves in much of the nonindustrial world. By the beginning of the twentieth century the world of the agricultural commodity market was divided between the developed, diversified, industrial economies of the consuming nations and the underdeveloped, monocultural agrarian economies of the producing countries.

The economies of most of the underdeveloped world remain dependent on a small number of primary agricultural products, and in many casès these products are the same as those produced in the previous century. Between 1959 and 1961 agricultural commodities contributed three-quarters of all non-petroleum exports of the countries of Latin America, Asia (excluding Japan), and Africa. Over 90 percent of these exports were destined for the developed market economies of the major industrial nations. Manufactures, by contrast, contributed only 10 percent of total exports from the underdeveloped world.[1] Petroleum exports contribute a growing share to exports from the under- developed nations, but at present these exports are overwhelmingly concentrated in a very few countries, notably, of course, in the Persian Gulf shiekdoms. With the exception of a few other mineral-exporting economies such as those of Chile, Zambia, and Bolivia, most countries of the underdeveloped world remain depen- dent on a few primary agricultural commodities which are their major source of foreign exchange, development funds, and internal economic activity. In 1959, coffee, the most important agricultural commodity in world trade, accounted for more than half the total exports of Brazil, Colombia, Costa Rica, Guatemala, Haiti, El Salvador, Angola, Kenya, the Ivory Coast, and Rwanda-Burundi. A similar proportion of total exports was accounted for by single crops, such as bananas in Honduras, Panama, Ecuador, and Somalia; cotton in Syria, Egypt, and the Sudan; rubber in Malaysia and Liberia; and sugar in Cuba and the Dominican Republic. A similar role is played by tea in Sri Lanka, jute in Bangla Desh, cocoa in Ghana, and rice in Burma. None of these monocultural export economies had any significant mineral or manufacturing exports, and in general, one or two secondary crops accounted for the bulk of the remaining exports. In a number of countries two or three major crops account for more than half of all exports, including rubber and rice in Thailand, Cambodia, and Vietnam; cotton and coffee in Uganda and the Central African Republic; palm, copra, and rubber in Indonesia; cotton, tobacco, and nuts in Turkey; and palm, rubber, and coffee in Zaire.[2] The economy of the typical underdeveloped country can be described as an agricultural export sector and its indirect effects.

Since agriculture is a labor-intensive activity, these agricultural export sectors exert a profound effect on large numbers of peasants and agricultural laborers in the underdeveloped world. The effects, however, are not spread evenly over the entire rural population, but instead tend to be concentrated in distinct commercial enclaves. These enclave economies are particularly likely if the export sector has been controlled by foreign corporations or colonial settlers. The dual economy of a commercial export enclave in the midst of a large sub- sistence population has been most fully described in Indonesia, where the export sector and the subsistence cultivators are located on different islands and can be easily distinguished.[3] Java, with most of Indonesia's population, remains a region of traditional Southeast Asian wet rice cultivation controlled by the indigenous village social system. Sparsely populated Sumatra produces the

[1] G. Blau, "Commodity Export Earnings and Economic Growth," in Edith H. Whetham and Jean I. Currie (eds.), *Readings in the Applied Economics of Africa* (London: Cambridge University Press, 1967), pp. 163–181.

[2] Export proportions calculated from data presented in United Nations Statistical Office, *Yearbook of International Trade Statistics* (New York: United Nations, 1959).

[3] Clifford Geertz, *Agricultural Involution* (Berkeley: University of California Press, 1971), pp. 12–47.

major export crops—palm, rubber, and copra. The system is a heritage of Dutch colonial rule but remains little changed today. The size of such export enclaves varies from country to country, employing, for example, much of the rural work force in Cuba or Sri Lanka and only a small fraction in Peru or Indonesia, but the dual pattern is characteristic of most agricultural nations. Whatever its size, the agricultural export enclave is usually one of the principal means by which the rural population is brought into contact with market forces and consequently a major source of economic and social change in rural areas.

The specialized agricultural organizations developed in the agricultural export sectors represent a sharp break with the pattern of subsistence cultivation. Frequently capital, technology, and even labor were imported from outside the host country, and the export sector developed in competition with, and at the expense of, the traditional agrarian social system. The expansion of the export sectors led to vast population movements including the international slave trade, massive expropriations of traditional landowners, the creation of armies of agricultural laborers, and the replacement of traditional communal social ties with commercial market relations. The new forms of export agricultural organization created new social classes and destroyed old ones and introduced new patterns of class conflict. Conflict developed between foreign owners of the new agricultural organizations and their wage laborers, between the new agrarian upper class and the old preindustrial landlords it replaced, and between landlords converted into commercial entrepreneurs and their former tenants now bound by ties of wages and rent. The strength of colonial and imperial political controls long prevented the political expression of these conflicts, but with the decline of colonial power in the postwar era, the commercial export sectors of the underdeveloped world have become centers of revolutionary social movements. This is not to say, of course, that the agricultural export economy is the only source of political change in rural areas or that peasants, sharecroppers, and agricultural laborers are the only classes or even the most important classes in all revolutions. Clearly, market mechanisms associated with the growth of cities and internal trade affect the social organization of traditional agricultural communities, and the success of revolutions depends on the actions of urban masses or elites even when these groups appeal directly to the countryside. Nevertheless, agricultural export sectors have been important sources of agrarian unrest in a number of areas of the underdeveloped world including Algeria, Angola, Kenya, Malaya, Guatemala, and most significantly Vietnam. The relationship of the rural population to the new forms of class cleavage and class conflict introduced by the agricultural export economy is essential in understanding the origin of this agrarian unrest in the developing world and in interpreting both the goals of its often anonymous peasant participants and the response of their political opponents both national and international. The purpose of this study, then, is to determine the effect of the agricultural export economy on the social movements of cultivators, those who perform the actual physical work of cultivation in the plantations and farms of the underdeveloped world. The study can be divided into two major parts: first, a cross-national statistical study of 135 agricultural export sectors in 70 underdeveloped nations and colonies in the period from 1948 to 1970, and second, case studies of three instances of major agrarian social movements—Peru, Angola, and Vietnam.

TYPOLOGIES OF EXPORT AGRICULTURE

The agricultural commodity market developed on a worldwide scale and is concentrated in a relatively small number of tropical products. As a result the new forms of agricultural organization it created tend to form regular repeating patterns in the underdeveloped world as a whole. Sugar, tea, and sisal plantations, for example, have remarkably similar characteristics whether located in Peru, Cuba, Tanzania, or Sri Lanka. In each case the plantation is owned by a legal entity or individual with substantial capital resources, the production techniques are based on industrial processing machinery, and the labor force consists of wage laborers resident on the estate. Similarly, commercial wet rice production tends to be organized in either small holdings or sharecropping systems throughout South and Southeast Asia and is never organized in the plantation form characteristic of sugar, sisal, and tea. These regularities in economic organization have led to a number of attempts to categorize the major types of export agriculture and to link these types with characteristic forms of social and class relations. Julian Steward and his associates, for example, developed a typology of rural subcultures based on the specialized form of agricultural organization developed for cash crop production in Puerto Rico.[4] Steward viewed the agricultural commodity market as the major source of social change in rural Puerto Rico. In the late 1940s and early 1950s market forces had led to concentration on a few cash crops, increased regional specialization, increased rationalization of production, and decreased emphasis on communal ties in both agricultural and social relations. Puerto Rico's principal cash crops at the time of Steward's research were coffee, tobacco, and sugar. Each crop had developed a specialized form of agricultural organization and a characteristic pattern of class relations and political organization. The three crops formed distinct regional enclaves in rural Puerto Rico. The coffee region of San José was still organized along preindustrial lines. This type of enterprise was used by Steward's associates, Eric Wolf and Sidney Mintz,[5] to illustrate the hacienda, or manorial, economy. In this system domain lands controlled by the estate owners

---

[4] Julian H. Steward, Robert A. Manners, Eric R. Wolf, Elena Padilla Seda, Sidney W. Mintz, and Raymond Scheele, *The People of Puerto Rico: A Study in Social Anthropology* (Urbana: University of Illinois Press, 1956).

[5] Eric R. Wolf and Sidney W. Mintz, "Haciendas and Plantations in Middle America and the Antilles," *Social and Economic Studies*, 6 (September 1957), 380–412.

are worked by laborers paid with the usufruct rights to small subsistence plots. The laborers on the San José coffee estates were paid a nominal wage, but their actual status was that of serfs bound to the land. The estate owner maintained his control by a combination of coercion, debt servitude, and periodic beneficence. The usufructuaries were not only required to work in the estate owner's coffee groves, but also to provide a variety of personal services at the convenience of the owner and his family. The vague open-ended quality of the serf's obligations and the estate owner's complete control over the subsistence plot made it relatively easy for the owner to control the political activities of his dependent serfs. Steward, Wolf, and Mintz reported no signs of overt conflict on the coffee haciendas of San José. Relations between lord and serf were ostensibly based on ties of personal trust and mutual aid. In actuality, the overwhelming power of the estate owner made any other form of relationship potentially dangerous for the serf.

The tobacco-growing regions of Puerto Rico were dominated by an entirely different form of agricultural organization—the small cash and subsistence farm worked by the owner and his immediate family. Tobacco was an important export crop, but it was easily combined with subsistence production and required a minimal investment. Thus many small peasant subsistence farmers could easily add tobacco to their regular crops. The tobacco area of Tabara was divided into many such farms, with relatively modest differences between large and small farms and few barriers to upward mobility through saving and investment in agricultural land. Traditional small holder virtues of saving, acquisitiveness, respect for property, and aversion to risk were pronounced in Tabara. All economic relations were on a cash basis, and the farmers were integrated into a variety of religious and educational organizations at the local level. The absence of any substantial class of large estate owners in Tabara eliminated any source of potential class conflict within the rural community, and the small tobacco farmers were generally politically conservative.

Sugar was Puerto Rico's primary export and was produced exclusively on large corporate and government-owned plantations employing resident wage labor. The immense investment required in the centrifugal processing of sugar led to an efficient, rationalized, bureaucratically administered organization and a homogeneous, landless labor force. There was little or no middle class, the possibility of upward mobility was zero, and relationships with the higher administrative classes were impersonal and economic. The workers were organized in strong labor unions, and there was a high degree of class solidarity and political participation. In the plantations owned by private corporations class-based organizations were particularly powerful and class conflict between the wage laborers and the plantation administration was overt and well understood by both sides. Despite the high level of class consciousness and density of political association in the corporate plantations, there were no signs of revolutionary, as opposed to reformist, class-based action. Of the three major types of commercial agricultural organization—the commercial hacienda, the small holding, and the plantation—only the latter showed any degree of class conflict. Even in this case, however, the conflict was hardly of revolutionary proportions.

A similar typology of commercial agricultural organization was also developed by Arthur Stinchcombe in an attempt to formulate a set of categories for worldwide comparative studies of rural class relations.[6] Although Steward's typology was based on an anthropological investigation of variation within a single society and Stinchcombe attempted to formulate a typology for worldwide comparisons, the forms of agricultural enterprise and their predicted consequences are remarkably similar. Three of Stinchcombe's five theoretical categories—the manorial, or hacienda, system, the family small holding, and the plantation—are identical to the corresponding Puerto Rican systems described by Steward and his associates. One of Stinchcombe's additional systems, the ranch, resembles the plantation in its substantial capital requirements and use of resident wage labor but differs in its more extensive use of land in grazing. The remaining system, the family-sized tenancy, does not resemble any of the Puerto Rican enterprises. Although Stinchcombe does not distinguish between rental property held by independent entrepreneurs and agricultural laborers paid with a share of the crop, it is clear from his examples—rice cultivation in Southeast Asia and cotton cultivation in Egypt—that the category refers to dependent sharecroppers. There was no equivalent form of agricultural organization in Puerto Rico, and sharecropping is in fact rare in Central and South America and the Caribbean.

Stinchcombe's analysis of the social consequences of these different systems resembles that of Steward, but is more directly concerned with class conflict and revolutionary social movements. Stinchcombe, like Wolf and Mintz, regards the serfs of the hacienda system as politically apathetic and incompetent, completely dominated by a sophisticated and culturally differentiated land-owning class. The internal economy of the hacienda is based on labor dues and subsistence agriculture, so that sensitivity to wages or prices is eliminated as a political issue. The politically dominant landed classes completely control the politics of their dependent serfs. Small holders in Stinchcombe's analysis have many of the social characteristics of the tobacco farmers of Tabara. They possess a reasonably high level of political affect and organization, but the isolation, spatial dispersion, and limited resources of small farmers make coherent long-term political action difficult. According to Stinchcombe, their political organizations tend to be short lived and easily dominated by outside interests.

Stinchcombe's descriptions of the political behavior of plantation workers, however, is distinctly different from the behavior reported by Steward for the workers on the south coast sugar plantations of Puerto Rico. According to Stinchcombe, plantation workers are characterized by political apathy, poverty

---

[6] Arthur L. Stinchcombe, "Agricultural Enterprise and Rural Class Relations," *American Journal of Sociology*, 67 (September 1961), 165–176.

of association, landlord domination of workers' organizations, and sporadic, extremist politics. In Puerto Rico, by contrast, plantation workers displayed intense class solidarity, high rates of association, disciplined labor unions, and active party participation. The sugar workers were the most class conscious and politically active of any agricultural group described by Steward, but according to Stinchcombe they resemble the serfs of a commercial hacienda. Stinchcombe's descriptions of ranch workers are roughly similar.

The family-sized tenancy, rather than the plantation, is the form of agricultural organization most likely to produce intense class conflict in Stinchcombe's typology. The conflicts over the share of the proceeds between cropper and landlord, the immense social distance separating them, the technical ability of the peasant, and the leadership of wealthier tenants combine to produce political sensitivity and effective leadership. The family-sized tenancy therefore produces not only intense class conflict but also overt revolutionary action. Stinchcombe cites evidence from a number of diverse regions to support his contention. He argues that the French Revolution was most enthusiastically received in areas in which feudal dues had been converted into cash rent, that the Chinese revolution had its origin in the high-tenancy areas of south China, that the Hukbalahap movement in the Philippines was concentrated in the high-tenancy areas of central Luzon, and that peasant rebellions in England during the Middle Ages were concentrated in Kent and the southeast, according to Stinchcombe, an area of extensive tenancy.

The relationship between the agricultural commodity market and revolution is also the subject of Eric Wolf's comparative study of twentieth-century peasant revolutions.[7] Wolf compared six revolutions which he considered to have involved peasant participation—Mexico, China, Russia, Algeria, Vietnam, and Cuba—and attempted to isolate the common elements in peasant revolution. Like Steward and Stinchcombe, Wolf regards the world market, which he refers to as "North Atlantic Capitalism," as the major motive force in revolutionary change. He differs, however, in his conclusions about the form of agricultural organization most likely to lead to revolution. His six revolutions occur in a wide variety of agricultural systems including the hacienda or manorial economies of Mexico and Russia, the sharecropping economies of China and Vietnam, the plantation economy of Cuba, and the migratory labor economy of Algeria. According to Wolf, however, none of these systems are likely to lead to revolution. In contrast to most previous theory on agrarian social structure, Wolf argues that it is the middle peasant who provides the mass base of revolutionary movements. This conclusion, of course, directly contradicts the observations of both Steward and Stinchcombe concerning the conservative and ineffective politics of small holders. It also stands in marked contrast to Marx's famous description of the political limitations of the French peasantry during the coup d'état of

---

[7] Eric R. Wolf, *Peasant Wars of the Twentieth Century* (New York: Harper & Row, 1969).

Louis Napoleon. Wolf argues, however, that the middle peasant is most vulnerable to the land expropriations, market fluctuations, high interest rates and foreclosures, and other changes introduced by the world market economy. As a result the middle peasant is receptive to revolutionary movements which promise the restoration of political order and economic stability. The middle peasant, according to Wolf, also has the independent economic base and tactical political resources that the landless sharecropper or plantation laborer lacks. Thus he has both the reasons and the resources to support a revolutionary movement. Wolf sees the marginal middle peasant as the carrier of the Chinese revolution during its long exile in Yenan, and as the major supporter of the Vietnamese revolution. In the case of China in particular he disagrees sharply with Stinchcombe, who claimed that the south China tenants, not the small holders of the north, were the main supporters of the revolution.[8] Wolf's theory is original and represents a sharp break with previous theorizing about agrarian class structure. Paradoxically the rural group considered by most anthropologists as the culturally conservative bearer of peasant tradition is also the major supporter of revolutionary change.

The three sets of typologies, of course, make three different predictions about the conditions most likely to lead to rural class conflict and revolution. In part, these differences reflect the different empirical evidence included in each study. There were no sharecropping systems in Puerto Rico, so that it is hardly fair to fault Steward for not anticipating their social consequences. Other differences, however, are clearly based on fundamentally different views about the effects of agricultural organization on rural class conflict. In Puerto Rico Steward found that plantations tended to produce the most intense class consciousness and strongest political organization and that small holding systems led to political conservatism. Stinchcombe agrees that small holders are conservative, but claims that plantation workers are politically apathetic and that sharecroppers are the principal revolutionary class. Wolf contends that *both* plantation workers and landless sharecroppers lack the independent political resources necessary for revolution and that the seemingly conservative small holders are actually the most revolutionary class. These differing conclusions reflect different implicit theories about the consequences of rural class relations. None of these studies, however, includes a formal theory of rural class relations, and none in fact makes any claims to have developed such a theory. Stinchcombe, for example, states at the outset that his study is concerned with "the description and analysis of empirical constellations of decision making structures" and notes the essentially "untheoretical nature" of such an approach.[9] Nevertheless, each of these studies has identified important regularities in the structure of agricultural organization and the nature of rural class conflict. The three studies are in fact typologies of agricultural organization and class relations,

---

[8] Wolf, however, is in agreement with Chalmers Johnson's interpretation of the Chinese revolution, in his *Peasant Nationalism and Communist Power* (Stanford, Calif.: Stanford University Press, 1962).

[9] Stinchcombe, "Agricultural Enterprise," p. 166.

not theories of the relationship between the two sets of variables. While the identification of empirical regularities is a necessary first step in the construction of theory, it cannot, of course, provide the theory itself. A theory of the effect of agricultural organization on the political and social movements of agricultural workers requires the abstraction of general principles from the empirical regularities identified in the typologies. This process requires two distinct steps. First, the casual variables underlying the structure of agricultural organization must be disentangled and separately defined. Second, the independent and dependent variables must be clearly distinguished. Independent variables describing economic organization must be separated from dependent variables describing political and social movements before causal propositions linking the two can be unambiguously stated. The empirical typologies frequently merged the two sets of variables, confounding cause and effect. Only when the underlying variables of the typologies have been disentangled is it possible to construct specific propositions about the causes of rural social movements.

A THEORY OF RURAL CLASS CONFLICT

Hubert Blalock has pointed out that social scientists frequently construct typologies when they hold an implicit theory about the interaction between two or more variables.[10] Each ideal type then represents a combination of particular values on these variables. When typologies are based on implicit notions of interaction, it should be possible to decompose the typologies into their constituent variables and state explicitly the combination of values which is expected to produce a given effect. The typologies of export agriculture and their predicted political and social consequences seem to be based on just such implicit theories of interaction between variables. Fundamentally the actions of peasants, sharecroppers, and agricultural laborers depend on their relationship with other agricultural classes, with whom they must share the proceeds of their labor. At the most general level the typologies suggest that social movements are the consequence of interaction between those classes which perform the actual physical work of cultivation and provide the mass base of an agrarian movement and those noncultivating classes which draw their income from agriculture but are frequently the targets rather than the initiators of agrarian protest. In Wolf's model, for example, the middle peasant is pressed by middlemen, banks, and tax collectors who threaten his hold over his land and therefore make him receptive to political radicalism. In Stinchcombe's theory the small tenant is engaged in conflict with the landlord over the share of agricultural production to be paid in rent. These typologies of agriculture are in fact expressions of recurring patterns of rural class conflict based on the interactions of the economic and political behavior of the cultivating classes on the one hand and that of the noncultivating

---

[10] Hubert M. Blalock, Jr., *Theory Construction: From Verbal to Mathematical Formulations* (Englewood Cliffs, N.J.: Prentice-Hall, 1969), pp. 30–35.

classes on the other. In this chapter an attempt will be made to propose a theory of rural class conflict which defines these recurring patterns of conflict in terms of interactions between the economic and political behavior of cultivators and that of noncultivators and predicts the circumstances under which these conflicts lead to cultivator social movements in general and agrarian revolution in particular. The fundamental causal variable in this theory is the relationship of both cultivators and noncultivators to the factors of agricultural production as indicated by their principal source of income. Thus the theory is based on a strict definition of class in terms of relations to property in land, buildings, machinery, and standing crops and financial capital in the form of corporate assets, commodity balances, or agricultural credit.[11] Both cultivators and noncultivators typically draw their income from a variety of different sources depending on the precise form of agricultural organization and its relations to commodity markets, but for purposes of understanding political behavior a broad distinction can be made between those cultivators and noncultivators who are largely or exclusively dependent on incomes drawn from landed property and those who are not. Noncultivators, who typically represent the upper class in most forms of agricultural production, may draw their incomes almost entirely from landed property and lack either capital in machinery and buildings or, often, any other financial assets beyond the land itself. On the other hand many agricultural upper classes are often dependent on incomes from the substantial capital invested in, for example, a corporate plantation, or on middleman profits in a small holding system, or on the profits to be made in exports from an underdeveloped country. Similarly cultivators, who generally represent the rural lower class, may draw their income from some set of rights to the land they work or may be paid wages in cash or in kind. Each of these distinctions actually represents a continuum; as market penetration and industrialization increase, the agricultural upper classes come to depend less and less on income from land ownership and more and more on income derived from control of processing, transportation, storage, and sale of agricultural commodities. It is obviously possible for some upper-class groups to draw income from both land and industrial or commercial capital. Similarly the cultivating class can be paid exclusively in rights to land, by some combination of land rights and wages, or exclusively in wages. In a commercial hacienda system, for example, dependent laborers are sometimes paid a nominal wage in addition to being granted usufruct rights to a subsistence plot. Similarly plantation workers are generally wage laborers but may sometimes be allowed to cultivate subsistence plots on plantation land to supplement cash wages. Whatever the income sources of cultivators and noncultivators, however, it is the noncultivators who typically control the critical means of production whether they be land, capital, or commercial marketing channels, and the two groups are separated by differences in function, control of resources, dependence, and

---

[11] Weber as well as Marx defined class in terms of relations to property. Max Weber, "Class, Status and Party," in Reinhard Bendix and Seymour Martin Lipset (eds.), *Class, Status and Power: Social Stratification in Comparative Perspective* (New York: The Free Press, 1966), pp. 21–27.

power. In some cases, such as the relationship between a village middleman and a small holder, the difference may be small, and in others, such as the contractual relationship between a corporation and a wage laborer, the difference may be much greater; nevertheless, there is usually a distinct vertical cleavage, with the cultivating class almost always in a less advantageous position. In most rural social systems noncultivating classes form the upper and cultivators the lower agricultural class.

The categories of cultivator and noncultivator both include groups which are conventionally thought of as distinct social classes, such as plantation laborers and commercial small holders, or corporate plantation owners and village middlemen, and there are obviously many possible principles by which these different social groups could be organized. It is the central role of land in agriculture, however, which gives rural class relations their unique character, and the relative importance of land versus either capital or wages sets limits on the direction and intensity of rural class conflict. Control over land affects the behavior of both cultivators and noncultivators, although in different ways, and the relative dependence of both classes on land is therefore critical in understanding both the political mobilization of cultivators and the response of noncultivators to this mobilization.

If the relative dependence on land versus either capital or wages is the most important determinant of the political and economic behavior of cultivators and noncultivators, then the interaction of the behaviors of the two broad classes should reflect this dependence. Figure 1.1 shows the income sources of both cultivators and noncultivators in dichotomous form in order to make these interaction effects clear. Although it should be remembered that dependence on

FIGURE 1.1 *Combinations of Cultivator and Noncultivator Income Sources, Typical Forms of Agricultural Organization, and Expected Forms of Agrarian Social Movements*

		CULTIVATORS	
		LAND	WAGES
NONCULTIVATORS	LAND	COMMERCIAL HACIENDA ——— REVOLT (Agrarian)	SHARECROPPING MIGRATORY LABOR ——— REVOLUTION (Socialist) (Nationalist)
	CAPITAL	SMALL HOLDING ——— REFORM (Commodity)	PLANTATION ——— REFORM (Labor)

land or capital or land or wages is to some extent a question of degree, the diagram in Figure 1.1 sets out the minimal logical possibilities of two dichotomous variables. The dichotomies are not, however, entirely artificial, and in fact, as the examination of particular forms of agricultural organization will make clear, particular combinations of cultivator and noncultivator income sources tend to be associated with discrete forms of agricultural organization identified in the earlier typologies. Figure 1.1 is intended as a mnemonic aid to keep the principal patterns of income source interaction and their associated political consequences clear. It is not intended to explain either why the income source of cultivators or noncultivators should affect their political behavior or why the interaction of these income sources should lead to any particular kind of social movement. To understand the consequences of rural property relations for agrarian revolution requires a theory linking income sources, economic behavior, and political behavior for both cultivators and noncultivators and a set of hypotheses expressing the effect of any combination of cultivator and noncultivator behaviors on the social movements of the cultivators themselves. The theory, therefore, must consider both the behavior of the two groups separately and the patterns of interactions between them.

THE NONCULTIVATING CLASSES.   The vertical dimension of Figure 1.1 represents a continuum between the two principal sources of income of the agricultural upper class—land and capital. The dimension reflects the transition from a landed upper class to a commercial or industrial elite through the penetration of the market into subsistence areas. The market transforms land, labor, and capital into commodities and demands rational calculation and efficiency in the organization of agricultural production. The landed upper classes represented in the upper half of Figure 1.1 are dependent exclusively on rent, labor dues, or profits from lands they work directly. In the extreme case, the landed upper class controls no expensive agricultural machinery or other industrial capital, has no control over the transportation or export of agricultural commodities, and has limited access to financial or commercial capital. The landed class is in fact often land poor, with few liquid assets and no fixed assets other than land and a few permanent buildings. Such an upper class tends to be found in types of agricultural organization such as the commercial hacienda described by Steward, the sharecropping system described by Stinchcombe, or the landed estate dependent on migratory labor as described by Wolf. The landed upper class depends on primitive agricultural technology, makes inefficient, even profligate, use of its labor force, and allows its lands to be worked extensively with little concern for their market value. The wealth and power of the landed upper class depends not on the efficiency of its estates, but on the area of land it controls. The greater the land area, the greater the wealth, the higher the standard of living of the landowners, and the greater their political and social influence. The landed upper class can expand its wealth only by acquiring new lands and can be impoverished only by the loss or division of its great estates. Since an upper-class income cannot be supported without vast tracts of land, the presence of a landed upper class leads to land concentration and the economic dominance of a few centralized estates. The large estates are profitable not because of any economies of scale, but rather because additional land is the only source of additional profit. The expansion of the large estates invariably involves the expropriation of small peasant landowners as well as conflict between the large estate owners themselves. The small landholder, however, is seldom in a position to resist the encroachments of the large estates, since he lacks the political and social resources associated with landed property. As a result the upper class tends to reduce small independent landowners to dependent laborers. The former landowners may become bound estate laborers, wage laborers migrating from areas of inferior land, tenant sharecroppers who have lost all rights to their lands, or small subsistence farmers who lack enough land to support themselves and are forced to supplement their own production by working on large estates. The dominance of the large estate and the reduction of the cultivating working class to dependent serfs or wage laborers are an inevitable consequence of an upper class exclusively dependent on revenues from land rather than capital.

Although all classes involved in production for export must by definition possess some minimal ties to the market, the strength of these ties varies considerably. In fact the greater the strength of market forces, the greater the likelihood that the landed upper class will be replaced by an agricultural upper class based on commercial or industrial capital. As agricultural production becomes more rationalized and efficient, the agricultural organization tends more and more toward the two specialized types in the bottom half of Figure 1.1—the small holding and the plantation. Both of these types involve an upper class dependent on capital other than land. It is apparent that the upper class of the corporate plantation as it is described by Steward or Stinchcombe is dependent on industrial capital. This class may in fact be composed of the stockholders of a diversified corporation which controls manufacturing and transportation companies as well as plantations. The nature of the upper class in the small holding system may seem more problematic. In this case there is obviously no agrarian upper class, since the land is owned by those who work it. There is, however, a substantial commercial and industrial upper class whose power and income is based on control of processing machinery, storage facilities, transportation, and finance capital. The small holder can therefore be considered a worker in an agricultural system controlled by urban financial interests. It was this view of the small holder–capitalist relationship which was expressed by Marx in his description of the nineteenth-century French peasantry; "The small-holding of the peasant is now only the pretext that allows the capitalist to draw profits, interest and rent from the soil, while leaving it to the tiller of the soil himself to see how he can extract his wages." [12] This view hardly describes the affluent

---

[12] Karl Marx, *The Eighteenth Brumaire of Louis Bonaparte* (New York: International Publishers, 1963), p. 127.

agribusiness of the American farm belt, but it is an accurate assessment of most small holders involved in export production in the underdeveloped world. Many such small holders are actually subsistence peasants producing cash crops only as a sideline. The processing, transportation, export, and of course eventual manufacture and sale of the finished commodity are all controlled by others. In Uganda, for example, cotton was grown exclusively by African small holders, but cotton gins were entirely controlled by Indian middlemen, and export was controlled by the British alone.[13] In the Belgian Congo the small holders not only did not control the profits in marketing their own cotton but were actually compelled to grow the crop according to individual quotas assigned by Belgian corporations.[14] Even in colonial Ghana, where cocoa is produced by a class of relatively affluent African small holders, the Cocoa Marketing Board bought up production at half the world price, sold at the world price, and retained the difference. Under colonial rule the board was controlled by the British and built up an enormous sterling balance in London banks which amounted to some 200 million pounds in 1955.[15] These examples indicate that the small holder of the agricultural export economy is properly regarded as a laborer who happens to control a small piece of land from which he "extracts his wages." The agrarian upper class is represented by the middlemen and financiers who control the marketing of the crop.

Both the small holding and the plantation are dominated by upper classes whose wealth is based on financial or industrial capital. They differ in that in one case the upper class surrenders control of the direct cultivation to a system of decentralized small farms, while in the other the upper class controls the agricultural enterprise directly, usually through a joint stock corporation. The centralized, corporate plantation engaged in direct cultivation, however, is relatively rare in agriculture, although it is more common in export agriculture than elsewhere. The industrial upper class of the corporate plantation is in fact dependent on the production parameters of a relatively narrow range of tropical crops. Philip Courtenay[16] has pointed out that the dominance of the corporate plantation in such crops is the result of two factors—the importance of primary processing machinery in export production and the continuous harvest possible in some tropical crops. Crops that require substantial mechanical processing before they can be exported create economies of scale by distributing the cost of processing equipment over many units. This advantage increases as a function of both the reduction of bulk possible during processing and the distance to the market. Tanganyikan sisal destined for European markets underwent a reduction

[13] Harold Ingrams, *Uganda: A Crisis of Nationhood* (London: H.M. Stationery Office, 1960), pp. 115–116 and 142–143.
[14] Gordon C. McDonald et al., *Area Handbook for the Democratic Republic of the Congo* (Washington: Government Printing Office, 1971), p. 301.
[15] Bob Fitch and Mary Oppenheimer, *Ghana: End of an Illusion* (New York: Monthly Review Press, 1966), pp. 40–45.
[16] Philip P. Courtenay, *Plantation Agriculture* (New York: Praeger, 1965), pp. 50–67.

to about 4 percent of its former bulk during the mechanical extraction of fibers.[17] Similarly Peruvian sugar destined for American markets underwent a bulk reduction to less than 5 percent of its former bulk during the extraction of refined sugar from cane.[18] Both of these crops were produced by plantations owned by wealthy individuals or corporations and involved industrial factory-like forms of organization. Economies of scale in processing cannot be realized, however, unless the expensive machinery can be kept in almost constant operation. This in turn requires a crop which can be harvested almost continually. Only a relatively small number of crops, including sisal, sugar, tea, and palm oil, satisfy the ideal conditions of bulk reduction and continuous harvesting which make the centralized factory organization of the plantation profitable. A number of other crops, such as rubber, coconuts, and bananas, have continuous or nearly continuous harvests but do not undergo substantial bulk reduction during processing. These crops are sometimes grown on plantations but can usually be efficiently produced by small holders. The agricultural upper class dependent on the industrial plantation is therefore confined to a relatively few crops.

In most cases the agricultural upper class must surrender its control over direct cultivation to small holders and realize its profits in the role of middleman or moneylender. In most crops centralized industrial organizations cannot compete with the small family farm. As market pressures increase, most agricultural systems tend toward the efficient organization of the small holding. The upper classes in an agricultural market economy are therefore more likely to rely on the income from commercial rather than industrial capital. The economic efficiency of the small holding has long been recognized by agricultural economists, although it continues to be a source of disappointment to Marxist theoreticians, who confidently await the centralization of agriculture to follow the centralization of industry.[19] The economic importance of land in the capital base of the productive unit gives a distinct advantage to the small holding in the production of most crops. First, it limits economies derived from specialization and hierarchical organization, since the difficulties of supervising a work force distributed over a large area are formidable. Second, it severely limits the use of machinery in planting, cultivating, and harvesting, since the machines must be brought to the raw materials rather than the other way round as is the case in industry. In highly mechanized American farms this problem is solved to some extent by the development of sophisticated mobile planting, cultivating, and harvesting ma-

---

[17] A. M. O'Connor, *An Economic Geography of East Africa* (London: G. Bell & Sons, 1966), p. 90.

[18] Estimated from figures presented in Eugene Burgess and Frederick Harbison, *Casa Grace in Peru* (Washington: National Planning Association, 1954), p. 28.

[19] For a conventional economic explanation of the competitive advantage of small holdings see R. L. Cohen, *The Economics of Agriculture* (London: Cambridge University Press, 1959). For an account of the long debate about the class status of the peasant in Marxist economic theory see David Mitrany, *Marx against the Peasant: A Study in Social Dogmatism* (Chapel Hill: University of North Carolina Press, 1951).

chinery, but this is a relatively late development in the history of commercial agriculture. Only a high-technology society can produce the complex devices necessary to handle perishable agricultural commodities while moving across open fields. The existence of such machinery in American agriculture, however, has tended to increase the degree of centralization of production and once again makes direct cultivation by large corporations economically profitable. Needless to say, most export economies have not reached this level of technological development and the division of labor and mechanization which lead to size concentration in industry are lacking in agriculture. In the absence of large-scale machinery the size of a farm tends to be limited to the land one man and his immediate family can work. Additional land and the labor to work it would not justify the additional costs in supervision and decline in labor quality.

In most export crops the small holding is the most efficient form of agricultural organization. In the few remaining crops plantations have a competitive advantage. Therefore upper classes dependent on commerical or industrial capital enjoy a distinct competitive advantage over upper classes dependent on landed property. Where there is a free market in land, labor, and capital, the landed upper class will be unable to compete effectively with the new type of organization dominated by commercial or industrial capital. The landed estate's inefficient use of land, labor, and agricultural technology should quickly eliminate it from the world commodity market. If the structure of agricultural organization were determined by economic factors alone, the landed estates in export agriculture would be replaced by small holdings or plantations. The economic analysis suggests that the types of agricultural organization in the upper half of the model in Figure 1.1 are economically unstable. In order to remain competitive in world agriculture, they should tend to be transformed into the types in the lower half of the diagram. This transformation, however, may not be a pleasant one for the landed upper class. The landowners may be able to adapt their estates to the centralized organization of the industrial plantation by investing in processing machinery, clearing their lands of tenants or serfs, and adopting a rational accounting of land and labor. It is more likely, however, that the landed upper class itself will be unable to find the necessary capital and will be replaced by large corporations that can. Such a process of change has been described in northeast Brazil by Charles Wagley and Marvin Harris[20] and by Harry Hutchinson.[21] In the 1950s traditional *engenho* plantations little changed from the days of slavery continued to cultivate sugar cane but lacked the expensive machinery necessary to process it. Instead they sent their cane to modern industrial (*usina*) plantations. Inevitably, however, economic and political power passed to the few wealthy families and corporations that controlled the *usina* plantations. The owners of the *engenho* plantations

[20] Charles Wagley and Marvin Harris, "A Typology of Latin American Subcultures," *American Anthropologist*, 57 (June 1955), 428–449.
[21] Harry William Hutchinson, *Village and Plantation Life in North Eastern Brazil* (Seattle: University of Washington Press, 1957).

were also under competitive pressure from industrial plantations in a new sugar region farther south. While a few members of the old landed aristocracy managed to survive the increased competitive pressure, most did not. The fate of the landed upper class in Peruvian sugar production was even less enviable. The Peruvian landed class was completely displaced by large foreign corporations which drove the less efficient estates into bankruptcy and bought up their lands.

The transition from a landed estate to a corporation plantation, however, is likely to be gentle in comparison to the transition to the small holding system. Such a transition can only come about through the breaking up of large estates and the liquidation of the landed aristocracy. Such, of course, was the fate of large landowners in the French Revolution. They found themselves replaced by peasant small holders who were both economically efficient and politically potent. Similar developments are described by Albert Hirschman in Colombia[22] and René Lemarchand in Rwanda.[23] In each of these cases serfs who had taken up cash crop production rebelled against the landed aristocrats and seized their estates, eliminating the landlords as a social class and establishing a system of small holdings.

Since free markets do not favor the landed upper class and more efficient forms of production threaten its existence as a class, it must adopt a rigid opposition to completely free markets. The continued existence of the landed upper class in the agricultural export economy depends, therefore, on political restrictions on the workings of the markets in land, labor, and capital. This attitude toward the market stands in sharp contrast to the attitudes of agricultural upper classes dependent on commercial or industrial capital. In both cases they profit from the unfettered workings of the market and are, in general, opposed to political intervention in the market unless it involves some direct consideration such as an export subsidy or a tax loophole. It is this fundamental difference in relations to the market which accounts for the divergent political behavior of landed upper classes on the one hand and commercial and industrial upper classes on the other. The landed upper class must rely on political power to prevent a free market in land, to protect itself against competition from small holders or plantations, to prevent expensive technological change from undermining its financial position, and to protect its huge underemployed labor force from the lure of higher wages in more efficient enterprises. The industrial and commercial upper classes benefit from an economically efficient allocation of the factors of production and can rely on market mechanisms to extract their profits. The economic weakness of the landed upper class forces it to rely on political means to attain economic objectives. The economic strength of the industrial and commercial classes makes such political controls much less essential. The relative economic power of the landed and commercial or industrial

[22] Albert Hirschman, *Journeys toward Progress* (Garden City, N.Y.: Doubleday Anchor, 1965), pp. 141–142.
[23] René Lemarchand, *Rwanda and Burundi* (New York: Praeger, 1970), pp. 93–177

upper classes in export agriculture leads to three basic differences in their political behavior which have critical consequences for their relations with the cultivating classes.

1. *A noncultivating class drawing its income from land tends to be economically weak and must therefore rely on political restrictions on land ownership. These restrictions tend to focus conflict on the control and distribution of landed property. A noncultivating class drawing its income from commercial or industrial capital is usually economically strong and requires fewer political restrictions on land ownership, and conflict therefore tends to be focused on the distribution of income from property, not on the ownership of property itself.* The presence of a landed upper class tends to focus conflict on control of the means of production, while the presence of a commercial or industrial agricultural upper class tends to focus conflict on the distribution of goods produced. The relationship between the presence of a landed aristocracy and conflicts over property is a direct result of the overwhelming importance of land as the source of upper-class income and the competitive disadvantages of large landed estates in export agriculture. Since land is the only important determinant of wealth, any change in the distribution of income between the upper and lower classes must depend on a redistribution of land. There is nothing else of any great value to become the focus of political attention. Thus in export sectors dominated by landed upper classes, conflicts over landed property are endemic. Since in a free market the landed aristocracy would quickly be bought out by more efficient small holders or plantations, the landed upper class inevitably develops some set of special land tenure privileges denied the rest of the population. The privileges may involve control of land through conquest, extortion or theft by a militarily dominant elite, systems of special land concession granted to metropolitan nationals in colonial dependencies, and systems of ethnic stratification which exclude most of the population from any access to the political and legal institutions controlling the ownership of property. Frequently, of course, these mechanisms may be used in combination. In the typical pattern of highland South America the dominant position of the Spanish and mestizo upper classes established by the conquest has been consolidated by the political disenfranchisement of the peasantry and by the extralegal upper class land expropriations. The peasantry in highland Latin America has been disqualified from politics by distinctions based on literacy, property, and race, and the mestizo upper classes control the courts and the land registry offices. In such a situation small landholders have no effective means of defending their claims, and extralegal encroachments on the lands of the indigenous peasantry are a chronic problem in most areas of Latin America where large estates exist.[24] No matter how efficient

---

[24] For a summary of land conflicts in Latin America see Ernest Feder, "Societal Opposition to Peasant Movements and Its Effects on Farm People in Latin America," in Henry A. Landsberger (ed.), *Latin American Peasant Movements* (Ithaca, N.Y.: Cornell University Press, 1969), pp. 399–450.

a small holder's production, he cannot grow crops on lands that have been stolen from under him. In colonial areas special land concessions enable nationals of the colonizing power to claim dominion over vast tracts of land which may already be occupied by the indigenous population. Such concession systems are particularly likely in colonial areas with large settler populations such as Algeria or Kenya. The indigenous population has no political power and consequently no legal recourse in such expropriations. The ethnic stratification systems which are inherent in colonial rule make it a practical impossibility for a member of the indigenous population to hold on to land in the face of pressure from members of the colonial elite. Landed property in agricultural export sectors seems a literal illustration of Proudhon's dictum that property is theft. In this case the theft is direct and land sales play a relatively small role in the dominance of the upper classes.

Since the legal or extralegal expropriation of land depends on the special privileges of the landed elite, conflicts over land often expand into conflicts over the control of the political system which makes the special land tenure privileges possible. Without the support of a landlord-dominated legal system the expropriations of *hacendados* in Latin America would be impossible. Deprived of the strength of colonial armies, settlers have been unable to hold on to their lands in most of the developing world. The conflict over landed property which is the fundamental political issue in any system dependent on a landed elite leads directly to conflicts involving the ultimate control of the political system. There are no other political options open to cultivators who are denied participation in politics, access to the legal system, or the right to engage in the pursuit of profit through small-scale farming. Such conflicts may not occur in all systems dependent on landed estates, but where such estates exist, the potential for violent conflict is always present. The conflict may involve both control of the means of production and control of the ultimate centers of political power in the society.

The economic strength of commercial and industrial classes in export agriculture makes special land tenure privileges considerably less essential. In fact in small holding systems the control of the land itself is not an issue, since the upper-class income depends on marketing, not producing the crop. In plantation systems the powerful corporate interests which constitute the agrarian upper class are clearly capable of buying out even powerful members of the landed aristocracy, to say nothing of small landholders. This is not to say, of course, that commercial or industrial interests will not take advantage of such concession if they are offered by a colonial regime or a pliable "independent" government. The Unilever plantations in the Belgian Congo depended on massive land concessions as did the Michelin plantations in Vietnam.[25] Such special privileges, however,

---

[25] On the Congo see Charles Henry Wilson, *The History of Unilever*, vol. I (London: Cassell, 1954), p. 180. On Vietnam see Charles Robequain, *The Economic Development of French Indo-China* (New York: Oxford University Press, 1944), pp. 195–216.

are essential for the survival of a landed upper class but not for the survival of an industrial or commercial upper class. Its economic success is assured by the workings of the free market. Its economic position can, of course, be damaged by nationalization or political restrictions imposed by other interest groups. Its overwhelming market power, however, tends to undermine its political opponents. The market price of cocoa, for example, is controlled by major chocolate manufacturers such as Nestle, not by the small holders of Ghana. Similarly, Firestone rubber dominates the economy of Liberia to such an extent that impeding production would threaten the major source of employment and government revenues and create a serious depression. The commanding economic position of the industrial and commercial classes in export agriculture, then, makes it less necessary for them to take a direct political role in restricting competition or expropriating the lands of the peasantry. In fact, these classes may actually find it profitable to encourage peasant production, supply funds for agricultural research, or sell their estates to native entrepreneurs. The major part of their profit does not depend on direct land ownership, and in many cases the political costs of ownership are not worth the additional profit. United Fruit, for example, adopted a policy of selling off its banana plantations in Central America while maintaining control over the "great white fleet" used in transporting bananas and of course maintaining control over marketing in the United States. United Fruit is therefore eliminating the image of "El Pulpo" (the octopus), which has been a target of left-wing propaganda in Central America for a half century, while maintaining control over the most profitable end of the banana business.[26] The commercial and industrial classes extract their profits not through special concessions, but through their control of scarce factors of production such as capital in processing machinery, transportation, and finance. Their relations with the lower class tend to be based on market ties, not on a battle over land ownership. Conflicts in export sectors dominated by industrial and commercial capital, therefore, tend to be focused on the distribution of income between the upper and lower classes, not on the ownership of property. Laborers may strike for higher wages, or farmers may demand lower interest rates, but neither group is likely to demand land expropriations or radical political change. This focus on the distribution of income tends to transform political conflict into economic bargaining. The economic weakness of the landed aristocracy tended to transform economic conflicts into political confrontations.

The economic and political consequences of a noncultivating class drawing its income from either land or capital are expressed in the upper causal pathway labeled hypothesis 1 in Figure 1.2. Figure 1.2 provides the specific causal linkages between income source on the one hand and political power on the other and therefore represents the intervening variables in the theory linking income sources and class conflict. As the upper pathway in Figure 1.2 indicates, land as the principal source of income for noncultivators leads to low economic power and dependence on political controls, which in turn lead to political conflict over

[26] *New York Times*, April 24, 1972.

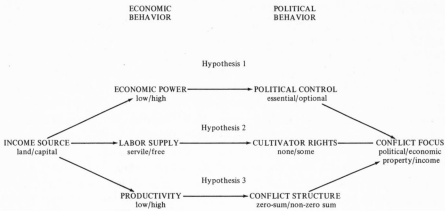

FIGURE 1.2   *The Effects of Principal Source of Income on the Economic and Political Behavior of Noncultivators*

property. Capital as the principal source of income for the noncultivating class, on the other hand, leads to greater economic power and less reliance on political control and consequently to economic conflict over income from property. The other causal pathways in Figure 1.2 also lead to the same ultimate political consequence for upper classes dependent on land or capital, but by two different intervening paths.

2. *A noncultivating class drawing its income from the land is usually dependent on servile or semiservile labor and cannot therefore permit the extension of political or economic rights to cultivators. As a result labor conflicts tend to be politicized. A noncultivating class drawing its income from industrial or commercial capital is usually dependent on free labor and can therefore more easily tolerate political and economic rights for cultivators. As a result labor conflicts tend to be economic rather than political.* Since the landed estate cannot compete with more efficient enterprises for labor, many of the same devices used to restrict the working of the market in land are used to restrict the market in labor. These restrictions may take the form of binding the workers to the land through hereditary serfdom, demanding compulsory labor directly through the intervention of colonial regimes, conscripting labor indirectly through devices such as the hut tax of colonial Africa, or relying on ethnic stratification to drive down the price of labor of the subordinate ethnic group. All these mechanisms depend on the political disenfranchisement of the population which is to supply the labor. This in turn requires an inequitable political system. The landed estate requires special privileges in the recruitment of labor as well as in access to land. In both cases the privileges are supported by a landlord-dominated political system.

To a greater or lesser degree the landed estate is dependent on semiservile labor. The labor supplied will, of course, be of low quality, and efficient production schedules will be impossible. In fact the landowner may consider himself fortunate if his laborers do not resist conscription by violent means. Such an intractable labor force is hardly useful in most industrial activities, but it is ideally suited to the inefficient, extensive cultivation of a landed estate. While it may be impossible to mine coal at the point of a bayonet, it seems to be possible to harvest coffee or grapes under a similar degree of compulsion. The low quality of the forced labor requires large numbers of laborers to compensate for the small amount of useful labor supplied by each. The landed estate is dependent on a labor force which is paid little or nothing, and works only under compulsion. The competitiveness of the landed estate in the world commodity market therefore depends in part on the difference between the price of free and of servile labor.

In such an environment a labor union or any other organization which threatens to increase the cost of labor is disastrous for the landowner. He cannot increase his labor costs without losing his competitive position in world agriculture. He cannot offset the cost of higher pay by employing fewer and more efficient workers, because the system depends on compulsion and compulsory laborers are inefficient laborers. He does not profit from the disciplined, responsible labor force that a labor union frequently produces. In the primitive agricultural technology of the landed estate efficient production is impossible and an efficient labor force, therefore, a luxury. Even if the workers were disciplined and efficient, they would be wasted on an enterprise which lacked the capitalization and rational organization of the industrial plantation. Thus the attitude of a landed upper class toward labor organization is one of absolute intransigence.

Neither industrial or commercial upper classes find collective action on the part of their workers particularly desirable. In the case of producers' cooperatives in small holding systems or labor unions in industrial plantations, the effect of such collective organization is to increase the share of the profits going to the workers. This may be costly for the upper classes, but it will hardly lead to economic ruin. In fact the upper classes may realize some potential gains from unionization or cooperative organization. The union provides a disciplined, efficient, responsible labor force which can be valuable in a capital-intensive organization like an industrial plantation. Sugar mills require a regular supply of cane for efficient operation, and irregular supplies of labor can lead to costly idleness. Banana production is subject to periodic disasters such as blow-downs in tropical storms and plant blights which threaten entire producing regions. Only determined, efficient, disciplined action by a large coordinated labor force can cope with these problems. If the banana crop is lost, the corporation's railways, docks and loading facilities, and refrigerated ships must all stand idle. In such an industrial environment a unionized labor force offers some advantages to offset the increased cost of labor. Labor organization will not lead to a disastrous weakening of the plantation's competitive position in the world commodity market.

Small holding cooperatives may provide some advantages to exporters and other middlemen by insuring regular output and avoiding mass bankruptcies of small producers. The commercial upper class has an economic interest in assuring that the small holders are protected from economic disaster. Admittedly this interest is long term, and in the short run the producers' association may succeed in retaining a greater share of its profits. On the other hand, producers' associations tend to be subject to the centrifugal political forces common in all small holding systems and seldom represent much of a threat to commercial interests. The upper class in the small holding system, like the industrial upper class of the plantation, is well able to withstand collective organization.

The fundamentally different attitudes toward labor of land- and capital-dependent upper classes lead to rigid, unyielding political repression on the one hand and a willingness to compromise on the other. Correspondingly the workers in a landed estate system can only protest through attempts to disrupt the workings of the forced labor system. Since this system, like the special land tenure privileges, is dependent on the control of the political system by the landed upper class, economic conflicts tend to become political. Like the situation created by land tenure privileges, the conflicts involve not simply a change of government, but the destruction of upper-class control over the state itself. In the case of both commercial and industrial upper classes, bargaining is possible and conflicts can be more easily confined to economic issues. This flexibility on the part of the upper class then leads to reformist action on the part of the working class. Violent seizure of the state may be the only way to end forced labor in a colonial state but is scarcely the only route to economic gains when an upper class is willing to bargain.

These intervening linkages between noncultivator income source and political behavior are summarized in the causal pathway labeled hypothesis 2 in Figure 1.2. Figure 1.2 indicates that land as the source of income leads to a servile labor force, which in turn leads to opposition to workers' rights and consequently politicized conflict. Similarly the figure indicates that capital as the principal income source leads to freer labor, less opposition to the cultivator rights, and, consequently, economic conflict over the distribution of income. Differences in labor recruitment as well as differences in economic power which depend on the source of upper-class income lead to similar patterns of class conflict although by different intervening causal chains.

3. *An upper class drawing its income from the land is associated with a static agricultural product and therefore creates zero-sum conflict between cultivators and noncultivators. As a result compromise in economic conflicts is difficult. An upper class drawing its income from commercial or industrial capital can increase production through capital investment and therefore expand the sum of agricultural income to be shared with cultivators, and conflict is therefore non-zero sum. As a result compromise in economic conflicts is possible.* This political difference is a direct result of the relatively greater importance of technology in agricultural systems controlled by industrial or commercial classes. In landed estate agriculture the total profits of the enterprise cannot be increased by more efficient organization, by increased use or fertilizers or insecticides, by the introduction of selective breeding to increase yields, or by the installation of

expensive machinery. All such technological innovations are usually beyond the resources of the landed estate owner. If he did possess such resources, he would of course no longer be the owner of a landed estate, but rather of a corporate farm or plantation. The profits from the landed estate are fixed, depending only on the price of the crop in the world commodity market. This price is, of course, beyond the landowner's control. The poverty and inefficiency of the landed estate would make it impossible for landed upper classes to grant economic concessions even if they were inclined to do so. The only economic concession possible is the redistribution of land, and this would, of course, require the sacrifice of the source of upper-class income and power. The upper and lower class in the landed estate are therefore locked in a zero-sum conflict over the control of land. There is no way to increase the income of either class except by decreasing the income of the other. In such situations compromise is difficult. When the zero-sum conflict involves the only major source of wealth in a society, such compromise is almost impossible.

The owners of industrial and commercial capital can, however, afford to make concessions to their workers. Advances in agricultural technology can lead to increases in productivity and a subsequent increase in profits. The industrial plantation can increase its efficiency by investment in machinery and can substitute machinery for labor. The owners of a corporate plantation may prefer a small highly paid labor force if new machinery makes it possible to decrease the total size of the labor force. Not only does the owner of the industrial plantation benefit from any improvements in agricultural technology, but he has the economic resources to invest in such improvements. The result is expanding rather than fixed revenues from the agricultural system. Similarly, commercial and industrial classes benefit from improvements in small holder production techniques. They may in fact be able to profit from the sale of tractors, combines, and other machinery to the small holder. Similarly, since their income depends on marketing, transporting, and processing primary commodities, technological improvements in any of these areas is likely to result in lower production costs and potentially greater profits. In the case of both industrial and commercial upper classes the total income divided between upper and lower classes is not fixed, but expands according to the rate of improvement in industrial and agricultural technology. This, in turn, makes it possible for upper classes to make economic concessions to their cultivators without lowering their own income. The expanding profits from technological change can be used to buy off rural social movements and divert them into reformist channels. The expanding income of workers or small holders in such a system also tends to increase commitment to the established property relations. The economic power of the industrial and commercial classes, therefore, encourages compromise efforts to avoid disrupting the technology which supports both upper and lower classes. In contrast to the landed estate systems, where the owner's loss is the worker's gain, the standard of living of both classes can improve in the industrial and commercial agricultural system.

These causal linkages are summarized in the lower path, labeled hypothesis 3, in Figure 1.2. As the figure indicates, land as the upper-class income source leads to low productivity, zero-sum conflict, and politicized conflict over property. Capital as the source of upper-class income, on the other hand, leads to higher productivity, non-zero sum conflict, and, as a result, economic conflict over the distribution of income from property. Once again differences in the economic behavior of noncultivating classes dependent on land or capital lead to differences in their political behavior and to differences in the pattern of conflict with cultivating classes.

In summary each of the three hypotheses of Figure 1.2 describing the effects of noncultivator income sources leads ultimately to the same pattern of class conflict for noncultivators dependent on land or capital. Where landed upper classes are present conflicts are focused on property, the upper classes are unyielding, and gains by one class can only be made at the expense of the other. The importance of political restrictions on the market in both land and labor tends to politicize economic conflict and frequently involves the state and the institutions of property it supports. When upper classes are dependent on commercial or industrial capital conflict is focused on the distribution of income, the upper classes are willing to compromise, and economic gains are possible for both classes. The dominance of market forces tends to depoliticize issues. In export agriculutre the presence of landed upper classes leads to insoluble political conflict over the means of production while the presence of industrial or commercial classes leads to economic conflicts over the distribution of income.

Clearly an agricultural system which tends to produce intractable conflict over the means of production and the control of the state should create the potential for violent revolution. The actual occurrence of revolution, however, depends not only on the economic and political characteristics of the upper classes but also on the political organization and power of the cultivating classes. If cultivators are weak and divided, even the most inefficient and oppressive landed upper class will be able to forestall revolution and preserve domestic tranquility. Repression is a powerful tool of political control and in the absence of countervailing power may be sufficient to contain the potentially explosive tensions of the landed estate. The explanation of the causes of agrarian revolution, therefore, requires an understanding of the political potential of the cultivating classes.

THE CULTIVATING CLASSES   The fundamental distinction underlying political behavior of cultivators as well as noncultivators is the importance of land revenues as a proportion of total income. In general, land will be used as payment in an agricultural enterprise either when the land itself is extensively cultivated and small patches for subsistence plots can be provided at low cost or when the small holding is the most efficient form of production and the upper class supports itself in commercial activities. Where land and standing crops are valuable or where industrial organization is economically efficient, laborers tend to be paid wages. In sharecropping systems land is usually considerably more valuable than in commercial hacienda systems. In Egyptian cotton cultivation, for example, land rents were sometimes two or three times the revenues which could be extracted by direct cultivation of the same area.[27] In this case share-croppers were employed, and they received no secure land rights of any kind. Their payment was simply a share of the crop. In the land-extensive hacienda systems of highland Latin America land is kept out of cultivation in part to pro-vide a cheap source of labor. Subsistence plots can therefore be turned over to usufructuaries with very little loss to the estate owner.[28] The usufructuary does not , of course, hold title to the land, but his right to cultivate a given plot may be permanent or even hereditary. The choice of payment in wages or in land rights is determined principally by the profit potential of the upper class. The choice of one form of payment over the other, however, has profound consequences for the poltical solidarity and organizational strength of cultivators. In general, land as the dominant source of income tends to divide the cultivating classes, while wages tend to unite them. This general principle is a result of the effects of both the economic interests of small landholders and the special situation of wage laborers in export agriculture. There seem to be three principal consequences of the differing forms of lower-class payment.

4. *The greater the importance of land as a source of income for cultivators, the greater their avoidance of risk and the greater their resistance to revolution-ary political movements. Correspondingly the greater the importance of wages in cash or in kind, the greater the acceptance of risk and the greater the receptivity to revolutionary appeals.* The conservative effect of the possession of even a small plot of land has long been recognized in studies of both subsistence peas-ants and commercial farmers. While peasant conservatism is sometimes attrib-uted to the restraining effect of the "culture of poverty" or some similarly backward ideology, it is usually recognized as a rational response to the economic conditions of peasant life.[29] The conservatism of small peasant subsistence farmers is a result of the precarious nature of peasant agricultural production and the bleak alternatives facing the landless in most peasant societies. As Eric Wolf[30] has pointed out, the peasant depends on a thin margin between maximum production and starvation. This margin is reduced by the extraction of the upper classes which are supported by peasants' production. In the commercial hacienda system the cultivator is essentially a small peasant producer whose surplus is

[27] Doreen Warriner, *Land Reform and Development in the Middle East: A Study of Egypt, Syria, and Iraq* (London: Oxford University Press, 1957), p. 26.
[28] See, for example, T. Lynn Smith, *Colombia: Social Structure and the Process of Development* (Gainesville: University of Florida Press, 1954), pp. 80–89, for a discussion of the workings of this process in Colombia.
[29] Oscar Lewis, "The Culture of Poverty," in L. Ferman, J. Kornbluh, and A. Haber (eds.), *Poverty in America* (Ann Arbor: University of Michigan Press, 1968), pp. 405–415.
[30] Eric R. Wolf, *Peasants* (Englewood Cliffs, N.J.: Prentice-Hall, 1966), pp. 4–6.

siphoned off through compulsory labor on the lands of the estate owner. Since both domain land and usufruct plot require simultaneous inputs of labor, the cultivator's chances of economic survival are reduced because he must abandon his own crops to attend to the lord's. The precise means of extracting this surplus varies from one peasant society to another, but invariably the extractions of the upper class leave the peasant with very little margin for error. His own primitive agricultural techniques are unlikely to yield any substantial increase in production, and even if such increase in production were possible, a major portion would be claimed by the upper class. The peasant finds himself locked into a dangerously marginal system of agriculture with no prospects for increasing his standard of living. If a peasant loses his lands, however, in a society in which land is the dominant source of cultivator income, his status is that of pauper and he may lose his position in the village and be forced into banditry or begging. Much of peasant conservatism derives from the peasant's slender survival margin, the stark alternatives facing the landless, and the risk of landlessness associated with any social or technological innovation. Marvin Harris's study of the village of Chimbarazo in Ecuador provides a pointed illustration of the dangers of change in peasant subsistence cultivation.[31] Well-intentioned Australian sheep experts persuaded a particularly progressive peasant to breed his ewes with merino stock provided by the Australians. The merino produces a much thicker coat and considerably more valuable wool than the ordinary Ecuadorian sheep. The progressive peasant followed the experts' advice and, just as they said, obtained a fine herd of valuable merinos. His good fortune was short lived. Some mestizos from a nearby town heard of his valuable animals and carried them off in pickup trucks in the middle of the night. Since most mestizos and a substantial number of his fellow peasants thought such sheep were too good for an Indian, the local authorities did not pursue the rustlers with much vigor. "Thus the progressive innovator was left as the only one in his village without sheep."[32] This amounted to complete economic disaster for the peasant and reduced him to a pauper without property. In most cases peasant resistance to political or technical change is based on a rational weighing of the probability of success against the risk of a disaster that could lead to the loss of property in lands and herds. This judgment reflects centuries of peasant experience with natural disasters and upper-class exploitation.

If productive technology is sufficiently advanced to convert the peasant into a small commercial farmer, a second source of conservatism becomes of increasing importance. As the small holder or former peasant becomes more affluent, he increasingly identifies his interests with those of the agrarian upper classes and correspondingly becomes fearful of movements which threaten property rights or draw too heavily on the support of landless peasants and laborers. This fact was clearly recognized by Mao Tse-tung in his analysis of

[31] Marvin Harris, *Culture, Man and Nature* (New York: Thomas Y. Crowell, 1971), pp. 478–479.
[32] *Ibid.*, p. 479.

classes in prerevolutionary Chinese society. The owner peasants or middle peasants, according to Mao,

> very much want to get rich . . . while they have no illusions about amassing great fortunes they invariably desire to climb into the middle bourgeoisie. Their mouths water copiously when they see the respect in which those small moneybags are held. People of this sort are timid, afraid of government officials and also are a little afraid of revolution.[33]

Mao argued that the middle peasants were unreliable allies because of their identification with the upper classes. The main carrier of the revolution was the semiproletariat of poor peasant sharecroppers. This group included both peasants who owned small amounts of land but were forced to become share-croppers or beggars to support their families, and completely landless share-croppers. Since the poor peasants had weak ties to the land and were barely able to survive from one harvest to the next, this group was the most receptive to Communist ideology and had the most to gain from revolution. In Mao's analysis the weaker the ties to the land, the greater the receptivity to Communist ideology.

Precisely the same argument can be made about more affluent small holders in developed market economies. In his *Agrarian Socialism*, Seymour Martin Lipset quotes Veblen's analysis of the commercial farmer's tendency to identifying his interests with those of large absentee landowners.

> His unwavering loyalty to the system is in part a holdover from that obsolete past when he was the Independent Farmer of the poets, but in part it is also due to the still surviving persuasion that he is on the way, by hard work and shrewd management, to acquire a "competence"; such as will enable him some day to take his due place among the absentee owners of the land and so come in for an easy livelihood at the cost of the rest of the community; and in part it is also due to the persistent though fantastic opinion that his own present interest is tied up with the system of absentee ownership, in that he is himself an absentee owner by so much as he owns land and equipment which he works with hired help—always assuming that he is such an owner in effect or in prospect.[34]

It should be noted that Lipset quotes Veblen disapprovingly. In his own study of Saskatchewan wheat farmers he argues that just such commercial farmers, not the industrial proletariat, had been the main support of socialist parties in both Canada and the United States. The Cooperative Commonwealth Federation studied by Lipset and populist and farmers' parties in the United

---

[33] Mao Tse-tung, *Analysis of the Classes in Chinese Society* (Peking: Foreign Language Press, 1967), p. 3.

[34] Quoted by Seymour Martin Lipset in *Agrarian Socialism* (Garden City, N.Y.: Doubleday Anchor, 1968), p. 33.

States have not been revolutionary or even particularly radical. In fact it could be argued that the CCF was neither agrarian nor socialist. Land ownership was not an important issue in the movement, and in fact the farmers of the CCF showed the same respect for landed property that is described in the quotation from Veblen. Their socialism was of a peculiarly limited quality. It was intended to control the middlemen involved in the marketing of wheat and was not concerned with government ownership of any other sector of the economy or even with welfare programs for the urban poor. The CCF was a reformist movement unconcerned with agrarian questions and certainly not revolutionary or even particularly socialist. The general principle that small holders are essentially conservative and resistant to revolutionary appeals seems to be supported rather than refuted by Lipset's study of "agrarian socialism."

In fact the evidence from studies of both peasants and commercial farmers indicate that the stronger the tie to the land, the greater the resistance to radicalism. This principal is expressed in the upper causal path labeled hypothesis 4 in Figure 1.3. The figure indicates that payment in land leads to an avoidance of any risk that might precipitate landlessness or lead to gains for the landless at the expense of property owners and that these economic characteristics in turn lead to political conservatism, identification with the interest of large landowners, and a corresponding resistance to political radicalism. Cultivators drawing their income from land therefore are not likely to form strong parties in their own interests, although they may support strong landowners' parties. Similarly Figure 1.3 indicates that payment in wages tends to increase workers' willingness to take risks, since they have little property to lose, and consequently cultivators paid in wages tend to be receptive to radical political ideologies. This in turn makes it possible for them to form strong parties based on cultivator rather than noncultivator interests.

FIGURE 1.3 *The Effects of Principal Source of Income on the Economic and Political Behavior of Cultivators*

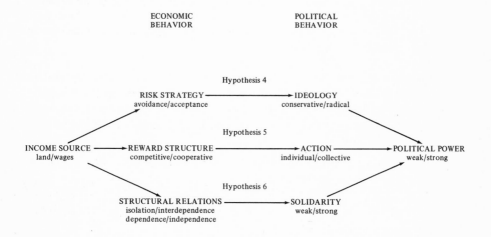

To argue that the weakening of ties to the land is a necessary precondition for class-based political organization does not necessarily mean that such organization will occur. The possibility of political mobilization of cultivators depends not only on what they may have lost in property rights but on what they may have gained in organizational potential through the replacement of payment in land with payment in cash or in kind.

5. *The greater the importance of land as a source of income for cultivators, the stronger the incentives for economic competition and the weaker the incentives for political organization. The greater the importance of wages as a source of income, the less the economic competition and the greater the incentive for political organization.* This principle of political behavior is a direct consequence of the fact that personal profit and upward mobility are possible through individual efforts in systems based on small landholdings while largely impossible in agricultural systems employing wage laborers. The relations between small landholders are governed by principles of economic competition whether the small holders are peasants or commercial farmers. While the competitive relations between commercial small holders may seem apparent, peasant communities are sometimes portrayed as cooperative rather than competitive societies. Ever since Robert Redfield described the peasant society of Tepoztlán as a "smoothly functioning and well integrated society made up of a contented and well adjusted people," [35] anthropologists have been steadily demolishing the image of organic interdependence and cooperation of Redfield's "folk" society. The peasant in these studies appears to be competitive, individualistic, envious, and distrustful. To know the peasant is apparently not necessarily to love him. Dwight Heath compiled a thesaurus of epithets applied to the Bolivian Aymara by various observers including such distinguished anthropologists as Harry Tschopik. The Aymara peasants were said to be

> anxious, apprehensive, brutal, careless, closed, cruel, depressed, dirty, dishonest, distrustful, doubtful, drunken, dull, fearful, filthy, gloomy, hostile, ignorant, insecure, irresponsible, jealous, malevolent, malicious, melancholic, morose, negative, pessimistic, pugnacious, quarrelsome, rancorous, reticent, sad, silent, sinister, slovenly, stolid, sullen, suspicious, tense, thieving, treacherous, truculent, uncommunicative, unimaginative, unsmiling, untrustworthy, violent, and vindictive.[36]

While some of these epithets reflect upper-class mestizo prejudices, some the perceptions of outsiders, and some are simply nonsense, there is an element of competitiveness, jealousy, and distrust which appears not only in this list but in many other descriptions of peasant communities. This set of attitudes has been

---

[35] Quoted in George M. Foster, "Interpersonal Relations in Peasant Society," *Human Organization*, 19 (Winter 1960–1961), 174.

[36] Dwight B. Heath, "Bolivia: Peasant Syndicates among the Aymara of the Yungas: A View from the Grass Roots," in Henry A. Landsberger (ed.), *Latin American Peasant Movements* (Ithaca, N.Y.: Cornell University Press, 1969), p. 179.

formalized by George Foster[37] as the "image of limited good" and by Edward Banfield[38] as "amoral familism." In both cases the basic attitudes involve a selfish interest in the property of an individual and his immediate family and intense suspicion of the acquisitive proclivities of others. The "image of limited good" is expressed by the attitude that valuable goods are always in short supply, that there is no way to increase that supply, and that consequently the only way an individual and his family can improve their position is at the expense of others. Foster points out that these attitudes are firmly rooted in the realities of peasant agricultural technology. Resources of land are absolutely limited if not actually declining because of population growth or hacienda land grabs. Peasant agricultural technology cannot improve because there is no way of protecting the profits derived from the improved technology. The situation of the peasant is in some ways parallel to that of the large landowner. The only way either can increase his income is by expanding his lands at the expense of others. Banfield's notion of "amoral familism" also reflects the dog-eat-dog tactics of the peasant subsistence economy. Banfield reduces the attitudes of amoral familism to a simple principle: "Maximize the material short-run advantage of the nuclear family; assume that others will do likewise." [39] Like the image of limited good, amoral familism can be viewed as a rational adjustment to a society with fixed resources liable to expropriation by a predatory upper class. These principles underlie a wide range of peasant behavior designed to protect the peasant's lands and flocks against the connivance, thievery, and outright violence of his neighbors. Marvin Harris reports that inquiries about peasant land ownership in Ecuador were met with extreme measures including the immediate disappearance of the landowner and his relatives, the abandonment of all work in the fields in question, and the stoning of government census takers.[40] The same pattern of behavior is illustrated in the following story told to Banfield by a resident of the south Italian peasant village of Montegrano.

> Dr. Gino tells a story about a peasant father who throws his hat upon the ground. "What did I do?" he asks one of his sons. "You threw your hat upon the ground," the son answers, whereupon the father strikes him. He picks up his hat and asks another son, "What did I do?" "You picked up your hat," the son replies and gets a blow in his turn. "What did I do?" the father asks the third son. "I don't know," the smart one replies. "Remember, sons," the father concludes, "if someone asks you how many goats your father has, the answer is you don't know." [41]

In a competitive economy in which land, flocks, and herds are the only important form of wealth, protection of property becomes almost an obsession.

[37] George M. Foster, "Peasant Society and the Image of Limited Good," *American Anthropologist*, 67 (April 1965), 293–315.
[38] Edward C. Banfield, *The Moral Basis of a Backward Society* (New York: The Free Press, 1958), pp. 83–101.
[39] *Ibid.*, p. 83.
[40] Harris, *Culture*, p. 476.
[41] Banfield, *Moral Basis*, p. 120.

Though economic gains cannot be made except at the expense of others, there usually exists a range of wealth even within the poorest peasant communities. This internal stratification is another important source of divisiveness. As long as such differences in wealth exist, it is always possible to imagine gaining wealth or status by outmaneuvering or outstealing one's neighbors. Similarly it is always possible to be reduced to poverty by the machinations of others. The wealthier members of the community, however, are likely to exert a major political and social influence over the behavior of other members. To be without property in land or herds is to have no social or political standing in the community. In the words of a Calabrian proverb, "He who has not, is not." [42] Informal influence and political power follow lines of internal stratification. The wealthiest and most conservative members of the community therefore usually provide the small amount of community cohesion possible in the competitive peasant world. These wealthier peasants frequently have close ties to the landed upper classes through fictive kinship and other forms of sponsorship, and act as a conservative brake on community action.

The internal stratification as well as the competitive internal economy of the peasant society are in no small measure dependent on the presence of a predatory landed upper class. The presence of this class discourages improvements in agricultural technology, threatens all peasants with land expropriations, and deprives them of any semblance of political control over their own villages. The economic base of "amoral familism" and the "image of limited good" depends on the continued hegemony of the landed upper classes. When these classes are weakened or destroyed, the economic impediments to cooperative peasant action are markedly reduced.

The social and political life of the small commercial farmer, like that of the peasant, is also based on relations of economic competition. Unlike the peasant, however, the small farmer can move up the "agricultural ladder" by reinvesting his profits in additional land and equipment. This does not mean that the commercial farmer is subject to less competitive pressure than the small peasant farmer. Although he is not involved in a zero-sum conflict with his neighbors, he is involved in classic free market competition. Each small holder is the idealized producing unit in a model free economy in which no individual producer can control prices, and profits and costs are determined by supply and demand. The most efficient producers can therefore drive less efficient producers out of business, especially during periods of depression or crop failures. Similarly each farmer can advance his economic position and attain additional land by increased efficiency. A competitive advantage can be translated into additional land and equipment and the prospect of increased future earnings. The commercial small farmers tend to be divided by competitive pressures similar to those that divide peasants. Like the peasant community, the farm community is likely to be dominated by its wealthiest members. The internal

---

[42] The proverb is reported by Joseph Lopreato in his article, "How Would You Like to Be a Peasant?" *Human Organization*, 24 (Winter 1965), 301.

stratification of the commercial small holding system is greater than in the peasant community, and therefore the prospects of upward mobility through individual effort are also greater. Although the economic conflict may not be as bitter as it is in the zero-sum world of the peasant, the real prospects for individual upward mobility discourage cooperative action to an even greater extent than in peasant communities. In both cases, however, the wealthiest members of the community dominate political organizations.

When agricultural workers are dependent on income from land, economic competition limits collective political organization, reduces class solidarity, and creates a conservative leadership dominated by the wealthiest landowners. Payment of wages in cash or in kind, however, creates economic incentives for collective political action, intense class solidarity, and leadership based on personal influence rather than wealth. Wage labor, however, does not in itself create incentives for political solidarity. In advanced industrial societies wage-based stratification systems create a pronounced emphasis on individual achievement and economic mobility. The agricultural export economy, however, creates a homogeneous, unskilled labor force with little or no internal stratification and no prospect for upward mobility. Agricultural wage laborers are exposed to competition for jobs, but export agriculture tends to equalize wages and working conditions at the same low level for all workers. Economic gains can seldom be realized at the expense of other workers but rather in most cases, only through economic pressure on the employer. The agricultural wage labor is by definition cut off from ties to the land and consequently has no incentive to invest his meager savings in permanent property. The divisive effects of individual property ownership are therefore largely absent. The agricultural wage laborer seems to illustrate the characteristics that Marx believed were essential for the mobilization of the industrial proletariat:

> But with the development of industry the proletariat not only increases in number; it becomes concentrated in greater masses, its strength grows, and it feels its strength more. The various interests and conditions of life within the ranks of the proletariat are more and more equalized, in proportion as machinery obliterates all distinctions of labor, and nearly everywhere reduces wages to the same low level.[43]

These economic characteristics were to lead to worker combinations against the upper classes, to class-based political parties and open class conflict, and, eventually, to revolution and the triumph of the proletariat. While it has become commonplace to observe that Marx's revolutionary prediction remains unfulfilled in industrial societies, this fact does not invalidate his original hypothesis concerning economic conditions and class consciousness. These conditions

---

[43] Karl Marx and Friedrich Engels, "Manifesto of the Communist Party," in Robert Freedman (ed.), *Marxist Social Thought* (New York: Harcourt, Brace & World, 1968), p. 185.

proved relatively transient in industrial societies. Increasing technological change leads to a more differentiated, not a more homogeneous class structure, and wages were increased, not reduced to the same low level. In the agricultural export economy, however, these economic conditions have persisted long after they have disappeared in industrial societies. The homogeneous poorly paid, concentrated mass of workers that Marx saw as the vanguard of the revolution are found not in industrial societies, but in commercial export agriculture in the underdeveloped world. It is in such societies that the greatest incentives for class-based organization and class conflict exist.

These characteristics of the agricultural wage labor force remain relatively constant whether the cultivator works as a plantation laborer, a seasonal harvest migrant, or even a cropper paid in a share of the crop. In each case upward mobility into the land-owning class is a practical impossibility, stratification within the cultivating class is minimal, and economic gains can be made only at the expense of the employer. There are no rich workers who could form the nucleus of a conservative leadership linked to the agrarian upper classes or provide a model of upward mobility through individual effort. Where all men are reduced to approximately the same level of poverty, leadership must depend on persuasion, charm, strength, cunning, or some other personal quality, not on the social status of accumulated property. All these characteristics of payment in wages are of course a result of the undifferentiated and largely unskilled occupational structure of wage labor in export agriculture, and other wage systems with greater prospects for upward mobility and greater internal stratification would establish incentives for individual, not collective action. In agricultural wage labor systems, however, the greatest gains are to be made only over the resistance of the employer, and overcoming this resistance requires collective, not individual effort.

These effects of the income sources of cultivators are summarized in the causal path labeled hypothesis 5 in Figure 1.3. This path indicates that payment in land tends to generate competition within the cultivator class and to discourage collective political organization and as a result leads to weak cultivator political organizations. Similarly payment in wages leads in general to less competition and more cooperation among cultivators and creates incentives for collective political action leading to strong cultivator political organizations. The nature of these organizations and their possibilities for success, however, depend not only on the interests of the wage workers but on the political power and economic interests of the agrarian upper class, although in agricultural systems in which land is the principal source of cultivator income the economics of production inhibit political organization whatever the nature of the agrarian upper class.

6. *The greater the importance of land as a source of income for cultivators, the greater the structural isolation or dependence on noncultivators and the weaker the pressures for political solidarity. The greater the importance of wages, the greater the structural interdependence of cultivators and the stronger*

the pressures for political solidarity. This political difference is a result of the fact that small cultivators tend to carry on their productive activities in relative isolation, while agricultural wage laborers are usually brought together in common work groups isolated from other classes. The relative isolation of small cultivators applies equally to peasants and commercial farmers. Peasant self-reliance was the basis of Marx's explanation of the absence of class-based political organization among the French peasantry:

> The small-holding peasants form a vast mass, the members of which live in similar conditions but without entering into manifold relations with one another. Their mode of production isolates them from one another instead of bringing them into mutual intercourse. The isolation is increased by France's bad means of communication and by the poverty of the peasants. Their field of production, the small-holding, admits of no division of labor in its cultivation, no application of science and, therefore, no diversity of development, no variety of talent, no wealth of social relationships. Each individual peasant family is almost self sufficient; it itself directly produces the major part of its consumption and thus acquires its means of life more through exchange with nature than in intercourse with society.[44]

Marx's observation about the self-reliance of the peasantry has been confirmed by anthropological investigations of peasant communities. Eric Wolf concludes that "a peasant's work is most often done alone, on his own land, than in conjunction with his fellows [*sic*]." [45] George Foster observed that "a peasant family potentially is the most independent of all social units. . . . Paradoxical as it may sound, their technology permits them a degree of independence denied members of more primitive and more advanced societies." [46] Even though systems of festival labor or reciprocal labor exchange may play a role in some peasant communities, they tend to rapidly disappear in any community exposed to the export market. Charles Erasmus points out that such cooperative labor seldom survives the economic reckoning introduced by the market.[47] Peasants participating in the market find reciprocal labor exchange and festival labor impractical because its cost is high, the work poor, and the laborers often unruly. As market forces enter peasant communities, each cultivator retreats into ever more isolated forms of production. The agricultural lower class that draws its income from the land usually does so in isolation. A peasant can neither expect nor demand labor from anyone other than the members of his immediate family. This economic self-reliance leads to restrictions on extending any kind

---

[44] Marx, *Eighteenth Brumaire*, pp. 123–124.
[45] Wolf, *Peasant Wars*, p. 289.
[46] George M. Foster, "Interpersonal Relations," p. 178.
[47] Charles Erasmus, "The Occurrence and Disappearance of Reciprocal Farm Labor in Latin America," in Dwight B. Heath and Richard N. Adams (eds.), *Contemporary Cultures and Societies of Latin America* (New York: Random House, 1965), pp. 173–199.

of aid or support outside the family. The sick, the injured, or the elderly peasant without lands or family is in desperate trouble in many peasant communities. The peasant community is divided by the economic self-reliance of its individual members who can get along perfectly well without the help of others and would be suspicious of such help even if it were offered.

Self-reliance and rugged individualism are also characteristics typically associated with the ideology of the commercial farmer. The self-reliance is more pronounced in some crops than in others, but most small farmers operate in isolation. The only outside help they require is a few hired men or some assistance from neighbors during a harvest. As is the case in peasant communities, the greater the market participation, the less frequent any form of community mutual assistance. Barn raisings and bringing in the sheaves may be a part of the folklore of rural America, but in most commercial farms labor is supplied by machines or hired help. The greater the self-reliance of the commercial farmer, the less his willingness to join in political associations with other farmers. In North America, populist and other radical farmers' movements have been most successful in the wheat belt of the great plains and relatively unsuccessful in the corn belt. Michael Rogin[48] notes that in general populism was more successful in wheat than in corn areas while, conversely, McCarthyism was more popular in the conservative corn belt. He reports that most studies of the economic organization of wheat and corn production have found that corn farmers are more dependent on their own individual efforts than are wheat farmers.[49] Wheat farmers are both more vulnerable to fluctuations in the international commodity markets and more susceptible to manipulation by middlemen than are corn farmers. Wheat farmers are also more vulnerable to the weather. The relatively concentrated demand for labor in wheat production usually requires wheat farmers to find additional part-time labor by hiring laborers or forming associations with other wheat farmers. Corn farmers on the other hand usually distribute their work evenly over the year, can always feed their corn to their hogs if the price is low, and are not subject to the same threat from the weather. Self-reliance tends to be an economic reality as well as an ideology for the corn farmer. Lipset makes similar observations about the political behavior of wheat and corn farmers.[50] In both Canada and the United States wheat farmers were more receptive to radical movements. Lipset argues that the fluctuations of the world grain market exerted a much greater effect in Canada than in the United States, and consequently the Canadian wheat farmers remained committed to radical political organization long after American wheat farmers had been pacified by the stabilization of the large American domestic wheat market.[51]

[48] Michael Rogin, *The Intellectuals and McCarthy* (Cambridge, Mass.: M.I.T. Press, 1967), p. 98.
[49] *Ibid.*
[50] Lipset, *Agrarian Socialism*, pp. 25–26.
[51] *Ibid.*, p. xiv (introduction to the Anchor ed.).

Cultivators drawing their income from the land are not only frequently isolated from one another but also dependent on structural ties to noncultivators who provide the social services, agricultural credit, and collective economic resources that the cultivators need but cannot supply themselves. Peasant subsistence communities are typically dominated by conservative politicoreligious hierarchies or by nearby landed estates, and peasants are linked to both the community and estate leadership through ties of fictive kinship, mutual aid, and coercion. A village notable or an estate administrator who controls the distribution of irrigation water or the allocation of work obligations on the estate can manipulate these structural ties to enforce loyalty to the noncultivating, *not* the cultivating classes. Similarly, commercial farmers are often dependent on banks, railroads, and export firms to provide economic services beyond the means of individual farmers and therefore are linked more closely to noncultivators than if such services were provided by cultivator cooperatives. These linkages to noncultivators therefore tend to reinforce the structural isolation of cultivators and make them both isolated and dependent.

In general, structural ties between cultivators paid in wages are stronger, and ties to noncultivators weaker, than among cultivators paid in land. The conditions of an agricultural wage labor force in fact closely resemble the isolated mass of industrial workers described by Clark Kerr and Abraham Siegel as the most prone to militant union activity and frequent strikes.[52] Like the miner or logger described by Kerr and Siegel, the plantation or estate wage laborer is isolated in an economic organization which is also a residential community. He is therefore dependent on his fellow workers for aid and assistance not only in economic matters but in social welfare as well. The agricultural wage laborer is typically cut off from other occupational groups and completely dependent on his fellow workers. Unlike the peasant or commercial farmer the agricultural wage laborer is typically part of a work gang, and his behavior may affect the work requirements and wages of others. In a homogeneous work group adherence to protective group norms established to limit the demands of the foreman or gang boss can easily be enforced by other workers. The interdependence of the work gang means that workers showing too much or too little enthusiasm for their work may find themselves increasingly isolated and under pressure from other workers, who can prevent them from fulfilling production quotas, create difficulties with management, or ostracize them from the estate or plantation worker community.

As Erving Goffman has pointed out, the plantation or landed estate is similar to a prison or other total institution.[53] The prisoner subculture can exert substantial pressure on individual prisoners and in fact runs a second

---

[52] Clark Kerr and Abraham Siegel, "The Interindustry Propensity to Strike," in Arthur Kornhauser et al. (eds.), *Industrial Conflict* (New York: McGraw-Hill, 1954), pp. 189–212.

[53] Erving Goffman, *Asylums: Essays on the Social Situation of Mental Patients and Other Inmates* (Garden City, N.Y.: Doubleday Anchor, 1962), pp. 1–124.

administration parallel to the formal structure of warden and guards. In agricultural organizations dependent on wage labor this second administration is often strong enough to offset the power of the formal administrative hierarchy, and in contrast to cultivators paid in land, cultivators paid in wages are often more strongly tied to one another than they are to the estate administration. The isolated production techniques of cultivators drawing their incomes from land make it possible for village or estate officials to control access to collective goods and sanctions and strengthen vertical ties between cultivators and noncultivators. In systems dependent on wage labor, however, the principal service of the noncultivators is to pay wages, the wage laborers typically have no access to the collective economic resources of the estate, which are controlled by its owner, and structural linkages to other workers therefore exert an important influence on their behavior. In any system of wage labor, then, coercive pressure from other workers can be used to enforce loyalty to the cultivator class, while in land payment systems these coercive resources are largely in the hands of the formal estate administrative structure or the conservative officials of a peasant village.

These economic and political consequences of payment in land or wages are illustrated by the causal path labeled hypothesis 6 in Figure 1.3. This path shows that payment in land leads to structural isolation and dependence and, consequently, to weak cultivator solidarity, which in turn inhibits effective political organization. Similarly payment in wages leads to greater independence of the estate administration, and consequently, agricultural wage laborers are capable of enforcing loyalty to the cultivating class. As a result cultivator political organizations are strengthened. Thus all three hypotheses illustrated in Figure 1.3 lead to the same general consequences for the behavior of cultivators. Payment in land tends to weaken and payment in wages tends to strengthen cultivator political organization. Nevertheless it is important to distinguish the three causal pathways because, as will become apparent in the case studies of Peru, Angola, and Vietnam, cultivators vary in the relative strength of the intervening economic variables in the model of Figure 1.3 and these differences exert a significant effect on their political behavior. In some cases, for example, economic incentives may favor cultivator political organization but political action may be inhibited by structural ties to noncultivating classes, or the political weakness inherent in a competitive economy may be temporarily overcome by a rapid loss of ties to the land and a consequent increase in willingness to accept economic and political risks. Hypotheses 1 to 6 concerning the behavior of both cultivators and noncultivators, then, express the consequences of payment in land in wages *in general*. Each pathway in Figure 1.2 and 1.3, however, represents a possible independent cause of political behavior, and each pathway may be influenced not only by the degree of dependence on land as a source of income but also by exogenous variables other than land. The complete causal model is therefore contained in the paths of Figures 1.2 and 1.3, not in the summary relationships of Figure 1.1, which simply restates the beginning and end of the causal chains in Figures 1.2 and 1.3 and shows both the income sources and the ultimate political consequences without specifying the intervening causal linkages.

Each of the cells in Figure 1.1 represents a combination of a particular pair of values on two different pairs of dichotomous variables. The upper half of each cell shows a representative type of agricultural organization defined by a combination of income sources for the upper and lower classes. The commercial hacienda, for example, may be conceived of as an agricultural organization which pays its labor force in land rights and supports an economically backward upper class dependent on land as its only source of income. The designation "commercial hacienda" is therefore placed in the cell formed by the intersection of land as the upper-class income source and land as the lower-class income source. Similarly combinations of upper- and lower-class income sources are represented by the other types of agricultural organization listed in the upper halves of the other three cells of the figure. The lower half of each cell describes the form of social movement which might be expected given a combination of the upper- and lower-class political behavior described in the headings for that cell. The social movement is conceived of as the outcome of the combination of the class conflict behavior of both cultivators and noncultivators created by the causal chains of Figures 1.2 and 1.3. For example, according to Figure 1.2, payment in land leads to noncultivator behavior which tends to focus conflict on the political control of property, and payment of noncultivators in land, according to Figure 1.3, leads to political passivity on the part of cultivators. The interaction of these two forms of political behavior should under normal circumstances lead to upper-class dominance and lower-class submission, although if conflict were to break out, it would be politicized and challenge the fundamental institutions of property itself.

The types of social movement expected for each cell can be inferred from logical combinations of the political characteristics associated with the corresponding income source for the row and column of that cell. Particular combinations of political behavior of cultivators and noncultivators are considered to lead to each of the major forms of social movements shown in the lower halves of each cell—revolt, reform, or revolution. Figures 1.1 to 1.3 do not, of course, explain how the political characteristics of the upper and lower classes interact to produce these movements, nor do they even define the various types of movements. Both of these problems require a separate examination of each of the cells of the fourfold table of Figure 1.1. There are four combinations of noncultivator and cultivator incomes sources which represent the exogenous variables in the theory: land and land, capital and land, capital and wages, and land and wages. Since each income variable (and therefore necessarily the corresponding political variable) is a dichotomy based on a variable with some continuous properties, it is also necessary to consider variations in the economic and political consequences of various types of agricultural organization within each of the four major combinations of income sources. Clearly, for example, within the broad category of noncultivators dependent on industrial capital some have vastly greater amounts of capital than others and therefore should display the economic and political consequences of capital income described in hypotheses 1 to 3 to a much greater extent than poorer capitalists who may draw some income from the land. Figure 1.1 is therefore to be considered a guide to the major patterns of interaction and thus the major patterns of rural class conflict. The specific predictions about both rural class conflict and social movements among cultivators require consideration of particular combinations of economic and political behavior within these broad categories and therefore depend on the specific causal chains expressed in hypotheses 1 to 6. The set of predictions for each of the major combinations of income sources will, however, be considered separately.

LAND AND LAND: THE AGRARIAN REVOLT

The combination of the upper and the lower agricultural classes drawing their income exclusively from land is characteristic of the commercial hacienda as described by Stinchcombe and Wolf and Mintz, as well as a number of closely related organizational forms. The *engenho* plantation of the Brazilian northeast as described by Wagley and Harris[54] clearly follows this pattern. Although sugar workers were paid wages, they remained largely dependent on subsistence plots on the estate or in the backlands. The closer the Brazilian sugar plantations resembled the dominant *usina* type, of course, the less the dependence of both classes on the land, and the more income sources were based on wages and industrial capital. The coffee *fincas* of Central America are seldom worked by the bound laborers characteristic of the commercial hacienda.[55] Instead they rely on small peasant subsistence farmers with inadequate land who work as daily wage laborers on the coffee estates. The income earned is a supplement to primary subsistence production, so the lower class is dependent on land rather than wages. The estate organization is primitive and seldom involves expensive processing machinery or corporate capital, so that the upper class is also dependent on income from land. A combination of small independent cultivators and large estates in close proximity may produce the same kind of class relations. The social and economic life of the community is usually dominated by the large estates. Even though the independent small holders do not formally work for wages or pay labor dues to the estates, they generally pay taxes or other forms of indirect tribute and are usually involved in land disputes with the estate owners. As long as one or the other of the two groups is involved in export production, the minimum theoretical criteria are satisfied. In this case the large estate and the small holdings would probably

---

[54] Wagley and Harris, "Subcultures."
[55] Robert C. West and John Augelli, *Middle America: Its Lands and Peoples*, (Englewood Cliffs, N.J.: Prentice-Hall, 1966), pp. 378–460.

be described as two different types of agricultural enterprise. This makes no difference as far as the theory is concerned unless the two groups have no economic or political relations with one another. Thus there are a number of systems other than the typical commercial hacienda which are dependent on land as the income source for both classes. For convenience, however, the term "commercial hacienda" will be used to describe any form of agricultural organization in which both classes draw their support from the land.

The nature of rural social movements in such commercial hacienda systems can be inferred from the combined effects of the political behavior of both upper and lower classes dependent on land. A landed upper class leads to intractable, zero-sum, political conflict over landed property and the control of the state. The upper class maintains itself through a system of special privileges based on the repression and disenfranchisement of most of the population. A cultivating class dependent on land is likely to be conservative, unable to organize collectively, and incapable of enforcing political solidarity. In short, it is politically incompetent. The social movements of any cultivating class depend on a collision between any immovable object in the form of the landed upper class and an all too easily resistible force in the form of a disorganized peasantry. The outcome of such a one-sided conflict seems apparent. There will be little or no peasant political activity. This is precisely the conclusion reached by Wolf and Mintz and Stinchcombe in their analyses of the commercial hacienda. It is clear that in any normal situation the overmatched peasants will face impossible odds. Commercial hacienda systems in Latin America have in fact survived for centuries with little apparent opposition. This apparent stability, however, has been purchased at considerable cost. Gerrit Huizer's study of peasant organization in El Salvador provides an illustration of the factors promoting stability in commercial hacienda systems.[56] In 1932 the world depression reached El Salvador and severely weakened the landed aristocracy. Sixty thousand peasants rose in rebellion and attacked the established system of landed property. The result was the slaughter of between 15,000 and 30,000 peasants and the immediate restoration of political stability. To insure that no similar situation would confront it in the future, the El Salvadorian landed elite passed a law making it a crime for more than five people to gather in any rural place for any purpose. Today El Salvadorian peasants are extremely reluctant to speak of the rebellion, although Huizer points out it is well remembered by those who would talk about it. While the personal ties between lord and peasant on the commercial hacienda sometimes encourage the notion that the system is based on reciprocal ties of organic solidarity, the slaughter in El Salvador should be a reminder that the commercial hacienda rests fundamentally on upper-class terrorism.

Although the combined political characteristics of upper and lower classes dependent on land seem to suggest that few rebellions of any kind should take

---

[56] Gerrit Huizer, *The Revolutionary Potential of Peasants in Latin America* (Lexington, Mass.: Heath, 1972), p. 27.

place, periodic uprisings have been a constant part of manorial economies from the German peasant wars to the Bolivian revolution of 1952. In addition, small-scale land invasions are a perennial problem in any system combining landed estates and a land-starved peasantry. When the revolts do occur, they are focused on just those issues specified by the theory—the control and distribution of property in land. Large-scale revolts seem to contradict the principle that peasants should lack the coherent political organization necessary to oppose the landlords. The conditions under which these revolts occur, however, indicate that no real contradiction exists. Peasant rebellions in commercial hacienda systems depend on the weakening of the repressive power of the landed aristocracy, the introduction of organizational strength from outside the peasant community, or both. As long as the aristocracy is willing and able to use force, it will be able to repress all but the strongest peasant movements. Strong political organization, however, cannot form in a competitive peasant subsistence economy. Political organization must depend on other forms of economic organization or on interest groups outside the peasant economy. The upper class is divided by its own predatory land acquisitions, and many of the small estate owners may find that more powerful neighbors are willing to take advantage of peasant unrest. Second, aristocracies are not known for their dedication to the work ethic. Their propensity for conspicuous consumption rather than asceticism and investment may lead them to economic ruin. Such weaknesses, of course, affect only individual members of the landed class, not the class as a whole. They may create localized peasant unrest but hardly major revolts. The landed aristocracy, however, may be threatened as a class by the withdrawal of its military power. Such sudden power deflations frequently occur after losses in major wars. Wolf argues that Russian defeats in World War I critically weakened the landed elite and made the peasant phase of the Russian Revolution possible.[57] Gerrit Huizer points out that the defeat of Bolivia in the Chaco war with Paraguay undermined the strength of the Bolivian landed elite and was therefore a contributing factor in the peasant revolt of 1952–53.[58] Similarly, landed upper classes supported by colonial powers may suddenly find themselves deprived of military backing after independence. Rene Lemarchand suggests that the end of Belgian rule in Rwanda was a critical factor in the overthrow of the Tutsi overlords by their Hutu serfs.[59] Such a sudden loss of military support not only limits upper-class terrorism but also dramatically changes the economic constraints on the peasantry. Since the competitive, conservative world of the peasant was in large part created by a predatory upper class, its removal makes rapid peasant mobilization possible. Such organization may be relatively short lived. Many peasant revolts which occur when a landed upper class has been critically weakened are little more than simultaneous land rushes by thousands of peasants bent on obtaining land

[57] Wolf, *Peasant Wars*, pp. 290–291.
[58] Huizer, *Revolutionary Potential*, pp. 88–89.
[59] Lemarchand, *Rwanda*, pp. 170–171.

that they may legally regard as theirs. Once this objective has been attained, the conditions of small commercial producers begin to exert a centrifugal influence on the movement, and it may once again relapse into political apathy. Once the agricultural workers in the commercial hacienda system have obtained land, they rapidly lose interest in politics. Even after the landed class has been weakened to the point that it can be liquidated by widespread peasant land seizures, the peasants themselves still lack the internal political organization to seize state power. Thus the form of social movement most common in the commercial hacienda system might be best described as an agrarian revolt—a short, intense movement aimed at seizing land but lacking long-run political objectives.

The balance of terror on which the commercial hacienda system rests can also be upset by political organization introduced into the peasant community from the outside. James Petras and Maurice Zeitlin, for example, have demonstrated that peasant radicalism in Chile was most pronounced in areas closest to mining centers, where strong left-wing unions could provide the organizational base the peasants lacked.[60] Even religious organizations may sometimes provide the organizational framework for conservative peasant movements. During the peasant movement in Pernambuco between 1960 and 1964, the Catholic church organised its own peasant syndicates.[61] Usually, however, the outside organization is provided by a socialist or reform political party. This party not only may provide the organizational framework the peasants lack but in addition may undermine the landlord's control over the political system. Thus it can eliminate both restraints on peasant political participation simultaneously. John Powell describes an example of such a peasant movement introduced from above in Venezuela.[62] In 1945 Rómulo Betancourt seized power in a coup d'état and established a regime based on the reformist Acción Democrática (AD) political party. The party drew its basic support from urban labor unions and intellectuals. Nevertheless the party established a peasant affiliate and set out to organize the countryside. Although the initial organizational attempt was cut short in 1948 by another coup, Betancourt returned to power in 1958, announced a dramatic land reform program, and again began organizing peasant syndicates. The organizational framework of the Venezuelan peasant movement was therefore provided not by the peasants themselves, but by an urban-based political party. Peasant political interests, however, remained focused on land, and small farmers with insufficient land remained the most politically active followers of the movement.[63]

Gerrit Huizer points out that a similar seizure of government power by a radical party was a necessary precondition for peasant land seizures during the

[60] James Petras and Maurice Zeitlin, "Miners and Agrarian Radicalism," *American Sociological Review*, 32 (August 1967), 578–586.
[61] Cynthia N. Hewitt, "Brazil: The Peasant Movement in Pernambuco, 1961–1964," in Landsberger, *Peasant Movements*, pp. 392–394.
[62] John Powell, "Venezuela: The Peasant Union Movement," in Landsberger, *Peasant Movements*, pp. 62–100.
[63] *Ibid.*

Bolivian revolution. Although peasant syndicates had been formed as early as 1936, they were generally repressed by landlord-dominated regimes. In the 1940s the Movimiento Nacional Revolucionaria (MNR), a leftist party which drew its support from tin miners and disaffected intellectuals, began organizing peasant syndicates. These peasant organizations were crushed almost as fast as they could be organized and the leaders sent to jungle prison camps. In 1952 the MNR, aided by armed miners and the defection of the national police, managed to seize power in La Paz. After a brief pause to determine the intentions of the new regime, the peasants acted. Guided by MNR activists, the Bolivian peasantry destroyed the entire system of landed estates in less than a year and a half of concentrated land invasions. Landlords fled to the cities, and most of the countryside passed into the hands of the peasants. The control of the central government by socialist or reformist parties seems in fact to be a necessary condition for a peasant revolt. Peasant movements have been associated with socialist or reformist political parties not only in Venezuela and Bolivia, but in Guatemala, Brazil, Chile, Mexico, and Peru.[64] Communist parties on the other hand have been relatively unsuccessful in organizing peasants in commercial hacienda systems. The peasants' dedication to private property in land makes them suspicious of parties threatening the abolition of all private property. The frequency of agrarian revolts in commercial hacienda systems does not alter the basic principles governing the behavior of upper and lower classes dependent on income from land. When successful peasant movements have taken place, they have been aided by socialist or reform parties that played an important role in both organizing the peasantry and neutralizing the power of the landed aristocracy. The peasants themselves before or after the revolution remain divided by the conditions of small cultivators, although the bitterness of economic competition may be lessened by the departure of the landlords. Nevertheless, the absence of the agrarian upper class allows the peasant to become a commercial farmer. Since he controls his own land, investments in permanent improvements will benefit him, not the landlord. Since he no longer pays labor dues, he can devote more time to his own plot. The size of his plot has usually increased to a practical size through the division of the lord's land. Thus the peasant is on his way to becoming a commercial farmer. The political consequences of this economic change, however, are likely to be slight. Commercial small holders, like subsistence peasants, are unlikely to form strong political organizations. Thus the peasant is unlikely to form a coherent political force either before or after an agrarian revolt.

The tactics and goals of a peasant revolt are paradoxically determined not by the economic circumstances of the peasant, but by the political behavior of the landed upper class. This class depends directly or indirectly on land-starved laborers or small farmers for its labor, expands its income through extralegal land seizures, and discourages improvements in agricultural tech-

---

[64] For descriptions of these movements see Huizer, *Revolutionary Potential*, p. 88–95, and Landsberger, *Peasant Movements*, *passim*.

nology which would increase total agricultural income. Thus when peasants do act, the only way in which they can improve their economic position is through the seizure of the lord's lands. The intransigence of the landed upper class and its inability to make economic concessions limits conflict to disputes over property. Thus the actions of landed estate cultivators are invariably focused on the redistribution of property. By the circumstances of upper-class control the only means at the disposal of the cultivators are illegal land seizures. The land seizures, in turn, may destroy the rural class structure and end the political power of the landed upper class. The acquisition of additional land, not the change of the political system, is the ultimate objective of cultivators who draw their income from the land. In fact the peasants are seldom the beneficiaries of the political changes they set in motion. It was reform or socialist parties that provided the political organization and opposition to the landed elite that the peasants themselves could not sustain. It is, therefore, usually those parties that fill the political vacuum left by the departure of the landlords. The characteristic forms of political behavior in systems in which both the upper classes and the lower classes are dependent on income from land are, alternatively, political apathy or agrarian revolt. The apathy of the peasant as described by Wolf and Mintz and Stinchcombe may persist for relatively long periods of time and consequently lead to the mistaken conclusion that the landed estate is free of political tension. The political consequences of the landed estate described in the theoretical propositions above suggest that an agrarian revolt is likely whenever the upper class is weak or the lower class can obtain organizational support. It is agrarian because the presence of a landed upper class focuses conflict on the distribution of landed property, and a revolt because moderate action will be repressed and revolutionary action is restrained by the political weakness of the peasants.

CAPITAL AND LAND: THE REFORM COMMODITY MOVEMENT

This combination differs from the previous one only in the change of income source for the upper class. The cultivating class remains dependent on land as its principal source of income, but the upper class is now dependent on commercial capital rather than land. This combination of income sources is characteristic of a variety of small holding systems from peasant subsistence plots producing a supplementary cash crop to commercial capitalist farms. Since the income source of the cultivators is the same as in the previous case, cultivator political behavior should also be similar. Cultivating classes dependent on land are politically conservative and unable to form strong political organizations based on class solidarity. This principle is as true in small holding systems as it was in commercial hacienda systems. Therefore small holders' political organizations should be weak and dependent on outside political parties and interest groups. In fact the instability and transience of small holders' political organizations have long been recognized. Mancur Olson remarks that "the most striking fact about the political organization of farmers in the United States is that there has been so little. . . . Many farm organizations have come and gone, but only a few have come and stayed." [65] John D. Hicks has pointed out that the populist movement was characterized by numerous splinter parties, and weak political leadership. The Greenback, Free Silver, Farmers Alliance and other populist parties came and went in rapid succession in the American farm belt.[66] Similarly, the electoral politics of commercial farmers have characteristically been more unstable than those of any other American occupational group. Campbell, Converse, Miller, and Stokes, for example, found that the electoral behavior of farmers was more unstable than that of even the least socially integrated and least educated urban occupational groups.[67]

Farmers are too divided by economic competition, internal wealth stratification, and structural isolation to be capable of generating strong political organization from within. Therefore, political organization usually forms around some organizational structure introduced from outside the agrarian community or developed for some other economic purpose. Olson argues that the development of the American Farm Bureau, the strongest and most persistent of all American farmers' movements, was largely the result of the direct efforts of the United States government.[68] According to Olson the Farm Bureau developed out of the agricultural extension program of the United States Department of Agriculture. County agents were hired by the Department to provide farmers with the technical information and educational resources developed in the land grant colleges. Many state governments required that farmers form organizations as an indication of interest before permitting the program to operate in their states. The Farm Bureau thus formed as an effort by individual farmers to take advantage of the valuable assistance of government technical experts. The power of the Bureau waxed and waned with the degree of federal involvement in agriculture and received a new impetus from New Deal farm programs. The county agricultural agent then became not only a source of technical information but the administrator of acreage allotments and subsidy payments. Olson argues that farmers would have been incapable of organizing a powerful lobby like the Farm Bureau in the absence of both the government backing and the strong economic incentives offered to individual farmers.[69]

The activities of the Illinois Farm Bureau as described by Olson indicate another fundamental principle of stable farmers' organizations. They may be

---

[65] Mancur Olson, *The Logic of Collective Action*, (Cambridge: Harvard University Press, 1965), p. 148.

[66] John D. Hicks, *The Populist Revolt* (Minneapolis: University of Minnesota Press, 1931).

[67] Angus Campbell, Philip E. Converse, Warren E. Miller, and Donald E. Stokes, *The American Voter* (New York: Wiley, 1964), p. 211.

[68] Olson, *Collective Action*, pp. 148–152.

[69] *Ibid.*

formed around commercial business organizations of one kind or another. Olson claims that the Illinois Farm Bureau became the nation's strongest because it was essentially a business organization which provided valuable services to farmers who became members. The most important of these benefits was low-cost automobile insurance, which could be provided because of the generally lower accident rates in rural areas. The Farm Bureau, therefore, was as much an insurance company as a political organization, and individual economic incentives rather than political solidarity drew farmers into the organization.[70] Olson contends that stable farmers' movements cannot exist unless they are based on some essentially external organization such as the government or an insurance company.

The alternative organization can also be provided by a political party, as was the case in commercial hacienda systems. Populist parties in the United States have been particularly prone to domination by other political interest groups, and of course were eventually incorporated by the Democratic party in the fusion campaign of William Jennings Bryan. Radical Communist or socialist parties have seldom had much success in overcoming the commercial farmer's devotion to property. Even when they have apparently succeeded, it has usually required the surrender of some of their more radical principles. Conservative parties, however, can provide the framework for a farmers' movement. Unlike the peasant of the commercial hacienda system, the commercial farmer is not typically confronted with a repressive landlord-dominated political regime. Farmers do not need the support of a political party to break the power of the landlords, but simply to provide the political coherence their organizations typically lack. Therefore even reactionary, landlord-dominated parties are capable of organizing small commercial farmers.

Whatever the nature of the external organization providing the framework for the movements of commercial farmers, their target is likely to be the middlemen who constitute the effective agricultural upper class. This conflict may take on political forms, but, given the political behavior of a commercial upper class, it is more likely to involve economic warfare over control of the commodity market. Lipset reports the initial organization of the Saskatchewan wheat farmers began with a wheat pool designed to break the power of the elevator operators and grain brokers.[71] The middlemen responded by trying to outbid the pool for the farmers' wheat, but the pool succeeded until the bottom fell out of the world grain market during the depression. The demands of American populist movements for free coinage of silver or paper currency can be understood as a form of economic warfare designed to lower interest rates by reducing the value of outstanding loans.

The focus of commercial farmers on such economic controversies is a direct result of their relations with an upper class consisting of middlemen and moneylenders. The relations between the two classes are based on jockeying

[70] *Ibid.*, pp. 153–159.
[71] Lipset, *Agrarian Socialism*, pp. 84–90.

for a greater share of the profits from the commodity market, not on an insoluble conflict over a limited amount of property in land. The small farmer already has access to the land, and he can usually count on expanding profits from agriculture technology to insure a gradually increasing income even given the extractions of middlemen. In times of depression, when the proceeds from agriculture shrink drastically, the small farmer may be inclined to support political movements aimed at restricting the middlemen. In general, however, the characteristics of the agricultural upper class tend to focus conflict on control over the commodity market. The upper class does not depend on the theft of property or the political disenfranchisement of the small farmer for its income. The share of profits from agriculture is large enough to permit the middlemen to tolerate some farmer organizations, and the conflict over the proceeds is usually not zero-sum. The typical movement produced by this combination of income sources for the upper and lower classes might be called a reformist commodity movement. It is focused on control of the market in agricultural commodities, does not involve radical demands for the redistribution of property or the overthrow of the state, does not lead to the demise of the agricultural upper class and is usually weakly organized in any case. It is moderate in its tactics and limited in its goals.

The typical social movement of cultivators dependent on land is an agrarian revolt when the upper class is dependent on land, but a reform commodity movement when the upper class draws its income from commercial capital. Since the income source of the lower classes is the same in both cases, this contrast must be a result of the differential effects of upper-class income. The intractable zero-sum conflicts over property which are inherent in the landed estate system generate agrarian revolts which frequently have radical social consequences. The greater flexibility, wealth, and negotiating ability of the upper class dependent on commercial income focus conflict on the market. Since the lower-class political behavior is roughly similar in both cases, it is the income of the upper class which determines whether it will be overthrown in a violent revolt or forced to yield a greater share of profits through an inflated currency.

CAPITAL AND WAGES: THE REFORM LABOR MOVEMENT

This combination of income sources is typical of agricultural organizations employing resident wage laborers and owned either by corporations or by individuals wealthy enough to afford expensive processing machinery. The form of social movements of agricultural workers can be inferred from the combined effects of upper- and lower-class political behavior associated with capital and wages, respectively. This combination of income sources produces a combination of political conflict focused on income from property rather than ownership of property, and strong working-class political organization. A radical, well-organized, class-conscious work force confronts an economically powerful upper class willing and able to bargain and make concessions. The most likely outcome of such a conflict is a reformist social movement focused on limited economic questions. Considering the combined effects of both upper- and lower-class political behavior leads to the apparent paradox of a radical class-conscious proletariat engaging in moderate labor union activities. In conventional Marxist theory such a politicized proletariat should, of course, lead to revolution rather than reform. Although Marx correctly anticipated the effect of homogeneous, concentrated mass labor on radical class consciousness, he underestimated the political acumen and economic power of the upper class. Rather than wait for the inexorable workings of the dialectic to produce their own gravediggers, the industrial upper classes have been willing to deploy their considerable economic power to subvert radical leadership and to divert revolutionary movements into reformist channels. If the declining rate of profit that Marx foresaw in the industrial future had lead to increasing rigidity on the part of the industrial upper class, then a revolutionary outcome might have been possible. Instead the increasing wealth of the industrial classes has made it possible for them to grant economic and political concessions to workers when faced with the unpalatable alternative of revolution. If the agro-industrial upper class of a plantation is willing to grant moderate wage gains in response to union pressure and permit the organization and political enfranchisement of the workers, revolution may seem a desperate and unprofitable action for the workers. The potentially lethal costs of revolution and its potentially large but unpredictable benefits must be weighed against the lower costs, greater certainty, and small gains of moderate reformist action. Thus the typical plantation proletariat has almost without exception chosen the moderate reformist course of bargaining with management over limited bread-and-butter questions. Since in this case, unlike the commercial farm, the labor rather than the commodity market forms the tie between upper and lower class, it is the price of labor which is the central focus of this bargaining. Thus a combination of an industrial upper class dependent on industrial capital and an agricultural working class dependent on wage labor creates a characteristic form of social movement which might be called the reform labor movement. The movement's goals are limited to questions of wages and working conditions, and it demands neither the radical redistribution of property nor the seizure of state power. It will not lead to dictatorship of the proletariat nor even in most cases to the nationalization of plantations. Even though the radical class consciousness of the workers frequently leads to a public commitment to left-wing ideologies, the realities of upper-class economic power almost invariably lead to reformist action.

The reformist labor movement based on a strong working-class solidarity and political organization was apparent in Steward's description of Puerto Rican sugar plantations. These characteristics, however, were not to be found in plantation systems according to Stinchcombe, who argued that plantation workers were either politically apathetic or extremist. Unfortunately for Stinchcombe most studies of corporate plantations or individually owned estates support the predictions of the theory of rural class relations and the observations of Steward. Strong class-based unions and worker political movements with reformist goals are found in the banana plantations of Central America,[72] in the sugar plantations of the Caribbean and lowland South America,[73] in the tea plantations of India, Ceylon, and Pakistan,[74] and in the sisal estates of Haiti and Tanzania.[75] There is, however, one striking exception to the predictions of the theory—the behavior of rubber plantation workers in Malaya. Immediately after Japanese occupation forces withdrew from Malaya at the end of World War II, a strong Communist union movement developed on the rubber estates and other plantations of Malaya. The rubber workers were the largest single occupational group in Malaya, and they formed the heart of the Pan-Malayan Federation of Trade Unions. The union in turn was dominated by the Malayan Communist Party. Initially the union's behavior seemed to follow precisely the predictions of the theoretical model. Even though the union was based on intense class solidarity, strong political organization, and a radical Communist ideology, it limited its initial actions to strikes aimed at union recognition and wage increase. Between 1945 and 1948 the union appeared to behave in conventional trade union fashion and concentrated on organizing other groups of workers and protecting the wage increases it had won. In mid-1948, however, the Malayan Communist party and most of the leadership of the Pan-Malayan Federation of Trade Unions called for a general strike, disappeared into the jungle, established liberated zones, and began a general insurrection aimed at expelling the British colonialists and seizing the export economy. While there is a debate about the origins of this decision, there is no doubt about the involvement of the plantation laborers, the labor union, or the Communist party or the reality of insurrection itself.

The revolutionary movement of the Malayan plantation workers seems to be a major exception to the predictions of the model of rural class conflict.

[72] Stacy May and Galo Plaza, *The United Fruit Company in Latin America* (Washington: National Planning Association, 1958).

[73] For Cuba see Lowry Nelson, *Rural Cuba* (Minneapolis: University of Minnesota Press, 1950); for Jamaica and the Caribbean generally, George L. Beckford, *Persistent Poverty* (New York: Oxford University Press, 1972); for British Guiana (Guyana), Raymend T. Smith, *British Guiana* (London: Oxford University Press, 1962); for Brazil, Wagely and Harris, "Subcultures," and Hutchinson, *Village and Plantation Life*; and for Peru, Solomon Miller, "The Hacienda and the Plantation in Northern Peru" (Ph.D. dissertation, Columbia University, 1964).

[74] International Federation of Plantation, Agricultural and Allied Workers, *Economic Surveys*, no. 1, *Tea*, (Brussels, 1960). Includes information on tea plantations in India, Ceylon, Pakistan, and East Africa.

[75] Tanzania: C. W. Guillebaud, *An Economic Survey of the Sisal Industry of Tanganyika* (Welwyn, England: Tanganyika Sisal Growers Association, 1958). Haiti: West and Augelli, *Middle America*, pp. 152–164.

Actually the special circumstances of the Malayan rubber economy created economic conditions which were quite unlike those in most industrial plantations. Rubber is in fact a marginal plantation crop and is frequently grown by small holders as well as by corporate plantations. The social organization of a rubber estate is far removed from the factory form of the typical plantation. Perhaps the atypical quality of rubber plantations can be best illustrated by a comparison of the rubber plantations of Malaya with the tea plantations of Ceylon. Superficially these two agricultural export economies shared many characteristics. Both were economically dependent on a single major crop, both were dominated by plantations owned by corporations based in the United Kingdom, and both were enclave economies in the midst of large populations of subsistence peasants engaged in rice cultivation. Both Malaya and Ceylon were British colonies, and in both cases the government was largely an extension of the planters' association of the dominant crop. Plantations in both systems were dependent on imported Tamil labor from southeast India, although in Malaya the Tamils were supplemented by imported Chinese laborers. In both cases the estate labor force was of a different religious and national background than the subsistence population and the plantation owners were, of course, also from a different religious and national group. The administration of the plantations was remarkably similar in the two colonies. In fact the rubber estate owners had originally migrated from the tea economy of Ceylon and brought their Tamil and Sinhalese administrators with them. In both cases the estates were isolated residential communities cut off from one another and from the indigenous subsistence population. In both cases Crown lands, or colonial land privileges, played a role in the establishment of the estate systems. In Ceylon, however, there was no Communist insurrection after World War II. There was instead a reformist labor movement typical of plantation economies.

In regard to the economic characteristics critical for upper-class political behavior the two systems are also at opposite ends of the plantation continuum. The propositions outlined above suggested that three economic characteristics of industrial upper classes were critical in determining their political behavior: (1) their economic and market strength including their control over exports and their possession of industrial capital, (2) their dependence on wage rather than servile labor, and (3) the constantly expanding incomes from agriculture, which are a result of advances in agro-industrial technology. It is these three characteristics which determine the flexible behavior of the industrial upper classes in plantation systems. The weaker each of these tendencies, the more the behavior of the plantation owner resembles that of the owner of the landed estate. That is, the more he must depend on legal or extralegal force to defend his estate and recruit labor, the less he can tolerate organization on the part of his laborers and the smaller the wage concessions he can make to his workers. The weaker these three tendencies, the greater the probability of the insoluble political conflicts characteristic of the landed estates. In each of the three characteristics the Ceylon tea plantations and the Malaya rubber plantations were at opposite extremes. Thus the theory predicts that their political behavior should be similarly opposed. Consider each of the propositions in turn:

1. Control of Industrial Processing Machinery and the Export Market The production parameters of tea and rubber require distinctly different forms of agricultural organization. Tea is one of the crops perhaps best suited to central-ized industrial production techniques. This is a result of two factors. First, tea must be processed immediately after it is picked, and processing requires a series of steps which depend on elaborate machinery. The tea must be withered, rolled, graded, and packed before shipment, and in almost all tea estates these pro-cesses are highly mechanized and have been so almost from the beginning of tea production. The typical tea estate usually contains a processing plant which looks like a small suburban factory in light industry. Small holders without pro-cessing equipment must sell their tea immediately to the processors and are in an extremely unfavorable bargaining position. Second, tea not only makes con-tinuous harvesting possible but makes it absolutely essential. Tea is actually a tree rather than a bush and therefore must be constantly pruned to keep it growing outward, maximizing its leaf area, rather than upward, maximizing the worthless trunk. Constant attention is necessary for the plant to continue pro-ducing. The harvest must be continuous because the new tea leaves, or "flush," are the most desirable for tea and must be picked in three days before they lose their flavor. If the trees are abandoned for any length of time, they stop producing anything of value. The trees usually require meticulous care and the liberal use of insecticides and fertilizers as well as constant pruning. A stable continuously employed labor force is absolutely essential for a tea estate. The factory can then be kept in continuous operation in coordination with the con-tinual harvest. As a result of these economies of scale, tea production in Ceylon tends to be dominated by large estates. In 1959 only 13 percent of Ceylon's tea was produced by small holders, and most of the rest was produced by British corporations that have traditionally supplied the capital necessary for the manufacturing installations and trees.[76]

Rubber, on the other hand, is also a tree crop in which continuous har-vesting is possible but unlike tea does not require any continuous input of labor. In fact the greater the harvest one year, the lower the harvest the next because of damage to the bark during tapping. It is therefore possible for small holders to easily combine rubber production with their other subsistence activities, tapping when the price is right and ignoring the trees the rest of the time. Also, in contrast with tea, no expensive processing machinery is necessary to process the latex at the estate. A little acid must be added to coagulate the latex, but the sheets can be pounded out with sticks or bare feet and dried in the sun. In Malayan estates these processes are usually carried out with the aid of rolling machines and smoke houses, but these facilities need not be located on the estate or even used at all. During the war in Cambodia, for example, the rubber

---

[76] Donald R. Snodgrass, *Ceylon: An Export Economy in Transition* (Home-wood, Ill.: Irwin, 1966), table A-38.

trade has continued undiminished even though the rubber plantations are under rebel control and the technical and administrative staff fled to Pnompenh. A tacit understanding between the government and the rebels permits the latex to be collected and shipped across government lines; it is then purchased by representatives of the French rubber companies that had previously run the estates. Except for bomb damage to the plantations the system seemed to work as efficiently during the war as it had before.[77]

Since processing machinery is superfluous and continuous harvesting unnecessary, small holders are strong competitors in rubber production. In 1959, for example, more than half of Ceylon's rubber estates were in holdings of less than 100 acres, and a quarter were in holdings of less than 10 acres.[78] In Malaya in 1959 small holders produced 40 percent of total production, and this proportion has remained relatively constant in the postwar period.[79] Thus the owner of a rubber plantation is in a competitive position very different from that of a tea estate owner. Since the economies of scale are much less in rubber, he must find other ways to compete with the family labor and entrepreneurial dedication of the small holder. The small holder is also better able to wait out fluctuations in the rubber market than is the estate owner and, since reduced tapping increases future yields, may actually gain a further competitive edge in production. The rubber plantation owners therefore find themselves in a position similar to that of the owners of landed estates. They must find some system of special privileges to protect their large estate against the more efficient small holder. The competitive position of the tea estate owner, on the other hand, is secure.

The Ceylon tea estates also hold a strong market position in the tea trade. Ceylon typically exports a third of the world's tea and thus has considerable influence on world prices. The major estates are linked in a few large companies and producers' associations, so their economic situation is actually one of oligopolistic control. The demand for tea is highly inelastic since it depends on the widespread caffeine addiction of European peoples. The tea estate owner is in the enviable position of the drug pusher with oligopolistic control of his markets. True enough no one has been seen carrying out a burglary to buy tea, but certainly the drug is at least habit forming. The rubber owner on the other hand is in a considerably weaker market position. First, of course, he must compete with the more efficient small holders. For the Malayan estate owners this means competing not only with their own small holders but with small holders elsewhere in Asia. Second, rubber is an industrial raw material dependent largely on the automobile market and hence subject to the price fluctuations of industrial economies. Most importantly, however, after World War II natural rubber faced competition from synthetic rubber developed in the United States

[77] *New York Times,* Oct. 17, 1972.
[78] Snodgrass, *Ceylon,* table A-38.
[79] Jin-Bee Ooi, *Land, Peoples and Economy in Malaya* (London: Longmans, 1963), p. 214.

during the war. By the time labor unions began to form on a large scale, synthetic rubber was already adding to the considerable competitive problems of the centralized rubber estate. In fact the economic weakness of the large plantations meant that they could not long survive without a colonial or client government which provided the economic environment they desired. As one Malayan union leader pointed out during heated negotiations in 1947, the workers were being used as "fodder to maintain an industry whose economy . . . had been rendered obsolete by world conditions."[80] The intransigence of the rubber planters' association was one element in the breakdown of these negotiations and the eventual end of the reformist labor movement. This intransigence came from the planters' need for political support to compensate for their ineffectual economic position. In 1948 this support came in the form of the continuation of colonial rule and the subjugation of the plantation workers' unions. In Ceylon, by contrast, plantations remained under British control even after independence in 1947, and in fact their immense importance to the economy has forestalled any attempt to nationalize them since. In 1958 a reformist party was elected on a platform promising nationalization. Sixteen years later this election promise has yet to be fulfilled. Given the efficiency, economic importance, and substantial capital requirements of the estate, it is unlikely that it ever will be.

    2. *Free and Servile Labor*   The political privilege of the greatest importance for the continued economic survival of the Malayan rubber estates was their control over indentured immigrant laborers. Although both Ceylon tea estates and Malayan rubber estates depended on imported Tamil labor, the laborers went to Ceylon more or less voluntarily, while they were shipped to Malaya as indentured labor. The difference in part reflects the differences in origins of the two estate systems as well as the different production parameters of tea and rubber. The Tamil labor force in Ceylon was attracted by the coffee boom of the 1830s. By the year 1880 the coffee boom had collapsed, but 200,000 Tamil estate laborers were already resident in Ceylon, and many had brought their families with them.[81] Thus from the late nineteenth century the tea estate relied on a stable labor force and operated in a moderately free labor market. In Malaya, by contrast, rubber estates did not begin on a large scale until the 1920s, and laborers were imported under servile conditions. Tamils were recruited by returned immigrants called *kanganys* who were paid a fixed wage for each day of labor they supplied to the estates. Chinese immigrants were supplied by independent contractors.[82] In both cases the laborer was forced to work off the cost of transportation, recruitment, and lodging before assignment to the estate. Many laborers in fact never worked off their indebtedness and were essentially slave laborers. There was a high rate of return to the

[80] Quoted in M. R. Stenson, *Industrial Conflict in Malaya* (London: Oxford University Press, 1970), p. 185.
[81] Snodgrass, *Ceylon*, p. 25.
[82] Stenson, *Malaya*, pp. 1–10.

country of origin in both cases. The rubber estates had no intention of giving up their privileged access to forced labor after World War II. Unfortunately for them the war had interrupted the source of supply, and the laborers had been freed from the estate discipline during the confused period surrounding the transition from Japanese to British rule. The laborers had no interest whatsoever in returning to the conditions of indentured servitude. The inefficient plantation could hardly survive without it. Consequently conflict between the two groups increasingly focused on control of the government, which, of course, backed the rubber planters in their attempts to reduce the workers to servitude. While the Ceylon tea estate owners had long dealt with wage laborers in an industrial environment, the rubber planters of Malaya created a servile society much like a landed estate.

3. Fixed versus Expanding Incomes   This characteristic of agricultural organization ultimately determines whether political conflict is zero-sum or non-zero sum. If agricultural income expands, then worker movements can be directed into reformist channels by the offering of small wage gains at little cost to the employer. Where income is fixed or declining, such concessions are impossible. In Ceylon not only were the manufacturing installations of the tea estates capable of technological improvements, but the capital resources of the owners made it possible for them to increase productivity through agricultural innovations. Donald Snodgrass points out that productivity in the Ceylon tea industry has risen almost continuously during the postwar period because of new fertilizers and new tea strains developed by the government agricultural experimental station.[83] These increases in productivity made it possible to increase wages. According to Snodgrass, between 1948 and 1951 wages rose 45 percent, although they leveled off after that point.[84] In 1956 the real wage index for Ceylon tea estate laborers was 75 percent above what it was in 1939.[85] Thus the Ceylon estate owners were able to keep the labor movement in reformist channels by providing a gradually increasing standard of living. Actually the greatest problem for the Tamil estate laborers came not from the plantation owners, but from the Sinhalese majority who became increasingly envious of their jobs in the underemployed agrarian economy of Ceylon.

In Malaya, by contrast, not only was there no way in which productivity could be increased by mechanization, but there was little that could be done to affect the yields of the trees. Wages could not be raised without making the inefficient estates even less competitive. After a brief rise in 1946, world rubber prices began to drop, and by 1949 the bottom had fallen out of the market. The introduction of synthetics and the end of military demand, as well as the postwar depression in the United States, all contributed to the precipitate decline. Thus instead of creating incentives for reformist action by increasing wages,

[83] Snodgrass, *Ceylon*, pp. 133–143.
[84] *Ibid.*, pp. 136–137.
[85] International Federation, *Tea*, pp. 46–47.

the plantation owners declared a 20 percent across-the-board wage cut and stepped up their drive against the labor unions.[86] Even reformist labor organization was seen as a threat to their survival. The estate owners called for drastic action against the unions. A representative of the incorporated society of planters called for the strict enforcement of restrictions on labor unions with "ruthless application of the sentences of death, banishment, and particularly flogging." [87] By 1948 the falling rubber prices and the union's militant reaction to the unilateral wage cut had increased the intensity of the planters' campaign for suppression of the union. The killing of three European planters on June 15, 1948, was used as a pretext for increased government intervention. As M. R. Stenson concludes in his analysis of labor conflict in Malaya, with the new government regulations "the essential outlines of the restrictive, paternalist, prewar regime were reestablished." [88] The restrictive prewar system of servile labor was, however, reimposed only after the political confusion of the British reoccupation had permitted strong workers' organizations to form. On rubber plantations located in countries which did not change hands during the war, semiservile labor continued with no interruption. Rubber plantations in Africa maintained servile labor both before and after the war. The laborers on these estates occupy much the same status as serfs on a commercial manor and are consequently unlikely to form strong political organizations. Rubber plantations are therefore not generally likely to lead to revolution or even strong labor movements. It was the political vacuum created by the Japanese withdrawal that permitted the rubber workers to organize. When the planters attempted to reestablish the prewar system, however, the workers were strongly organized and capable of resistance.

Figure 1.4 shows the effects of rubber and tea production on the economic and political behavior of noncultivators in Malaya and Ceylon in terms of hypotheses 1 to 3. This diagram makes clear that the behavior of a noncultivating class dependent on income from rubber estates shares many similarities with the behavior of an upper class dependent on land. The rubber estates owner's limited economic power and competition from small holders make him dependent on political, particularly colonial, protection and therefore resistant to political change. The indentured labor supply of the rubber estates in Malaya leads to the repression of workers' organizations just as did the semiservile labor force of the typical landed estate. Finally the declining profits of rubber production immediately after World War II limited the share of agricultural production which could be given to workers just as the stagnant technology of the landed estate limited worker economic gains. As a result the Malayan rubber estate owners are a distinctly marginal category sharing many of the characteristics of the landed estate, and their overall political behavior, like the behavior of land estate owners, leads to politicized conflict over the property.

[86] Stenson, *Malaya*, pp. 184–185.
[87] *Ibid.*, p. 162.
[88] *Ibid.*, p. 233.

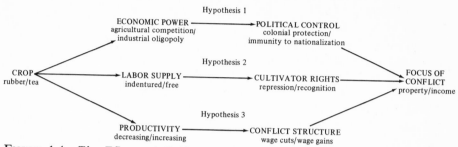

FIGURE 1.4 *The Effects of Rubber and Tea Production on the Economic and Political Behavior of Noncultivators in Malaya and Ceylon*

The Ceylon tea estate owners, on the other hand, have the economic power, the free wage labor, and the increasing productivity that the Malayan rubber estates lack, and as Figure 1.4 indicates, these economic characteristics lead to immunity to political change, including nationalization, recognition of limited rights for works, and gradually increasing wages. Collectively these characteristics shift conflict from politics to economics and from the control of property to the distribution of income from property. The comparison of Ceylon and Malaya therefore indicates that the greater the capitalization of the plantation, the more flexible its administration, and that the lesser the capitalization, the more noncultivator behavior resembles the rigidity of the landed estate. It also indicates that hypotheses 1 to 3 are essential in understanding political behavior within the broad interaction categories of Figure 1.1.

In Malaya, although not in most other world rubber export sectors, the politically inflexible estate owners were confronted with a well-organized class-conscious plantation workers' union which had coalesced during the power vacuum created by the Japanese withdrawal. With all reformist avenues cut off by the unyielding position of the rubber estate owners, the workers turned to revolt. In Malaya, then, the classic Marxian conditions seem to be realized. A radical class-conscious proletariat faced a rigid unyielding bourgeoisie burdened with a declining rate of profit. The fact that the proletariat and the bourgeoisie faced one another in a rural setting does not change the nature of Marx's prediction of class-based revolution. Thus the apparent exception of Malaya actually supports the underlying principles governing the political behavior of upper and lower agricultural classes. Revolutionary movements are most likely to occur when cultivators can form strong, radical, and cohesive political organizations, but noncultivators are unable to grant political and economic concessions because they must rely on legal or extralegal force to maintain their position. With the exception of Malaya this combination of upper- and lower-class political characteristics is seldom found in plantation environments. It is, however, considerabily more common in the fourth and remaining combination of income sources in Figure 1.1.

LAND AND WAGES: AGRARIAN REVOLUTION

The form of social movement expected from this income combination can be inferred from the combined effects of upper- and lower-class political behavior dependent on the income sources for the corresponding row and column for this cell in the diagram in Figure 1.1. The social movements of cultivators will therefore be determined by the conflict between a radical, well-organized, class-conscious work force and an upper class unable and unwilling to grant any political or economic concession and dependent on legal or extralegal force for its economic survival. This combination of upper- and lower-class characteristics is precisely the same as in the Malayan rubber estates. The political consequences too are likely to be similar: a powerful revolutionary movement focused on wrenching control of both landed property and political power from a violent and unyielding upper class. The economic weakness of the upper class leads it to close off all avenues of social action except violent resistance. In contrast to the situation in a commercial hacienda system, however, the upper class is not opposed by a divided and politically incompetent mass of bound laborers. Instead it typically faces a powerful worker organization which has the incentive to attack the system of special privileges that supports the landlords and the political coherence to seize the state power that maintains those privileges. The typical form of social movement in systems dependent on landed property and wage labor is revolutionary. Such movements involve not only violent conflict over landed property and direct attack on the rural stratification system, but also a coherent political effort to seize control of the state by force. Since neither party is likely to compromise and both usually command considerable military power, long guerilla wars are the likely result. None of the other combinations of upper and lower income sources has this potential for revolutionary war. In landed estates where laborers are dependent on land there is violent conflict over property, but the conflict is likely to be sporadic, short lived, and focused on the redistribution of land, not the seizure of the state. In most industrial plantation systems a strong, cohesive, radical workers' political organization is capable of making demands on the upper class. The upper class, however, is dependent on its economic, not its political power and is therefore able to compromise and begrudgingly grant small gains to the workers. The presence of an economically powerful upper class diverts the powerful plantation workers' organizations into conventional trade union activities such as strikes over wage demands. The combination of a commercial upper class and a working class dependent on land characteristic of small holding systems possesses neither intense conflicts over property *nor* cohesive working-class organizations. They therefore tend to be the most stable of all systems. They do not lead to revolt, to revolution, or even to particularly powerful reform movements. It is only when strong working-class political organizations is combined with a weak upper class dependent on force that revolution is likely. This combination occurred in Malayan rubber plantations but is atypical of world plantation systems. It is, however, typical of many though not all landed estates dependent on wage labor.

There are two distinct forms of agricultural organization which combine a landed upper class and a working class dependent on wage labor, and each has different consequences for revolutionary movements of agricultural workers. Both sharecropping systems and landed estates dependent on migratory wage labor combine a landed upper class and wage laborers. Although both types of systems may under some conditions create powerful cultivator political organizations, the basis of lower-class solidarity is dramatically different in the two systems. In sharecropping systems the basis of group solidarity is economic class status, and the corresponding revolutionary movements tend to be based on socialist or Communist ideologies. In landed estate systems dependent on migratory wage labor the work force is only partly dependent on wages for its support. Since it must return to subsistence agriculture for the off season, it remains dependent on the traditional peasant or tribal village. When revolutionary movements do form in such systems, they are therefore likely to combine both wage laborers and traditional communal organizations. The ideology uniting these disparate elements cannot be based on class but can be based on national or racial hatred of a settler class. Settler-owned estates affect not only the wage laborers but the traditional subsistence cultivators they frequently displace. Thus revolutionary movements in migratory wage labor estate systems are likely to involve coalitions based on communal ties. The differences between the two forms of movement are fundamentally a result of the way in which the market affects the traditional community. In sharecropping systems the traditional upper class often become the new landed elite in the export economy. In the migratory estate it is usually foreign settlers who form the landed elite, and consequently both workers and the traditional landed elite are likely to suffer. The differential effects of the market on the traditional structure in the two systems thus leads to fundamentally different forms of revolution.

SHARECROPPING AND REVOLUTIONARY SOCIALISM   Sharecropping systems frequently develop through the gradual growth of markets in stratified peasant societies. The traditional agrarian upper class responds to new urban and export markets by intensifying pressures on the peasantry for higher rates of production or forcing the peasants to adopt new crops valuable in the export markets. The landlord then claims the export crop and pays his tenant with a share of what he himself has produced. In a precommercial society with few market outlets, the extractions of the landlord are usually limited to what he and his retine can consume. When an export market becomes available, however, the demands of the landlord become almost limitless. The market therefore progressively undermines the paternalistic relationship between landlord and tenant and converts it into a commercial contract based on a calculated division of the peasant's surplus. The contract is one sided, however, since only the landlord has the power to enforce its terms, and consequently his share tends to be substantial and the position of the tenant precarious. Such systems are particularly common in labor-intensive annual crops. In such crops there is usually nothing to be gained from processing at the point of production, and brief intense inputs of labor are required during planting and harvesting. These crops are perfectly suited to production by small holders and cannot be produced competitively on large estates in free market situations. The agricultural upper class therefore must manipulate the political system to gain economic advantage. Sharecroppers have virtually no legal rights in disputes with landlords and can be dismissed at any time. They are usually politically disenfranchised, since the landlord could not long survive a government dominated by the more numerous sharecroppers. The upper-class control over the land rests on special access to the courts and the extralegal maneuvers customary in landed estate systems. The sum of the proceeds of the enterprise is fixed, since neither landlord nor tenant has any incentive for investing in new technology. The economic characteristics of the landlord in the sharecropping system lead to the now familiar pattern of intractable zero-sum conflict over landed property.

The sharecropper resembles the plantation wage laborer in the three economic characteristics critical for his political behavior—weak ties to the land, working-class occupational homogeneity, and work group interdependence. The sharecropper has no legal right to the land and may not even have a stable claim to occupy it in practice. In fact, instability of tenure is chronic in many sharecropping systems. In preindependence Burma farmers frequently went from one plot to another, each time becoming indebted to Indian banking houses and each time losing their lands through bankruptcy.[89] In Vietnam tenant refugees unable to meet the extractions of the landlord or pay off the loans he had advanced made up a large part of the population of the frontier regions along the Cambodian border.[90] In India the sharecropper is formally a "tenant at will" and can be dismissed any time the landlord wishes.[91] Thus sharecroppers are generally reduced to absolutely minimal ties to the land which they work.

The extractions of landlords, middlemen, and moneylenders usually reduce most sharecroppers to the same low level of wages. It is impossible to accumulate property in such systems, and any property which is accumulated usually must be mortgaged to pay off debts. Whatever the sharecropper produces in addition

89 Erich H. Jacoby, *Agrarian Unrest in Southeast Asia*, (New York: Columbia University Press, 1959), pp. 78–88.
90 Pierre Gourou, *Soil Utilization in French Indochina* (New York: Institute of Pacific Relations, 1945), pp. 346–347.
91 Donald S. Zagoria, "The Ecology of Peasant Communism in India," *American Political Science Review*, 65 (March 1971), 144–160.

to his normal crop will be taken by the landlord. Whatever improvement he makes in his land will only raise its market value, increase his rents, and make his eviction more likely. The improvements will benefit the landlord and the next tenant. Individual mobility in such a system is an absurdity and economic initiative a waste of time. The only way in which economic gains can be made is by limiting the landlord's extractions. This fact creates a strong incentive for collective political action.

Finally, sharecroppers are usually more interdependent than other kinds of small cultivators. Their production affects the landlord's expectations about the production of others, and therefore group pressure may be exerted to hold back part of the harvest. Also, sharecroppers are usually found in areas of extremely high land values where cultivation is intense and population density high. Donald Zagoria reports that in India areas of high population density were also areas of high rates of tenancy and suggests that the high population density might create the kind of concentration found in some industrial organizations.[92] Zagoria also notes that sharecropping systems are also found in systems of irrigated cultivation, particularly of rice. In fact, irrigated wet rice sharecropping is the dominant form of agricultural production in much of Southeast Asia. There are in fact direct economic connections between irrigation, population density, and sharecropping. High population densities can only be supported if land is intensively cultivated. In most areas of poor tropical soils intensive cultivation can only be accomplished through irrigated agriculture. Irrigation works, in turn, increase the value of the land, making its possession more desirable for the landlords. These economic characteristics are particularly pronounced in rice cultivation. Clifford Geertz has provided a detailed description of the ecology of rice production in Indonesia which suggests its profound consequences for economic and social organiaztion.[93] Rice is grown not in the soil, but in a biotic medium suspended in irrigation water. The techniques of paddy cultivation (called *sawah* in Indonesia) resemble those of modern experimental hydroponics rather than traditional agriculture. The rice paddy is actually a tank for holding the nutrient medium in which rice grows, and the irrigation systems are the pipeline by which the nutrients are transported. In Indonesia these characteristics have permitted the almost indefinite expansion of rice production on a relatively constant area by ever more elaborate terracing and paddy construction in a process Geertz calls "agricultural involution."

Water rather than soil is therefore the critical element in wet rice production, and water is considerably more subject to human control than is physical terrain. As Karl Wittfogel has pointed out, however, the control and distribution of irrigation water require coordinated action which is in general beyond the resources of individual farmers or even entire villages.[94] In most areas of wet

---

[92] *Ibid.*
[93] Geertz, *Involution*, pp. 28–37.
[94] Karl Wittfogel, *Oriental Despotism* (New Haven, Conn.: Yale University Press, 1957), pp. 22–29.

rice cultivation cooperative artificial irrigation works are poorly developed, and in much of monsoon Asia the level of water in paddies is determined almost entirely by rainfall. This is true even in Indonesia, where less than half the Java rice fields have anything more than the most primitive artificial irrigation works. The barriers to artificial irrigation are not only the absence of organizational resources but frequently the resistance of large landowners who fear that canals will be dug across their lands and that their own short-run economic welfare will be sacrificed for the good of others. If such resistance can be overcome, however, the rewards of artificial irrigation in terms of increased and more regular yields are considerable, so that the possibility of irrigation greatly increases incentives for collective action. In systems such as Vietnam where landlords are a substantial barrier to collective irrigation, political organizations capable of eliminating the landlords immediately obtain a major collective good in the form of artificial irrigation water to distribute to the politically worthy. Artificial irrigation can, however, produce such collective goods only in decentralized systems in which small village farmers, not large estates, benefit from improvements in irrigation. Obviously, if a centralized estate or a plantation employs irrigation extensively, this simply increases the economic power of the estate owner and does not lead to additional incentives for cultivator collective action. Irrigation, then, affects the prospects for cultivator organization differentially, depending on the organization of the agricultural enterprise.

Decentralized sharecropping systems in general and irrigated rice production in particular, however, are likely to create a homogeneous landless peasantry with strong incentives for collective action and intense pressure for group solidarity. These economic characteristics should in turn lead to political radicalism, powerful organizations, and intense class solidarity. Thus an organized class-conscious proletariat is the likely consequence of sharecropping systems. In fact, areas of tenancy have shown a pronounced attraction to left-wing, particularly Communist, ideologies and a surprising potential for powerful political organization. Zagoria reports that those areas of India which have the highest population densities, highest rates of tenancy, and greatest dependence on irrigation also show the highest level of Communist voting.[95] Kerala and West Bengal have long been areas of both wet rice production and rural Communist strength. Similarly the Italian "red belt" in the provinces of Emilia, Tuscany, and Umbria, north of Rome is the area of the highest rates of share tenancy in the country.[96] The area has produced consistent Communist majorities in rural areas since World War II. Unlike the politics of peasants dependent on individual subsistence plots, these political affiliations are internally generated, not introduced by outside urban-based parties. In fact, Mattei Dogan has pointed out that in Italy the rural Communist organization is increasingly responsible for Communist strength in

[95] Zagoria, "Peasant Communism."

[96] Mattei Dogan, "Political Cleavage and Social Stratification in France and Italy," in Seymour Martin Lipset and Stein Rokkan (eds.), *Party Systems and Voter Alignments* (New York: The Free Press, 1967), p. 146.

urban areas, a relationship which reverses the usual pattern of urban-to-rural political influence.[97] The organizational potential of sharecroppers was clearly recognized by Mao Tse-tung in Hunan as early as 1927. Irrigated rice share-croppers were almost entirely responsible for the phenomenal growth of radical peasant associations in Hunan in 1927. Mao reports that more than a million members were recruited by the associations in October and November of 1927 alone.[98] In situations where landlord repression is weakened, sharecroppers are capable of amazing organizational efforts.

The sharecropper therefore shares with the plantation wage laborer a tendency to participate actively in workers' associations and strong Communist parties. The demands of the sharecroppers, however, are unlikely to be limited to the moderate reformist concerns of the plantation wage laborer. The share-cropper confronts not an economically powerful industrial upper class, but a weak landed aristocracy rigidly committed to maintaining its privileged economic position by force. Therefore the strong Communist parties are likely to make radical political and economic demands. At minimum these demands include the expropriation of the landlords and the distribution of their lands, at maximum the revolutionary overthrow of the state which supports landed property. The two demands are often intertwined, since the landlords are not likely to give up their lands without a fight. Revolutionary Communist movements in rural areas have been almost exclusively associated with sharecropping in general and irri-gated rice sharecropping in particular. Edward Mitchell has demonstrated that Hukbalahap activity in central Luzon is concentrated in areas of rice share-cropping,[99] Zagoria demonstrated a correlation between wet rice sharecropping and the rural Communist vote in India, and as will be demonstrated in Chapter 5, the Communist revolution in Vietnam had its origin in commercial, irrigated, rice sharecropping areas of the Mekong delta. The intense interdependence created by community control of irrigation technology and the high rates of tenancy associated with rice cultivation are particularly likely to lead to revolu-tionary socialist movements.

There is, however, one notable exception to this general association between sharecropping and Communist revolution. The cotton plantations of the Ameri-can South are based almost exclusively on sharecropping, yet they have been remarkably resistant to any form of political organization. During the depression the Southern Tenant Farm Workers Union made a determined and initially successful effort at unionization based on the moderate socialism of H. L. Mitchell. The attempt was crushed, and the tenants, both black and white, relapsed into their former apathy.[100] This phenomenon seems hardly to be the

[97] *Ibid.*, p. 187.

[98] Mao Tse-tung, *Report on an Investigation of the Peasant Movement in Hunan* (Peking: Foreign Language Press, 1967), p. 17.

[99] Edward J. Mitchell, "Some Econometrics of the Huk Rebellion," *American Political Science Review*, 63 (December 1969), 1159–1171.

[100] Vera Rony, "Sorrow Song in Black and White," *New South* (Summer 1967).

result of the special problems created by racial divisions in the South. In Egypt, Syria, and Turkey cotton cultivation is also organized in sharecropping systems and workers show similar patterns of political apathy. It seems that it must be some feature of cotton sharecropping generally rather than the peculiar cultural circumstances of the southern United States which accounts for the passivity of Southern plantation workers.

One contrast is immediately apparent when the cotton sharecropping systems are contrasted with the revolutionary irrigated rice sharecropping systems. Cotton sharecropping is almost always organized in centralized estates as it is in the American South. Rice sharecropping, on the other hand, is almost invariably decentralized. Individual sharecroppers work their own plots, and the lands of a given owner may be scattered across several villages or even provinces. The landowner provides no centralized direction or control. In cotton production the lands of sharecroppers are consolidated and the plots may be worked as a unit even though the cropper's pay ultimately depends on his own designated area. In the so-called through and through method common on many Southern cotton estates the croppers may be organized in work gangs and function much like workers under an industrial plantation system. At first glance such a system would seem more, not less, likely to lead to working-class solidarity. The workers are concentrated and work in interdependent work groups on cotton plantations, but are dispersed in individual plots in rice sharecropping. The other economic characteristics of cotton estate sharecropping, however, clearly indicate its inhibiting effect on worker organization. First, while most sharecroppers are exposed to a considerable turnover and insecurity of tenure, cotton sharecroppers are remarkable stable. The plots may in fact be inherited, much in the way usufruct plots are passed down from father to son. The sharecroppers of a typical cotton estate are most similar to laborers bound to the land by debt servitude. In fact they are seldom out of debt to the plantation store, which in the American South is often a lucrative sideline for the plantation owner. As cotton plantations become more fully rationalized in response to market forces, they usually evict the sharecroppers and adopt wage labor. When increased market penetration occurs in rice sharecropping systems, it leads to *increased,* not *decreased* rates of tenancy. Most cotton estates can be considered similar to backward commercial haciendas where the work force is bound to the land. The control of the holdings of cotton sharecroppers creates the same kind of conservatism found in the bound laborers of commercial haciendas and inhibits radical political organization.

The interdependent work organization of the cotton estate paradoxically tends to decrease, not increase worker solidarity because the work organization is dominated by the plantation owner. In commercial wet rice sharecropping the local village community is responsible for the maintenance of any irrigation works, and the landlord plays a peripheral if not obstructionist role in management. He may in fact not even be resident near the lands he controls. On the other hand, on irrigated cotton estates such as those of Egypt, the water is firmly under the control of the centralized estate management and can be distributed according to the economic productivity and political reliability of the workers. Thus the collective organization required for irrigation works creates incentives for class-based associations in decentralized rice sharecropping systems but tends to reinforce the power of the central administration on cotton estates. In addition, the cotton estate owner usually controls the ginning of cotton, which provides him with an overwhelming economic advantage in dealing with his workers. In most decentralized rice sharecropping systems hulling is controlled by middlemen and the landlord is again seldom involved. The decentralized rice sharecropper therefore is not dependent on the landlord for the marketing of his crop, while the cotton sharecropper usually is. Finally, the concentration of workers provides the estate management with greater powers of surveillance. The decentralized sharecropping system common in rice cultivation, on the other hand, distributes the workers of a given owner over a wide area, complicating problems of social control for the landlord.

Thus cotton and rice sharecroppers differ on two of the three factors that hypotheses 4 to 6 indicated were critical for strong cultivator political organization. The economic and political consequences of the two crops are illustrated in Figure 1.5, which indicates that in some respects the behavior of cotton sharecroppers more closely resembles the behavior of cultivators paid in land rather than wages, while the behavior of rice sharecroppers is much closer to that of landless laborers. Cotton sharecroppers have firmer ties to the land because of the weaker market influences and greater paternalism of centralized cotton estates, while market fluctuations and indebtedness lead to frequent insolvency and high turnover in rice tenancies. This difference in turn leads to greater conservatism on the part of cotton sharecroppers, who fear the loss of their long-term tie to the estate, while rice sharecroppers, whose ties to the land are minimal

FIGURE 1.5   *The Effects of Cotton and Rice Sharecropping on the Economic and Political Behavior of Cultivators*

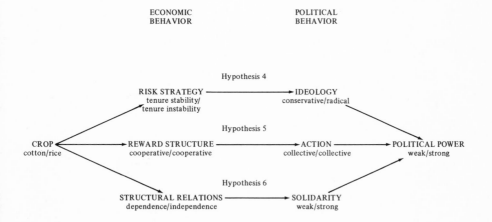

in any case, are more inclined to accept political risks. Thus according to hypothesis 4 rice sharecropping should produce stronger political organizations than cotton sharecropping. The variables specified in hypothesis 5 do not differ significantly in the two systems, since both minimize opportunities for individual mobility and require collective action to realize gains against landlord resistance. The most important differences between the two systems are those specified in hypothesis 6. Cotton sharecroppers are considerably more dependent on land-lords than are rice sharecroppers, and this fact tends to undermine cultivator solidarity and encourage commitment to the conservative estate administration. The strength of vertical ties in the cotton sharecropping system, then, is the critical determinant of the political passivity of cotton sharecroppers. Decen-tralized sharecropping systems and particularly those in wet rice cultivation com-bine weak ties to the land, strong incentives for collective organization, and structural independence from landlords, making these systems the most likely to lead to revolutionary Communist movements.

THE MIGRATORY LABOR ESTATE AND REVOLUTIONARY NATIONALISM
Like the sharecropping system the migratory labor estate is characterized by an upper class dependent on land and a lower class dependent on wages. The agricultural lower class, however, differs significantly in both the form of wage payment and its relation to the commodity market. Sharecroppers producing for export are fully integrated into market mechanisms and have usually lost all ties with subsistence cultivation. In the migratory estate system, how-ever, the laborer, although paid in wages, remains in part dependent on sub-sistence production. The laborer typically spends much of his time in traditional subsistence agriculture and usually migrates to work on the estate during the harvest. The worker's relative dependence on subsistence production rather than wages is in part determined by the harvest length of the crop and in part by the laborer's mobility. Some migratory laborers follow the harvest as it proceeds geographically across a crop-producing region and may even work more than one crop. In this case they are almost exclusively dependent on wage labor and return to subsistence production only briefly. In other cases the migrant will appear only for a month-long harvest and return immediately to subsistence production. In this case, of course, his economic characteristics are similar to those of a subsistence peasant rather than those of a wage laborer.

The migratory labor estate, like the sharecropping system, tends to be concentrated in crops which are more efficiently produced by small holders and do not permit any appreciable economies of scale. The migratory labor system is used most frequently in perennial tree crops, particularly coffee and grapes, which cannot be easily adopted to sharecropping. Sharecropping is impractical for the estate owner because of the value of standing crops which might be damaged by overzealous exploitation in a cropper's tenure. Nevertheless estate cultivation is not an economically competitive form of production even in peren-nials like coffee and grapes. In both cases most of the labor is demanded in a relatively short harvest period, usually of two to four months duration. Although grapes require more year-round attention than coffee, neither crop approaches the continuous harvest characteristic of ideal plantation crops. Similarly, neither crop requires expensive processing machinery. Coffee beans can be dried in the sun before shipment, and wine can be pressed barefoot where more elaborate machinery is not available. Both crops can easily be combined with subsistence production, and in many export economies coffee is regularly grown as a sideline by subsistence farmers. Since the migratory labor estate does not depend on economies of scale, the upper class cannot depend on economic power to secure its position. Like landowners in sharecropping and commercial hacienda systems the estate owners must use a variety of political devices to secure land and labor at below market cost. The economic and political characteristics of the owners of the landed estate are identical to those of the owners of commercial haciendas or of landlords in sharecropping systems. They are economically weak, dependent on servile labor, and supported by a backward agricultural technology. Consequently, like other landed estate proprietors they tend to rely on legal and extralegal force to secure land and labor, adopt an intransigent attitude toward labor organization, and are unable to make wage concessions to workers.

Migratory labor estates were found in grape cultivation in colonial Algeria, in coffee cultivation in colonial Kenya, and continue to exist in grape and lettuce cultivation in California. In each of these systems the agrarian upper class has relied on a series of ingenious manipulations of the legal system or on outright force to secure the necessary land and labor for its inefficient estates. In Algeria the French simply declared that all lands belonging to the Algerian ruler, the Bey, were French by right of conquest and parceled them out to French nationals. The Bey's lands consisted of most of the valuable and well-irrigated land in Algeria.[101] In Kenya similar large-scale land concessions were granted to British settlers, and members of the indigenous population unfortunate enough to live on the settlers' new lands were declared to be squatters and moved to "native reserves" on inferior land.[102] In California land concessions were based on the often fraudulent manipulation of claims to former Mexican land grants.[103]

The techniques for recruiting labor were no less ingenious. In Algeria the deprivation of all irrigated land in the colony forced much of the population to become wage laborers simply to survive.[104] In Kenya the hut tax, the poll tax, and direct conscription were all used to satisfy the settlers' demand for labor.[105] In California illegal or quasi-legal immigration from Mexico was the preferred method.[106] In each case the tactics created a disenfranchised, politically power-less agricultural labor force which was paid almost nothing. In each case the

101 Wolf, *Peasant Wars*, pp. 211–212.
102 Carl G. Rosberg, Jr., and John Nottingham, *The Myth of Mau Mau: Nationalism in Kenya* (New York: Praeger, 1966), pp. 18–19.
103 Carey McWilliams, *Factories in the Fields* (Boston: Little, Brown, 1939), pp. 12–15.
104 Wolf, *Peasant Wars*, pp. 217–218.
105 Rosberg and Nottingham, *Mau Mau*, pp. 45–46.
106 Ernesto Galarza, *Merchants of Labor* (Santa Barbara, Calif.: McNally & Loftin, 1964).

formal political devices of labor recruitment were reinforced by ethnic stratification systems which reserved all high-paying jobs for the dominant ethnic group and drove down the wages for the subordinate group. This was particularly clear in California, where competition between foreign agricultural laborers and the white population has been a constant source of racial conflict and hatred.[107]

The upper classes of the migratory estate behave in precisely the manner to be expected of upper classes dependent on landed property. The migratory wage labor force, however, would seem to lack the usual economic characteristics of an agricultural working class dependent on wage labor. Unlike the sharecropper, the migratory laborer seems an unlikely recruit for radical political action. His ties to the land are often substantial and he can always return to subsistence production if estate labor is unreliable. Since he returns to a subsistence community, he is subject to the same individualistic competitive pressures and hopes for individual mobility that characterize the subsistence peasant. The longer he remains in the subsistence milieu, the more his political behavior resembles that of a member of an agricultural working class dependent on land—conservative, apathetic, and badly organized.

The migratory labor pattern also tends to undermine any possible pressure for group solidarity based on work group interdependence. The constant turnover inherent in the migratory system weakens the worker community. The migrant is seldom dependent on other workers for welfare assistance, since he can always return to his subsistence community for aid. In California, for example, the presence of large numbers of foreign migrants has always hindered labor organization, and the Farm Workers Union was only organized after the Mexican border had been effectively closed to migrant farm labor by the end of the *bracero* program. Similarly, workers on Kenyan estates were limited to terms of 30 days and then were compelled to return to their reserves, thus preventing the formation of a stable worker community.[108] Even though a migratory wage labor force is not divided by internal stratification and wages are uniform and low, the weak pressures for group solidarity and ties to the subsistence economy make class-based organization impossible in migratory systems.

It is clear, on the other hand, that migratory estates in colonial areas have been subject to violent revolutionary movements similar in strength, if not in ideology, to those of sharecropping systems. In Algeria, Kenya, and Angola, major rural revolts against the colonial regime were based in large part on migratory wage laborers. The explanation of these revolts, like the explanation of revolts in commercial hacienda systems, must depend on the introduction of political organization from outside the workers' community. The workers themselves are too divided to provide the coherent political organization necessary for an armed insurrection.

Revolutionary movements in migratory estate systems depend on the traditional agrarian elite. The interests of this normally conservative group of land-

[107] McWilliams, *Factories, passim.*
[108] William A. Hance, *The Geography of Modern Africa* (New York: Columbia University Press, 1964), pp. 396–397.

owners would seem to be closer to those of the owners of the migratory labor estates than to those of the workers. Under some circumstances, however, their interests come to parallel those of the workers. This occurs when the landed estates are developed by settlers who threaten the continued political survival of the traditional agrarian leadership by the expansion of their estates. The organizational framework of the traditional subsistence community, then, may provide the organization that the workers lack. It is an organization based on the economics of subsistence production rather than specifically directed at political ends, but it can provide the same organizational coherence as a political party or an economic organization.

This pattern is particularly apparent in Kenya. The traditional tribal structure of the Kikuyu was dependent on the control of land by lineage groups, and the authority of tribal leaders ultimately derived from their allocation of community lands. The expansion of settler coffee estates in the midst of the areas of highest Kikuyu population density displaced the tribal leadership as well as most of its followers. Land disputes became a chronic problem in Kenya, especially as a growing population further diminished the available land in the reserves. Many of the wage laborers working on the estate were also Kikuyu and sometimes worked the very lands that had been stolen from their lineage or clan. The massive land expropriations which established the white highlands and the Kenyan coffee export economy simultaneously undermined the authority of the traditional authorities and created a large, unorganized semiproletariat from the same tribe. While the economic interests of these two groups were not parallel, they were clearly united in their opposition to the estates. As both Rosberg and Nottingham and Barnett and Njama[109] have pointed out, the so-called Mau Mau movement was a more or less direct consequence of the chronic land disputes between the Kikuyu and the English settlers. The Kikuyu tribal structure provided the organizational framework the migratory wage laborers lacked and made a revolutionary movement possible. The inflexibility of the Kenyan settlers made any other kind of political action impossible. As was the case in sharecropping systems, a well-organized political party of agricultural workers faced an inflexible elite dependent on force rather than economic power. The results were a revolutionary uprising, but the ideology was provided, not by a class-conscious workers' organization, but by the Kikuyu tribal social structure. Thus the movement took on a nationalist rather than a Communist ideology, although its goals were equally revolutionary. Only a nationalist ideology could unite the diverse economic interests of the traditional subsistence cultivators, tribal leaders, and migratory wage laborers which formed the basis of Mau Mau strength.

A revolutionary nationalist movement, such as the Mau Mau, can only occur if the migratory estates develop in a settler economy and create a threat to the landholdings of the traditional elite. Even then the periods in which such a

---

[109] Rosberg and Nottingham, *Mau Mau*, p. 248; Donald Barnett and Karari Njama, *Mau Mau from Within* (New York: Modern Reader, 1966), pp. 31–35.

revolt can occur are short. If the estates expand sufficiently, they will break the power of the traditional elite and reduce the migratory laborers to impotence. Only in colonial areas where the estate system has not completely eliminated the power of the indigenous landed classes can a revolutionary nationalist movement occur. The migratory wage laborer, like the laborer on a commercial hacienda, is incapable of providing the organizational strength to oppose the power of the landlords.

Under some circumstances both the sharecropping and migratory labor estate systems can create a combination of strong political organization on the part of the agricultural working class and political conflict over property and the control of the state. In the case of decentralized sharecropping systems the organization is based on a Communist party organized from within the worker community. In the case of the colonial migratory labor estate the organization is dependent on the traditional structure of the agrarian society. While both systems combine upper- and lower-class political behavior leading to revolution, the nature of the political organization of the working class creates a Communist movement in one case and a nationalist movement in the other. Only those agricultural organizations, however, which combine an upper class dependent on land rather than capital and a lower class dependent on wages rather than land create the political conditions necessary for revolution.

The theory of rural class conflict demonstrates that the social movements associated with various types of agricultural organization are fundamentally a result of the interaction between the political behavior associated with the principal source of income of the upper and lower agricultural classes. Combinations of income sources are associated with particular types of agricultural organization and lead to particular forms of social movement. The predictions of the model of rural class conflict can be summarized in the following set of hypotheses:

A. A combination of both noncultivators and cultivators dependent on land as their principal source of income leads to an agrarian revolt. This combination of income sources is typical of commercial haciendas and closely related systems. An agrarian revolt is directed at the redistribution of landed property and typically lacks broader political objectives. The typical tactic of such movements is the land invasion. An agrarian revolt is most likely when a socialist or reform party has weakened landed-upper-class control of the state and provided the organizational framework lacking among cultivators dependent on land.

B. A combination of noncultivators dependent on income from commercial capital and cultivators dependent on income from land leads to a reform commodity movement. Such a combination of income sources is typical of small holding systems. The reform commodity movement is concerned with the control of the market in agricultural commodities. It demands neither the redistribution of property nor the seizure of state power. The typical tactic of such movements is a limited economic protest. The greater the sensitivity to markets in small holding systems, the greater the probability of a reform commodity movement.

C. A combination of noncultivators dependent on income from capital and cultivators dependent on income from wages leads to a reform labor movement. Such a combination of income sources is typical of plantation systems. The reform labor movement is concerned with limited economic demands for higher wages and better working conditions. It demands neither the redistribution of property nor the seizure of state power. The typical tactic of such movements is the strike. Reform labor movements are most likely in industrial plantation systems.

D. A Combination of noncultivators dependent on income from land and cultivators dependent on income from wages leads to revolution. Such a combination of income sources is typical of sharecropping and migratory labor estate systems. The revolutionary movement demands the redistribution of landed property through the seizure of the state. The typical tactic of such movements is guerrilla war. In sharecropping systems the dominant ideology is likely to be Communist, while in migratory labor systems the dominant ideology is likely to be nationalist. Revolutionary socialist movements are most likely in decentralized sharecropping systems, and revolutionary nationalist movements are most likely in colonial settler estate systems.

CHAPTER 2

World Patterns

ANALYSIS OF THE distribution of political resources between noncultivators and cultivators suggested that the nature of rural social movements depends fundamentally on the type of agricultural organization. This chapter considers the empirical relationship between agricultural organization and rural social movements in a population of 135 export sectors of 70 developing nations in the period from 1948 to 1970. The analysis correlates the dominant type of agricultural organization for each export sector with the number of acts of rural protest observed in that sector. This same general method was also used in the case studies of Peru, Angola, and Vietnam reported in Chapters 3, 4, and 5. The case studies, however, consider variation within export sectors and involve measures of rural protest based on primary newspaper sources for each of the three countries. In the comparative analysis only the dominant type of organization is coded for each export sector, internal variation is ignored, and measures of rural protest are based on secondary press sources with broad international coverage. The more reliable measures and finer units of analysis in the case studies reduce problems of measurement error, but considering one case at a time limits the generality of the findings. The comparative analysis depends on somewhat cruder and less reliable measures but permits generalization about a world population rather than a single case.

The method of the comparative analysis closely resembles the approach of cross-national studies of collective violence such as those of Ivo and Rosalind Feierabend, Ted Gurr, and Bruce Russet.[1] In these studies a variety of quantita-

---

[1] Ivo K. Feierabend and Rosalind Feierabend, "Social Change and Political Violence: Cross-national Patterns," in H. D. Graham and T. R. Gurr (eds.), *Violence in America: Historical and Comparative Perspectives* (New York: Praeger, 1969), pp. 632–687; Ted Gurr, "A Causal Model of Civil Strife: A Comparative Analysis Using New Indices," *American Political Science Review*, 62 (December 1968), 1104–1124; Bruce M. Russet, "Inequality and Instability: The Relation of Land Tenure to Politics," *World Politics*, 16 (April 1964), 442–454.

tive and qualitative characteristics of nation-states were correlated, with event counts derived from secondary newspaper sources. Russet, for example, examined the relationship between an index of civil disorder, deaths by domestic violence, and national indices of tenancy and inequality in land distribution and found significant positive correlations with both agricultural measures when percent of the national labor force in agriculture was controlled. Both the Feierabends and Gurr found significant correlations between indices of political instability based on newspaper sources and various measures of economic deprivation computed from national accounts data.

These statistical comparative studies have in general used the nation-state as the unit of analysis even when their theories have been phrased in regional or even individual terms. This approach has simplified data collection, since most sources with broad international coverage aggregate data at the level of the nation-state. It has, however, complicated problems of inference when the nation-state is not the unit of analysis specified by the theory. The Feierabends, Gurr, and Russet, for example, all rely on the psychological concept of "relative deprivation" to explain patterns of collective violence but, instead of measuring individual psychological states, rely on national indices of economic conditions. The intervening variables linking national characteristics and individual psychological states are neither fully explained nor directly measured. Unless national units can be considered relatively homogeneous with respect to the hypothetical psychological state, it is always possible to conceive of potential sources of spuriousness involving third variables correlated with the explanatory variables. This is, of course, a problem inherent in aggregate data analysis and in a somewhat less general form is frequently referred to as the problem of spurious ecological correlation. In Russet's study of land tenure and collective violence, for example, it might be argued that high rates of tenancy are always associated with highly developed urban sectors, and that the observed collective violence occurs in the cities, while the countryside is tranquil. While alternate explanations of this kind can never be completely eliminated in aggregate data analysis, they can be reduced by selecting a sufficiently homogeneous unit of analysis. If Russet had, for example, included only rural areas in his measures of civil disorder, explanations which relied on spurious correlation between tenure forms and urban characteristics would have been ruled out.

The unit of analysis in this study was selected to minimize these problems of spurious correlation. The unit, which will be called the agricultural export sector, is defined by the major producing regions for a given export crop within a given country. This unit is more homogeneous than the nation-state and permits measurements of agricultural organization to be made directly rather than inferred from aggregate national data. Each agricultural export sector is identified by a particular country, crop, and geographic region. The tea-producing central hill districts of Sri Lanka would, for example, constitute a single agricultural export sector as would the coffee-producing highlands of Kenya. Such a unit of analysis obviously requires data on crop production within countries, but in other respects the method of analysis is similar to that of the usual cross-national study.

The world population of agricultural export sectors on which the comparative analysis is based was selected in three steps. First a list of predominantly agricultural countries was constructed. Second, the principal export crops for each of these countries were determined. Third, the major producing regions for each export crop were identified. The list of countries included all independent states and colonies which satisfied the following criteria: (1) a population of 1 million or more in 1968, (2) non-Communist for at least 10 years between 1948 and 1970, (3) at least 25 percent of the labor force in agriculture in 1965, (4) total value of agricultural exports greater than US$2 per member of the agricultural work force in 1965. These criteria were designed to select a population of countries which would include most of the politically significant export sectors of the underdeveloped world. Communist countries were excluded because the social and political effects of agricultural export sectors depend on the workings of a free rather than a controlled market. The requirement that 25 percent or more of the work force be employed in agriculture effectively excludes all industrial nations and limits the population to the underdeveloped areas of Latin America, Africa, the Middle East, and South and Southeast Asia. Only the peripheral, least industrialized areas of Europe are included. The requirement that total agricultural exports exceed $2 per member of the agricultural work force excludes most states of the Sahara and Saudi Arabian deserts and land-locked agrarian states such as Bolivia and Afghanistan. A total of 70 states and colonies satisfied all four criteria and were included in the list from which the export sectors were selected.[2]

Export crops for each of the 70 countries were included in the study population if they satisfied one or more of the following criteria: (1) contributed a median of 15 percent or more of a country's total agricultural exports in the period from 1948 to 1968,[3] (2) contributed a median of 2 percent or more of the total agricultural exports of the macrostates of Brazil, Italy, Indonesia, India, and Pakistan, (3) contributed 15 percent of total agricultural exports for a continuous period of five years or more between 1948 and 1968. These rules were intended to include as many export crops with potential political significance as possible but to exclude minor crops which would generate data insufficient to make classification of agricultural organization possible. The total of 135 export crops from the 70 countries which satisfied one or more of these criteria constitute the study population and are listed by world region in Appendix 1. Thirty countries contributed only one export crop to this population, another 30 contributed two each, and 10 (including the five macrostates)

---

[2] Laos was also excluded from the population on the grounds that no stable state existed through most of the 1948 to 1970 period. This procedure follows that of Gurr in "Causal Model of Civil Strife."

[3] The data for 1969 and 1970 were not available in published United Nations statistics in 1971 when the population of export sectors was selected.

contributed three or more export crops. The small number of export crops for each country is, of course, a result of the high degree of concentration of agricultural exports. The crop with the largest median proportion of agricultural exports contributed between 76 and 100 percent of the total in 13 countries, between 51 and 75 percent in 25 countries, between 26 and 50 percent in 28 countries, and between 0 and 25 percent in only four countries.

The utility of the agricultural export sector as a unit of analysis depends on the stability of these agricultural exports over the period selected for the study. If old crops disappeared or new crops appeared in the export statistics for any country during the period from 1948 to 1968, then it is possible that the corresponding export sector could be lost from the population for the period in question. There are two situations which can bring about such changes in export statistics, and each has somewhat different consequences for the analysis. First, a new export crop may be introduced or an old export crop may disappear because of economic or ecological changes. Second, a crop may still be produced on a large scale but no longer be exported because all production is consumed internally. In the first instance the agricultural export sector is lost from the population for the period before or after it appears in the export statistics. Obviously no observations can be made about the form of agricultural organization if the export system simply does not exist. These cases will appear as missing data in the coding of agricultural organization. In the second instance the crop is no longer exported, but the agricultural system producing it continues to exist and can be coded. In this case disappearance from the export statistics does not mean that the case must be dropped from the population. If substantial numbers of crops either appeared or disappeared in the period from 1948 to 1968, however, the population would be too unstable to carry out a meaningful analysis. Fortunately such major changes in agricultural exports are extremely rare within the time span considered in the study. A major change in export statistics was considered to have occurred if any crop in the study population contributed less than 5 percent of total agricultural exports for any continuous period of five years or more.[4] In only 5 of the 135 cases did such changes in export statistics occur. In two instances (cotton in Guatemala and coffee in Peru) the change in export statistics was a result of the introduction of a new export crop on a large scale. These two cases are treated as missing data for the period before the crop was introduced. In no case was the change in export statistics the result of the abandonment of a previously exported crop. In two cases (vegetables in Portugal and rice in Korea) the changes were the result of the export of a widely produced staple which had formerly been consumed internally. In one case (rice in Vietnam after 1965) a previously exported crop falls below 5 percent of total agricultural export for a period of five years or more even though it continued to be produced for internal consumption. In these three cases the form of

---

[4] Since the criterion for selection in the case of the five macrostates was a median of 2 percent of agricultural exports, in these cases the rule was relaxed to less than 1 percent for a continuous period of five years or more.

agricultural organization can be determined even for the periods when the crop was not exported, and the cases can therefore be included in the population. The relatively small number of major changes in agricultural exports, however, indicates that the agricultural export sector is a stable unit of analysis which can be used in studies involving relatively long time periods.

The geographic boundaries of the agricultural export sector were defined by the areas of maximum production for each of the 135 export crops. The boundaries were approximated by combining first-order political subdivisions (provinces, departments, states) which produced a substantial proportion of the total crop. First-order political subdivisions were ranked by their contribution to total production and selected successively until the accumulated total production exceeded 75 percent of the national total. In the small number of cases in which a single first-order subdivision is involved in the production of two or more export crops, the subdivision is excluded from the analysis altogether unless there is clear evidence of a two to one ratio in the value of one crop as opposed to the other.[5] Internal production data were seldom available for the entire 1948 to 1968 period, and it was usually necessary to rank provinces by production data for whatever year happened to be available. When data for more than one year were available, the year closest to the midpoint of the period was selected. Limitations of climate and geography usually produce well-defined and relatively stable zones of maximum production for each export crop. When fluctuations in area do occur, they usually involve marginal lands on the periphery of the principal producing areas. It was not possible to empirically assess the stability of the boundaries over time because of the temporal limitations of the data. It is unlikely, however, that the fluctuations in the total area could have been much greater than the fluctuations in the total exports of a particular crop, and the major exports remained relatively stable from 1948 to 1968.

MEASURES OF AGRICULTURAL ORGANIZATION

In the comparative analysis of agricultural export sectors it is assumed that a given crop is grown according to a single form of agricultural enterprise throughout the sector area. This assumption is usually justified, since within any single country the political, economic, and ecological determinants of agricultural organization are likely to be relatively constant in all areas producing a given export crop. Each agricultural export sector was categorized according to the dominant type of agricultural enterprise in the sector. In practice the dominant form was considered to be the enterprise type controlling a plurality

---

[5] In two cases, the Ivory Coast and Togo, the growing areas for the major export crops, coffee and cocoa, were indistinguishable. In these two cases the more important crop (coffee in both cases) was included in the analysis and the other crop was ignored.

of the area in which the crop was cultivated. Classification of the dominant enterprise type required both a rigorous definition of the agricultural enterprise and a set of rules for assigning an enterprise to the appropriate type.

The choice of definition of the agricultural enterprise affects the size of the unit and the class position of the agricultural work force. In the United States Agricultural Census, for example, it has been customary to define a farm as all the land under the control of one person or partnership, and this control may be exercised through ownership, lease, rental, or sharecropping arrangements. This definition reduces a Mississippi valley cotton estate to an aggregate of independent farms each run by an operator who becomes the classificatory equivalent of the independent entrepreneur who rents a Midwestern wheat farm. Schulman reports that a similar practice is followed in many South American agricultural censuses with similar results.[6] Control over both the use of land and the disposal of crops is the critical issue in a definition of an agricultural enterprise and its operator. Smith argues that the sharecropper in the southern United States does not legally hold residual rights to the crop, does not determine the productive uses of his parcel, and is therefore better classed as an agricultural laborer than as an independent entrepreneur.[7] This usage shifts the controlling unit from the sharecropper's plot to the estate as a whole. Thus a renter who controls the disposal of his crop and decides on the productive use of his land would belong in the class of independent small holders, and a sharecropper would belong to the category of agricultural laborers. The enterprise in which the sharecropper works consists of all parcels under the control of a single landlord. An agricultural enterprise can therefore be considered to be a personal or corporate entity with the right to control the use of a given parcel of land and to dispose of the crop made on that land, subject only to specific contractual obligations with any other parties who may have an interest in the land. This definition would, for example, lead to the classification of each of the following systems as a single agricultural enterprise:

1. The land controlled by a single cotton irrigation scheme in the Sudan. In this system cotton lands are owned and irrigated by the government. Tenants who are the former owners of the lands supervise the operation of their plots, but crop rotation, irrigation timing, and the use of fertilizer and insecticides are all controlled by the government. The tenants are responsible for cultivation but frequently hire migratory laborers from outside the cotton zone to perform most of the manual labor. The effective unit in the control of the crop is the entire irrigation scheme rather than the individual tenant plot even though the latter is the effective unit for labor administration.

[6] Sam Schulman, *A Sociological Analysis of Land Tenure Patterns in Latin America* (Gainesville: University of Florida Press, 1954).
[7] T. Lynn Smith, *The Sociology of Rural Lile* (New York: Harper, 1953), pp. 279–288.

2. The land owned by a single landlord in the Mekong delta of Vietnam. The landlord controlled land use and crop disposal and frequently provided seed and capital equipment. The tenant had no written contract and received a share which was usually less than half the crop. Even though the tenant worked without supervision, he still had no real economic independence, and hence all tenant units under the control of a single landlord constituted the agricultural enterprise.

Once the agricultural enterprise had been identified, the dominant enterprise type was determined for each agricultural export sector. The classification was based on information on agricultural organization in English, French, and Spanish sources in the University of California, Berkeley, libraries. The complete list of sources consulted for each country is presented in Appendix 4. Bilingual graduate research assistants assembled the materials for each country and coded the structure of the dominant form of agricultural enterprise.[8] The nature of ownership, administration, and labor organization of the dominant agricultural enterprise was classified according to the categories listed on the code sheets in Appendix 2. The owner of a particular enterprise was considered to be the group or individual that had effective control of the land and of crops grown on it for at least 20 years. Long-term lease holders are therefore considered owners for purposes of this classification. The administrator or operator is the individual or group that exercises effective rights to the land or the crop or the designated agent of such individual or group. Laborers are those individuals performing the actual physical work of cultivation. When more than one source of labor was employed in a particular enterprise, the source contributing the greatest total number of man-days per year was the source coded. Once the type of ownership, operation, and labor organization had been determined, it was possible to define the dominant enterprise type. The actual coding was based on the detailed categories of ownership, operation, and labor organization described in Appendix 2, and the system type was defined by simple combinations of these characteristics.

The social consequences of the form of agricultural organization depend on the distribution of resources between owners and workers, and the typology of agricultural organization is therefore defined by combinations of type of ownership and type of labor organization. The five types of agricultural organization described in general terms in Chapter 1 are defined below in terms of the coding categories for ownership and labor organization.

[8] Jacques Brissy coded the form of agricultural organization for the Middle East and North Africa, French Sub-Saharan Africa, South and Southeast Asia (except India and Indonesia) and Northern Europe. Ronald Royce coded Central America. Fernando Uricoechea coded British Africa, Southern Europe, India, and Indonesia. Lea Ybarra coded South America and Portuguese Africa. The research bibliographies in App. 4 were assembled by these coders for the countries in their assigned regions. Sources in languages other than English, French and Spanish were used for statistical purposes only.

1. The commercial manor or hacienda. An individually owned enterprise which lacks power-driven processing machinery and is worked by usufructuaries, resident wage laborers, or wage laborers who commute daily from nearby subsistence plots.
2. The sharecropped estate. An individually owned enterprise which lacks power-driven processing machinery and is worked by sharecroppers or share tenants.
3. The migratory labor estate. An individually owned enterprise which lacks power-driven processing machinery and is worked by seasonal, migratory wage laborers.
4. The plantation. An enterprise owned either by a commercial corporation or government body, or by an individual if the enterprise includes power-driven processing machinery, and worked by wage laborers resident for continuous terms of more than one year.
5. The family small holding. An individually owned enterprise worked by the owner and his family.

These definitions make it clear that the various type of agricultural organization differ principally in the method by which the labor force is organized. The commercial hacienda and the sharecropped and migratory labor estate all have the same form of ownership and differ only in the form of labor organization. In each case the owner is an individual whose relatively limited financial resources are indicated by the absence of expensive processing machinery on the estate. The plantation differs in both ownership and labor organization from the other systems. In the family small holding, of course, the roles of owner and laborer are combined. These combinations of ownership and labor organization do not, of course, exhaust all logical possibilities. It is possible, for example, to combine corporate ownership with sharecropping or migratory wage labor. Economic considerations, however, make such combinations extremely unlikely. In 1948 there were only three systems which did not fall into one of the five types of agricultural organization. Cotton in the Sudan was produced on government-controlled irrigation projects which employed migratory laborers supervised by tenants. Indonesian sugar was produced in a complex sharecropping arrangement involving both corporate control and partial ownership of the sugar lands by adjacent villages. Cotton in Mozambique was produced in a system of compulsory sharecropping controlled by large Portuguese companies. In 1970 two additional cases (Tunisia, grapes; Guinea, bananas) did not fit the typology. In both cases postcolonial regimes established government-controlled cooperatives to supplant estates owned by Europeans. In the entire population of export sectors, however, such cooperative control is extremely rare. Even in Mexico the major exporting areas are controlled by commercial haciendas rather than the cooperative *ejidos* which are widespread in subsistence agriculture. The five categories of agricultural organization defined above are therefore not only mutually exclusive but, in effect, exhaustive of the world population of agricultural export sectors.

The major types of agricultural organization in the population of 135 export sectors are remarkably stable over the period from 1948 to 1970. Between the beginning of the 23-year interval in 1948 and the midpoint in 1959 only one change in enterprise type occurred. Between 1959 and 1970 there were an additional eight changes, and since no export sector changed more than once, there were a total of nine changes for the entire 1948 to 1970 period. In addition, six plantation systems were nationalized during the period, but in these cases only the ownership changed. The structure of the enterprise and the organization of the work force remained the same.

There seem to be three principal reasons for the stability of agriculture enterprise types. First, technological and economic changes are much less likely in agricultural than in industrial organizations. In part this fact reflects the greater importance of the unchanging factors of terrain and climate in agriculture. Agriculture is also relatively little influenced by technical innovations, particularly mechanization, until very late in the course of a nation's industrial development. Technological change is, in fact, more likely to affect demand for raw materials (e.g., the substitution of synthetic for natural rubber) than the nature of agricultural products themselves. Genetic innovations may produce increased yields or more disease-resistant strains but seldom produce a large enough effect to alter the type of agricultural enterprise. The recent development of the so-called miracle grains is a notable exception, since their greater yields and requirements for fertilizers and pesticides tend to favor wealthier farmers and drive poorer small holders into sharecropping. The discovery of miracle crops is, of course, by definition a rare event. In the world population of agricultural export sectors only one change in enterprise type can be attributed to technological change. In Syrian cotton at the beginning of the 1960s the traditional sharecropping system which had been used for both export and subsistence crops was replaced by a migratory estate system employing wage laborers. The change was a result of an influx of urban capital, an increased use of tractors, and the opening of new irrigated cotton lands. The more highly capitalized tractor farmers found that it was more efficient to consolidate their estates, eliminate resident sharecroppers, and put all their irrigated lands into cotton production. In the other export sectors technological change of this kind either did not take place or took place on too small a scale to influence the form of agricultural enterprise.

The second reason for the stability of agricultural enterprise types lies in the immense economic and social importance of these systems in most agrarian nations. Export crops are frequently the single most important source of foreign exchange, the most important source of government revenues, and the major source of cash income and employment for much of the rural population. A minor fluctuation in prices, let alone a major change in the form of agricultural organization, would disrupt the entire economy. In Kenya, for example, the Mau Mau movement and much nationalist agitation concerned the coffee estates of English settlers in the "white" highlands. The nationalist Kenyatta government however, did not break up either the coffee estates or the British tea plantations after independence. To do so without insuring some equally efficient management would have caused the collapse of the Kenyan economy, which is almost completely dependent on export agriculture and lacks major mineral or manufacturing sectors. Instead of attacking the export sectors directly, Kenyatta broke up English-owned estates in areas of mixed farming and redistributed the land to peasant subsistence cultivators. This strategy relieved much of the intense internal land shortage while at the same time leaving the export economy functioning at preindependence levels. The tea and coffee estates were attacked indirectly by government encouragement of competitive production in peasant small holdings. By 1967 African small holders had taken a decisive lead in coffee production, and it is likely that the share of European estates will continue to decline as African producers become more efficient. The relatively long unproductive period in tea, however, has permitted the British to remain in almost complete control of production while the plantings on African holdings mature. By the mid-seventies the importance of European estates should be diminished even in tea. During the 1948 to 1970 period, however, the Kenyan tea sector was classified as a corporate plantation system, although the coffee sector changed from a migratory labor to a small holding system after 1966. Similar policies of encouraging small holder competition with European estates caused changes in enterprise type in the export sectors of two other countries. In the Cameroons, postindependence government policies made it possible for small holders to assume the major proportion of export production and displace European estates. In Guinea the government intervened more directly by establishing banana cooperatives which gradually forced a decline in the number of European estates. In each of these cases a major political change—the transition from colonialism to independence—was required before even a gradual change in the dominant form of agricultural enterprise could occur.

In addition to these technological and economic factors there are usually substantial political and social barriers to changes in enterprise type. Land reform or nationalization in predominantly agrarian countries is frequently a revolutionary action. Effective land reform requires a radical redistribution of an agrarian country's major form of wealth and the liquidation of one of its most important political interest groups—the large landowners. Frequently an alliance of landowners and the military can stifle effective land reform indefinitely. Despite the existence of numerous land reform laws in many agrarian nations, remarkably little real land redistribution has taken place in the world's major agricultural export sectors. Redistributive land reform involving the dissolution of large estates and the creation of a class of small holders had taken place in only 3 of the 135 export sectors since 1948. In 1949 the Chinese Nationalists occupied Taiwan and initiated a largely successful reform which converted most of the island's commercial rice area from sharecropping to small holdings. After World War II the Indian moneylenders who had held most of Burma's commercial rice land in a sharecropping system were unable to return. Although tenants continued to pay at least nominal rents until as late as 1965, the rice export sector eventually became a small holding system. In Rwanda

Hutu serfs had occupied the position of usufructuaries on lands dominated by Tutsi overlords. In 1959–60 the Hutu revolted, massacred the Tutsi and transformed the manorial land-owning system into one of independent small holdings. A number of export sectors were nationalized during the postwar period, but in only two cases did the nationalization create a new type of agricultural enterprise. In both Tunisia and Algeria postcolonial regimes nationalized the vineyards of European *colons*. In Algeria a migratory labor estate system was replaced with government-run cooperative plantations in which the work was performed by resident wage laborers. In Tunisia the vineyards were also nationalized, but a system of migratory labor on relatively small estates persisted even under government control. The remaining instances of nationalization involved simple changes in ownership and management without any essential change in structure. In Indonesia the Sukarno government nationalized Dutch sugar, tea, palm, and rubber plantations. In Cuba the Castro government nationalized the sugar plantations, and in Peru a nationalist military government also seized control of the sugar plantations. While these land reforms and nationalizations do not include all attempts at land reform in the postwar period, they do include all successful land reforms in the world's major export sectors. The small number of changes of all kinds, amounting to only 9 of 135 export sectors, indicates that these sectors are immune to almost anything but profound political change. In all but one of the 9 cases of changes in enterprise type and in all cases of plantation nationalization, a revolutionary change in government, in most cases a transition from colonialism to independence, was necessary before a change in agricultural organization could occur.

It is also interesting to note the direction of these changes in agricultural organization. Almost all cases involve a change from a politically unstable form of enterprise to a politically stable form. The greatest number of changes in organization are observed in the sharecropping and migratory labor estate systems, which are the most likely to generate conflicts which can only be resolved by revolutionary violence. Similarly the small holding system, which creates a conservative interest in private property and discourages revolutionary movements, has the smallest number of changes. Of the 18 migratory estates coded in 1948, 5 had been transformed into a different enterprise type by 1970. Similarly 3 of the 23 sharecropping systems had changed type. Of the 47 small holding systems recorded in 1948, however, *none* had changed enterprise type by 1970. Similarly, even though 6 of the 25 plantation systems had been nationalized, none had been broken up into small holdings or changed in other essential respects. Only 1 of the 17 commercial hacienda systems recorded in 1948 had changed type by 1970. Of the nine new enterprise types resulting from these changes, however, five were small holdings, two were mixed cooperative types, one was a plantation, one a migratory estate, and none were sharecropped estates. The general pattern is a transformation from the more unstable sharecropping and migratory labor estate systems into the stable small holding and cooperative forms.

elds. This relationship is clear both from the crops listed in Table 2.
.42 correlation between annual crops and the dummy sharecroppin,
Table 2.2. Even within this range of crops, however, sharecroppin,
e exclusive or even dominant form. While some sharecropping sys
dministered in a centralized operation similar to a commercia
frequently sharecroppers work in a decentralized system and ar
ependent of one another. In this case the landlord is simply a ren
and the sharecropper carries out many of the managerial functions o
holder without, of course, holding any legal right to the crop or the
hich he works. In such a situation it is clear that there are no economic
s in sharecropping, and as the data in Table 2.1 indicate, small holdings
qually likely alternative in most annual crops where sharecropping
are numerous. From an economic standpoint the small holding is con-
y more efficient, since the small holder will be more concerned with
mprovements to increase his yields in future years. As was the case for
lowners in the commercial hacienda and migratory labor estate systems,
recropped estate owner is in a precarious economic position and survives
rough the impoverishment and disenfranchisement of the peasantry. The
ant rents of sharecropping systems would not long persist under a repre-
ve government, which would be influenced by the majority interest of
s. In a completely free market with no barriers to entry, small holders
prevail in most export sectors where sharecropping systems are now
nant. The small holding is in fact competitive through a wider range of
than any other system and is adaptable to both annuals and perennials.
in crops which require substantial pretransport bulk reduction does the
ll holding suffer a competitive disadvantage. The persistence of centralized
ns of production in other crops is not a consequence of their economic
ciency, but rather of the political hegemony of the land-owning classes. It is
fact that tends to transform economic conflicts over the division of the pro-
ds from agriculture into political conflicts over the ultimate instruments of
ntrol in the society.

MEASURES OF RURAL SOCIAL MOVEMENTS

The sociological description and measurement of social movements are
limited by the ambiguous boundaries of the phenomenon itself. Social movements seldom create the kind of repeated observable structures which make
measurement convenient. Their institutional structure, tactics, and ideology
change continually, their limits in time and space are illdefined, and their range
of support is often difficult to determine. Some definitions of social movements
such as those of Ralph Turner and Lewis Killian, and Hans Toch are suffi-

EXPORT CROP AND AGRICULTURAL ORGANIZATION The relative competitiveness of various types of agricultural organization is an important determinant of their ability to survive political transformations and, therefore, an
indirect determinant of the degree to which the land-owning classes depend on
political hegemony to control the agricultural working class. As was indicated
in Chapter 1, the greater the independent economic power of agrarian upper
classes, the greater their reliance on negotiation and indirect economic influence.
The weaker their economic position, the greater their reliance on force. The
economic position of the estate and plantation owners depends on the competitiveness of centralized production. Much of the stability of estate and plantation systems over the 1948 to 1970 period depends on their political influence.
This political power is reinforced, however, if the dissolution of the plantations
or estates would lead to a disruption of the export economy. The greater the
economic justification for a centralized form of production such as an estate or
plantation, the greater its resistance to political change. Since in most export
sectors centralized organizations are not the most efficient producers, political
factors must explain the dominance of the estates in these systems.

The data in Table 2.1 and 2.2 show the relationship between crop production parameters and the relative competitiveness of the five major types of agricultural organization in the year 1948.[9] These data make clear that the highly

TABLE 2.1   *Export Crop and Agricultural Organization*

EXPORT CROP	AGRICULTURAL ORGANIZATION						
	CH	SC	MLE	PL	SH	Other	Total
Sisal	0	0	0	2	0	0	2
Tea	0	0	1	5	0	0	6
Sugar	1	0	0	5	2	1	9
Palm	0	0	0	2	0	0	2
Rubber	0	0	0	7	1	0	8
Copra	0	0	0	0	2	0	2
Bananas	1	0	2	3	1	0	7
Grapes	0	0	3	0	2	0	5
Coffee	9	0	7	1	9	0	26
Cocoa	2	0	0	0	5	0	7
Cotton	5	7	0	0	4	2	18
Tobacco	0	1	2	0	4	0	7
Fruits and nuts	0	2	0	0	4	0	6
Groundnuts	0	1	0	0	2	0	3
Vegetables	0	3	0	0	3	0	6
Grains	0	8	1	0	4	0	13
Livestock	1	0	2	0	2	0	5
Other	0	0	0	0	3	0	3
Total	19	22	18	25	48	3	135

[9] For the two systems which did not exist in 1948 (Guatemala cotton and
Peru coffee) the enterprise type listed is the first observed after 1948. Rice in
Taiwan is listed as the small holding system it became after 1949 rather than
as the sharecropping system which existed for the year 1948 only.

TABLE 2.2   *Intercorrelations of Agricultural Organization and Crop Production Parameters*

VARIABLE	(2)	(3)	(4)	(5)	(6)	(7)	(8)
1. Bulk reduction	−.18	.26	−.10	−.17	−.10	.60	−.21
2. Annual		−.29	−.05	.42	−.13	−.33	.08
3. Harvest period			−.10	−.16	−.17	.53	−.12
4. CH				−.18	−.17	−.20	−.31
5. SC					−.18	−.21	−.33
6. MLE						−.20	−.31
7. PL							−.37
8. SH							—

centralized factory-like form of the plantation is economically competitive over a very narrow range of crops even though it is almost completely dominant within this range. As the correlations in Table 2.2 make clear, the principal determinants of plantation organization are bulk reduction in processing, a long harvest period, and a perennial as opposed to an annual crop. The dummy plantation variable in Table 2.2 is correlated .60 with a variable indicating crops which undergo substantial bulk reduction in processing. The plantation variable is also correlated .53 with the length of the harvest and −.33 with annual crops. Crops such as sisal, sugar, tea, and oil palm, which undergo a bulk reduction of 90 percent or more during primary processing, obviously produce immense economies in transportation costs if processing is carried out at the point of production. As the data in Table 2.1 make clear, these crops are almost entirely produced by plantations. In addition, all these crops have a continuous, 12-month harvest which makes the maintenance of a permanent wage labor force practical. There are a number of other crops, including rubber and bananas, which do not undergo substantial bulk reduction but can be harvested continuously and therefore also favor plantation production. Plantations are almost never found in crops with harvest periods of six months or less and are never found in annual crops which require two brief, intense inputs of labor for planting and harvest. Actually the principal determinants of plantation organization are bulk reduction and continuous harvesting. The addition of the annual versus perennial crop variable to the other two adds little predictive power. The multiple correlation for the regression of the dummy plantation variable on bulk reduction and harvest period is .71, while the multiple R for all three variables is .72, an increase in explained variance of a little more than 1 percent. The equation for the regression of the dummy plantation variable on the bulk reduction and harvest period variables, ignoring the error term, is as follows:

$$Z_7 = -.12 + .49\,Z_1 + .40\,Z_3$$

where Z_7 equals the standardized score for the dummy plantation variable and Z_1 and Z_3 equal the standardized scores for the bulk reduction and the harvest

length variables respectively. This equation
exert approximately equal influence on
systems. Crops with long harvest which requ
therefore, provide the conditions which m
efficient than small holdings.

Both the commercial hacienda and the
centrally organized, but they lack the competi
system. In both cases workers are supervised
and estate lands are cultivated as a single uni
competitive in the range of crops with continuou
reduction. As the data in Table 2.1 indicate, these
a narrow range of crops which share some but
which lead to the centralized plantation organiz
perennial short-harvest crops like coffee or grapes
cotton which require some preliminary processing
crops like coffee make the migratory estate system p
that large amounts of labor be recruited only once a
harvest period. There is no annual planting to deman
labor. The system obviously requires a large subsistence
will be forced to support themselves during the peri
employed on the estates. Cotton tends to be produc
hacienda system rather than the migratory labor estates b
and the inputs of labor required for both planting and
easily supplied by usufructuaries or by wage laborers who
sistence plots. Even in the narrow range of crops such as
which these two systems are numerous, they are far from do
cases could easily be displaced by small holdings. As the
indicate, grapes, coffee, cotton, and tobacco, the principal
crops, are produced in only slightly lower proportion by smal
estate owners. In fact the proportion of small holders in these
mately the same as for the total population of export sectors (a
Clearly, then, these systems do not have the decisive economic ad
would create the kind of market control enjoyed by plantation
owners of these systems are consequently much more vulnerabl
movements demanding the dissolution of their estates. Small holde
replace the estate even in a monocultural export economy withou
disrupting the economy.

Sharecropping, like small holding, is usually a decentralized fo
duction, but unlike small holding it is restricted to a relatively narrow
crops. Sharecropping is limited to annual crops which have no permane
to be damaged during the cropper's tenure. The insecurity of the croppe
provides no incentive to improve standing crops, and in fact his best in
served by exploiting the crop as fully as possible even at the cost of

ciently broad to encompass any series of collective acts aimed at changing the social order.[10] More restrictive definitions such as those of Neil Smelser and Stanley Milgram limit the phenomenon to noninstitutional actions and usually require some shared intention or belief among the members of the movement.[11] This study will follow the more restrictive definitions and consider collective acts which take place outside the established institutional framework and involve participants who are united by some shared sense of identity.

Many social movements produce little in the way of documentary evidence, and what they do produce is frequently fragmentary and variable in quality. Unless social scientists are able to collect data during or immediately following major outbreaks of collective behavior, it may be difficult to obtain quantitative data on many forms of social movements. Survey research techniques have increasingly been used to study collective behavior during outbreaks of racial rioting in the 1960s, but this method offers little help in historical studies. Historical information is, however, available in pamphlets and circulars, in the memoirs of movement leaders, in the accounts of contemporary observers including newspaper reporters, and in the records of internal security forces, and such data may form the basis for quantitative measurement. George Rudé, for example, has used arrest records to study the composition of Parisian crowds during the French Revolution,[12] and Eric Hobsbawm and Rudé have used similar constabulary records to study the spread of the rural swing movement in nineteenth-century England.[13] The most common source of data for quantitative studies of social movements, however, has been contemporary newspaper reports. Charles Tilly and his associates, for example, have constructed systematic event counts of incidents of collective violence reported in French newspapers for the nineteenth and twentieth centuries and are extending such studies to nineteenth-century Italy.[14] Stanley Lieberson and Arnold Silverman used incidents of racial rioting reported in the *New York Times* to study the precon-

[10] Ralph Turner and L. M. Killian, *Collective Behavior* (Englewood Cliffs, N.J.: Prentice-Hall, 1957), p. 38; Hans Toch, *The Social Psychology of Social Movements* (Indianapolis: Bobbs-Merrill, 1965), p. 5.

[11] Neil Smelser, *Theory of Collective Behavior* (New York: The Free Press, 1962), p. 71; Stanley Milgram and Hans Toch, "Collective Behavior: Crowds and Social Movements," in L. Gardner and E. Aronson (eds.), *The Handbook of Social Psychology*, vol. IV (Reading, Mass.: Addison-Wesley, 1969), p. 584.

[12] George Rudé, *The Crowd in the French Revolution* (London: Oxford University Press, 1959).

[13] E. J. Hobsbawm and George Rudé, *Captain Swing: A Social History of the Great Agrarian Uprising of 1830* (New York: Pantheon, 1968).

[14] See James Rule and Charles Tilly, "Measuring Political Upheaval," Center for International Studies, Princeton University, 1965 (Mimeo.); Charles Tilly, "Collective Violence in European Perspective," in H. D. Graham and T. R. Gurr (eds.), *Volence in America: Historical and Comparative Perspectives* (New York: Praeger, 1969), pp. 4–44; and David Snyder and Charles Tilly, "Hardship and Collective Violence in France," *American Sociological Review*, 37 (October 1972), 507–519.

ditions of urban race riots.[15] Seymour Spilerman and Terry Clark have also used newspaper sources to study the distribution and determinants of racial disorders in the United States.[16]

Quantitative cross-national studies of collective behavior have also relied on newspaper sources. The handbooks of cross-national data assembled by Charles Taylor and Michael Hudson, and Arthur Banks include counts of events of political instability coded from the *New York Times* and other newspaper sources.[17] Harry Eckstein, Rudolph Rummel, and Raymond Tanter have all conducted cross-national studies of collective violence using events reported in the *New York Times*.[18] Ivo and Rosalind Feierabend based their index of political instability on data coded from *Deadline Data on World Affairs*,[19] and Ted Gurr estimated rates of political violence from these sources and a number of regional press summaries such as the *Asian Recorder*, the *Africa Diary*, and the *Hispanic American Report*.[20] These studies have indicated that the coding procedures for such data are reliable and that the resulting indices are relatively unaffected by systematic bias introduced by press censorship or international attention focused on a particular country.

Newspaper reports are the basic source of information about rural social movements in the comparative analysis of the world population of agricultural export sectors and in the case studies of Peru, Angola and Vietnam. The principal sources used in the comparative analysis are the *New York Times,* the *Times* of London, the *Hispanic American Report,* the *Africa Diary,* and the *Asian Recorder.* Each of these sources provides international coverage and each is indexed, greatly reducing time spent in searching for instances of rural protest. Their principal disadvantages are a relative absence of detail and a tendency to report only those events with relatively high levels of activity. Many agrarian events are summarized briefly, and many are not reported at all unless there are

[15] Stanley Lieberson and Arnold R. Silverman, "The Precipitants and Underlying Conditions of Race Riots," *American Sociological Review*, 30 (December 1965), 887–889.

[16] Seymour Spilerman, "The Causes of Racial Disturbances: Tests of an Explanation," *American Sociological Review*, 36 (June 1971), 427–432, and William R. Morgan and Terry Nichols Clark, "The Causes of Racial Disorders: A Grievance-Level Explanation," *American Sociological Review*, 38 (October 1973), 611–624.

[17] Charles Lewis Taylor and Michael C. Hudson (eds.), *World Handbook of Political and Social Indicators*, 2d ed. (New Haven, Conn.: Yale University Press, 1971); Arthur S. Banks (ed.), *Cross-Polity Time Series Data* (Cambridge, Mass.: M.I.T. Press, 1971).

[18] Harry Eckstein, "Internal War: The Problem of Anticipation," in The Smithsonian Institution, *Social Science Research and National Security: A Report Submitted to the Research Group on Psychology and the Social Sciences* (Washington, 1962), pp. 102–147; Rudolph J. Rummel, "Dimensions of Conflict Behavior within and between Nations," *General System Yearbook*, 8 (1963), pp. 1–50; Raymond Tanter, "Dimensions of Conflict Behavior within and between Nations, 1958–1960," *Journal of Conflict Resolution*, 10 (March 1966), 41–64.

[19] Feierabend and Feierabend, "Social Change and Political Violence."

[20] Gurr, "Causal Model of Civil Strife."

substantial numbers of deaths, substantial property damage, or large numbers of participants. These biases, however, tend to be relatively constant from one country to another and therefore are unlikely to introduce systematic bias. While the national newspapers used in the case studies provide greater detail and a lower threshold of reported activity, it would be prohibitively expensive to assemble a file of such sources for all 70 countries in the world comparative study. Since few of these papers have indexes, time spent in examining even a few years of issues would be enormous. The enumeration of acts of rural protest in every issue of a single Angolan newspaper for a six-month period of the year 1961, for example, required as much time as the coding of rural protest for the entire 23-year period between 1948 and 1970 from all the secondary sources for approximately one-fifth of the world population. The comparative analysis therefore relies entirely on secondary sources. The *New York Times* index was consulted for instances of rural protest for all 70 countries for the entire 23-year period between 1948 and 1970. The regional press summaries could only be used for the more limited periods in which they were published. The *Hispanic American Report* was consulted for the period from 1948 to 1964, the *Africa Diary* for the period from 1961 to 1970, and the Asian Recorder for the period from 1955 to 1970. The London *Times* was consulted for all African, Asian, and Middle Eastern countries for the periods not covered by regional press summaries and for all European countries for the entire 1948 to 1970 period. With the exception of the six-year period from 1965 to 1970 for Central and South America, social movement information for all countries is based on two independent sources. One of these two sources was always the *New York Times*, and the other was either a regional press summary or the London *Times*, depending on the country and time period in question.

These newspaper materials represent the raw materials for measures of social movements for all agricultural export sectors in the world population. In general, newspaper articles report a particular action or summarize a series of actions involving the participants in a social movement. These reports of overt acts constitute the behaviorial evidence of a social movement. For purposes of measurement a social movement was considered to be composed of a series of such observable actions, and movements which did not produce such evidence are obviously excluded from the analysis. For purposes of tabulation the action sequences reported in newspaper articles were broken up into relatively homogeneous clusters of behavior called events. An event is any act or series of actions occurring on the same day or successive days in the same export sector and the same or a contiguous first-order political subdivision. This definition specifies a continuous series of actions in a particular geographic region. A new event occurs whenever a continuous action is interrupted by a period of one day or more or when the locus of the action changes to a noncontiguous administrative division or to a different export sector. It is possible, therefore, for some events to extend for days or even weeks and include major parts of a given country. This tends to be the case, for example, when the event is a major battle in a revolutionary movement and the fighting involves many engagements spread over a broad front. Most events, however, are more limited in time and space. Frequently events last no longer than a single day and involve only one political subdivision of a particular country. Most land invasions, small-scale guerrilla attacks, and riots follow this pattern. The overt actions which constitute an event could obviously be divided into even finer units by specifying smaller time intervals or smaller geographic areas. The event definition used in the world comparative analysis, however, is well suited to the summary articles found in secondary newspaper sources. The general quality of these accounts seldom permits finer temporal or spatial resolution of the sequence of action. In the case studies of Peru, Angola, and Vietnam, however, more detailed reporting permitted more restricted event definitions and correspondingly greater powers of resolution.

If an event is considered to be the basic behavioral unit of a social movement, then the actions included in an event obviously must share the general defining characteristics of a social movement. In this study a social movement is understood to be composed of collective acts which are outside the normal institutional framework of a society and involve participants who share some common sense of identity. Therefore events were included in the study population if they (1) were collective, (2) were noninstitutional, and (3) involved solidary groups. An event was considered to be collective if a source mentioned more than 10 participants or if there was indirect evidence of group participation through the use of words connoting collective action such as "rally," "march," "demonstration," "riot," "strike," "revolution," "uprising" or words referring to collectivities such as guerrilla bands, unions, leagues, parties, or factions. An event was considered to be noninstitutional if it was either illegal or not sanctioned by established societal institutions. Evidence of violence initiated by either event participants or social control forces and involvement of illegal parties or other illegal organizations were considered indicators of noninstitutional actions. Similarly, regularly scheduled conventional collective actions such as church services, sports events, or patriotic assemblies on national holidays were not included in the population of noninstitutional events. Strikes are a marginal case, since they may be legally sanctioned but are irregular and surrounded with controversy. All strikes whether legal or illegal were considered instances of noninstitutional behavior.

Only those noninstitutional collective events which involved some common sense of identity on the part of participants were considered constituent elements of a social movement. Panics, crazes, fads, mass migrations, and similar noninstitutional actions by large numbers of people acting in pursuit of individual interests were excluded. The determinants of such actions are likely to be the opposite of those involved in the development of solidary social movements. The divisive effect of individual land ownership, for example, tends to inhibit organized political and social movements among small farmers but increases the likelihood of market panics and other individualistic forms of mass behavior.

The focus of the theoretical analysis is on the conditions under which cultivators overcome their individual economic interests and form collectivities for united political action. The population of noninstitutional collective events therefore excludes all action which do not involve group solidarity.

Since the focus of this analysis is on rural social movements, the population of events was restricted to those actions which involved individuals who perform the physical work of cultivation. References to peasants, agricultural laborers, sharecroppers, plantation workers, harvest migrants, and similar rural occupational groups were considered evidence of participation by cultivators. Similarly, explicit references to nonagrarian occupational groups such students, miners, or government workers were considered indications of the absence of rural support. When mixtures of agricultural and nonagricultural occupations were reported for a particular event, the event was included in the analysis only if a clear majority of the participants were rural workers. Foreign invasions and actions by owners and administrators (unless they were also cultivators) were also excluded. Blanquist, or guerrilla *foco*, movements are a marginal case. In movements of this kind a small group of urban intellectuals, students, or workers retreats to the countryside and wages guerrilla war against the government. The leaders of such movements frequently claim peasant support and sometimes have it. Since the determinants of guerrilla *foco* movements would seem to lie in urban areas rather than in the countryside, all such movements have been excluded from the analysis unless there is overwhelming evidence that most of the fighting force was made up of peasants or agricultural workers. Where evidence is ambiguous or debatable, the guerrilla *foco* movement is excluded. Guevara's ill-fated Bolivian expedition of 1967, for example, would not be included in the analysis because he recruited few peasants from the Bolivian countryside.[21] Movements of regional secession have also been excluded from the analysis if there is clear evidence that the movement is based on urban commercial or industrial interest groups or if it involves a coalition between urban groups and the rural upper classes. The American Civil War would not be considered a rural social movement by this criteria, nor would the Nigerian civil war or the Katanga secession. Explanations of these movements might be derived from theories of elite behavior rather than theories of mass political mobilization. If the occupation or class status of the participants in a particular event could not be determined, however, then any event occurring in a rural area was included in the analysis.

The event is the unit of observation in the coding of newspaper materials, but the agricultural export sector is the basic unit of analysis in the statistical manipulation of the data. Thus some set of rules is necessary for associating events with agricultural export sectors. In conventional ecological analysis such association would depend on the location of an event. If an event was reported to have occurred in the geographic area of a particular agricultural export sector,

---

[21] See Richard Gott, *Guerrilla Movements in Latin America* (Garden City, N.Y.: Doubleday, 1972) for an account of Guevara's expedition as well as descriptions of other guerrilla *focos* in Latin America during the 1960s.

then ecological analysis would correlate characteristics of the sector with characteristics of the event. The data reported in newspaper articles, however, make it possible to link events and export sectors more directly. The articles sometimes provide information on both the crop and the occupation group involved in an agrarian protest. The mapping of events onto export sectors used this information as well as the event location. If, for example, the article noted that Ceylon tea plantation workers in the district of Kandy went on strike, it would be clear from an examination of the coded data on Ceylonese export sectors that the tea sector controlled by British corporate plantations was the appropriate match. If the article simply noted that a rural strike occurred in Kandy province in Ceylon, then the event would be matched with the same export sector, but in this case the matching process would be reduced to simple ecological correlation. Any single characteristic or combination of characteristics could be used to associate a given event with a given agricultural export sector. When two of the three types of information were available but in conflict, crop information was given priority over occupational information, which in turn was given priority over location information. If two types of information were in conflict with a third, then the discrepant type was discarded. If an event spread over two or more export sectors, then the system which contributed the largest portion of the event area was the system linked to that event. This problem, however, arose in less than 1 percent of all matched events. A total of 1,601 events were associated with the 135 agricultural export sectors according to these rules. Thirty-three percent of these events were matched by using all three types of information in combination. Another 13 percent were matched on the basis of a combination of two of the three types of information. The remaining 64 percent were matched on the basis of one type only, and 48 percent of the total were matched on the basis of location information alone. Thus approximately half the events were matched with export sectors on the basis of the conventional ecological criterion, while the remaining matches involved combinations of occupational, crop, and location information.[22]

EVENT TYPES   The characteristics of each rural collective event identified in the newspaper source were coded according to the sets of categories listed in Appendix 3. When possible coders noted the date, location, duration, number of participants, number of casualties, and amount of property damage for each event. The coders also recorded a number of qualitative event characteristics in order to provide information to test the hypotheses outlined in Chapter 1. The qualitative characteristics included the organization, tactics, and ideology of the participants in each event. The organization codes concerned the manner in which the active participants in an event were deployed and the administrative apparatus controlling that deployment. The participants in a particular event might form a loosely organized crowd, a disciplined mass formation, or a military or paramilitary band. These acting formations might in turn be controlled by

[22] Less than 2 percent of all events had insufficient information on all three matching characteristics.

other organizations including unions, peasant leagues, political parties, and tribal groups. The tactics of the event participants were coded according to both the action pattern and the target of the event. The actions themselves included strikes, land seizures, riots, and acts of warfare, and the targets of these actions included settlers, landowners, and units of internal control forces. The ideology of the event participants was inferred from their actions or public pronouncements and was based on the specific demands made in any given event. These demands could include economic, political, and communal concerns, so that any single event could be categorized by more than a single demand. Finally the coders indicated the political party affiliations, if any, of the participants in the event. More detailed descriptions of these categories and coding instructions are presented in Appendix 3.

The most important codes for purposes of determining the effect of agricultural organization on rural social movements are those concerned with the ideology of the movement. The theoretical analysis suggested that, in general, a single type of movement should be associated with each type of agricultural organization—revolutionary socialist movements with sharecropping systems, revolutionary nationalist movements with migratory labor systems, agrarian movements with commercial hacienda systems, labor movements with plantation systems, and commodity movements with small holding systems. These five types of movements were distinguished primarily on the basis of their goals. Revolutionary socialist and nationalist movements are directed at fundamental political and social change. The objectives of both types of movements include the overthrow of the existing political system and the destruction of rural class structure. In revolutionary socialist movements the old political system is to be replaced by a socialist state and the old agrarian class structure abolished through collectivization or nationalization of agriculture. The revolutionary nationalist movement shares the socialist movement's concern with fundamental political change, but in this case the existing political leadership is to be replaced by a new national, regional, ethnic, or racial group. The revolutionary nationalist movement always involves fundamental political change, but it may or may not involve parallel economic change. When such economic changes do occur, the agrarian upper classes may simply be replaced by members of the new ethnic group, or the upper class may be destroyed and replaced by small holders from the new ethnic group. The revolutionary socialist movement aims at fundamental economic change through the seizure of the state apparatus. The revolutionary nationalist movement aims at the replacement of one ruling ethnic group with another. Even though the participants in a revolutionary nationalist movement are frequently motivated by economic discontent, the primary goals of their movement are usually communal rather than economic.

The agrarian movement shares the nationalist and socialist movements' demands for the radical transformation of the rural class structure. It differs, however, in its more limited political objectives. Both revolutionary nationalist and socialist movements demand a transformation of the political system, but the objectives of the agrarian movement are limited to the immediate problem of the control and redistribution of land. The agrarian movement lacks any long-range political goals and frequently dissolves when its immediate demands for land have been satisfied. The agrarian movement may destroy the political power of the rural upper classes, but it seldom possesses the political coherence to organize the seizure of state power. The agrarian movement, therefore, typically leads to revolt rather than revolution.

Labor and commodity movements are reformist and challenge neither the power of the state nor the existing rural class structure. In both cases the movement's objectives are limited to altering the distribution of income between the rural upper and lower classes. Labor movements demand a greater share of the profits, while commodity movements demand limitations on the power of the financial and commercial classes which control the disposition of the smaller farmer's production. Although both movements may adopt radical political ideologies, their actual demands are usually limited to the redistribution of income from rural property and do not include the redistribution of the property itself.

Since rural social movements have been defined as a series of collective events, the tendency of a given export sector to generate a given type of movement is a function of the number of events of a given type observed in that sector. If the participants in a large number of events in a given export sector were, for example, to share a commitment to revolutionary socialist goals, then the sector would be inferred to have a high propensity for revolutionary socialist movements. The problem of categorizing types of social movements can therefore be reduced to the problem of categorizing types of events. The receptivity of any given export sector to any of the five major types of movements can be expressed as a function of the number of events of each major type observed in that sector. The categorization of the objectives of participants in particular events depends on two sets of coding categories: (1) the specific demands of the event participants and (2) the ideology of any political party with which they are affiliated. The five types of events corresponding to the five types of movements can each be defined by a combination of demands and party affiliations. Specific definitions of each type and illustrative descriptions from newspaper sources are presented below.

1. The Revolutionary Socialist Event   Any event in which the participants are associated with a revolutionary socialist party and demand either unconstitutional political change, radical transformation of the rural class structure, or both. A revolutionary socialist party is any Communist or Trotskyist party, including both the Moscow and Chinese variants of Communism. Inferences about the Communist affiliations of event participants were restricted to direct evidence from statements of movement leaders or from the title of the party itself. References to Communists by opponents of the movement were not considered evidence of Communist participation. Unconstitutional political demands included both demands for the suspension of civil liberties or the extralegal replacement of a regime and demands for fundamental changes in the ideology legitimating the political community. Usually such demands were associated with demands for the violent overthrow of the existing political system. Demands for the radical transformation of the rural class structure included both demands for land redistribution and demands for nationalization or collectivization of agriculture. More moderate economic demands such as for lower rents, more secure tenure, better wages, or lower interest rates were not considered indications of an attempt to transform the rural class structure. Only those events which combined both Communist or Trotskyist party affiliation and radical economic or political demands were included in this category. Strikes called by Communist-dominated banana plantation workers' unions in Costa Rica in the 1950s, for example, were not considered revolutionary socialist events even though a Communist party was clearly involved. These strikes were focused on wages and other bread-and-butter issues and demanded neither the nationalization of the plantations nor the establishment of a socialist state. A land invasion led by Naxalite Communists in West Bengal, however, would be considered a revolutionary socialist event, since both a Communist party and demands for land redistribution were involved. A typical revolutionary socialist event is reported in the article excerpted below from the *New York Times* of March 31, 1950. The event is one of a series involving the White Flag Communist party in lower Burma during the confused period immediately after World War II. A four-sided civil war had broken out involving the central government, and rebel armies under the command of the Karens, a chronically dissident ethnic group, and two Communist factions, the Red Flags and the White Flags. The two Communist parties had split over ideology and tactics, with the White Flags adhering to a more moderate Stalinist line and the Red Flags adopting a radical Trotskyist position. Both parties, however, fielded armies against the central government, and both clearly attempted to seize power by violent means. The event reported in the *Times* describes one of a large number of military engagements involving the White Flag armies.

BURMA FORCES WIN TOWN, CLEAR WAY TO MANDALAY

RANGOON, Burma, March 30—The Burma Army has captured Pyinama from the Communists, clearing the railroad to Mandalay. Government troops, driving down from the north, entered the city last night, army dispatches said.

The retaking of Pyinama, 244 miles north of Rangoon, clears 500 miles of rail on the Rangoon-Mandalay line and opens the way for resuming internal surface communications, bottled up by the insurgents since February 1949.

Details of the victory of the Government forces were meager but earlier reports had suggested that probably the White Flag Communists who had held the city were withdrawing and were not expected to offer strong resistance.

RANGOON, March 30 (Reuters)—Thakin Than Tun, Premier of the newly formed Communist rebel government at Prome 160 miles north of here, today proclaimed martial law and imposed a dusk to dawn curfew in the territory he holds.

This event clearly involves military units of a Communist party attempting to overthrow the state and establish its own government. The military unit is directed by the White Flag rebel government of Thakin Than. The tactics involve guerrilla war, and the immediate target is clearly the government armies. Even when government forces initiate an event, the activities of insurgent forces are always coded. This particular description gives little definite information on the duration, number of participants, or number of casualties in the event. Nevertheless the qualitative information clearly indicates that it is a revolutionary socialist event.

   2. *The Revolutionary Nationalist Event*   Any event in which the participants are associated with a nationalist or communalist party and demand either unconstitutional political change, radical transformation of the rural class structure, or both. A nationalist or communalist party is any party organized for political action on the basis of ethnic group ties. This category includes anti-colonial and anti-imperial nationalist parties, secessionist or separatist parties, and parties advocating regional, tribal, or racial autonomy within a federated political system. Religious parties, including the religious arms of radical sects and cults, were not considered nationalist or communalist parties for purposes of this classification even if they advocated secession or federated autonomy for their religious group. Nationalist parties with strong economic ideologies including Communist and moderate socialist parties were classified according to their economic rather than their nationalistic goals. The category of nationalist and communalist parties, then, includes only pure nationalist parties whose formal ideology is based almost entirely on ethnic group solidarity. Not all such nationalist parties, however, are associated with revolutionary nationalist events. Only those events which combined nationalist party affiliation and radical political or economic demands fall in this category. The radical political and economic demands are the same as those defining revolutionary socialist events, but in the case of revolutionary nationalism the demands are, of course, more likely to be political than economic. It is possible, however, for an event whose participants are affiliated with a pure nationalist party to make radical economic demands. While such demands may not be the principal goal of the party, they may be a secondary concern in a number of events in the nationalist movement. In fact the argument linking migratory labor systems with revolutionary nationalist movements suggested that such movements were based on the economic disruption of an expanding estate economy. The principal political expression of this discontent, however, is a movement for national autonomy rather than a movement for specific economic change. Only ethnic solidarity can span the diverse economic interests which make up the revolutionary nationalist coalition. The Mau Mau movement in Kenya is typical of revolutionary nationalist move-

ments. Although the expropriation of Kikuyu lands by settlers in the "white" highlands was a major contributing factor in the revolt, Mau Mau ideology emphasized tribal solidarity and militant opposition to white rule. The following article from the *New York Times* of September 29, 1952, presents a description of a typical event in the Mau Mau movement.

NEW RAIDS IN KENYA
Dread Mau Mau Native Group Kills 2 African Chiefs

NAIROBI, Kenya, Sept. 28 (AP)—The police announced today the murderous native Mau Mau society had struck again, killing two African chieftains and slaughtering 350 cattle and sheep owned by white settlers in the foothills of Mount Kenya.

The latest blow of the anti-white society—sworn to drive the British out of Africa—took place while the colonial legislature was considering emergency laws to crack down on the terrorists.

The raided district is about 100 miles from Nairobi. The Mau Mau struck after a night meeting, slaughtering the livestock with spears, swords, and knives. They cut telegraph lines to hamper police action, but authorities said about 100 suspected members had already been rounded up.

The organization of this event involves a guerrilla band directed by the quasi-political Mau Mau organization. The party affiliations of the participants were classified as revolutionary nationalist because of the nationalist political aspirations of the Mau Mau and their close ties with other Kenyan nationalist groups including Jomo Kenyatta's Kenya African Union. Since the Mau Mau clearly sought to change the political community through violence, the event includes a radical political demand. The tactics are terrorism, and the primary targets of the action are the traditional African chiefs. The event takes place in Central District Kenya's principal coffee-growing area and in a region in which much Kikuyu land had been expropriated by white settlers.

3. *The Agrarian Event* Any event in which the participants demand the expropriation and redistribution of land, but do not make any other radical political or economic demand and are not affiliated with a revolutionary socialist or nationalist party. Agrarian events therefore include only those events focused exclusively on the redistribution of land. Although the expropriation and redistribution of land may lead to a radical change in the rural political system, the participants in agrarian events are not concerned with the indirect political consequences of their actions. Events in which the participants demand land but also make unconstitutional political demands or demands for the nationalization of private property do not qualify as agrarian events. Similarly demands for land by adherents of a revolutionary party attempting to overthrow the state do not qualify as agrarian events. The participants in an agrarian event may be affiliated with a political party, but it must not adhere to revolutionary goals. Thus land invasions sponsored by the Venezuelan Peasant Federation, which had close

ties to the reformist Acción Democrática (AD) political party, would constitute agrarian events, since AD was a constitutional party which did not advocate fundamental constitutional change. The Land invasion sponsored by the Indian Communist party, on the other hand, would not constitute agrarian events, but rather revolutionary socialist events, even though a demand for land redistribution was clearly involved. Most agrarian events, however, involve no formal political parties and frequently represent little more than a group of squatters moving onto temporarily unused lands of a nearby estate. This is a familiar form of peasant protest throughout Latin America and in other areas where large commercial manors are found. One typical agrarian event occuring in Nicaragua is described in the following item from the *Hispanic American Report* of May 1963:

> About 1,000 agricultural workers invaded and settled on 2,000 manzanas (1 manzana = 1.74 acres) of uncultivated cotton land in Chinandega Department. The farmers claimed that the government had promised to distribute the lands and that they acted to take advantage of the dry season to avoid being cheated of their land by local politicians.

The participants in this event apparently constitute simply a loosely organized crowd, and no administrative organization is involved. The tactic is obviously a land invasion, and the immediate target is the owner of the uncultivated cotton lands. The absence of any demands other than the distribution of land and the evident acceptance of the legitimacy, if not the efficacy, of the government land reform program indicate that the participants clearly do not have any revolutionary goals in mind. There are no demands for the overthrow of the state or for the collectivization of agriculture, and no political parties revolutionary or otherwise are involved. In fact the peasants seem to accept the political structure, being concerned only with the graft of the local incumbents. The action therefore satisfies all the criteria of an agrarian event.

4. The Labor Event   Any event in which the participants demand higher wages, better working conditions, or the right to organize but do not demand unconstitutional changes in government, nationalization, or land redistribution. The participants in labor events may be affiliated with any political party including revolutionary socialist and nationalist parties. In fact the participants in labor events are frequently associated with radical socialist or Communist parties even though their demands must, by definition, be reformist. An event involving participants affiliated with a Communist party would, of course, be classified as revolutionary socialist if the participants made radical rather than reformist demands. The seizure of six British-owned plantations by Communist-led plantation workers in Indonesia would, for example, be classified as a revolutionary socialist rather than a labor event because an implicit demand for nationalization was involved. Strikes by Cuban sugar plantation workers, on the other hand, were coded as labor events even though they were directed by Communist-affiliated unions. In all cases the unions demanded better wages or working conditions and did not strike to bring down the government even during Castro's final military offensive against the Batista regime. The defining characteristics of the labor event are its reformist concern with income redistribution and its reluctance to challenge either property or polity. A typical labor event is described in the following article from the London *Times* of December 16, 1958:

WAVE OF STRIKES
ON SISAL ESTATES
GOVERNOR ASKED TO INVESTIGATE
From our Correspondent
DAR-ES-SALAAM, Dec. 15

The Governor of Tanganyika, Sir Richard Turnbull is being asked today for an investigation of the situation in the sisal industry territory, following a series of strikes.

They began after the biggest wage award, totaling £250,000, had been negotiated by the joint central council of the industry on which both management and workers are represented. The sisal plantation workers union refused to recognize it saying that the workers' delegates on the council had been chosen by the employers.

Since the agreement, a series of strikes had taken place, including a 20-day stoppage on the important Mazinde estate at Tanga. When the management threatened to dismiss 100 workers a day until the strike ended, the union began a lorry shuttle service to take 2,000 workers from the estate to various parts of the province. The union was to feed them, but now shops have stopped credit some workers are existing on two or three mangoes a day. The union allege a lock out, but the management say the men were taken from the estate before even collecting the money due them.

The work stoppage at the Mazinde estate involved a disciplined mass action directed by a labor union. The tactic of the event is, of course, a strike, and the target is the sisal industry management. The demands of the strikers are limited to questions of wages and representation. There is no evidence in this article or in others concerning the Tanganyikan sisal workers' union that any Communist or other radical socialist party was involved. Even if such a party had been involved, however, the strike would have been classified as a labor event, since no radical political or economic demands were made.

5. The Commodity Event Any event in which the participants demand changes in the workings of the market in agricultural commodities. This category includes demands for controls on credit through lower interest rates, government-financed loans, or cheap money, demands for controls on middlemen through government ownership of processing machinery or storage facilities, and demands for control of marketing and prices through producers' associations, government marketing boards, price support programs, or compulsory restrictions on production. Demands for control over the commodity market also include attempts to prevent undesirable government intervention through prices, controls, taxes, or compulsory cultivation programs. The demands of a commodity event must be limited to such market concerns and not include demands for unconstitutional political change or radical transformations of the rural class structure through nationalization or land redistribution. The participants in a commodity event may be affiliated with any political party including revolutionary socialist or nationalist parties. Such political affiliations are, however, extremely unlikely. Even when socialist parties are ostensibly involved, they are usually committed to property rights and must, of course, by definition eschew radical political or economic demands. The socialism of Saskatchewan wheat farmers, for example, extends only to controls over the marketing of wheat and does not include any desire to nationalize private property or alter the ownership of individual farms. Similarly protests of the African Farmer's Union in Uganda were closely associated with the African nationalist movement but were concerned with Asian and British ownership of cotton gins rather than the expulsion of the colonial regime. The commodity event, like the labor event, is part of a reformist movement, and even when such events are associated with radical parties, their demands are limited to the redistribution of income. The two types of events differ in their participants' concern with the labor market in one case and the commodity market in the other. A typical commodity event is described in the following article from the London *Times* of October 20, 1966:

IRISH FARMERS PROTEST

DUBLIN, Ireland, Oct. 19 (AP)—Thousands of protesting farmers tied up town traffic today in a march on government buildings to demand an economic "new deal." Their noon parade was orderly but noisy. The farmers are demanding a program of minimum prices for cattle and sheep and a farmer-controlled meat-marketing board.

The farmers in this event are organized into a disciplined mass formation, but there is no apparent coordination of their activities by any formal administrative organization. Their tactic is obviously a protest march, and the target of their actions is the national government. The farmers' demands are limited to controlling the meat market, and no revolutionary demands or revolutionary parties are involved. The limited demands and the farmers' concerns with the meat market identify this action as a commodity event.

EVENT DISTRIBUTIONS   The five types of events are mutually exclusive and together include most events observed in the world population of agricultural export sectors. There were 1,572 events on which enough information was available to classify event type, and 84 percent of these events were included in one of the five event types.[23] An independent coding of press sources from 10 of

[23] Of the remaining 16 percent, 91 events, or approximately one-third, were accounted for by the Colombian civil war of 1948 to 1955. This war involved rural upper- and lower-class groups on both sides and, even though some agrarian issues may have been involved, represents a marginal instance of a

the 70 countries in the study population indicated intercoder reliabilities of between .82 and .99 for the five major event types.[24] Most of the events in the study population were revolutionary, socialist, or nationalist, which together accounted for 70 percent of the total. The absolute number of events of different types is not as important as the theoretical relevance of the categories themselves. The distribution of each type of event is, however, significant for the analysis. In theory particular event types should cluster in particular types of agricultural export sectors. The null hypothesis would therefore predict that events are randomly distributed and do not tend to cluster in any one type of export sector. Such a distribution of events would be produced if the probability of the occurrence of one event did not affect the probability of the occurrence of another. These are the defining conditions of a poisson process. The distribution generated by a poisson process is characterized by a single parameter λ equal to the mean of the distribution. In a poisson distribution with no event clustering, the mean is equal to the variance and both are equal to the parameter λ. The greater the degree of clustering of events within particular sectors, the greater the ratio of the variance to the mean. The variance/mean ratio I is therefore often used as an index of clustering or as a measure of deviation from the poisson assumption of independent events.[25] In a poisson distribution with mean equal to variance, equal to λ, this ratio will be one, and the larger the degree of clustering, the larger the value of the ratio. The data in Table 2.3 present the variance/mean ratio for the distribution of each major type of event and for the distribution of all rural collective events. It is clear that in each case the cluster index is significantly greater

---

rural social movement. Similarly a number of events which did not fall into one of the five movement types were instances of banditry, again a marginal instance of collective behavior. It is debatable whether the bandit is a rebel or a conventional criminal. There were also a number of tribal fights which involved communal ties but no political parties. Again, these events may be considered feuds rather than instances of noninstitutional behavior.

[24] The 10 countries—Ireland, Costa Rica, Brazil, Lebanon, Yemen, the Philippines, Senegal, the Ivory Coast, Angola, and Malawi—represent a simple random sample of the study population stratified by world region and median event activity in the original coding. The reliability coefficients are the product moment correlations between the total number of events of a given type in a given country recorded by two independent coders. The correlations over the ten countries for each type of event are as follows: revolutionary socialist, $r = .99$; revolutionary nationalist, $r = .99$; agrarian, $r = .97$; labor, $r = .91$; commodity, $r = .82$.
The validity of secondary newspaper sources is discussed in the case studies, which compare statistically the secondary sources with the primary news sources for each of the three countries Peru, Angola, and Vietnam. In general correlations between the geographic distribution of particular event types in the two sets of sources range between .71 and .97, although in the case of Vietnam, the correlation for revolutionary socialist events is only .34. See the discussions of secondary source validity below: Chap. 3, pp. 137–139; Chap. 4, pp. 263–266; and Chap. 5, pp. 329–330.

[25] J. K. Ord, "The Negative Binomial Model and Quadrant Sampling," in G. P. Patil (ed.), *Random Counts in Scientific Work*, vol. 2, *Random Counts in Biomedical and Social Sciences* (University Park: Pennsylvania State University Press, 1970), p. 158.

TABLE 2.3   *Cluster Indices for Principal Event Types*

Event Type	Mean	Variance	I Ratio
All events	12.04	1,066.41	88.6
Rev. socialist	4.54	609.25	134.20
Rev. nationalist	3.87	389.94	100.76
Agrarian	.75	4.69	6.25
Labor	.62	2.58	4.16
Commodity	.26	1.24	4.77

than one. In the cases of revolutionary socialist and nationalist events in particular the index exceeds 100, indicating a high degree of clustering. It is clear that events of all types are not randomly distributed according to poisson assumptions, but are significantly clustered within particular export sectors.

There are two equally plausible interpretations of this clustering. The clustering may indicate heterogeneous conditions in various agricultural export sectors. Some sectors may be particularly event prone just as some individuals may be considered to be particularly accident prone. Or the export sectors may be homogeneous with respect to event proneness, but the occurrence of one event may increase the probability of additional events by some contagion process. It has often been demonstrated that both of these assumptions lead to formally equivalent distributions,[26] and there is in fact no way to distinguish one process from the other on the basis of the data in Table 2.3 alone. It is, however, important to distinguish the contributions of the two processes in the empirical analysis. The theory clearly made predictions about heterogeneity rather than contagion. In theory certain forms of agricultural organization should be prone to generate particular types of events.

Although it is not possible to determine the relative importance of heterogeneity versus contagion on the basis of overall event distributions, it is possible to make such distinctions by inspecting the temporal sequence of events within particular export sectors. Inspection of those systems with large numbers (over 100) of events revealed a substantial contagion effect. The best predictor of the number of events in a given month was the number that occurred in the previous month. This contagion effect is not the principal interest of this study, although it can, of course, be examined as an empirically distinct phenomenon. In this study contagion effects represent a source of error. The effects of rural class structure on the receptivity of the agricultural population to a particular form of social movement is measured by between-system heterogeneity, not within-system contagion. In a statistical analysis, contagion will tend to cause systems with large numbers of events to be weighted more heavily than their actual receptivity to a particular type of movement would warrant. A simplifying assumption was introduced in order to correct for this statistical artifact. Each

[26] For a discussion of the history of such distributions see James Coleman, *Introduction to Mathematical Sociology* (New York: The Free Press, 1964), pp. 299–301.

movement was assumed to be governed by an exponential growth function such that the rate of increase in the number of events per unit time was proportional to the number of events which had already occurred. There are a number of plausible sociological conditions which could create event contagion of this form. The occurrence of one event in a social movement simultaneously serves as an example of successful protest to other potential actors and complicates problems of social control. The greater the number of events, the greater the strength of the example and the greater the problems for the social control forces. Thus as the number of events grows, the social control forces are progressively overwhelmed, making it increasingly difficult to stop additional outbreaks of collective behavior. Such a process seems to be at work in some of the large revolutionary socialist and nationalist movements with the highest levels of event clustering. Rebel forces begin with a few small-scale attacks on isolated outposts which are not successfully contained by the police. More widespread attacks follow, and the social control forces are spread thin attempting to control the new outbreaks. In the final stages the rebels overwhelm local government units, secure territory, establish an army, obtain foreign aid or even recognition, and move to large-scale warfare. If some such exponential growth process is assumed to account for the apparent contagion in the event data, then an index which takes this effect into account would provide an index of heterogeneity. The equation describing the exponential growth process is

$$X_t = X_0 e^{rt}$$

where X_t equals the total number of events observed during some time period t, X_0 equals the number of events which had already occurred at the beginning of the period, and r is a parameter equal to the rate of growth or spread of the disturbance in a particular sector. If we assume that one event has already occurred in each sector at the outset of the period of observation and that t is some unitary constant, the equation reduces to

$$X + 1 = e^r$$

or

$$ln(X + 1) = r$$

The natural logarithm of the number of events observed in some unit of time (+ 1) is equal to the rate of spread of events of that type in that system. The parameter r then can be considered an index of receptivity of a given sector to a given type of event. A logarithmic function of the number of observed events then provides a measure of system heterogeneity, while the simple total number of events is a function of both system event proneness and the increase in number of events due to the exponential contagion process. The logarithmic function therefore will be the fundamental unit of measurement used in the analysis of the effects of agricultural organization on a population's receptivity to a particular type of rural social movement. All variables involving numbers of events of any kind will actually be based on the $\log_e$ of the number of events plus one.

RESULTS OF THE WORLD ANALYSIS

The relationships between the five major types of agricultural enterprise and the five types of movements are presented in Table 2.4.[27] Each type of agricultural organization is represented by a dummy variable and each movement type by the natural logarithm of the number of events of that type (+ 1). The correlations in Table 2.4 indicate the effects of agricultural organization on the major forms of social movements in the world population of agricultural export sectors. The table shows correlations between the type of enterprise coded for the year 1948 and the $\log_e$ of the total number of events observed in the secondary newspaper sources between 1948 and 1970. The type of enterprise observed in 1948 was the best predictor of the total number of events observed over the entire 1948 to 1970 period. The major enterprise types changed little between 1948 and 1970, however, so that it makes little difference which year is chosen to represent the value of the agricultural variable.

TABLE 2.4 *Intercorrelations of Types of Events and Types of Agricultural Organization for World Population of Export Sectors*

VARIABLE	EVENTS				AGRICULTURAL ORGANIZATION				
	(2)	(3)	(4)	(5)	(6)	(7)	(8)	(9)	(10)
1. Rev. socialist	−.07	.12	.00	.07	.39	−.11	−.07	−.12	−.07
2. Rev. nationalist		−.17	−.14	−.06	−.09	.49	−.09	−.16	−.10
3. Agrarian			−.01	.08	.12	−.04	.51	−.17	−.29
4. Labor				−.01	−.02	−.16	−.12	.59	−.26
5. Commodity					−.04	−.14	.00	−.12	.23
6. SC						−.18	−.18	−.21	−.33
7. ML							−.17	−.20	−.31
8. CH								−.21	−.33
9. PL									−.36
10. SH									—

The data in Table 2.4 indicate that the major types of social movements are relatively independent of one another. This is also true of the major types of agricultural organization. In the latter case, however, the independence is an artifact of the mutually exclusive quality of the categories themselves. No export sector can be classified according to more than one type of enterprise at any point in time. The independence of the major types of social movements is not

[27] The Malaysia rubber plantation system has been excluded from this analysis. As was indicated in Chap. 1, the Malaysian rubber plantations are a special case, atypical of plantation systems generally. Since this sector experienced the greatest number of events of any sector in the population (almost all revolutionary socialist), including it would tend to give disproportionate weight to this exceptional case and distort general trends in the other 134 cases in the population.

an artifact of mutually exclusive categories. It is possible for sectors with large numbers of events of one type to simultaneously have large numbers of events of another type even though no one event can be classified according to more than one type. It might, for example, be the case that large numbers of agrarian events invariably occurred in sectors which also experienced large numbers of revolutionary socialist events. It is also possible that sectors with large number of events of one type would be significantly less likely to have events of another type. In this case, the occurrence of one type of movement would inhibit the occurrence of others. Neither of these situations occurs in the data. All the correlations between the $\log_e$ number of events of each type are insignificant or weak. It would seem, therefore, that the major types of movements are not only mutually exclusive and exhaustive but also orthogonal. Systems which show systematically high or low scores on one type of event do not show systematically higher or lower scores on others.

The theoretical analysis suggested that in general the following pattern of enterprise type and event type should exist in the data:

Enterprise Type	*Event Type*
Sharecropping	Revolutionary socialist
Migratory labor estate	Revolutionary nationalist
Commercial hacienda	Agrarian
Plantation	Labor
Small holding	Commodity

The correlations assessing these relationships form the diagonal of the rectangular matrix formed by the intersection of the set of event variables and the set of agricultural organization variables, and are underlined in Table 2.4. If the hypotheses are correct, these five correlations should be strong and positive, while all other correlations in the rectangular enterprise-event type matrix should be weak or negative. The results follow precisely this pattern. Revolutionary socialist events are moderately correlated ($r = .39$) with sharecropping systems, revolutionary nationalist events are strongly correlated with migratory labor systems ($r = .49$), agrarian events are strongly correlated with commercial hacienda systems ($r = .51$), and labor events are strongly correlated with plantation systems ($r = .59$). The remaining correlation along the diagonal— between small holding systems and commodity events—is considerably weaker than the others ($r = .23$), although it too is statistically significant ($p < .01$) and in the expected direction. None of the off-diagonal correlations in Table 2.4 are positive, indicating that no enterprise-event type relationship exists other than the predicted ones. Not only is there a distinct tendency for the predicted event types to cluster in the predicted systems, but there is no tendency for any other system to generate that type of event. In a few cases enterprise types appear to weakly inhibit the occurrence of event types other than the appropriate ones. Small holding systems are significantly less likely than other systems to generate either agrarian events ($r = -.29$) or labor events ($r = -.26$), and plantation

TABLE 2.5a   *Intercorrelations of Revolutionary Socialist Events with Sharecropping and Decentralized Sharecropping*

VARIABLE	(2)	(3)
1. SC	.76	.39
2. Decentralized SC		.51
3. Rev. socialist		—

systems are slightly less likely to generate agrarian events ($r = -.17$). With these exceptions, events seem randomly distributed across all systems other than the one in which they were predicted to cluster.

The analysis of agricultural organization in Chapter 1 suggested not only that particular types of agricultural organization would be prone to particular types of movements but that within each type certain sectors should be more prone to these events than others. These hypotheses are examined in Tables 2.5a to 2.5e and Figures 2.1a to 2.1d. Table 2.5a shows the relationship between revolutionary socialist events and dummy variables representing both all sharecropping systems and decentralized sharecropping systems only. Centralized sharecropping systems are operated as a single unit with sharecroppers working under the supervision of the estate management. In decentralized systems croppers work on separate, physically dispersed plots and manage their own work schedules. In neither case, however, is the cropper anything more than a laborer paid in kind. In Chapter 1 it was suggested that the centralized sharecropping system closely resembles the commercial hacienda in the degree of landlord control over workers and that decentralized sharecropping system would be more likely to generate revolutionary socialist movements. The data in Table 2.5a make clear that the decentralized system typical of rice production is considerably more likely to create revolutionary socialist events than is the sharecropping category as a whole. The correlation between the dummy variable for all sharecropping systems and revolutionary socialist events is .39, while the correlation with the decentralized systems only is .51. In fact the partial correlation between revolutionary socialist events and sharecropping controlling for decentralized sharecropping ($r_{13.2}$) is equal to zero, indicating that the entire effect of sharecropping systems on revolutionary socialist events is accounted for by the decentralized systems. The economically weak absentee landlords of the decentralized sharecropping systems are apparently an essential factor in the growth of revolutionary socialist movements.

A similar economic distinction affects the probability of revolutionary nationalist movements. The coalition of small holders and migratory wage labor which is critical for the success of the revolutionary nationalist movement can form only if the small holders have not been completely liquidated as a class. When migratory labor estates expand, they frequently displace small holders, who then become either wage laborers on the lands they had formerly owned, discontented former landowners now reduced to poverty, or small landowners

TABLE 2.5*b*   *Intercorrelations of Revolutionary Nationalist Events with Migratory Labor Estates and Colonial Regimes*

VARIABLE	(2)	(3)	(4)
1. MLE	.23	.81	.49
2. Colonial regime		.40	.38
3. (1) × (2)			.63
4. Rev. nationalist			—

facing increased pressure on their remaining lands. These circumstances do not persist long after the estate consolidation process has ended. Once the small holders have been liquidated or brought under the control of the estate owners, the wage laborers are too divided by their migratory work patterns to organize a coherent nationalist movement. In the world population of agricultural export sectors the migratory labor estates with persisting conflict between estates and small holders are largely found in colonial areas with large settler populations. In most migratory estate systems in Central America, for example, small holders have either been liquidated or incorporated into the commercial hacienda system, and neither the small holders nor an independent agrarian upper class exists to lead a revolutionary nationalist movement. Even though long-range migratory labor patterns exist in Central America, the other necessary conditions for a revolutionary nationalist movement are absent. In colonial states with relatively recent settler immigration, however, conflicts between small holders and estates persist and create the conditions necessary for a revolutionary nationalist movement. Colonial migratory estate systems should therefore be most likely to generate revolutionary nationalist events. Table 2.5 *b* shows the effect of the combination of migratory labor estates and colonial regimes on the number of revolutionary nationalist events. A colonial regime is any regime which has been under colonial control for a year or more since 1948. The interaction variable in Table 2.5*b* therefore indicates agricultural export sectors organized in migratory labor estate systems and subject to colonial rule for some period since 1948. These are the settler estate systems, which should have the highest rates of nationalist events. Table 2.5*b* also shows the zero-order correlations of nationalist events with colonialism and migratory labor estates separately. It is clear that the interaction variable has the highest correlation with revolutionary nationalist events ($r = .63$). It is also clear, however, that there is a significant correlation between revolutionary nationalist events and colonialism ($r = .38$) as well as a correlation between nationalist events and migratory labor estates ($r = .49$). This pattern of results raises two possible alternative explanations of the data. First, the effect of migratory labor estates may be a spurious consequence of its correlation with colonialism. Colonial regimes alone may lead to revolutionary nationalist events, and the form of agricultural organization may be irrelevant. This alternative hypothesis is simple and persuasive, since the revolutionary nationalist movement is usually directed at a colonial regime and therefore may be explained by political factors alone. Even if this hypothesis is false, it is still possible that colonialism exerts some independent effect in addition to the effect of agricultural organization. Both colonialism and migratory labor estates may exert independent, additive effects and no interaction term may be required to explain revolutionary nationalist events. In this case the additive model would be preferred to the interaction model on grounds of parsimony. Ignoring the constant and error terms, the additive model is described by the equation

$$Z_4 = Z_1 + Z_2$$

and the interactive model by

$$Z_4 = Z_1 + Z_2 + Z_3$$

where Z_1 is the dummy migratory labor estate variable, Z_2 is the dummy colonization variable, Z_3 is the interaction term, Z_4 is the $\log_e$ of the number of revolutionary nationalist events, and all four variables are expressed in standardized form. The additive model accounts for 31 percent of the observed variance in revolutionary nationalist events, while the interactive model accounts for 42 percent, a gain of 11 percent in variance explained. This increase in explained variance due to the interaction variable is substantial and statistically significant ($F = 20.37$, $p < .001$). Thus in terms of explanatory power the interactive model is to be preferred to the simple additive model. The interactive model is shown in the path diagram of Figure 2.1a. This diagram makes clear that the interaction between migratory labor estates and colonial regimes accounts for the correlations of both variables with nationalist events. There is no significant direct effect of colonial regime on revolutionary nationalist events ($p_{42} = .15$). Since the colonialism variable itself has no significant direct effect, the correlation between migratory labor estates and nationalist events cannot be accounted for by its spurious correlation with colonial regimes. The sum of all indirect paths from migratory labor estates to nationalist events via colonialism ($r_{12}p_{42} + r_{12}p_{32}p_{43}$) is equal to only .07. The direct path from migratory estates to nationalist events, however, is also close to zero ($p_{41} = .02$). The indirect path from migratory estates to nationalist events via the interaction term clearly accounts for most of the observed correlation between the two variables ($p_{31}p_{43} = .44$). It is clear, therefore, that a combination of migratory labor estates and colonial political systems is required for a revolutionary nationalist movement.

The same general logic can be applied to the analysis of the relationship between commercial haciendas and agrarian events. In theory commercial haciendas are unlikely to generate any strong political organization because of the divisive effects of individual land ownership. Since strong political leadership cannot be produced internally, it must be introduced from outside if an agrarian movement is to succeed. Usually this leadership is provided by a powerful socialist or reformist party with a strong interest in agrarian problems. The

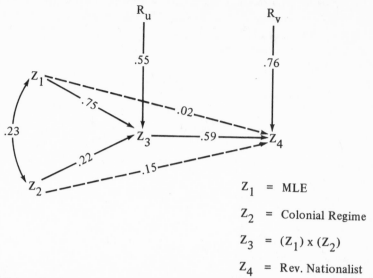

Z_1 = MLE

Z_2 = Colonial Regime

Z_3 = $(Z_1) \times (Z_2)$

Z_4 = Rev. Nationalist

FIGURE 2.1*a*   *Path Diagram of Effects of Migratory Labor Estates, Colonial Regime, and Interaction Term on Revolutionary Nationalist Events*

reform parties of Betancourt in Venezuela, Belaúnde in Peru, and Arbenz in Guatemala, for example, all encouraged the organization of peasant syndicates and advocated far-reaching land reform programs. In each case the reform party's ascension to power was associated with a widespread agrarian movement among the peasantry. If such parties are essential in the organization of an agrarian movement, then agrarian movements should occur only in those commercial hacienda systems located in countries where socialist or reform parties play a significant role in government. As was the case in the analysis of migratory labor estates, an interaction effect would be expected. The combination of commercial haciendas and socialist or reform parties should affect the probability of an agrarian movement, but neither factor alone should have an independent effect. The relationship between commercial haciendas and agrarian events as a function of the national political environment is presented in Table 2.5*c* and Figure 2.1*b*. The political variable is based on Charles Anderson, Fred von der Mehden, and Crawford Young's classification of the importance of socialist or related reform parties in the political systems of developing countries.[28] The classification indicates whether socialist or related reform parties had been the ruling party or the principal opposition party and logical successor to the ruling party at any time during the postwar period. The classification also considers the commitment to socialism of parties of each type. The Bandaranaike regime

[28] Charles W. Anderson, Fred R. von der Mehden, and Crawford Young, *Issues of Political Development* (Englewood Cliffs, N.J.: Prentice-Hall, 1967).

TABLE 2.5c *Intercorrelations of Agrarian Events with Commercial Haciendas and Socialist or Reform Parties*

VARIABLE	(2)	(3)	(4)
1. CH	.00	.74	.51
2. Soc. or reform		.25	.18
3. $(1) \times 2$			.58
4. Agrarian			—

in Ceylon, for example, was considered an example of an avowedly socialist party which had held power for some period since World War II. The Belaúnde Terry regime in Peru was considered a social reform rather than a socialist movement. The political variable in Table 2.5c simply indicates whether or not any socialist or reform party has held power or been the logical successor to the ruling party at any time since World War II. The data in Table 2.5c indicate that the combined effect of commercial haciendas and socialist or reform party participation in government is stronger ($r = .58$) than the effect of either commercial haciendas ($r = .51$) or reformist or socialist party participation ($r = .18$) separately. A comparison of the additive and interactive models again indicates that the interactive model is superior. The simple two-variable additive model accounts for 29 percent of the variance in agrarian events, but the interactive model accounts for 36 percent, a gain of 7 percent. The addition of the interaction term creates a statistically significant additional effect ($F = 13.73$,

FIGURE 2.1b *Path Diagram of Effects of Commercial Haciendas, Socialist or Reform Party, and Interaction Term on Agrarian Events*

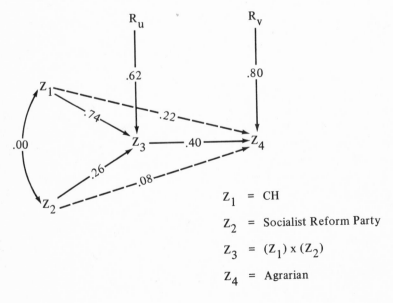

Z_1 = CH

Z_2 = Socialist Reform Party

Z_3 = $(Z_1) \times (Z_2)$

Z_4 = Agrarian

p $<$ .01). The path diagram in Figure 2.1b indicates that the interaction term accounts for most of the correlation between the dummy commercial hacienda variable and the number of agrarian events. The coefficient of the direct path from the commercial hacienda variable to the agrarian events variable (p_{41}) is an insignificant .22, while the coefficient for the indirect path through the interaction term ($p_{31}p_{43}$) is equal to .30. Since there is no correlation between commercial haciendas and the party system ($r_{12} = .00$), there can be no spurious relationship through the effects of the party system. In any case the party system exerts only a trivial and insignificant effect on agrarian events (direct path $p_{42} = .08$). The path analysis indicates that a combination of a commercial hacienda system and the participation of a socialist or reformist party in government is necessary for an agrarian movement.

The analysis of the structure of plantation systems suggested that the principal determinant of labor movements on plantations was a large, regimented, permanent labor force in an industrial environment. Not all crops grown on plantations are equally amenable to industrial technology and a large resident labor force. Crops like rubber, palm, and copra, for example, are closer to forest products than to agricultural products and do not require the large, regular inputs of labor necessary in agriculture. Rubber, palm, and coconut trees can grow wild without insecticides or fertilizer and with little attention to weeding or pruning. The trees' longevity also makes frequent plantings unnecessary. Rubber in particular actually gains from neglect, since harvesting tends to reduce future yields. All three of these crops can be produced by small independent entrepreneurs who are actually gatherers rather than agriculturalists. In the case of the oil palm the small producer simply collects palm kernels from semispontaneous growths. Palm products form an important part of the exports of both Sierra Leone and Nigeria, but neither system was included in the world population of agricultural export sectors because in both cases production techniques are based on gathering rather than agriculture. Coconuts are usually cultivated by small holders and are seldom produced on plantations. Rubber is frequently produced on plantations, but in most rubber export sectors, particularly in Malaysia, Indonesia, and Ceylon, small holders make an almost equal contribution to total exports. Rubber trees can be harvested continuously, but no other production characteristic favors centralized production. Latex need only be compressed and smoked before shipment, and although power-driven machinery is used for this process on large estates, small holders can accomplish the same end with simpler equipment. Since no expensive processing machinery is required, there are no financial barriers to entry by small holders. Rubber, palm, and coconut harvesting operations resemble forestry operations with small independent gangs or even individuals working separately and frequently paid on a piece rate. The tight labor discipline and carefully controlled harvest schedules required on a sugar or banana plantation are unnecessary for tree crops. The production of tree crops is not labor intensive, does not require a large, stable, disciplined wage labor force, and, in the case of rubber and copra,

TABLE 2.5d   *Intercorrelations of Labor Events with Plantations and Industrial Crops*

VARIABLE	(2)	(3)	(4)
1. PL	.56	.76	.59
2. Ind. crops		.78	.50
3. (1) × (2)			.68
4. Labor			—

does not require estate-owned processing machinery. Most plantation crops including bananas, sugar, sisal, and tea, however, do require large continuous inputs of disciplined labor working under industrial conditions. Since these are the plantation characteristics critical in the development of a labor movement, the plantation crops produced under industrial conditions should account for most of the labor events observed in plantation systems. The tree crop plantation should, correspondingly, not lead to large numbers of labor events.

The data in Table 2.5d show the relationship between plantation organization, crops produced in an industrial environment (bananas, sugar, sisal, tea) and labor events. It is clear that industrial plantations producing nonforest crops are significantly more likely to be associated with labor events ($r = .68$) than are the plantation systems considered collectively ($r = .59$). There is, however, also a strong zero-order correlation between industrial crops and labor events ($r = .50$), so that it is at least possible to argue that an additive rather than interactive model is appropriate. It could be argued, for example, that properties of the industrial crops lead to labor events when they are not grown on plantations. If this were true, it could mean that the effects of industrial crops and plantation organization are additive or even that the effects of plantation organization are a spurious consequence of the plantation industrial crop correlation ($r = .56$). These alternative hypotheses do not seem likely, but they can be examined in exactly the same manner as for the interaction effects involving other dependent variables. Comparison of the additive and interactive models indicates that the former accounts for 38 percent of the variance of labor events while the latter accounts for 48 percent, a gain of 10 percent. The increase in variance contributed by the interaction term is significant at the .001 level ($F = 24.04$). It is clear that an interaction effect rather than some additive effect of crop and agricultural organization is involved. The path diagram in Figure 2.1c indicates that the interaction term accounts for most of the correlation between plantation systems and labor events. The coefficient of the direct path from plantation to labor events (p_{41}) is a statistically insignificant .18, while the coefficient of the indirect path via the interaction term ($p_{31}p_{43}$) is equal to .28. The industrial crop variable alone exerts almost no direct effect on labor events ($p_{42} = -.07$). Thus it is clear that the effect of plantation systems on industrial events is almost entirely accounted for by the industrial plantation crops. The plantation tree crops, therefore, make almost no contribution to the

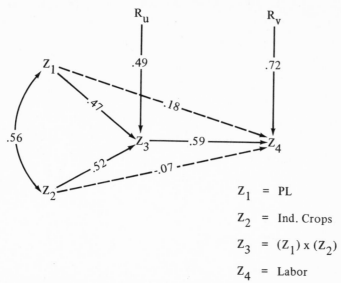

Z_1 = PL

Z_2 = Ind. Crops

Z_3 = $(Z_1) \times (Z_2)$

Z_4 = Labor

FIGURE 2.1c *Path Diagram of Effects of Plantation, Industrial Crops, and Interaction Term on Labor Events*

plantation-labor event correlation. Within the category of plantation systems, the mean score on the labor event variable for industrial crops is more than three times that for tree crops (1.30 versus .35, t for difference = 3.21, $p < .001$).

Economic differences also affect the relationship between small holdings and market events. Since the commodity event is, of course, concerned with the market in agricultural commodities, one would expect to find that greater market participation leads to greater participation in commodity movements.[29] Many small holders are primarily subsistence farmers who produce a small amount of an export crop for sale. Others, however, are almost completely dependent on market sales for subsistence. Table 2.5e shows the relationship between commodity events and market participation for small holding systems. The market participation variable indicates whether the farmer is almost completely dependent on the market, dependent in part on the market and in part on subsistence farming, or almost completely dependent on subsistence farming. The interaction variable in Table 2.5e represents the arithmetic product of this market variable with the dummy variable for small holding systems. It is clear that small holding systems with high rates of market participation are most likely to experience commodity events. The low ($r = .09$) correlation between market participation

[29] Since labor events are directed at changes in the labor market, the same general argument could be made concerning labor events and plantation organization. In this case, however, almost all workers are completely dependent on the market, so that there is insufficient variance in market participation to make comparison on this variable meaningful.

TABLE 2.5e   *Intercorrelations of Commodity Events with Small Holding and Market Participation*

VARIABLE	(2)	(3)	(4)
1. SH	−.21	.82	.23
2. Market part.		.17	.09
3. (1) × (2)			.31
4. Commodity			—

and commodity events indicates that this variable is not a likely source of spuriousness. A comparison of the additive and interactive models involving market participation and small holdings indicates that the interaction model is once again superior. The increase in variance explained due to the interaction term is relatively small, 2.3 percent ($F = 5.74$, $p < .05$). The interactive model still explains only a little more than 9 percent of the variance in the dependent variable—a considerably weaker relationship than those involving other combinations of agricultural organization and event types. The path analysis in Figure 2.1d, however, indicates that almost all the rather modest correlation between small holdings and commodity events is accounted for by the path via the interaction term (direct path $p_{41} = -.03$; indirect path $p_{31}p_{43} = .28$). Thus the effect of small holding systems on commodity events is confined to those systems with high rates of market participation.

FIGURE 2.1d   *Path Diagram of Effects of Small Holdings, Market Participation, and Interaction Term on Commodity Events*

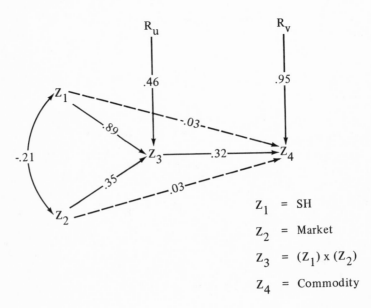

Z_1 = SH

Z_2 = Market

Z_3 = (Z_1) x (Z_2)

Z_4 = Commodity

In each of the five relationships between agricultural organization and event type the relationship is mediated by some characteristic of internal economic or external political organization. In each case the interaction terms are better predictors than the original variables. The resulting relationships between agricultural organization and types of social movements can be summarized as follows:

Decentralized sharecropping	Revolutionary socialist	$r = .51$
Settler estates	Revolutionary nationalist	$r = .63$
Hacienda/socialist reform	Agrarian	$r = .58$
Industrial plantation	Labor	$r = .68$
Commercial small holding	Commodity	$r = .31$

The typology of social movements was based primarily on the goals of the participants in a movement's constituent events. The actions of the participants in each event could also be coded from newspaper sources. Table 2.6 shows the results of a factor analysis of the coded actions of event participants. Each variable in Table 2.6 represents a logarithmic transformation of the number of events observed in a given export sector with a given action characteristic. The first set of variables in Table 2.6 is concerned with quantitative measures of event intensity, including the number of participants, the amount of property damage, and the number of casualties and arrests. The remaining sets of variables are nominal classifications of other action characteristics. The basis of group solidarity in each event represents the minimum group which provides a sense of social psychological unity for event participants. Group solidarity could be based on membership in the same ethnic group or on membership in various occupational groups such as peasants, workers, or farmers. The individuals' participation in a particular event were also classified according to the nature of the organization they formed while carrying out their actions. The acting formations included crowds, bands, disciplined mass formations, and military units. These groups in turn could be administered by complex organizations including peasant leagues, market associations, labor unions, and legal and illegal parties. The direction of the action taken by the organized or unorganized mass of participants was also coded. The tactics of an action included demonstrations and other peaceful displays of group strength, land seizures, attacks on the persons of landowners, fights with police, strikes, and warfare. The target of the action was considered to be the individual or group on which demands were made, against which actions were directed, or that was regarded by demonstrators as directly responsible for the conditions which made their actions necessary. These individuals and groups included settlers, social classes, including landowners and managers, government agencies, the police, and the regular army or national guard. When the targets of the action were members of the same ethnic or class groups as the event participants, the target was classified under the general category of "collaborators." From the perspective of the event participants

TABLE 2.6   *Factor Analysis of Tactical Event Codes: Varimax Factor Pattern*

	FACTOR				
VARIABLE	1	2	3	4	5
Intensity					
Number events	.75	.36	.33	.35	.15
Property damage	.68	.41	.07	.24	−.12
Killed	.75	.35	.04	.21	−.11
Injured	.83	.32	−.05	.13	−.13
Arrests	.65	.43	.10	.33	.11
Man-days	.46	.30	.61	.36	.10
Number participants	.44	.33	.61	.38	.11
Solidarity					
None	−.09	.33	−.02	.45	.07
Ethnic	.57	.65	−.08	−.27	−.02
Peasant	.30	−.14	−.02	.80	−.01
Farmer	.02	−.06	.08	.01	.90
Worker	−.14	−.08	.94	−.06	.07
Acting formation					
Crowd	−.04	.82	.02	.25	−.06
Irregular band	.38	.46	−.04	.07	.01
Disciplined mass	.05	.08	.69	.49	.39
Military unit	.92	.01	−.08	−.01	.06
Administration					
None	−.03	.76	−.03	.13	−.08
Local group	.35	.60	−.02	−.16	.04
Peasant league	−.03	.01	.02	.78	.19
Market Association	.00	−.02	.07	.03	.90
Labor union	−.14	−.08	.93	−.04	.07
Legal party	.19	.13	.03	.40	−.09
Illegal party	.90	−.11	−.08	.05	.02
Tactic					
Displays	.11	.28	.25	.36	.66
Land seizures	−.09	.13	.08	.84	.07
Antilandowner	.23	.20	.03	.16	−.13
Riots	.12	.82	.02	.16	.04
Repel police	.35	.55	.04	−.08	.11
Strikes	−.08	−.04	.91	−.08	.04
Warfare	.95	.08	−.07	.07	.04
Target					
Collaborators	.86	.10	−.04	.01	.14
Settlers	.70	.31	−.04	−.21	.03
Social classes	−.06	−.03	.66	.62	−.04
Gov. agencies	.46	.10	.16	.48	.33
Police	.36	.56	.05	.12	.17
Regular army	.92	.06	−.06	−.04	.03

these are groups that have failed to side with the rebels and are implicitly supporting the established order. The category of collaborator included strikebreakers, serfs on invaded lands, and peasants who failed to support a rebel army.

The varimax factor analysis solution presented in Table 2.6 identified five principal factors which together accounted for 70 percent of the communality of the original matrix. The first two factors are very similar to the "internal war" and "turmoil" dimensions identified by Rummel and Gurr in their cross-national studies of collective violence.[30] Their studies, however, were concerned with elite as well as mass political violence and included incidents in both rural and urban areas. The remaining three factors in Table 2.6 seem to be specific to agrarian movements, and consequently it is not surprising that no similar factors appear in the Rummel and Gurr studies.

The first factor in Table 2.6 clearly makes the greatest contribution to the intensity of the movement in a given export sector. The total number of events observed in an export sector, the total amount of property damage, the total number killed and injured, and the total number of arrests all have high loadings on factor 1. The remaining event characteristics with high factor loadings indicate that this factor clearly resembles the internal war dimension of the Rummel and Gurr studies. The acting formation with the highest factor loading is the military unit (.92), and the form of administration with the highest loading is the illegal party or alternative government (.90). The tactical variable with the highest loading is, of course, warfare (.95), and the targets with the highest loadings include settlers (.70), regular army troops (.92) and collaborators (.86). The last category is a function of guerrilla terrorism directed at the civilian population. The most important factor and the one contributing the greatest number of rural collective events to the total for any export sector is warfare.

The second factor in Table 2.6 also corresponds closely to the second factor in the Rummel and Gurr studies. This factor, which Rummel calls "turmoil," might simply be called "rioting" in terms of the event characteristics of Table 2.6. The characteristics with the highest factor loadings include crowds as the acting formation in the event (.82), the absence of any formal administrative apparatus directing the event (.76), and rioting as the principal tactic (.82). No specific targets have high loadings on this factor. The overall pattern suggests diffuse crowd violence with a variety of objectives.

The third factor clearly includes the identifying features of a strike. The event characteristics with the highest factor loadings include worker solidarity (.94), administration by a labor union (.93), and, of course, strikes as the principal tactic (.91). This factor also has significant loadings on the total number of participants (.61) and the total number of man-days (.61) as well

[30] Rummel, "Dimensions of Conflict Behavior," and Gurr, "Causal Model of Civil Strife."

as the participation by disciplined mass formations (.69). This factor, then, seems to describe strike events involving relatively peaceful mass actions by large numbers of workers directed by a labor union.

The fourth factor clearly includes the characteristics of a land invasion. The event characteristics with the highest factor loadings include peasant solidarity (.80), peasant leagues as the administrative organization (.78), seizures of land as the principal tactic (.84), and, to a somewhat lesser extent, social classes, in this case landowners, as the target (.62). It is interesting to note that attacks on landowners as opposed to simple seizures of land have a very low loading on this factor. In this population of export sectors, land invasions seem to be generally peaceful and do not involve the violence of the peasant *jacquerie*. The typical factor 3 event would be a peaceful peasant land invasion.

The remaining factor clearly describes events involving protests over conditions in the commodity markets. The event characteristics with the highest factor loadings include the occupational identity of farmers as the basis of group solidarity (.90), commodity market associations as the administrative apparatus directing the event (.90), and demonstrations as the principal tactic (.66). The event characteristics with the highest loadings suggest peaceful organized protest by farmers who are members of a commodity-based association.

The total number of event characteristics can be reduced to a small number of discrete actions—wars, riots, strikes, land invasions, and market protests. The data in Table 2.7 show the relationship between these five types of action and both types of social movements and types of agricultural organization. The hypotheses outlined in Chapter 1 suggested that a particular pattern of action should be associated with each type of social movement and, correspondingly, particular actions would be more common in particular types of crop systems. In particular, revolutionary socialist and nationalist movements were to be associated with warfare, agrarian movements with land invasions, labor movements with strikes, and commodity movements with market protests. Correspondingly both decentralized sharecropping systems and settler estates should be associated with warfare, commercial haciendas in reform political systems should be associated with land invasions, industrial plantations should be associated with strikes, and small holdings should be associated with market protests. The data for testing the first of these two sets of hypotheses are presented in the rectangular submatrix formed by the intersection of movement type variables 1 to 5 and action type variables 6 to 10 in Table 2.7. The action variables are the highest loading items on the corresponding factor in Table 2.7. It is clear that all the predicted relationships exist in the data. Warfare is associated with both revolutionary socialist ($r = .56$) and revolutionary nationalist ($r = .63$) movements. Agrarian movements are strongly associated with land invasions ($r = .75$) and labor events with strikes ($r = .75$). Commodity movements are, of course, associated with market protests ($r = .70$). Rioting seems to occur as part of a number of different types of movements and is not strongly associated with any one.

TABLE 2.7   *Intercorrelations of Event Tactics, Event Objectives, and Type of Agricultural Organization*

VARIABLE	(2)	(3)	(4)	(5)	(6)	(7)	(8)	(9)	(10)	(11)	(12)	(13)	(14)	(15)
1. Rev. socialist	-.07	.12	.00	.07	.56	-.05	-.05	.24	.03	.51	-.11	-.03	.10	.01
2. Rev. nationalist		-.17	-.14	-.06	.63	.27	-.15	-.11	.01	-.06	.63	-.11	-.11	-.13
3. Agrarian			-.01	.08	-.05	.27	.04	.75	.10	.05	-.10	.58	-.10	-.18
4. Labor				-.01	-.14	-.10	.88	.10	.12	.05	-.15	-.09	.68	-.22
5. Commodity					.02	.22	-.01	.06	.70	.02	.01	-.07	-.11	.31
6. War						.01	-.19	.01	.01	.23	.40	-.08	-.16	-.05
7. Riots							-.05	.28	.04	.02	.17	-.04	-.16	-.05
8. Strikes								.05	.08	-.02	-.16	-.04	.63	-.21
9. Land seizures									.08	.23	-.13	.39	-.14	-.18
10. Market protests										.06	-.09	.06	.02	.11
11. Decentralized SC											-.11	-.10	-.12	-.11
12. Settler estate												-.10	-.12	-.21
13. Hacienda/reform													-.11	-.19
14. Ind. plantation														-.22
15. Com. small holding														—

The data for the second set of hypotheses concerning the relationship between agricultural organization and action characteristics is presented in the rectangular submatrix formed by the intersection of action variables 6 to 10 and agricultural variables 11 to 15 in Table 2.7. It is clear from this matrix that warfare is associated with both settler estates $(r = .40)$ and decentralized sharecropping systems $(r = .23)$. The multiple R for the regression of warfare on both settler estates and decentralized sharecropping is equal to .48. These two systems, both of which combine an economically weak upper class with a wage labor force with unstable ties to the land, are the major sources of revolutionary warfare. Land invasions are associated with the commercial hacienda/reform or socialist party variable $(r = .39)$. It is clear, however, that land invasions also occur in decentralized sharecropping systems $(r = .23)$. Strikes are almost exclusively associated with industrial plantation systems $(r = .63)$. There is no significant association between market protests and commercial small holding systems even though these systems are associated with commodity movements. Apparently the tactics used in commodity movements are too variable to permit a simple correlation with agricultural organization. With this exception the pattern of correlations in Table 2.7 conforms to expectations.

CONCLUSIONS

The overall pattern of results supports the general theory of rural social movements outlined in Chapter 1. Revolutionary movements tend to occur in systems in which the principal source of income of the upper classes is land ownership and the principal source of income of the lower classes is wages paid either in cash or in kind. In such a system the upper classes cannot depend on the power of financial or industrial capital to maintain their competitive position or to recruit and control their labor force. As a result the upper classes are unable or unwilling to grant economic or political concessions to workers. The agrarian upper class is too poor to concede a substantial share of the income from agriculture to its workers and cannot concede the land itself without undermining the base of its power. It cannot yield political power without diminishing its ability to recruit labor through coercion and to protect its lands against invading peasants. The attitude of the upper class, therefore, must be unyielding. Agricultural wage laborers, however, are increasingly able to organize collective opposition to demand change. In sharecropping systems the market splits the traditional agrarian social structure along class lines and the agricultural workers are progressively converted into a rural proletariat paid in kind. The weaker their ties to the land, the less individual economic action can provide a means of upward mobility and the greater the likelihood that economic gains will be sought through collective political action. An organized working class therefore confronts an economically weak and politically rigid upper class. The result is a revolutionary war. It is warfare organized along class lines with a distinct socialist ideology. Revolutionary socialist war is particularly likely in decentralized sharecropping systems, in which the landlords' coercive power is diminished by the physical dispersion of individual cultivators and their economic power is weakened by middleman control of processing. Decentralized sharecropping systems therefore create the conditions for a social movement based on revolutionary socialism as the dominant ideology and warfare as the dominant tactic.

The migratory labor estate system shares with the sharecropping system the economic weakness and political rigidity of the estate owners and their dependence on land as their only source of income. It also includes an agricultural labor force whose ties to the land have been considerably weakened by migratory wage labor. The migratory labor estate differs, however, from the sharecropping system because the development of the market does not split the traditional agrarian social structure, but may actually reinforce traditional communal ties. The migratory wage laborer finds that he must depend on the traditional peasant society for support during the long periods when he is not employed on the estate. The traditional leadership and individual small holders find themselves under increasing economic pressure from the land expropriations of the estate owners. As long as the traditional leaders and small holders exist as a significant political force, they can combine with wage laborers to form a powerful revolutionary coalition with a common interest in destroying the estate owners. This coalition can only form where an estate system is in the early stages of development and the small landowners and traditional leadership have not been completely liquidated. These conditions are most likely in colonial settler economies. The settlers are no more able to concede political or economic power than were the landlords in the sharecropping system. Like the landlords in the sharecropping system they face a powerful political coalition that would benefit from their demise. The result is a revolutionary nationalist movement aimed at seizing state power and eliminating the estate system that it supports. The diversity of economic goals in the revolutionary coalition and the ethnic divisions between settlers and the indigenous population create a movement based on communal rather than class ties.

The agrarian upper class in the commercial hacienda system, like those in the sharecropping and migratory labor estate systems is dependent on land as its principal source of income. The workers in this system, however, share this dependence on land. The usufructuary or small peasant working as a wage laborer retains an interest in his individual plot which stimulates economic competition and discourages collective political organization. The control of even small amounts of property also inhibits the appeal of revolutionary movements threatening the abolition of private land ownership. The hacienda worker is interested only in obtaining land and lacks broader political or social objectives. Since internal political organization is largely absent and parties with revolutionary economic programs can make little progress, peasant movements in commercial hacienda systems depend on socialist or reformist parties with an important role in national government. Even in this case, however, the peasant's enthusiasm for a social movement is likely to dissipate as soon as his immediate hunger for land has been satisfied. The peasants of a commercial hacienda system are therefore the least likely of any agricultural working class to become the beneficiaries of the political changes their movements set in motion. The widespread land seizures of an agrarian movement may destroy the political power of the landed aristocracy, but the resulting political vacuum will be filled by urban interest groups who possess the long-term political objectives and coherent political organization that the peasants lack. The commercial hacienda therefore establishes the conditions for a short-lived agrarian revolt.

The principal source of income for the upper classes in both the plantation and small holding systems is industrial or financial capital rather than land, and the basic source of their power is therefore money rather than force. Conflict in both systems tends to be focused on the distribution of income, not on the ownership of income-producing property itself. As a result rural social movements in both systems tend to be reformist rather than revolutionary. Even the workers of an industrial plantation whose ties to the land are completely severed and who form the homogeneous class-conscious proletariat of classical Marxian theory are unlikely to create a revolutionary movement. The prospects for successful negotiations and the resulting incremental gains in income must be weighed against the dangers and uncertainty of revolution. Since the owners of plantations have both the resources to make concessions and the incentive to create a disciplined labor force, they are likely to respond more flexibly to working-class demands than would an upper class whose wealth depended entirely on land. The industrial plantation therefore creates the conditions for revolutionary class consciousness but reformist action. The small holding system shares with the plantation system an economically powerful upper class whose income is based on commercial and industrial capital. The small holder, however, like the peasant in a commercial hacienda system, is tied to his individual farm and as a result is committed to the pursuit of individual rather than collective economic goals. Political action of any kind is unlikely, but when such action does take place, it is likely to be concerned with minor changes in the market for agricultural commodities rather than major changes in the institutions of property.

When landed property is the only source of income for the agrarian lower classes, conflicts over the ownership of property and the control of the state are the result. When industrial and financial capital are the major source of upper-class wealth, concessions can always be made and rural social movements diverted before they reach revolutionary proportions. Revolution begins not among the class-conscious proletariat of the industrial plantation, but among the proletarianized sharecroppers and migratory laborers of the landed estate.

The general relationships revealed in the analysis of the world population of agricultural export sectors are considered in individual export systems in the case studies of Peru, Angola, and Vietnam in Chapters 3, 4, and 5. Four of the five major relationships between agricultural organization and social movements are considered: the relationship between the industrial plantation and the labor movement, between the commercial hacienda in a reformist political environment and the agrarian movement, between the settler estate and the revolutionary nationalist movement, and between the decentralized sharecropping system and the revolutionary socialist movement. Only the relationship between small holdings and commodity events has not been considered, in part because of the very absence of any large social movements in small holding systems. Chapter 3 considers both labor and agrarian movements in Peru. The labor movement occurs in the industrial sugar plantations of the coast, and the agrarian movements occur in the commercial hacienda systems of both the coast and the sierra. The Peruvian agrarian movements all took place during a period when the central government was controlled by a reformist party committed to land reform. Chapter 4 considers a revolutionary nationalist movement, the Angolan revolution, in a settler-based coffee export economy. Finally Chapter 5 considers the war in Vietnam as an instance of a revolutionary socialist movement. The analysis attempts to show the relationship between the revolutionary movement and the decentralized sharecropping system of the rice export economy. Each of these cases was selected from the world population of agricultural export sectors because it had experienced a particularly well-known and well-described movement and because each promised to provide detailed knowledge of the general principles linking types of agricultural organization and types of rural social movements.

CHAPTER 3

Peru: Hacienda and Plantation

IN A PHRASE which has become a favorite among writers on Peru, Antonio
Raimondi described the country as a beggar sitting on a bench of gold. The
popularity of his description derives as much from its reference to the deep
divisions of Peruvian economic and social life as it does from its patriotic affirmation of the country's development potential. Peru is in fact split into two distinct
economic sectors, and this division is accompanied by similar divisions in culture,
politics, and social organization. The division is particularly apparent in the
agricultural economy, which includes both a small, highly developed export
sector and a vast, backward subsistence sector. As is the case in other dual
economies, economic development and cultural change have been concentrated
almost exclusively in the export enclaves, and much of rural Peru changed little
from the time of the Spanish conquest until the second half of the twentieth
century. These extremes of agricultural organization and economic development
closely parallel and are in part dependent on the dramatic extremes of Peruvian
geography. In few other places on earth are such diverse environments found in
such close proximity, and an understanding of Peruvian geography is essential
for explaining both the development of the agricultural export economy and the
pattern of rural social movements.

Peru is usually divided into three natural regions; the coast, the sierra, and
the *selva,* or jungle. The regional divisions form three roughly parallel strips
running in a northwest to southeast direction from the Ecuadorian to the Chilean
frontiers. The coast is a strip of desert ranging from 50 to 100 miles in width
and ending abruptly in the steep upthrust of the Andes, which in some places
extend almost to the Pacific. The sierran highlands include snow-capped mountains, some of which reach 20,000 feet, broad highland plateaus at 10,000 to
12,000 feet, and numerous canyons and valleys which are cut far below the level

124

of the surrounding plateau. The *selva* is a tropical and semitropical forest in the upper reaches of the Amazon and remains largely a frontier area. The regions are usually distinguished on the basis of altitude, although frequently vegetation, climate, topography, and even social organization seem to play some part.

The coastal region is considered to extend to about 6,500 feet, and usually a distinction is made between the *costa baja,* or coast proper, at altitudes less than 850 feet and the *costa alta* at altitudes from 850 to 6,500 feet, where the coast merges with the sierran highlands.[1] The Peruvian coast is one of the driest areas on earth, and in many places years may pass with no rain at all. Agriculture would be impossible except for the presence of 52 rivers which extend back into areas of higher rainfall in the Andes and provide water for irrigation. Even so, only a dozen of these rivers have a year-round flow, and many of the others have too little water for practical use. The soils of the coast are surprisingly fertile once irrigated, and the most productive agriculture in Peru is located in the coastal oases. The extreme aridity of the coast is a result of the offshore upwelling of the Humboldt, or Peruvian, current, which cools the prevailing westerly winds off the Pacific and deprives them of their moisture content before they reach the coast. The current is critical to the delicate ecology of the Peruvian coastal economy, and when a film of wind-blown warm water moves in over the cold current, a linked series of ecological disasters occur which threaten both the agricultural and fishing industries of the coast. The upwelling of the Peruvian current pulls nutrients toward the surface, where they support vast numbers of anchovies, which are the basis of Peru's fish meal industry, a major source of export earnings. The fish are in turn fed upon by sea birds which deposit guano on offshore islands, where it is mined and used for fertilizer in the coastal oases. When warm water covers the current, the fish are deprived of nutrients and disappear, the birds die off, reducing the supply of fertilizer, and the warm moisture-laden winds continue on over the coast, where their moisture precipitates, causing disastrous flooding and blocking out the intense sunlight necessary for coastal agriculture. Without the presence of the cold Peruvian current the coastal region would probably become a tropical rain forest similar to adjacent areas in Ecuador, and coastal agriculture would be impossible.

The coast forms three separate subregions for agricultural purposes. The northern third of the coast is a flat plain more than a hundred miles wide and is exposed to almost continual sunlight. The middle third is narrower as the Andes gradually constrict the coastal plain, but it is cut by numerous rivers whose alluvial fans provide a favorable environment for agriculture. The central coast is frequently cloudy, although here as in the north little rain actually falls and hardier plants which can take advantage of limited sunlight are grown. The southern third of the coast is almost completely without moisture, and little agriculture is possible in this region.

[1] David A. Robinson, *Peru in Four Dimensions* (Lima: American Studies Press, 1964), p. 157.

The sierran region is formed by the highlands of the Andes, which lie between the coast and the jungle. The topography of the Andes is extremely complex but can be roughly described as three parallel mountain chains running along the same axis as the coastal strip. The chains are separated by rivers which join to flow into the Amazon and are broken by many smaller streams which have cut deep, transverse canyons, forming largely inaccessible pockets. Rainfall is more abundant than it is on the coast, but it is distinctly seasonal, and in most places irrigation would be necessary for efficient agricultural production. Most of the land which does not actually lie on precipitous slopes, forms the *puna,* a desolate highland plateau covered by short grass and scrub. Much of this plateau lies at altitudes of between 12,000 and 15,000 feet, and since little agriculture is possible above the 12,000-foot level, most of this area is used for extensive grazing. In 1961 only 1.7 million hectares were under cultivation in the sierra, while more than 9 million hectares were used for grazing.[2] Agriculture is possible in the broad river valleys, some of which lie as much as 5,000 feet below the high plateau, and on small patches of land in the steep-walled transverse canyons. The rugged terrain and the scattered agricultural land make transportation difficult, and except in a few regions close to major rail or road routes, sierran agriculture remains at a subsistence level.

The third major region, the *selva* or *montaña,* begins on the lower slopes of the eastern Andes, but its boundary is marked as much by its typical forest vegetation as by altitude alone. In general, two zones are distinguished: the *selva baja,* or low jungle—a dense, tropical rain forest found at altitudes less than 1,500 feet—and the *selva alta,* or high jungle, sometimes called the *ceja de montaña,* or "eyebrow of the forest," because of its characteristic bushy forest growth, which in places extends as high as 5,000 feet up the Andes. The low jungle is an extension of the Amazon basin and is in closer contact with the Atlantic through river transport than it is with much of Peru. It is sparsely populated by nomadic hunter gatherers and has been of little economic importance since the collapse of the turn-of-century rubber boom. The high *selva* is a region of broken sloping terrain crossed by numerous ravines and river beds which impede overland transport and tend to isolate the area from the rest of the country. The heavy rainfall and semitropical climate of this region make it possible to grow a number of industrial crops. Coca has been grown in the region since the time of the Incas, and this area still supplies most of the coca leaves chewed as a stimulant by many sierran Indians. Tea is also produced, but the major cash crop is coffee, which began to be produced in volume in the late 1950s. It is grown exclusively on the eastern slopes of the Andes at altitudes between 2,500 and 6,500 feet, and the rapid increase in production has stimulated considerable migration into the high *selva* region.

[2] Comité Interamericano de Desarrollo Agrícola (CIDA), *Tenencia de la Tierra y Desarrollo Socio-Económico del Sector Agrícola: Perú* (Washington: Pan American Union, 1966), pp. 3–4.

Since the low *selva* is largely uninhabited, the principal social and economic contrast in Peru is between the coast and the sierra. The high *selva* can be considered part of the sierra for purposes of this crude social division, although there are some significant differences in agricultural organization between the two regions. The coastal region is responsible for most of Peru's modern economic activity, while the sierra remains a subsistence economy. With the exception of the mining in the central sierra all industry is concentrated on the coast, and the few major towns in the sierra are more administrative than commercial centers. The indigenous Indian societies of the coast were destroyed by the invading Spaniards, and coastal society developed in response to an expanding export economy in the late nineteenth and early twentieth centuries. As in most export economies most of the capital, entrepreneurial skill, and even the labor supply were originally imported from abroad, and few traces of indigenous culture remain on the coast. In the sierra an imported manorial economy was imposed on the indigenous communal land-holding patterns, and many elements of indigenous culture survive to the present. While Spanish is almost universally used on the coast, there are many areas in the sierra in which only the indigenous Indian languages, Quechua and Aymara, are understood. Traditional dietary practices, modes of dress, ceremonial observance, and community organization persist in the Indian sierra while they have almost vanished on the Hispanicized coast. Literacy, urbanization, communication, political participation, and modernization in general are considerably more advanced on the coast. The sierran population, cut off from outside influences by the cordillera of the Andes, remained until the 1960s a separate society with little or no participation in national life.

Both the agricultural economy and the pattern of rural social movements follow this fundamental division between sierra and coast. The agricultural export sector is almost entirely concentrated on the coast, while the subsistence sector is confined to the sierra. Coastal agriculture is capital and land intensive, oriented toward outside markets, and based on irrigation and mechanization, while sierran agriculture is land extensive, poorly capitalized, and based on an agricultural technology little changed from the time of the Incas. The manorial economy of the sierra is based on forced labor by dependent serfs and expands through the acquisition of additional landholdings rather than through technical improvements. Investment by either internal or external capital is limited to a few modern ranches. Coastal agriculture is based on wage labor and expands through investments in machines, fertilizers, and irrigation works. In 1960 the Peruvian agricultural development bank reported that more than 75 percent of its outstanding loans were to coastal agricultural enterprises, even though the coast contains only 23 percent of the country's agricultural land.[3] Most sierran agriculture lacks any form of mechanization and in many places is carried out

[3] Perú, Superintendencia de Bancos, *Memoria y Estadística* (Lima: Imprenta Casa Nacional de Moneda, 1960), p. 57.

with human muscle power aided only by the traditional Incan foot plow. In 1961, 84 percent of the 6,950 tractors in Peru were concentrated on the coast, and in most places in the sierra 30 to 40 percent of all agricultural units lacked even animal traction.[4] These differences in capitalization and labor organization are reflected in immense differences in productivity. In 1960 the largely coastal agricultural export sector employed less than 4 percent of the economically active population in agriculture but contributed almost 40 percent of national agricultural production. The production per person employed in the agricultural export sector was more than eight times greater than in the subsistence sector.[5]

The world population of agricultural export systems includes three Peruvian cases, and, as might be expected, two of the three are located on the coast. Both cotton and sugar are grown in coastal oases and represent both the major form of agricultural production and the major source of employment for the rural coast. The single sierran system involves coffee grown in the high *selva* region and forms a tiny commercial sector in the midst of a much larger population of subsistence cultivators. The dominant form of agricultural enterprise in both sugar and cotton production closely resembles the world pattern for these crops, but the organization of coffee production differs significantly from the world pattern. Sugar is typically produced in corporate plantations employing resident wage labor and utilizing expensive processing machinery. All these features are present in the dominant agricultural enterprises in Peruvian sugar production. Cotton is produced in centralized commercial estates in Peru as it is elsewhere in the world, but the Peruvian cotton is cultivated by wage labor rather than sharecroppers. Since the estates typically lack processing machinery, the system was classified as a commercial hacienda in the world analysis. Although the organization of Peruvian coffee production was also classified as a commercial hacienda system for the purposes of the world analysis, it actually differs significantly from both the coastal cotton estates and from coffee estates elsewhere. In the centralized, market-oriented cotton estates of the coast the cash crop is cultivated on domain lands, while in the sierra coffee is produced on usufruct plots and domain lands continue to be used for grazing. Actually the sierran coffee system includes both commercial manors with dependent usufructuaries bound to the estate by custom or law and independent small holders in regions of large estates. While many of the latter hold nominal title to their land, they are under the political and economic control of large landowners and many in fact work part time on the haciendas to supplement the inadequate earnings of their own plots. The differential use of domain and usufruct lands in the cotton and coffee systems leads to significant differences in social organization despite their classificatory similarities.

Both cotton and sugar have been major Peruvian exports since the beginning of this century, and they continued to contribute a substantial fraction of total agricultural exports during the 1948 to 1970 period. Coffee production

[4] CIDA, *Perú*, p. 328.
[5] Perú, *Boletín del Banco Central de Reserva del Perú* (Lima, 1962), p. 64.

TABLE 3.1   *Principal Agricultural Exports as a Percentage of Total Agricultural Exports 1948–1970*[a]

YEAR	Sugar	EXPORT Cotton	Coffee	Wool
1948	43	53	1	2
1949	—	—	—	—
1950	28	64	0	7
1951	25	63	0	10
1952	28	67	2	2
1953	32	60	5	2
1954	29	57	6	7
1955	30	52	7	5
1956	24	63	7	6
1957	35	48	9	7
1958	26	57	12	5
1959	28	53	12	7
1960	32	50	13	5
1961	36	46	13	4
1962	29	52	13	5
1963	33	48	13	6
1964	31	45	18	6
1965	26	40	21	8
1966	28	50	17	5
1967	36	35	19	6
1968	42	24	21	9
1969	29	35	23	8
1970	39	23	30	3

[a] United Nations Statistical Office, *Yearbook of International Trade Statistics* and *World Trade Annual and Supplements.*

began only in the late 1950s but has made an increasing contribution to total agricultural exports since 1960. As the data in Table 3.1 indicate, the contributions of cotton and sugar remained relatively constant over the postwar period, while coffee exports, which were virtually nil at the beginning of the period, almost equaled the contribution of the traditional crops by the late 1960s. The median share of agricultural exports over the 1948 to 1970 period was 50 percent for cotton and 29 percent for sugar. The median figure for coffee was only 12 percent, but the coffee system was included in the world population because exports exceeded the 15 percent mark for a continuous period of more than five years (1964 to 1970). Wool contributed a median of 6 percent of total agricultural exports in the 1948 to 1970 period, and since the largest contribution in any one year was 10 percent, the wool export sector was not included in the world population of country crop systems. Peruvian exports are considerably more varied than those of most countries in the study population, and agriculture as a whole has made up a decreasing fraction of total exports in recent years. In 1948 cotton and sugar were the only agricultural exports of any importance, but agriculture still contributed 50 percent of total exports, while in 1970, even with increased coffee exports, agriculture contributed only 15 percent of exports.

The relative decline of agriculture is accounted for by the expansion of the fish meal industry and the opening of new copper and iron deposits. The absolute value of agricultural exports actually increased from 80 million dollars in 1948 to 150 million dollars in 1970. For most of the period before 1960 agriculture hovered around half of total exports, and for the entire 1948 to 1970 period agricultural exports were concentrated in either two or three major crops. The agricultural export sectors continued to be the focus of intense social and political conflict throughout the postwar period. Despite their declining economic importance and small proportion of the agricultural work force they have been the major source of social change in rural areas. Social movements in both the coast and the sierra have been closely tied to the export systems in sugar, cotton, and coffee.

The social movement data for Peru from the *New York Times* and the *Hispanic American Report* provide a general overview of the major pattern of events in the Peruvian agricultural export sector. The sources report a total of 36 events forming two distinct movements—a rural labor movement on the coast and an agrarian movement in the sierra. The coastal labor movement is represented by six events—five in the sugar system and one in the cotton system. The agrarian movement includes a total of 30 events, with 22 of these associated with the coffee system, three with the cotton system, and two with subsistence areas. An additional three agrarian events, all of which occurred in the central sierra, could not be associated with any of the systems in either the export or the subsistence population. The labor events associated with the coastal sugar plantations follow the typical pattern of a rural labor movement. The events are all strikes organized by labor unions, and are directed at limited economic objectives. There are no strikes calling for nationalization, although in the early part of the period riots occurred in at least two cases when strikes were declared illegal and police were called in. The labor unions are affiliated with the Peruvian APRA party (*Alianza Popular Revolucionaria Americana*), which, despite the reference to revolution in the party's name and its early Marxist affiliations, has become a reformist democratic party which contests elections and in many respects resembles the traditional parties of the Peruvian upper class. All the strikes involve wage issues, and none of them make any political demands of the government or even attack the property rights of the plantation owners. The rural labor events are concentrated in the relatively brief period between the end of legal suppression of labor unions in 1956 and the relatively unfavorable organizational environment of the military regime which took power in 1968. The first event took place in 1957 and the last in 1963, and they are relatively evenly distributed over the intervening years.

The agrarian movement of the sierra shares neither the reformist tactics nor the respect for property of the coastal sugar workers. The sierran movement represented the first major challenge to traditional patterns of land ownership since the beginning of the republican era. In less than three years of concentrated assault the peasants of the sierra left the manorial economy in ruins and broke the political power of the hacienda owners. While the demolition was neither as rapid nor as complete as it was in neighboring Bolivia, the peasant movement left a fatally weakened rural elite which has proved unable to resist new initiatives for land reform. Despite the massive effect of the movement much of it was carried out with relatively little bloodshed. The primary tactic of the peasant was land invasion, and when invasions were not repelled by the police, hacienda owners were seldom subjected to abuse. Most of the 30 recorded agrarian events involve land invasions rather than land invasions accompanied by attacks on persons, and only 9 of the 30 involve any kind of violence, including violence initiated by the police. The invasions were organized by peasant leagues, but with a few notable exceptions they were not motivated by revolutionary ideology. The peasants' interest was solely in gaining and defending land, and once this objective had been attained, they showed no interest in continued political action. In contrast with the relatively continuous economic action of the coastal workers, the highland peasants carried out their invasions in one immense outburst which reached peak intensity in the period surrounding the 1962–63 elections. The invasions themselves were carried out by relatively small groups of neighbors or members of the same community, and despite the fact that many peasant leagues were affiliated with national peasant organizations, there was almost no administrative coordination of their actions.

All but three of the reported agrarian events took place in the sierra, and most of these were associated with the coffee system. The three remaining events were all associated with the coastal cotton system and closely resembled the land invasions of the sierra. The cotton system also included a single labor event, a riot over wage demands. Agrarian events were therefore associated with commercial manors in both the sierra and the coast, while labor events were almost all associated with the coastal sugar plantations. This pattern is of course representative of the results of the world analysis of agricultural export sectors. These results are based on a crude event count in secondary sources and a rough division of Peru into crop-producing areas. This chapter will attempt to develop a more complete description of Peruvian social movements based on primary source materials and a more detailed statistical picture of the country's agricultural organization. While this analysis is directed at determining the exact empirical relationships between agricultural organization and the organization of social movements, it also permits a comparison of the results of the worldwide analysis based on secondary sources with those obtained from primary Peruvian materials.

STATISTICAL DATA ON PERUVIAN AGRICULTURE AND RURAL EVENTS

In the world analysis the agricultural export sector was the fundamental unit of analysis, and each system was defined in terms of first-order political subdivisions. Although this unit is adequate for cross-national generalization, it is not useful for an internal analysis of Peruvian agrarian structure. Peru is divided into three export sectors and one subsistence sector in the world population, and these units are made up of varying numbers of departments, the first-order political subdivision. There are a total of 24 departments if the constitutional province of Callao is counted as a separate department (Map 3.1). Unfortunately the boundaries of the departments bear little relationship to the geographic divisions of Peru and a number of departments contain areas in more than one natural region. In addition, three of the departments fall in the low *selva* region and are of little interest in any analysis of agrarian structure. The second-order political subdivisions, termed provinces in Peru, are considerably more convenient for statistical purposes, and many agricultural data are reported at this level in government sources. There were 144 second-order political subdivisions in Peru in 1960 if the constitutional province of Callao is again counted as both a province and a department. With the exception of the province of Chancay, which includes extensive areas in both the coast and the sierra, each of the remaining 143 provinces can be unambiguously assigned to one of the three natural regions. Since the wide economic and cultural differences among the natural regions and particularly the differences between the coast and the sierra effect both the pattern of agricultural organization and the pattern of social movements, it is essential that the regional effects as well as the effects of agricultural organization be considered in any statistical analysis. For this reason each of the 144 provinces was assigned to one of the natural regions on the basis of altitudes indicated in topographical maps presented by Robinson.[6] This procedure assigned 28 provinces to the coastal region, 97 to the sierra and high *selva* regions, and 18 to the low selva. The province of Chancay was singled out and analyzed separately. This division of the primary unit of analysis by natural region makes it possible to consider both differences between regions and the correlations between agricultural organization and event distributions within regions.

The analysis of course requires independent measures of agriculture and social structure on the one hand and the distribution of events on the other. Fortunately, adequate data on both variables are available. Peru conducted its first population census of modern times in 1940 and a second census in 1961. The results of the 1961 census appeared originally by department only, but more recently the National Office of Statistics has issued a five-volume summary of the results presenting data by province.[7] These volumes present information on demography, migration, work force participation, occupation, education, literacy, housing, health, and even dietary practices and patterns of dress. The first 11 volumes of an additional series showing breakdowns by third-order subdivisions (districts) has also been published, but these data are not likely to be available for the entire country in the immediate future, and the provincial data are adequate for statistical purposes. Peru also conducted its first agricultural census in 1961, and the Statistical Office has published results showing

[6] Robinson, *Peru*, pp. 31–66.
[7] Perú, Dirección Nacional de Estadística y Censos, *Sexto Censo Nacional de Población*, vol. 1, books 1–5 (Lima, 1965).

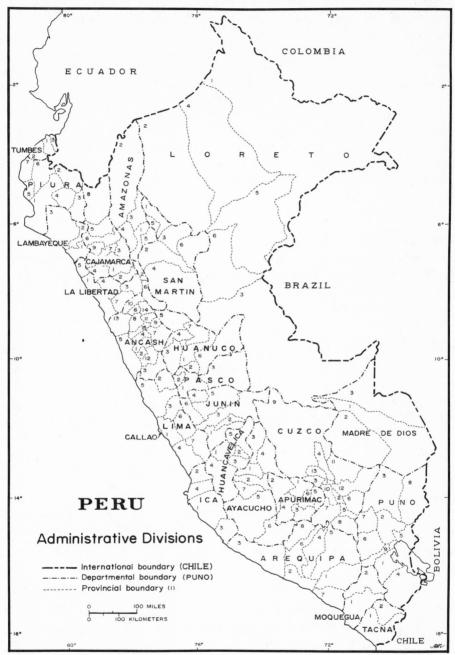

PERU

Administrative Divisions

- ▬ ▬ ▬ International boundary (CHILE)
- ▬ · ▬ · ▬ Departmental boundary (PUNO)
- ▬ ▬ ▬ ▬ Provincial boundary (I)

| 0 | | 100 MILES |
| 0 | | 100 KILOMETERS |

MAP 3.1

133

KEY TO MAP 3.1

(C = Coast, S = Sierra, J = *Selva*)

01 AMAZONAS
  01 Chachapoyas   S
  02 Bagua   J
  03 Bongará   J
  04 Luya   S
  05 Rodríquez de   J
     Mendoza

02 ANCASH
  01 Huaraz   S
  02 Aija   S
  03 Bolognesi   S
  04 Carhuaz   S
  05 Casma   C
  06 Corongo   S
  07 Huari   S
  08 Huaylas   S
  09 Mariscal Luz.   S
  10 Pallasca   S
  11 Pomabamba   S
  12 Recuay   S
  13 Santa   C
  14 Sihuas   S
  15 Yungay   S

03 APURÍMAC
  01 Abancay   S
  02 Andahuaylas   S
  03 Antabamba   S
  04 Aymaraes   S
  05 Cotabambas   S
  06 Grau   S

04 AREQUIPA
  01 Arequipa   S
  02 Camaná   C
  03 Caravelí   C
  04 Castilla   S
  05 Caylloma   S
  06 Condesuyos   S
  07 Islay   C
  08 La Unión   S

05 AYACUCHO
  01 Huamanga   S
  02 Cangallo   S
  03 Huanta   S
  04 La Mar   S
  05 Lucanas   S
  06 Parinacochas   S

  07 Víctor Fajardo   S

06 CAJAMARCA
  01 Cajamarca   S
  02 Cajabamba   S
  03 Celendín   S
  04 Contumazá   S
  05 Cutervo   S
  06 Chota   S
  07 Hualgayoc   S
  08 Jaén   S
  09 Santa Cruz   S

07 CALLAO
  01 Callao   C

08 CUZCO
  01 Cuzco   S
  02 Acomayo   S
  03 Anta   S
  04 Calca   S
  05 Canas   S
  06 Canchis   S
  07 Chumbivilcas   S
  08 Espinar   S
  09 La Convención   S
  10 Paruro   S
  11 Paucartambo   S
  12 Quispicanchis   S
  13 Urubamba   S

09 HUANCAVELICA
  01 Huancavelica   S
  02 Acobamba   S
  03 Angaraes   S
  04 Castrovirreyna   S
  05 Tayacaja   S

10 HUÁNUCO
  01 Huánuco   S
  02 Ambo   S
  03 Dos de Mayo   S
  04 Huamalíes   S
  05 Marañón   S
  06 Pachitea   S
  07 Leoncio Prado   S

11 ICA
  01 Ica   C
  02 Chincha   C
  03 Nazca   C

  04 Pisco   C

12 JUNÍN
  01 Huancayo   S
  02 Concepción   S
  03 Jauja   S
  04 Junín   S
  05 Tarma   S
  06 Yauli   S

13 LA LIBERTAD
  01 Trujillo   C
  02 Bolívar   S
  03 Huamachuco   S
  04 Otuzco   S
  05 Pacasmayo   C
  06 Pataz   S
  07 Santiago de   S
     Chuco

14 LAMBAYEQUE
  01 Chiclayo   C
  02 Ferreñafe   C
  03 Lambayeque   C

15 LIMA
  01 Lima   C
  02 Cajatambo   S
  03 Canta   S
  04 Cañete   C
  05 Chancay   C–S
  06 Huarochirí   S
  07 Yauyos   S

16 LORETO
  01 Maynas   J
  02 Alto Amazonas   J
  03 Coronel Portillo J
  04 Loreto   J
  05 Requena   J
  06 Ucayali   J

17 MADRE DE DIOS
  01 Tambopata   J
  02 Manu   J
  03 Tahuamanu   J

18 MOQUEGUA
  01 Mariscal Nieto   C
  02 General Sánchez S
     Cerro

19 PASCO		01 Puno	S	04 Mariscal Cáceres	J
01 Pasco	S	02 Azángaro	S	05 Riojo	J
02 Daniel Carrión	S	03 Carabaya	S	06 San Martín	J
03 Oxapampa	S	04 Chucuito	S		
20 PIURA		05 Huancané	S	23 TACNA	
01 Piura	C	06 Lampa	S	01 Tacna	C
02 Ayabaca	C	07 Melgar	S	02 Tarata	C
03 Huancabamba	C	08 Sandia	S		
04 Morropón	C	09 San Román	S	24 TUMBES	
05 Paita	C			01 Tumbes	C
06 Sullana	C	22 SAN MARTÍN		02 Contralmirante	C
07 Talara	C	01 Moyobamba	J	Villar	
21 PUNO		02 Huallaga	J	03 Zarumilla	C
		03 Lamas	J		

provincial data on land tenure, land use, size of holding, and access to irrigation water.[8] In 1962 the Inter-American Committee for Agricultural Development (CIDA)[9] also conducted an exhaustive study of land tenure arrangements in Peru, and while its report presents illustrative case studies rather than systematic data, it provides valuable background information for the approximate period of the agricultural census.

No compilation of events as they are defined in this monograph is available, so that it was necessary to compute event counts directly from newspaper sources. This task was considerably simplified by the excellent archives maintained by the two principal Lima dailies *El Comercio* and *La Prensa*. *El Comercio* maintains a staff of six archivists, who systematically cull the columns of most Lima dailies and classify materials by topic. *La Prensa* also maintains an archive, but it concentrates on articles from its own pages and is much less complete. The archives at *El Comercio* extend back to 1955, so that it was possible to search the entire period from 1955 to 1970 for all major Lima papers by simply consulting a few major categories in the index. The time period covered by the archive includes both the agrarian movement in the sierra and the labor movement on the coast. Agrarian events were generally listed under the general heading "Indigenous Communities" in the *El Comercio* archives, although reports were not limited to actions by members of such communities. This category included most of the land invasions and closely associated events. The listings under "Agriculture" and the headings for various crops were also searched but with relatively little success. Some agrarian events were also listed under the general heading "Guerrillas," which included a number of instances of organized violence by peasant bands. Labor events appeared under the general heading "Strikes." Almost all agrarian and labor events were found in the archives of *El Comercio,* and the *La Prensa* archive was used as a supplement.

[8] Perú, Dirección Nacional de Estadística y Censos, *Primer Censo Nacional Agropecuario* (Lima, 1963).
[9] CIDA, *Perú.*

The Peruvian press provided detailed coverage of strikes and land invasions despite the controversial nature of both topics. The press has in general been remarkably free of government censorship, and a wide range of political views from the extreme right to splinter parties of the left are represented. The major Lima dailies are, however, controlled by members of the Peruvian oligarchy and reflect the conservative views of their owners. News and comment are usually clearly distinguished, but both editorial writers and reporters adhere closely to the dominant political line of the owners. Both *El Comercio* and *La Prensa* have close ties to the landowners of the coastal export economy, and while both papers gave extensive coverage to the invasions, both clearly supported the land-owners against the peasants. *El Comercio* is the oldest continuously publishing Peruvian daily, having been founded in 1839, and is controlled by the Miró Quesada family. The paper runs about 30 pages in length and has a circulation of 75,000. Its large news staff provides extensive coverage of internal political and economic matters. While *El Comercio* usually advocates a conservative position on economics, its current editor, Luis Miró Quesada, is intensely nationalistic, and the paper occasionally takes more radical positions toward foreign economic interests. At times the paper's major political philosophy seems to be opposition to APRA. This attitude is in part a consequence of the assassination of two members of the Miró Quesada family by *Apristas* during the 1930s. *El Comercio* frequently portrayed the land invasions as an APRA plot and called for their suppression. When not accusing APRA, *El Comercio* persistently described the invasions as the work of anonymous "reds" (*rojos*). The paper took a more moderate line toward strikes, although they were usually lamented because of their adverse effect on production. Despite its opposition to the invasions *El Comercio* supported the moderate land reform measures of Fernando Belaúnde Terry and provided detailed coverage of the invasions.

La Prensa like *El Comercio* is a major Lima daily, with a circulation of 65,000. Its ties to the coastal landowners are even closer than those of *El Comercio*. Its owner, Pedro Beltrán Espantoso, is a member of the National Agrarian Society, the principle interest group of the large land owners of the coast. Beltrán also served as premier in the conservative presidency of Manuel Prado (1956 to 1962), and the paper reflects his orthodox views on politics and economics. *La Prensa* does not share *El Comercio's* aversion to APRA and in fact supported the presidential candidate of an APRA-based coalition in the 1962 presidential elections. It is, however, ardently anti-Communist and even editorially accused *El Comercio* of becoming the "voice of *Fidelismo*" in Peru for its reporting of the land invasions. While *La Prensa's* reporting is more objective in tone, its opposition to the land invasions was as intense as that of *El Comercio*. Like *El Comercio,* however, it continued complete coverage of the invasions even after it was attacked in the Peruvian Senate for, of all things, encouraging invasions by reporting them.

While the coverage of *El Comercio* and *La Prensa* was by far the most detailed, a number of other Lima papers provided some accounts of invasions and strikes. Some of the most sympathetic reporting was carried by *Expreso,* a new daily founded in 1961. Although its owner Manuel Mujica Gallo is a millionaire, the paper adopted a liberal editorial policy and consistently condemned police violence against peasant invaders. *Expreso* assigned Hugo Neira, a sociologically sophisticated reporter who had studied with the French Peruvianist François Bourricaud, to cover the invasions from Cuzco in the southern sierra. Neira's collected reports, published as a book, *Cuzco: Tierra y Muerte,* provide the best single account of the southern phase of the sierra agrarian movement. *La Tribuna,* the party organ of APRA, also carried accounts of invasions, but its limited staff and political format made it much less useful than the major dailies. APRA initially gave qualified support to the invaders but quickly reversed itself and condemned most of the later invasions. The other papers catalogued in the *El Comercio* archives include *Última Hora,* an evening tabloid owned by Pedro Beltrán, *El Gráfico,* the Miró Quesada family's entry in the evening field, and *La Crónica,* another tabloid with heavy sports and crime coverage.

The criteria for selecting an event from these newspaper sources were similar to those used in the analysis of secondary sources. In order to take advantage of the greater detail available in the Peruvian press, the temporal and spatial boundaries of an event were tightened. An event was defined as a continuous action by a single formation which took place in a given province on one day or successive days. Unlike the event definition in the world analysis, this definition distinguished the action of different formations in the same general area and also separated events occurring in adjacent areas in different second-order political subdivisions. This definition permitted considerably greater powers of resolution than would have been possible with the more encompassing definitions suitable for summary articles in secondary press sources. Since most newspaper stories carried only a few items of information about each event, a simplified coding scheme was adopted to take advantage of the information which was presented. The newspapers consistently distinguished the occupational group of participants, and this information was recorded in three main categories: *obreros,* or wage laborers, *campesinos,* or peasants, and *comuneros,* or members of indigenous Indian communities. The distinction between *campesinos* and *comuneros* was essential for the analysis of Peruvian social movements, although this distinction is not included in the categories for the world analysis. Events were also classified by type of event according to the typology of movements outlined in Chapter 2, although only two types, agrarian and labor events, were observed. A preliminary coding was also made of tactics, although almost all labor events were strikes and almost all agrarian events were land invasions. There were a total of 463 agrarian events and 122 labor events recorded for the entire 1955 to 1970 period in the newspaper sources catalogued in the *El Comercio* archives. While the numbers of both labor and agrarian events are an order of magnitude greater than those recorded from the *New York Times* and the *Hispanic American Report,* the differences in the event definitions tend to exaggerate the numbers of events reported in the Peruvian sources. Most of the events coded in the secondary sources are summaries of activity extending over a long period of time in several Peruvian departments, while those coded from primary sources include only actions taken by a single formation in a single province on the same day or successive days. Nevertheless it seems clear that even if this difference were eliminated, there would still be a considerably greater number of events reported in the Peruvian press sources. The effect of this difference on the overall results of the worldwide analysis, however, depends not only on the absolute number of events but on how representative the limited number of events coded in secondary sources are of the greater number of events coded from primary sources. Obviously there would be little damage to the analysis if the secondary source events were a representative sample of the larger population of events in primary sources. If, however, the events in the secondary sources were selected in such a way as to systematically distort either the number or spatial distribution of certain types of events, then the validity of the world results could be affected. The relationship between events in the two sources can be examined in the data presented in Table 3.2. These data indicate the correlations between primary and secondary source event counts by department for the 1955 to 1970 period covered by both sources. Even though the number of agrarian and labor events recorded in the primary sources is considerably greater, it is clear that the spatial distribution of both types of events is roughly similar. The correlation between the number of events in primary and secondary sources for each department is .75 for labor events and .95 for agrarian events. The data in Table 3.2 also indicate that the degree of association between the two types of events and the three major crop systems included in the world population is also roughly similar for the two sources. The correlations in the table show the relationships between sugar, cotton, and coffee production by department and the number of events in both primary and secondary sources observed in that department. The only major discrepancy in the pattern of correlations for primary and secondary sources is for considerably greater association between cotton and labor events for primary sources. The correlation between labor events and sugar production is correspondingly higher for secondary sources than it is for primary sources. The correlation between the number of agrarian events and coffee production is almost identical in the two

TABLE 3.2 *Intercorrelations of Primary and Secondary Source Measures of Labor and Agrarian Events with Sugar, Cotton, and Coffee Production by Department*

VARIABLE	(2)	(3)	(4)	(5)	(6)	(7)
1. Labor events, primary	.75	.12	−.03	.68	.43	−.23
2. Labor events, secondary		−.08	−.15	.97	.03	−.23
3. Agrarian events, primary			.95	−.10	.02	.46
4. Agrarian events, secondary				−.16	−.03	.45
5. Sugar					−.03	−.23
6. Cotton						−.19
7. Coffee						—

sets of sources: .45 for secondary and .46 for primary. At least in the case of the sugar and coffee systems the secondary sources provide a reasonable approximation to the results which would have been obtained in the primary sources and the overall event distributions for both sources are roughly comparable. In terms of the description of events by type and location the two sources are in enough agreement to indicate a fair amount of validity for the secondary source material. The correlations in Table 3.2 are, of course, based on first-order political subdivisions and do not provide as accurate a picture of the true pattern of relationships as an analysis based on the 144 second-order subdivisions. In the remainder of this chapter the lower-level divisions will be the basis for the analysis, and an attempt will be made to examine in more detail both the agricultural organization of Peru and the ecology of rural social movements. Since both agricultural organization and rural events differ in the coast and the sierra, each region will be considered separately.

THE COAST: PLANTATION AND HACIENDA

The pattern of social movements in agricultural areas of the coast reflects the fundamental division between the corporate plantation system in sugar and the commercial manor system in cotton. The economic and political interests of both owners and laborers reflect this division, and an understanding of the pattern of coastal events requires a more detailed consideration of the agricultural organization and labor relations of the two systems.

THE CORPORATE PLANTATION   The northern coast of Peru is ideally suited to the production of sugar cane because of its constant sunlight, slight temperature variations, broad alluvial plains, and easily controlled irrigation water. As the data in Map 3.2 indicate, the provinces of Trujillo in the department of La Libertad and Chiclayo in Lambayeque accounted for 86 percent of national production in 1970.[10] Smaller amounts are produced further south in the province of Santa in Ancash and Chancay in Lima, but decreasing sunlight and decreasing areas of flat land make production less efficient in the south. Cane cultivation is concentrated in irrigated oases in the major river valleys of Chicama and Santa Catalina in Trujillo, Lambayeque and Zaña in Chiclayo, Nepeña in Santa, and Pativilca and Huacho in Chancay. Peruvian yields are among the highest in the world. In the Chicama oasis in Trujillo, which produces 40 percent of the national total, yields as high as 12 tons an acre have been attained. This compares favorably with yields in Hawaiian fields, which are the most productive in the world.

---

[10] Sugar production by province in Map 3.2 was calculated from data presented in *Estadística Azucarera del Perú* (Lima: Central de Cooperativas Agrarias de Producción Azucareras del Perú Ltda., August 1971), table 1.

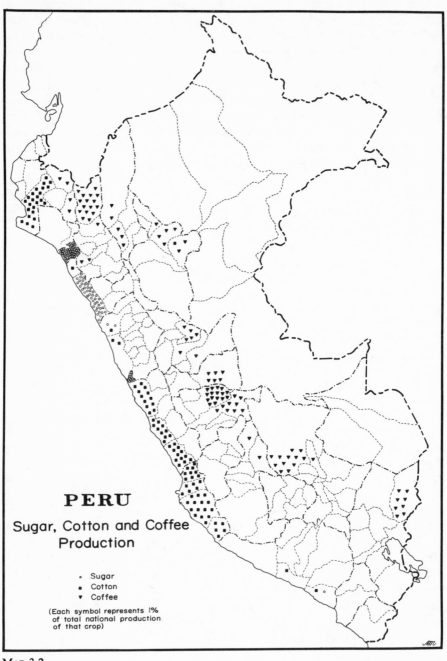

PERU

Sugar, Cotton and Coffee Production

- ○ Sugar
- ■ Cotton
- ▼ Coffee

(Each symbol represents 1% of total national production of that crop)

MAP 3.2

140

The attractiveness of the north coast has justified substantial capital investment in sugar production, and crop production parameters are ideally suited to industrialized production techniques. Peruvian sugar can be harvested year-round rather than in two or three campaigns, as is the case in many other sugar areas, and a single planting produces for 10 or 11 years, rather than two or three as is the case elsewhere. Since cutting is continuous and planting need take place only once a decade, it is possible to provide stable employment for a year-round labor force, make maximum use of milling facilities, and provide a regular supply of raw materials for subsidiary manufacturing industries. Peruvian sugar mills run on a 24-hour-a-day year-round schedule and are shut down for two months a year for routine maintenance rather than because of inadequate supplies of cane. All aspects of sugar production except planting and harvesting are mechanized. While the flat landscape of the north coast would seem ideally suited to mechanical cane cutters, the grooves of irrigation channels in the fields interfere with their operation and cane cutting is not fully mechanized. Oversized tractors are used for plowing and planting, and most of the larger plantations have their own internal railways and cranes to perform the heavy work of cane transport. Most plantations are run as single integrated enterprises, each with its own mill and administrative staff, although some of the smaller estates send their cane to the refineries of larger estates nearby. The most highly developed plantations bear little relationship to an agricultural organization and are more like industrial installations.

The favorable environment for the industrialization of cane production has led to substantial economies of scale, and the history of Peruvian sugar production in this century has been one of increasing concentration of more and more land in fewer and fewer units. The CIDA made a detailed study of this process in the Chicama oasis in Trujillo.[11] In 1962 four plantations controlled 85 percent of the agricultural land in the valley, and the largest, Casa Grande, controlled 51 percent of the total. The expansion of the sugar estates has come largely through the consolidation of traditional subsistence haciendas, although indigenous communal landholders and minifundists have also been all but wiped out. The 65 original haciendas in the Chicama valley in the nineteenth century had been concentrated into only seven holdings by 1918, and these in turn were consolidated into the four plantations remaining in 1962. Only a scattering of small holders and a single indigenous community survived, and the Chicama oasis is for the most part one continuous cane field. The efficiency of the large estates gave them an overwhelming economic advantage over smaller producers, but the consolidation of their holdings was also carried out by harassing smaller landholders, particularly by withholding supplies of essential irrigation water.

The consolidation of the sugar estates and the industrialization of production required substantial amounts of capital and received their initial impetus from the profits of the nineteenth-century guano boom.[12] The collapse of the

[11] CIDA, *Perú*, pp. 19–23.
[12] Jonathan V. Levine, *The Export Economies* (Cambridge, Mass.: Harvard University Press, 1960), pp. 118–122.

Peruvian economy after the disastrous War of the Pacific (1879 to 1884) led to a temporary halt in sugar exports and the drying up of internal supplies of capital. After World War I the expansion of the sugar industry resumed, but this time financed almost entirely by foreign capital. While some large plantations continued to be controlled by Peruvian nationals, the largest landholdings and the most efficient producers were foreign owned. Casa Grande, the largest single producer contributing 30 percent of the national total, was owned by Gildemeister and Co. before it was nationalized by the revolutionary military regime in 1969. While Gildemeister had its headquarters in Lima it was actually controlled by Dutch capital. The Peruvian land reform information office reported that at the time it was nationalized 55 percent of its invested capital was Dutch, 9 percent Swiss, 6 percent German, 4 percent American, and only 26 percent Peruvian.[13] The Casa Grande estate in fact bought out its largest competitor in the Chicama valley, the Negociación Roma owned by Víctor Larco Herrera, a Peruvian national.[14] Larco went bankrupt attempting to equip his estate with modern machinery in order to withstand economic pressure from Casa Grande. He contracted a large debt with the Bank of Lima and had invested a substantial amount in new machinery when he was caught by falling sugar prices in 1925 and forced to default. Gildemeister's reserves of foreign capital enabled it to pick up his note and take control of Roma at a very favorable price.

Before the nationalizations of 1969 the second largest producer in Peru was the W. R. Grace Corporation, which contributed about 18 percent of the national total. The corporation is wholly owned by Americans and has its headquarters in Connecticut. Together Gildemeister and Grace controlled almost half of the sugar produced in Peru. The Grace Corporation, or Casa Grace as it was known in Peru, was the dominant force in sugar even though it was not the largest producer. It controlled 75 percent of the refined sugar destined for the export trade and provided processing facilities for some of the smaller estates. It operated the Cartavio estate in the Chicama valley and also the Paramonga installation in the Pativilca valley in Chancay province. Casa Grace is typical of the large corporate interest involved in the most fully rationalized forms of export production. It is in fact a holding company, with assets of 182 million dollars in 1953, of which 60 million were invested in Latin America.[15] Although the corporation was originally founded by William R. Grace as a marine supplies business in Callao, it now has substantial operations throughout Spanish America and its major interests are in shipping (Grace Lines). The total capital involved in its sugar installations at Cartavio and Paramonga amounted to some 9 million dollars at the time they were nationalized by the military government.[16] While this sum represents an immense amount of capital by Peruvian standards,

13 Perú, Dirección de Difusión de la Reforma Agraria, *Del Latifundio a la Cooperativa* (Lima: Industrialgrafica, S.A., 1970), p. 15.
14 CIDA, *Perú*, pp. 21–22.
15 Eugene Burgess and Frederick Harbison, *Casa Grace in Peru* (Washington: National Planning Association, 1954), p. 3.
16 Perú, *Latifundio*, p. 15.

it was only one-half of 1 percent of Casa Grace's total assets. Grace also controls diversified enterprises throughout Peru, including textiles, paper, industrial chemicals, paints, foods, ore concentrates, distribution, and internal transportation. Grace continues to dominate cargo and passenger shipping from Peruvian ports and has substantial control over wharves and lighterage facilities in many of the coastal sugar areas. While the growing of sugar cane was certainly a significant part of Grace's Peruvian activities, it actually made most of its profits from refining and related manufacturing activities. Significantly the military regime specifically exempted Grace's manufacturing installations at Paramonga from its 1969 nationalization decree after protests from Grace executives. Grace's interests in transport and manufacturing continue to make it a major factor in the Peruvian economy.

The Grace installation at Paramonga was the most highly industrialized of all plantations in Peru, and sugar production is only part of its diversified activities. Molasses from the centrifugal sugar process was used to manufacture rum for export, and bagasse, the cane fiber by-product of cane milling, was used in manufacturing paper. The processes led to both a rum and alcohol, and a paper-manufacturing plant at Paramonga. Since the paper did not have a wide market in Peru, Grace developed its own box-manufacturing plant at Paramonga and in 1953 controlled 100 percent of Peruvian box production.[17] Similarly Grace discovered that the converting of bagasse to paper required substantial quantities of caustic soda, which were unavailable in Peru. Consequently an additional plant was established to manufacture caustic soda from salt mined 40 miles from Paramonga on the coast. This additional manufacturing process led to chlorine gas as a by-product, and Paramonga entered the chemical business. The Paramonga plantation became as much a manufacturing installation as a sugar plantation. All these manufacturing activities associated with the plantation remained under Grace's control even after the sugar plantation itself was placed under government management.

The nature of labor organization, like the technology of production, reflects industrial influences. In the 1960s sugar plantations were worked exclusively by resident wage laborers, and the work force was relatively stable and employed year-round. Originally the plantations were worked by Negro slave labor and after the abolition of slavery in 1849 by imported Chinese coolies. Since the expansion of the sugar industry after World War I, however, the industry had come to depend exclusively on migrants from the Indian sierra. Originally these laborers were recruited by labor contractors who entrapped sierran peasants by advances of cash, alcohol, or cocaine and then turned them over to the plantation owners in a condition of virtual debt servitude. This system, called *enganche,* is now formally illegal, but it had been abandoned on most large plantations largely for economic reasons. The increasing scarcity of land in the sierra has prompted a substantial voluntary migration, and while peasants frequently returned to the sierra during festivals or to harvest their fields, the declining opportunities in the

[17] Burgess and Harbison, *Casa Grace*, p. 4.

sierra and the availability of wage labor on the coast have created a large permanent labor supply in the coastal oases. While many of the coastal plantations maintained recruiting offices in the sierra or even purchased sierran haciendas in order to provide a stable labor supply, Solomon Miller[18] reports that by 1958 most of these offices had been closed and the plantations relied entirely on resident rather than even partially migratory labor. Actually the advances of mechanization and the natural increase of the resident population meant that by the 1960s most of the plantations had a distinct labor surplus, which began creating significant social problems in the oases.

Since the plantations are located in isolated deserts far from any towns, virtually all economic and social services are provided by the plantation administration. The plantations are in fact residential communities of several thousand persons including workers and their dependents. In 1970 Casa Grande and its annexes had a resident population of 32,000 and an economically active population of 4,500. Paramonga had a resident population of 20,000 and an economically active population of 2,000.[19] Richard Patch, who visited Paramonga in 1959,[20] divided the resident population into four main groups: (1) the management living in a separate district in free-standing houses called chalets, (2) white-collar employees with professional and technical skills who lived in hacienda-built brick houses, (3) foremen and skilled workers who lived in traditional plantation adobe houses, and (4) unskilled laborers living in the rear blocks of adobe housing or in mat and stick shacks. Since unskilled laborers made up 80 percent of the work force, the living conditions for most of the workers were squalid. Patch pointed out that within the unskilled workers' living quarters assignments were made by an authoritarian major domo who insisted on being called "Capitán" and assigned housing on the basis of the assimilation of the worker. Recently arrived migrants from the sierra received the shacks on the hillside, while long-term acculturated workers were assigned the better adobe houses. The neat prosperous appearance of the workers' quarters from the roads running through the hacienda is deceptive because of the blocks of inferior housing behind them.

The plantations also provided clothing, food, electricity, medical care, and welfare funds. They also ran a variety of community services with greater or lesser enthusiasm. At Paramonga, Grace maintained parks, recreational facilities, including the local movie theater, Cine Paramonga, athletic fields, kindergartens, a day nursery, and even paid for the local Catholic church. The plantation also supported a resident detachment of the *guardia civil* to maintain order in the community. Since virtually all land was used for cane, workers were not provided with subsistence plots and were completely dependent on plantation

18 Solomon Miller, "The Hacienda and the Plantation in Northern Peru" (Ph.D. dissertation, Columbia University, 1964), p. 118.
19 Perú, *Latifundio*, pp. 37 and 42.
20 Richard Patch, "The Role of a Coastal Hacienda in the Hispanization of Andean Indians," *American University Field Staff Reports*, West Coast of South America Series, 6 (March 1959), 5–7.

wages and fringe benefits. Although the benefits were of some value to the workers, they were sometimes capriciously administered. Indebtedness to the company store was common, and workers were frequently discharged before they had attained rights to benefits, or their work records were doctored to show that they had worked "extra" hours which did not count toward benefits. Although wages averaged only 40 cents a day for field workers at Paramonga when Patch visited it, the sugar workers represented something of a labor aristocracy in Peru and earned more than twice as much as workers on coastal cotton estates.

The maintenance of community services became increasingly burdensome to the plantations as the resident populations increased and worker organizations demanded the services as rights rather than gifts. Shortly before the 1969 nationalizations community services had been reduced on some coastal plantations.

The economic interests of both labor and management on the plantation lead directly to an organized labor movement as the dominant form of action by rural workers. In the early 1950s the sugar plantations practiced a kind of industrial paternalism and were intensely suspicious of union organizers. Thomas Ford,[21] who visited the Grace installations at Cartavio and Paramonga and the Casa Grande plantation, reported that administrators were hostile to unions and claimed that generous plantation benefits made them unnecessary. Ford himself was probed about his political views, apparently under the suspicion that he was a union organizer. Publicly the plantation management seemed to adopt the position that labor unions were an unpleasant but unavoidable by-product of industrialization.[22] While the plantation owners were scarcely any happier than any other industrialists at the prospects of unionization, there are a number of characteristics of the sugar installations that suggest that they have little to fear and some possible gains from rural labor organization.

Consider the management position:

1. Grace and Gildemeister are diversified enterprises, and agriculture does not represent their total livelihood. In fact, given the small importance of cane growing to their total profits, the loss of cane lands or even government nationalization or workers' control is not the total tragedy that it is for a small estate owner.

2. Their capital assets, particularly Grace's control of transport facilities, make them relatively invulnerable to political action by either governments or organized groups of agrarian workers. Whoever grows the cane in Peru will likely require technical assistance in processing it or, at minimum, must ship it on Grace Lines. It is possible that a radical regime could begin by nationalizing industrial enterprise, and this course has been followed in Chile. It does not seem

[21] Thomas Ford, *Man and Land in Peru* (Gainesville: University of Florida Press, 1955), pp. 58–59.

[22] See the discussion of manpower problems in Burgess and Harbison, *Casa Grace*, chap. 4, for one expression of the management position.

as likely a course as the distribution of land to peasants which is favored even by moderate regimes. Initially the Peruvian revolutionary regime nationalized only land, not industrial installations in Peru, although eventually foreign industries were affected.

3. No radical labor organization is likely to demand that the plantations be split up into subsistence plots. This would be impractical given the economies of scale in sugar production, and the coastal oases would not support their current resident populations if they were entirely given over to subsistence farming. In any case land distribution is not a significant demand of resident wage laborers. In fact the Peruvian land reform program operates the plantations as units, and while they were eventually turned over to workers' cooperatives, the immediate effect of the reforms was simply to substitute government employees for company managers.

4. Substantial capital substitution is possible. The large plantations continually work to increase efficiency through new plantings, insecticides, fertilizers, and machines. Since 1960 much cane harvesting is being done by machine and the labor force has been declining. Patch[23] found 4,600 laborers at Paramonga in 1959, while there were only 2,000 employed in 1970. This reduction in labor force has of course been an indirect consequence of demands for higher wages on the part of unions. But it represents an important strategy for the plantations to deal with increasing union demands. Capital substitution is also possible by shifting the primary emphasis of the plantation from its sugar growing to subsidiary manufacturing activities, as was the case at Paramonga.

5. The greater the degree of mechanization of agriculture, the more the plantation management requires a disciplined, reliable, stable labor force. While the *enganchador* with his advances of alcohol and cocaine may have provided men, his recruits could hardly be expected to be reliable or even sober. In fact the plantations would probably benefit from business unionism which controlled and disciplined errant workers and, most important, prevented them from returning to the sierra for fiestas and harvests. The substantial demands of the mills for regular supplies of cane require the regular and predictable performance of trained workers. While cane cutting is not skilled labor, it does require some training. Untrained workers continually cut too high on the stalk, significantly reducing the sugar content of the cane.

6. The more the plantation owner can reduce the labor force by mechanization, the fewer benefits he pays. A small efficient group of workers is much more valuable than a large unskilled group of part-time migrants, especially if expenses of the workers' dependents must be provided for.

7. The plantation managers are unlikely to feel that their livelihoods are threatened by wage increases or even by nationalization. In fact managers of the nationalized plantations simply walked out of their offices without a fight and permitted the owners to pursue the matter with the government.

23 Patch, "Coastal Hacienda," p. 5.

8. The increasing mechanization of production provides the management with a valuable tool to control workers. In fact Grace avoided unionization for several years by giving across-the-board wage increases. Needless to say this strategy did not work in the long run, but it indicates that last-ditch resistance to union demands may not always be necessary.

9. The expansion of the sugar plantation has also eliminated the last possible source of conflict with the agricultural working class by eliminating most of the small holders and indigenous communities that might attempt to reclaim lands taken from them by the plantations. They might well have some legal rights to these lands, but they do not exist as an effective social or even demographic factor in areas of large sugar estates. The industrialization of sugar production both created a rural proletariat and liquidated the peasant class of the coastal oases.

While none of these economic and political factors mean that plantation management is likely to favor unionization or even tolerate it without active resistance, they do indicate that plantation managers have alternatives open to them which are closed to the owners of subsistence or commercial haciendas. When the economic position of landowners is weak, they must rely almost exclusively on physical coercion and the disfranchisement of workers to protect their interests. When the economic position of management is as strong as it is in Peruvian sugar plantations, indirect economic control can be substituted for direct coercion.

If management can tolerate political and economic organization on the part of workers, then the workers in turn have less need to attempt revolutionary political change to defend their interests. In fact the workers in Peruvian sugar have seldom shown any interest in nationalization, land reform, or other measures which would threaten landed property and have concentrated on demands for improvements in wages and working conditions. There are a number of characteristics of the social organization of sugar plantations which encourage this orientation to limited economic goals and union organization.

1. Upward mobility through means other than collective action is not a practical possibility. Since most agricultural workers are unskilled cane cutters and only a small percentage work in factories or refineries, there is little possibility for upward mobility within the hierarchy of the plantation. In addition the physical isolation and controlled economy of the sugar oasis preclude any occupational groupings outside the plantation hierarchy and therefore eliminate traditional routes to upward mobility through the status of small businessman or shopkeeper. The immediate effect of the expansion of the plantations in the twentieth century was to eliminate the embryonic middle class in most sugar areas. With both internal and external opportunities for individual mobility structurally eliminated, the worker has little choice but to undertake collective action if he wants to improve his economic position.

2. Ties to the land, particularly the association with land ownership in the sierra, are increasingly tenuous on most plantations. When migratory labor was

common, the worker viewed himself as a sojourner and hoped to earn enough money in a relatively short period of time to obtain or expand landholdings in the sierra. Migratory workers with close ties to sierran peasant communities have traditionally been used as strikebreakers. Their pronounced interest in individual land ownership exerts potent divisive influence on worker solidarity on the sugar plantations. With the increasing dependence of the plantations on resident wage labor, however, this source of division has largely been eliminated and workers are completely oriented toward the wage market and have little interest in subsistence plots.

3. The residential community of the hacienda is dominated by the sugar workers, and consequently off-the-job social relationships become an important source of influence over workers unwilling to join a union. The worker who resists a union strike call loses not only the friendship of his immediate circle of work associates but also the support of the welfare and personal assistance network of the plantation residential community. These personal relationships may be an important source of social insurance for workers, and the community is able to exert considerable coercive control over the behavior of its members. It is in fact not uncommon for unions to establish disciplinary units to fight strikebreakers and enforce solidarity. Union control over worker solidarity is also enhanced by the ethnic stratification of the hacienda, since the management is for the most part upper-class mestizo while the field workers maintain at least a partly Indian cultural identity. Betrayal of the union is thus betrayal of the Indian working class to the mestizo overlords.

4. The continuous harvest provides the workers with a means to apply gradual economic pressure to the plantation owners without threatening them with economic disaster. While a strike during a relatively short harvest may appear to be a potent economic weapon, its very destructiveness and its relatively short duration encourage landowners to take drastic and often violent measures to stop such strikes at all costs. Since a work stoppage does not mean the total loss of the sugar crop, strikes can be carried out during negotiations with losses to management gradually mounting as the strike continues.

5. The relative affluence of the sugar economy means that workers can afford a dues check-off system to support full- and part-time union workers. This in turn provides an important source of occupational mobility for the most articulate and intelligent workers and provides individual incentive for them to begin organizing efforts.

6. The sensitivity of foreign capital to political influence gives the workers an important additional weapon. Strikes or demonstrations in Peruvian sugar are usually the subject of close government scrutiny because of the immense economic importance of the industry, and the potential for nationalization tends to moderate the actions of foreign corporations toward worker organization.

THE COMMERCIAL HACIENDA   The economic interests of both workers and managers suggest a strong labor movement in the coastal sugar areas. The interests of both classes in the coastal cotton areas, on the other hand, are almost the reverse of those in the sugar areas. The agricultural organization of cotton production is much less fully rationalized, and many cotton estates retain characteristics of traditional subsistence haciendas. These differences in class interests and agricultural organization reflect differences in both the production parameters of cotton and sugar and the coastal environments in which the two crops are produced. In general cotton is produced in areas in which sugar cannot compete effectively because of a lack of sunlight, irrigation water, or both. Sugar cane requires several times as much water as cotton, and the sugar content is significantly reduced by limited sunlight. Most cotton production is concentrated in three areas, the province of Piura in the Piura department, the provinces of Chancay, Lima, and Cañete in Lima, and the provinces of Ica, Chincha, Nazca, and Pisco in Ica (see distribution in Map 3.2).[24] As was the case in sugar production, cultivation is limited to irrigated river valleys and the highest yields are attained in the Piura valley in Piura province, the Rímac valley in Lima, and the Cañete valley in Cañete. These are the areas in which the most fully rationalized and most efficient producers are to be found. Further south in Ica where water is scarcer, yields are generally lower and production is less efficient. Two principal cotton varieties are grown: Peruvian Tanguis, or extralong-staple cotton, a perennial, and Peruvian Pima or Karnak, or ordinary long-staple cotton, an annual. The extralong-staple varieties are grown in Piura, while the ordinary long-staple is grown in Lima and Ica. The perennial long-staple is generally planted every two or three years, and after harvesting the cotton stalks are cut 2 or 3 inches from the ground in a process called ratooning. While the perennial nature of Tanguis cotton suggests that centralized production might have distinct economic advantages, in fact ratooning causes significant losses due to insect infestation and has generally fallen into disuse on estates. Tanguis, like Pima and Karnak, can be considered an annual crop for purposes of understanding agricultural organization. The harvest period for both varieties is typical of cotton generally and runs about four months in the north and five months in the central region. Most of the crop in both areas is harvested in a concentrated period of about two months, creating a substantial seasonal demand for labor. While the bulk of labor on the estates is provided by resident wage laborers, an almost equal amount is provided for by seasonal day laborers from the sierra. The day laborers in fact substantially outnumber the permanent workers, but since they work only during the harvest, more than half of the total number of man-hours required annually are contributed by the resident laborers. Thus the Peruvian cotton system has been classified as a commercial hacienda. While some phases of cultivation have been mechanized, harvesting and planting are still carried out by hand. In most estates power-driven pumps for irrigation and the scientific use of fertilizers and insecticides are essential for efficient production. Most estates have tractors and in the most modern areas, such as the San Lorenzo oasis in the north, aircraft are used for crop dusting.

[24] Cotton production by province in Map 3.2 was calculated from data presented in Perú, Cámara Algodonera del Perú, *Memoria Anual* (Lima: República del Perú), app. 10.

Nevertheless the concentrated nature of the harvest means that it is not possible to make efficient use of processing machinery on a year-round basis, and only the very largest estates own their own cotton gins. Eugene Hammel, who worked in the Ica valley in 1957,[25] reported that there were a total of seven gins, only two of which were located in rural areas, and only one of these was on an estate. Most processing was carried out in two large urban mills. The seasonal demand for labor and the absence of processing machinery on the estates means that there are few economic advantages in centralization, and consequently the average estate size is considerably smaller in cotton than in sugar. In the Chancay valley José Matos Mar found that estate sizes ranged from 300 to a maximum of 1,900 hectares,[26] and similar magnitudes are reported by Claude Delavaud in the Piura valley in the north.[27] Casa Grande by contrast controlled over 100,000 hectares, and Paramonga controlled 18,000.[28] There is in fact little economic justification for even the current degree of centralization, and small holders would be effective competitors in cotton if they were able to obtain sufficient land and credit. Economic considerations do, however, lead to considerable centralization in the processing and marketing of the cotton crop. There were a total of 54 cotton gins in Peru in 1969, and 14 of these were controlled by just two companies, both foreign owned. Together these companies produced 35 percent of Peruvian ginned cotton.[29] There is a similar degree of concentration in the export of the cotton crop, and in 1960 two export houses controlled almost half of all exports.[30] One of these was the American-controlled Anderson Clayton company, which also has substantial cotton interests elsewhere in Latin America, notably in Brazil. While processing and exports are controlled by corporate interests, neither the capital investment nor the degree of foreign control is as great as it is in sugar. The cotton estates themselves are frequently owned by families or family-run corporations, and almost all of them are controlled by Peruvian nationals. The absence of substantial economies of scale and the more limited capital requirements have made it possible for members of the Peruvian landed aristocracy to convert their estates to commercial cotton production without becoming dependent on foreign capital.

The smaller size, lower capital requirements, and lesser degree of industrialization in cotton have led to a land use pattern in the cotton oases different from that in the sugar areas. The sugar estates expanded to encompass most of the arable land in their oases, consolidating smaller haciendas into gigantic holdings and destroying most of the original small holders and indigenous com-

[25] E. A. Hammel, *Power in Ica* (Boston: Little, Brown, 1969), p. 39.

[26] José Matos Mar, "Las Haciendas en el Valle de Chancay," in *Les Problèmes Agraires des Amériques Latines* (Paris: Centre National de la Recherche Scientifique, 1967), p. 343.

[27] Claude Collin Delavaud, *Les Régions Côtieres du Pérou Septentrional* (Lima: Institut Francais d'Études Andines, 1968), p. 426.

[28] Perú, *Latifundio*, pp. 37 and 42.

[29] Julio Cotler and Felipe Portocarrero, "Peru: Peasant Organizations," in Henry A. Landsberger (ed.), *Latin American Peasant Movements* (Ithaca, N.Y.: Cornell University Press, 1969), pp. 297–322.

[30] Perú, *Memoria Anual*, app. 9.

munities. The owners of traditional coastal haciendas expanded their cotton acreage by putting unused waste land and swamps into cultivation and left many of the original small holdings intact. While the cotton estates dominate the arable land of the valleys almost to the same extent as the sugar plantations, much of this concentration of ownership reflects the traditional latifundia-minifundia complex of the coastal subsistence economy. In Chancay valley 54 percent of the cultivated area is devoted to cotton, 29 percent to citrus fruits, and 17 percent to foodstuffs. Some 77 percent of the cultivated land in the valley is the property of 18 cotton estates. In the upper part of the valley, however, live some 32,000 people belonging to 27 indigenous communities.[31] In addition, Faron[32] reports that in the lower Chancay valley there were a number of different types of small peasant landholders including *comuneros,* sharecroppers, independent freeholders, and settlers in a government-supported farm colony. In Piura large cotton estates control most of the land area, but the population of the indigenous community of San Juan de Catacaos makes this one of the most densely populated areas on the north coast.[33] In Ica there are substantial pockets of small holding peasants as well as a few communal landholders in cotton areas.[34] While irrigation water is a constant source of contention between the cotton estates and the small holders and *comuneros,* the cotton estate owners have not used their political and economic power to cut off the flow of water to small holders as was frequently done in sugar areas. This of course hardly reflects their greater benevolence, but rather the economic limitations of estate size in cotton areas. The owner of a cotton hacienda can usually obtain enough land to run a profitable estate without dispossessing the surrounding small holders, who in any case controlled marginal land which would be expensive to irrigate. The class structure of the typical cotton valley is considerably more complex than a typical sugar oasis and includes small holders and *comuneros* as well as resident and migratory wage laborers.

While commercial cotton cultivation did not lead to the expropriation of small landholders, the dependent serfs of the haciendas did not fare as well. Originally most coastal estates were worked in a traditional form of share-cropping called *yanaconaje.* With the advent of cotton production in the nineteenth century this form of tenancy was adapted to cash crop production and a system of centralized sharecropping developed. Tenants had customary rights of tenure but lacked written contracts and were forced to provide free labor to the estate owner as well as pay half of their crop as rent. The liberal Bustamante regime in 1947 passed a law attempting to regulate the rights of tenants, provide written contracts, and limit the share rent. The effect of this measure is a good illustration of what might be called Ford's law of Peruvian land tenure. Thomas Ford pointed out that the law's effects were exactly the opposite of its nominal

---

[31] Matos Mar, "Chancay," pp. 319–320.
[32] Louis C. Faron, "The Formation of Two Indigenous Communities in Coastal Peru," *American Anthropologist,* 62 (June 1960), 437–453.
[33] Delavaud, *Régions Côtieres,* p. 433.
[34] Hammel, *Ica,* pp. 12–13.

intent and suggested that the surest way to perpetuate a practice by landowners in Peru was to pass a law forbidding it.[35] The precarious tenure and exorbitant rents under traditional sharecropping arrangements made the system economically attractive to the landowners. When they found their normal exploitative methods restricted by the new regulations, they set about ridding themselves of the restrictions by ridding themselves of the sharecroppers. In most cotton areas at present sharecropping has been almost entirely replaced by wage labor, and only a few favored tenants remain on the land. While the new system of wage labor required greater cash expenditures, the owners had little difficulty in financing it out of rising cotton revenues. In fact the 1947 law was the final blow to sharecroppers, who had been gradually replaced by wage laborers since the 1930s. The expiration of the sharecroppers led to an increased number of landless peasants living in rural slums or concentrated in the cotton valley towns. Delavaud reports that in the lower Piura valley, for example, 78 percent of all families had no land at all and only 17 percent had more than 2 hectares. The pressure on available land of course increased with the natural increase of population and in most of the cotton valleys generated conflicts between the cotton estates and the rural lower class.

The typical cotton estate at present includes a professional administrator, a supervisory staff, a semiskilled group of mechanics and irrigators, a larger group of permanent workers, and a much larger group of migratory workers. In Piura Delavaud found that on eight medium to small cotton estates there were a total of 100 mechanics and irrigators and 178 other permanent workers employed year-round, 386 weeders employed for five months, and 1,010 harvest pickers employed for two months.[36] Matos Mar reported that on the 17 large estates he studied in Chancay there were a total of 2,086 permanent workers, presumably including both semiskilled and unskilled workers, and 3,500 seasonal workers.[37] Most estates employ professional administrators, although many owners continue to live at least part of the time on their estates and some play an active role in management. Relations between estate owner and worker are paternalistic, and the *patrón* may attend the festivals and weddings of his employees, advance them small sums of money, and share medical and burial expenses. Fictive coparenthood (*compadrazgo*) is still practiced in the cotton areas, although it has almost vanished in the sugar areas, and the estate owner may become the godparent or sponsor (*padrino*) of the children of especially favored workers. The permanent workers are the principal beneficiaries of the *patrón*'s favor, and the migratory sierran Indians are usually assigned the worst jobs and treated with little consideration. While labor contractors and the *enganche* system have declined in importance, migrants continue to constitute an essential source of labor for the cotton estates even though they are no longer an important factor on sugar plantations.

[35] Ford, *Man and Land*, p. 84.
[36] Delavaud, *Régions Côtieres*, p. 278.
[37] Matos Mar, "Chancay," p. 320.

The ownership of a cotton estate is closely tied to upper-class life styles and the traditional position of the landed aristocracy in the rural social structure. In Ica Hammel provides two contrasting profiles of cotton estate owners which serve to define the range of upper-class behavior.[38] The first and more established landowner was a descendant of the Hispanicized coastal aristocracy and managed an estate that had been held in his family since the early 1800s. He maintained a luxurious manor house and a staff of servants and spent part of the year in Lima, where he belonged to the exclusive Club Nacional. Educated in the United States, he tended to model himself after the image of a British country squire. His attitude toward his workers was kindly, almost apologetic, and he invariably phrased his orders as requests for favors. The second owner also maintained an affluent life style but was less clearly a part of the coastal gentry. His attitude toward his workers was harsh, even brutal, and the workers were privately contemptuous of his behavior. His father had once whipped a worker into town for misdirecting irrigation water. The cotton estates of both these men support a standard of living which would require an annual income of $30,000 to $50,000 in the United States, and clearly cotton cultivation was as much a social status as a business enterprise for both of them. Nevertheless both estate owners are rational businessmen who are constantly attempting to lower costs and increase production on their estates. Both men would probably like to mechanize their operations and reduce their work force, but the difficulties of mechanizing cotton picking and their limited capital resources mean that such mechanization would probably require substantial financial support from outside sources. The less successful of the two owners had in fact already contracted a substantial debt with one of the cotton mills and, although he had paid it off, was unable to obtain additional credit for necessary improvements.

The limited mechanization and capital resources of most cotton estates and the greater importance of land ownership as a source of income make the attitudes toward labor organization of the cotton estate owners considerably different from those of the owners and administrators of sugar estates. The cotton estates are not diversified enterprises, and agriculture represents their only profit-making activity. Estate owners must therefore use their political and economic influence to maintain control over their land and to insure adequate supplies of irrigation water. They cannot respond to protests by either agricultural workers or subsistence peasants by expanding the industrial aspects of cotton production, for these activities are entirely under the control of the great cotton-exporting companies. Even if cotton picking could be mechanized and large estates became economical, it is unlikely that the current Peruvian owners would be the beneficiaries of such changes. Instead, given the limited capital resources of the Peruvian economy, it would be likely that foreign capital would gain an increasing amount of direct control over cotton estates. In fact extensive mechanization could lead to developments similar to those on the coastal sugar

[38] Hammel, *Ica*, pp. 65–77.

plantations, where Peruvian nationals were forced to sell to competing foreign firms with more adequate financing. The absence of any notable economies of scale in their present operations means that cotton estates could be split up by a revolutionary regime without necessarily disrupting cotton production. The large corporations which control processing and export could as easily deal with small holders and in fact might be able to negotiate more favorable terms than they can with the politically influential estate owners. While any land reform which distributes land to the peasant would lead to an immediate drop in cotton production because of the conversion of cotton lands to subsistence plots, it would be technically possible to split up estates into efficient producing units if adequate capital and marketing facilities were provided by the government. The commanding economic position of Grace or Gildemeister, based on its control of processing and export, rests with the cotton-exporting firms, not with the cotton estate owners. Furthermore, in the cotton valleys there are substantial numbers of peasants and agricultural laborers who retain an interest in obtaining land and could in fact put the cotton estate lands to their own uses. The interests of the sugar plantation proletariat, on the other hand, are likely to be focused almost entirely on wages. The cotton estate owners are therefore vulnerable to agrarian movements because they have no technological substitutes for economic power which passes to workers or peasants. The limited prospects for further mechanization of cotton production also mean that movements of agricultural workers cannot be controlled by raising wages to defuse discontent. Wage gains cannot be offset by gains in worker productivity, and therefore wage increases are likely to be seen as a sacrifice of the owners' standard of living to the workers.

The estate owners also gain little from a trained and disciplined labor force, and therefore would profit little from unionized labor. In fact their extensive use of migratory labor makes them dependent on an unskilled, compliant labor force and provides them with a weapon to use against their resident workers. The relatively short cotton harvest will continue to require large amounts of labor for a few months each year, and any gains that might accrue from a more disciplined labor force would be more than offset by the costs of paying a wage that would support workers in the off season. At present the sierran peasants subsidize the estate by supporting themselves in subsistence agriculture for most of the year. The migrants also provide the estate owners with a ready tool either for breaking labor movements or for heading off their demands. Sierran migrants are frequently given the jobs that the permanent workers refuse, and such agreements are sometimes the subject of explicit negotiation between owner and worker. This split in the labor force allows the estate owners to play the two groups off against one another and avoid unionization.

The cotton workers both permanent and temporary actually have few resources to bring to bear on estate owners during negotiations. The migratory workers always have the option of returning to the sierra if conditions are too bad on the coast. The permanent workers can demand that the more unattractive jobs be transferred to the migrants. Furthermore there is usually a division of interests between the permanent wage laborers and the remaining sharecroppers, the former concerned with wages, the latter with land ownership. The unity of interest in wages and working conditions found in the sugar plantation proletariat is completely absent on the cotton estates. In addition, collective action is not the only route to upward mobility for individuals. There is usually a considerable group of craftsmen, petty traders, and shopkeepers in most of the cotton valleys, and these occupations represent an alternative to wage labor. Hammel[39] notes that in Ica many sierra migrants set up fruit stands in the towns and hope to move out of agricultural labor, and Delavaud[40] reports that the town of Piura was an important center of cottage hat manufacture. While the cotton estates themselves are a tightly knit society, it is a society ruled by an estate owner, who can use the differential distribution of his favor to control and discipline his laborers. The laborers themselves therefore cannot depend on the community of workers for social and economic support as they can in sugar areas. They may in fact have important ties to social groups outside the estate community, and these groups can provide assistance in emergencies.

The workers have few tactical and organizational resources useful in collective bargaining. In fact the resident workers who would seem the most likely to unionize actually have the least power to inflict economic damage. A strike by the harvest workers is not a realistic possibility, since additional workers can easily be recruited in almost indefinite numbers from the sierra. A strike at any other point of the production cycle can be easily waited out with relatively little cost. The continuous harvest of the sugar estate provides the workers with a mechanism for gradually increasing costs to the owners, but in the cotton estate most year-round work can be deferred without substantial production losses. In addition, the smaller size of the cotton estate work force makes coordination of strike activity considerably more difficult than on the gigantic sugar plantations. The weakness of the workers and the relatively limited resources of the estate owners keep wages low, and the low level of wages makes it difficult to provide dues check-off systems for workers and hence to support union organizers or provide careers in unions for ambitious workers. The more highly paid mechanics and irrigators do provide the nucleus for union organization, and despite the obstacles to collective action on cotton estates much unionization has taken place. The unions are, however, weaker and less prone to strike than those in sugar areas.

While the cotton estate owners may face a weaker resident work force than do the sugar plantation owners, there is another potential source of movements of social protest among the rural lower class in the cotton valleys. Peasant small holders, the members of indigenous communities, and the few remaining sharecroppers all function under the political and social domination of the estate owners, and all are faced with the general scarcity of land and water in the

[39] *Ibid.*, p. 104.
[40] Delavaud, *Régions Côtieres*, p. 435.

cotton valleys. Many of the displaced sharecroppers have at least a moral claim to the lands of the estate owners, and many of the indigenous communities are involved in land disputes with the haciendas which predate the cotton economy. Small holders or *comuneros* who have insufficient land to support themselves may be compelled to work as day laborers on the cotton and in many respects resemble the usufructuaries of sierran estates. In fact Faron reports that in Chancay landlords assisted two indigenous communities in obtaining legal recognition in order to insure themselves an adequate supply of labor.[41] The cotton valleys are of course areas of high market penetration, and both the international cotton market and national and local produce markets exert an important influence on the nonstate peasantry. Even the indigenous Indian communities on the coast are more like commercial cooperatives or modern towns than they are like traditional Indian villages, and most of them have discarded Indian behavior patterns and have been fully assimilated into the Hispanic coastal culture. The owners of the cotton estates therefore face a group of nearly landless peasants who are closely tied to market agriculture and who resemble dependent serfs rather than commercial small holders. These conditions are of course precisely those which should be most likely to lead to an agrarian movement. While on the sugar estates a labor movement is the most likely response of workers and an agrarian movement is highly unlikely, the reverse should be the case on the cotton estates. These predictions are of course consistent with the general pattern of results for the world analysis of agricultural export sectors. The predictions can easily be tested in the event data from Peruvian press sources.

COASTAL EVENTS   A total of 166 events were coded from Lima press sources in the *El Comercio* archives for the 29 coastal provinces in the period from 1955 to 1970. The spatial distribution of both labor and agrarian events for all Peruvian provinces, including the coastal sugar and cotton areas, is shown in Map 3.3. Labor events outnumber agrarian events by two to one in the coastal provinces (115 labor and 51 agrarian). Of the agrarian events, 33 were the actions of *comuneros,* seven of *campesinos,* and the rest either could not be classified as to occupation or involved participants from several occupation groups. The correlation between the number of events of each type and the total production of sugar and cotton for coastal provinces is presented in Table 3.3 and can be roughly estimated by comparing the event distributions in Map 3.3 with crop distributions in Map 3.2. It is clear that the pattern of correlation conforms to the results which would have been expected given the nature of agricultural organization in cotton and sugar. Labor events are strongly correlated with sugar production ($r = .81$) and weekly correlated with cotton production ($r = .17$). The pattern of correlations for agrarian events is just the reverse. The total number of agrarian events is correlated .64 with cotton pro-

[41] Faron, "Two Indigenous Communities," p. 440.

TABLE 3.3   *Intercorrelations of Labor and Agrarian Events with Cotton and Sugar Production for Coastal Provinces*

VARIABLE	(2)	(3)	(4)	(5)	(6)
1. *Comunero* agrarian events	.48	.94	.22	.04	.61
2. *Campesino* agrarian events		.63	.13	−.11	.50
3. Total agrarian events			.24	.01	.64
4. Labor events				.81	.17
5. Sugar					−.11
6. Cotton					—

duction but is not correlated at all with sugar production ($r = .01$). It is clear that the two effects are independent of one another, since there is no significant correlation between cotton and sugar production ($r = −.11$). The strength of the correlation indicates not only that strikes tend to occur in sugar valleys and land invasions in cotton areas but also that the number of strikes and invasions is roughly proportional to the amount of cotton or sugar produced in each province. These correlations, particularly the association between sugar and strikes, correspond to results reported by Cotler and Portocarrero, who analyzed strikes reported by the Peruvian Ministry of Labor. They found that the ratio of unions reporting strikes to those not reporting strikes was 1.17 for sugar, .29 for cotton, and .18 for other crops.[42] In the cotton areas both *comunero* and *campesino* agrarian events tend to occur, and the correlation between the number of events involving each of the two groups and total cotton production is approximately the same ($r = .61$ for *comunero* events and $r = .50$ for *campesino* events). The two types of events frequently occur in the same area as the .48 correlation between *comunero* and *campesino* events indicates. In fact a number of agrarian events which were not classified in either of these two categories actually involved joint actions by *comuneros* and *campesinos*.

The labor events in the sugar areas are large strikes with several thousand participants and affect almost all the largest plantations. Several major strikes were reported at both Casa Grande and Paramonga and at a number of large plantations in the principal sugar areas including Cartavio and Laredo in the Chicama valley, San Jacinto in the Nepeña valley, and Cayaltí, Pomalca, Patapó, and Pucalá in the Lambayeque and Zaña valleys. Most of the strikes were peaceful, although in several cases strikers were fired on by police and in one case, at Casa Grande,[43] a battalion of infantry was dispatched from Lima to aid local police and a cavalry detachment already on the scene. Many of the strikes involved the residential community of the plantation as well as the agricultural workers. At Cayaltí[44] wives destroyed the company store during a strike, and at Casa Grande[45] 800 wives and children of strikers demonstrated against

[42] Cotler and Portocarrero, "Peru," p. 301.
[43] *La Prensa*, Sept. 9, 1959; *El Comercio*, Sept. 9 and 10, 1959; *La Crónica*, Sept. 9, 1959.
[44] *El Comercio*, Apr. 25, 1958.
[45] *La Prensa*, Aug. 20, 1958.

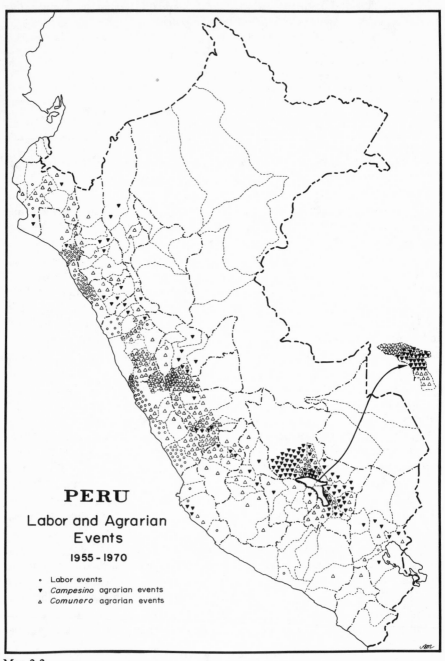

PERU

Labor and Agrarian Events

1955 - 1970

- ○ Labor events
- ▼ *Campesino* agrarian events
- △ *Comunero* agrarian events

MAP 3.3

158

strikebreakers. Cane fields were burned in at least two of the strikes, but other than attacks on company stores there was little damage to permanent facilities. No attacks on industrial machinery or sabotage of field equipment were reported, although the troops sent to Casa Grande were supposedly sent to prevent the workers from occupying the sugar refinery. There was considerable coordination of the strikes by the Sugar Workers' Federation of Peru (FTAP), and in several instances the entire work force in the sugar industry went out on strike. Sympathy strikes by workers at plantations in the same valley or in annexes of a struck plantation were also common. The sugar workers were also involved in two national general strikes called by the Federation of Peruvian Workers (CTP), one of which protested military intervention in the 1962 presidential elections.[46] The sugar workers' federation and the national workers' federation are both closely tied to the APRA party, and the workers have long been the basic source of APRA strength in the north. The military intervened to prevent APRA from taking power, and the strike represented political retaliation by the workers. The vast majority of strikes, however, are either concerned with salary increases or other job-related matters such as the installation of time clocks or the displacement of workers by mechanization.

Strikes by cotton workers are smaller and less frequent than those involving sugar workers and usually involve a few hundred workers on a single hacienda. In Chancay and Cañete in the department of Lima, however, cotton workers seem to be considerably more militant and provincial federations of cotton workers are able to coordinate mass strikes by several thousand workers in each valley. The cotton workers' organizations are affiliated with the Rural Workers' Federation of Peru (FENCAP) rather than with an industry-wide labor union as is the case in sugar, and newspaper accounts invariably refer to cotton workers as *campesinos* (peasants), while sugar workers are called *obreros* (workers). The militance of the Chancay and Cañete cotton workers is a result of both the relatively high degree of rationalization of production in Cañete and the influence of strong urban unions in nearby Lima. Strikes are considerably less frequent in both Piura and Ica, but one Iquenian strike involved the entire department. While strikes are concentrated in the department of Lima, land invasions are concentrated in Piura and Ica. The Piura invasions involve for the most part the actions of the large indigenous community of San Juan de Catacaos, which made repeated attempts to invade nearby cotton haciendas. The best known of the coastal invasions was carried out by San Juan de Catacaos, small subsistence farmers, and other residents of Catacaos district on January 14, 1964.[47] There were approximately 12,000 people involved in the invasion, which was one of the largest carried out anywhere in the country. The invaders occupied the cotton lands of at least 20 different haciendas claiming

[46] *La Tribuna,* July 20, 1962.

[47] For newspaper accounts of this invasion see *La Prensa,* Jan. 14, 15, 17, 1964; *El Comercio,* Jan. 14, 1964; *La Tribuna,* Jan. 14, 1964; *La Crónica,* Jan. 14, 1964; *Expreso,* Jan. 17, 1964.

legal title dating to colonial times. The invasion itself was carried out with almost military precision, and the invaders sealed off the area by cutting bridges and telegraph wires. They were reportedly led by local government officials and a national deputy as well as the leaders of the community itself. Showing considerable political sophistication, the *comuneros* carefully avoided the lands of Juan Languasco de Habich, minister of the interior and police. After the land had been seized, the *comuneros* methodically conducted a cadastral survey and divided the land into plots to be assigned to families by community authorities. A detachment of 180 assault police was flown in from Lima on three planes, but when they attempted to retake the lands, they were met with fierce resistance by peasants armed with shotguns and slingshots. A detachment of police was ambushed by 100 *comuneros* on the outskirts of the town of Catacaos, and attempts to drive off the invaders with tear gas failed. Finally police opened fire, and at least nine *comuneros* were wounded. The peasants were finally forced off the lands but sent a delegation to Lima to demand action from the new land reform administration and made several later and less ambitious attempts to retake the land once the police had left. While conflicts between indigenous communities and haciendas are endemic in Peru, the situation in Piura was exacerbated by the opening of a large new area of irrigated cotton land and the subsequent diversion of water from traditional landholders to the new cotton estates.

There were also a number of invasions by indigenous communities in the Chancay valley, and in most cases the *comuneros* were accompanied by residents of nearby towns. In general, communities moved down the Chancay valley into the cotton area to seize lands. In Ica invasions were carried out for the most part by *campesinos* and in one instance by sharecroppers, but *comuneros* were also involved. The largest of these invasions involved a mass rally of 2,000 *campesinos* in Ica and an attempt to seize control of six haciendas; but the rally was broken up and the invasion attempt petered out.[48] In Ica peasants destroyed irrigation canals diverting water to cotton estates.

The strong correlations between sugar and strikes and between cotton and land invasions strongly confirm the overwhelming influence of the technological organization of agriculture on the social movements of agricultural workers. The industrialization of sugar production clearly provided economic and social conditions conducive to labor organization at the same time that it eliminated any peasant class in the sugar oases which might have threatened an agrarian movement. The expansion of the cotton haciendas produced a weak union movement capable of organizing large-scale strikes only when aided by urban workers and at the same time increased the population of land-starved peasants who might attempt to claim estate lands for their own use. While the rise of the export market was the fundamental cause of both movements, the differing production parameters of cotton and sugar caused the traditional hacienda complex of the

---

[48] *El Comercio,* Aug. 13, 1963.

coast to evolve in two different directions—in the case of sugar toward industrialization, in the case of cotton toward an elaboration of the traditional manor. The pattern of both social movements and technological organization reflected the ecological division of the coast between cotton and sugar.

THE SIERRA: HACIENDA AND *COMUNIDAD*

The export agriculture of the coast developed in the late nineteenth and early twentieth centuries, and consequently both cotton and sugar production are based on modern agricultural technology. The subsistence economy of the sierra, on the other hand, is based on land tenure patterns established at the time of the conquest and has changed little since the consolidation of the hacienda system at the beginning of the republican era. On the coast agricultural production is divided between the corporate plantation and the commercial hacienda, while in the sierra it is divided between the traditional hacienda and the so-called *comunidad indígena,* or indigenous community of highland Indians. Both forms of sierran land tenure have been significantly effected by export crop production, and the peasant movements of the 1960s are as closely tied to the export economy in the sierra as they were on the coast. Both haciendas and indigenous communities, however, exist in commercial and precommercial forms, and the export economy of the sierra, unlike that of the coast, still employs a small fraction of the total rural population.

The history of sierran land tenure is based on a one-sided struggle between haciendas and communities for control of a limited amount of arable land. For almost half a millenium the haciendas have continuously expanded at the expense of the indigenous communities. When Francisco Pizarro seized control of the Inca empire in a military coup against the last Inca Emperor, Atahualpa, in 1532, most sierran land was held by communal groups called *ayllus.* While the exact kinship structure of the *ayllu* is a subject of debate and in fact by the time of Pizarro it may have evolved into an endogamous residential community rather than a lineage organization, it is clear that the *ayllu* held and worked land collectively. While individual plots were periodically redistributed to family heads and families retained rights to their own production, the land itself was the inalienable property of the *ayllu.* The Inca nobility did not control the agricultural production of the *ayllu* directly, but rather siphoned off labor through a corvée system called the *mita.* The initial system of Spanish exploitation here as elsewhere in the New World was the *encomienda,* a grant of administrative responsibility over a specified group of indigenous inhabitants called the *repartimiento.* The *encomienda* represented a marginal solution to the problem of colonial administration in an agrarian bureaucracy with limited resources. The *encomendero* was charged with collecting royal tribute and Christianizing the Indians under his control and, in lieu of salary, was given the right to recruit labor and exact tribute on his own behalf. The fundamental land-holding unit remained the *ayllu,* and agricultural production was carried out much as it had been under the Incas. The *mita* was vastly expanded in the colonial period to obtain labor for the silver and mercury mines, and the escalating demands of the *encomenderos* and the diseases introduced by Europeans combined to decimate the indigenous population. Within a century after the conquest the population of the Inca empire, which has been estimated to have been as high as 6 million, declined to slightly more than a million.[49] While the Spanish Crown attempted to limit the power of the *encomenderos* and defend the Indian subjects of the king, the power of the *encomenderos* continued to expand. As in all agrarian bureaucracies the system became increasingly corrupt as the titular administrative officials of the Crown became warlords controlling vast numbers of Indians and administering immense amounts of territory. The *encomenderos* diverted more and more of the tribute of the *repartimiento* to their own ends and in the face of a precipitously declining Indian population redoubled their demands for *mita* labor. While the *encomienda* did not include control of Indian lands, the indirect effect of corvée labor and tribute brought many communities to the brink of economic disaster, and many were forced to sell off lands to meet the ever-expanding demands of the *encomenderos.* The abuses of the *encomienda* system led Viceroy Toledo to initiate a series of reforms in the 1570s to reduce the power of the *encomenderos* and to exert greater direct control over the Indian population. Toledo ordered the consolidation of the Indian population in settlements called *reducciones* which included both administrative centers and agricultural land to support the new community. The concentration of one or more *ayllus* in a single *reducción* did in fact lead to tighter administrative control but at the same time produced a general expropriation of the original *ayllu* land. As was to be the case in every attempt at reform of highland land tenure, Viceroy Toledo's measures had the effect of increasing the power of the Spanish overlords at the same time that they seemed to be limiting it. The colonists quickly claimed title to abandoned *ayllu* lands and, despite the feckless efforts of the distant sovereign to protect the rights of the Indians, expanded their holdings at the expense of the newly created *reducciones.* As the Spanish Crown became increasingly impoverished in the later colonial period, it began to rely more and more on direct grants of lands to settlers in the hopes of luring more revenue-producing agriculturalists to the New World. While the *encomienda* system of indirect control of Indian communities exacted tribute while leaving agricultural organization unchanged, the land grants were exploited directly by binding Indian communities to the land in a system of villein tenure transplanted from the manorial economy of Spain. Indian communities whose lands had literally been stolen from under them by the colonial grantees were permitted usufruct rights to a portion of their former lands in exchange for labor services on domain lands

---

[49] George Kubler, "The Quechua in the Colonial World," in Julian H. Steward (ed.), *Handbook of South American Indians* (Washington: Government Printing Office, 1946), pp. 331–410.

claimed by the new Spanish owners. The colonists invariably worked the better bottom lands themselves and forced the Indian communities to accept the usufruct of rocky hillsides or barren *puna*. The Indian communities, however, maintained the social structure of original *ayllu* under the hacienda system as well as in the *reducciones*. Although the haciendas controlled Indian labor directly, the nominally independent communities of the *reducciones* continued to work collectively. The Indian communities of the haciendas, the *reducciones*, and the few remaining *ayllus* continued to exist side by side in the sierra. In fact all were under the direct control of landowners who dominated local politics and usually controlled the appointment of the leaders of Indian communities. The uneasy coexistence of haciendas and communities continues down to the present. The distinction between Indian communities on and off the haciendas, however, depends only on the degree of independence, not on any absolute difference in agricultural organization.

The end of the colonial epoch in 1832 signaled if anything the acceleration of land seizures by the owners of haciendas. The laissez faire economic ideas of Bolívar and San Martín led to reforms aimed at turning the highland population into a nation of Jeffersonian small farmers. Land was to be freely bought and sold, and Indians were free to dispose of formerly inalienable community land. Given the dominant political position of the landowners, however, absurdly one-sided bargains ensued and the upper classes rapidly cheated the Indians out of much of their remaining land. While the disastrous reforms were quickly rescinded, the pace of land seizures hardly slowed. The artificial land scarcity created by the expropriations of the republican era was exacerbated by the growth of the Indian population, which, reversing its long decline in the colonial period, increased dramatically in the nineteenth century. The increasing pressures of population on available land forced the communities to higher altitudes and increasingly marginal lands. In many places communities were compelled to leave agriculture entirely and adopt pastoralism suitable to the barren *puna*. The scarcity of community land created divisive economic interest within the community, and as the pressure on land increased, communal work practices fell into disuse and more and more residents of communities became individual landowners. The communities were also forced to turn to crafts and commercial activity to supplement their declining income from agriculture, and in some cases communities came to exist with no lands whatsoever. The increasing pastoralism and commercialization of the communities initiated in the early republican era and increasing in the nineteenth century was to have a profound effect on their adjustments to the export economy of the twentieth century and on their final act of retribution against the *hacendados* in the peasant revolt of the 1960s.

In the nineteenth and twentieth centuries communities lost most of their communal characteristics and continued to exist only to defend their members' land against the haciendas. The community leadership continued to exercise some of its traditional functions, including the annual adjudication of boundary disputes between members, but its authority was hopelessly compromised by the domination of the *hacendados*. While the community leaders claimed legitimacy on the basis of their ties to the administrator of the traditional *ayllu* and carried the staff of office which was the symbol of authority under the Incas, in fact they were appointed by political representatives of the landowners and exerted little real influence except in religious matters. Despite political domination first by Spanish colonists and later by mestizo landowners, the communities managed to maintain remnants of their traditional culture and have not been fully assimilated even at present in most of the sierra. Quechua, the *lingua franca* of the Inca empire, is still in general use in the sierra, and in many places it is the only language understood. In the area around Lake Titicaca in southern Peru, Aymara —a language which predates the Incas—continues to be spoken. While systematic colonial campaigns against idolatry have had considerable success and the Indian population is fully Catholicized, many elements of traditional religion persist, particularly in festival observances. Traditional Indian patterns of dress such as the wearing of ponchos by men and the *lliklla*, or shawl, by women are common in the sierra. Agricultural technology has also made few concessions to the innovations in land tenure introduced by the Spaniards. While the Incan foot plow now usually has a steel rather than a stone blade, the foot plow and the Incan adze hoe are still the principal implements of cultivation in most Indian communities. Haciendas generally have greater access to animal traction than communities and, since they are located on the better bottom lands, make greater use of irrigation technology, but there is remarkably little difference in cultivation techniques on and off the haciendas. Both communities and haciendas continue to produce subsistence crops, particularly barley, wheat, and potatoes, and very little of the production is sold even in local markets.

Legislation in the twentieth century has attempted to protect the rights of the remnants of the original Indian communities, but this legislation has been as ineffectual as that of the early republican era. The largely illiterate Indian population has not the legal, political, or financial resources to defend itself against the continued land seizures of the *hacendados*. The 1912 constitution created a legal identity for the Indian communities and provided mechanisms for formal recognition of the community and registration of title to its lands. The term *comunidad indígena* (indigenous community) was officially reserved for those communities which had obtained formal legal recognition, but this term has come into general use to describe almost any Indian community which is not actually located on the lands of a hacienda. Indigenous communities, then, include remnants of *ayllus* and *reducciones,* communities without lands, groups of Indians who have banded together to protect themselves against encroaching haciendas, and even commercial centers and towns of predominantly Indian composition. Most of these types of communities are involved in struggles with large landowners over ancient land claims, and even official recognition as a *comunidad indígena* does not insure any degree of protection against the expansion of the *hacendados*. Since the only means of expending agricultural income in the sierra is through the acquisition of additional land, communities are continually threatened with the expropriation of what little land they have remaining. The *hacendados* rely on shady lawyers, political deals, or outright force to expand their lands, and the peasants of the sierra have come to refer to the hacienda owners and their allies as *gamonales,* which literally means "boss," or *cacique,* but in its usage in the sierra has a meaning closer to "gangster." The tactics of *gamonalismo* depend ultimately on the political power of the national government, which has long backed the sierran *hacendados* with force when their power was seriously threatened by communities attempting to reclaim their lands.

By the 1950s and 1960s the alliance between the central government dominated by members of the coastal oligarchy and the hacienda owners of the sierra was beginning to weaken, and the power of the *hacendados* over the communities correspondingly decreased. In 1956 the military regime of General Odría was replaced by the civilian government of Manuel Prado. Under Odría and his predecessors peasant and union organizations had been repressed and peasants who attempted to reclaim land illegally controlled by haciendas were ordered to vacate the lands and shot down by police if they refused. While Prado was a conservative representative of the coastal export oligarchy, he permitted peasant and union organization and allowed APRA to operate openly for the first time since 1946. Peasants' organizations began in many areas of Peru, and by the time of the 1962 presidential elections land reform was a dominant political issue. In the world analysis of the population of agricultural export sectors peasants in hacienda systems were unable to initiate actions against hacienda owners unless central governments were controlled by liberal or reformist elements. This general principle applies to Peru as well. The parties in the 1962 election actively competed for the peasant vote and stimulated wide interest in land reform. During the period from 1960 to 1962 peasant land invasions began on a small scale in some areas of Peru. While the 1962 election was invalidated by a military intervention on July 18, new elections were held a year later in which Fernando Belaúnde Terry, a moderate architect with little previous political experience, won with a platform emphasizing land reform. For the first time in Peruvian politics direct appeals were made to the Peruvian peasantry, and in fact Belaúnde's Acción Popular and APRA were actively competing for peasant support. Belaúnde's inauguration on July 28, 1963, touched off a massive wave of peasant land invasions which may represent one of the largest spontaneous peasant movements in recent Latin American history. The Peruvian press data indicate that a total of four invasions took place in 1960, eight in 1961, and 39 in the election year of 1962. In the first seven months of 1963, before Belaúnde took office, only 16 invasions occurred. After July 28 a total of 91 invasions took place, spreading over most of the highlands, and in 1964 there were a total of 95 additional invasions. After 1964 the invasions tapered off in response to Belaúnde's promises for land reform in the central sierra and his active repression of the invaders in southern Peru. Altogether in the period between 1955 and 1970 a total of 463 land invasions and closely related agrarian events were reported in Peru, with 75 percent of these concentrated in the years 1962 to 1964. The dependent serfs of haciendas and the residents of indigenous communities were both involved in the invasions, and of the total of 418 events in which the occupation group of the participants could be determined, 139 were carried out by the serfs of haciendas and 279 by residents of communities. Ninety percent, or 376 of these 418 events, were carried out in the sierra, 130 by *campesinos* and 246 by *comuneros*. The distribution of the two types of events by province is shown in Map 3.3. Following the usage in the Peruvian press the agrarian events engaged in by the dependent serfs of haciendas are called *campesino* events, while those engaged in by residents of indigenous communities are called *comunero* events. The press does not reserve the term *comunero* for residents of legally recognized *comunidades indígenas,* so that these events include actions by both registered and unregistered Indian communities. It is clear from Map 3.3 that the distributions of the two types of events do not overlap, and in fact, while *comunero* agrarian events are widely distributed over much of the sierra, *campesino* agrarian events are concentrated in the department of Cuzco. Of the 130 *campesino* agrarian events shown in sierra provinces in Map 3.3, 94, or 72 percent, are concentrated in the department of Cuzco and 56 of these occur in the valley of La Convención and adjacent areas of the provinces of Anta, Urubamba, Calca, and Paucartambo. With the exception of the *campesinos* of Cuzco, the dependent Indians of the highland haciendas were surprisingly passive even though they were mostly directly exposed to the coercive labor practices of the haciendas. In most areas it was the independent communities that carried out the attacks on the hacienda system. In fact in many areas the targets of the *comunero* invasions were actually resident *campesinos* on invaded haciendas. Pitched battles between *campesinos* and *comuneros* were common in some areas and increasingly frequent as the *comuneros* became more successful in obtaining hacienda land. In 1964, for example, *campesinos* fought pitched battles with invading *comuneros* in Calca and Anta provinces of the department of Cuzco. In most areas of the sierra the *campesinos* felt their interests were parallel to those of the *hacendados*. In fact *campesinos* were frequently evicted along with the owner when the *comuneros* finally seized control of the land. Only in Cuzco did the serfs themselves rise up against their masters, and the problem of understanding the mobilization of *campesinos* becomes one of understanding why they threw in their lot with the landowners in all areas of Peru except Cuzco yet in this department were the most active and even revolutionary of any peasants on or off the haciendas.

THE HACIENDA: CALLEJÓN DE HUAYLAS AND LA CONVENCIÓN   The original land tenure system of La Convención is not indigenous, but it was imported into the region from nearby areas in the sierra and shares most of the features of the highland hacienda. The typical hacienda in the sierra at the time of the CIDA study, which was carried out just before the peasant uprisings, had changed little from the nineteenth century. Dependent serfs usually called *colonos* (although the term *arrendire* was used in La Convención) were permitted the usufruct of subsistence plots in exchange for assuming a variety of obligations to the *patrón* called *condiciones*. The most important of these obligations was to donate a fixed number of days per month (*días de condiciones*) to the lord's domain lands. In most places in the sierra these days varied from 10 to 15 a month—about 100 working days a year—and labor was from sunrise to sunset. While the timing of the work varied from place to place, the method preferred by the *patrón* was to maintain a peremptory right to the labor at the time of his own choosing. Since the agricultural cycles of the domain and usufruct lands were identical, the *patrón's* demands came at precisely those times when the *colono* most needed to work on his own plot. Frequently this meant that the *colonos* were forced to abandon their fields until dangerously late in the harvest period and often lost their own crops while harvesting those of the *patrón*. In exchange the serfs were paid a nominal wage of less than 3 cents a day, apparently so that the *patrón* could claim that no one worked for nothing. In addition, the *patrón* could use the obligatory days of labor to rent out his *colonos* to other estates or to mestizo businessmen in nearby towns and pocket the difference between the price of free and servile labor. The *colono* and his family were also required to provide domestic services (*pongaje*) in the *patrón's* household, and the *colono* might be required to supply the labor of his wife and children at particularly critical times, for example during the harvest of the coca crop. In most areas crops harvested on domain lands had to be transported to the *patrón's* residence even if he lived in town and the trip required days. If the *colono* had no pack animals, he was compelled to transport the harvest on his back. The penalties for not fulfilling these obligations were generally the loss of animals from the *colono's* herd, the confiscation of agricultural implements or seed, and not infrequently flogging or incarceration in the hacienda jail. In pastoral areas the serf was given permission to graze his own animals on the *patrón's* pasture in exchange for acting as shepherd for the *patrón's* flocks. If the *patrón's* flocks did not multiply at the expected rate, the peasant was required to make up the difference from his own animals, and peasants usually found that a large increase in their own herds was immediately susceptible to confiscation by the *patrón* on the ostensible grounds that the *colono* had not been paying enough attention to the *patrón's* flock. The *colonos* of a particular estate were referred to as the Indians of the hacienda; they were bought and sold along with the land, and their labor services were figured in the cost of purchase or rental. Serfdom was frequently hereditary, although in practice any *colono* could be evicted at the whim of the *patrón*. The *patrón* held life-or-death judicial authority over his dependent serfs, and the murder of peasants or the violation of their wives and daughters was not uncommon. The mestizo overlords regarded the peasants as little better than animals and actively discouraged education or the use of Spanish on the sound assumption that it might create aspirations beyond servile labor.

In almost all the sierra the hacienda was a purely subsistence enterprise and the *colono's* production usually left him at the verge of starvation. The precarious nature of usufruct agriculture and the overwhelming power of the *patrón* combined to create an intense, almost pathological conservatism on the part of most Indians resident on haciendas. In all areas outside the valley of La Convención this *colono* passivity persisted even in the face of a general peasant uprising. The hacienda Vicos in the valley of Callejón de Huaylas in the province of Carhuaz is typical of the highland subsistence hacienda and illustrates the reasons for the deeply ingrained conservatism of the *colono*. Vicos is the best-known and most intensely studied hacienda in Peru because it was the site of the Cornell Peru Project, an ambitious effort to combine social research with carefully measured efforts to initiate social change. Vicos has been described in numerous publications, some of the more detailed of which are those of the project's originator, the late Allan Holmberg, and its Peruvian director, Mario C. Vázquez, who went on to become director of the Bureau of Peasant Affairs under the revolutionary military regime.[50] One of the more candid views of the project in its early stages is provided by the ubiquitous Richard Patch,[51] who also wrote a detailed account of a coastal sugar estate described above. In 1952 Cornell University became the *patrón* of the hacienda Vicos by leasing it from its owners, a charitable organization called the Benefit Society of Huaraz. For an annual rent of about $500 Cornell obtained a medium-sized estate of 10,000 to 20,000 hectares, about 1,000 hectares of which were cultivated, and acquired title to the approximately 1,800 serfs resident on the hacienda. At the time Cornell assumed control, about 90 percent of the land was held in usufruct plots and the remaining 10 percent, which included almost all the valuable bottom land, was worked directly by the hacienda. Custom required that the *colonos* pay a labor tax of three days a week working the hacienda lands and also serve as cooks, shepherds, and servants from time to time as the *patrón* required. They were paid approximately 5 cents a day and could also be rented out to local businessmen. In fact any Vicosino who risked traveling to the nearby town could be ordered to work by any mestizo, and the intervention of the *patrón* might be required to save him from more extended bondage. The *colonos* were members of a captive Indian community of about 400 families, and all spoke Quechua and dressed in a local variant of traditional Indian dress. Only 23 persons could speak Spanish, and illiteracy was total. The hacienda *patrón* controlled the work organization of the hacienda through an appointed

50 For summaries of this project see Henry F. Dobyns, Paul L. Doughty, and Harold D. Lasswell (eds.), *Peasants, Power and Applied Social Change: Vicos as a Model* (Beverly Hills, Calif.: Sage, 1971), particularly articles by Holmberg and Vázquez; Allan R. Holmberg, "Changing Community Attitudes and Values in Peru: A Study in Guided Change," in Richard N. Adams et al., *Social Change in Latin America Today* (New York: Council on Foreign Relations, 1960), pp. 63–107; and Henry F. Dobyns, Carlos Monge M., and Mario C. Vázquez, "Summary of Technical Organizational Progress and Reaction to It," *Human Organization*, 21 (Spring 1962), 109–124.

51 Richard Patch, "A Hacienda Becomes a Community," *American University Field Staff Reports*, West Coast of South America Series, 4 (October 1957), 1–14.

administrator, a mestizo outsider, and also employed three mestizos as foremen. The foremen in turn controlled eight straw bosses, who were selected from the Indian community after long years of demonstrable subservience. The straw bosses administered the work of approximately 380 men employed on the hacienda lands and handled technical matters such as fertilization, irrigation, and field drainage. The work organization of the hacienda was paralleled by the hierarchical organization of the Indian community. The community was controlled by a group of elders called the *varayoc* who worked their way up the organizational hierarchy by scrupulous adherence to traditional religious practices and the generous provision of festivals and small loans to the less fortunate of the community. While the *varayoc*'s principal functions were religious, it did play an important role in settling disputes between members of the community over land and cattle and administered sanctions for the hacienda managers. While the officials were supposedly appointed from within the community, they were actually controlled by the *patrón,* and in fact reliable performance as a *vara* was the usual route to the position of straw boss in the hacienda work organization. The *varayoc* had the power to confiscate land or cattle, to determine when work obligations to the hacienda had been fulfilled, to recruit labor for public works projects, and to decide which women would be compelled to serve in the *patrón*'s house. Combined with their role in settling internal community disputes, these powers created a petty despotism constrained only by fear of retaliation from envious members of the community. Nevertheless the *varayoc* were able to enforce both moral piety and responsible work habits on the members of the community. Returning veterans or others who had left the community for any length of time were quickly forced back into the hacienda control structure. Despite the payment of wages, the hacienda relied on forced labor backed up by the coercive power of the *patrón* and his political allies in local administrative centers. While in theory flogging had been abolished at Vicos in 1928 after the intervention of the central government, it was still practiced on other estates in the vicinity and Vicos itself maintained its own jail for recalcitrant workers. A series of graduated sanctions ranging from the loss of seed or agricultural implements or the confiscation of animals to eviction, flogging, or death were available to the *patrón* through his foremen, the village administration, or his government allies. Even the most extreme sanctions could be imposed for seemingly trivial offenses. Serfs on a hacienda adjoining Vicos who had been impressed by the reforms introduced by the Cornell administration began constructing a new school building and petitioned the ecclesiastical authorities who held title to the land to allow them to work hacienda waste land communally. The *patrón* of the estate, a hereditary renter, responded to these modest initiatives by summoning a 15-man detachment of the national police and personally leading them to the area of the estate worked by the *colonos.* The police attempted to arrest the peasants, then opened fire, killing three and seriously wounding five others. In this case the local official who ordered the patrol was forced to resign, but it is unlikely that any such action would have been taken without the considerable local political influence of Cornell. The labor supply of the hacienda in Vicos and elsewhere in Peru depended ultimately on the threat of force.

While the coercive methods of the *patrón* did insure that *colonos* would from time to time appear in his fields, the work supplied was reluctant to the point of outright obstruction. The *colonos* demanded and received as many as six 15-minute coca breaks a day on the grounds that work in those altitudes required the stimulus of regular coca chewing. There was no similar enthusiasm for the narcotic, however, when the *colonos* worked their own lands, and usually they limited the time to two five-minute breaks a day. The *colonos'* families were permitted the gleanings from the fields after the formal harvest had been completed, and the *colonos* themselves became skilled at carefully marking areas that might have been "overlooked" by the harvesters so that their wives and children could later carry out a more meticulous harvest. With the primitive cultivation techniques available to the *patrón* and his limited access to investment capital or transportation to market, this low-quality labor was adequate and the *patrón* preferred an unreliable but subservient labor force to a more skilled and demanding one.

The structure of Vicos at the time that Cornell took control established a balance of material and coercive resources that made peasant mobilization only a remote possibility. This was hardly a result of the fact that *colonos* were socially isolated and cut off from adequate communication since Vicos was a more tightly knit community than the typical coastal cotton estate or certainly the semiurban sugar plantation. The long-term stability of Vicos depended on a balance of the interests of the *patrón* with the interests of the *colonos* themselves.

1. The *patrón's* labor supply depended on a politically disenfranchised group of dependent serfs who supplied the bare minimum of labor necessary to carry out subsistence production. While much has been made of the irrationality of the estate owners, their dedication to traditional agrarian life styles, and their resistance to modern technology, in fact the isolated valleys of the sierra have no markets for crops, no sources of outside funds, and little mechanization. Highland subsistence crops are annuals, cultivation enjoys no appreciable economies of scale, and most crops would be considerably more efficiently produced by small holders. While in areas close to rail lines in central Peru some commercialization has taken place, capital investment in a highland hacienda would in most cases represent a waste of money. Trips to Europe, expensive vacations, or the purchase of American goods are actually considerably more rational ways of spending money than investment in agricultural production, for which there are no ready markets and no available technology. With no prospects for rationalization of production the *patrón* gains little or nothing from a responsible unionized labor force, and the increased cost of unionization cannot be offset by gains in productivity through investment in machinery. In fact in a free market situation the inefficient *patrón* would rapidly lose out to small holders, and consequently the *patrón* would maintain his coercive apparatus

both to discourage small landholders and to propel his reluctant *colonos* into the fields. The presence of *colonos* on the lands of the hacienda is itself an indication of inefficient agricultural production. If sierran lands could be economically exploited by modern agricultural technology, the usufruct plots would likely be cultivated directly by the *patrón,* and a considerably smaller but more efficient labor force would be maintained on a wage basis. In fact the first step taken by landowners attempting to modernize their estates for livestock production in the central sierra is a local variant of the enclosure movements in which the *colonos* are coerced into abandoning their plots. The coexistence of *colono* and *patrón* therefore depends on their mutual inefficiency. Any expansion of market production on either side would threaten the balance of coercion and subsistence which maintains the traditional hacienda. The relationship between *patrón* and peasant is however one of zero-sum conflict, and the expansion of the lands or agricultural production of one are invariably at the expense of the other. The enfranchisement or unionization of the serf class would mean the demise of the *patrón,* and the modernization of the hacienda would mean the liquidation of the *colono.* In such a situation any change in the status quo is dangerous to both sides.

2. *Colonos* who might conceivably gain from the *patrón's* demise are not inclined to pursue collective action since it might disrupt their own marginal subsistence activities. The typical Vicosino lives on bread for a few months of the year immediately after the harvest but is quickly reduced to stretching his remaining food supply in a thin soup for the rest of the year. The intense conservatism of the Vicosino which has been noted by almost all observers of the estate depends fundamentally on the slim margin between maximum production and starvation on the usufruct plots. The insecure tenure of the *colono* means that he has nothing to gain by capital improvements, and by custom such improvements, called *mejoras,* are the property of the *patrón. Colonos* are extremely reluctant to invest any time in improvements, and Patch points out that in the area of Vicos it is commonly said that a man who paints a board which is not his own loses both the paint and the board. Since technical improvements in *colono* cultivation will not occur given the insecure tenure arrangements, the Vicosino's marginal level of production has remained unchanged for generations. Even the introduction of new crops carries with it substantial risks. The Cornell group seemed puzzled by the Vicosinos' reluctance to adopt a new breed of potato introduced by the Americans, who guaranteed that it would produce high yields. While resistance to increased agricultural yields may seem irritational to representatives of an American farm extension service, it makes a good deal of sense in the economy of the sierra. Even if the odds that the new variety of potato will succeed in the first year are as good as nine to one, the peasants' pay-off matrix may still dictate retaining traditional crops if the one chance of failure means death by starvation and the nine chances of success mean at most a small increase in production which will likely be siphoned off by mestizo middlemen in nearby towns. The risks of organizational innovations such as unioniza-

tion are even greater, and the *colono* who shows signs of potential radicalism such as learning Spanish or wearing shoes will not long remain on the hacienda.

3. While the majority of Vicosinos were poor to the point of near starvation, there nevertheless existed considerable stratification within the community, and the prospects for individual rather than group mobility were therefore considerable. Patch estimates that the wealthiest serfs of Vicos controlled 10 times as much wealth as the poorest.[52] Vázquez points out that there was a distinct peasant upper class of approximately 8 percent of the families who held herds as large as 10 to 20 animals and controlled enough liquid resources to advance loans to other members of the community.[53] The prospects for increasing one's wealth at the expense of other members of the community lead to dog-eat-dog economic relations and endemic thievery, particularly of livestock. In fact when the Cornell researchers attempted to control cattle rustling by branding livestock, they were met with solid resistance from the wealthier members of the community, whose own herds obviously could not stand careful scrutiny. The wealthier members of the community were actually better off than many mestizo townsmen and in fact maintained close ties to the mestizo ruling class through *compadrazgo* relationships. The peasant upper class of Vicos was always vulnerable to theft, witchcraft, or malicious gossip, but it provided a model of upward mobility through conservative community leadership and faithful obedience to the *patrón*. The divisive influence of the distribution of wealth in Vicos stands in marked contrast to the leveling influence of wage labor among agricultural workers of either the sugar or the cotton estates.

4. The limited financial resources of the community and their unequal distribution made political organization outside the hacienda administrative structure a practical impossibility. In the plantation communities of the coast class-based interests could be reinforced by community control over an informal network of mutual assistance and social support. In the sierran hacienda the traditional Indian leaders used the delegated coercive powers of the *patrón* to play the economically divided *colonos* off against one another. The dual structure of hacienda and community organization meant that *colonos* more frequently sought assistance from their superiors rather than from equals in a situation that William F. Whyte has aptly described as a triangle without a base.[54] Organizational ties ran from the *colono* upward to the peak of the administrative hierarchy of the hacienda, but the base of the triangle, the *colonos* themselves, were not connected by ties of social or economic interest. The formation of an associational interest group among the serfs would therefore depend on displacing the compromised authority of the *varayoc* and the development of new organizational ties among the *colonos* themselves. The Cornell administration

[52] *Ibid.*
[53] Mario C. Vázquez, "The Interplay between Power and Wealth," in Dobyns, Doughty, and Laswell, *Peasants*, pp. 65–84.
[54] William F. Whyte, "Rural Peru: Peasants as Activists," *Transaction*, 7 (November 1969), 37–47.

actively encouraged such alternative organizations, and one of the key events in the reorganization of Vicos occurred when a land dispute was taken to elected community officials rather than to the community elders of the *varayoc*. Without the active intervention of the Cornell project, however, it seems unlikely that the *colonos* would risk retaliation from the dual power structure of the hacienda and attempt to establish their own organization. Given the domination of the foreman and the *varayoc,* a talented leader had little choice but to work his way upward through the existing structure and could find only a temporary dangerously exposed position as a peasant organizer within the Vicos community. The isolation of the hacienda increased the control of the traditional community leaders and made it even more difficult for a peasant organization to develop an independent resource base. While the isolation of a sugar plantation had been an advantage for union organizers since it tended to reinforce the common economic interests of the workers, the isolation of the hacienda simply increased the power of the hacienda administration and reinforced economic divisiveness within the *colono* community.

5. Even if the divisive economic interests and organizational weakness of the hacienda could be overcome, there was relatively little to be gained from collective action. While it might seem possible to organize a harvest strike in exchange for higher pay or reduced labor dues, actually such a strike would come at a time when the *colonos* themselves were most vulnerable to retaliation. Since the harvest periods of the hacienda and the usufruct plots overlap, eviction, arrest, or even confiscation of agricultural implements would result in the loss of the *colonos'* harvest. While some strikes were organized by *colonos,* they were usually immediately countered by the arrest of the leaders and the subsequent impoverishment of their families. The marginal economic position of the *colono* made him unwilling either to risk mass economic action or to aid those who had attempted it and suffered the consequences. Even if a strike were successful, however, the gain to the *colono* would be slight. He might be freed from some of the more onerous *condiciones,* particularly the requirement that his wife and children work in the *patrón*'s residence, or he might secure more time for his own plot. While these issues are of great social and psychological importance to both *colono* and *patrón,* the economic gains from such limitations on the *patrón*'s power would be marginal. Although the colono and his family might be able to devote more time to their own plot, the marginal return from this additional labor would hardly justify the risks of participating in a strike. Most *colono* plots are already so intensively cultivated that the soil fertility is in danger of total depletion, and more work would simply accelerate this process. Without a valuable cash crop to justify the added attention to the usufruct plot, the gains from collective labor action would be minimal. The only immediate means for the *colono* to increase his income in the subsistence hacienda is to follow the example of the *patrón* and sieze any land not in cultivation. Needless to say, the most likely target, the uncultivated hacienda lands, is also the most jealously defended. Peasant seizures of hacienda lands would, of course, lead to

the loss of the *patrón*'s income and the demise of the hacienda system. In most areas of Peru land seizures provoke violent retaliation. If the divided economic interests and organizational weakness of the *colonos* make even a labor union too risky, it seems unlikely that peasant solidarity could be maintained in the face of the Draconian measures likely to be used by a *patrón* threatened with the loss of his lands. While the potential gains of a land seizure are certainly greater than the potential gains of a strike, the penalties too are correspondingly greater. While attempts by dependent serfs to take control of the hacienda through either litigation or direct action are not unknown in the highlands, they have seldom enjoyed more than short-run success. The attempt of the Vicos *colonos* to purchase the hacienda and thus obtain the use of domain lands illustrates the general futility of such action in the political climate of Peru before the revolution of 1968. In 1957 the Cornell researchers began encouraging the Vicosinos to save money toward a future purchase when the Cornell lease expired. The proceeds of the hacienda lands were turned over to the community in order to provide financial backing for the project. With an apparent financial opening to actual ownership and the political sponsorship of Cornell, the Vicosinos' economic divisions vanished and they managed to save the phenomenal sum of $30,000 in a little over five years. The political resistance mobilized against this seemingly moderate plan for reform ranged from the local Rotary Club, which accused the Cornell researchers of communism, to the prime minister of Peru, who felt it might set a precedent for land reform measures throughout the country. Since the prime minister at the time was one Pedro Beltrán, editor of *La Prensa* and himself one of the largest landowners in Peru, the resistance was not unexpected. The Benefit Society of Huaraz immediately increased the price of the hacienda by a factor of 10 on the grounds that community buildings and other improvements built by the communal labor of the *colonos* in projects sponsored by Cornell made it much more valuable than the annual rent would have indicated. At this point the peasants, who had been told for almost a decade that they were to receive the hacienda, held an angry meeting and threatened to buy arms and resist the reimposition of the hacienda system by force. Despite peasant threats, the political influence of the university, and the intervention of the United States ambassador it is still unlikely that the Vicosinos would have gained control except for the extraordinary personal intervention of the brother of the President of the United States. In 1961 Edward Kennedy, then a private citizen, visited the Callejón de Huaylas, toured much of the valley, and talked with the serfs of Vicos. Kennedy was evidently much impressed by rural conditions in the valley and on his return to Lima requested an interview with President Manuel Prado and demanded the sale of the hacienda to the Vicosinos. In July 1962 the sale was finally consummated with the aid of a loan from the national government. It might be added that Kennedy's intervention and the period of the sale corresponded to the beginning of the peasant land invasions in the sierra, and by the time of the actual sale the land invasions were beginning to present a widespread threat to the sierra ruling classes.

While the Vicos experiment is usually portrayed as a model of moderate agrarian reform in Latin America, it actually illustrates the limits of effective land reform in the absence of radical political change or peasant mass action. There seems little doubt that the Vicosinos would ever have obtained control of the hacienda without the personal intervention of the brother of the President of the United States, and in fact on at least three earlier occasions similar efforts had been swiftly repressed by the *patrón* and his government allies. While some peasants may still believe that the United States President like the Pope is a semidivine figure who can be relied upon to intervene on behalf of the poor and meek, the Cornell researchers might be expected to know better. Neither the introduction of a new variety of potato, the organizational innovations of the anthropologists, the community building projects, nor any of the other reforms introduced by Cornell were able to create a self-sufficient community in the absence of intense political pressure. What the Cornell project did conclusively illustrate, however, is that peasant culture does not inhibit change when restraining political forces have been eliminated. The Vicosinos were constrained not by the culture of poverty, but by repression. A change in the balance of political forces, the support of powerful patrons outside the community, and the diversion of the proceeds of domain land to the community were sufficient to convert a distrustful, divided group of peasants into a cohesive political force in the space of less than five years. The experiment of Vicos indicates both the delicate local balance of coercion and material interests which maintain the stability of the highland hacienda and the massive national social forces which hold that balance in place.

In the absence of the extraordinary political alliance which made the transformation of Vicos possible the serfs of the Callejón de Huaylas and most other highland valleys of Peru remained tied to the subordination and minimal security of the hacienda system even during the peasant uprisings of the 1960s. In the valley of La Convención in the department of Cuzco, however, the hacienda system collapsed under the impact of a mass movement organized by the serfs themselves with no help whatsoever from local or national political authorities. The movement attracted international attention, particularly after the leadership was assumed by Hugo Blanco, a radical Trotskyist organizer who was portrayed in both the Peruvian and American press as a new "Fidel of the Andes." Actually, as Blanco himself has pointed out,[55] neither the peasant methods nor goals were revolutionary and both were focused on changes in the agricultural organization of the valley. The widespread interest in the movement has prompted a number of firsthand accounts of the politics and land tenure system of La Convención. The CIDA included La Convención as its principal illustrative case study in its section on land tenure in the *seiva* region.[56] The dis-

---

[55] Interview with Blanco reported in Wesley Craig, "Peru: The Peasant Movement of La Convención," in Henry A. Landsberger, *Peasant Movements*, p. 292.
[56] CIDA, *Perú*, pp. 206–216.

tinguished Marxist historian Eric Hobsbawm visited the valley at the height of
the movement and provided both an overview of the principal events and an
analysis of the agrarian structure as a form of "neo-feudalism."[57] A detailed
chronology of peasant actions was constructed by Hugo Neira in his reporting
for *Expreso*,[58] and a detailed sociological study of the valley was carried out
by Wesley Craig, who systematically surveyed the peasant communities which
eventually displaced the hacienda system.[59]

All these accounts make clear that the organization of the traditional
hacienda system of La Convención was in many respects identical to that of the
Callejón de Huaylas and other areas of the sierra even though its history and
ecological circumstances were distinctly different. The valley of La Convención
begins a few miles from the Incan ruins at Machu Picchu and lies along the
Urubamba River, which flows north, eventually joining the Amazon. The valley
slopes from about 5,000 to less than 700 feet, and most of it lies in the zone of
high jungle rather than in the sierra proper. In its northern reaches it was
inhabited by forest Indians rather than Indian *ayllu* communities and was
sparsely populated at the time of the conquest. Land concentration in La Convención dates to the colonial era, but labor has always been scarce in the valley
and both the labor supply and the hacienda system were imported from the
sierra. The large landowners of the valley at first tried to solve their labor
problem by entrapping forest Indians and when this failed relied on *engancha-
dores* for temporary wage laborers. Eventually they evolved the system called
arrendire, which in most respects resembles the *colono* system of the sierra. In
exchange for accepting work obligations, a serf, or *arrendire,* received the
usufruct rights to a small, generally inferior plot of hacienda land. The *condiciones* were similar to those in the Callejón de Huaylas and included obligatory
labor for 15 to 18 days a month on hacienda lands, provision of additional
family labor during the harvest, gratuitous service in public works projects,
transport of hacienda produce, and preferential sale of usufruct crops to the
patrón. All the private agricultural land in the valley was controlled by 136
estates which ranged in size from 2,000 to 152,000 hectares, with a sizeable
number in the 30,000 to 40,000 hectares class.[60] The hacienda land monopoly
was broken only by the site of the provincial capital, Quillabamba, and immigrants to the valley could only obtain land by becoming *arrendires* on one of the
estates. Despite the vast size of the properties very little land was actually
cultivated because of the rugged terrain of the high *selva* region. In the 1930s a

[57] E. J. E. Hobsbawm, "A Case of Neo-Feudalism: La Convención, Peru,"
Journal of Latin American Studies, 1 (May 1969), 31–50. See also Hobsbawm's "Problèmes Agraires à La Convención, Pérou," in *Les Problèmes
Agraires des Amériques Latines* (Paris: Centre National de la Recherche
Scientifique, 1967), pp. 385–393.
[58] Hugo Neira, *Cuzco: Tierra y Muerte* (Lima: Problemas de Hoy, 1964).
[59] Wesley W. Craig, *From Hacienda to Community: An Analysis of Solidarity
and Social Change in Peru,* Cornell University, Latin American Studies Program, Dissertation Series, no. 6 (Ithaca, N.Y., September 1967).
[60] CIDA, *Perú,* p. 208.

malarial epidemic decimated the valley population and created a temporary land surplus. By 1960, however, Craig reports that all available land was under intense cultivation and much of it was beginning to show signs of soil depletion.[61] The haciendas monopolized the first-class agricultural land along the valley floor, and the *arrendires* were left to carve out usufruct plots on ingeniously terraced hillsides. Despite the poor quality of this land there was considerable migration into the valley even after the population losses of the malarial epidemic had been offset, and latecomers found land increasingly scarce. Most of the immigrants came as individuals, and consequently the typical communal village of the sierran hacienda was absent in La Convención. Like most of the high *selva* the valley is an isolated frontier area, and until the completion of a railroad to Machu Picchu in 1928 and the extension of a road to Quillabamba in 1930 transportation out of the valley was limited to a narrow mule track. Some cash crops including sugar, tea, and coca were grown on hacienda lands, but the immense transportation problems discouraged investment, and agricultural techniques and work organization were among the most backward in Peru.

The hacienda owners maintained tight control over the *arrendires,* who were themselves widely scattered over the hacienda lands and had little contact with one another or with *arrendires* from other estates. In contrast to the hacienda Vicos there was no parallel village administrative structure, and both secular and religious affairs were controlled by the hacienda owners. As was the case in the sierra, judicial authority was exercised by the *patrón,* and the isolated frontier quality of the area seems to have encouraged particularly abusive behavior on the part of the *hacendados.* Flogging was common, and Hobsbawm reports instances of shooting of trespassers and squatters and rapes of Indian women.[62] *Hacendados* scrupulously avoided speaking to their serfs in Spanish and ridiculed any Indian who tried to affect mestizo dress. While the hacienda system is not based on active Indian communities as it is in the sierra, most of the *arrendires* continue to speak Quechua and follow traditional Indian patterns of dress. Census figures indicate that the proportions of Quechua speakers and wearers of traditional Indian dress are approximately the same in La Convención as they are in adjacent areas of the sierra.[63]

The traditional structure of the La Convención hacienda was no more likely to generate a successful peasant movement than was the structure of hacienda Vicos. In some respects the situation of the La Convención *arrendire* was even less favorable than that of the Callejón *colono*. The haciendas exerted total control over the valley of La Convención, while in most areas of the sierra indigenous communities and mestizo towns at least offered some alternatives to hacienda power. The *arrendire* tenure was precarious, usually for a fixed period and, in the migratory labor situation in La Convención, was unlikely to be

61 Craig, *Hacienda to Community*, p. 17.
62 Hobsbawm, "Problèmes Agraires," pp. 386–387.
63 Perú, *Sexto Censo Nacional de Población*, vol. 1, Book 3. pp. 2–3, Book 5, pp. 5–8.

hereditary. If the *hacendado* could find someone willing to sell himself more cheaply, he could easily replace his current *arrendire*. There was considerable stratification within the *arrendire* class, particularly between early arrivals, who had obtained relatively generous grants of land, and more recent arrivals, who found themselves left with small plots of marginal land. The absence of strong traditional Indian communities on the hacienda had a mixed effect on the possibilities for peasant organization. Although it eliminated the conservative influence of the *varayoc,* it correspondingly increased the direct control of the *hacendados*. The limited agricultural possibilities of the *selva* suggested that little could be gained from increased subsistence production on the usufruct plots, and even the *hacendados* were indifferent to technical improvements on their estates. The balance of material and coercive resources seemed to suggest a future of stagnation for the valley social structure.

The development of export crop production in the postwar period, however, dramatically altered the economic relations of the hacienda system and tipped the balance of resources in the *arrendire*'s favor. After 1945 the world price of coffee rose dramatically, and in Cuzco it increased by a factor of 12 between 1945 and 1954. Coffee is ideally suited to the middle altitudes and bountiful rainfall of the high *selva*, and production expanded along the entire eastern slope of the Peruvian Andes. In La Convención production increased sixfold between 1945 and 1960. Most of this production, particularly in its early stages, came from the usufruct plots of the *arrendires*. The *arrendire* of La Convención was no more inclined to take risks than the *colono* of Vicos and operated at the same marginal subsistence level, but coffee offered distinct advantages for the usufructuary. It could easily be interspersed with food crops, and a relatively small amount of additional attention would insure both a minimal food supply and a possible cash crop. While the *arrendire* risked losing his coffee bushes to the *patrón* just as he might lose any capital improvement, at least he had an opportunity to make a quick profit when the initial crop was harvested. In addition the *arrendires* held a distinct ecological advantage over the *hacendados*, since their plots were located on the hillsides, where cooler temperatures and higher rainfall were better suited to coffee. The relatively short harvest period of coffee also favors small holder production particularly in areas where it can be combined with food crops. In contrast to the development of export crop production on the coast, in the *selva* crop production parameters favored the small holder, and the *hacendados* found themselves with neither suitable land nor sufficient seasonal labor to start competitive production.

The economic possibilities of increased coffee production made it profitable for the *arrendire* to find ways to spend more time on his own plot and less time working for the *hacendado*. Instead of a marginal gain in production and a possible decline in the fertility of his plot, he could gain a substantial return on his labor. Initially the conflict between the *condiciones* of the hacienda and the time required for coffee cultivation was solved by hiring subtenants called *allegados* to fulfill the work obligations of the *arrendire* while he devoted himself to making money in the coffee business. In general the *allegado* assumed a third or less of the *arrendire*'s land and assumed some proportion of the *arrendire*'s work obligation. Some of the *arrendires* found the coffee trade profitable enough to acquire as many as a dozen subtenants, and their wealth began to rival that of the smaller *hacendados*. Subtenancy was not customarily permitted by the *hacendados*, but they initially tolerated the practice because it seemed to provide a larger pool of labor. When even this system failed to produce sufficient labor, the *arrendires* and even some *allegados* began hiring wage laborers to fulfill their work obligations or to work directly on the coffee harvest. The rise of the cash economy and the transformation of *arrendires* into small businessmen made the conflict between the free and compulsory economies increasingly apparent. Hobsbawm estimates that by 1960 the profits of inefficient hacienda agriculture depended on the difference between the prices of free and forced labor.[64] While the *arrendire* was paid a wage of 5 cents a day to work in the lord's fields, he was forced to contract for free labor at a rate of up to 50 cents a day to work his own field. Even allowing for a reasonable cash rent for the use of the usufruct plot, such extractions appeared increasingly unreasonable to the *arrendires*. One ingenious *hacendado* used his right to preferential sale of usufruct crops to buy coffee from his *arrendires* at a price of 28 cents a kilo while the free market price across the river from his estate was 44 cents a kilo. His 16-cent margin of profit was assured by assigning armed guards to patrol his side of the river and intercept "smuggled" free market coffee.[65]

Much to the surprise of the *hacendados* their serfs had come into the possession of an important income-producing property over which they had temporarily lost control. The relationship between lord and serf in the traditional manor had been based on the precarious assumption that given the general inefficiency of production, neither could demand much more from the other. The coffee economy suddenly made the marginal hillsides valuable, and the *hacendados* moved to reclaim the land and go into the coffee business themselves. Contracts with *arrendires* were found to have expired prematurely, *condiciones* were not adequately fulfilled, and one *patrón* insisted that his expanding family required the use of all his land including the usufruct plots. The scramble for land was accompanied by a scramble for labor, since the coffee harvest required simultaneous inputs of labor on both usufruct and domain lands.

The *hacendados'* efforts to reclaim lands threatened individual coffee producers, and increasingly the *arrendires* began to turn to collective legal action. Unlike the serfs of the subsistence manor they had both the prospect of substantial economic gains and the economic resources to hire legal help. Craig points out that the coffee farmers of La Convención created a minor boom for the Cuzco legal profession as large numbers of lawyers were hired to protest the forced labor conditions of the haciendas.[66] The *arrendires* had at least one legal

---

[64] Hobsbawm, "Neo-Feudalism," pp. 45–48.
[65] CIDA, *Perú*, pp. 214–215.
[66] Craig, *Hacienda to Community*, p. 39.

point in their favor, since the forced labor obligations of the *arrendire* agreement were formally illegal. This law had of course been of little use to the *arrendires* as long as the *hacendados* controlled the local legal system. It was usually used to evict *arrendires* on the grounds that they paid no rent and hence had no legally recognized right to the lands. Now, however, it could be used to argue that it was the obligatory work which was in fact illegal. The first peasant syndicates in La Convención were formed as early as 1952 to hire lawyers and place demands with the authorities in Cuzco. The demands included reductions in the number of days of forced labor, a reduction in the number of hours worked per day, and an end to preferential sales and assignment of improvements to the hacienda owners. The relative wealth of the coffee farmers and the economic benefits to be gained from an end to forced labor led to collective organization. By 1958 virtually the entire valley was organized in the Federación Provincial de Campesinos de La Convención y Lares.

The development of the coffee export economy had completely reversed the economic interests of the dependent serfs and upset the stability of the traditional highland hacienda. Coffee could be produced on usufruct plots without risking the loss of traditional food crops, and consequently the intense conservatism of the serf based on his marginal subsistence activities vanished. The cultivation of coffee made the *arrendire*'s labor on his own plot increasingly valuable and time spent on forced labor increasingly costly. The coffee crop was coveted by both the *arrendire* and the *hacendado*, and its increased value disrupted the balance of economic interests between them. The increasing economic resources of the *arrendires* made organizational leadership an increasingly attractive role for the more ambitious peasants and even for lawyers and radical students from Cuzco and made possible an organizational framework independent of the traditional hacienda. The economic gains from collective resistance to the work demands of the *hacendado* were substantial, and individuals who could avoid the *días de condiciones* and spend more time on their crop made substantial gains. The isolation of the haciendas made it possible for the wealthier and more powerful *arrendires* to enforce collective conformity on weaker *arrendires* and *allegados*. It was in fact the wealthier members of the peasant community who had the most to gain from collective action. The peasant movement of La Convención was in fact a bourgeois revolution in which the economic power of a growing class of small-scale capitalists confronted the declining authority of the feudal *hacendados*.

The *hacendados* had, of course, one remaining card to play—their traditional control of the police and military. The organization of the approximately 30,000 *arrendires* and *allegados* into a cohesive political force made local coercive resources inadequate, and the *hacendados* appealed for help from the departmental *guardia civil* and the national army. It is possible that even at this point the peasant organizations could have been crushed by a sanguinary military campaign, but the 136 *hacendados* of this obscure valley in the jungle appeared increasingly expendable to the members of a coastal oligarchy faced with the threat of a peasant revolution spreading throughout the sierra. In the election of 1962 the voting power of the peasant federation nullified the traditional political influence of the *hacendados,* and the central government became increasingly reluctant to side decisively with the landowners. In December 1961 the peasant federation declared a general strike in the entire valley and simply refused to fulfill the compulsory work obligations of the *condiciones.* This tactic left the peasants in de facto control of their usufruct plots and forced the landowners to appeal for a mass eviction of the *arrendires.* Instead the Prado regime issued a curiously redundant decree declaring the forced labor obligations illegal in the valley (they were in any case illegal under existing law as the peasants had long pointed out).

The evident weakness of the landowners led the peasants to increasingly radical tactics. In May of 1962 Hugo Blanco, the son of a Cuzco lawyer who had become an *allegado* on a La Convención valley estate, was elected president of the peasant federation and the intensity of the peasant movement dramatically increased. In late 1962 and early 1963 the peasants shifted from defensive measures aimed at eliminating the *condiciones* to offensive actions aimed at increasing their share of the valley land. Craig points out that the change in tactics and the election of Blanco reflected the demands of the *allegados* rather than those of the *arrendires* and created a split in the movement.[67] The *allegados* felt land scarcity more acutely and were prepared to rally behind Blanco's slogan "Tierra o Muerte" to claim hacienda land. More than 80 haciendas in the valley were successfully invaded, and several of them, particularly the Chaupimayo estate, formerly part of the largest single holding in the valley, became centers of revolutionary activity and staging areas for assaults on haciendas both in the valley and in nearby areas in the sierra. The increasing intensity of the movement and Blanco's revolutionary image finally led the oligarchy to intervene in a bloody military campaign which led to Blanco's capture in May of 1963. Despite the military presence and the massacre of at least one group of peasant invaders, the peasant federation remained in possession of much of the land it had seized. While the military effectively ended the expansion of the La Convención movement, it did not succeed in reestablishing the status quo in the valley. Craig points out that by 1965 the few *hacendados* who had not been chased out by their own serfs were passively awaiting the expropriation of their estates by the government land reform program.[68] Their power over their labor force had vanished along with their political influence. Despite the abusive practices of the La Convención hacienda owners surprisingly few were actually harmed by the peasants, and most were allowed to leave their lands peaceably taking their possessions with them. In fact before the intervention of the military there was remarkably little violence associated with the movement. In the hacienda system of La Convención violence was the economic tool of the *hacendados,* while the market economy was the revolutionary instrument of the peasants. The relative absence of

[67] Craig, "Peru," p. 291.
[68] Craig, *Hacienda to Community,* pp. 47–48.

violence in the early stages of the La Convención movement was a result of the political weakness of the landowners and underscores the fact that in most peasant movements violence is initiated from above, not from below.

It is clear from the case studies of La Convención, particularly Craig's careful survey of crop distributions within the valley, that the coffee export economy was a necessary precondition for the rise of the peasant movement.[69] While it is true that La Convención was both a major center of coffee production and a major center of agrarian protests by *campesinos*, it is also clear that there are many other areas of intensive coffee production which lack any similarly intense peasant movement. While the increase in coffee production in La Convención may have appeared a unique change to those concentrating their research in the valley, actually coffee cultivation was widespread in the high *selva* region. As the crop production data in Map 3.2 indicate, several other provinces equaled or surpassed the production of La Convención.[70] The province of Jaén in Cajamarca was actually the leader in national production, accounting for 20 percent of the total, Tarma in Junín was second with 16 percent, and La Convención was actually third with 12 percent. Substantial amounts of coffee were also produced in Jauja in Junín, Oxapampa in Pasco, Sandia in Puno, and Leoncio Prado in Huánuco. As the distribution of *campesino* agrarian events in Map 3.3 makes clear, none of these major coffee-producing areas (except La Convención) had any substantial numbers of agrarian events. In the provinces of Tarma and Jauja in Junín, *comunero* events did occur in substantial numbers but were located in the high *puna* area rather than in the selvatic coffee-producing areas (compare the event and crop distributions for the department of Junín in Maps 3.2 and 3.3). In fact when land invasions did occur in the coffee areas of Junín, they involved *comuneros* attempting to confiscate the coffee harvests of large haciendas rather than *campesinos* attempting to defend their coffee against hacienda owners. The absence of any overall relationship between coffee and *campesino* agrarian events can be summarized by the small .26 correlation between total coffee production and total number of *campesino* events in a province. While the center of *campesino* agrarian events, La Convención, is a center of coffee production, not all centers of coffee production are centers of agrarian events. The correlation between coffee production and *comunero* agrarian events is even lower, an insignificant .05.

The response of the *campesinos* of La Convención and the nearby provinces of Calca and Paucartambo to the coffee economy depended on the peculiar organizational characteristics of coffee production in this region. Coffee produc-

---

[69] Craig demonstrates that the solidarity of peasant communities established on the former haciendas was closely related to the amount of coffee grown. Communities which continued to cultivate coca, a traditional selvatic crop, were considerably less likely to receive high scores on Craig's index of solidarity than were communities which had shifted to coffee cultivation. Craig, *Hacienda to Community*, pp. 85–87.

[70] Coffee production by province in Map 3.2 was calculated from data presented in Carlos Martínez Claure, *La Producción de Café en el Perú* (Lima: privately published, 1967), p. 31.

tion increased dramatically throughout Peru during the 1950s, and almost all production took place in frontier areas of the high *selva*. In La Convención, however, a combination of processing methods and estate size both increased the material resources at the command of the peasants and limited the opportunities for expanded production. The *arabica* coffee grown in Peru is processed through two distinctly different methods which vary considerably in their profitability to the small producer.[71] Processing is required to separate the inner coffee grain from a dual outer shell before it can be sacked for export. In the so-called *lavado*, or wet, process the outer shell of the bean is removed by friction rolling in a small mechanical mill, and the inner shell is removed through fermentation in specially constructed tanks. The coffee is raked several times during fermentation to remove the sticky fermented inner coating. The coffee is then dried, usually in open sunlight but sometimes in specially constructed ovens. This process obviously requires expensive processing machinery, and only about 1,000 of the largest producers can afford the complete wet processing installation. Smaller producers can, however, form cooperatives to purchase machinery and share the cost of processing. The wet processing of coffee raises its value by almost $10 a *quintal*, or about 30 percent. The other method, the so-called natural, or dry, process, follows the procedure used in Brazil and other areas producing low-grade coffee. Coffee beans in varying stages of ripeness are spread out to dry in an open courtyard, and the outer shell is removed by hand threshing. The dry-processed coffee brings a low price, and the final step in the decortication process is carried out by exporting companies in Lima, which sell the final product at a substantial profit. Small producers are the principal users of the dry method, but since the wet method requires abundant supplies of water, dry processing is used by larger producers in arid areas, particularly in Cajamarca in the north.

Most wet-processed coffee is grown on large estates of from 10 to 100 hectares, while most dry coffee is grown on small holdings, some of which are smaller than 3 hectares. Below about 3 hectares coffee production is not an economically rational proposition, and in fact producers of this size closely resemble subsistence farmers. When the size of a coffee holding is below about 3 hectares, family labor is used exclusively, but above this level migratory wage labor is employed, so that 3 hectares represent the boundary between the family farmer and the estate owner. The valley of La Convención is unique in combining extremely small plots with an average size of 2.28 hectares with wet processing of coffee.[72] Thus the peasant of La Convención is in the paradoxical position of being a wealthy, land-starved small holder. In the major coffee-producing areas of the departments of Junín and Pasco large estates of 100 hectares are not uncommon, wet processing is used, most estates own their own machinery, and owners are part of the upper class.[73] In Cajamarca in the north no wet processing

---

[71] This description is based on Claure, *La Producción de Café*, chap. 2.
[72] *Ibid.*, p. 70.
[73] *Ibid.*, pp. 66–68, 70.

is used, but estate size is again large,[74] since this is one of the few areas in Peru in which a sizeable middle peasantry exists despite the hacienda system. In Sandia in the department of Puno there are many small holders[75] in a region dominated by large estates, but coffee is processed by the dry method only, and the subsistence qualities of the hacienda system remain intact.

The more valuable wet-processed coffee produces an economic interest in collective action when it is combined with a size of holding too small to support processing machinery. The peasants of La Convención would have sound economic reasons for forming cooperatives to control coffee processing even if they were not threatened with eviction by the haciendas. The greater profits of wet-processed coffee increase the prospects of supporting a leadership cadre, paying legal costs, and providing other material resources necessary for successful organization. Thus it seems likely that the peasant mobilization of La Convención depended not so much on the expansion of the coffee market but on the peculiar form of agricultural organization which developed in the valley. Growing conditions in the southern end of the valley are ideal, and rainfall is more than sufficient for wet processing. Only the economic limitations of small plot size prevented realization of the more substantial profits of wet-processed coffee. Collective peasant organization could both overcome this economic constraint and reduce the demands of the haciendas for compulsory labor. If this argument is correct, it suggests that less favorable growing conditions or an inadequate supply of water might have encouraged the *arrendires* to eke out a minimal subsistence income, even with the addition of coffee, and the economic justification for the movement of La Convención would have been diminished.

The overall relationship between the various types of coffee production and the distribution of agrarian events is presented in Table 3.4. While it should be kept in mind that this table essentially contrasts La Convención with all other provinces, it is clear that only wet-processed coffee produced on small estates has any significant correlation with either *campesino* or *comunero* agrarian events. The correlations between wet-processed coffee grown on small estates and *campesino* agrarian events is actually a substantial .77, although correlations with

TABLE 3.4 *Intercorrelations of Agrarian Events with Coffee Production by Type of Processing and Size of Holding for Sierran Provinces*

VARIABLE	(2)	(3)	(4)	(5)	(6)	(7)
1. *Comunero* agrarian events	.06	.05	—	.13	−.07	−.05
2. *Campesino* agrarian events		.26	.77	−.05	−.06	−.04
3. Coffee total			.42	.70	.18	.62
4. Coffee, wet, 3 ha. or less				−.03	.22	−.02
5. Coffee, wet, more than 3 ha.					−.05	.13
6. Coffee, dry, 3 ha. or less						−.05
7. Coffee, dry, more than 3 ha.						—

[74] *Ibid.*, pp. 59–60.
[75] *Ibid.*, pp. 81–83.

all other combinations of estate size and processing technique are negligible. The comparative analysis of provincial data for the entire sierra region suggests that the social organization of coffee production, not the expansion of production itself, was the source of the peasant movement of La Convención. This qualification nevertheless supports the general principal that peasant organization occurs as a rational response to economic and political opportunities provided by the new forms of agricultural organization created by a developing export economy.

THE INDIGENOUS COMMUNITY: HUALCAN AND SAN PEDRO DE CAJAS
With the exception of the province of La Convención, dependent hacienda serfs seldom carried out land invasions, and in fact more than two-thirds of all invasions in the sierra were carried out by members of the indigenous communities (*comuneros*). As the event distributions in Map 3.3 make clear, the *comunero* invasions were widely distributed throughout the highlands rather than concentrated in a single region as were *campesino* events. While the peasant movement in La Convención reached its peak intensity in 1962 and early 1963, the *comunero* invasions did not begin on a large scale until after the inauguration of Belaúnde Terry on July 28, 1963. Smaller-scale *comunero* invasions had, however, begun much earlier. The first invasion reported in the Peruvian press occurred on January 20, 1960, when the *comuneros* of San Antonio de Rancas began a series of invasions of the Paria estates of the Cerro de Pasco corporation in the department of Pasco.[76] Invasions continued on a small scale in Pasco and in neighboring Junín between 1960 and 1963 while the movement in La Convención was reaching its peak. After July 1963, however, the *comunero* movement exploded into a massive series of invasions beginning in the original areas of unrest in the departments of Junín and Pasco but rapidly spreading throughout the central sierra. At its peak the movement involved invasions by over a hundred distinct communities and may have involved as many as 300,000 individuals. The largest numbers of invasions were recorded in the central sierra provinces of Pasco and Daniel Carrión in the department of Pasco and the provinces of Huancayo, Jauja, Tarma, and Yauli in Junín. Substantial numbers also occurred in adjacent areas of the department of Lima, particularly in the provinces of Cajatambo and Yauyos. The provinces of Bolognesi, Recuay, and Yungay in Ancash and the province of Huancavelica in the department of the same name were also major centers of activity. In general the pattern of events in Map 3.3 suggests a widening circle of activity spreading outward from the initial centers of unrest in the central provinces of Junín and Pasco. While the central region remained the area of most intense activity, scattered invasions were reported throughout the sierra (see Map 3.3). The department of Cuzco also experienced a large number of land disputes involving *comuneros*, but most of these were distinctly different in form from the central region invasions. As the event distributions in Map 3.3 make clear, most of the Cuzco *comunero* events took place in areas of high *campesino* activity, while in the rest of the

[76] *La Prensa*, Jan. 4, 1962.

sierra the two kinds of events seldom occurred together. In most Cuzco provinces and particularly in the province of Anta adjacent to La Convención the
invasions involved *campesino* organizations attempting to seize community lands
or battles between liberated *colonos* and nearby communities. The southern
Cuzco phase of the *comunero* movement seems to have been a more or less
direct response to the mounting pressures for land from the *campesino* movement centered in La Convención.

Virtually all the *comunero* agrarian events were land invasions in the
central sierra, and many adopted the slogan of the Cuzco *campesinos,* "Tierra o
Muerte," and were clearly interested in regaining lands in dispute with adjoining
haciendas. The peasants took pains to demonstrate their piety and patriotism,
frequently holding religious services on invaded haciendas and prominently dis-
playing the Peruvian national flag. Eighteenth- and nineteenth-century peasant
uprisings, particularly the famous revolt of Túpac Amaru in 1780, had a pronounced Indian nationalist ideology and were clearly as much ethnic as economic struggles. The *comunero* invasions of the 1960s, however, were almost
devoid of references to Indian cultural identity and instead focused exclusively
on land rights. The relative absence of either communal demands or a distinct
nationalist ideology among the *comuneros* may seem an exception to the general
proposition that indigenous land-holding groups are likely to emphasize communal rather than class interests. In fact, the Peruvian "indigenous community"
of the 1960s was neither indigenous nor communal and, despite vestigial remnants of Incan language and culture, had been submerged in the sierra peasant
class and left with little or no autonomous political or social identity. While
some Peruvian intellectuals have long insisted that the indigenous community
is either the embodiment of the native virtues of the Incas or, on the contrary,
the precursor of some Peruvian collective farm, most serious anthropologists
who have actually visited Indian communities have come away with very different impressions. There is very little land in Peru that is actually held communally, and most indigenous communities are in fact aggregates of marginal
small holders who own and work their land individually. Traditional communal
work practices such as festival labor or reciprocal labor exchange have fallen
into disuse in most areas of the sierra to be replaced by daily wage labor. The
internal structure of most communities is neither homogeneous nor egalitarian,
and most have internal class divisions similar to those of the hacienda communities. The administrative structure of the indigenous community is appointed and controlled by the mestizo upper class of the area even when the
community is not directly the property of a particular hacienda. Since sierran
land is increasingly scarce, many community residents have been forced to
assume obligations as *colonos* on nearby haciendas to supplement the limited
production of their plots on community land. In most respects in fact the traditional subsistence community of the sierra closely resembles the economic and
social organization of the hacienda community. In fact the operational definition

of an indigenous community in the sierra seems to be a group of serfs who do not happen to live on a hacienda. A number of observers have suggested that the preservation of the indigenous community is simply a means of maintaining a politically disenfranchised, economically depressed pool of labor for the sierra haciendas.[77] As Kubler pointed out, a long series of exploiters from the Inca nobility and the *encomenderos* to the hacienda and commercial estate owners of the present have found it advantageous to maintain the community, and it is likely that indigenous communities will continue to exist only so long as there are economic interests which profit from exploiting them.[78] As the export economy of the coast attracted more and more sierran labor in the twentieth century, the sierran *hacendados* have found that the guarantee of a small amount of land for communities enabled them to draw upon servile laborers as closely bound to the land as their own *colonos.*

The protective legislation enacted in the twentieth century has bound the communities even more tightly to the soil but has hardly halted the predation of the sierran upper classes. The legal protection extended to Indian communities in the constitutions of 1912 and 1933 illustrate the effects of Ford's law of Peruvian land tenure with a vengeance. The constitutional provisions implementing presidential decrees in 1936 and 1938 created a legal identity for communities and made community lands inalienable.[79] While the intent of these laws was to provide communities with legal protection against hacienda expropriations, their effect was to bind the *comuneros* more closely to the land by eliminating the possibility of economic escape from the sierra through the proceeds of a sale. The protective legislation did not effectively stop the expansion of haciendas, and by guaranteeing a supply of semiservile labor in the communities, it actually perpetuated the power of the hacienda system that it was designed to check. The process of recognition provided for in the new legislation was difficult if not impossible for most communities because it required the services of a lawyer, knowledge of Spanish, local political influence, and a long and expensive process of survey and registration. While the legislation created a Bureau of Indian Affairs in 1927 to supervise the legal recognition of communities, as late as 1955 the Bureau had only one employee who could speak Quechua[80] and seldom initiated efforts to register communities. If a community wanted to obtain legal recognition as a *comunidad indígena*, it would have to collect enough money from limited community resources to send a delegation to Lima with the neces-

---

[77] See Richard Patch, "How Communal Are the Communities," *American University Field Staff Reports,* West Coast of South America Series, 6 (June 1959), pp. 1–18, and Henry F. Dobyns, *The Social Matrix of Peruvian Indigenous Communities* (Ithaca, N.Y.: Cornell University, Department of Anthropology, Cornell Peru Project, 1964), pp. 13–22.

[78] Kubler, "Quechua," p. 409.

[79] Dobyns, *Indigenous Communities,* pp. 1–2.

[80] Julio Cotler, "The Mechanics of Internal Domination and Social Change in Peru," in Irving Louis Horowitz (ed.), *Masses in Latin America* (New York: Oxford University Press, 1970), pp. 407–444.

sary supporting documents. These economic and cultural barriers to recognition meant that only the most economically advanced Indian communities could apply for recognition, and by 1959 only 1,500 of the more than 5,000 Indian communities in Peru had obtained the legal designation *comunidad indígena*.[81] Actually, since recognized communities are the most economically advanced, the more likely a community is to have obtained legal recognition, the less likely it is to have retained any traditional Indian cultural or economic practices. Many of the so-called indigenous communities are in fact towns of mixed cultural orientation or simply groups of farmers who have banded together to attain legal recognition for its advantages in lawsuits. Insofar as the law extends any legal protection at all to the Indian population, it extends it to the most thoroughly assimilated and wealthiest sectors. The reforms of the early twentieth century created the legal fiction the *comunidad indígena*, which held out the hope of legal protection to the mass of the Indian population of the sierra but in fact extended it only to communities which had lost most of their Indian characteristics.

Even legal recognition as a *comunidad indígena* is no guarantee against further expropriations by haciendas or commercial estates. The reforms made it possible for a recognized community to register its lands by conducting a cadastral survey, but Peru maintains no uniform system of surveys or title registration and in practice land boundaries are often wherever local mestizo authorities choose to place them. The constitutional provisions gave communities the right to sue to protect their lands, but given the corrupt legal system of the sierra this provision has simply tied up astounding amounts of community funds in endless litigation. The CIDA reports that in the department of Puno as much as 9 percent of the income of a typical community went for legal expenses in contrast to less than 5 percent spent on education.[82] Litigation is as continual as it is fruitless. Dobyns reports a survey of registered indigenous communities which indicated that 73 percent were involved in land disputes of one kind or another and that some of these disputes had been in the courts for as long as 40 years.[83] Even successful suits, however, do not necessarily lead to control of land. Patch reports that one community after years of litigation with an adjacent hacienda finally obtained a favorable judgment in the courts of the departmental capital. The hacienda, however, simply ignored the decision and continued in possession of the lands.[84] The legal protection of the new reforms has done nothing to prevent the haciendas from gradually slicing off additional portions of community lands. Patch also describes a community which adjoined two immense haciendas originally created entirely from community lands. The community members suddenly found that one of the haciendas had made them an offer to sell them several thousand hectares of what they had thought was their own communal

[81] R. Maclean y Estenos, *Sociología del Perú* (Mexico City: Instituto de Investigaciones Sociales, 1959), p. 262.
[82] CIDA, *Perú*, p. 190.
[83] Dobyns, *Indigenous Communities*, pp. 33–34.
[84] Patch, "How Communal," pp. 12–13.

pasture. When the *comuneros* resisted this patent attempt at extortion, the hacienda owners simply looked for mestizo buyers and ignored the land titles of the *comuneros*.[85]

While the predatory ingenuity of the hacienda land grabbers is impressive, their activities are dwarfed by the expropriations of the large commercial interests of the central sierra. This region, the center of the *comunero* agrarian movement, was also the area of the most extensive commercialization and the most widespread land expropriations during the twentieth century. In 1915 associates of J. P. Morgan founded the Cerro de Pasco corporation to exploit the copper and other mineral deposits of the departments of Pasco and Junín. The company eventually expanded to become Peru's largest mineral exporter, and its mining activities had a profound effect on the economy and land-holding patterns of the central sierra. The company's original mines were located at Cerro de Pasco, and it built an immense smelting center at La Oroya in Tarma, Junín. According to the CIDA account of land tenure in the central sierra, the opening of the La Oroya installation in 1922 had immediate and disastrous effects on the surrounding area.[86] The fumes from the smelter contained lethal amounts of arsenic, lead, zinc, and hydrogen sulfide, and a number of human deaths could be traced directly to the smelting operation. The effects on plants and animals, however, were even more profound, and the fumes eventually created a desert of approximately 700,000 hectares in the center of what had been one of the most productive stock-raising and agricultural areas of Peru. A number of indigenous communities adjacent to the smelter were totally ruined, and the fumes severely curtailed both hacienda and community agriculture throughout the province of Junín. The company was eventually faced with protests, lawsuits, and executive decrees demanding compensation for landowners and immediate installation of pollution control equipment. The company responded by buying out all landholders within a radius of 30 kilometers from the smelter. The lands were, of course, practically worthless at the time of the purchase, and with the exception of the lands of one large and politically powerful Peruvian stock-raising company, all were bought at drastically reduced prices. The company finally installed pollution control equipment in 1942, 20 years after the smelter had gone into operation. Since the equipment made the surrounding area once again suitable for ranching, the company opened a huge commercial stock-raising enterprise on the formerly barren lands. The stock-raising activities seem to have developed as an incidental consequence of the company's attempt to eliminate protests by buying out surrounding landholders, but the results were so favorable to the company that many Peruvians continue to believe that the pollution was intentional and the company had conspired to steal the land all along. The destruction of the haciendas and communities in the department of Junín created a large landless proletariat which could then be employed in Cerro de Pasco's mines and refining operations. The stock-raising

[85] *Ibid.*
[86] CIDA, *Perú*, pp. 23–26.

enterprise on the adjacent land provided a cheap source of food for the workers in the mines and smelters. The export of wool turned a substantial profit which more than offset the cost of the pollution control equipment. Since the stock-raising activities required very little labor, they neither interfered with the demand for labor in the mines nor required the maintenance of a large inefficient population of *colonos* on company land. The company also developed commercial stock-raising activities on its large landholdings around its mine at Cerro de Pasco and became a major wool exporter and the largest single landowner in the central sierra. The success of the Cerro de Pasco corporation's commercial livestock operations attracted other companies and Peruvian individuals who opened their own ranches in the area. The new ranches further displaced the remaining traditional haciendas and communities. These immense properties, particularly the Cerro de Pasco corporation's holdings in Pasco and Junín and the Algolán corporation's large modern ranches in adjacent Cajatambo province in Lima, became the primary target of the *comunero* agrarian invasions of the 1960s.

The expansion of the modern ranches was not the only consequence of mining operations in the central sierra. Mining operations required an extensive transportation infrastructure including major rail and road links between the mining centers and the coast. The Cerro de Pasco corporation constructed its own railway from Cerro de Pasco to La Oroya, where it joined the central rail line to Lima constructed in the nineteenth century. The line extended south as far as Huancavelica and brought the entire central sierra region in close contact with the money economy for the first time. The transportation network lowered the costs of agricultural products throughout the central sierra and made commercial agriculture a real possibility for the first time. While the principal beneficiaries of these opportunities were the large ranches, many of which were owned by the Cerro de Pasco corporation itself, small haciendas and some indigenous communities were able to increase their production of cash crops. Since most of the land in the departments of Junín and Pasco is high *puna* at altitudes above 13,000 feet, opportunities for agriculture are limited and in most places commercial activities were confined to stock raising. Although the southern sierra, particularly the province of Puno, continues to be the major source of wool for export, the herding economy of Puno continues to be based on an inefficient hacienda system while the livestock operations of the sierra were based on scientific breeding and pasturage. Thus a second element in the transformation of the central sierra and the rise of the *comunero* movement was the presence of a major export commodity, in this case wool, which provided a source of outside income for many indigenous communities. Like the coffee boom in La Convención, the wool economy of the central sierra was to radically alter the organizational interests of peasant communities.

The involvement of Indian communities in the money economy depended not only on their proximity to transportation but also on their access to agricultural land. Paradoxically those communities with the least access to usable land had the best opportunity to participate in the money economy. As Mishkin has pointed out, in the late 1940s the increasing population of indigenous communities forced *comuneros* to turn pastoralism as an alternative to declining agricultural income.[87] The expropriations of the haciendas had already deprived many communities of land in the river valleys where agriculture was possible, and many communities were rapidly converted from agriculture to pastoralism. Pastoralism represented a temporary solution to the problems of population pressure in most areas of the sierra, since the increasing flocks and herds eventually exhausted the pasturage just as the increasing human population had threatened the exhaustion of agricultural land. As Mishkin points out, however, pastoralism brought the communities into contact with the money economy, and the sale of wool became the major source of outside income for many communities.[88] On the high *puna* of the central sierra pastoralism had always been a necessary adaptation to the altitude, but the availability of inexpensive transport to Lima and world markets transformed many marginal pastoral communities into profitable enterprises. In areas of the sierra which lacked adequate transportation and access to outside markets the rise of pastoralism marked simply another stage in the exhaustion of community resources and the decline of the community as a viable economic unit. In the central sierra, however, the same economic change created a new tie to the export economy.

The central sierra therefore combined large-scale expropriations by modern ranches with the growth of commercial communities based on the export of wool. Both the pressures of the expanding ranches and the organizational resources created by the wool economy were to have a pronounced effect on the intensity of the *comunero* agrarian movement in the central sierra. In most of the southern and northern sierra, however, Indian communities remained outside the export economy in wool and remained cut off from modern political or social influences of any kind. Although these communities were faced with continual expropriations by haciendas and commercial estates, they were as internally divided as the serfs of the hacienda Vicos and were never able to organize to reverse the direction of expropriations. While many of the communities of the central sierra were transformed into modern economic units, most sierran Indian communities remained as they had always been—loose groupings of individual subsistence cultivators. These differences in economic organization and their consequences for political action can be seen clearly in the contrast between the communities of Hualcan and San Pedro de Cajas. Hualcan is the subject of a detailed ethnography by William Stein and is perhaps the best described of any traditional Indian community of the sierra.[89] It is located in the province of Carhuaz, department of Ancash, in the Callejón de Huaylas not far from the hacienda Vicos. Stein worked with the Cornell group and chose the community

[87] Bernard Mishkin, "The Contemporary Quechua," in Julian H. Steward (ed.), *Handbook of South American Indians* (Washington: Government Printing Office, 1946), pp. 411–470.

[88] *Ibid.*, p. 429.

[89] William W. Stein, *Hualcan: Life in the Highlands of Peru* (Ithaca, N.Y.: Cornell University Press, 1961).

because he hoped to contrast community and hacienda organization. Unlike most communities studied in the sierra, Hualcan is not officially registered as a *comunidad indígena* and retains many of the characteristics of a traditional Indian community. The province of Carhuaz was not a center of activity during the *comunero* movements of 1960 to 1963, and in fact only one community in the province (Ecas) was reported to have carried out invasions. San Pedro de Cajas, on the other hand, is located in Tarma, Junín, at the center of the most intense *comunero* activity and in fact holds the distinction of having initiated the large-scale phase of the movement by invading the hacienda Chinchausiri at 4 A.M. on July 29, 1963, the day after Belaúnde Terry was inaugurated. Since this was the first invasion under the new government, all the major Lima dailies covered the event, and it is the most fully described of any of the invasions of the postinaugural period. San Pedro de Cajas was one of the first communities to take advantage of the legal reforms of the 1912 constitution and registered as a *comunidad indígena* on January 29, 1926. Its legal existence, in fact, predates the establishment of the Bureau of Indian Affairs. In contrast to Hualcan, San Pedro de Cajas is a modern community which is fully integrated into the wool export economy, and while it maintains some Indian features, it has been greatly influenced by Hispanic culture radiating outward from Lima and the coast. The two communities, one of which carried out an invasion and one of which did not, are in fact typical of invading and noninvading communities in general. A more detailed description of each will indicate clearly the importance of the wool economy and community economic development in the genesis of the central sierra invasions.

The community of Hualcan is located on the north bank of the Chucchín River about 10 miles from the mestizo town of Carhuaz. Since the community is located in a river valley, it is predominantly agricultural rather than pastoral and most of the community lands are located at the 10,000-foot level or below. While Hualcan's lands extend well up into the region of *puna* vegetation, which begins at about 13,000 feet in this area, most land under cultivation, and all the most valuable land, is located well below the upper limits of agriculture. The town plaza itself is located at 9,000 feet, 4,000 feet below the beginning of the *puna* zone. While most families own herds of sheep and some wool is produced, almost none of it is sold outside the community. The production of local herds is usually used for homespun clothing or occasionally bartered with local mestizo townsmen. Land is individually owned, and in the typical minifundia pattern of the sierra the plots of a single individual are frequently scattered widely over the land held by the community. Agricultural technology is primitive, and while fertilizer and a rudimentary crop rotation system are used, these techniques simply make the difference between bare subsistence and crop failure. Irrigation is used on some of the bottom land along the river, but much of the land is too rocky or inaccessible. The land shows signs of soil depletion, plant blights and crop failures are common, and the *comuneros* rely more on prayer than on planning for successful harvests. There is no interest in improving yields through technical innovations. Wealth accumulated by community members is rapidly dissipated through the fiesta system rather than invested in agriculture. The agricultural technology is approximately the same as that of hacienda Vicos and creates the same pressures toward conservative interest in individual subsistence plots.

The community's only access to the outside world is via a narrow trail to Carhuaz, which is an hour to an hour and a half away by foot. The only other means of transportation is a few burros owned by some community members. Even if the lands of Hualcan would support more intensive agriculture, the inadequate transportation facilities would inhibit the sale of products in outside markets. As long as the physical isolation of the community persists, it is unlikely that the stagnant subsistence economy will change. Stein in fact quotes Ralph Beal's observation that in matters of economic development one road is worth three schools or 50 government administrators.[90] Without a road commercial activity is limited to barter at local markets, and the community economy is for the most part completely self-contained. While the *comuneros* show a distinct interest in buying machine-made goods whenever they acquire any cash, their lack of salable resources limits their outside purchases. Most community members therefore dress in traditional Indian garments, including the poncho for men and the *lliklla*, or shawl, for women and wear homemade rather than machine-made clothing. Sandals made from old rubber tires are purchased outside the community, but they are considerably cheaper than machine-made shoes worn in wealthier mestizo areas. The only signs of advanced technology in the village are a few sewing machines. The absence of technical or commercial activity in the community has led to a total disinterest in education and indifferent attendance at the local school. Almost no one in the community has learned Spanish, and the few literates read Quechua.

The community lands are inadequate to support its current population, and only about 50 percent of the *comuneros* could exist without some form of outside employment. Almost all community members work at some time during the year as day laborers in Carhuaz and on nearby haciendas. Like the community of Vicos, Hualcan is deeply divided by an unequal distribution of property. The owners of irrigated lands along the river form a subcommunity of relatively affluent, independent landowners who could, if necessary, support themselves entirely from their own agricultural activities. The landowners on the rocky hillsides, however, have had insufficient land for many years, and most have been forced to contract with nearby haciendas for additional lands. These *comuneros* assume the *condiciones* associated with hacienda labor throughout the sierra and become part-time *colonos*. Thus one half of the community is a group of relatively independent landowners while the other half is actually a group of semi-

[90] *Ibid.*, p. 15.

serfs. The wealthier bottom land owners dominate community politics and are dedicated to maintaining the status quo. The *comuneros* of the hillsides who might profit from land invasions are unlikely to gain political control of the community.

In Hualcan as well as in Vicos, internal stratification, individual plots, and a strongly developed sense of personal property lead to intense economic competition, jealousy, suspicion, and endemic thievery. Most *comuneros* find it necessary to build huts in their fields to guard crops at harvest time. Even so, Stein estimates that half of all crops are lost to thieves.[91] Some farmers have gone so far as to diversify their crops to spread out the harvest and avoid the total loss of their food supply in a single theft. Most of the wealthier citizens in particular take pains to disguise their true wealth, and articles of any value are immediately hidden. Most litigation in Hualcan is actually between members of the community, and as in the community of Vicos there seems little possibility that the individualistic economy would permit collective political action. In fact even cooperative labor for community projects is difficult if not impossible to mobilize. While festival labor and reciprocal labor exchange are still practiced, they are disliked by laborers and employers, who both prefer explicit daily wage contracts.

Collective action is also inhibited by the organizational structure of Hualcan, which again parallels that of hacienda Vicos. The community *varayoc* are selected from the wealthier members of the community, which usually means the conservative landowners along the river bottom. The chief of the *varayoc*, called the *comisario* in Hualcan, is appointed by the mestizo authorities in the town of Carhuaz and is forced to report to them on a weekly basis under penalty of fines. He in turn appoints the remaining *varayoc*, who are therefore all dependent on the Carhuaz officials. The *varayoc* perform most of the functions of the leaders of the Vicos community and in addition are responsible for recruiting corvée labor for public works on the behalf of mestizos. The indirect rule structure of the *varayoc* is reinforced by the direct appointment of an official of the local government (*teniente gobernador*), who is the legal representative of the authorities in Carhuaz. This individual is backed by local police power and wields considerable influence, since he is responsible for rounding up recruits for the army. Finally the *comuneros* who have entered into *colono* arrangements with the nearby haciendas are controlled by *mayorales* much as are the serfs of Vicos. This triple alliance of conservative community authority makes it almost impossible to develop an organizational structure which might oppose the mestizo elite. As was the case in Vicos, talented *comuneros* are diverted into a conservative leadership role or are driven from the community altogether. The community's resources permit no independent peasant organizations. Beyond the town of Carhuaz the community has no connections at all with the political system, and most community members are largely ignorant of national politics.

[91] *Ibid.*, p. 19.

Finally the community is not directly threatened by any hacienda encroachments. The community lands are separated by a wide gorge from the hacienda area, and the worst lands are closest to the haciendas. The haciendas themselves are as agriculturally backward as the community and unlike the commercial stock-raising enterprises of the central sierra have little to gain from displacing indigenous communities. *Comuneros*, in fact, provide a substantial portion of the labor force on hacienda land. The same balance of mutual inefficiency which discourages enclosure movements by *hacendados* or technical improvements by *colonos* preserves the integrity of community lands in Hualcan. The *comuneros* have as little to gain from moving against the haciendas as the haciendas have from moving against the community. The conservative owners of the bottom lands who have the most to lose from any conflict with the haciendas are the best protected by distance from hacienda encroachments and the least radical of any peasants in the community. Their vested interest in protecting their marginal advantages over the rest of the community undermines collective solidarity. The wealthy peasants of La Convención found enough financial reward in protest actions to drag weaker members of the community into collective action on their behalf. The same principle works in reverse in Hualcan. The wealthier members support the mestizo structure of direct and indirect rule and prevent radical action by the hard-pressed *comuneros* of the hillsides.

Hualcan shares all the political and economic characteristics which made collective political action by the serfs of hacienda Vicos unlikely and even irrational. Its backward economy provides a slim margin of survival which could easily be threatened by either technical innovations in agriculture or changes in the political structure of the community. Precarious agriculture and tiny dispersed plots create the same kind of economic conservatism that was found at Vicos. The internal stratification of the community, particularly the division between the bottom lands and the hillside, creates an atmosphere of individualistic economic competition which inhibits cooperative economic or political action. The administrative structure of the *varayoc*, the *teniente gobernador*, and the hacienda *mayorales* insure that conservative organizations will co-opt or suppress independent peasant leadership. The limited financial resources of the community make it unlikely that union organizers could be supported from dues or other contributions of community members. Hualcan, like most of the traditional subsistence communities of the sierra, had little rational reason to participate in the *comunero* movements of the 1960s and, like almost all of them, remained uninvolved.

The community of San Pedro de Cajas is the precise opposite of Hualcan in respect to all these characteristics and is in fact more similar to an agricultural cooperative or a local branch of a farmers' union than it is to a traditional Indian community. The lands of San Pedro de Cajas are located on the high *puna* of Junín at altitudes above 13,000 feet, while almost all land worked in Hualcan was below 10,000 feet. Since the barren *puna* is suitable for extensive grazing and little else, San Pedro de Cajas is almost exclusively a pastoral community.

Hualcan, on the other hand, concentrated almost entirely on subsistence agriculture. San Pedro de Cajas numbered approximately 3,000 people in 1960 yet controlled less than 1,000 hectares of cultivated land or less than a third of a hectare per inhabitant.[92] The community controlled 9,000 hectares of pasture land, however, and its flocks of 13,000 sheep made it the second largest sheep-raising community in the province of Tarma.[93] The *puna* pasture lands were not valuable enough to encourage individuals to attempt to claim sections for their exclusive use but were valuable enough to require defense against expropriations by nearby commercial stock-raising haciendas. Consequently the pasture land continued to be held communally even though the tiny subsistence plots were owned by individuals. The herding economy like the pasture lands themselves is a community enterprise, and in 1947 a communal grange was established with 374 shareholders to undertake commercial wool production for sale outside the community.[94] In contrast to the individually owned subsistence plots of Hualcan the communal grange of San Pedro de Cajas is a successful cooperative commercial enterprise and nets the community over $40,000 in cash in a typical year.[95]

The commercial success of the pastoral economy of San Pedro de Cajas is based not only on its extensive grazing lands but on its proximity to major transportation centers. The community is connected by dirt access roads to the paved central highway which leads to both La Oroya and Cerro de Pasco, where it connects with terminals of the central rail lines to the coast. The access roads are well maintained by community labor, and in contrast to the physical isolation and nonexistent transportation facilities of Hualcan, San Pedro de Cajas not only maintains the roads but operates a transportation cooperative with buses which run between the community and the cities of Tarma and La Oroya.[96] It also owns its own trucks, which can be used for the transport of wool for sale in urban markets. San Pedro de Cajas has used its location and its access to the transportation facilities generated by the mining activities of the central sierra to become a successful commercial enterprise. While the wool export economy is the community's major source of outside income, it is not sufficient to support the community, and many community members must work elsewhere. In contrast to the *comuneros* of Hualcan, however, the residents of San Pedro de Cajas are not employed as *colonos* on nearby haciendas, but rather travel to Cerro de Pasco or La Oroya to work in the mines or smelters of the Cerro de Pasco corporation. The haciendas adjoining San Pedro de Cajas are in fact modern sheep ranches which provide limited employment activities in general and do not permit *colonos* to use their land. Exposure to employment in the mining

[92] Perú, Ministerio de Trabajo y Asuntos Indígenas, *Atlas Comunal: Comunidades Indígenas Reconocidas Oficialmente* (Lima, August 1964).
[93] *Ibid.*
[94] Dobyns, *Indigenous Communities*, p. 75.
[95] *Ibid.*
[96] *Ibid.*, p. 46.

economy has had a substantial effect on the cultural orientation of the community, and many community members came in contact with both mestizo culture and *Aprista* political organizers while working in the mines.

In contrast to the pronounced economic individualism and distrust in Hualcan, San Pedro de Cajas has carried out a number of cooperative projects in addition to its communal grange and transportation facilities. In 1957 it formed a corporation wholly owned by community members and installed a hydroelectric plant at a cost of over $10,000. The plant is now in full operation and provides the community with electricity for 16 hours each day.[97] The community organized to build a primary school using building materials donated by the Cerro de Pasco corporation and also erected a community meeting hall through the use of cooperative labor. In contrast to the hostility to education in Hualcan the *comuneros* of San Pedro de Cajas even built a school for girls, which was opened in 1962.[98] In most areas of the sierra in general and Hualcan in particular, women were expected to avoid the Spanish language or any other sign of formal education. Most of the *comuneros* of San Pedro de Cajas, of both sexes, were bilingual in Spanish and Quechua as are many members of indigenous communities in the central region.

The internal organization of the community and the cooperative work projects are based on modern economic organizations such as the corporation or the agricultural cooperative and bear no resemblance to the traditional communal work practices in subsistence communities. The political organization of the community is also modern in form and provides a distinct contrast to the dependent political leadership of the *varayoc* in Hualcan. The community is tightly linked to APRA through its ties with Francisco Espinoza, who was the legal representative, or *personero*, of the community during its phase of cooperative expansion in the late forties and early fifties. Espinoza's success in organizing San Pedro de Cajas brought him to the attention of national officials of APRA, and in the mid-1960s he became secretary general of the Federation of Communities of the Center, a component of the APRA Rural Workers' Federation of Peru (FENCAP).[99] Espinoza has close ties with the powerful *Aprista* Senator Ramiro Prialé from Huancayo in the Junín department and exerts a substantial influence on national FENCAP policy. He was sent to the United States to study agricultural practices by the National Farmers Union and worked for a short time as an official of the United States Agency for International Development in Peru. AID has been helpful to San Pedro de Cajas and loaned the community funds to purchase new vehicles when its community transportation

[97] *Ibid.*, p. 70.
[98] *Ibid.*, p. 54.
[99] Espinoza's leadership position in San Pedro de Cajas and his role in FENCAP are described in Susan Carolyn Bourque, "Cholification and the Campesino: A Study of Three Peruvian Peasant Organizations in the Process of Societal Change" (Ph.D. dissertation, Cornell University, 1971), pp. 149–151.

facilities ran into financial difficulties. While Francisco Espinoza's direct influence on the community was probably not great at the time of the invasions, a member of the Espinoza family still held the position of *personero* in 1963, and presumably the community had considerable influence within FENCAP and APRA. When the community carried out its invasion APRA's party organ *La Tribuna* gave it favorable coverage and made its offices available for a press conference called by a delegation of community officials.

By the time San Pedro de Cajas carried out its land invasion, it had already developed an extensive organizational apparatus based fundamentally on its financially successful herding operations. The communal pasturage and grange provided an economic basis for cooperative action in other areas. The community's cooperative public service activities and effective political organization were both fundamentally dependent on economic structures which had been developed originally to exploit opportunities in the wool trade. The cooperative nature of this form of agricultural activity and its substantial profits made it possible for San Pedro de Cajas to support a political apparatus independent of the mestizo authorities of the towns. The success of the herding economy gave community members a substantial vested interest in cooperative action against further encroachments by haciendas and a substantial incentive to expend their activities if more land could be acquired. The outside employment of the *comuneros* of San Pedro de Cajas led not to another level of control by local mestizo *hacendados*, but rather to closer ties to *Aprista* labor unions in the mines.

By the early 1960s, therefore, San Pedro de Cajas had both the organizational framework and the economic incentive to initiate protest actions against neighboring haciendas. It also had a long-standing dispute with the neighboring hacienda of Chinchausiri, which had acquired a title to a large section of community lands in 1927.[100] Both Chinchausiri and San Pedro de Cajas are in the radius of the area affected by the fumes of the La Oroya smelter,[101] and the hacienda acquired the land during the period of devaluation which followed the opening of the smelter. In 1963 the hacienda was owned by the Sociedad Ganadera del Pacífico, a commercial sheep-raising enterprise which was a subsidiary of a large Lima textile-manufacturing concern.[102] The administrator of the hacienda, José Carpena, was vague about how title to the land had been acquired but admitted in newspaper interviews that he and his brothers had acquired ownership "fourth hand." [103] In any event it is clear that hacienda Chinchausiri operations were part of the general movement toward commercial stock-raising operations initiated by the Cerro de Pasco corporation in Junín. The community carried out a long series of expensive legal actions against Chinchausiri for more than 30 years to no avail. In the three years immediately preceding the invasion the San Pedro de Cajas legal representative had petitioned

[100] *El Comercio*, July 31, 1963.
[101] CIDA, *Perú*, map facing p. 24.
[102] *Expreso*, July 31, 1963.
[103] *La Prensa*, July 31, 1963.

the local director of indigenous affairs for a hearing on the community's land titles. The *personero* claimed that the community's land titles dated to grants made by members of religious orders to the community in 1627 and that the community had never recognized Chinchausiri's claims. The director of indigenous affairs scheduled three separate hearings at which representatives of the community and the hacienda were to have appeared, but the hacienda owners simply ignored the director's requests and only the *personero* of San Pedro de Cajas appeared.[104] In the years since the Sociedad Ganadera del Pacifico had acquired the lands, it had developed a highly successful stock-raising business, grazed more than 20,000 head of sheep on its estate, and clearly had no intention whatsoever of returning the land to the community.

While it is unclear exactly how the invasion of Chinchausiri was planned, it seems unlikely that timing the invasion to occur in the early morning hours on the day after Belaúnde Terry's inauguration was coincidental. The presidential election campaign itself had generated intense interest in land reform, and Belaúnde Terry carried much of the southern sierra. Although San Pedro de Cajas was solidly APRA, it voted unanimously for Belaúnde Terry on the basis of his promises for land reform. It seems likely that the timing of the invasion was as much designed to keep pressure on Belaúnde as it was a result of the exhaustion of legal remedies. In any event, the invasion itself was carried out with precision and dispatch, and by sunrise on the first day of his term of office Belaúnde Terry was confronted with a *fait accompli*. During the night at least 1,500 members of the community occupied 8,000 hectares of the Chinchausiri estate, all of which were apparently part of the Corina section which the *comuneros* had claimed. The land occupied by the *comuneros* ran roughly parallel to the main rail line from La Oroya to Cerro de Pasco and included about half the Chinchausiri estate. The site of the invasion was about two miles from the hacienda house and no hacienda personnel were affected.[105] The *comuneros* arrived in trucks and buses as well as on foot, and it seems apparent that the cooperative transport service of San Pedro de Cajas had been put to a somewhat different use than its AID sponsors had originally intended. The invasion was orderly and without violence or property destruction except for the tearing down of fences in order to gain entry to the estate. The photographs in Plates 1 and 2 were taken during the first day or two after the invasion and indicate clearly both the tactics and organization of the invasion.[106] The first photograph (Plate 1*a*) shows the trucks used to drive from San Pedro de Cajas to Chinchausiri, a distance of about 10 miles. The mobility of motor transport obviously gave the *comuneros* the tactical advantage of surprise. The prefect of police for the central region did not even arrive on the scene until hours after the invasion was completed. The trucks and buses were used to ferry the remaining members of the community to the hacienda, eventually leaving the original community site

[104] *El Comercio,* July 31, 1963; *Expreso,* July 31, 1963.
[105] Accounts of the invasion were carried in all the Lima dailies; see particularly *Expreso* and *La Prensa,* July 31, 1963.
[106] Photographs courtesy of *Expreso.*

PLATE 1*a*   *Section of Fence of Chinchausiri Estate at Point at which Comuneros Entered*

PLATE 1*b*   *Comuneros of San Petro de Cajas Constructing Sod Huts on Chinchausiri Lands*

PLATE 2*a*   *Comuneros of San Pedro de Cajas on Chinchausiri Lands*

PLATE 2*b*   *Worship Service Held on Invaded Lands at the Tent Shrine of Saint Peter, Patron Saint of the Community*

deserted. The *comuneros* erected about 100 tents and began building what would eventually total 500 sod huts on the reclaimed land, (Plate 1*b* shows one of the huts under construction). The invaders organized themselves into four sections for defense in case of attempted eviction and set up their own police force to keep order. One of the sections assumed responsibility for the hacienda herds grazing on the occupied land. The *comuneros* established a small tent shrine for the patron saint of the community (Plate 2*b*) and held religious services which, one report suggests, increased their sense of community solidarity. The Peruvian national flag was prominently displayed for photographers (see the somewhat staged photograph, Plate 2*a*), and the *comuneros* insisted that they were only interested in taking what had belonged to them under Peruvian law. Strict discipline was enforced, and one of the *comuneros'* slogans was "with morals and without alcohol."

The photographs also indicate that abstinence from alcohol was not the only way in which the *comuneros* of San Pedro de Cajas deviated from the usual cultural behavior of highland Indian communities. The hut-building picture makes clear that substantial numbers of men owned machine-made modern clothing, and one man in the foreground seems to be wearing loafers and jeans (Plate 1*b*). This modern dress is in stark contrast to most pictures of traditional Indian dress, in which homespun materials and traditional styles predominate. Most notably, all the men and even women and children in the photographs are wearing shoes rather than sandals. While it may seem peculiar to suggest that wearing shoes is unusual in the Andes at an altitude of 13,000 feet, in fact most highland Indians are forced to go barefoot or at best wear rubber tire sandals similar to those worn in Hualcan. Wearing shoes and manufactured clothing is another indication of the relative affluence of San Pedro de Cajas. Nevertheless, the pictures also indicate that the community maintains some traditional Indian characteristics. In the staged formal photograph (Plate 2*a*) most of the men are wearing the traditional Indian poncho. One man in the picture is clearly a former miner, as is indicated by his mine worker's hard hat. The dress of the *comuneros* of San Pedro de Cajas indicates a combination of traditional and modern elements which characterizes many communities of the central region. The modern economy has allowed them to purchase machine-made clothing, shoes, and even trucks and buses, but they remain devoted to the patron saint of the community and still consider the poncho appropriate dress for religious and formal occasions.

The reaction of government authorities to the invasion was distinctly moderate, which reflects both the *comuneros'* excellent timing and their considerable influence in local politics. The prefect of Junín sent out two of his deputies to investigate the situation and later reported that the invasion had been orderly. The prefect publicly defended the *comuneros* against accusations that there had been violence and property destruction. Only five police appeared on the estate, and no effort was made to evict the invaders. Both the local chief of police and the departmental prefect prudently decided to await instructions from Lima. The government, represented by Prime Minister Oscar Trelles, declared the invasion "an orderly occupation of lands in litigation" and suggested that the dispute be transferred to the institute for land reform. The *comuneros* remained in possession of the land, and the Belaúnde government eventually declared most of central Junín and Pasco a land reform area. The prime minister did suggest that the land reform program depended on the orderly process of law, and later in the year, after a tour of the area by Trelles himself, most of the *comuneros* were convinced that they should withdraw and await the land reform program.

The contrasting economic and social characteristics of Hualcan and San Pedro de Cajas suggest that the invasion of Chinchausiri and other invasions in the central sierra can be traced fundamentally to the rise of the export economy in wool.[107] Just as was the case with the development of the coffee economy in the high *selva* areas, the development of the wool economy destroyed the equilibrium between *hacendados* and peasants and gave each group an incentive to increase land expropriations at the expense of the other. The contrast between Hualcan and San Pedro de Cajas also indicates that the dynamics of the *comunero* invasions are similar to those of *campesino* invasions. In most respects the contrast between the two communities parallels the contrasts between the subsistence haciendas of the Callejón de Huaylas and the commercial haciendas of La Convención. The *comuneros* of San Pedro de Cajas and the *arrendires* of La Convención were both able to overcome the conservatism and divisiveness of a marginal subsistence economy by transforming their lands into commercial farms. Both therefore could realize considerable economic gains from collective action, and both eventually developed political organizations which offset the power of the estate owners and made these gains not only valuable but politically practical. The *comuneros* and *arrendires* differed at least superficially in the nature of the political structure that eventually led to land invasions. In La Convención the peasants found it necessary to establish peasant leagues completely independent of the traditional subsistence hacienda organization. In San Pedro de Cajas the traditional structure of the indigenous community was adapted to serve the new changing economic and political interests of the community members. It should be kept in mind, however, that the community organization of San Pedro de Cajas was no closer to the traditional structure of the Indian *ayllu* than the Federación Provincial de Campesinos de La Convención y Lares was to the structure of the traditional hacienda. Both were modern associational interest groups formed on the basis of economic rationality rather than communal traditions. San Pedro de Cajas had in fact at least one important advantage in collective organization that was absent in the valley of La Convención. Its economic organization itself was cooperatively organized, and therefore political action could be based on a stable community of economic interests. In La Convención the interests of individual coffee farmers are fundamentally competitive, and

---

[107] For an alternate explanation of the *comunero* invasions emphasizing cultural modernization see Howard Handelman, "Struggle in the Andes: Peasant Political Mobilization in Peru" (Ph.D. dissertation, University of Wisconsin, 1971).

when the power of the landowners was broken, the peasants rapidly became individualistic small farmers. In San Pedro de Cajas it might be expected that the
communal grange economy would continue to create pressure for cooperative
action even after the encroaching haciendas had been destroyed. San Pedro de
Cajas may in fact represent a Peruvian version of a collective farm, but collectivization came about not through the preservation of the traditional Indian *ayllu*,
but by the destruction of the Indian community and the building of an agricultural cooperative.

If the contrasting economic organizations of Hualcan and San Pedro de
Cajas are representative of invading and noninvading communities generally, it
should be possible to demonstrate this fact statistically in the same manner as
was done in the case of the sugar, cotton, and coffee economies. The argument
above suggests that the social and political differences between Hualcan and San
Pedro de Cajas rest fundamentally on their different economic organization and
that this in turn is a result of the rise of the wool export economy in the central
sierra. Thus it should be possible to correlate some measure of community wool
export production in each province with the number of *comunero* agrarian
events observed in that province. Unfortunately it is not possible to measure
community involvement in the export economy directly in all sierran provinces.
While statistics are available on the number of head of sheep and the amount of
wool produced in each sierran province, these data do not distinguish between
community and other forms of production, nor between production for local or
for international markets. Wool is produced not only in commercial estates like
Chinchausiri, but also on subsistence haciendas in the southern sierran department of Puno. Even if a distinction could be made between community and
hacienda production, there would still be no adequate measure of commercial
production, since many communities produce exclusively for their own use.
These considerations make it necessary to construct an indirect measure of community involvement in the wool export economy. The 1961 census of agriculture
reports the total landholdings of registered indigenous communities in all of
Peru's provinces and also distinguishes between land held by individual *comuneros* and land held by communities.[108] The census data also indicate that
almost all land held collectively by communities is pasture land, while almost all
cultivated land is held by individual *comuneros*.[109] Thus the proportion of land
in a given province held collectively by communities is a rough measure of the
importance of pastoral communities in that province. The proportion of land
held by individual *comuneros*, on the other hand, is an indication of community
agriculture, not pastoralism. While almost all community-held land is pasture,
not all pasture land is used for the commercial production of wool. Many backward subsistence communities continue to graze large flocks on community-held
lands without selling any of their production to outside markets. Thus it is necessary to distinguish between pastoral communities which do or do not participate

108 Perú, *Primer Censo Nacional Agropecuario*, pp. 14–43.
109 *Ibid.*, p. 68.

in the market economy. Again an indirect measure is the only one available in published statistics. Manufactured consumer goods can only be purchased by communities which earn cash income by the sale of agricultural products outside the community. The only source of cash income for almost all sierran communities is the sale of wool. Consequently the greater the value of consumer goods purchased outside the community, the greater the community's cash earnings from the sale of wool. Thus a measure of the distribution of consumer goods provides an indirect measure of commercial wool production. One convenient index of consumer purchases is the acquisition of shoes in the rural sierra. In most areas of the sierra members of the rural population either go barefoot or wear sandals and the purchase of machine-made shoes is one of the first signs of affluence in indigenous communities. The importance of shoe purchases as an indirect measure of involvement in the cash economy is also apparent in the comparison between Hualcan and San Pedro de Cajas. Most members of the Hualcan community either went barefoot or bought simple rubber-soled sandals; as the photographs in Plates 1 and 2 make clear, almost everyone in San Pedro de Cajas wore machine-manufactured shoes. Any number of consumer goods would serve equally well as a measure of involvement in the money economy, but shoes are likely to be one of the first purchases of *comuneros* confronted with the bitter cold and rocky trails of the Andean highlands, and consequently should provide a minimum measure of consumer activity. The number of rural residents wearing shoes in each province in Peru can easily be obtained from the 1961 population census, so that this measure is both simple and practical.[110] Provinces which have many communities involved in the production of wool for market should be provinces which have both large proportions of their land held by pastoral communities *and* large numbers of rural residents who wear shoes. The combination of pastoral communities and shoe wearing suggests that a statistical interaction effect should be expected. Provinces with a large proportion of their land held by pastoral communities may or may not participate in the money economy. Provinces in which large numbers of rural residents wear shoes may be expected to have many small commercial farmers, but they may or may not be involved in the pastoral economy. Only those provinces which have both a high proportion of community pastoralism, as indicated by a large amount of land held collectively by communities, and high rates of participation in the money economy, indicated by large numbers of rural residents wearing shoes, might be expected to have large numbers of communities participating in the wool export economy. Although this indirect measure is not as satisfactory as a direct measure based on the amount of wool sold by communities in Lima or other urban centers, it is a reasonable approximation given the assumption that the major source of outside income for any community is the sale of wool.

The expansion of the wool export economy not only reorganized the internal structure of Indian communities but also had an equally significant effect on surrounding haciendas. As was apparent in the disputes between Chinchausiri

[110] Perú, *Sexto Censo Nacional de Población*, vol. 1, book 5, pp. 1–8.

and San Pedro de Cajas, the central sierra was a region in which conflicts between commercial estates and commercial communities were common. The vast estates of the Cerro de Pasco and Algolán corporations, which were the primary targets of land invasions, were modern stock-raising ranches which threatened the communities with continued expansion. Obviously land invasions will not occur in the absence of land to be invaded, and consequently only those regions of the sierra in which large estates predominate might be expected to have invasions. In many areas of the central sierra and particularly in the lower Mantaro valley communities exist in areas in which there are no large commercial estates or subsistence haciendas to compete for available pasturage. Even though communities in these areas are economically developed and well organized, the absence of friction with surrounding estates eliminates one of the basic causes of land invasion. The wool economy of the central sierra upset the balance between subsistence hacienda and subsistence community by giving each a substantial incentive for expansion at the expense of the other and by eliminating the symbiotic *colono* relationship which had made the preservation of communities advantageous for the large haciendas. Community pastoralism and involvement in the money economy are not in themselves sufficient to account for *comunero* invasions. A third element, the presence of large estates, is also necessary. *Comunero* invasions, then, should be expected in areas which have the following three characteristics: (1) a large proportion of land held collectively by pastoral communities, (2) a large proportion of rural residents who have used their involvement in the money economy to purchase shoes, and (3) a large proportion of land controlled by large estates. Only if all three conditions are present would the balance between hacienda and community be upset and the communities be capable of invasions. In the central sierra, the development of a transportation network and the rise of the wool export economy created all three conditions simultaneously. A province which has a high rate of *comunero* land invasions should therefore be a province in which a high proportion of the land is held by large estates and pastoral communities and in which most rural residents wear shoes. This hypothesis requires that a triple interaction effect be demonstrated statistically, since all three conditions must be included for invasions to occur and any one condition or pair of conditions is insufficient.

The data for assessing the adequacy of this hypothesis are presented in Table 3.5 and in the path diagram in Figure 3.1. Table 3.5 indicates the correlation between *comunero* and *campesino* agrarian events and indices of community and estate land ownership and consumer purchases for the sierra provinces. The correlations have been computed for all sierran provinces with the exception of the province of Anta adjacent to the valley of La Convención, since in this province it is clear that most *comunero* agrarian events involve disputes between *comuneros* and La Convención *campesinos* and are clearly more closely related to the La Convención movement than to the *comunero* movement elsewhere in the sierra. Table 3.5 includes measures of each of the three preconditions of *comunero* agrarian events and an interaction variable which is simply the arith-

TABLE 3.5 *Intercorrelations of Agrarian Events with Community Land, Estate Land, Shoe Wearing, and Interaction Variable for Sierran Provinces*

VARIABLE	(2)	(3)	(4)	(5)	(6)	(7)
1. *Comunero* agrarian events	.06	.01	.37	−.05	.40	.60
2. *Campesino* agrarian events		.13	−.17	.19	−.12	−.15
3. Community land, individual			−.28	.13	−.04	−.22
4. Community land, collective				−.57	.35	.79
5. Estate land					−.23	−.17
6. Shoe wearing						.52
7. (4) × (5) × (6)						—

metic product of the three variables. It is apparent that the highest correlation with *comunero* agrarian events is produced by the triple interaction variable ($r = .60$). The correlation between *comunero* agrarian events and the proportion of land in a province held collectively by communities, and hence the proportion of community pastoral land, is considerably lower ($r = .37$). It is also interesting to note that there is no relationship between the proportion of land held by individual *comuneros* and the number of *comunero* agrarian events. Thus the number of *comunero* events in a province is not simply an artifact of the number of registered communities in the province. Only when communities hold land collectively, which in most cases means when they work communal pastures, is there any effect on the propensity to engage in land invasions. There is no direct effect of the proportion of land held in large estates when this variable is considered alone ($r = -.05$). The peasant class in a region in which land was held exclusively by large estates would consist of *colonos*, and there would be few *comuneros* available to engage in land invasions. The proportion of land held by large estates was roughly determined by subtracting the total area of community landholdings of 5 hectares or more from the total area of all landholdings of 5 hectares or more and dividing this area by the total area of agricultural land in the province. While 5 hectares may seem a modest definition of a large estate, this is an adequate cutting point given the latifundia-minifundia pattern of sierran landholdings. Most peasants hold plots smaller than 5 hectares, and these small holders make up the bulk of rural landowners other than estates. Since there is no appreciable class of middle-size farmers in the sierra, almost all land held by agricultural units over 5 hectares in size is held by large estates of 500 hectares or more. Thus 5 hectares is a reasonable cutting point for determining the amount of land held by large estates. It would have been simpler to use some larger size of holding, but agricultural census statistics do not provide provincial breakdowns on estate size beyond the distinction between land held in units of 5 hectares or more and land held in units of less than 5 hectares. The index of participation in the money economy, the proportion of rural residents wearing shoes, does show a positive correlation with the number of *comunero* agrarian events in a province ($r = .40$), but again this correlation is considerably less than that of the triple interaction variable.

The zero-order correlations presented in Table 3.5 are not in themselves sufficient to test the interactive relationship between the commercial export economy in wool and the rise of the *comunero* agrarian movement, since it is possible that a simple additive model might have equivalent explanatory power and would therefore be preferred on grounds of parsimony. This alternative hypothesis can be simply tested by comparing the variance explained by the triple interaction model and by various additive models. In comparison to a three-predictor-variable additive regression equation the interaction term increases the variance explained by 14.2 percent, a difference that is significant at beyond the .001 level ($F = 21.81$). No other regression model involving the three constituent variables and any *pairwise* interaction term, on the other hand, adds any appreciable predictive power to the original additive model, and all are significantly weaker than the equation containing the triple interaction term. In fact the interaction term is almost as powerful a predictor alone as it is in combination with its three constituents in a four-variable regression model, and the additional variance explained by these three constituent variables collectively is statistically insignificant ($F = 1.78$).

The greater predictive power of the triple interaction term in comparison with its constituent variables is also apparent in the path diagram in Figure 3.1. This diagram makes clear that each of the three exogenous variables—percent wearing shoes, percent community land, and percent large estate land—affects the value of the triple interaction term but only the interaction term exerts any

FIGURE 3.1   *Path Diagram of Effects of Community Landholding, Estate Land-holding, and Shoe Wearing on* Comunero *Agrarian Events and Triple Interaction Term*

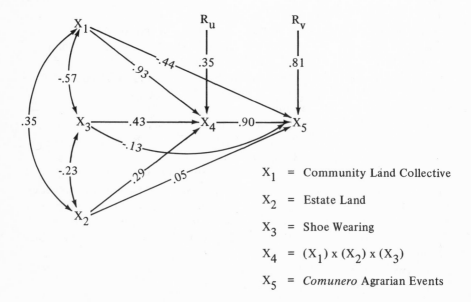

X_1 = Community Land Collective

X_2 = Estate Land

X_3 = Shoe Wearing

X_4 = $(X_1) \times (X_2) \times (X_3)$

X_5 = *Comunero* Agrarian Events

direct positive effect on the number of *comunero* events. The direct path coefficient from the triple interaction term to the *comunero* event variable is .90, while the direct paths from both percent wearing shoes and percent large estate land are both negligible and the direct path from percent community land is actually negative (− .44). This strong negative relationship between community land and invasions in the absence of indicators of modernization or estate encroachments reemphasizes the fact that traditional pastoral communities of the sierra are involved in intense internal economic conflict because of their declining prospects in agriculture and therefore lack the collective incentives and organizational resources to carry out invasions. The path diagram makes clear that the zero-order correlations between *comunero* events and both percent wearing shoes and percent community land are actually entirely accounted for by their contribution to the triple interaction term. The third variable, percent of land in large estates, is not correlated with *comunero* events directly, but the path analysis makes clear that it does exert a significant indirect effect through the interaction variable. The regression analysis indicates conclusively that it is the combination of three variables and not any one of them singly that creates the conditions for land invasions by *comuneros.*

The results of the statistical analysis also confirm the general impression derived from the comparative analysis of Hualcan and San Pedro de Cajas and reaffirms the importance of the export economy in the central sierra as the critical determinant of the *comunero* movement. It was the export economy that made pastoralism an economically practical form of community enterprise, and it was the export economy that provided the funds necessary to both purchase consumer goods and transform the communities into modern agricultural co-operatives. At the same time the export economy created the major competitor for pasture land, the large commercial estate. The three elements taken together, then, made peasant land invasions both organizationally possible and economically profitable. The changing national political climate finally provided an opening for direct collective action, but it was only those communities which had been transformed by the export economy which were in a position to take advantage of the political change.

On both the sierra and the coast, the agricultural export economy transformed traditional agriculture and created new forms of agricultural organization which both created the preconditions for rural social movements and shaped the directions these movements would take. The exact form of agricultural organization depended in turn on both the production parameters of the export crop and the preexisting structure of subsistence agriculture. The expansion of the sugar economy created immense corporate plantations which both eliminated surrounding subsistence small holders and communities and created a wage labor proletariat that formed the basis for an organized labor movement. The cotton economy developed within the organizational framework of the traditional coastal hacienda. It left many communities and small landowners in possession of some lands in the cotton valleys, but it created new population pressures through the displacement of sharecroppers and led to new conflicts over water and land. In the sierra it was the small farmer rather than the estate owner who profited from the export economy. In La Convención the hacienda system was undermined by the development of cash crops on usufruct rather than domain lands and by dependent serfs rather than modernizing *hacendados*. Finally the wool economy created opportunities for both large estates and some Indian communities. Those communities which were physically situated on the high *puna* in close proximity to transportation facilities were able to take advantage of the new opportunity and build cooperative economic enterprises which then provided the political framework for land invasions and other political action.

In each of these four cases—sugar, cotton, coffee, and wool—the traditional structure of Peruvian subsistence agriculture based on the tenuous coexistence between *hacendados* and *colonos* or *comuneros* was upset by the introduction of cash crops which gave both lord and serf new economic possibilities and new organizational resources. The response of the peasant class to these new opportunities varied depending on the structure of the agricultural organization created by the export crop. In each case, however, the response was based on a rational assessment of the political and economic resources available to itself and to its opponents. In the case of the corporate plantation this process led to labor organization and strikes aimed at limited wage demands; in the case of cotton, coffee, and wool it meant land invasions aimed at ending the domination of the haciendas and destroying the land-owning classes. Neither these actions nor the generations of conservative inaction that preceded them provide any reasons to believe that the *colonos, comuneros*, and workers did not act in their own best interest or that they did not both understand and adapt to the economic and political realities established by subsistence agriculture on the one hand or an export economy on the other. The case study of Peru indicated, as did the world analysis of agricultural export systems, that the social movements of cultivators are based on the nature of the economic conflict between cultivators and noncultivators and the primary determinant of this conflict is the distribution of political and economic resources established by new forms of export agricultural organization.

CHAPTER 4

Angola:
The Migratory Labor Estate

PIZARRO ARRIVED in Peru with less than 200 men in 1532 and by 1533 had taken the Incan capital of Cuzco. Within a decade he had defeated the last major rebellion of primary resistance. By 1580 the last vestiges of Incan resistance had been eliminated and the reforms of Viceroy Toledo had consolidated colonial control throughout Peru. Angola was first discovered by the Portuguese explorer navigator Diogo Cão in 1483, but no permanent settlement was established until the founding of Luanda in 1576, and for most of Angola's 450-year history Portuguese occupation was limited to less than 150 miles into the interior. The military occupation of what is now Angola did not begin in earnest until the twentieth century, and the major battles against the indigenous African kingdoms were fought during the first decade of the century. The last rebellion of the primary resistance movement was not ended until 1919, military control of many areas of eastern Angola was not established until the 1930s, and the administrative organization of the colony dates only to 1922. Thus while the traditional political and agrarian structure of Peru was incorporated in a system of feudal social classes almost from the date of the conquest, most of Angola remained beyond even effective military, let alone economic, control until the twentieth century. While the last movement which betrayed any characteristics of Incan nationalism was the revolt of Túpac Amaru in 1780, the indigenous kingdoms of Angola have remained the focus of political conflict down to the present and, despite their much diminished importance under Portuguese rule, have remained centers of political organization and resistance. In 1961, less than a half century after the suppression of the last primary resistance, the Portuguese were again faced with a major uprising. This most recent and most serious threat to their rule combined currents of modern nationalism with the traditional concerns of the African kingdoms. The revolt of 1961, however, unlike the uprisings of a half century earlier, was a response to modern economic forces and, like the peasant revolt in Cuzco a few months later, was tied to radical changes in agricultural organization brought about by the rise of a new form of export production. The parallel between the Peruvian sierra and the Angolan forests is, however, even closer. The rise in world coffee prices which led to the rapid expansion of coffee production in Cuzco had a similarly dramatic effect in Angola, and in the decade between 1950 and 1960 both Peru and Angola became major coffee exporters. Angola became the largest producer in Africa and one of the three or four largest producers in the world. The expansion of the coffee economy created the largest and in some respects the only economic boom that the colony had seen in its long history. The coffee economy of Angola, however, did not develop in an independent nation with a long-established manorial system and a diversified export economy, but rather in one of the most backward colonies in Africa. The modern political history of Angola began with the consolidation of Portuguese rule in the 1920s, but the modern economic history of the country did not begin until the rise of the coffee economy in the 1950s. It is difficult to underestimate the economic stagnation of the Angolan colony before the sudden rise in coffee exports, but during the 1950s Angola became the Cinderella colony of the Portuguese empire and many politicians in Lisbon dreamed of a new Brazil. The northern tropical forests and savanna once considered a frontier region even within Angola became the focus of rural economic activity and the scene of a major land rush. The economic changes brought about by the sudden expansion of coffee exports created new sources of political organization and conflict just as they had done in Cuzco. Differences in both the social organization of coffee production and the nature of the political system between the two countries, however, created the preconditions for a class-based agrarian movement in Cuzco but for a communal, revolutionary nationalist movement in Angola. The 1961 uprising was put down by Portuguese troops at a cost of 30,000 to 40,000 African lives, but the revolutionary nationalist movement continued. In 1974 after 13 years of guerrilla war the centers of the 1961 uprising were still contested, and fighting had spread to a new front opened by rebels infiltrating from newly independent Zambia to the east. By 1974 a Portuguese expeditionary force of 50,000 men was spread out over vast areas of forest and savanna, and the long chain of inconclusive battles which have marked the history of Portuguese military efforts in Angola seemed to have resumed.

A variety of explanations have been advanced for the contrast between the rapid Iberian conquest of Latin America and the protracted Portuguese struggle for Angola, but the reasons most frequently cited are the inhospitable physical environment of Africa and the military effectiveness of the indigenous African kingdoms.[1] Angola presented formidable environmental problems for early

---

[1] David Birmingham, *Trade and Conflict in Angola* (London: Oxford University Press, 1966), p. 10, suggests four reasons: (1) tropical disease, (2) African hostility, (3) an arid coastal climate unsuitable for agriculture, (4) the slave trade. Douglas Wheeler, in Douglas Wheeler and René Pélissier, *Angola* (New York: Praeger, 1971), p. 35, adds a fifth reason to Birmingham's four: the inferior quality of Portuguese colonists. James

Portuguese soldiers and settlers. Geographically the country forms a region of transition between the tropical rain forests of the Congo basin to the north and the deserts and savanna of the great South African plateau to the south. A narrow coastal plain extends from the mouth of the Congo River in the north to the South-West African border in the south. The plain is broadest in the north, reaching its greatest width of 100 miles in the Cuanza River valley just south of the Angolan capital of Luanda. In the south the plain narrows and disappears entirely in some places. Malaria is endemic on the coast, and before the widespread use of quinine in the late nineteenth century the coastal lowlands were a formidable barrier to Portuguese military operations. In the first 20 years of the Portuguese campaigns in Angola more than 2,000 troops died of fever in the coastal lowlands, and throughout the period of the early conquests more troops were lost to fever than to enemy action.[2] Even in the 1960s more than 150,000 cases of malaria a year were reported in Angola, and only in the area immediately surrounding Luanda has the disease been eradicated by spraying mosquito-breeding areas.[3] Sleeping sickness is also common in the coastal lowlands, particularly in the north, and although cavalry were found to be as effective against African mass armies as they had been against the mass armies of the Incas, it was difficult to keep the horses alive long enough to use them. While the African population suffered from outbreaks of unfamiliar diseases, it seems to have had much greater resistance to common European diseases than did the New World Indians, and the biological warfare that had worked to the Europeans' advantage in the New World worked to their distinct disadvantage in Africa. As long as the Portuguese were confined to the coastal lowlands, much of the effect of their superior military organization was neutralized by heavy losses of men and animals to tropical disease.

The interior plateau of Angola is considerably more favorable for European settlement, particularly in the south central region, where the climate is almost temperate, but the plateau is separated from the coastal strip by a steep escarpment. In the north the transition from coast to plateau is gradual, with level areas and rolling hills separating the scarp faces, and the interior plateau reaches an altitude of only 3,000 to 4,000 feet. In the center and south the escarpment rises abruptly from the coast in two steps characterized by sheer rock faces rising to heights of 1,000 feet or more. Much of the central plateau lies at altitudes of

---

Duffy, *Portuguese Africa* (Cambridge, Mass: Harvard University Press, 1961), p. 79, mentions tropical disease, the inaccessible African plateau, and the formidable opposition of African tribes. Marvin Harris, "Portugal's Contribution to the Underdevelopment of Africa and Brazil," in Ronald Chilcote (ed.), *Protest and Resistance in Angola and Brazil* (Berkeley: University of California Press, 1972), pp. 209–223, argues that while disease and African resistance were important, the major reason for the absence of conquest was the political instability created by the slave trade.

[2] Wheeler and Pélissier, *Angola*, p. 35.

[3] Allison Butler Herrick et al., *Area Handbook for Angola* (Washington: Government Printing Office, 1967), p. 166.

5,000 to 6,000 feet, and the altitude leads to a more moderate climate and a lower incidence of tropical disease. Despite the favorable climate, the south central escarpment has long been a barrier to Portuguese penetration of the interior, and the central plateau was the last area to be explored and occupied. Until the nineteenth century the Portuguese held only a single fort on the edge of the plateau, and even this degree of military penetration required the cooperation of the local African monarch. Most of the early Portuguese military efforts on the plateau were limited to slave raids or brief punitive expeditions, and Portuguese traders were forced to operate under the jurisdiction of various African kingdoms. With twentieth-century improvements in transportation the central plateau became a major center of European settlement and the site of ambitious agricultural colonization programs, but in the period of initial contact the escarpment presented too great a barrier.

In the north the plateau is lower, the ascent from the coast is less abrupt, and the land slopes gradually toward the lowlands of the Congo basin so that the escarpment is not an important barrier to military operations. The north, however, is a region of semitropical forests and savanna and is subject to the same tropical diseases as are the coastal lowlands. While dense tropical rain forests are found only in the extreme north, semitropical vegetation is found in scattered patches in river valleys and sheltered areas where it is watered by dense fogs. The tsetse fly is found throughout the northern forests, and the incidence of all tropical diseases is considerably higher in the northern interior than it is on the central plateau. While the north was the first region to be explored by the Portuguese, the region was not occupied until the late nineteenth century, and there was little European settlement until the coffee boom in the 1950s. Further south the forest patches become more widely spaced until the northern region merges with the savanna vegetation of the south central plateau. Angola's most important river, the Cuanza, forms a rough dividing line between the northern forest and the south central savanna. While most rivers in Angola are navigable for only 10 to 15 miles, the Cuanza is navigable for 120 miles from its mouth. The availability of water transport on the Cuanza, the presence of fevers in the northern forest, and the steep escarpment in the south focused early Portuguese military effort in the lower Cuanza valley. The limits of navigable water on the Cuanza marked the limits of effective Portuguese control until the pacification of Angola in the twentieth century.

In addition to the problems of climate and terrain the Portuguese were handicapped by the persistent and well-organized resistance of the indigenous African kingdoms. The Portuguese faced three major groups of African peoples —the Bakongo in the northern forests, the Mbundu in the center along the Cuanza valley, and the Ovimbundu in the south on the high plateau. All these peoples were organized in politically centralized kingdoms with Iron Age technology and formidable armies raised by corvées administered by district governors or other agents of the king. Firearms were acquired by some African peoples as early as the late sixteenth century, and the Ovimbundu in particular seem to have made extensive use of muskets in establishing their control over the central plateau in the eighteenth century.[4] The sale of firearms in Angola and other areas in West Africa was actually essential to the economy of the slave trade, and although the Portuguese initially prohibited the sale of arms, they found that their embargo was easily circumvented by other European nations. By the late eighteenth century the Portuguese found they still faced African armies armed with muskets but had gained none of the benefits of the arms trade and consequently authorized the limited sale of firearms by Portuguese nationals.[5] The Portuguese were forced to sell arms to the very people they would later attempt to conquer, and the trade in firearms both stimulated the political centralization of the African kingdoms and reduced the military advantage of the Portuguese. The wholesale provision of firearms to African peoples ended with the demise of the slave trade, but as late as 1914 the peoples of southern Angola were able to obtain repeating rifles from the German colony of South-West Africa and put them to use in opposing the final pacification of the region.[6] In some of the early battles European musketeers fought on both sides and African kingdoms formed military alliances with European powers attempting to break the Portuguese trade monopoly in Angola. In the middle of the seventeenth century the Dutch allied themselves with both the Bakongo in the north and the Mbundu peoples in the center and succeeded in seizing Luanda and reducing the Portuguese presence to a few interior strong points. A large military expedition from Brazil was required to rescue the remaining Portuguese garrisons and restore the colony to Portuguese control. The military strength of the African peoples was such that as late as 1802 the colonial government prohibited the import of mares on the grounds that it might make it possible for the African armies to acquire cavalry.[7] While no effective cavalry units were developed by the African kingdoms, mass armies of thousands of men could be raised. The Bakongo kingdom, the largest and most powerful of the African states, was reported to be able to raise an army of 80,000 men in the seventeenth century.[8] African warfare lacked the logistical support and tactical direction of European military operations and at times displayed elements of ritual war. The combination of manpower and firearms, however, made the battles for Angola resemble interstate wars rather than colonial police operations. Only in the late nineteenth century with the neutralization of malaria and the introduction of modern weaponry did the military advantage shift decisively in favor of the Portuguese.

[4] Gladwyn Murray Childs, *Umbundu Kinship and Character* (London: Oxford University Press, 1949), p. 195.

[5] David Birmingham, *The Portuguese Conquest of Angola* (London: Oxford University Press, 1965), pp. 45–46.

[6] Wheeler and Pélissier, *Angola*, p. 75.

[7] Jan Vansina, *Kingdoms of the Savanna* (Madison: University of Wisconsin Press, 1966), p. 184.

[8] Basil Davidson, *The African Slave Trade: Precolonial History 1450–1850* (Boston: Little, Brown, 1961), p. 138.

Both the physical location and the political organization of the African peoples exerted a profound effect on the direction of Portuguese military effort and, consequently, on both the political relationships established under colonial rule and the direction of the nationalist movement of the 1960s. The Bakongo were the first of the African peoples reached by the Portuguese explorers, but their political strength and their location in the northern forests and the Congo basin made initial conquest unattractive. The Bakongo kingdom was a politically centralized territorial bureaucracy divided into six great provinces, each ruled by a governor appointed by the king. In the seventeenth century the Bakongo kingdom itself had a population of 2,500,000[9] and maintained tributary relationships with other states to the north and south. The kingdom was ruled by a despotic monarch, the Manikongo, who maintained an elaborate court in a fortified capital at São Salvador. Provincial governors were summoned to the court annually to present tribute to the king, and a courier service maintained contact with the territorial administration. At the time of initial Portuguese contact in the 1490s the kingdom was at the height of its power and was capable of coordinating the military actions of all its constituent provinces and enlisting allies from tributary states. In many respects the political organization and military strength of the kingdom were comparable to those of Portugal, although its economy was based on swidden cultivation rather than true agriculture and its extensive trade relations did not include maritime commerce.

The Portuguese at first treated the kingdom as a sovereign state and attempted to establish diplomatic and trade relations. The Manikongo was receptive to Portuguese influence and was converted to Catholicism, assuming the Portuguese Christian name João and the title Dom. While initial Portuguese contact had been limited to trade in ivory and cloth, the rapid expansion of the overseas slave trade, first for the sugar island of São Tomé in the Gulf of Guineau and later for Brazil, led to increased Portuguese involvement in the Kongo kingdom. The Portuguese intervened directly in the succession struggle following the death of João I and succeeded in installing the pro-European Dom Afonso I as King. The Kongo monarchy came under increased European influence, and a Portuguese adviser or confessor became an integral part of the court at São Salvador and an important figure in the royal administration.

The slave trade was both the major reason for Portuguese interest in the Kongo kingdom and the eventual cause of its downfall. The Kongo monarchy, aided by the Portuguese, was at first able to establish a lucrative monopoly of slaves shipped through the mouth of the Congo River from the port of Mpinda. The rapid increase in the slave trade, however, led to increased warfare with Mbundu peoples to the south and generated intense political conflict within the Kongo kingdom. In the late sixteenth century the weakened kingdom was invaded by a fierce tribe of warriors from the interior, and Portuguese assistance

[9] George P. Murdock, *Africa: Its Peoples and Their Culture History* (New York: McGraw-Hill, 1959), p. 292.

was required to drive out the invaders and recapture São Salvador. The Portuguese themselves invaded the Kongo kingdom in 1665 and defeated the Kongo armies of Ambuila and beheaded the ruling monarch. While this battle marked the end of effective centralized control by the Kongo monarchy, it did not lead to the assumption of direct rule by the Portuguese. The remnants of the Kongo kingdom were still a military threat, and the northern forests were regions of fevers and unattractive to European settlers. The Portuguese withdrew from the region and for much of the next two centuries maintained only intermittent contact with the kingdom. The capital of São Salvador was occupied by the Portuguese from 1859 to 1870, but they then abandoned the region once again until the annexation of the Kongo kingdom by the colony of Angola in 1888. After the defeat of the Kongo armies at Ambuila and the death of the ruling monarch the kingdom disintegrated into independent subunits controlled by African warlords who maintained bands of military retainers and controlled the local flow of slaves. By the end of the eighteenth century the largest effective unit of administration was the chiefdom, which usually consisted of a capital town of some 200 huts and several villages of 50 huts. The largest chiefdoms were no more than 12 miles across.[10] In the late nineteenth century the churches and fortifications of São Salvador were in ruins and the king himself was little more than a local chief living in a small village surrounded by a wooden palisade. In the twentieth century a visiting British traveler found that King Dom Pedro VII was reduced to supplementing a Portuguese retainer by cultivating rice and coffee in his own garden.[11] Despite the impecunious state of the monarchy it remained an important symbol of political unity for the Bakongo people, and bitter succession struggles continued even in the twentieth century. In 1913 Tulante Álvaro Buta, a minor chief in the region of São Salvador, led a revolt against the ruling monarch, who he felt had cooperated too readily with Portuguese attempts to recruit forced labor for the plantations of São Tomé. The revolt was put down with the aid of Portuguese troops but not before it had spread to most of northern Angola. Buta's rebellion marked the last effective military resistance by remnants of the old Kongo kingdom, but its defeat did not end conflict over the kingship. In 1955 the death of Dom Pedro VII led to a renewed struggle, first to appoint a king independent of the Portuguese, and then to control the king's council of ministers. While this effort did not lead directly to open rebellion, the principal figures in the negotiations over the kingship were to become a significant faction in the growing nationalist movement in the Bakongo areas of Angola. The relatively late assumption of direct rule in the areas of the old Kongo kingdom left remnants of the traditional political apparatus which could provide the framework for the nationalist revolt of the 1960s.

[10] Vansina, *Kingdoms*, p. 190.
[11] F. Clement and C. Egerton, *Angola in Perspective* (London: Routledge & Kegan Paul, 1957), p. 176–177.

To the south of the Kongo in the Mbundu kingdom of Ndongo the Portuguese destroyed the indigenous political apparatus with a thoroughness which left no traditional framework to form the basis for a later nationalist movement.[12] The kingdom of Ndongo was located in the coastal lowlands along the Cuanza, and since the river provided the Portuguese with their principal route into the interior, the Ndongo became the first African kingdom to be conquered by Europeans. Nevertheless, it still required a long series of military campaigns beginning in 1575 and lasting for a century before the old area of the Ndongo kingdom was subdued, and remnants of the Ndongo ruling classes carried on periodic warfare against the Portuguese from strongholds further inland for a considerably longer period. The Portuguese had first been attracted to Ndongo by tales of silver mines at Cambambe on the Cuanza, but later, when the mines proved imaginary, their interest shifted to the capture of slaves. As long as Kongo maintained its slave monopoly, the Portuguese were forced to rely on trade through African agents, and as the slave trade undermined the power of the Kongo, the supply of slaves became increasingly unreliable. At the same time the trade undermined the power of the Kongo kingdom, it increased the power of Ndongo, which was founded around 1500 and derived its power from its ability to control the trade between the Portuguese on the coast and the slaving states of the interior. Faced with increased competition from other European nations and declining supplies of slaves, the Portuguese attempted to eliminate the African middlemen and capture the slaves themselves by direct military action. The demand for slaves led to increasing conflict with the Ndongo king, the Ngola, and eventually to the conquest of the entire kingdom. The Portuguese established a new state in the area of the Ndongo kingdom, which came to be called the kingdom of Angola after the name of the Ndongo ruler. The kingdom of Angola was for 300 years simply one of a number of states competing for control of the slave trade. The Portuguese kingdom attempted to establish vassalage relationships with neighboring African states, but these relationships were actually uneasy alliances which were frequently upset by the interminable warfare of the slave trade. While Ndongo was destroyed, other Mbundu kingdoms which were less accessible to Portuguese armies retained a considerable degree of autonomy. In the interior, the kingdom of Matamba was conquered by remnants of the Ndongo kingdom fleeing the Portuguese and remained beyond Portuguese control until the nineteenth century. The kingdom of Dembos, which had once been a tributary state of the Kongo even though it was populated by Mbundu peoples, was located only 70 miles from Luanda, but its rugged, mountainous terrain and dense forest vegetation provided a natural barrier against Portuguese armies. Dembos was capable of inflicting disastrous defeats on Portuguese expeditions as late as the beginning of the twentieth century, and 15 successive campaigns were required before it was finally defeated in 1919. Dembos, like the kingdom of the Kongo, retained a traditional political apparatus

---

[12] For a detailed account of Portuguese campaigns against the Mbundu see Birmingham, *Portuguese Conquest.*

which could provide the framework for a nationalist movement, while the former area of Ndongo became the most thoroughly assimilated area of Angola.

On the central plateau inland from the port of Benguela the steep escarpment limited Portuguese contact to trading missions until the end of the nineteenth century. The Ovimbundu kingdoms of the plateau seem to have formed at least in part as a result of the stimulus of trade with the Portuguese, and they maintained their autonomy for a longer period than either the Bakongo or the Mbundu kingdoms. The Ovimbundu states organized great caravans to transport slaves and other trade goods from the interior to the Portuguese settlements on the coast and after the collapse of the slave trade actually strengthened their commercial position through trade in ivory, wax, and rubber. By the nineteenth century the Ovimbundu kingdoms dominated trade on the plateau, and Portuguese merchants operating without the support of European armies found themselves increasingly unable to compete with African traders. While some traders had managed to establish themselves on the plateau by the nineteenth century, many were forced to live much as did their African counterparts and gradually merged with the indigenous population. The Ovimbundu gained the reputation of being the shrewdest and most aggressive traders in Angola, and conflicts over the Ovimbundu treatment of Portuguese traders eventually led to Portuguese military occupation of the plateau in 1890. A decline in rubber prices and a large influx of Europeans after the occupation led to a major rebellion in 1902 by the Bailundu kingdom, the most powerful of the Ovimbundu states. The suppression of this rebellion in 1904 marked the end of effective primary resistance on the plateau, and the Portuguese rapidly expanded their occupation to control the entire area.

The Bakongo, Mbundu, and Ovimbundu were the African peoples first exposed to Portuguese influence and have been the most deeply affected by modernizing influences. The agricultural export economy, particularly the coffee economy of the postwar period, has also had its greatest effect on these peoples. The remaining African peoples are located far from coastal markets or Portuguese settlements in the Zambesi basin or in the deserts of the South-West African border areas. The Lunda-Chokwe peoples are a product of the same state formation processes which led to the centralization of the Mbundu and Ovimbundu kingdoms and were deeply involved in the slave trade. Unlike the peoples of the coast and interior plateau, however, the Luanda-Chokwe have not been greatly affected by either the nineteenth-century trade in rubber or ivory or the twentieth-century agricultural export economy and remain traditional agriculturalists. The Nganguela and Nyaneka-Humbe peoples who live to the west and south of the Ovimbundu are also isolated from modernizing influences and are among the most conservative of the African peoples. Of the remaining African peoples the most important are the Ambo, particularly the Cuanhama tribe, whose members live on both sides of the South-West African border. The strategic position of the Cuanhama and their warrior culture have made them an important factor in Angolan military history. Before they were conquered in

1915 they carried out frequent raids against neighboring peoples including the Ovimbundu and fought with the Germans against the Portuguese in World War I.

By 1930 the Portuguese had secured effective military control over the interior of Angola and had defeated the last rebellions of the African peoples. The modern administrative organization of the colony dates from this period and was formally established in the Colonial Act of 1930 and the Portuguese constitution of 1933. In the revised constitution of 1951, Angola's status was formally changed from colony to "overseas province," but it remained a political dependency of Portugal. As James Duffy has pointed out[13] such changes have occurred frequently in Angolan history without changing the realities of Portuguese rule. In 1971 the title of the colony was once again changed, this time to "overseas state" in an attempt to relieve international pressures for political independence, but the change was as cosmetic as those that had preceded it. Angola is, in fact, governed by the Portuguese minister of overseas affairs (formerly the minister of colonial affairs) who appoints the governor general of Angola and whose administrative decisions have the binding effect of law in Angola. Local administration within Angola is organized in a system of centralized direct rule under the control of the governor general and the Overseas Ministry and staffed by a cadre of professional colonial administrators. The administrative structure is composed of first-order political subdivisions called districts and second-order political subdivisions called townships (*concelhos*) or circumscriptions (*circunscrições*). Second-order political subdivisions are composed of administrative posts, the fundamental organizational unit in the control of the African population. In 1961, after an administrative reorganization following the northern uprising, there were a total of 15 districts. The governor of each district reported to the Angolan governor general but was appointed by the overseas minister. The second-order political subdivisions are usually distinguished by the number of European inhabitants, with townships generally including more Europeans than circumscriptions. Recent increases in European immigration to Angola and the insecurity of Portuguese rule since 1961 have led to frequent reorganization of the second-order administrative structure. In 1950 there were a total of 75 townships and circumscriptions, in 1961 there were 84, and by 1966 the number had increased to 117. Map 4.1 shows the 85 townships and circumscriptions and the 15 districts of Angola as they are listed in 1960 census publications and represents the actual administrative divisions as they existed after the 1961 reorganization. Since the administrative divisions used in the reports of the 1960 census are approximately those that existed at the time of the 1961 uprising, it will be convenient to use the boundaries presented in Map 4.1, in discussing both agricultural organization and rural events.

[13] James Duffy, *Portugal in Africa* (Cambridge: Harvard University Press, 1962), p. 68.

While the formal administrative structure of Angola suggests an integrated political system, the formal structure bears little resemblance to the actual pattern of Portuguese colonial rule in Angola. Except in areas around towns with large European populations such as Luanda or Nova Lisboa the Portuguese administration is more like a network of military outposts of an occupying army than it is like a working political system. The fundamental unit of the Portuguese administration structure, the administrative post, consists of little more than a post chief (*chefe de pôsto*) aided by two or three native police (*sipaios,* or sepoys), an interpreter, and a native clerk. The post chief may be the nominal administrator of several African villages or a few European plantations or trading posts, and the administrative post itself is seldom more than a small village or trading community. Post chiefs are transferred frequently, seldom learn the local African dialects, and normally visit the African villages under their control only once a year. The *chefe*'s main contact with the African population is through collecting taxes, administering punishment and fines, and recruiting forced labor for road repair and other public works. Since Angola has no system of native courts, the *chefe* is also responsible for adjudicating disputes which cannot be settled by customary practices in the villages under his control. The combination of administrative, judicial, security, and penal functions of the *chefe* makes him the effective embodiment of Portuguese colonial rule, and his remoteness and arbitrary authority have made him a figure viewed with fear and mistrust by most of the African population. In general the *chefe,* on arrival at his post, attempts to establish good relations with settlers and traders in the area and is frequently more responsive to the interests of the local European population than to the abstract principles of colonial administration enunciated in Lisbon or Luanda. While the authority of the *chefe* can be supported by military force in extreme cases, in general he depends on native police and whatever paramilitary assistance he can recruit from the local settler population. Before 1961 the authority of the *chefe* was seldom seriously challenged, but his reliance on the arms as well as the good will of the local European population reinforces his essentially local interests.

The *chefe* maintains liaison with the African population through African chiefs called *regedores,* who are sometimes traditional leaders but are almost invariably selected by the *chefe* and paid a salary by the colonial administration. The *regedor* serves at the pleasure of the *chefe* and has little real authority, serving largely as a conduit for Portuguese instructions. In Ovimbundu country, for example, Adrian Edwards[14] reports that the *regedor* had to report on a weekly basis to the *chefe* and was severely punished if he failed to satisfy administrative demands for taxes or labor. Frequently the punishment took the form of beatings with the *palmatória,* a flat wooden paddle with beveled holes drilled in the surface, which was brought down on the outstretched palm of the offending

---

[14] Adrian C. Edwards, *The Ovimbundu under Two Sovereigns* (London: Oxford University Press, 1962), p. 41.

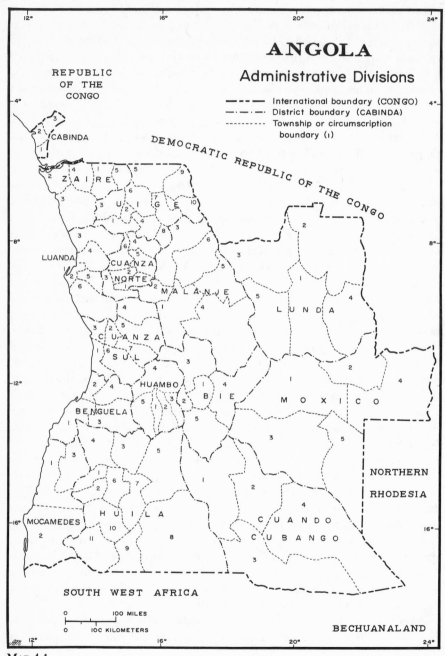

ANGOLA

Administrative Divisions

— · · — International boundary (CONGO)
— · — · — District boundary (CABINDA)
— — — — Township or circumscription
boundary (1)

REPUBLIC
OF THE
CONGO

CABINDA

DEMOCRATIC REPUBLIC OF THE CONGO

ZAIRE

UIGE

LUANDA

CUANZA
NORTE

MALANJE

LUNDA

CUANZA
SUL

HUAMBO

BIE

MOXICO

BENGUELA

NORTHERN

RHODESIA

MOCAMEDES

HUILA

CUANDO

CUBANGO

SOUTH WEST AFRICA

0   100 MILES

0   100 KILOMETERS

BECHUANALAND

MAP 4.1

222

KEY TO MAP 4.1

01 CABINDA
 01 Cabinda
 02 Cacongo
 03 Maiombe

02 ZAIRE
 01 São Salvador
 02 Santo Antonio do
  Zaire
 03 Ambrizete
 04 Nóqui
 05 Cuímba

03 UÍGE
 01 Uíge
 02 Songo
 03 Bembe
 04 Negage
 05 Zombo
 06 Damba
 07 Pombo
 08 Alto Cauale
 09 Cuango
 10 Macocola

04 LUANDA
 01 Luanda
 02 Viana
 03 Ambriz
 04 Dande
 05 Icolo e Bengo
 06 Quiçama

05 CUANZA NORTE
 01 Cazengo
 02 Golungo Alto
 03 Cambambe
 04 Ambaca

 05 Quiculungo
 06 Dembos

06 CUANZA SUL
 01 Novo Redondo
 02 Amboim
 03 Porto Amboim
 04 Libolo
 05 Quibala
 06 Seles
 07 Cela

07 MALANJE
 01 Malanje
 02 Cacuso
 03 Duque de Bragança
 04 Songo
 05 Bondo e Bângala
 06 Cambo

08 LUNDA
 01 Saurimo
 02 Chitato
 03 Camaxilo
 04 Cassai Sul
 05 Minungo

09 BENGUELA
 01 Benguela
 02 Lobito
 03 Ganda
 04 Balombo

10 HUAMBO
 01 Huambo
 02 Vila Nova
 03 Bela Vista
 04 Bailundo
 05 Caála

11 BIÉ
 01 Bié
 02 Chinguar
 03 Andulo
 04 Camacupa
 05 Alto Cuanza

12 MOXICO
 01 Moxico
 02 Dilolo
 03 Luchazes
 04 Alto Zambeze
 05 Bundas

13 CUANDO CUBANGO
 01 Menongue
 02 Cuito Canavale
 03 Baixo Cubango
 04 Cuando

14 MOÇÂMEDES
 01 Moçâmedes
 02 Porto Alexandre
 03 Bibala

15 HUÍLA
 01 Lubango
 02 Chibia
 03 Caconda
 04 Quilengues
 05 Ganguelas
 06 Alto Cunene
 07 Capelongo
 08 Baixo Cunene
 09 Cuamato
 10 Gambos
 11 Curoca

chief with considerable force. The *regedores* administered the villages under their control with the aid of locally appointed village headmen and traditional tribal councils. Hélio Felgas reports that in northern Angola these secondary administrative officials were frequently selected from the nobility of the old Kongo kingdom and retained some of their traditional authority.[15] While the *regedores* were hopelessly compromised by their services to the local administrative post and shared the *chefe*'s unpopularity, the local village officials enjoyed slightly greater autonomy and correspondingly greater prestige among the African population. In fact, the Portuguese seldom attempted to reorganize the

[15] Hélio Felgas, *As Populações Nativas do Congo Português* (Luanda, 1960), p. 33.

social and economic structure of the villages, and customary legal practices and patterns of land ownership persisted under colonial rule. The administrative control of the Portuguese was never as tight as the mestizo administration of the sierran Indians in Peru, and there was seldom a large class of Portuguese settlers to maintain much direct economic control over the African population. As long as the periodic demands for labor and taxes were met and no signs of political deviance were reported by the *chefe*'s village spies, the African population was permitted to govern itself with little outside interference. Unlike the indigenous community of highland Indians in Peru, the communal land-holding and political practices of the African population remained essentially unchanged under Portuguese rule. The tribal social structure, while considerably weakened, remained a viable source of economic opportunities and political authority for Africans cut off from white society.

The regulations enforced by the *chefe* depend fundamentally on the legal distinction between the European and indigenous population. This principle was embodied in the so-called Native Statute of 1954, and while this law was formally repealed in 1961, it continues to express the reality of Portuguese colonial administration in Angola. Despite the explicit Portuguese ideology of an assimilationist, multiracial society the Native Statute formally recognized a special status for citizens who were Negroes or descendants of the Negro race. All such citizens who did not as yet "possess the level of education or the personal and social habits which are a condition for the unrestricted application of the public and private law pertaining to Portuguese citizens" [16] were confined to the status of *indígena,* or member of the indigenous population, and were to be governed by customary tribal law. Only Europeans and those Africans who had acquired the proper social habits and become assimilated to European ways (*assimilados*) were granted the rights of the *não-indígena* status, which included the full protection of Portuguese law. Later statutes specified that *não-indígena* status could be granted to any African who was over the age of 18, could speak Portuguese, had attained a suitable level of education, earned a cash income sufficient to support his family, and did not have a criminal record. *Não-indígena* status was also extended to anyone who could demonstrate that he had served in the colonial administration, was a licensed merchant, or was a partner in a business firm. In practice an African attempting to become an *assimilado* might also be expected to show a suitably deferential attitude toward Portuguese authority or pay a bribe to local officials. Despite the Portuguese emphasis on assimilation, the 1950 census listed only 30,089 *assimilados* out of a total African population of more than 4 million.[17] While the *indígena* status was ostensibly designed to preserve customary law for those Africans living in a traditional village milieu, its actual effect was to deny legal protection to 95 percent of the

---

[16] United Nations, General Assembly, 16th Session, *Report of the Sub-Committee on the Situation in Angola,* supplement no. 16, A/4978 (New York, 1962), p. 58.

[17] Duffy, *Portuguese Africa,* p. 295.

population and establish an invidious system of special privileges for the European minority. The benefits of property ownership, trade franchises, labor recruitment contracts, and land concessions were reserved for Europeans or *assimilados,* while the burdens of forced labor, restricted mobility, and payment of the native tax were confined to the indigenous population. In the agricultural export economy the legal distinctions have affected the pattern of land ownership, the methods of labor recruitment, and the relative competitiveness of European and African production. The legal distinction between European and African and the system of direct colonial rule were both essential to the development of the settler-based agricultural export economy of Angola in the 1950s. Without the legal advantages of *não-indígena* status and the protection of the *chefe de pôsto* export agriculture would have been unlikely to attract settlers from Portugal, and the export economy might well have developed as a system of family small holdings as it did in other major African producers such as Uganda and the Ivory Coast. As it was, these distinctions provided a crucial economic prop for the settlers, and their preservation whether in law or in fact became one of the major issues of the Angolan war.

THE COFFEE EXPORT ECONOMY

The military pacification of Angola and the establishment of a colonial administration in the twentieth century did little to rescue the colony from the long period of economic stagnation which followed the collapse of the slave trade. Portugal's mercantilist economic policies discouraged foreign investment, and the backward metropolitan economy generated little venture capital for overseas investment. Angola's only contribution to the Portuguese economy was as a limited market for textile manufactures, but the small European population and the poverty of most Africans limited consumption. What little economic development which had taken place in Angola before 1950 was largely the result of foreign investment undertaken despite Portuguese capital restrictions. In 1903 British associates of Cecil Rhodes began work on the Benguela railway, which was eventually extended to the Katanga minefields in the Belgian Congo in 1931. In 1920 Belgian and British interests associated with Union Minière established Diamang (*Companhia de Diamantes de Angola*) to exploit the diamond fields of Lunda and obtained a concession which gave them virtual state power over much of the district. Neither of these developments had much effect on either the African or the Portuguese population, and by the 1920s the colony was virtually bankrupt. With no industry, with mining limited to Diamang activities, and commercial agriculture attracting little outside capital, Angola appeared an unpromising area for European settlement. Despite ambitious colonization schemes proposed by successive colonial administrations few Portuguese settlers were attracted to Angola before World War II. In the 1920s Duffy reports that fewer than a thousand Portuguese settlers a year emigrated to all of

Portuguese Africa, while 10 to 20 times that number emigrated to Brazil.[18] Despite colonial policy aimed at establishing a population of small European farmers on the central plateau, few immigrants actually remained in agriculture, and most eventually drifted to the towns or became involved in petty trading activities.

The development of the coffee economy radically changed the internal economy of Angola, altered its relationship with the metropolitan and world economies, and stimulated the first large wave of European settlement in Angolan history. While coffee had been exported as early as 1830 and the first commercial estate was established in 1837, most of these early ventures were economically marginal. Most coffee was gathered from semispontaneous growth by Africans and sold to Portuguese bush traders. During the nineteenth century exports expanded gradually, reaching a high of 11,000 tons in 1895, but increased competition in world markets reduced exports to 3,000 to 4,000 tons annually in the first two decades of the twentieth century.[19] Production increased gradually in the twenties and thirties, but as late as 1938 Angola exported only 19,000 tons and coffee made up less than 19 percent of Angola's agricultural exports.[20] The principal agricultural export commodity before World War II was maize grown by Ovimbundu small holders on the central plateau. The rise of the coffee economy in the postwar period was initiated by rapidly rising prices touched off by the acute commodity shortages of the Korean war period. As the data in Table 4.1 indicate, the average price of coffee f.o.b. Angola almost tripled from 8.6 escudos in 1948 to 23.7 escudos in 1951 and reached an all-time high of 29.4 escudos in 1954.[21] Production figures did not reflect the dramatic price increases until the end of the decade, since some time elapsed between the news of the huge profits in Angola and renewed immigration from Portugal and several years are required to bring new coffee bushes into full production. The area devoted to coffee, however, expanded from 120,000 hectares in 1948 to 500,000 in 1961, and exports increased from 53,000 to well over 100,000 tons in the same period. By 1961 at the outbreak of the nationalist revolt, settlers who had come hoping to take advantage of the high prices of 1955 found themselves with substantial investments in new plantings just coming into full production at a time when a world coffee surplus had begun to undermine prices. The rapid expansion of coffee production was not, of course, limited to Angola, and the additions of substantial African supplies to the traditional Latin American coffees brought about a chaotic price situation. In 1958 Angola signed the world

[18] Duffy, *Portugal in Africa*, pp. 144–145.

[19] A. Baião Esteves and F. Santos Oliveira, "Contribuição para o Estudo das Caracteristicas dos Cafés de Angola," in Portugal, Junta de Investigações do Ultramar, *Estudos, Ensaios e Documentos*, no. 126 (Lisbon: Junta de Investigações do Ultramar, 1970), p. 21.

[20] United Nations Statistical Office, *Yearbook of International Trade Statistics* (New York, 1953), p. 29.

[21] 28.75 escudos = US$1. All coffee export prices represent the average price of total coffee exports including coffee residues and shelled and unshelled beans.

TABLE 4.1   *Coffee Exports from Angola 1948–1970[a]*

YEAR	Value, Million Escudos	Weight, Thousand Tons	COFFEE EXPORTS Price, Escudos per kilo	Percent Agric. Exports	Percent Total Exports
1970	3880.0	180.6	21.48	61.0	31.9
1969	3232.8	182.8	17.69	62.2	30.4
1968	3530.5	188.6	18.72	75.7	45.3
1967	3546.8	196.5	18.04	88.3	51.9
1966	3058.4	156.4	19.55	67.0	48.1
1965	2687.1	159.2	16.88	70.5	46.8
1964	2859.1	138.7	20.61	71.8	48.7
1963	1894.8	136.4	13.89	62.0	40.5
1962	1864.1	156.9	11.88	63.1	43.7
1961	1398.5	118.1	11.84	57.5	36.1
1960	1264.0	87.2	14.49	53.5	35.4
1959	1387.5	89.0	15.59	60.3	38.7
1958	1539.4	79.6	19.33	67.5	41.7
1957	1454.8	74.9	19.42	68.3	43.3
1956	1603.5	89.8	17.86	67.3	48.8
1955	1275.6	60.1	21.22	62.8	45.5
1954	1340.2	45.6	29.39	61.5	41.9
1953	1882.0	71.5	26.32	68.6	53.2
1952	1137.6	47.7	23.83	53.3	41.3
1951	1527.7	64.5	23.69	57.9	47.9
1950	746.6	37.5	19.91	42.2	34.4
1949	551.5	46.4	11.98	37.3	30.8
1948	459.8	53.4	8.61	39.6	30.9

[a] United Nations Statistical Office, *Yearbook of International Trade Statistics.*

coffee agreement which included most major producers and consuming nations and allocated fixed quotas to participating nations and stabilized prices. The effects of the agreement were not immediate, however, and prices dropped after 1958, reaching a level of slightly more than a third of their 1954 high by 1962. Thus the Angolan coffee boom was compressed into a single decade from the Korean war commodity boom to the collapse of world coffee prices in the late fifties. Despite its brief duration it brought about a profound change in Angola's economy. Since Angola had few significant exports of any kind before 1950, the rise in coffee production converted the colony into a monocultural export economy. Between 1948 and 1970 coffee contributed a median of 62 percent of Angola's agricultural exports and a median of 41 percent of total exports. Even after the period of the boom, coffee continued as the mainstay of the economy. Not until 1965, when restrictions on foreign capital were lifted, did expanded iron and petroleum production begin to reduce this dependence on coffee. Since none of the other agricultural exports contribute more than a small fraction of total agricultural exports, Angola contributes only one export sector to the world population of agricultural export sectors.

The coffee boom also had a pronounced effect on Angola's trade relations with the metropole and with foreign nations. In the mid-fifties coffee was not only Angola's leading export but the most important single export of the entire escudo zone, including metropolitan Portugal. Coffee even displaced cork as Portugal's most important source of foreign exchange. Since more than half of the Angolan coffee crop was sold in the United States, the export economy redirected trade patterns and the United States replaced Portugal as the colony's major export market in a number of postwar years. The export earnings of coffee enabled Angola to continue to run substantial trade deficits with Portugal while continuing to show a balance-of-payments surplus for most of the postwar period. The profits from the coffee trade generated new commercial expansion in Luanda, which became the principal coffee port. Profits also flowed back to Lisbon, where according to Irene van Dongen they created a substantial building boom along the Avenida de Roma, the capital's principal artery.[22] The new economic opportunities created by the coffee boom finally attracted settlers to Angola in substantial numbers, and in the 1950s the rate of Portuguese immigration reached 10,000 per year. The expanding European population and the increasing wealth of the colony created an enlarged market for Portuguese manufacturers, and despite changes in the pattern of Angolan exports Portugal remained the principal source of Angolan imports. By the time of the 1961 revolt the coffee economy had become a major determinant of economic growth, not only in Angola but in metropolitan Portugal as well.

Even though substantial numbers of African small holders and laborers were involved in the increased coffee production, the economic benefits of the boom were almost exclusively confined to the European population. Settler production increased much more rapidly than African production, and the proportion of total production contributed by Africans declined from 39 percent in 1941 to 26 percent in 1958.[23] The dominance of European producers in the postwar period led to the classification of the Angolan coffee export sector as a migratory estate system despite the presence of substantial production by both African small holders and corporate plantations. The production parameters of Angolan coffee, however, do not provide any substantial economic justification for the dominance of settler-owned estates. Almost all Angolan coffees are low-grade robusta. The relatively lower price of robusta seldom justifies the elaborate wet processing technique used for the higher-grade arabicas produced in Peru and elsewhere in Latin America. Even the largest Angolan estates use the less

[22] Irene S. van Dongen, "Coffee Trade, Coffee Regions, and Coffee Ports in Angola," *Economic Geography*, 37 (October 1961), 320–346.

[23] United Nations, General Assembly, 21st Session, Special Committee on the Situation with Regard to the Implementation of the Declaration on the Granting of Independence to Colonial Countries and Peoples, *Supplementary Report of Sub-Committee I: The Activities of Foreign Economic and Other Interests Which are Impeding the Implementation of the Declaration on the Granting of Independence in the Territories under Portuguese Administration*, app. II, "Agricultural and Processing Industries in Angola," A/AC. 109/L. 334/add. I (New York, 1966), p. 60.

expensive dry processing technique exclusively. Since the only machinery required in the dry process is a small, inexpensive friction mill for removing the outer shell of the dried berry, processing expenses are a minor part of total production costs, usually contributing less than 3 percent of the total. Most European estates have their own processing machines, and small producers without machines can pay to have their coffee processed by independent entrepreneurs who tour the coffee regions with small mills in the backs of pickup trucks. Drying the berries is usually accomplished by simply spreading them in the open, sometimes on especially constructed brick or adobe courtyards but more frequently on the ground or on an open surface composed of tightly packed ant heaps. Needless to say, little capital is required for such processing, and the dominance of settler estates is hardly a result of any efficiencies of scale. Most of the other production characteristics of Angolan coffee also favor small holder rather than estate production. The coffee harvest is concentrated in a single four-month campaign between July and September, and more than half of total labor input is required during this period. Large European estates are usually confronted with an acute labor shortage during the harvest, while African small holders simply mobilize slack family labor resources. Coffee can easily be combined with subsistence production, so there is little risk in tending a few coffee trees in addition to the staple food crops of manioc or maize. The small African producer is therefore usually more diversified than the settler estate and can withstand market fluctuations by reverting to subsistence production. At the outset of the coffee boom the principal coffee regions were essentially areas of open resources in which slash-and-burn agriculture and traditional communal tenure arrangements were the rule, so that the African cultivator could usually establish control over a few coffee bushes at little cost either to himself or his kinsmen. Coffee is a semispontaneous crop which forms part of the natural vegetation in much of northern Angola. In the initial stages of the coffee boom no investment was required in standing crops already in partial production. While newly planted coffee bushes require three to five years to come into full production, the African producer need not convert entirely to coffee and could easily wait until the trees began to yield. Coffee cultivation in Angola is extraordinarily labor intensive, since the areas most favorable for coffee are also most favorable for other tropical vegetation. Efficient production requires that large shade trees be removed or thinned out, and this process encourages the growth of secondary vegetation which competes with the coffee. Coffee bushes in most of Angola are continually in danger of being strangled by forest creepers or submerged in fast-growing tropical grasses or waste shrubs, and continual weeding is necessary for the plants to survive. Since the substantial cost of supervising this labor and the generally low quality of the underpaid Angolan labor force are not offset by any substantial advantages in centralized production, the small producer again gains an advantage. Finally, transportation and export are under the control of large private companies rather than estate owners. It is clear that the export companies could deal effectively with either small holders or estate owners and therefore that the estate owners do not owe their position to any form of control over export markets. In fact many African small holders easily adapted to commercial production both before and during the period of the coffee boom and during the 1950s. There were an estimated 50,000 Africans growing coffee on plots of one to two hectares. Despite the favorable production parameters for small holders, they continue to produce only approximately a quarter of the crop, with the remainder accounted for by European estates. The dominance of the estates, however, clearly does not depend on economies of scale or on control of export or processing, but on the legal and political advantages of European settlers under colonial rule.

European estates are organized in two distinct regional enterprise types which reflect the history and ecology of robusta coffee production north and south of the Cuanza River.[24] In the north robusta production is concentrated in the districts of Uíge and Cuanza Norte, and European production is organized in migratory labor estates. In 1958 there were over 800 European growers in the northern region, and most of these were Portuguese settlers who owned medium-sized holdings of from 100 to 300 hectares. While a few estates were controlled by absentee owners living in Luanda or Salazar, most owners lived on their estates and supervised their workers directly. In the southern region robusta coffee is limited to the district of Caunza Sul, and although in 1958 over 500 European growers were officially recorded in the district,[25] three-quarters of all production came from a few large corporate plantations. Half of all southern robusta was in fact produced by a single corporation, the *Companhia Agrícola de Angola* (CADA), which controlled 18 coffee plantations and operates the largest plantation in Angola, Boa Entrada, at Gabela in the township of Amboim. In 1963 Boa Entrada was reported to control about 60,000 hectares and employed 11,580 Africans and 280 Europeans.[26] The large plantations of the southern region were established in the first two decades of the century, and the effects of the coffee boom were greatest in the northern region, where relatively few estates had been established before World War II. In 1948, 65 percent of total national robusta production was contributed by the northern region and 35 percent by the southern region. By 1958 the effects of the boom had increased the share of the northern region to 78 percent, and the share of the southern region had declined to 22 percent.[27] The distribution of robusta production by region in the latter year is shown in Map 4.2.

[24] See van Dongen, "Coffee Trade," for a discussion of differences between the two regions. The northern and southern regions correspond to zones 3 and 16 respectively of the agricultural regions of Angola defined in the 1960 census of agriculture. The characteristics of each zone are described briefly in Eduardo Cruz de Carvalho, "Esbôço da Zonagem Agrícola de Angola," *Fomento*, vol. 2, no. 3 (1963), pp. 67–72.

[25] Angola, Direção dos Serviços de Economia e Estatística Geral, *Anuário Estatístico 1959* (Luanda: Imprensa Nacional, 1960), pp. 94–95.

[26] United Nations, "Agricultural and Processing Industries in Angola," p. 58.

[27] Angola, *Anuário Estatístico 1959*, pp. 94–95.

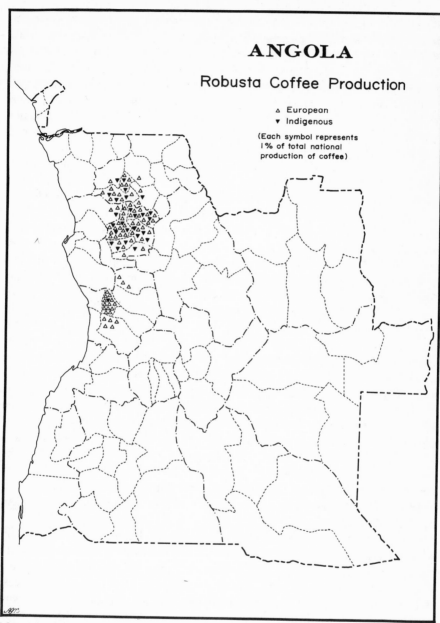

ANGOLA

Robusta Coffee Production

△ European
▼ Indigenous

(Each symbol represents
1% of total national
production of coffee)

MAP 4.2

231

Coffee is produced in both regions on the subplateau between the coastal lowlands and the interior plateau at altitudes between 1,300 and 3,300 feet. The more abrupt rise of the escarpment in the south, the narrowness of the sub-plateau, and the greater altitude of the interior plateau have concentrated coffee cultivation in a relatively narrow band close to the coast. In the north the more gradual ascent, the greater width of the subplateau, and the more moderate height of the interior plateau have permitted coffee cultivation to extend over a wider area farther inland. As the data in Map 4.2 indicate, southern production is concentrated in a narrow arc including the western portions of the townships of Amboim, Seles, and Libolo, which all lie close to the coastal strip. In the north the principal producing townships are Uíge, Ambaca, and Dembos, which surround and include areas of the Malanje plateau, the northern extension of the interior plateau. Since the effective maximum altitude for robusta production in both the north and the south is approximately 4,500 feet, the lower plateau in the north has permitted cultivation in valleys around its fringes, while no robusta is cultivated on the plateau in the south. The differences in the geography of the two regions had important consequences for the development of European agricultural organization. In the south corporate plantations were originally established to produce sugar on the coastal lowlands long before the period of the coffee boom. Sugar is, of course, typically produced on highly capitalized corporate plantations, and the initial estates in this area were organized for sugar rather than coffee production. Sisal and oil palms are also grown in the lowlands, and in the extreme south some cattle are grazed in areas adjacent to what is now the coffee zone. All these agricultural products tend to produce a more centralized enterprise than does coffee, and the corporate plantation organization in the south depends on these crops of the coastal lowlands. When increasing prices made coffee attractive, these estates simply diversified their activities, continuing the cultivation of plantation crops in the lowlands and adding coffee trees on the adjacent subplateau areas. Coffee plantations in the southern zone continue to be more diversified than those in the north and usually produce either sugar, sisal, or cattle, as well as coffee. In the north most estates concentrate exclusively on coffee, and little centralization is required for efficient production.

The plantations in the south were first established at the turn of the century when concessions to Europeans were typically granted on a massive scale with only vaguely defined boundaries. CADA's initial concessions, for example, were said to include an area of some 17,000 square kilometers.[28] In general, concessions were made with little regard for the rights of any African cultivators who happened to be living in the designated area. Before 1921 Portuguese colonial land policies permitted concessionaires to expropriate African lands if they either paid compensation or relocated Africans in native reserves established outside the concession. The corporate interests attempting to establish sugar plantations

[28] Kavalam Madhu Panikkar, *Angola in Flames* (New York: Asia Publishing House, 1962), p. 59.

on the coast generally displaced most of the indigenous population in those sections of the concessions which they actively exploited. When their activities extended to coffee cultivation, they managed to claim most of the available land and remove many of the indigenous inhabitants early in the century. The exportations in the south were facilitated by the relatively low population densities on the coast and subplateau. The major population concentrations and the major kingdoms of the Ovimbundu were located on the high plateau far from the areas useful for plantation crops or robusta coffee. These early expropriations and the lower population densities in the southern coffee zone left relatively few African small holders in possession of valuable coffee land by the time of the coffee boom in the 1950s. Farther inland on the high plateau where few large agricultural concessions were granted at the beginning of the century, African commercial production is still significant. Robusta varieties do not grow at altitudes above 4,500 feet, but arabicas can be produced on the high central plateau. Two-thirds of the small amount of arabica produced on the plateau is accounted for by Ovimbundu small holders.

In the southern plantation region coffee is not as significant a part of the natural vegetation as it is in the north, and most coffee bushes have been planted and cultivated by estates. In the north there has been a substantial amount of semispontaneous coffee since its introduction in the 1830s. Before the period of the boom much of the northern crop was gathered from wild bushes. During the boom many of the former African coffee gatherers became small holders when higher prices justified more attention to cultivation. At the beginning of the boom there was a substantial class of small holding African producers in the north which was almost entirely absent in the south. European coffee cultivation in the north is centered in areas of maximum indigenous population density and, consequently, areas of maximum land used by subsistence cultivators. The areas of maximum coffee production surrounding the Malanje plateau in the townships of Uíge, Ambaca, and Dembos include large number of villages of the two most important tribal groups of the north, the Bakongo and the Dembos. The expansion of European production during the period of the boom therefore was inevitably at the expense of both small African coffee producers and traditional African subsistence farmers. While coastal plantations developed in the north as they had in the south, they are located relatively farther from the current centers of coffee production than they are in the south. As a result land expropriations for coastal plantation agriculture did not reduce the indigenous population density in the coffee areas as they had done in the south. As a result of these ecological and population differences between the northern and southern coffee zones, African small holders, particularly before the 1961 revolt, contributed a much larger fraction of robusta production in the north than in the south. As the data in Map 4.2 indicate, by 1958 African small holders produced less than 5 per cent of the robusta coffee in the southern zone but 37 percent in the northern zone. The early development of sugar plantations in the south eliminated conflicts with African small holders by eliminating the relatively few small holders in the plantation region. In the north the coffee boom exacerbated conflict between the substantial class of African small holders and European estate owners by providing each with an incentive to expand production.

Coffee plantations in the south, particularly those which also produce sugar or sisal, are likely to be much more highly capitalized and much less labor intensive than coffee estates in the north. CADA had a registered capital of 225 million escudos (US $7.8 million) in 1963, and another large southern producer, Mário Cunha, had assets of 10 million escudos (US $350,000) at the same time.[29] Most northern producers have little capital other than land and standing crops, and in many northern estates the small estate trading post is a more important capital asset than the coffee plantation itself. The southern estates make greater use of machinery in both cultivation and processing than do the northern estates. The most important labor-saving device is the mechanical weeder, which is routinely used on southern estates but almost never used in the north. Since weeding is the most labor-intensive aspect of production other than the harvest, the mechanization of weeding leads to a relatively smaller labor force in the south. The average number of laborers required to produce a ton of coffee in the north is almost twice that of the south (north 1.46 laborers per ton, south 0.74 laborers per ton in 1958).[30] The large southern estates still rely on dry processing as do estates in the north. The southern estates, however, usually have additional equipment for sorting the dried berries on the basis of specific gravity. This additional process produces a more uniform product and consequently a higher export value. Other forms of agricultural machinery are also more common on the southern plantations. These differences are apparent not only on the large plantations such as those of CADA or Mário Cunha but even on moderate-sized estates in the south. Afonso Mendes's research on agricultural organization in Angola provides detailed descriptions of mechanical equipment employed on typical coffee estates in both the northern and southern coffee zones.[31] Mendes describes one typical estate in the district of Cuanza Sul which produced 350 tons of coffee, grazed 200 head of cattle, and employed 326 laborers. Its mechanical equipment included four tractors, five rotating plows and harrows, a mechanical weeder, machinery for leveling and ditch digging, and a half dozen small trucks. By comparison an estate in Quiculungo in the northern zone which employed 650 laborers exclusively in coffee production had only two tractors, three small trucks, and a hulling machine. Scientific cultivation techniques are also considerably more advanced in the south, and CADA in particular maintains a staff of agricultural technicians and an experimental farm. CADA obtains yields of over 500 kilograms per hectare, while

[29] United Nations, "Agricultural and Processing Industries in Angola," pp. 58–59.

[30] Calculated from data presented in Angola, *Anuário Estatístico*, 1959, pp. 94–95.

[31] Afonso Mendes, *O Trabalho Assalariado em Angola* (Lisbon: Universidade Técnica de Lisboa, Instituto Superior de Ciências Sociais e Política Ultramarina, 1966), pp. 160–170.

northern yields seldom exceed 300 to 400 kilograms per hectare. The greater efficiency of the southern plantations and their lower labor requirements generally enable them to produce at a lower cost than the northern settler estates, and their diversified crops enable them to survive temporary drops in the price of coffee. The southern plantations were therefore able to maintain profitable coffee operations even before the period of the boom, while many of the northern estates were profitable only during the period of inflated coffee prices in the 1950s and suffered accordingly during the period of declining prices at the end of the decade.

The dominant characteristics of the northern coffee estates are their chronic lack of capital and their economic marginality. Most of the early European farmers were in fact small bush traders who bought up coffee gathered by Africans. The Portuguese have always been active in petty trade activities in Angola, and bush traders made up the most important class of Europeans outside the towns before the coffee boom. As Gladwyn Childs has pointed out,[32] the marginal trading peoples such as the Hausa, Indians, Syrians, Armenians, and Greeks who dominate petty trade elsewhere in Africa are entirely absent in Angola and their role is filled by the Portuguese themselves. In fact many menial urban jobs which in other European colonies would have been filled by Africans or members of other ethnic groups are dominated by the Portuguese in Angola. The Portuguese involvement in petty trade and other low-status jobs is a direct reflection of the poverty of the metropole and the low economic status of most Portuguese immigrants to Angola. Most of the petty traders and early coffee farmers in northern Angola migrated from the poorest rural areas of Portugal and exchanged a marginal existence as peasant farmers for a precarious existence in the African bush. The traders' profits came from advancing credit at the trading post at interest rates of 30 to 40 percent a year against coffee, manioc, or palm products collected by Africans. The traders, however, were in turn deeply in debt to trading houses in Luanda which extended them credit and supplied their trade goods in exchange for the small amount of primary agricultural products they were able to collect. Before the coffee boom most traders were forced to subsist on manioc or on game they shot themselves, and their standard of living was only marginally superior to that of the African population. The typical trading post consisted of a small two-story wooden frame building with the post store on the first floor and the trader's one- or two-room living quarters on the second. The only appreciable advantage held by the Portuguese trader was his *não-indígena* status, which enabled him to obtain a trading license and establish financial arrangements with other Europeans. Before the postwar rise in coffee prices few small traders had the financial resources to start direct production, and most new immigrants had little money when they arrived. As the price of coffee increased, however, the traders began to see the possibility of greater profits in direct cultivation of coffee which had formerly been collected by Africans. Traders in the northern region began to claim coffee trees near

[32] Childs, *Umbundu Kinship*, p. 191.

their trading posts as their own property and hired African contract laborers to clear the underbush and harvest the crop. Financing of direct cultivation was usually secured by using the trading post as collateral, although later the colonial agricultural development bank advanced loans against the potential crop. During the initial period of the boom many of the traders invested heavily in new plantings and expanded their claims to include any African holdings which happened to be nearby. At coffee prices of the mid-fifties direct cultivation became immensely lucrative, especially in comparison with profits from trade. In 1958 Alfredo de Sousa[33] estimated that the average cost of production in direct cultivation was 15.37 escudos per kilogram. At the average price f.o.b. Angola of 19.33 escudos per kilogram (see Table 4.1), in 1958 this would have yielded an average profit of almost 4 escudos per kilogram. Assuming the same production costs for the peak-price year of 1954 yields a net profit of 14 escudos per kilogram. Since the typical northern producer in this period had a yield of approximately 350 kilograms per hectare and the typical estate was approximately 250 hectares in size, the net profit for a producer in 1958 would have been 350,000 escudos, or approximately US $12,000.[34] The same estimation procedure in terms of 1954 prices yields an incredible profit of 1,225,000 escudos, or approximately US $42,600. For the Portuguese bush trader or peasant immigrant even the lower 1958 figure was more money than he was likely to see in a decade, and the profits touched off a scramble for new acreage and a wave of new immigration to the coffee area. Most of the immigrants were relatives of the original bush traders, and many took jobs as foremen on established plantations and then branched out to establish their own estates. The European population of the principal coffee areas expanded dramatically. The European population of the township of Uíge, for example, increased from 342 in 1950 to 2,462 in 1960, and the township of Dembos increased from 317 to 1,247.[35] The town of Uíge in the center of the northern coffee area, which had only 11 commercial establishments and a few brush and mud buildings in 1946, expanded to a sizeable town with 179 commercial establishments, modern buildings, and electricity by 1956.[36] Many bush traders felt that after years of unrewarding trade the millenium had finally arrived and rushed to invest in consumer goods including foreign automobiles and even refrigerators, which, considering the absence of electrification in the area, were of limited utility. Most traders

---

[33] Alfredo de Sousa, *Ensaio de Análise Económica do Café,* Junta de Investigações do Ultramar, Estudos de Ciêncas Políticas e Sociais, no. 17 (Lisbon, 1958), pp. 25–36.
[34] The United Nations Sub-Committee on Foreign Economic Interests in Portuguese Territories used slightly different figures and estimated the net income of a coffee estate at US $7,000 in the year 1957. See United Nations, "Agricultural and Processing Industries in Angola," p. 71.
[35] Calculated from data presented in Angola, Direção dos Serviços de Estatística, *Recenseamento Geral da População 1950,* vol. 2 (Luanda: Imprensa Nacional), pp. 68–85; *1960,* vol. 1, pp. 35–42.
[36] Richard J. Houk, "Recent Developments in the Portuguese Congo," *Geographical Review,* 48 (April 1958), 201–221.

expanded their trading posts or built new ranch style villas on the site of their new coffee groves and of course invested large sums in improving their estates. Jorge Vieira da Silva, a former secretary of agriculture for Angola, visited a small bush trader near Uíge in 1952 at the beginning of the boom. The trader, who had been subsisting largely on manioc before the boom, offered Silva an elaborate lunch on the porch of his trading post and declared that he now felt northern Angola was the new garden of Eden.[37] The expansive prosperity of the boom years was of course short lived. By 1959 prices had fallen to the level of production costs, and they continued to fall, reaching the disastrous level of 11.88 escudos per kilogram in 1962. Since most of the bush traders had gone into substantial debt to take advantage of the seemingly limitless profits of the boom years, these price levels meant bankruptcy. The outbreaks of the nationalist revolt in 1961 threatened the entire coffee crop, and from that point on the maintenance of the small northern growers became as much political as an economic question. The Ministry of Agriculture continued to advance loans even to owners who were in default on previous harvests, and more than 80 percent of northern producers became dependent on government support for their survival. The price of labor increased 40 percent between 1960 and 1962, largely as a result of labor reforms introduced after the rebellion, and the prices prevailing in the 1960s returned coffee production to its previous marginal position in the northern region.

Even the substantial profits of the boom years, however, were based on two aspects of agricultural organization which were inextricably linked to colonial rule—the forced expropriation of native lands at little or no cost and the forced recruitment of African labor. Land at the beginning of the boom was virtually free for the taking by any European, and the initial capital requirements would have been substantially increased if the lands had been purchased from Africans. Similarly, the cost of indigenous labor would have been greatly increased had there been anything resembling a free labor market for Africans in Angola. Even de Sousa admits that the profitability of Angolan estate production depended on an artificially depressed price of labor, and he includes in his calculations fringe benefits seldom paid by northern producers.[38] Colonial policies toward indigenous land and labor made the settler estate possible, and without them African small holders would have been the principal beneficiaries of the boom.

LAND POLICY   The fundamental objective of colonial land policies in Angola has always been to attract a large settler population by offering special privileges to Portuguese immigrants. Although the Portuguese government is publicly committed to an uncompromising defense of lands habitually occupied by the indigenous population, this principle has frequently been sacrificed for the convenience of Portuguese settlers. Colonial administrations have encouraged the development of African family farms, but settler agriculture has always been

[37] Interview, Berkeley, Calif., June 1973.
[38] Sousa, *Económica do Café*, p. 31.

seen as a primary determinant of Angolan development, and land legislation has reflected this emphasis. The current land policy of Angola dates to 1901, when all land which was not considered private property under Portuguese law was declared state domain. Uncultivated lands could be claimed by settlers under a system of state-supervised concessions designed to discourage speculation and encourage orderly development. The concession system, however, applied only to Portuguese citizens and Africans who had satisfied the requirements of *assimilado* status, and the fundamental colonial distinction between the indigenous and nonindigenous populations became the basis for two distinctly different systems of property rights. Under land legislation for the nonindigenous population most agricultural land was governed by a system of concessions called *aforamento*, which granted limited usufruct rights until development requirements had been satisfied. Any Portuguese settler or other European willing to abide by Portuguese law could apply for an *aforamento* concession simply by filing a claim with the land survey office. The claim included a rough outline map of the boundaries of the claim and, if the request was for 100 hectares or more, a description of the plans for development and the financial resources of the applicant. After a cadastral survey by the claims office the land could be recognized as a provisional concession which gave the holder the right to occupy and exploit the land in exchange for a nominal quit rent of from 1 to 10 escudos per hectare per year. A provisional concession could be converted into a definitive concession after a period of five years if the holder of the concession demonstrated that he had satisfied development requirements. Before 1961 these requirements were satisfied if at least 10 percent of the land was under cultivation or if permanent structures for specialized economic purposes had been erected on the land. The definitive concession gave the holder in effect complete private property rights, and the land could be freely bought and sold, used as collateral for a loan, and bequeathed to heirs.

In theory no concession was to infringe on the traditional land rights of the indigenous population, and before the provisional concession was granted, the land survey office was required to determine whether the concession included any African lands. While traditional African land rights were recognized in the 1901 legislation, they were vaguely specified, and a 1919 Angolan decree further weakened African claims. The decree permitted expropriations of native lands if the native population were resettled in reserve areas or if it was simply moved to another area within the concession. Most of the large plantations established at the turn of the century were based on these vague specifications, and land expropriations reached a large scale by 1920. In 1923, however, Norton de Matos, the high commissioner for Angola, recognized the abuses of the system and issued a decree which specified that the land rights of the indigenous population extended to an area five times that which they traditionally occupied and such lands could not be included in a concession. Land in these reserves was to be governed by traditional custom and usage, could not be sold to outsiders, and remained under the control of lineage and tribal authorities. In the areas of indigenous occupation, land was held under traditional communal tenure, and usufruct rather than absolute property rights were recognized. The specifications of habitual occupation provided at best an ambiguous definition of traditional zones of African cultivation. Most traditional agriculture both in the manioc areas of the north and maize areas of the central plateau is based on shifting, slash-and-burn techniques which made continuous cultivation the exception rather than the rule. Typically forest and grass are burned off and the ashes used for fertilizer. The land is then planted with subsistence crops which are rotated annually for three or four years before the area is left to fallow. The fallow period in the fragile tropical soils of Angola may need to be as long as 10 or 20 years, and during this period the land reverts to its natural vegetation with little or no sign of human occupation. The slash-and-burn system requires that villages be moved frequently so that neither cultivated fields nor permanent structures may be present to delineate areas of traditional African lands. These substantial ambiguities in legislation concerning indigenous land rights were not a serious problem as long as Portuguese settlement was largely urban and most agricultural concessions were limited to a few coastal plantations. The hinterland could be considered an area of traditional African exploitation, and the few concessions requested could be decided on an ad hoc basis. During the land rush of the coffee boom, however, the legislation proved to be almost worthless in protecting the African population.

While some effort was made to guarantee traditional communal land rights, individual landholding by Africans was extremely limited both in law and in practice. The Native Statue of 1954 which codified the distinction between indigenous and nonindigenous status also specified the conditions under which Africans could come into possession of individually owned land. They could of course opt for Portuguese law but only if they had attained *assimilado* status. Africans living in the traditional milieu could only obtain property rights by completing a lengthy and complex process of title registration. The conditions for obtaining title were considerably more stringent for Africans than for Portuguese citizens. While a Portuguese citizen needed to demonstrate only five years occupation of a provisional concession, an African had to demonstrate that he had cultivated an area for a continuous period of 10 years. Even a single-year break in cultivation could cause forfeiture of all rights. In addition, the African was required to keep the entire area of his potential property under cultivation, while the Portuguese citizen was required to cultivate only 10 percent of his provisional holding. Cultivation in this instance meant not simply tending a few spontaneous coffee bushes or practicing slash-and-burn agriculture, but keeping land permanently cleared and planted in crops or converting spontaneous growths to cultivated crops with proper spacing and weeding. Even if an African cultivator could satisfy these conditions he was still required to produce an official document (written, of course, in Portuguese) describing the area in question, have this document validated by a colonial official, and finally have the claim certified by the land survey office. At this point the African was issued a certificate of title, called the *Môdelo J*. Even the *Môdelo J,* however, did not represent full title, but usufruct rights only. In order, according to one Portuguese source, to counteract the "peculiar improvidence of the primitive peoples," [39] land held under *Môdelo J* title could not be used as collateral for a loan and could not be sold to a member of the nonindigenous population without the consent of the colonial administration. These limitations effectively eliminated any incentive to develop the land, since few Africans had any collateral other than land. Needless to say, few Africans ever satisfied the formidable requirements for individual ownership, and in fact it is doubtful if they were ever intended to do so. The policy of encouraging African small holders was in direct conflict with the need for labor on public works and on the coffee estates. An African farmer who had obtained the *Môdelo J* was exempt from forced labor and therefore the greater the number of recognized indigenous cultivators, the smaller the amount of labor available for European farms. The local *chefe de pôsto* was responsible for enforcing both land and labor regulations, and he was likely to be receptive to settlers' interests, if not actually directly bribed by them. As a result conflict between property rights for Africans and forced labor for Europeans was usually resolved in favor of the latter. The conflict between small holder certification and labor requirements was particularly acute in the northern coffee zone. Malcolm McVeigh, a Methodist missionary who served in the area between 1958 and 1961, reports that local administrators were extremely reluctant to grant the *Môdelo J* because of pressure from settlers for cheap labor.[40] While administrative regulations required that an African with 5,000 coffee plants be classified as a individual landowner, McVeigh found many Africans with 10,000 to 12,000 coffee plants in the Dembos township who were unable to obtain the *Môdelo J*. They were therefore forced to work on European coffee estates for about 35 cents a day. McVeigh claimed that the only way that an African coffee farmer could actually obtain the *Môdelo J* was to obtain the consent of his employer, which, naturally enough, he was extremely reluctant to grant. Even Portuguese sources document the limited prospects of individual land ownership for African farmers. The *Boletim Geral do Ultramar* reported that by the year 1957 only 155 African cultivators in the township of Uíge (which at that time included the townships of Uíge, Songo, and Bembe as they are shown in Map 4.1) had obtained the *Môdelo J,* even though the same source estimated that there were 9,688 indigenous coffee producers in the township at the time.[41]

Whatever the legal merits of the colonial land regulations, they seem to have had very little practical effect in northern Angola during the period of the

---

[39] A. de Sousa Franklin, "The Portuguese System of Protecting Native Landed Property," *Journal of African Administration,* January 1957, p. 20.
[40] Malcolm McVeigh, "Labor in Chains," *Africa Today,* 8 (October 1961), p. 9.
[41] Portugal, Agência Geral do Ultramar, "A Demarcação de Terrenos do Estado no Distrito do Congo," *Boletim Geral do Ultramar,* 35 (March 1959), pp. 63–70.

coffee boom. During the 1950s the process of certification of European concessions fell hopelessly behind the actual demand for land, and many coffee farmers worked their lands for years without any legal certification or inspection by the colonial government. The *Boletim Geral do Ultramar's* report on land concessions in the district of the Congo (which included the districts of Uíge and Zaire in Map 4.1) documented the collapse of the land registration process. Between 1954 and 1957, 989 requests for concessions were filed with the land survey office, almost all of them for coffee cultivation, but only 53 provisional concessions were granted in the same period.[42] In the principal coffee-producing areas land was frequently occupied by force and estate owners and traders generally annexed whatever coffee land they thought they could successfully defend. Most estate owners were armed with heavy elephant guns and maintained small staffs of professional hunters for their estates. Shoot-outs between these small-scale armies were not uncommon. The northern land rush resembled the California gold rush of a century before, complete with claim jumping, shoot-outs, and frontier justice.[43] The tiny Portuguese colonial administration in the northern region was hard pressed to keep track of the complicated litigation and conflict arising out of the land claims and could do little to control them. Despite the land conflicts coffee production expanded rapidly, and as the United Nations report on land tenure in the Portuguese territories observes, "an anomalous situation resulted in which Angola reached a high level of prosperity largely based on the illegal occupation of land." [44]

Since even Portuguese land claims depended on force, the unarmed African producers were at an overwhelming disadvantage. Even in the unlikely event that they appealed to the *chefe de pôsto* for help against settler expropriations, the settlers could always argue that the African claim was not registered or that the land had been abandoned. Without arms or legal protection the African population saw vast areas of its property pass into Portuguese hands in a remarkably brief period of time. In the township of Uíge (1961 boundaries), the leading coffee-producing township, there were a total of 116 requests for provisional concessions in the year 1955. The total area of the concessions, 19,366 hectares in this year alone, represented 10 percent of the *total* land area of the township.[45]

---

[42] *Ibid.*

[43] I am indebted to Jorge Vieira da Silva, former minister of Agriculture for Angola, and Eduardo Cruz de Carvalho, former director of the Angolan agricultural census for valuable background information on social conditions in the coffee regions during this period.

[44] United Nations, General Assembly, 20th Session, Special Committee on the Situation with Regard to the Implementation of the Declaration on the Granting of Independence to Colonial Countries and Peoples, *Report of the Special Committee*, chap. V, "Territories under Portuguese Administration," app. II "Concession, Occupation and Settlement of Land in Angola and Mozambique" A/6000/add. 3 (part II), agenda item 23 (New York, 1965), p. 31.

[45] Calculated from data presented in Angola, *Boletim Oficial de Angola*, Suplemento: Repartição Central dos Serviços Geográficos e Cadastrais, Series 3, no. 52 (Luanda, December 1957).

Since the rate of concession remained relatively constant between 1954 and 1957, the total area claimed by settlers in that period would have represented 40 percent of the total land area of the district. Obviously such large-scale land expropriations must have caused substantial displacements of the indigenous population. Assuming that the 477,888 indigenous inhabitants of the district were evenly distributed and that the concessions were actually put into cultivation, almost 5,000 Africans would have been displaced in the year 1955 alone. The situation in the Dembos township of Cuanza Norte, the second most important coffee-producing township, was even more disastrous for the African population. In 1955 almost 16 percent of the total land area of the district was claimed in concession applications. Again assuming equal population distribution and complete cultivation, these expropriations would have resulted in the displacement of 10,000 Africans in 1955. If the same rate persisted through the peak years 1954 to 1957 almost two-thirds of the township land area would have been claimed and almost 40,000 people displaced. Actually not all European claims were worked, and some were held for speculative purposes. On the other hand, land concessions were not limited to the years 1954 to 1957, and population tended to be concentrated in areas close to trading posts and hence to the sites of future coffee estates, so that these estimates may be conservative.

While the *chefe de pôsto* would seldom be of any help to Africans attempting to defend their lands, he could be of considerable assistance to settlers attempting to clear African "squatters" from their concessions. Official colonial policy in northern Angola had favored the consolidation of African villages along the principal roads outside the coffee groves located in forested areas.[46] Initially these relocations were justified as a means of asserting greater administrative control over the dispersed indigenous population and later as part of a campaign to eradicate sleeping sickness, which was endemic in the northern forests. Resettlement was also encouraged by the colonial policy of discouraging slash-and-burn cultivation and encouraging stable communities of agriculturalists. Any combination of these reasons could therefore be used to justify administrative intervention in settlers' attempts to separate Africans from their lands. The *chefe de pôsto* could order villages moved from prime coffee areas on the grounds that he was combating sleeping sickness, encouraging stable agriculture, or facilitating taxation and be amply justified under colonial regulations. The settlers, of course, would be the beneficiaries of these administrative moves. In 1957 a group of African dissidents from São Salvador in the district of Zaire in northern Angola complained of just such practices in a protest directed to the Secretary General of the United Nations.[47] They complained that entire villages were moved by administrative authorities and that villages whose inhabitants could not move themselves were burned to the ground. Standing crops belonging

---

[46] Jorge Vieira da Silva, interview, Berkeley, Calif., June 1973.
[47] "Statement to the Secretary General of the United Nations," in Ronald H. Chilcote (ed.), *Emerging Nationalism in Portuguese Africa: Documents* (Stanford, Calif.: Hoover Institution Press, 1972), p. 47.

to the inhabitants of the former villages were then seized by the Portuguese under the pretext that they were abandoned properties. The protest indicates that these practices had begun in the 1930s and had continued to the date of the protest (1957). The officially recorded actions of the colonial government itself reveal similar instances of administrative assistance in resettling Africans in the coffee regions. While the concept of native reserve had long existed in colonial theory, few such reserves were actually established until the 1950s. In the mid-fifties five African reserves were established on the fringes of the main coffee areas and substantial numbers of Africans were resettled in them. In the township of Quiculungo in Cuanza Norte, for example, 5,300 Africans were resettled in a native reserve consisting of only 4,100 hectares.[48] These reserves served to relieve some of the pressure in the coffee regions, but large numbers of Africans found that they had suddenly become squatters on European estates and were faced with the alternative of moving to whatever free land they could find or becoming estate laborers. Given the immense demand for labor in the principal coffee regions and the coercive power of the settlers, many of the former landowners were in fact forced into the role of laborers on lands that had recently belonged to them. Many Africans lost their coffee groves to Europeans, although the protection of the Angolan coffee board enabled a substantial minority of small holders to continue production.

LABOR POLICY   The land expropriated by Portuguese settlers would have been of little value in estate agriculture without an assured supply of low-cost labor. To a large extent this labor was supplied by a system of direct or indirect administrative compulsion applied to the indigenous population. While forced labor was not uncommon in colonial Africa, Portugal tended to continue such practices longer than other colonial powers, and the extent of compulsory labor in Angola has long been a subject of international controversy. In part this controversy reflects the close alliance between Portugal and England, since much of the criticism has come from English missionaries and reformers. While Portugal formally abolished slavery in its colonies in 1878, an English critic, Henry Nevinson, charged in 1906 that a form of slavery persisted in labor recruitment for the cocoa island of São Tomé.[49] The publication of his criticisms initiated a popular campaign to force English chocolate manufacturers to boycott São Tomé cocoa. A similar controversy was stirred up by Edward Alsworth Ross's report to the League of Nations in 1925 which charged that forced labor amounting to slavery and involving women and children was widely used in both public and private enterprises in Angola.[50] The British muckraking tradition was revived in 1955 by the journalist Basil Davidson, who charged that forced labor continued to be recruited by colonial authorities on behalf of commercial in-

[48] United Nations, Special Committee, "Concession, Occupation, and Settlement of Land in Angola and Mozambique," p. 29.
[49] Henry W. Nevinson, *A Modern Slavery* (London: Harper, 1906).
[50] Edward Alsworth Ross, *Report on Employment of Native Labor in Portuguese Africa* (New York: Abbott Press, 1925).

terests.[51] In 1959, in part in response to growing international pressure, Portugal ratified the forced labor convention of the International Labor Organization which was to take effect in Angola one year later, in November 1960. Three months later the government of Ghana filed a complaint with the ILO charging that forced labor practices continued in Portuguese Africa in contravention of the convention and demanded an investigation. The ILO conducted an exhaustive inquiry which included a trip to the Portuguese colonies and a long list of witnesses on both sides of the issues.[52] As had been the case in past controversies involving forced labor, Portuguese spokesmen denied all charges and maintained that whatever abuses had existed had been rectified by recent changes in colonial regulations. While the ILO report might have been expected to provide a relatively objective examination of compulsory labor in Angola, it actually produced a very limited set of findings dealing only with the period since the forced labor convention had taken effect, i.e., from November 1960 to the date of the report, April 1962. While most complaints by Angolan Africans, British missionaries, and representatives of African governments focused on forced labor conditions in the northern coffee regions in the mid-fifties, the ILO report excluded both the period and the region from its final recommendations. The ILO delegation did not visit Angola until December 1961, nine months after a substantial rebellion had broken out in the coffee regions, a rebellion based in part on just those labor abuses which had been mentioned in the Ghana complaint. Because of the revolt Portuguese colonial officials insisted that they could not provide security in the northern coffee region. The only coffee estate actually visited by the commission was CADA's Boa Entrada, the largest and most modern estate in Angola. As Irene van Dongen has pointed out, CADA's labor policies are unusual not only for Angola but for tropical Africa as a whole, and it has acquired a reputation for providing medical treatment, education, and housing for its workers in addition to paying reasonable wages and maintaining acceptable working conditions.[53] Labor in the northern coffee regions of Angola has not in fact been studied by any non-Portuguese since the beginning of the 1961 rebellion.

After the 1961 revolt the relatively liberal Overseas Minister Adriano Moreira introduced a series of reforms designed to eliminate forced labor entirely and establish a free labor market for the African population. While Moreira's 1962 labor code included stiff penalties for administrators who used compulsion in the recruitment of labor for any purpose, it is debatable whether these latest reforms have had any substantial effect in practice. Moreira himself was fired as overseas minister in December 1962, and Portuguese colonial policy since that time has become more oriented toward military pressure than to inter-

---

[51] Basil Davidson, *The African Awakening* (London: Alden Press, 1955).
[52] International Labour Office, "Report of the Commission Appointed under Article 26 of the Constitution of the International Labour Organization to Examine the Complaint Filed by the Government of Ghana Concerning the Observance by the Government of Portugal of the Abolition of Forced Labour Convention, 1957 (No. 105)," *Official Bulletin*, 45 (April 1962).
[53] Van Dongen, "Coffee Trade," pp. 338–339.

nal reform.[54] In 1972 the Angola Committee of the Netherlands published what it claimed was a secret report to the Portuguese government from Afonso Mendes, who from 1962 to 1970 was director of the Angolan Labor Institute established by the Moreira reforms.[55] According to the committee the report had been written to suggest counterinsurgency strategies to the colonial administration. In the report Mendes points out that forced labor abuses supposedly eliminated by the 1962 reforms continued on a large scale despite stiff penalties and suggests, reasonably enough, that these continued abuses were a major source of rebel support in Angola.

Whatever the status of indigenous labor within Angola since the ratification of the forced labor convention in 1960 or the adoption of Moreira's labor code in 1962, it seems reasonably clear that in the period of the coffee boom a system of at least indirect forced labor was an important factor in the economic survival of the northern coffee estates. The labor legislation of this period is based on the native labor codes of 1899 and 1928, which expressed the fundamental principle of Portuguese colonial labor policy—the moral obligation to work. In the words of the 1899 labor code, "All the natives of the overseas Portuguese provinces are subject to the moral and legal obligation of acquiring through work the means they lack, to subsist and improve their own social condition. They have complete liberty to choose the mode by which they fulfill this obligation, but if they do not fulfill it in some way, public authority can impose its fulfillment." [56] Like colonial land policy, the labor code was based on the distinction between the indigenous and nonindigenous population, and the "moral and legal obligation" to work applied only to the latter. While in practice the labor code established a system of compulsory labor for the benefit of the nonindigenous population, in colonial theory it was justified as part of the civilizing mission of the Portuguese. J. M. da Silva Cunha, colonial labor expert for the Salazar regime, wrote in 1949 that state compulsion was justified, since "the state imposes with the threat of death many other obligations which are less legitimized by the interests of civilization, so why should it not impose this obligation on these rude Negroes of Africa, on these ignorant pariahs of Asia and on these half-savages of Oceania." [57] Under the native labor codes the "rude Negroes" of Angola were required to demonstrate that they were employed or face compulsory labor. The 1928 labor code required that every member of the indigenous population subject to recruitment carry a "native work book" (*caderneta indígena*) which contained a complete record of his tax and work status. The *caderneta* could be requested by any colonial official, and, if the work on tax records was unsatisfactory, the bearer could be subjected to forced labor. Since

[54] John Marcum, *The Angolan Revolution*, vol. 1, 1950–1962 (Cambridge, Mass.: M.I.T. Press, 1969), pp. 314–315.

[55] Angola Comité, *Petition by the Angola Comité, Concerning the Report of Mr. Pierre Juvigny Regarding the Implementation of the Abolition of Forced Labour Convention, 1957 (No. 105) by Portugal,* annex II, "The Reality in Angola" (Amsterdam, 1972).

[56] Quoted in International Labour Office, "Report of the Commission," p. 147.

[57] Joaquim Moreira da Silva Cunha, *O Trabalho Indígena* (Lisbon: Agência Geral das Colónias, 1949), p. 157, translated by Robert Stam.

the employer, whether state or private, was responsible for making entries in the *caderneta*, the worker was ultimately dependent on his employer for protection against forced labor. The 1928 code restricted forced labor to healthy males between the ages of 14 and 60, and later regulations provided exemptions for any indigenous inhabitant who could demonstrate that he had been employed by a European for nine months or more in a given year or who had satisfied the Agricultural Ministry's requirements for certification as a stable cultivator. The 1928 code also restricted the application of administrative compulsion to public works. Any use of administrative authority for recruiting labor for private enterprises was to be strictly forbidden. The long list of applicable public activities, however, provided a considerable number of loopholes for local officials with an interest in satisfying private demands for labor. Administrative compulsion could be used to recruit labor for repairs during natural calamities, for the cleaning of native living quarters, for water conservation in native areas, for the maintenance of roads between native settlements, for the extermination of harmful insects, and for the cultivation of areas in the indigenous reserves.[58] The last provision in particular was used by private companies to institute a system of compulsory cotton cultivation in the district of Malanje.[59] Forced labor could also be ordered for any violation of the criminal statutes and in lieu of voluntary payment of the native tax. In fact the head of the Angolan Native Affairs department admitted that as late as 1959 a worker might be forced to work from 65 to 100 days a year if he lacked the cash to pay the native tax.[60] All these provisions of the native labor code remained in effect until at least 1960. The labor code provided no mechanism for redress of African grievances and provided even less protection for Africans than did the system of land regulations. According to Afonso Mendes, in his book *O Trabalho Assalariado em Angola*, laborers were typically rounded up by sepoys attached to the local administrative post, or the local *regedor* was pressured by the *chefe de pôsto* to produce the requisite numbers. Even Mendes, writing as a head of the Angolan Labor Institute, admits that the system led to considerable violence. Other sources including British missionaries and journalists are considerably more explicit and describe beatings of *regedores* by *chefes*, nighttime raids of sepoys on villages, and brutal treatment of laborers.[61] In fact Mendes points out that administrative authorities frequently used the threat of recruitment for forced labor to control African behavior they considered questionable. Whatever relief the African population enjoyed under the native labor codes came more from the slack demand for labor than from any explicit protection under the law. Before the coffee boom there was little demand for labor outside of public works, and internal improvements were in general limited to those necessary for administrative control.

[58] *Ibid.*, p. 256.
[59] *Ibid.*, pp. 257–260.
[60] International Labour Office, "Report of the Commission," p. 174.
[61] McVeigh, "Labor in Chains," pp. 9–11; Davidson, *African Awakening*, pp. 197–214; and Sid Gilchrist, *Angola Awake* (Toronto: Ryerson Press, 1968), pp. 25–33.

During the period of the boom, however, the demand for labor reached extraordinary proportions. At the same time that massive land expropriations were taking place in the northern coffee regions, vast numbers of additional laborers were needed to work the new estates. The numbers recorded in official Portuguese statistics suggest that in the most important coffee-producing townships virtually the entire male labor force must have been mobilized to satisfy the demands of the coffee estates. In 1958, for example, in the township of Uíge, there were reported to have been a total of 9,444 laborers on European estates out of a total male indigenous population which amounted to only 25,237 at the time of the 1960 census.[62] since only about half of the Angolan population falls into the legally recruitable age range of 14 to 60, these figures indicate that more than three-quarters of all eligible males in the township were involved in labor on coffee estates. At the same time, however, there was a total of 2,928 tons of coffee produced in the township by indigenous cultivators.[63] Since the typical African cultivator holds at most 2 hectares and African yields are lower than European, the typical African would produce at most about half a ton of coffee. If this estimate is correct, there would have been approximately 5,800 individual African coffee producers in the Uíge township in 1958. Thus the total number of individual African coffee cultivators plus the total number of laborers on European estates considerably exceeded the African male population between the ages of 14 and 60. Settlers would therefore have found it necessary to either recruit women, children, and old men or force some of the indigenous coffee cultivators to work part time on their estates. It is likely that all these sources of labor were used to some extent, and the number of laborers recorded in official statistics does not count transients needed for the four-month harvest period. Since the total labor force more than doubles during this period, the harvest must have required the mobilization of almost the entire adult population of the township, the recruitment of outside labor, or both. Similar computations for the Dembos township in Cuanza Norte indicate that the demand for labor was, if anything, even greater than in Uíge.[64] In the northern coffee region virtually the entire population was affected by the demand for estate labor, and there would have been very few families without someone involved in estate labor for at least part of the year.

The extraordinary demand for labor required vastly expanded recruitment efforts by both estate owners and their allies in the colonial administration. Most of the abuses cited by witnesses in the ILO commission hearings involve labor recruitment in the northern coffee regions at the height of the boom.[65] One witness testified that he had seen *chefes de pôsto* round up Africans for European

[62] Angola, *Anuário Estatístico 1959*, pp. 94–95; Angola, *Recenseamento Geral da População 1960*, vol. 3, pp. 34–37.

[63] Angola, *Anuário Estatístico 1959*, pp. 94–95.

[64] The figures are 16,313 coffee laborers in 1958 out of a male indigenous population of 35,652 in 1960 and an estimated 7,090 African coffee producers in 1958.

[65] International Labour Office, "Report of the Commission," pp. 178–180.

employers every year from 1952 to 1958 in the area of the Bembe coffee plantations. A number of witnesses stated that in the northern coffee regions *chefes*
were regularly bribed to provide laborers for the settler estates. A substantial
number of witnesses described beatings of *regedores* who failed to provide the
necessary number of laborers. Other witnesses testified that the aged, women,
and children were regularly recruited for work on coffee plantations. The Portuguese colonial authorities responded that such practices were, of course, forbidden by law and, in any event, had not come to the attention of the relevant
Angolan authorities. It seems likely that some such measures were in fact used
in the coffee regions, since the total mobilization of the population could hardly
have been accomplished without them.

While direct administrative intervention by the colonial authorities and the
use of native auxiliaries to round up laborers were formerly illegal under the
1928 labor statutes, the law did not prevent local officials from using the forced
labor regulations to place indirect pressure on reluctant workers. Since the demands of the estates were rapidly exhausting the available population in the
northern region, to say nothing of the available labor supply, a class of independent labor recruiters developed to import contract laborers from other areas in
Angola. The labor contractors used methods remarkably similar to the *enganche*
system in Peru. The contractor would advance small loans, provide potential
workers with expensive gifts, particularly bicycles, or get them drunk on palm
wine before inviting them to sign a labor contract. A bonus called the *mata-bicho*
which amounted to from two to four months salary was paid for singing the
contract. The term of the contract was usually for one year, and the labor code
permitted penal sanctions to be applied to workers violating its terms. In general,
the independent contractors attempted to establish good relations with both the
local Portuguese and African authorities and often followed the traditional
African practice of sponsoring a substantial feast for the inhabitants of a village
before attempting to recruit laborers. While the recruitment was supposedly
voluntary and, unlike the activities of the *chefe*, did not involve the direct application of force, it depended on the implicit threat of forced public labor. Labor
recruiters frequently bribed local authorities to increase their demands for public
works labor in order to encourage workers to sign up as contract laborers on
the coffee estates. Since the estate labor was generally less onerous and better
paid than work on the roads or other public works, most Africans who could
not otherwise avoid recruitment elected to sign "voluntary" contracts with labor
recruiters. The numerous legal justifications for the use of forced labor for public purposes provided the local administration officials with a variety of techniques for aiding the contractors while appearing to enforce the colonial labor
regulations. As one former Portuguese colonial official notes, "A very demanding
civil servant in any area was a great asset for a contractor, and so the civil servant was paid to be demanding. . . . If you know how the [legal] system works
it is very easy to see how it could be put to use for a second purpose." [66]

[66] Eduardo Cruz de Carvalho, interview, San Francisco, Calif., June 1973.

The labor contractor was an essential link between the estate owner and the laborer, and his importance increased as labor began to be sought at greater and greater distances from the coffee regions. While no precise figures are available on the number of migratory contract laborers at work in the coffee regions in the 1950s, the number was presumably substantial, given the ratio of coffee laborers to total local population in the principal producing townships. It is possible to roughly estimate the proportion of laborers from the Ovimbundu areas of Angola for 1960 from linguistic data in the 1960 census.[67] While contract laborers at first had been recruited from among the Kikongo-speaking tribes of the northern districts of Uíge and Zaire, the greatest population densities and largest untapped supply of labor were to be found among the Umbundu-speaking Ovimbundu on the central plateau. During the 1950s several disastrous maize harvests and a steadily increasing population combined to create greater incentives for contract labor in this region than elsewhere in Angola. By 1960 the census data indicate there were a total of 750 Umbundu-speaking males in the township of Uíge. Since there was no similar number of Umbundu-speaking women, it is reasonable to assume that almost all these men were migratory contract laborers rather than permanent settlers, who would have brought their families with them. Thus approximately 8 percent of the coffee labor in the Uíge township was supplied by Ovimbundu migrants. Similar calculations indicate that 55 percent of the total coffee labor force in the Dembos township was recruited from Umbundu-speaking areas. The proportion of Umbundu-speaking contract laborers increased dramatically after the 1961 uprising as Kikongo-speaking tribesmen native to the northern region fled across the border to the former Belgian Congo and were replaced by contract laborers from the central plateau. By 1964 Mendes reports that only 14 percent of the agricultural labor force in the Uíge district and 12 percent in the Cuanza Norte district were locally recruited.[68] Most of the remainder were Umbundu-speaking Ovimbundu from the central plateau. Most contract laborers, whether recruited from the central plateau or from the periphery of the northern coffee region were single males who viewed themselves as reluctant captives sentenced to a one-year term of duty. As Afonso Mendes points out, "The workers regard their work much as a young recruit regards military service—an obligation rather disagreeable, during which he will expend the minimum effort necessary. . . . [T]his state of mind, plus the eagerness to go home, contributes to the low productivity, which in turn contributes to the hostility and suspicion of the employers." [69] Despite the efforts of the labor contractors and colonial officials many of the "voluntary" contract laborers succeeding in escaping from the estates and returning home before the expiration of their one-year term. Mendes estimates that in the mid-fifties more than 64 percent of the labor force on the coffee estates he studied was replaced during the year.[70] The substantial turnover and the one-year term of the labor

[67] Angola, *Recenseamento Geral da População 1960*, vol. 3, pp. 84–93.
[68] Mendes, *O Trabalho Assalariado*, p. 60.
[69] *Ibid.*, p. 167.
[70] *Ibid.*, pp. 136–137.

contract inhibited class-based labor organizations, and most workers remained closely tied to their traditional tribe or language group, even during their period of work on the coffee estates. The tribal and linguistic division could be exploited by the estate owners, and during the 1961 uprising in particular the Portuguese claimed that Ovimbundu migrants, as well as settlers, were being attacked by the rebels. The Ovimbundu were the most vulnerable to such tactics since they were an isolated minority in the Bakongo and Mbundu coffee areas.

The involvement of both labor contractors and colonial authorities in recruiting labor for the coffee estates was a consequence of the failure of the prevailing wage rates to attract sufficient numbers of workers. Estimates of the daily wage paid in the northern coffee regions during the late 1950s range from 6 to 10 escudos, or from 20 to 35 cents, in cash and an approximately equal amount in food.[71] This wage is approximately the same as that prevailing on the sugar plantations in Peru at the same period, but the Peruvian plantations were able to attract workers even without the services of the *enganche*, while the coffee estate owners required both contractors and administrative sanctions. This difference between the two systems is a result of differences in the supply of labor under situations of open and closed agricultural resources. While in Peru plantation laborers were forced to accept subsistence wages because of the scarcity of sierra land, in Angola most Africans were able to support themselves in subsistence agriculture without outside employment. As Afonso Mendes has pointed out,[72] the prevailing wages in agricultural labor were hardly sufficient to attract Africans who could support themselves in subsistence agriculture with considerably less effort. In addition, the labor contracts required long separations from lineage and family groups and involved the harsh and often brutal discipline of the estate foreman. In the coffee regions the European land rush deprived many Africans of lands for subsistence, but at the same time many African coffee producers were increasing their earnings sufficiently to make estate labor even less attractive. It is apparent that compulsion will remain an integral part of the Angolan labor system as long as sufficient land is available to support subsistence production or until industry expands sufficiently to make higher wage levels possible. By the late 1960s land in the central plateau region was becoming scarce enough so that at least some workers were forced into contract labor for purely economic reasons. In most other areas of Angola, however, subsistence agriculture was still a viable alternative to wage labor.

[71] Sousa, *Económica do Café*, p. 31, estimates the monthly wage for coffee workers at 200 escudos in cash and an equal amount in food, clothing, and medical assistance. Sousa assumes 25 days of work per month, which would lead to a daily wage of 8 escudos in cash and an equal amount in other benefits. Mendes, *O Trabalho Assalariado*, p. 57, indicates that the average monthly cash salary for rural workers was 145.78 escudos in 1958. Assuming 25 working days per month, this could represent a daily cash wage of approximately 6 escudos. McVeigh, "Labor in Chains," p. 9, indicates an hourly cash wage of 35 cents, or 10 escudos per day.

[72] Mendes, *O Trabalho Assalariado*, pp. 43–46.

It is apparent that in a completely free labor market, either the labor contractor would be unnecessary or his role would be reduced to that of an employment bureau. In Angola in the 1950s, however, coffee estates were unable to pay a wage sufficient to attract voluntary laborers and still produce coffee cheaply enough to compete with small holders in Angola and elsewhere in Africa. Thus the importance of the contractor reflects the inefficiency of the northern coffee estates and the coercive quality of the Angolan labor market. The discrepancy between the free and forced labor markets is apparent in the relative size of the labor contractor's fee and the worker's wage. The labor contractor is paid 1,500 escudos per worker, while the average monthly salary of a coffee laborer is approximately 200 escudos in cash. The recruiter's fee represents more than seven months salary for the African worker. It is apparent that the recruiter was paid for his ability to manipulate the colonial administration and entrap laborers rather than for simply locating and transporting them. Even if the labor contractor had been eliminated and his fee paid directly to the worker, it is questionable whether many voluntary laborers would have appeared. If this had been the case, the estate owners would obviously have preferred to pay the higher wage and attract voluntary workers rather than the reluctant and unreliable conscripts provided by the labor recruiter. The absence of economic incentives required the direct or indirect application of force. The control of this force, like the control over land concessions, rested ultimately on the perpetuation of Portuguese colonial rule.

The contract laborers on the coffee estates were organized in a tightly disciplined chain of command similar to that of a military unit. A typical estate in the northern region employed from 300 to 500 workers organized into work gangs of from 10 to 15 men under the direction of an African overseer. The overseers in turn reported to a half dozen foremen responsible for organizing the daily work schedule and enforcing discipline in the work gangs. Foremen were usually Portuguese or *assimilados*, although sometimes Africans from remote tribes would be recruited as foremen. Pastoral Ovambo peoples were particularly favored as foremen, since they were contemptuous of sedentary peoples in general and northerners in particular. The foremen generally exercised political as well as economic control over the work force and were the effective representatives of the colonial administration on the estate. Disputes that were not handled by the workers themselves were settled by decree by the foremen. While foremen varied considerably in the severity of their discipline, corporal punishment, particularly beatings with the *chicote*, or leather whip, was not uncommon. Most foremen were conscious of tribal and lineage relationships among the workers and generally permitted kinsmen to work together in the same gangs. This policy reinforced the local and communal interest of the workers and tended to offset broader worker organizations. The work itself was organized in a system of prescribed daily tasks (*tarefa diária*) which in theory permitted the workers to complete their work at their own speed in a reasonable length of time. The system is well adapted to compulsory labor, since it tends to minimize the need for close supervision or highly motivated workers. Each worker was given a daily work quota which varied from one stage of the coffee production cycle to another and was permitted to stop work whenever the task was finished. In the Uíge district a typical daily task called for picking three 80-kilogram bags of coffee. There is considerable disagreement about how much time was actually required to complete the *tarefa diária*, with Portuguese sources claiming five to eight hours while African and missionary sources claim that 12 hours or more were required.[73] During the harvest period in particular the work was rigidly supervised, since failure to provide an adequate distribution of berries would lead to disruption of the hulling process and substantial crop losses.

Most estates maintained company stores or canteens, which were frequently simply the original trading post. As a result most workers saw little actual cash during their year term, and few returned with anything more than the initial bonus they had been paid to sign the contract. The estates maintained a revolving-door policy in which workers were paid at one end of the trading post and encouraged to buy consumer goods at the other. Frequently cash wages went no farther than the company store, and advances and indebtedness further reduced the worker's ability to profit from his term on the coffee estate. In fact some Portuguese officials actually justify this system on the grounds that it prevented the African workers from misusing the money in gambling or similar irresponsible pursuits.[74] In theory the workers' renumeration included housing and medical benefits, but in fact workers were often required to build their own huts when they arrived at the estates. Workers generally lived in traditional fashion, preparing their own meals and constructing their own local versions of village life.

SETTLERS, LABORERS, SMALL HOLDERS, CHIEFS

The organization of production, the land tenure system, and the forced labor practices in the northern coffee regions established economic and political interests on the part of estate owners, laborers, and African small holders which limited their interaction to a narrow range of alternatives. Consider first the interests of the coffee estate owner:

1. The northern coffee estate does not exist because of any appreciable economies of scale. Its labor organization is inefficient, and it controls no expensive processing machinery. From a purely economic standpoint the estates are inferior to small holdings, and the overall production of Angolan coffee would be unaffected if the estates were divided up into plots controlled by individual family farmers. In fact, given the inefficiency of the forced labor system, the demise of the estates might actually lead to an increase in production.

[73] International Labour Office, "Report of the Commission," pp. 208–212.
[74] Cruz de Carvalho, Vieira da Silva, interview, Berkeley, Calif., June 1973.

The productive efficiency of the northern estates cannot be improved by mechanization, since there is no practical way to apply machinery to coffee cultivation in the northern region. Wet processing techniques are not economically viable for robusta coffee, and the rough jungle terrain of the northern region makes the mechanization of weeding impractical. The relatively brief harvest period reduces the advantages to be gained from investments in processing machinery which must stand idle for two-thirds of the year. The northern region is not ecologically suited to combining coffee with traditional plantation crops such as sugar cane, so that evolution toward the plantation-like southern form of agricultural organization is unlikely. The northern estate owner, then, is confined to an inefficient productive organization with no practical alternatives for substituting capital for labor. An organized agrarian movement could demand the breakup of the estates without any loss in production, and the gains of an organized labor movement could not be offset by the installation of more efficient machinery. Thus any form of even moderate collective protest will be viewed as a threat to the continued economic survival of the northern coffee estates.

2. Even if the efficiency of the northern estates could be increased by improvements in the coffee groves themselves, the typical northern coffee farmer lacks the capital resources to carry out the improvements. Since the coffee farmers are either former bush traders or recent Portuguese peasant immigrants, they are invariably too poor to make capital improvements without increasing their indebtedness to either the coffee-exporting houses or the agricultural development bank. The period of coffee boom profits was too brief to permit extensive substantial accumulation of capital. The chronic scarcity of capital in the northern coffee region is reflected by the persistence of part-time trading activities by most estate owners. The scarcity of capital reduces the economic advantages of the Portuguese settler over the African small holder and limits his ability to replace laborers with machines. The poverty of the traders and settlers serves to increase their conflicts with both small holders and laborers.

3. The economic opportunities available to the Portuguese settler outside his estate are extremely limited. Even after the period of the boom the typical estate owner was able to afford a comfortable house and a staff of servants which would be beyond his means elsewhere. He held a position as a manager or proprietor and before the outbreak of the rebellion was assured of a reasonable degree of economic security. Without the coffee estate the owner would be faced with the prospects of returning to the role of bush trader, seeking employment in urban areas of Angola, or returning to metropolitan Portugal. The first option would obviously lead to the same precarious standard of living from which many of the estate owners had so recently escaped, and the other two alternatives are scarcely an improvement. The low level of economic development in Angola produces few middle-class occupational positions, and in most urban areas petty trade and service occupations are already oversupplied with Portuguese workers. Economic opportunities in the metropole are only slightly better, and in fact much of the Portuguese industrial labor force consists of migrants in more

industrialized areas of Europe. With no skills outside agriculture and with few contacts with commercial interests in Angola or Portugal, the estate owner's prospects for maintaining his status without his estate are negligible. Settlers from other European colonial powers were able to return to expanding industrial economies, but for settlers in Angola returning to the metropole was not a real option. For them Angola represented their last chance for economic success, and they had endured primitive frontier conditions and, in many cases, years of poverty to develop their estates. The limited options of the estate owners explain their stubborn resistance to any reforms which might threaten their position.

4. The economic marginality of the coffee estates, the general scarcity of capital, and the absence of economic opportunities outside agriculture forced the estate owners to rely on the system of ethnic stratification embodied in the Native Statute and expressed in the discriminatory system of land and labor regulations. Without the special privileges of land concessions and compulsory labor the northern coffee estates could not exist. Since these privileges rested in turn on the distinction between the indigenous and nonindigenous status, the settler estates could not survive in a political system controlled by the African majority. Thus the estate owner found it necessary to resist any attempts to share political power with the African population even at the cost of an indefinite period of guerrilla war. While large-scale plantation agriculture and major European corporations could find investment opportunities in Africa even under independent governments, the Angolan coffee estate owner had little to offer an independent regime and would be unlikely to survive a transfer of political power.

5. The substantial contribution of labor to total production costs and the need for compulsory labor led to a zero-sum conflict situation between owner and worker that could only be resolved by the direct application of force. The forced recruitment of labor and the *tarefa diária* system permit the owner to extract a minimum amount of low quality labor from a reluctant labor force. If increasing labor costs or falling prices threaten the owner's profit margin or adequate labor cannot be attracted, the only alternatives available to him are to increase the coercion of the system. There are a number of points at which pressure can be applied, including forced recruitment by administrative authorities, the tightening of labor discipline on the estate, or the expansion of the required daily task, but invariably such tactics will lead to increased rates of defection, poorer task performance, and sabotage and other acts of retaliation by workers. These problems in turn can only be controlled by a still greater application of force. The estate owner is therefore caught in a vicious circle of escalating violence whenever his profit margin is threatened. While in the short run the settler may be able to extract the necessary labor, in the long run he simply reinforces the violence of the colonial system and limits worker protests to a response in kind.

6. The use of force by settlers in either land seizures or labor recruitment is unlikely to be opposed by economic interests in either Angola or the metropole.

In Angola there are no substantial industrial interests which might favor more enlightened labor policies as the price of political stability, and the land-owning interests in the coffee regions represent the most important local interest group in the colony. In Peru the abuses of the sierran *hacendados* were ultimately checked by the growing political power of the industrial and commercial interests of the coastal export economy. In Angola settlers were faced with no similar internal opposition. Similarly, domestic political opposition in most European colonial nations made it difficult for settlers to demand substantial military support. In Portugal, until the coup of 1974, there was no domestic opposition to raise objections to indefinite colonial wars. Before the coup, the military and political elite of Portugal remained committed to the settlers in Angola even after the 1961 uprising. Military and political leaders in both the colony and the metropole displayed remarkable unanimity in carrying out what grew to become an immensely costly war. For 13 years the Angolan war evoked neither the internal political conflict nor the divisions in the military elite that accompanied the French involvement in Algeria. The existence of the northern coffee region became an extension of military policy, and the colonial government encouraged the settlement of former soldiers on abandoned estates for reasons of both security and economics. Despite their economic inefficiency and isolation the northern settlers had sufficient military backing to remain in control of their estates as long as Portugal did not withdraw its troops. Their survival after a Portuguese withdrawal, however, is unlikely in the extreme.

Ultimately, the use of military force by both the settlers and the Portuguese government is a reflection of economic weakness. Force was used by the settlers to establish estates which could not be maintained by economic means alone. Any economic or political threat had to be met with still greater applications of force. Falling prices required intensified labor coercion to reduce costs. The high price of legitimately acquired coffee land precipitated forced expropriations on a massive scale. The situation of open resources made a paid labor force impractical and created the legal obligation to work. Failure of local African authorities to cooperate with the forced labor system required more severe coercive pressure. Portugal was willing to hold on to its colonies even at the cost of indefinite warfare because the metropolitan economy lacked the capital necessary to compete with other foreign investors in independent Africa. In neighboring Zambia, British interests maintained a substantial control over copper mining even after independence and received lucrative management contracts even under a system of partial government control. Since even Diamang and the Benguela railroad are controlled by non-Portuguese capital, the Portuguese economic position in Angola is likely to be reduced to almost nothing if political control is surrendered to the African majority. As Basil Davidson has pointed out, increased foreign investment after 1965 has revealed clearly the dependent position of Portugal, itself, in the world economy.[75] Restrictions on foreign in-

[75] Basil Davidson, *In the Eye of the Storm: Angola's People* (Garden City, N.Y.: Doubleday, 1972), pp. 305–321.

vestment were relaxed in 1965 in order to provide additional revenues to partially offset the cost of the war. By 1974, however, Portugal had found itself in the unenviable position of fighting an expensive war to protect non-Portuguese economic interests.

Inevitably the settlers' attempt to attain economic objectives through military force has severely limited the tactics of the African opposition. A labor movement in the northern coffee estates is a logical contradiction. Since the principal weapon of the labor movement, the strike, involves withholding labor and Angolan labor is compulsory, it would be impossible for the laborers to strike without risking immediate penal sanctions. In any case, strikes are illegal in metropolitan Portugal, to say nothing of the colonies, and any attempt at a militant labor organization is likely to meet the fate of the brief strike of African dock workers in Portuguese Guinea in 1959. Portuguese troops fired into the strikers, killing more than 50. Land invasions would meet with a similarly sanguinary fate. Since the settlers used force to remove Africans from the land in the first place, they would hardly hesitate to use it to remove any Africans foolish enough to return to their original lands. The local colonial administration would not be likely to oppose violent eviction of land invaders, even if it did not actively assist the settlers. Market actions by the small number of African small holders would only work to the advantage of the dominant settler estates and are equally impractical. The African population then finds itself limited to the unappealing alternatives of acquiescence or violent resistance.

A number of considerations suggest that not only is revolutionary violence a probable consequence of the economic situation in the northern coffee region, but that this violence should be organized along communal rather than class lines. That is, the movement would be classified as revolutionary nationalist, rather than revolutionary socialist.

1. Since a relatively brief period of time elapsed between the consolidation of colonial rule and the expansion of the coffee economy, the traditional African political apparatus could still provide the organizational framework for a nationalist movement. Since the Portuguese administrative staff in the northern coffee regions was small and spread out over a large area, and few Europeans settled in the region before the boom, local political affairs were conducted largely by the Africans themselves with little outside interference. The traditional framework of family, lineage, and tribe remained an important element in land ownership, social structure, and to a lesser extent political organization until the beginning of the coffee boom. The African kingdoms of the northern coffee region had not been incorporated into any form of modern economic organization before the boom. The Portuguese demands for labor and land rapidly undermined the traditional tribal structure, but it remained powerful at the beginning of the coffee boom, particularly in those areas farthest from the ancient Portuguese kingdom of Angola. The Bakongo, the descendants of the ancient African kingdom of the Kongo, were the most important tribal group in the northern coffee region, and Bakongo leaders organized the most important nationalist

group in the north, the União das Populações de Angola (UPA). According to John Marcum, the UPA was formed by two factions of Bakongo exiles living in the Belgian Congo.[76] Both factions had been involved in the power struggles which surrounded the traditional Kongo monarchy. One faction had emerged from the struggle to appoint a king, independent of the Portuguese, at the death of Dom Pedro VII in 1955. The other faction was led by Manuel Barros Necaca, the son of Miguel Necaca, who had attempted to mediate the dispute between the Kongo monarchy and the rebel chief, Tulante Álvaro Buta, during the latter's 1913 rebellion. Manuel Necaca's nephew, Holden Roberto, eventually emerged as the leader of the Bakongo exiles in the Congo. At first the exiled Bakongo hoped to restore the ancient kingdom of the Kongo, and the party's original title, União das Populações do Norte de Angola, reflects this local and tribal emphasis. Later, under pressure from other African nationalists, the party changed its name and broadened its goals to include independence for all the African peoples of Angola. Nevertheless, the UPA's close ties to the Kongo monarchy limited its appeal to areas of Bakongo dominance, and it was never able to command support in either the heavily populated homeland of the Ovimbundu on the central plateau or in the Mbundu hinterlands of Luanda. The UPA did establish some influence in the areas of the former Mbundu kingdom of the Dembos, which like the Bakongo retained remnants of its original political apparatus and was subject to the economic pressures of the coffee economy. The UPA was essentially a rural, communal party whose origins reflected the persistence of traditional African political and social institutions in sparsely settled northern Angola. Significantly the UPA's principal rival in the Angolan nationalist movement, the Movimento Popular de Libertação de Angola (MPLA), developed in urban Luanda and among the Mbundu of the old kingdom of Angola, where assimilation was most advanced, few remnants of tribal social structure remained, and large numbers of Africans were involved in the money economy. The MPLA leadership was recruited from the ranks of urban intellectuals and *assimilados* and, unlike the UPA, stressed class rather than race as the basis of anti-Portuguese solidarity. The divergent social base and ideology of the two parties led to frequent clashes including at least one major military skirmish during the period of the guerrilla war. At the time of the 1961 uprising the MPLA remained largely an urban party, and the peasants and agricultural laborers of the northern coffee region were closely tied by kinship and tribal affiliation to the UPA. The migratory labor system and forced labor conditions of the coffee estates discouraged the development of a class-based associational interest group among the estate workers, so that the only effective organization available to direct resistance to the Portuguese was the traditional tribal structure or the communal party organization of the UPA.

2. The dominance of the African traditional authorities was reinforced by the system of communal land rights which persisted under colonial rule. Outside areas of European settlement, land continued to be controlled by lineage or tribe.

[76] Marcum, *Angolan Revolution*, pp. 56–64.

No individual property rights were recognized, and an individual's access to land depended ultimately on his kinship ties. The Portuguese land regulations tended to reinforce these traditional practices by making individual land ownership a practical impossibility for most Africans and by establishing the legal concept of native reserves in which customary law was to prevail. Until these policies were hastily jettisoned for the convenience of the settlers in the coffee regions, they tended to support communal rather than individual land ownership. In contrast to the indigenous Indian communities of Peru, the traditional tribal communities of Angola were not merely aggregates of individual small holders held together by a legal fiction, but were real communities based on collective ownership of land. Even African coffee growers depended in part on kinship to support their claims to their groves, since they could find little protection under Portuguese land law. The collective nature of the African subsistence economy tended to support a collective political organization, and no individual subsistence plots existed to create divisive economic interests. The resulting interest groups, however, were tribal and lineage organizations, not class-based associational interest groups. The development of the coffee export economy might have rapidly undermined this communal solidarity if it had led to the development of a small holder rather than an estate economy. Colonial land policies, however, undermined any security of tenure which might have permitted individual economic mobility, and reinforced the collective nature of the economy.

3. The development of the agricultural export economy did not split the social structure of African subsistence communities along lines of class or wealth. The traditional African kingdoms were stratified by class, and the royal lineage formed a distinct upper-class minority. The importance of these distinctions decreased under colonial rule, but divisions of wealth and access to land persisted and might have led to class cleavages within the African community. In the Ovimbundu regions of the central plateau, the coffee economy tended to reinforce the gap between ruling lineages and the rest of the population. *Regedores* and other tribal notables could earn substantial sums by assisting labor contractors and administrators in recruiting contract labor for the northern estates. They could either accept bribes from the contractors for finding laborers or extort payments from villagers for protection from labor recruitment. In the northern coffee regions such relationships tended to be disrupted by wholesale land expropriations which accompanied the expansion of the coffee economy. Without control over village lands the traditional leadership found its power rapidly declining. The wealthier members of the community then found themselves exposed to pressures from the same estate owners who were attempting to recruit poorer and less influential members of the community as forced laborers. The expansion of the settler-based coffee economy, therefore, tended to reinforce solidarity between rich and poor members of African communities and encourage organization based on tribe or lineage rather than class.

4. The system of migratory labor created by the contract system and the seasonal demand for harvest labor tended to direct the interests of individual

workers toward their home villages rather than toward their fellow workers. Workers tended to view whatever earnings they were able to sequester during their term on the estates as resources to be used to advance their position in the tribal social structure. The most frequent motive for what little actual voluntary labor existed under the contract system was to earn sufficient money for a bride price. The contract laborer earning money to pay a bride price or to purchase cattle in his home village would not be receptive to organizations stressing mobility through collective labor organization. In any case, such collective class-based mobility was impossible because of the poverty of the estate owners and the military discipline of the estates. The orientation toward village and tribe was reinforced by the Portuguese policies of permitting related Africans to work together but fanning tribal resentment whenever it was useful to them. The residential community of the coffee estate was a dangerous and barren environment for the worker, and assistance and security would be found not on the estate, but in his home village. Injured or sick workers or those in difficulty with the estate organization had to depend on kinsmen in their home villages for help. When the workers were recruited from relatively short distances, the possibility of social support tended to create solidarity between village and worker. This was particularly true of Bakongo working on coffee estates in Bakongo regions of northern Angola. For Ovimbundu contract laborers from the central plateau this dependence on tribal ties meant acute social isolation and exposure to considerably greater risk. The Ovimbundu was isolated in what, for all practical purposes, was a foreign country, and he was forced to rely on the limited good will of his Portuguese overseers or the assistance of his fellow workers. The migratory labor system in Angola tended, as it did elsewhere in the world, to undermine class solidarity and increase the strength of communal ties.

5. A class-based movement in the Angolan coffee regions would have involved uniting economic interest groups with divergent interests—the estate laborers and the African small holders. The development of pronounced proletarian or farmer economic interests was inhibited by the forced labor system and the insecurity of tenure created by European land expropriations. It is clear, however, that in a more highly developed market economy the interests of wage laborers and small holders would tend to diverge. The greater the degree of market penetration, the greater the divergence of interest and the greater the likelihood of competing political organizations based on conflicting economic interests. Given the weak market forces affecting the African landholders and laborers, however, it was possible to span these interests by appealing to communality of tribe or race. Communal interests were reinforced by the Portuguese *indígena* status, which affected both landholders and wage laborers. The principles of colonial rule itself made possible a broad communal coalition including both workers and small holders.

6. Finally the communal interests of the Africans in the northern coffee region were reinforced by potential alliances with other Africans outside of Angola. This consideration was particularly critical for the Bakongo, who by an

accident of colonial boundary demarcation lived in approximately equal numbers in both Angola and the Congo. There was always considerable migration across this border, especially by Bakongo attempting to escape Angolan forced labor practices. During the early 1950s the colonial regime of the Belgians was somewhat more liberal than that of the Portuguese, and it was possible for exile groups to organize in the Belgian Congo while they remained outlawed in Angola. The independence of the Congo in 1960 vastly expanded opportunities for exile political organization. After the suppression of the 1961 uprising, the guerrilla war was carried on largely by exile groups based in the Congo and Zambia. The existence of these groups was in turn dependent on the support or, at minimum, the tolerance of two African governments whose economic policies and ideological orientations were very different. Solidarity between these independent African governments and the Angolan rebels could be based on pan-African solidarity or anticolonialism but not on common economic ideology. The presence of important exile political groups in newly independent African countries and the aid of the African governments themselves reinforced the communal rather than the class characteristics of the revolutionary movement.

Although the economic and political pressures created by the expanding coffee economy would seem to lead to an inevitable confrontation between the Portuguese settlers and the African majority, it is possible to imagine the coffee economy reaching a certain degree of stability after the initial expropriations had ended. If the land expropriations had been consolidated and the military superiority of the Portuguese remained unchallenged, the expropriated landholders would eventually have been forced to find a source of subsistence outside the northern coffee regions. Many might have migrated to the Congo or joined the large mass of unemployed Africans in Luanda, or other major Angolan towns. The estate owners could then have imported large numbers of Ovimbundu laborers from the central plateau and the possibility for a communal-based coalition between displaced landowners and coffee estate laborers would have been eliminated. In fact, just this kind of development seems to have taken place after the 1961 uprising. Several hundred thousand Bakongo are believed to have fled across the border into the Congo, and as the labor statistics reported by Mendes indicated,[77] most have in fact been replaced by Ovimbundu. The Ovimbundu are cut off from political or social support from their home region but remain closely tied to the traditional tribal structure by the migratory nature of the labor system. It is unlikely, therefore, that they could form a class-based or a communal-based revolutionary movement.

These changes, however, had not taken place before the 1961 uprising, and the displaced small holders and tribal communal landholders of the northern coffee regions remained an important political force. Three critical events intervened to trigger the northern uprising before the liquidation of the African landholders could create the possibility of political stability in the coffee areas. First, the independence of the Congo in June 1960 liberated half of the Bakongo

[77] See p. 249 above.

while leaving the other half under colonial rule. The precipitous exit of the Belgians from the Congo encouraged Angolan nationalists to believe that the Portuguese would rapidly yield to the pressures of guerrilla war. Second, in November 1960 the United Nations agreed to take up the question of independence for Portuguese colonies and a Security Council debate on the situation in Angola was held in early March 1961. The UN action may not have had the mass impact of the independence of the Congo, but it encouraged UPA leaders in the belief that they might expect Western support in their efforts to oust the Portuguese. Both of these expectations, of course, proved disastrously exaggerated, since the Portuguese tenaciously resisted the initial uprising, and no aid was forthcoming from the West. In early 1961, however, these possibilities exerted a significant effect on the nationalist leadership. Finally, by 1960 sharply falling prices had brought the northern coffee economy to the point of economic collapse. At 1961 prices estate owners in the northern region stood to lose almost as much as they had made during the height of the boom. Furthermore, many producers who had established their estates in the mid-fifties were just beginning to realize returns on their investments when they found themselves faced with massive losses. In the coercive economy of northern Angola the reverses of the estate owners were certain to be passed on to the African population in the form of even lower wages or increased demands for forced labor. Since labor represented the single largest cost to the estate owner and the only one over which he could exert any significant control, the pressures of falling prices led to an increase in the coercive nature of the estate system and consequently to a cycle of escalating violence. At the same time that the African population was becoming increasingly aware of the possibilities of independence, the estate owners were faced with the prospect of an economic disaster, which could only be prevented by tightening the system of colonial rule. By the beginning of 1961 these political and economic changes increased the probability of an uprising. The analysis of the structure of the coffee export economy and its effect on estate owners, agricultural laborers, and African small holders suggests that the movement should be nationalist in form and should be concentrated in areas of maximum coffee production. More specifically the analysis suggests:

a. The northern rather than the southern coffee region should have been the site of the uprising, and the intensity of the conflict should have been roughly proportional to the amount of coffee produced. Only in the north were there direct conflicts between estate owners and small holders, and only in the north did land concessions take place on a large scale in the 1950s. In addition, labor requirements increased at a much faster rate in the north than in the south, and labor required to produce a given amount of coffee was also substantially greater in the north. The greater the reported coffee production in the area, the greater the demand for forced labor and consequently the greater the intensity of the nationalist movement.

b. The greater the area of land concessions in an area, the greater the intensity of the nationalist movement. Expropriations of both African coffee producers and communal landholders were an important element in establishing the coalition between estate laborers and African villagers. The large population displacements caused by the land concessions created a large number of refugees with an interest in reclaiming tribal lands. The greater the degree to which traditional communal tenure arrangements were undermined by European concessions, the greater the tendency of traditional African leaders to ally themselves with estate laborers and ordinary villagers against the Portuguese.

c. The greater the demand for forced labor in an area, the greater the intensity of the rebellion. The estate laborers represented the second critical element in the anti-Portuguese coalition. The greater the proportion of the local population affected by labor recruiting for the coffee estates, the broader the base of the anti-Portuguese coalition.

d. Both land concessions and labor recruitment should be correlated with the amount of coffee produced in a region. The argument above suggested that all three elements—estate coffee production, land concessions, and forced labor recruitment—should be necessary for the development of a revolutionary nationalist movement. The analysis of the Angolan agricultural economy of the 1950s, however, also indicates that coffee production was almost totally responsible for both the rate of land concessions and the rate of labor recruitment. Thus while in theory an interaction effect might be expected, in fact the three variables are likely to be too highly correlated to demonstrate any significant interaction.

COFFEE PRODUCTION AND REVOLUTIONARY NATIONALIST EVENTS

These hypotheses can be tested empirically by computing ecological correlations between measures of the coffee export economy and measures of revolutionary nationalist events for political subunits within Angola. The world analysis data on Angola involved only first-order political subdivisions, the districts, but the internal analysis is based on second-order political subdivisions, the townships and circumscriptions. The boundaries of the 85 townships and circumscriptions and 15 districts in Angola in 1961 are shown on Map 4.1, and all data are computed in terms of these boundaries.

Data on revolutionary nationalist events were obtained from newspaper sources supplemented by the chronology of the 1961 uprising contained in Hélio Felgas's *Guerra em Angola*.[78] Primary newspaper sources were considerably less useful for Angola than they were for Peru because of the strict censorship imposed by the Portuguese government. All news in both Angola and metropolitan Portugal has been censored since the 1930s, and information in Angola itself is tightly controlled by the Center of Information and Tourism of Angola (Centro de Informação e Turismo de Angola, or CITA). All Angolan newspapers are subjected to prior government censorship, and all reflect the

---

[78] Hélio Felgas, *Guerra em Angola* (Lisbon: A. M. Teixeira, 1962).

policy of the colonial government. The largest Angolan newspaper. *Diário de Luanda,* with a circulation of 15,000, is controlled by the Portuguese news agency ANI (Agência de Notícias de Informações). ANI is a private news organization based in Lisbon but is closely controlled by the Portuguese government. *Diário de Luanda* was the only Angolan source coded for agrarian events for the period of the 1961 uprising. *Diário* is a Luanda-based tabloid running approximately 15 pages and concentrating on European and Portuguese news of interest to Portuguese settlers. The front page is typically dominated by official policy statements and news of visits to Angola by government officials or other distinguished Portuguese citizens. Many of the remaining pages are devoted to human interest stories and cultural and sports news. Photoreproduction is poor and usually limited to pictures of European movie starlets. *Diário* has no permanent network of correspondents outside of Luanda, although eventually a reporter was dispatched to the northern region to cover the guerrilla war. *Diário* scrupulously observed the two-day news blackout imposed by Portugal at the onset of the 1961 uprising and in fact carried little more than news releases of the Portuguese military and reports of heroic resistance by local adminstrative posts until the tide of battle had shifted decisively in favor of the Portuguese. Coverage was extremely guarded and limited to information about the fate of Portuguese settlers and officials in the northern region who might be known to Portuguese in Luanda. After an initial period of sketchy coverage, reports of combat and ambushes became more frequent and a reasonable chronology of events began to emerge. Editorially the paper voiced hysterical opposition to the rebels, alternately condemning them as Communists, tribal cultists, or Protestants, all of whom the paper viewed with approximately equal distrust.

The military history of the northern rebellion by Hélio Felgas, the former governor of the northern province of the Congo (now the districts of Uíge and Zaire) is equally one sided in its interpretation of events but considerably more objective in tone and is the most detailed chronology available on the northern uprising. Felgas describes both the initial military success of the rebels and the later Portuguese campaign to recapture the northern region. Felgas's book is a valuable source of information for rural events especially for the period at the beginning of the revolt, when coverage in *Diário* was sketchy.

The nature of the revolutionary nationalist movement in Angola required a slightly different coding strategy than that used in the world analysis. The rebellion broke out simultaneously in several different townships of Angola on the morning of March 15, 1961, and much of the action was concentrated in the first two or three days. After the initial uprising military factors played an increasingly important role in the distribution of events. This was particularly true after the beginning of the Portuguese counteroffensive in May of 1961. After the first two or three weeks the rebellion became a military struggle in which terrain, proximity to foreign sanctuaries, and the deployment of Portuguese forces were the major determinants of event location. Thus to determine the social base of the movement, it is necessary to concentrate on the early period of the rebellion. The event definitions used in the world analysis treat the entire period from March 15 to March 21, 1961, as a single event which extends geographically to include most of northern Angola. In order to provide a more detailed picture of this critical period of the rebellion, event boundaries were limited to actions of the same formation, against the same target, in the same township, on the same day or successive days. This definition greatly increased the number of discrete events which could be recorded in the period at the outbreak of the rebellion and permitted a more accurate plotting of the social base of the movement. The event definition for the Angolan analysis was the same as that used in the case study of Peru except for the added qualification of action directed at the same target. Since many of the attacks on the first day of the revolt may have been actions of closely associated collectives, it seemed advisable to differentiate areas of maximum activity on the basis of the number of continuous attacks as well as the number of discrete formations.

These event definitions were used to record the number of events reported in all issues of *Diário de Luanda* in the first six months of 1961 and in those portions of Felgas's *Guerra em Angola* describing the same period. Events described in both sources were coded only once. All rural events reported in both these sources were revolutionary nationalist events. Most of the events consisted of terrorist attacks on farms or isolated European settlers, rebel assaults on towns and administrative posts, ambushes of Portuguese patrols, or small-scale battles between rebels and Portuguese troops. A total of 366 discrete events were recorded for the period from March 15 to June 15, 1961. The spatial distribution of the 60 events recorded for the first month of the uprising (March 15 to April 15) is shown in Map 4.3. No events were reported by *Diário* prior to March 20, 1961, and Felgas, of course, is concerned only with the period of the uprising itself. A total of 10 events were coded from the *New York Times*, the London *Times*, and *Africa Diary* for the same period, and eight of these occurred between March 15 and June 15. The coding of the secondary sources, of course, included the entire 1948 to 1970 period, but the difficulties of searching every page of *Diário* and the temporal limitations of Felgas's book made the more extended time period impractical for the primary sources. The secondary source data included a total of 39 events, all but one of which were classified revolutionary nationalist and almost all of which reflected the continuation of the Angolan war after the initial uprising. Since the social geography of the rebellion is reflected by the distribution of events in the first weeks of the movement, a more extended time period would add little to the Angolan case study.

A comparison of the spatial distribution of events for the period in which the two sets of sources overlap indicates a considerable degree of agreement despite the much larger number of events recorded in the primary sources. As was the case in the analysis of Peruvian event data, the larger number of events coded in primary sources reflects the more restricted event definitions used for primary sources and a tendency toward summary articles in secondary sources.

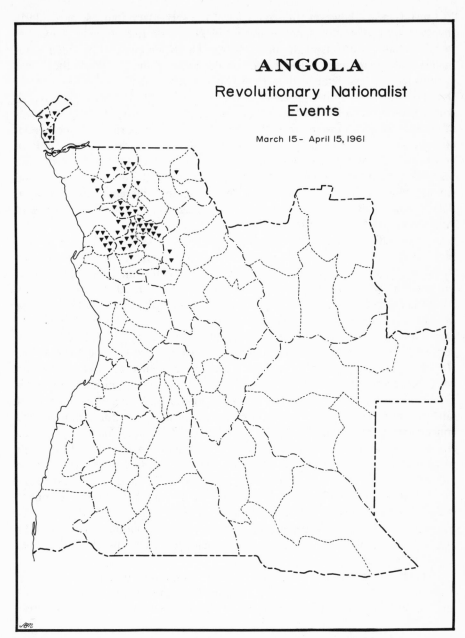

ANGOLA

Revolutionary Nationalist
Events

March 15 - April 15, 1961

MAP 4.3

265

In some respects, however, the coverage of the secondary sources, particularly the *New York Times*, is superior to that of *Diário de Luanda*. The *Times* reported detailed accounts of the uprising from the beginning and included statements by Angolan nationalists as well as Portuguese officials. While the *Times* is considerably less detailed than Felgas, it provides a better overall picture of the movement than the principal Angolan paper. Nevertheless the overall correlation between the number of events recorded by district in the two sets of sources is an almost perfect .97. This figure is comparable to the spatial correlation of .95 for primary and secondary sources for agrarian events in Peru and is higher than the .75 intersource correlation for labor events in Peru. The high correlation reflects the concentration of events in the districts of Uíge and Cuanza Norte in both sets of sources. Whatever the differences in policy and detail in the various sources, there was little disagreement about which areas of Angola were the centers of rebel activity.

Information on agricultural organization on Angola is not based on a complete agricultural census but is adequate to describe the major variables affecting the export economy. Angola began an agricultural census in 1960, but the outbreak of the rebellion made it impossible to survey the northern coffee region. The data on the southern coffee region have been published along with a number of volumes describing other areas of Angola,[79] but data are presented by natural agricultural regions rather than by political divisions, so that it is difficult to compare the agricultural census information with other statistical data. The *Angolan Statistical Annual (Anuário Estatístico)* regularly publishes figures on coffee production by township and until 1959 listed European and indigenous production separately. The 1959 statistical annual also includes numbers of laborers employed in coffee production in each township.[80] Information on land concessions is reported periodically in supplements to the *Boletim Oficial de Angola*,[81] and annual summaries list concessions individually and indicate their precise location, tenure status, and area. Angola conducted its first modern population census of the indigenous population in 1960, and in contrast to the earlier 1940 and 1950 census population data were based on a complete enumeration rather than simply estimated from tax records on file at administrative posts. Volumes have been published showing population distributions by age, sex, nationality, race, language, and religion for each township and sometimes administrative post for all of Angola.[82]

The relationships between measures of agricultural organization derived from these sources and revolutionary nationalist events are shown in Table 4.2 and can be inferred from a comparison of the distribution of coffee production

[79] Portugal, Ministério do Ultramar, Missão de Inquéritos Agrícolas, *Recenseamento Agrícola de Angola* (Lisbon, 1964).

[80] Angola, *Anuário Estatístico 1959*, pp. 94–95.

[81] Angola, *Boletim Oficial de Angola,* Suplemento: Repartição Central dos Serviços Geográficos e Cadastrais, Series 3, no. 52 (Luanda, December 1957).

[82] Angola, *Recenseamento Geral da População 1960*, vols. 1–3.

TABLE 4.2 *Intercorrelations of Revolutionary Nationalist Events with Coffee Production, Language, Religion, and Population by Second-Order Political Subdivisions*

	E_2	E_3	C_1	C_2	W_1	W_2	A_1	A_2	L_1	L_2	L_3	L_4	R_1	R_2	R_3	P_1	P_2	P_3	P_4
E_1 Events mo. 1	.49	.39	.59	.74	.71	.72	.44	.75	.23	.25	-.18	-.27	.17	.41	-.35	-.10	-.06	.05	-.12
E_2 Events mo. 2		.79	.29	.45	.40	.52	.32	.49	.58	-.05	-.23	-.31	.00	.77	-.39	-.11	-.07	.11	-.13
E_3 Events mo. 3			.23	.33	.32	.35	.21	.39	.57	-.03	-.24	-.32	.10	.62	-.40	-.12	-.08	.12	-.11
C_1 Robusta Eur.				.81	.95	.87	.48	.75	-.01	.22	.08	-.26	.15	.20	-.22	-.06	-.03	.06	-.01
C_2 Robusta ind.					.93	.95	.53	.83	.07	.30	-.11	-.24	.18	.31	-.30	-.08	-.04	.09	-.05
W_1 Coffee labor						.96	.56	.88	.04	.26	-.02	-.26	.16	.30	-.28	-.07	-.03	.08	-.03
W_2 % laborers							.53	.84	.12	.25	-.07	-.28	.15	.38	-.32	-.08	-.04	.09	-.07
A_1 No. conc.								.71	-.05	.03	.23	-.18	.13	.34	-.28	.15	.08	-.01	.31
A_2 Area conc.									.09	.23	.03	-.27	.11	.44	-.32	-.02	.03	.10	.03
L_1 Kikongo										-.32	-.33	-.38	.25	.57	-.50	-.14	-.11	.12	-.32
L_2 Kimbundu											-.26	-.37	.21	-.15	-.09	.08	.12	-.05	.00
L_3 Umbundu												-.33	.27	.03	-.23	.11	.08	-.08	.55
L_4 Other													-.67	-.45	.77	-.04	-.08	.00	-.19
R_1 Catholic														.10	-.86	.18	.19	.00	.10
R_2 Protestant															-.60	-.06	-.03	.04	.09
R_3 Pagan																-.11	-.14	-.02	-.13
P_1 White 1950																	.98	-.06	.33
P_2 White 1960																		.01	.31
P_3 Inc. white																			-.15
P_4 Black 1960																			—

in Map 4.2 and the distribution of events in Map 4.3. Indigenous and European robusta coffee production as it is shown in Map 4.2, and summarized statistically in Table 4.2 is based on data reported in *Anuário Estatístico* for the year 1958. The number of laborers employed in coffee production for each township and circumscription in 1958 was reported in the same sources, and the percent of males employed in coffee labor was computed by dividing the 1958 employment figures by the total male "black" (*preta*), or indigenous, population reported in that township or circumspection in the 1960 census. The number and area of land concessions were computed for the year 1955, which represented the peak of the land rush. The number and area of requested concessions reported in the *Boletim Oficial* were summed for each of the geographic areas included in the township and circumspection boundaries as they are shown in Map 4.1. Only requested concessions which had not been surveyed or granted provisional *aforamento* status were included in the tabulations. Since requested concessions were for the most part occupied without formal grants from the land survey office, this variable measures the extent of illegal land expropriations during the year 1955. Only concessions of 1,000 hectares or less were considered, since most larger concessions are intended for either mineral exploration or cattle ranching in the sparsely populated southern desert. Agricultural concessions in areas where substantial indigenous population displacement might take place are therefore generally concessions of 1,000 hectares or less.

It is clear that the pattern of correlation in Table 4.1 supports the general line of argument and the specific hypotheses outlined above. First, the number of nationalist events coded from *Diário de Luanda* and *Guerra em Angola* for the period of March 15 to April 15, 1961, is correlated .59 with European robusta production and .74 with indigenous robusta production. Second, the number of events recorded from March 15 to April 15 is correlated .75 with the area of concessions requested in 1955. Third, the number of events in this period is correlated .72 with the percent of indigenous males employed on coffee estates. It is also clear from a comparison of event distribution in Map 4.3 with the distribution of European and indigenous robusta production in Map 4.2 that the correlation between robusta production and number of nationalist events is entirely accounted for by events in the northern region. No events were recorded in the southern coffee townships in the district of Cuanza Sul. This fact explains the relatively lower correlation between European robusta production and events than between indigenous production and events. European and indigenous production are, of course, highly correlated ($r = .81$), but this correlation is almost entirely explained by the northern region. In the north indigenous production is roughly proportional to European production, while almost all production in the southern district is from European estates. For this reason the distribution of indigenous production in Angola can be taken as an index of the areas in which *both* European and indigenous production occur. If the correlation between European and indigenous production is partialed out of the correlation between European production and events, this correlation is reduced to zero. Only in those coffee areas in which there are substantial numbers of *both* indigenous and European producers are there any substantial numbers of events. This relationship is also apparent in a comparison between the data on production in Map 4.2 and the data on events in Map 4.3.

Table 4.2 also makes clear that the effects of coffee production, land concessions, and labor recruitment are not independent of one another. All are highly intercorrelated. The correlation between indigenous coffee production and percent indigenous males in coffee labor is .95, the correlation between indigenous coffee production and area of land concessions is .83, and the correlation between labor and land concessions is .88. It is clear that the greatest demand for coffee estate labor and the greatest area of land expropriations were in just those areas where indigenous producers were most numerous. Land concessions are concentrated in the northern region, and the southern zone townships have in general only one-tenth the area of requested concessions of the northern coffee townships. The overall pattern of results strongly supports the hypotheses derived from the analysis of the northern coffee zone and supports the predicted difference between the social effects of differences in the organization of robusta production north and south of the Cuanza River. Only in areas where settler estates were in direct competition with the local population for land and labor were there any substantial numbers of events in the first month of the uprising.

The data in Table 4.2 also indicate that the correlation between characteristics of the coffee economy and the number of events generally decreases after the first month of the uprising. This phenomenon is apparent in the first three rows of correlations for each variable associated with the coffee economy. The second row indicates correlations with the number of events in the second month of the uprising, and the third row indicates correlations with the number of events in the third month. In most cases the correlations decline from one row to the next. The correlation between indigenous production and the number of events, for example, declines from .74 in the first month to .45 in the second month to .33 in the third month. This decline in the strength of the relationship is a result of the spread of the movement outward from the initial centers of the uprising. This phenomenon is apparent in Felgas's account of the movement, particularly in his map of the military situation in June of 1961.[83] The rebels initially secured much of the coffee area and overran many of the farms and administrative posts in the region in the first few days of the revolt. From that point they attempted to extend their control northward toward the Congo border and westward toward Luanda. By the beginning of May the distribution of events also begins to reflect the beginning of the Portuguese counterthrust, which, of course, starts at the fringes of the coffee regions. Thus the apparent

[83] Felgas, *Guerra*, map facing p. 96.

decline in the influence of the coffee economy on the later stages of the rebellion is actually a result of the initial success of the rebels in the areas of their greatest strength in the northern coffee regions.

The data in Table 4.2 also indicate that the correlations between measures of the coffee economy and numbers of events are not simple artifacts of the size of the indigenous or European population or of the rate of increase in the number of settlers. There is no significant correlation between the size of the indigenous population and either coffee production or number of events. Similarly there are no significant correlations between the number of events and the size of the European population in either 1950 or 1960, or between the number of events and the percent increase in the European population in the decade. It is not the influx of European settlers itself that created the preconditions for revolt during that decade, but rather the form of economic organization established by settlers in the northern coffee regions. This fact is also reflected in the relatively lower correlations between the *number* of requested land concessions and the number of first month events as opposed to the *area* of requested concessions and the number of first month events. The former correlation is .44 while the latter is .75, even though the number of land concessions and the area of land concessions are correlated .71. The number of concessions in a township or circumscription is an approximate measure of the number of European agricultural settlers of all kinds in the area. It is in fact a better measure of the influx of Europeans into rural areas than is the increase of the total European population, since most European immigrants settled in Luanda or other urban areas. While large numbers of settlers claimed land in areas of Angola outside the northern coffee region, particularly on the central plateau, most of these requests were for 1 or 2 hectares, indicating that the settlers probably intended to work as small holders and cultivate much of the land themselves. Most concessions in the northern coffee regions were for 250 hectares or more, could only be worked by contract labor, and would result in a much greater displacement of the indigenous population. Since the number of concessions is not as highly correlated with the number of events as the area of concessions, it was clearly not the presence of settlers, but rather the land expropriations and labor demands of the coffee estates which were the critical factors in the uprising.

ALTERNATIVE THEORIES

The data in Map 4.3 and Table 4.2 also provide a means of assessing the value of alternative explanations of the northern uprising. The most frequently expressed alternative theories attribute the revolt to some mixture of three principal causes—outside agitators from the Congo, Bakongo tribalism, or Protestant sectarianism. Each of these theories has some evidence in its favor, and all have been actively proposed by the Portuguese government at one time or another. Further scrutiny of both the statistical data and the events of the rebellion, however, tends to indicate that all three theories are largely false.

1. The outside agitator theory is probably the most popular explanation of the revolt among Portuguese commentators. This was the official position of the Portuguese government expressed in news releases during the first week of the rebellion. The government charged that foreign terrorists had infiltrated across the Congo frontier and denied that the uprising reflected any widespread opposition to Portuguese rule by Angolan Africans.[84] This position is also supported by Felgas, who admits that substantial numbers of coffee estate laborers and African coffee farmers were involved in the uprising but paradoxically concludes that the rebellion was the work of rebels from the Congo.[85] The Portuguese journalist Pieter Lessing reached similar conclusions and describes how "a terrible army . . . swept across the frontier from the Congo." [86] Even René Pélissier's reasonable objective analysis concludes that "it was not a spontaneous revolt against poverty as claimed, but a series of operations organised by the UPA." [87] Pélissier suggests that the leading events of March 15 included "attacks on the Congolese frontier to give free passage to UPA commandos who included not only Angolans but a sizeable number of troublemakers from the Leopoldville population." [88]

It is clear that the UPA exile organization in the Congo was involved in planning the timing of the uprising and that UPA organizers entered northern Angola to encourage the revolt. There are a number of factors, however, that suggest that local economic tensions in the coffee regions rather than troops from across the border were the major source of the rebellion's strength. First, the distribution of events in the initial stages of the revolt does not suggest that rebel activity radiated outward from the Congo border. As the event data in Map 4.3 make clear, the greatest number of events in the first month of the uprising occurred in the township of Uíge in the Uíge district, the townships of Ambaca and Dembos in the Cuanza Norte district, and the township of Dande in the Luanda district. All these areas are closer to the Angolan capital of Luanda than they are to the Congo frontier. Attacks closer to the frontier in the Zaire district circumscription of Cuímba and townships of Ambrizete and São Salvador may have been initiated by rebels crossing from the Congo. A number of these attacks, however, notably assaults on the McBridge and Primavera coffee plantations in Cuímba, involved collusion with local plantation workers. Only in the Cabinda enclave does there seem to be any reason to conclude that foreign rebels played the most important role in the uprising. Descriptions of

---

[84] *New York Times*, Mar. 18, 1961.
[85] Felgas, *Guerra*, pp. 33–37.
[86] Quoted in Marcum, *Angolan Revolution*, p. 130.
[87] Wheeler and Pélissier, *Angola*, p. 177. In the first half of this jointly written book, however, Wheeler suggests that the coffee economy was at least a contributing factor in the revolt; see pp. 136–141.
[88] *Ibid.*, p. 181.

these attacks indicate that infiltrators were relatively well armed,[89] there is little coffee produced in the enclave, and it is, of course, surrounded on three sides by the Congo. The major centers of the Angolan rebellion, however, were not located near the frontier, but in the heart of the northern coffee region. Second, the weapons and tactics used scarcely suggest a well-planned invasion. Most reports of attacks on *fazendas* or Portuguese outposts indicate that the principal rebel weapons were *catanas* (machetes), or *canhangulos* (primitive, homemade firearms). Atrocity pictures of slaughtered European settlers, which are included in a number of Portuguese accounts of the uprising, also suggest that most wounds were inflicted at close quarters with primitive weapons. With the exception of the attacks in the Cabinda enclave there is little hard evidence, even in Portuguese sources, of modern weapons imported from outside Angola. A military attack on the scale of the northern uprising would certainly have deployed a more substantial number of arms than were reported by the Portuguese.

Finally there is a surprising amount of agreement on the nature of the events of March 15 which touched off the uprising. Felgas describes the attack on the *fazenda* Zalala on the morning of March 15 as follows:

> The personnel presented themselves in the usual way. Nothing seemed irregular. Only a few workers were missing. Each worker had a *catana* in his hand, the *catana* which he usually worked either trimming the coffee trees, or cutting grass or hay, or cutting down trees. The *catana* in fact serves every purpose for the native. It had not as yet served the purpose of cutting up white people, however.
>
> Suddenly a whistle was heard and then, the throng, with *catanas* raised, advanced on black and white foremen, who were unarmed and very surprised. Some ran to the houses to arm themselves and warn their families. Others fell there immediately. The killing of the whites and their native friends didn't take long, since the murderers were numerous and they knew the jungle well, and disappeared into it after the revolting deed.[90]

Felgas goes on to report that the same method of attack was repeated in numerous other coffee *fazendas* in the townships of Dembos and Uíge. A very similar description is presented in Bernardo Teixeira's *The Fabric of Terror*,[91] a polemical defense of Portuguese heroism and attack on alleged African savagery. Teixeira's cousin owned a coffee estate in the township of Ambaca which was attacked on the morning of March 16. Teixeira visited the *fazenda* shortly after the Portuguese reoccupation and obtained a transcript of an interview with the estate's assistant foreman, who was the only European to survive the attack. As

---

[89] See Felgas, *Guerra*, p. 68, and *Diário*, April 14, 1961.

[90] Felgas, *Guerra*, pp. 28–29. Translated by Robert Stam.

[91] Bernardo Teixeira, *The Fabric of Terror* (New York: Devon-Adair, 1965), chap. 2.

was the case at *fazenda* Zalala, African laborers reported for work in the morn-ing in the usual way, bringing their *catanas* with them. The foreman noted that some of the Ovimbundu contract workers seemed to be missing and asked the Bakongo *capataz*, or overseer, where they were. The *capataz* told the foreman that the missing workers were sick, but when the foreman sent a servant to in-vestigate, the assembled workers attacked. Led by the Bakongo *capataz* they massacred the estate's entire European population, including Teixeira's cousin and his family.

The most widely reported account of the beginning of the revolt from the nationalist side is Holden Roberto's description of the uprising at the Primavera coffee plantation in the circumscription of Cuímba, 65 miles from the Congo frontier.[92] According to Roberto, the contract laborers gathered before the plantation manager's house to demand six months back wages. The manager refused and opened fire on the crowd of workers. The workers attacked the manager with their *catanas* and slaughtered him and his family. The uprising rapidly spread as other Portuguese, hearing of the killings, began shooting Africans on sight and Africans responded by attacking *fazendas*, burning houses, and blocking roads. Except for the emphasis on specific economic grievances and the significant assertion that the Portuguese manager initiated the violence, Roberto's account is identical to those of Felgas and Teixeira. It would seem that whatever coordination or outside help was supplied by UPA exiles, the initial uprising was touched off by estate laborers and then rapidly expanded to other Africans in the northern coffee regions. This conclusion is also supported by descriptions of attacks on administrative posts, notably the famous massacre at Quitexe in Ambaca township, described by both Felgas and Teixeira and re-ported in *Diário de Luanda*.[93] According to Teixeira's account Africans from surrounding farms and villages appeared at the town's trading posts early on the morning of March 15 and appeared to be simply coming to purchase trade goods. Neither Felgas, Teixeira, nor *Diário* mentions any outsiders. Teixeira specifically mentioned that the attackers lived in the region and frequented the local trading posts. Felgas indicates that the massacre was assisted by servants in European homes who slit the throats of their own masters. As was the case in the *fazenda* attacks, the principal weapon used was the *catana,* and no evidence of rebel firearms was reported in any of the sources. According to *Diário* a total of 27 Portuguese civilians were killed during the attack, but Teixeira describes a trader and his daughter who were able to stand off the attackers armed only with hunting rifles. Thus the outbreak of the rebellion seems clearly to have been the work of the local population, and neither foreign arms nor infiltrators seem to have been involved on a large scale.

Although the timing of the attack and the simultaneous outbreaks in widely dispersed areas on March 15 suggest that the UPA probably was involved to some degree in coordinating the actions, it is also possible that even this degree

[92] Recounted in Marcum, *Angolan Revolution*, p. 134.
[93] Felgas, *Guerra*, p. 27; *Diário*, Mar. 28, 1961; Teixeira, *Terror*, chap. 3.

of organization is an exaggeration. Clifford Parsons, a Baptist missionary in northern Angola, claimed that there was "no clear indication of an overall plan of campaign, and it appears likely that there was little coordination between the different bands of guerrillas that went into action on 15 March." [94]

The Angolan revolt, then, seems to more closely resemble a popular uprising than it does an armed attack by guerrilla infiltrators. In this respect it seems to differ significantly from the guerrilla fighting in Portuguese Guinea and Mozambique which involved much better-armed rebels and more extensive use of border sanctuaries.

2. A number of commentators including Felgas, Pélissier, and Eduardo dos Santos argued that the rebellion was confined to Bakongo tribesmen and involved atavistic tribal religious practices.[95] *Diário de Luanda* frequently praised the "loyal Bailundos" who were said to be supporting the Portuguese against the rebels. "Bailundo" refers to Bailundu tribesmen and is the term commonly used to describe members of any Ovimbundu tribe. According to both *Diário* and Felgas the "Bailundo" contract laborers in the north remained loyal to the Portuguese and were the target of terrorist attacks by Bakongo rebels. Pélissier argues that the UPA's tribal sects limited its appeal to the Bakongo peoples alone. Santos suggests that use of fetishes, particularly the belief that water with magical properties (*"maza"*) would ward off bullets, indicated that the revolt was rooted in Bakongo tribalism. The data in Table 4.2, however, do not support a simple ethnic interpretation of the uprising. In the first month of the revolt the number of events is much more highly correlated with the distribution of coffee production than it is with the distribution of Kikongo-speaking peoples. In fact the number of events is approximately equally correlated with both the proportion of Kikongo speakers ($r = .23$) and proportion of Kimbundu speakers ($r = .25$). The linguistic boundary between the Kikongo-speaking Bakongo tribes and the Kimbundu-speaking Mbundu roughly follows the southern boundaries of the districts of Zaire and Uíge in Map 4.1. Census data indicate that 99 percent of the population of the districts of Zaire and Uíge speak Kikongo. South of the boundary line only one township, Ambriz in Luanda, has more than 5 percent Kikongo speakers. South of the linguistic boundary, in the centers of rebellion in the townships of Dande in Luanda and Dembos and Ambaca in Cuanza Norte, more than 80 percent of the population speak Kimbundu and the remainder are largely Umbundu-speaking Ovimbundu contract laborers. Thus the area of the initial uprising includes both Bakongo and Mbundu territories which do not share a common language but were equally affected by the coffee economy. It is clear from the correlations in

[94] Clifford Parsons, "The Makings of a Revolt," in Institute of Race Relations, *Angola: A Symposium: Views of a Revolt* (London: Oxford University Press, 1962), p. 66.

[95] Felgas, *Guerra*; Wheeler and Pélissier, *Angola*; Eduardo dos Santos, *Maza: Elementos de Etno-História para a Interpretação de Terrorismo no Nordeste de Angola* (Lisbon: Edição de Autor, 1965).

Table 4.2 that as the rebellion progresses, more and more of the action tends to be concentrated in exclusively Kikongo-speaking areas, but as has already been indicated, this fact reflects the importance of purely military considerations at later stages of the war. Although it is true that the rebellion never spread to the Ovimbundu south of the Cuanza River, it is also clear that the effects of the coffee economy were not felt in this region either. The distribution of events at the beginning of the uprising is more closely associated with coffee production than with tribal boundaries.

3. Catholicism had always been closely associated with the civilizing mission of the Portuguese, and the colonial administration in Angola tended to view Catholic missions as an important element in the pacification of the African population. While Protestant missions were tolerated and even thrived in some areas of Angola, they were always distrusted by colonial authorities. As John Marcum has pointed out, Protestant missionaries became scapegoats for the 1913 rebellion of Tulante Álvaro Buta, and in 1961 the Portuguese once again attempted to blame the Protestants for their difficulties.[96] According to Marcum, Protestant Africans became fair game for Portuguese troops and Protestant missionaries were expelled from Northern Angola. The official Portuguese position is summed up in an editorial from *Diário* which reads as if it were a tract of the Counter-Reformation period rather than a modern political document.

> Protestantism was born of feeling of pride and rebellion which always divide men. Protestantism cannot help build our world, cohesive and unified, integrating diverse races and dispersed territories. Protestantism in its own essential bases, makes people hostile, contrary to the unity of the nation. It is like a tumor among us that disturbs the equilibrium of the healthy body where it is introduced, but which is neither attached nor absorbed.[97]

While the role of Protestantism in Angolan rebellions was frequently exaggerated by Portuguese authorities, the close association between Catholicism and colonial rule made Protestantism a natural ideological alternative for Africans opposed to Portuguese rule. Protestant missions in northern Angola and the Congo were frequently the source of charismatic religious leaders who founded cults combining elements of Protestantism and traditional African religion. As Wheeler has pointed out,[98] since 1919 at least four major prophets have appeared in northern Angola and the adjacent areas of the Congo, all named Simon and all preaching forms of syncretic African Protestantism. In Angola the most important of these movements was that of Simon Gonçalves

[96] Marcum, *Angolan Revolution*, pp. 147–154.
[97] *Diário*, May 2, 1961.
[98] Wheeler and Pélissier, *Angola*, p. 153.

Toko,[99] who was educated at a Baptist mission in Maquela do Zombo in northern Angola. The doctrines of Tokoism represented an ingenious strategy for limiting the demands of Portuguese rule while at the same time building an alternate status system for Africans. Tokoists believed in a separation between the secular world of the Portuguese and the spiritual world of the African. Only the latter was significant, so that Tokoists were instructed to adhere to the letter of colonial regulations. This particular doctrine, of course, created considerable difficulties for colonial administrators, who had never taken the colonial regulations protecting the African population very seriously. Tokoists gained a reputation similar to that of jailhouse lawyers and became skilled at using the Portuguese' own rules against them. The movement had become a sufficient threat by 1949 that its major leaders were exiled, and Simon Toko himself was eventually sent to the Azores. The movement continued to have a strong appeal to Africans displaced from tribal society, and it continued to be viewed by the Portuguese as a potentially dangerous source of rebellion.

Neither Tokoism nor, of course, more orthodox Protestant denominations preached rebellion against colonial authorities, and there seems to be little evidence that Protestant sects were involved in the 1961 uprising. The areas of greatest Tokoist strength and their major churches were all located in the township of Zombo, which had no major events in the first month of the uprising (Map 4.3). The Tokoists also tended to have their greatest success among educated Africans in urban areas, and the 1961 rebellion was almost entirely rural. The Zombo peoples were the major ethnic supporters of Tokoism and, though they were Kikongo speaking, remained largely uninvolved during the uprising of other Bakongo.

While Protestant missionary efforts were most successful in Bakongo areas of northern Angola, the areas of greatest Protestant influence do not correspond to the areas of most intense rebellion. The data in Table 4.2 indicate that the correlation between events in the first month and the proportion of African Protestants in a township is .41; some of this correlation, however, is accounted for by the correlation between Protestantism and indigenous coffee production ($r = .31$). The independent effect of Protestantism partialing out the effect of coffee production is not strong ($r = .28$). The correlation tends to increase as the rebellion moves northward into the Bakongo Protestant strongholds, but as has already been indicated, the distribution of events in the first month of the rebellion is the best measure of the social base of the movement. It is clear from the data in Table 4.2 that the coffee economy rather than Protestant ideology is the more important determinant of the number of nationalist events in the first month of the uprising.

[99] For accounts of the Tokoist movement see Alferdo Margarido, "The Tokoist Church and Portuguese Colonialism in Angola," in Ronald H. Chilcote (ed.), *Protest and Resistance in Angola and Brazil* (Berkeley: University of California Press, 1972), pp. 29–52; and Silva Cunha, *Aspectos dos Movimentos Associativos na África Negra*, Portugal, Junta de Investigações do Ultramar, Estudos de Ciêncas Politicas e Socials, no. 23 (Lisbon, 1959).

Comparison of the ecology of Angolan coffee production with the distribution of nationalist events indicates that the social and economic consequences of the coffee export economy were the primary causes of the uprising even though the resulting movement was based on a communal, nationalist ideology. The rapid expansion of the coffee export economy between 1950 and 1960 led to the expropriation of African lands and the growth of a migratory labor system, and these economic changes in turn created the possibility of a political coalition between coffee laborers, African coffee farmers, and traditional tribal authorities. The poverty of the Portuguese estate owners and the marginal economic character of the estates themselves made coercion an integral part of the coffee economy. The racial distinctions enforced by colonial rule were necessary to insure land and labor for the estates, but land concessions and forced labor were major sources of African discontent. As was the case in other colonial migratory systems the expansion of the export economy initiated a revolutionary nationalist movement. In Angola the speed with which the economy developed and the economic weakness of Portugal combined to create one of the most persistent of all nationalist wars.

CHAPTER 5

Vietnam: Sharecropping

THE AGRICULTURAL economy of Vietnam is the product of two periods of foreign domination. The traditional village subsistence economy of northern and central Vietnam reflects the impact of over a thousand years of Chinese rule, but the agricultural economy of southern Vietnam developed in response to the world economy introduced during less than a century of French colonial rule. The disparate influences of the Chinese and French occupations produced a dual agricultural economy similar to those of Peru and Angola. In the Red River delta in what is now North Vietnam and in the river deltas of the coastal lowlands that span the two independent Vietnamese states, an economic and social organization modeled on that of ancient China persisted even during the French colonial period. In the Mekong delta of what is now South Vietnam the influence of the traditional village economy introduced by the Chinese was weaker, and the French occupation created an agricultural export economy based on commercial rice production. These two economic sectors persisted throughout the colonial period and remained a clear division in Vietnamese rural society even after the end of French rule. The Chinese and French occupations created two distinct societies with different relationships to the world economy and different responses to the period of war and revolution which accompanied the end of French colonialism. Vietnam remains to the present a predominantly agrarian society and the problems of public administration and agricultural production were similar for both foreign occupiers. Their solutions to these problems reflected the conditions of an agrarian bureaucracy on the one hand and capitalist colonial administration on the other.

From the long experience of Chinese rule the Vietnamese absorbed the agrarian technology, bureaucratic organization, and state morality of ancient China. The Chinese introduced the techniques of irrigated wet rice cultivation which formed the material base of their own civilization and began the construction of an elaborate dike network to protect the delta against the violent

278

floods of the Red River. The Chinese also introduced the organizational techniques necessary for the construction and maintenance of complex hydraulic works. The centralized bureaucracy of the Chinese mandarinate became the model for the administrative structure of an independent Vietnam, and shortly after the Chinese withdrawal the Vietnamese emperors established a fixed hierarchy of officials, an academy to train civil servants, and a system of competitive examinations for public office. The highest officials in the Vietnamese mandarinate survived an arduous series of local and regional competitions to reach the final contest at the imperial court. The examinations themselves emphasized Chinese classics to the almost total exclusion of Vietnamese history and culture. The Vietnamese imperial administration became so thoroughly Sinicized that court landscape painting depicted scenes in southern China and ancient Chinese persisted as the official language of the mandarinate long after it had become a dead language in China itself.

The Vietnamese imperial administration also inherited the problems associated with a centralized agrarian bureaucracy. A large bureaucracy is expensive and could seldom be financed out of state revenues directly. Since the fundamental form of wealth in any agrarian society is land, there was an inevitable temptation to substitute land grants for salaries. Members of the royal family, important court officials, highly placed mandarins, and successful military commanders were rewarded with large land grants, by the right to collect rent from a number of villages, or by the officially ignored diversion of taxes from a local area. Although the land grants were intended to buy the loyalty of important officials, they inevitably undermined the central authority they were intended to promote. A direct land grant or the right to collect rents provided an ambitious mandarin with the resources to recruit and support a sizeable army and hence to establish an independent base of political power. As a result the Vietnamese empire was continually faced with centrifugal pressures leading to the erosion of imperial authority and to interminable civil war. A vigorous dynasty could limit the power of landed property by increasing state revenues and replacing landowners with salaried officials. But crop failures, foreign invasions, or peasant revolts could easily drain the treasury and require a return to the land grant system, further weakening the already threatened imperial power.

This problem became particularly acute as the Vietnamese empire expanded from its traditional centers of power in the Red River delta southward along the narrow coastal strip between the Annamite mountain chain and the sea. In the course of 800 years the Vietnamese gradually pushed back the Indianized kingdoms of Champa and Cambodia, reaching the Mekong delta in what is now South Vietnam at the end of the eighteenth century, only a half century before the arrival of the French. The military occupation of an area was gradually followed by the settlement of villages of landless peasants fleeing the land scarcity and population pressures of the older settled areas. In some cases, particularly in the period of expansion against the Champa kingdom, the peasants themselves gradually infiltrated a new area and began cultivation. Each area added to the Vietnamese empire reproduced the agrarian base, village organization, and bureaucratic administration of the traditional areas of Vietnamese power. Each new conquest required that new commanders be rewarded and new mandarins created, and each new territory created a new basis for political fission. In the sixteenth century the influence of wealthy land-owning families split the empire into two kingdoms which persisted until the reunification of Vietnam at the beginning of the nineteenth century.

The Vietnamese empire as it existed just before the French conquest had attained the greatest level of centralized control in its long history. Aided by foreign military technology, the emperors had finally become powerful enough to eliminate the independent power basis created by land grants and bind officials to the imperial treasury by paying them directly in money or rice. The nineteenth-century emperors also moved to restrict the power of large land-owners by setting limits on the maximum size of holdings and initiating a land reform to strengthen small holders and landless peasants at the expense of the gentry. The local village organization was similarly strengthened by decrees requiring the return of illegally acquired village land and the redistribution of this land every three years to needy members of the community. The imperial attempts to curtail the power of large landowners invariably strengthened the power of villages and placed more land in the hands of small holders. In the settled areas of northern and central Vietnam this pattern of land owner-ship and village organization was firmly established by the time of the French conquest. In the Mekong delta of southern Vietnam, however, the process of settlement and village formation had barely begun when it was cut short by French occupation. Land ownership and village organization in the Mekong delta therefore developed in response to the political and economic influences of the world economy rather than through contact with the Sinicized areas of traditional Vietnamese social and economic organization.

The French arrived in Vietnam in force in the nineteenth century seeking a river route to the markets of southern China and mercantile advantage in Vietnam itself. At first French interest centered on the Mekong as the hoped-for route to China. The French navy seized Saigon in 1859 and three years later forced the weakened Vietnamese emperor to cede the three easternmost provinces of southern Vietnam. In 1867 the French seized the three remaining western provinces and established the colony of Cochinchina in southern Vietnam. After expending immense sums in conquest and pacification, the French found that they had conquered a largely unsettled frontier region whose dominant feature was its miles of uncultivated swamps. The Vietnamese mandarinate had departed at the order of the emperor when the French seized power, so that there was no indigenous political organization through which the French could rule. They were therefore forced to undertake the additional expense of recruiting and paying French nationals to administer the colony.

From its outset the French colonial administration in Cochinchina adopted the narrow fiscal objective of balancing the colonial budget, paying the ever-expanding French administrative cadre, and if possible creating a profitable economy which would justify the costs of conquest and administration. But in order to create the conditions for stable economic growth, the French had to establish firm control over the indigenous population and eliminate the remaining centers of violent resistance. Most of the Vietnamese population joined the mandarins in refusing to cooperate with the colonial administration, so that it was essential the French find some inducement to collaboration if they were ever to govern effectively and make the colony profitable. The cost-conscious French administration was therefore led to a policy which closely resembled the pattern of imperial rule in the older areas of Vietnam—the payment of collaborators in large land grants. A substantial amount of land was available in the Mekong delta, since it was sparsely settled. In addition the French had initiated an ambitious canal-building project at least as much for military as for economic reasons, but the canals had the important economic consequence of improving drainage and making cultivation possible over wide areas of the delta. The land either was given directly in the form of concessions to French nationals or to deserving Vietnamese who had loyally served the French or was auctioned off in large lots to defray the cost of canal building. The French short-run fiscal and political interests therefore combined to cause them to create a new landed elite indebted to French power. The large landowners, who had often served in the French colonial bureaucracy, converted to Catholicism, adopted French manners and language, and formed a new aristocracy which displaced the old mandarinate. From the French point of view they combined the advantages of loyalty and low cost. The new Vietnamese elite simplified problems of French rule, and the payment of land lowered the cost of administration.

The French emphasis on making the economy pay and the increasing influence of French merchants in the colony led to a second radical change in the structure of Vietnamese society—the large-scale export of rice. The export of rice had been forbidden by the emperor on the ostensible grounds that reserves were necessary to feed the poor and prevent famine. Although the emperors were in fact concerned about the support of the poor, they also feared the independent economic power and foreign alliances which a large export trade would have created. The Vietnamese mandarinate also regarded commercial activities as a possible threat to their control and generally used their influence to restrict the activities of indigenous Vietnamese entrepreneurs. The French on the other hand were anxious to increase the revenues of the colony, and French nationals controlled the export trade. Thus one of the first acts of the French administration after the capture of Saigon in 1859 was to authorize the export of rice. The demand of foreign markets and the new lands opened by French canals combined to make possible a dramatic increase in rice cultivation and exports. In 1860 only 57,000 tons were exported from

Cochinchina. By 1870 exports had increased to 229,000 tons, and 522,000 hectares of rice land were in cultivation. By 1929 exports had reached 1,223,000 tons, and the area in cultivation had almost quadrupled to over 2 million hectares.[1] Vietnam became, along with Burma and Thailand, one of the three largest exporters of rice and maintained this position until war and revolution disrupted production. After World War II exports never reached more than 346,000 tons, and by 1965 Vietnam had become a net importer.[2] The economic organization created by the colonial export economy, however, continued to influence political events in Vietnam even after exports themselves ceased.

There is of course no economic reason why the rice export economy need have been combined with large landholdings. Rice production enjoys no appreciable economies of scale and is usually carried on in small units worked by either sharecroppers or small holders. In fact with the exception of a few modern French holdings the technology of rice production in Cochinchina was similar to that practiced in traditional areas of Vietnam, and most cultivation continued to be carried out in small units worked by sharecroppers. French exporters could have dealt as easily with dispersed small holders as with large landowners, since most exported rice was channeled to the Saigon market by Chinese middlemen. Distribution of land to small holders would have tended to increase consumption and decrease the surplus available for export, and eventually population growth in the Mekong delta of Cochinchina would have consumed the marketable surplus just as it had already done in the older settled areas of Vietnam. But at the outset of the French occupation the delta was sparsely populated, and a substantial surplus would have been available for export even if the land had been controlled by small holders. The presence of large landholdings in the export economy of Cochinchina was a consequence of politics, not economics.

The French colonial administration in Cochinchina had been established for more than 20 years before the French proceeded to the conquest of the remainder of Vietnam. In 1884 they took control of central and northern Vietnam as the protectorates of Annam and Tonkin. In both regions the political and economic impact of French rule was weaker than it had been in Cochinchina. In Annam the French retained an emasculated imperial court at Hué and continued to rule through the traditional mandarinate. Each mandarin at the provincial level, however, was assigned a French adviser who actually exercised final authority. French economic penetration of Annam was not extensive, the land had long been occupied by a dense population of small holders, and French colonial policies did not create a new land-owning class. In Tonkin French economic involvement was more extensive, especially in

[1] Pierre Gourou, *Land Utilization in French Indochina* (New York: Institute of Pacific Relations, 1945), p. 331.
[2] Robert L. Sansom, *The Economics of Insurgency in the Mekong Delta of Vietnam* (Cambridge: M.I.T. Press, 1970), p. 262.

areas devastated by fighting during the conquest. In these areas large blocks of land were granted to deserving Vietnamese just as had been done in Cochinchina. The land concessions were, however, never as extensive as they were in Cochinchina, and Tonkin remained a region of miniscule peasant holdings. In both Annam and Tonkin the patterns of land ownership and village organization established by the last emperors of an independent Vietnam persisted under colonial rule. In Cochinchina in general and in the Mekong delta in particular land ownership and village organization developed under the impact of the world economy, and the relationships of tenancy and indebtedness replaced the traditional ties of the village. Annam and Tonkin remained largely a traditional subsistence sector, while Cochinchina was transformed into an agricultural export sector.

This fundamental economic and social division between the Mekong delta in Cochinchina and the Red River delta and central lowlands of Tonkin and Annam persisted throughout the period of colonial rule. After Vietnam was partitioned in 1954, the dividing line between the two sectors of the rural economy fell in the territory of the Republic of Vietnam south of the 17th parallel. The Democratic Republic of Vietnam north of the 17th parallel included the areas of traditional Vietnamese social and economic organization in Tonkin and northern Annam. South Vietnam included both the southern provinces of Annam and the entire area of the former colony of Cochinchina. In terms of the 1960 administrative divisions of South Vietnam shown in Map 5.1 the coastal lowlands from the province of Quang Tri south to Binh Thuan were part of the protectorate of Annam, and they continue to form an area of traditional Vietnamese subsistence agriculture. The provinces of South Vietnam's central highlands from Kontum in the north to Quang Duc and Lam Dong in the south were also a part of Annam. The malarial jungles of this mountainous region were avoided by the Vietnamese on their march to the south, and the area is sparsely populated by tribal groups. The remaining provinces of South Vietnam were formerly part of Cochinchina. The Mekong delta proper is usually considered to begin in Long An province south of Saigon and includes all provinces south to the South China Sea and west to the Cambodian border. The remainder of the former territory of Cochinchina north of Saigon forms a transition zone between the delta and the southern plateau of the central highlands. Much of this region is covered with lateritic soils poorly suited to intensive cultivation of food crops. This area, particularly the provinces of Binh Long and Long Khanh, is the site of vast French-owned rubber plantations which contribute the second of Vietnam's major export crops. In recent years with the decline in rice exports rubber has become Vietnam's leading export. Most of the rural population, however, remains in either the subsistence or the export sector of the rice economy. In colonial Vietnam the two sectors were represented by the Red River delta and the coastal lowlands on the one hand and the Mekong delta on the other. In an independent South Vietnam the contrasting zones are the truncated central lowlands and the Mekong delta. It was

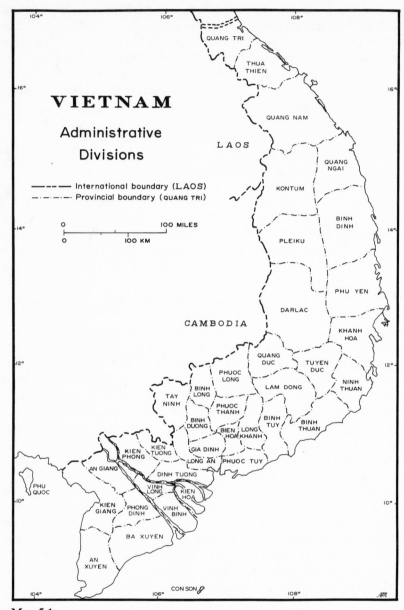

VIETNAM

Administrative

Divisions

— - — - — International boundary (LAOS)
— · — · — Provincial boundary (QUANG TRI)

0   100 MILES
0   100 KM

QUANG TRI

THUA
THIEN

QUANG NAM

LAOS

QUANG
NGAI

KONTUM

BINH
DINH

PLEIKU

PHU YEN

DARLAC

CAMBODIA

KHANH
HOA

QUANG
DUC

TUYEN
DUC

PHUOC
LONG

LAM DONG

NINH
THUAN

BINH
LONG

TAY
NINH

PHUOC
THANH

BINH
DUONG

BINH
TUY

BINH
THUAN

BIEN
HOA

LONG
KHANH

KIEN
PHONG

KIEN
TUONG

GIA DINH

AN GIANG

LONG AN

PHUOC TUY

PHU
QUOC

DINH TUONG

VINH
LONG

KIEN
HOA

KIEN
GIANG

PHONG
DINH

VINH
BINH

BA XUYEN

AN
XUYEN

CON SON

MAP 5.1

284

in the Mekong delta that new forms of economic and social organization radically changed the political interest and organization potential of the Vietnamese peasantry and at the same time created a class of large landowners which was unknown in traditional Vietnam. This contrast between the Mekong delta and the other regions of Vietnam is critical in understanding both the historical sources of agrarian discontent in colonial Vietnam and the origins of the current war in the south.

THE RED RIVER DELTA AND THE COASTAL LOWLANDS

The fundamental unit in the administrative structure of rural areas under both imperial and French colonial rule was the Vietnamese *xa*, the peasant village or commune. In northern and central Vietnam this social unit was a closed corporate community whose separation from the outside world was emphasized by a densely nucleated village structure and by the thick bamboo hedge which surrounded the village. Although the precise political and social organization of the *xa* varied in different historical periods and in different geographical locations, certain basic elements appear in most Vietnamese villages from the fifteenth century onward in most of northern and central Vietnam.[3] Each village was an aggregation of peasant families with a legal identity and a collective responsibility to the central government. Each village had a ranked social hierarchy of notables, and although the system of ranking and the criterion of advancement varied, the senior notables were invariably the most influential individuals in the community. Advancement through the order of precedence could come with age or through mandarinal connections, but wealth in landed property was usually a prerequisite for notable status. The village council was selected by co-optation from the upper ranks of the hierarchy of notables rather than outside appointment. The council of notables, either directly or indirectly, held final authority in the administration of the internal affairs of the village. It controlled the allocation of land and head taxes, the administration of the military draft and the corvée, the adjudication of internal disputes, and the maintenance of internal security. The notables usually controlled the selection of the village chief (the *xa truong* or *ly truong*), who occupied the strategic but unenviable position of liaison between the village council and the local mandarinate. The notables also had important religious functions, which were symbolized in semiannual ceremonies held at the village *dinh,* a building which served both as a temple and a communal meeting house. The *dinh* was the center of the cult of the village spirit and

[3] For a description of the historical evolution of the Vietnamese village see Nguyen Xuan Dao, "Village Government in Vietnam: A Survey of Historical Development," annex to Lloyd W. Woodruff, *The Study of a Vietnamese Rural Community: Administrative Activity*, vol. II (Michigan State University Viet-Nam Advisory Group, May 1960).

represented the local embodiment of the national agrarian cult headed by the emperor. At the founding of a new village the future inhabitants petitioned the emperor to invest a guardian spirit, and no village was complete until the cult of its guardian spirit had been established. In northern and central Vietnam most villages controlled inalienable communal lands (*cong dien*), which were generally redistributed to registered members of the community every three years by the council of notables. The village maintained a list of individuals who appeared on the mandarinal tax roles, and these individuals constituted the registered inhabitants. Originally the mandarinal roles were to include all male inhabitants between the ages of 18 and 60, but the registration list usually reflected local ingenuity in tax evasion rather than the actual demographic composition of the village.

In many respects the typical Vietnamese communes closely resemble the indigenous communities of the Peruvian sierra described in Chapter 3. Like the Peruvian communities the Vietnamese *xa* is a legally recognized aggregation of peasant subsistence farmers controlled by a civil religious hierarchy ultimately responsible to outside authorities. As was the case in Peru, however, there is disagreement about the reality of communal life within the *xa*. Just as some Peruvian intellectuals regarded the *comunidad indígena* as either the embodiment of primitive Incan communalism or the precursor of a Peruvian version of the collective farm, some students of the Vietnamese commune regard it as a collective enterprise which combines the sacred community of the *dinh* and the secular organization of agrarian socialism. This theme is particularly evident in the writings of Paul Mus and his students John McAlister and Frances FitzGerald.[4] Mus, McAlister, and FitzGerald, for example, all see great significance in the fact that the Vietnamese phrase for socialism, *xa hoi*, echoes the word *xa,* which connotes the spiritual unity of the village. Mus and McAlister suggest that "*Xa Hoi* sees the future of Viet Nam as being dependent on its past and on a tradition which predates the French occupation," [5] and FitzGerald contends that Ho Chi Minh's use of the phrase *xa hoi* linked "the future distribution of wealth with the sacred communal traditions of the village." [6] In their writings the social and moral structure of the village was shaped by the cult of the guardian spirit and reaffirmed by ceremonial observances at the *dinh.* They argue that this traditional unity was destroyed under French colonialism and as a result revolutionary socialism can appeal to the Vietnamese peasantry through its implied promise to restore the spiritual unity of the village. Most observers of the economics and political organization of the traditional Vietnamese village, however, have reached very different conclusions about this putative unity. The French geographer Pierre Gourou and

---

[4] See John T. McAlister, Jr., and Paul Mus, *The Vietnamese and Their Revolution* (New York: Harper & Row, 1970), and Frances FitzGerald, *Fire in the Lake: The Vietnamese and the Americans in Vietnam* (New York: Random House, 1972).

[5] Mus and McAlister, *The Vietnamese,* p. 124.

[6] FitzGerald, *Fire in the Lake,* p. 295.

Americans with extensive field experience in Vietnam such as Samuel Popkin and Terry Rambo describe a world in which social and economic conflict are endemic and unity and communal solidarity are a result of either stalemated conflict or oligarchic control.[7] This view does not deny the intense religious feeling and frequent communal ceremonies emphasized by Mus and his students. It does, however, suggest that land tenure and economic organization reveal a very different village than that solemnly portrayed in ceremonial observances at the *dinh*.

Despite its appearance of collective solidarity, the traditional Vietnamese village was actually an aggregation of small holders engaged in isolated subsistence production and united only by desire to gain precedence in the hierarchy of the village. In this respect the villages of northern and central Vietnam resembled traditional villages of the Peruvian sierra such as Hualcan in which collective solidarity was largely a legal fiction and land ownership and agricultural production were individual matters. In Vietnamese communes there was no collective economic organization that provided the cohesion and political unity of modern Peruvian communities such as San Pedro de Cajas. Just as was the case in Peru the precarious subsistence agriculture, pronounced internal stratification and conservative village oligarchy of the traditional community might be expected to inhibit collective action in both economics and politics. In Peru it was the modern cooperatively organized communities like San Pedro de Cajas which participated most actively in the Sierran agrarian movement, while traditional indigenous communities like Hualcan remained largely inactive. In Vietnam it seems unlikely that similarly organized traditional communities would actively support a revolutionary socialist movement. In contrast to the views of Mus and his students, the success of revolutionary socialism in Vietnam could not have been a response to socialism's evocation of the unified village of precolonial Vietnam, since no such unity seems to have existed. An examination of the economics and politics of northern and central Vietnamese villages indicates that only under unusual conditions would they likely be responsive to either revolution or socialism.

The presence of communal lands within the Vietnamese village might seem a possible economic base of communal solidarity, but in fact these lands seldom promoted cooperation. In contrast to the Peruvian village, however, most Vietnam villages actually did control substantial amounts of communal

[7] The definitive work on the village in the colonial period is Pierre Gourou's *The Peasants of the Tonkin Delta* (New Haven, Conn.: Human Relations Area Files, 1955), originally published as *Les Paysans du Delta Tonkinois: Étude de Géographie Humaine* (Paris: Editions d'Art et d'Histoire, 1936). For accounts by American field workers see Samuel L. Popkin, "Corporatism and Colonialism: The Political Economy of Rural Change in Vietnam," paper presented at the South East Asia Development Advisory Group, Rural Development Panel Seminar, Savannah, Ga., June 1974, and A. Terry Rambo, "A Comparison of Peasant Social Systems of Northern and Southern Viet-Nam: A Study of Ecological Adaptation, Social Succession, and Cultural Evolution" (Ph. D. dissertation, University of Hawaii, 1972).

land. The French colonial survey of landholdings conducted between 1929 and 1931 under the direction of Yves Henry found that communal lands constituted 21 percent of the cultivated rice area in Tonkin and 25 percent of the rice area in Annam.[8] The distribution of this land was uneven, however, with some villages holding almost all their land in common while others held little or no communal land. Pierre Gourou's data on communal lands in the Tonkin delta strongly suggest that the largest concentrations of communal land were usually found in areas where cultivation was least promising.[9] Large areas of communal lands were found in coastal marshes and riverine mud flats, where unstable soil and hydraulic conditions made permanent cultivation and occupation of the land difficult. In areas where most lands could be put into permanent cultivation, most land was individually held. As was the case in the Peruvian sierra, where only pastoral lands were held in common and agricultural land was individually owned, in colonial Vietnam the common lands were also the least desirable.

Even though the communal lands were administered collectively by the council of notables, they were worked in small units by the same techniques used in individual subsistence plots. The cooperative organization and collective agricultural techniques of the commercial pastoral communities of the Peruvian sierra were entirely absent. Communal lands were divided into tiny plots which added only a small additional parcel to each family's private holdings. In Tonkin delta the average communal plot amounted to only 360 square meters.[10] In many cases this was too small an amount of land to justify the capital costs of cultivation, and landless villagers often rented their shares to large landowners who then worked them either directly or with sharecroppers. The small plots received by small landholders were worked just as intensively as the families' own lands, but the communal plots added nothing to community economic cooperation or solidarity.

Not only did communal lands not lead to economic cooperation, but they often led instead to intense political conflict within the village. Village notables generally viewed their control of communal lands as an opportunity to enrich themselves and used a variety of devices to manipulate the distribution to their advantage. Even though in theory the lands were to be passed out to the poor and landless, in fact they were usually distributed to registered members of the community in order of their precedence.[11] Those with close political or family ties to the notables typically received the most desirable plots, while the poorest lands generally went to the poorest members of the community. This process tended to discourage capital improvements, since a poor member of the com-

[8] Yves Henry, *Économie Agricole de l'Indochine* (Hanoi: Gouvernement General de l'Indochine, 1932), p. 213.
[9] Gourou, *Tonkin*, p. 385.
[10] *Ibid.*, p. 389.
[11] Popkin, "Corporatism and Colonialism," p. 14.

munity knew that any improved lands would likely go to friends of the notables at the next distribution. Notables also used their control over registration lists to inflate the number of recipients of communal lands and then either retained the additional shares or sold them at a profit.[12] Much community land was rented ostensibly to support village feasts and to maintain the *dinh* and other public buildings, but the bidding for the plots was frequently rigged by the notables, who auctioned off the lands in large lots to exclude most of the poor villagers and pocketed the difference between the low public bids and the much higher private payments.[13]

Most land in the villages of central and northern Vietnam was individually rather than communally owned. Centuries of continuous habitation and partible inheritance had created a mosaic of tiny dwarf holdings fragmented into even smaller dispersed parcels. The rural landscape of northern and central Vietnam is crisscrossed by the field dikes, or bunds, which mark the boundaries of each parcel. In the most densely settled areas of the Tonkin delta the process of division had gone so far that 2 to 3 percent of the land area was covered by the bunds, and some villages in Tonkin had more parcels of land than entire provinces in Cochinchina.[14] Imperial restrictions on large landholdings were effective in northern and central Vietnam, and most land was owned by marginal subsistence farmers. French colonial policies, particularly the increased demands for taxes in cash and rice, forced many small holders into debt to moneylenders or larger landowners and increased the rate of tenancy. By the time of Yves Henry's study of land tenure at the beginning of the 1930s, however, tenancy and land concentration were not apparent in northern or central Vietnam, and a 1960 sample census conducted by the South Vietnamese government found similar patterns of land ownership and tenancy in the central lowlands.[15] The central lowlands which had formerly been part of colonial Annam were in both 1932 and 1960 a region of small landholdings worked by their owners.

Henry's study found that in Tonkin 91.5 percent of all holdings were of less than 1.8 hectares—the maximum size of holding which could be worked without hired labor.[16] At the other extreme there were only 252 landholdings of over 36 hectares.[17] Despite the absence of large landholdings there was still considerable stratification within the population of peasant small holders. Almost a million small holders with less than 1.8 hectares controlled only 36.6 percent of the land, but 60,000 medium peasant proprietors with from 1.8 to

[12] Gourou, *Tonkin*, pp. 389–390.
[13] Popkin, "Corporatism and Colonialism," pp. 14–15.
[14] Gourou, *French Indochina*, p. 276.
[15] Republic of Vietnam, Department of Rural Affairs, Agricultural Economics and Statistics Service, *Report on the Agricultural Census of Viet-Nam* (Saigon, 1962).
[16] Henry, *Économie Agricole*, pp. 108–109.
[17] *Ibid.*

3.6 hectares controlled 26.6 percent, and 30,000 large proprietors controlled an additional 16.6 percent.[18] Thus less than 8 percent of the landholders controlled more than a third of all land. With the exception of the largest holdings, the land was worked by the owner and his family with the aid of some hired labor in the case of the medium peasant owners. The largest holdings, those with over 3.6 hectares, were worked at least in part by tenants, but together they accounted for less than 17 percent of the land, and this area therefore represents the maximum amount of land that could have been in tenancy.

In Annam Henry found that small holders of less than 2.5 hectares constituted 93.8 percent of all holdings and there were only 51 holdings of over 50 hectares.[19] In most provinces of Annam 70 to 95 percent of the holdings were worked by their owners, although in the provinces of Quang Nam and Binh Dinh the proportions of owner-operated holdings were 65 and 70 percent respectively.[20] These patterns of land ownership are also apparent in the data of the 1960 South Vietnamese agricultural census. In the provinces of the central lowlands which had formerly been part of Annam 95.4 percent of all holdings were of less than 2 hectares, and together these holdings constituted 88.2 percent of the cultivated area.[21] Almost 90 percent of the holdings were at least in part owner operated, and rented lands constituted only 32.3 percent of the total land area.[22] The pattern of land ownership established under the last Vietnamese emperors persisted through both the French colonial period and, at least in South Vietnam, after independence.

The dense population and dwarf holdings of northern and central Vietnam created an intense competition for arable land within the village. Each peasant proprietor defended his own holding at almost any cost and attempted to expand it at the expense of his neighbors if at all possible. Gourou notes the strength of this "peasant mentality" in Tonkin in particular, where each peasant "is strongly attached to his land, dreams of increasing it, patch by patch as a result of whatever savings he can realize." [23] In the long-settled areas of northern and central Vietnam all available land had long been in cultivation, and attempts were even made to sow rice in the main channels of major delta streams on the chance that it might be harvested before the current swept it away.[24] Since it was difficult if not impossible to purchase land outside of the village, the expansion could only occur through conflict with other members of the village. The peasants of Tonkin and Annam were notoriously litigious and were willing to risk financial ruin over seemingly trivial amounts of land. Litigation was at least as frequent as it was in the indigenous communities of the Peruvian sierra, but in Vietnam the adversaries were individual villagers

[18] *Ibid.*
[19] *Ibid.*, pp. 144–145.
[20] *Ibid.*, p. 47.
[21] Republic of Vietnam, *Agricultural Census*, p. 25.
[22] *Ibid.*, p. 27.
[23] Gourou, *French Indochina*, p. 331.
[24] Gourou, *Tonkin*, p. 405.

rather than the village and encroaching estate owners. Since the village cadastre was usually out of date and often fraudulent, there were ample opportunities to contest land titles and plot boundaries outside the legal system. Rambo provides one particularly vivid example of the intensity of this extralegal conflict. Village gardens were surrounded by small bamboo hedges which formed the effective boundaries of the plot. By trimming the inside of the hedge while allowing new shoots to grow on the outside, a villager could gradually expand his garden and encroach on the adjacent plot.[25] The internal political economy of the village was greatly dependent on concealment of its activities from outside authorities, and the exposure of any of the numerous irregularities in village affairs could be an important weapon in a land dispute. Denunciations of one villager by another were in fact a major source of administrative control of village affairs. The French, for example, maintained an official state monopoly on the production and sale of alcohol, but the protection of the village provided a lucrative opportunity for an illegal local commerce in alcohol. When illegal stills were located by the French, it was usually the result of denunciations by those seeking tactical advantage in village conflicts.

Although disputes over land boundaries and titles were a central part of village life, Gourou argues that the capital preoccupation of the villagers was their position in the order of precedence.[26] Once a villager had increased his plot from the modal 1.8 hectares to what for Tonkin represented a comfortable plot of 3.6 hectares, he could begin to participate in the political intrigues and public ceremonies which were essential to advancement in the village hierarchy. Notable status gave the villager the opportunity to participate in the rigged bidding of communal lands, the traffic in illegal tax cards, and the manipulation of fraudulent registration lists that were the chief economic rewards of village life. As a result most villagers would bear substantial expenditures and even go deeply into debt to move up in the hierarchy. Each advancement in rank involved a feast requiring the sacrifice of an ox.[27] Since an ox represented a major piece of capital equipment, sponsoring such a feast precipitated a financial crisis for most peasants. Despite the frequency of these feasts there is no evidence that the ceremonial expenditures associated with notable status had any appreciable redistributive effect within the village. Popkin points out that villagers viewed the expense of the feast as an investment which they would have ample opportunity to recoup through their increasing access to community graft.[28] The opportunities provided by the sponsorship of community ceremonies were therefore jealously guarded, and no notable willingly gave up his role in such ceremonies. There was, nevertheless, a substantial turnover in the families controlling positions in the hierarchy, and there was

[25] Rambo, "Peasant Social Systems," p. 187.
[26] Gourou, *Tonkin*, p. 305.
[27] Rambo, "Peasant Social Systems," p. 34.
[28] Samuel Popkin, "The Myth of the Village," University of Texas, Austin, 1974, (Mimeo.), p. 18.

no permanent hereditary aristocracy in the village. Although upward mobility was difficult, downward mobility was always a distinct possibility. Partible inheritance, unstable hydraulic conditions, and financial insecurity made it difficult for notables to maintain their holdings and their positions intact for several generations. In the words of a popular Chinese proverb adopted by the Vietnamese, "No one stays rich for three generations and no one stays poor for three generations." No matter how small the peasant's plot, he could still dream of increasing it through subterfuge or luck until he acquired the financial resources necessary to participate in the high intrigues of the council of notables.

For most peasants, however, such upward mobility would remain simply a dream. Their principal concern was to avoid the financial or agricultural disaster which would prompt the forced sale of their lands. Without land the position of the Vietnamese villager was precarious in the extreme. Opportunities in agricultural wage labor within the village were limited by the relatively small number of medium and large owners who could afford hired help. Even this employment was usually seasonal and often unpredictable from one year to the next. There were a small number of opportunities in village crafts, but a rigid guild structure maintained monopolistic control over their trade secrets. The loss of a peasant's lands could even force him to leave the village and place himself in a dangerously exposed political position. Those who were outside a village and could not produce a tax card showing their village affiliation were assumed to be bandits under both imperial and French rule and were subject to immediate arrest. Even if the peasant was willing to accept the political risks, opportunities for wage labor were scarcely better outside the village than within. The coal mines of Tonkin provided some employment, as did a small textile industry, but the major employers of wage labor in colonial Vietnam were the rubber plantations of Cochinchina. Labor on the rubber plantations, however, was largely involuntary, and a landless villager risked impressment by a village notable acting as a labor contractor for a French plantation. The work in the malarial jungles of the rubber areas was so unhealthy that during the colonial period less than half of all workers survived the three-year term of service. The bleak opportunities for laborers without land in northern and central Vietnam created a conservative interest in the protection of even a minimal subsistence plot and a consequent resistance to both political and technical innovation. The peasants of Tonkin and Annam adopted a strategy of minimizing the maximum loss they could suffer from any possible change in their fortunes. Much of their resistance to change is a result of the variety of risks to which they were exposed and the small margin between maximum production and an economic disaster which might lead to landlessness.

In northern and central Vietnam the cultivated area was barely adequate to support the population at a subsistence level, and the margin between maximum production and economic disaster correspondingly narrow. Approximately 240 kilograms of paddy are necessary to provide a minimal daily diet of 1,500 calories,[29] and in central and northern Vietnam total production per capita seldom reached this level. In 1932 Henry reported that the production of paddy per capita was 217 kilograms in Tonkin and 233 kilograms in Annam.[30] By 1960 the disruptions of war and revolution and a growing population had lowered the per capita production to 139 kilograms in the central lowlands of what had been Annam.[31] Even these minimal per capita supplies did not indicate the actual level of consumption, since a considerable portion of a peasant crop was sold immediately to meet debts, taxes, gambling losses, and ceremonial expenses. Meeting these obligations often forced the peasant well below the subsistence minimum, so that he was usually forced to supplement his rice diet with less desirable crops such as manioc or sweet potatoes. Not infrequently the entire rice crop went to meet taxes and debts and the peasant was forced to live entirely on secondary crops. Needless to say, this level of rice production left no surplus for export and from the colonial period to the present these areas have never exported substantial amounts of rice.

The development of a commercial rice economy was inhibited not only by the consumption needs of a growing population but by the absence of a transportation network in either the Tonkin delta or the dispersed river deltas of the central lowlands. As Rambo has pointed out, the Tonkin delta village and field system was poorly suited to modern transport.[32] The only flat noncultivated land which was not regularly flooded was on the tops of the major dikes. The small field dikes which crisscrossed the delta were suitable only for pedestrian traffic. Major rivers were navigable only with difficulty and in any case were not accessible from most villages. The French rail network was built to connect major urban centers and was not suitable for local paddy transport. The absence of any means of transporting the principal agricultural product of the village almost completely eliminated participation in the cash economy. Gourou estimated that the total outside commerce of a typical village in Tonkin in the 1930s amounted to less than 50 francs a year.[33] The minimal demand for consumer goods was almost entirely satisfied by village craftsmen, and the wealthier landowners in the village were the major source of credit. Many transactions were based on payment in rice, and the peasants' major need for cash was to pay colonial taxes. The heavy French colonial taxes did force the peasant into the cash economy and exposed him to fluctuations in the price of rice, but the involvement was considerably weaker than it was in Cochinchina. More importantly it focused economic conflict on the question of taxation instead of on the internal class structure of the village. Colonial taxes tended to increase

[29] Sansom, *Economics of Insurgency*, p. 37.
[30] Henry, *Économie Agricole*, p. 332.
[31] Calculated from data presented in United States Operations Mission to Vietnam, Program Office Research and Statistics Section, *Annual Statistical Bulletin*, no. 4 (Saigon, May 1961), pp. 7 and 71.
[32] Rambo, "Peasant Social Systems," p. 66.
[33] Gourou, *French Indochina*, p. 257.

stratification within the village and provided the notables with still another opportunity to enrich themselves by controlling the internal distribution of the tax. Nevertheless the colonial tax was generally viewed as an external demand on the village as a whole.

Agriculture in Tonkin and Annam was almost entirely for subsistence, and the absence of any commercial rice trade prevented even wealthier peasants from acquiring chemical fertilizers, modern pumps, or other expensive agricultural technology. Agriculture was a struggle to defend a narrow subsistence margin with traditional techniques of wet rice cultivation which had changed little from the time they were introduced by the Chinese. This struggle was made more difficult by the unstable hydraulic environment of the northern and central coastal deltas. The climate of Vietnam is dominated by the monsoons, which divide the agricultural calendar into distinct wet and dry periods. In northern Vietnam there are two monsoon periods; the summer monsoon brings heavy rains from the southwest, and the winter monsoon brings a light drizzle and fog from the northeast. The heavy rains of the summer monsoon would inundate the Tonkin delta if it were not protected by a network of dikes. The Red River in particular is characterized by violent and irregular changes in flow and breaches in the dikes and flooding are a perpetual problem throughout the rainy season. This season also brings typhoons, which devastate coastal areas and can also cause severe inland flooding. The danger from both typhoons and flooding is considerably greater in northern and central Vietnam than it is in the Mekong delta, and the risk to the peasant subsistence margin correspondingly greater. Similarly, although the winter monsoon in northern and central Vietnam permits the growing of a second rice crop, the rainfall in both monsoon periods is highly variable. In southern Vietnam there is in general only one monsoon period, but the rainfall is regular and constant from one year to the next. The irregularity of rainfall in the north and center adds the problem of drought to the risks of flooding and typhoons. As Rambo has pointed out, much of the intensity of the agricultural techniques of northern and central Vietnam can be understood as an attempt to reduce the risk associated with this unstable hydraulic environment.[34] The tiny dispersed parcels of the region actually protect the peasant against a localized hydraulic disturbance which otherwise could reduce him to landlessness or starvation. Intensive cultivation of each small parcel is necessary not only to achieve maximum total production but to insure a minimal crop if most of the parcels are destroyed.

A dense population, tiny dispersed plots, and irregular climatic conditions led to intensive agricultural techniques which required an extravagant amount of labor. Additional labor was applied as long as some increase in total production could be obtained without regard to its marginal cost. The large labor input led Gourou to characterize Tonkinese cultivation techniques as "horticulture: hand labor, a small plot cultivated by each peasant, minute and individual care

---

[34] Rambo, "Peasant Social Systems," p. 70.

of the plants." [35] Gourou estimated that a hectare of double-cropped rice land required 400 man-days per year in Tonkin.[36] Much of this time was spent in tedious hand labor designed both to minimize risk and to bring every corner of every field into cultivation. The rice crop was actually harvested twice in order to insure that the valuable grains were not lost to flooding or storms. The peasant first harvested the heads with a hand sickle and then harvested the stalks separately. In preparing the paddies for transplanting, any corners the plows had missed were carefully hoed by hand, and the entire paddy was frequently rearranged in small mounds to facilitate aeration of the soil. Since men and oxen competed for a limited food supply, most of this work was done without the aid of animal traction. Dumont reports that two or three Tonkinese farmers would drag a harrow through the muddy cold paddies themselves rather than hire an expensive bullock.[37]

The immense labor requirements of this system of cultivation and the prevalence of small-scale land ownership in northern and central Vietnam have produced a distinct set of personality characteristics which clearly differentiate the hard-working northern Vietnamese from the more easygoing southerners. These characteristics are well-known cultural stereotypes in Vietnam and are mentioned by almost all outside observers. The peasants of northern and central Vietnam are characterized by a commitment to the work ethic, by frugality verging on stinginess, and by a pronounced aversion to risk. At the same time the northerners' dedication to their own plots even at the expense of their neighbors' welfare has produced a reputation for individualism and reserve. Charles Robequain, for example, notes that because of this reputation large southern landowners were reluctant to accept northerners as tenants even though they regarded them as harder workers than native southerners.[38] Disciplined hard work, the cautious protection of property, and rugged individualism were useful adjustments to the agricultural environment of the north, but they proved a distinct handicap to cooperative political or economic organization within the village.

All phases of rice cultivation were carried out by individuals or families, and there was relatively little cooperative labor even at harvest and transplanting, when such cooperation would greatly reduce labor costs. The absence of cooperation is particularly striking in irrigation, where the technological and economic incentives for collective action would appear to be greatest. Villagers were responsible for the collective maintenance of the local dike network, which was constantly eroded by running water and undermined by vegetation, but these works were entirely protective in nature. There were no artificial irrigation systems of ditches and canals to move water from the

[35] Gourou, *French Indochina*, p. 295.
[36] *Ibid.*, p. 284.
[37] Rene Dumont, *Types of Rural Economy: Studies of World Agriculture* (New York: Praeger, 1957), p. 140.
[38] Charles Robequain, *The Economic Development of French Indo-China* (London: Oxford University Press, 1944), p. 72.

principal streams of the delta to the local fields. Most Vietnamese rice fields were dependent on impounded rain water and standing water in village ditches and ponds for the maintenance of adequate water levels. Standing water was lifted short distances to the paddies in conical bamboo scoops or baskets at an immense expenditure of muscular effort with no mechanical aid and little mechanical advantage. This primitive irrigation system required almost no cooperation, and some of the scoops or baskets could be worked by a single man. Despite the chronic problems of drought and inadequate standing water, the immense amount of water readily available in nearby channels, and the substantial increase in production and economic security that irrigation would have made possible, no cooperative irrigation systems were developed in Vietnam at the local level. In Tonkin the successful use of river water would have required large-scale cooperation because of the turbulence and rate of flow of the principal streams and the irregular terrain of the delta. The organizational resources necessary to overcome the divisive interests of a local village of small landowners were not available. Gourou concludes his analysis of the problems of local water shortages with the observation that "all these difficulties will disappear when they have set up irrigation networks which make everywhere available to the peasant water in virtually unlimited quantities." [39] The social structure of colonial Vietnam was, however, incapable of the collective organization successful irrigation required.

Only after 1954, when the traditional village structure was destroyed by revolution and a new cooperative organization drew reluctant peasants into a communal economy, were the organizational resources of communities sufficient to carry out collective irrigation. The North Vietnamese government established agrarian cooperatives after 1959 and began work on both defensive irrigation works and smaller dikes, penstocks, and bridges to rationalize the delivery of irrigation water to the villages. Even the victorious revolutionary regime found it difficult to lure the individualistic villagers into the cooperatives. Two important arguments that the Communist cadre could offer, however, were the demonstrable advantages of a second rice crop made possible by the new irrigation works and the long-range stability in the face of flooding made possible by defensive dikes around each village. [40] In the colonial period and before the establishment of a strong central power there was no means for overcoming the peasants' dedication to their individual plots and their unwillingness to surrender either the land or the labor necessary for these collective works.

Since the provision of flowing irrigation water to village fields was beyond the organizational resources of the commune, irrigation water within the community invariably became a scarce fixed resource much like communal lands. The total amount of water in the village was arbitrarily fixed by the accumula-

---

[39] Gourou, *Tonkin,* p. 109.
[40] For a description of the appeal of collective irrigation see Gérard Chaliand, *The Peasants of North Vietnam* (Baltimore: Penguin, 1969), pp. 98–101.

tion of rainfall in all paddies, ditches, and ponds, and this fixed sum, of course, declined in periods of drought. New catchment basins could have been constructed, but in comparison to the additional water that could have been brought in from rivers the expansion in total water resources would have been minor. New ditches and pools also raised the insoluble question of whose lands would be sacrificed to the common good. The fixed amount of water invariably led to redistributive conflicts within the village, and these conflicts were exacerbated in times of drought when the need for irrigation water in paddies increased while the supply of standing water decreased. In an economy in which villagers would use the gradual growth of a bamboo hedge to steal 2 inches of adjacent land the theft of water from adjacent paddies or ponds was a continual problem. Although elaborate rules were devised to regulate these conflicts, they were rarely successful. All that was required to steal water was a single breach in a field dike, which could be accomplished and repaired in a few minutes. Like communal land, communal water was a more important source of conflict than of cooperation in Vietnamese villages.

Popkin argues that the relatively large public sector of the northern and central Vietnamese villages in the form of communal lands and standing water was both an important reward in community power struggles and an important source of power for the victorious faction.[41] Much of the apparent solidarity of the villages of Tonkin was the result of the notables' monopolistic control over vital community resources and their willingness to sanction uncooperative villagers by limiting their access to these resources. This power of the notables had existed before the French colonial period, but, according to Popkin, French authority both increased stratification within the village and reinforced the power of the village elite. In contrast to the views of Mus and his students who contend that colonialism caused the collapse of internal village government, Popkin argues that the council of notables became even more secure because French military power made it effectively immune from retaliation from poorer members of the village and French colonial taxes provided it with a powerful additional sanction. The notables represented the large land-owning interest in the village and formed a conservative oligarchy which could be effectively resisted by other wealthy landowners but not by most poor villages. Direct and indirect sanctions were used by the notables to maintain community solidarity, although as Gourou states, "a strict tyranny is the concomitant of this solidarity." [42] Notables were not above shaking down villagers for contributions to support the semiannual festivals at the *dinh* and arresting villagers who were too poor to contribute to this expression of the spiritual unity of the village. Failure to purchase tax cards at the inflated rates offered by the notables in control of the village tax system could result in beatings or ostracism. The notables were also able to effectively direct the power of outside authorities against other villagers. Just as was the case in land battles, denunciations to outside authorities

[41] Popkin, "Corporatism and Colonialism," p. 7.
[42] Gourou, *Tonkin,* p. 314.

were an important tool of the notables in their efforts to enforce community solidarity. Gérard Chaliand provides one example of such tactics in an interview with a North Vietnamese party secretary who had been a landless peasant during the colonial period. His landlessness was a result of pressure from village notables. The notables first planted liquor in his family's home and then tipped off the local authorities to dispossess one uncle.

> In 1943 the village notables decided to put pressure on my family and I shall never forget the experience. At their bidding a man came to my uncle's house, feigned insanity and set fire to the place. Luckily the flames were soon extinguished, but the "lunatic" had smashed everything in reach. The two notables accompanying the "lunatic" were seized and bound, but my two uncles were arrested for laying hands on the notables. There was pandemonium at the district court. In the end, my uncles had to sell all they owned to pay for the trial and were sentenced to three months imprisonment. We had already lost three saos as a result of the liquor incident and now the last four saos had to be sold. We had nothing left.[43]

The tyranny of the notables explains the otherwise puzzling fact that the greater community cohesion of northern and central villages made them much more subject to control than the much less cohesive villages of Cochinchina. The greater the community cohesion, the more secure the notables' grip and the more readily administrative demands could be communicated to the local population. Although, in the words of an oft-quoted Vietnamese proverb, "the law of the emperor yields to the customs of the village," in fact the village had a collective responsibility to both the imperial and French administrations and was free only to allocate the distribution of outside demands within the village. The law of the emperor yielded only if the village met these collective responsibilities; if not, intervention by outside authorities was likely. In imperial times the discovery of a corpse on community lands could lead to the uprooting of the village and the banishment of its members, and failure of the community to meet its tax obligations could lead to the confiscation of the property of the wealthier notables.[44] In a symbolic manifestation of these imperial controls the punishment for sheltering a dissident in times of rebellion was the destruction of the bamboo hedge around the village, ending its nominal autonomy. As was the case in the indigenous communities of highland Peru, Vietnamese peasants had been consolidated into communes to facilitate administrative control and the extraction of peasant surpluses. In Vietnam the surplus was extracted by the state organization rather than by large landowners, but in both cases the autonomous corporate village was a convenient administrative fiction. The Vietnamese

---

[43] Chaliand, *North Vietnam*, pp. 94–95.
[44] Dennis J. Duncanson, *Government and Revolution in Vietnam* (London: Oxford University Press, 1968), p. 57.

village continued to exist only so long as there were groups which profited from its exploitation. The communal solidarity of the traditional Vietnamese village was imposed from above and was not a product of the fundamentally individualistic subsistence economy.

The small proprietors, marginal subsistence agriculture, the competition for communal land and water, and the tyranny of the notables created a constellation of coercive and economic forces which would lead to collective political action only under unusual circumstances. The danger of landlessness forced the peasant to tenaciously defend his small plot and made him suspicious of any political program which might benefit the landless at the expense of his own meager holding. The threatening ecology of the northern and central deltas and the narrow subsistence margin required an intensive agriculture which consumed most of the time and attention of cultivators but required little cooperation. The surest solution to problems of minimal subsistence was to be found not in redistributing the minimal amount of land in large holdings or in decreasing the surplus extracted by the notables and moneylenders, but in ever more intensive cultivation of existing subsistence plots. The struggle of the peasants in northern and central Vietnam was primarily with the natural, not the social environment, and their solutions to their economic problems were therefore individual struggles against nature rather than a collective revolt against oppression. In fact other small holders were seen as potential competitors for the limited community land and water rather than as allies in collective action against the notables. Upward mobility through the order of precedence in the village remained a hope for all but the poorest peasant, but such mobility could only be secured by a conservative emulation of the attitudes and behavior of the established community elite. Once an elite position had been assured, it was possible to join the spoils system of community politics, but poor peasants whose interests might have been served by a collective peasant organization did not have access to the political resources required for this competition and in fact ran substantial risks by opposing the tyranny of the notables. The sanctions based on control of community land and water, the manipulation of registration lists and tax records, and the threat of beatings or ostracism quickly integrated even rebellious members who had long been absent from the village back into the conservative order of precedence.

Even if the problems of divisive individual plots, individual mobility, and a conservative oligarchy could have been overcome, there was relatively little to be gained from collective action in the northern Vietnamese village. Land reform would not lead to the dramatic increase in property ownership that would be possible in less densely settled and more extensive agriculture areas. There was simply not enough land to be distributed. This fact placed a severe limit on the land reform program adopted by the North Vietnamese government after independence. According to Bernard Fall the North Vietnamese land reform classified a peasant with a holding of 0.21 hectares as a rich farmer and a peasant with 0.12 hectares as a medium farmer.[45] Obviously, small amounts of land could be taken from these "rich" and "medium" peasants without reducing them to landless laborers. Most of the large landowners and redistributable land were actually in the south outside the control of the revolutionary regime in the north. Although collective action in irrigation could lead to dramatic increases in production, the results of this action became apparent only in the long run and lacked the immediate political appeal of the redistribution of large estates to those who tilled them. In the short run the peasants of northern and central Vietnam had much to lose and relatively little to gain from collective political action.

The political stability of the traditional Vietnamese village was, however, based on a delicate balance of economic and coercive forces which could easily be disturbed by political or ecological disaster. In such situations the formerly docile and conservative peasantry were remarkably transformed into a revolutionary mass dedicated to the overthrow of the notables and the end of the taxes, tribute, and political interference of the national administration. The stability of the village depended on maintaining sufficient production so that only individuals, not whole villages or regions, were forced below the subsistence minimum and into landlessness. Once the agricultural base of the traditional village was disturbed over a wide area, the interests of the peasantry dramatically changed. Drought, typhoons, floods, and civil war all had this potential for breaking up the economic structure of the traditional village. In these situations differences in wealth tended to diminish as the value of devastated land fell and more and more peasants were forced into bankruptcy by massive crop failures. Lands themselves could be rendered worthless, and the patient labor of adding to a subsistence plot in gradual increments became pointless in the midst of flood or drought. Even wealthy peasants were forced into landlessness in such situations, so that the economic interest in the protection of property which normally divided them from the poor and landless peasants was markedly, if temporarily, reduced. The intensive cultivation of isolated subsistence plots was a rational strategy only so long as the subsistence margin could be maintained. If drought wiped out the possibility of even minimal subsistence production, intensive labor and a tenacious hold on a subsistence plot became less useful adjustments. In most periods money was found to pay taxes because it was still possible to protect the subsistence minimum and meet tax bills. In disaster situations taxes might require the sale of the entire harvest, the seed rice, the capital equipment of the farm, and even the land itself. In this situation taxes forced the peasant into the market for agricultural commodities, capital equipment, and land against his will. Having temporarily lost the endless battle with nature, the peasant had the immediate problem of reducing the external tax demand and preventing the liquidation of his remaining agricultural assets. The cash nexus between the peasant and the local and national administration became consider-

---

[45] Bernard Fall, *The Two Vietnams: A Political and Military Analysis* (New York: Praeger, 1963), p. 159.

ably more apparent and much more difficult to tolerate in periods of natural disaster. At the same time that the disaster undermined the basis of peasant economic stability and conservatism, it lowered the coercive resources of the village administration. Access to communal water is of no value if the water has vanished in a drought, and the distribution of communal lands is not an important source of community power if the lands are inundated by salt water in a typhoon. Similarly a disaster may make it more difficult for the notables to call on outside support, since the resources of the central administration will be similarly strained. Typhoons in central Vietnam, for example, made it impossible to land emergency grain shipments along the coast to relieve the acute food crisis resulting from the inland flooding associated with the typhoon. Finally incentives for collective action and the relative costs and benefits changed dramatically in periods of natural disaster. In a situation in which marauding bands of bandits or starving villages might mount attacks on a village and military units might be necessary to collect taxes, collective political action became essential to individual safety. The disruptions of the disaster also lowered the possibility of retaliation by the notables and provided an opportunity to erase all past debts and obligations by destroying the community records and governing structure.

Thus in natural disasters the economic conservatism, individual mobility, and tyranny of the notables simultaneously disappeared, and a peasant revolt was the result. Mandarins were assassinated, village notables attacked, and registers and tax lists destroyed and commercial granaries looted. Such peasant revolts were a continual problem in imperial Vietnam and persisted in the colonial period. Areas which combined frequent natural disasters and a narrow subsistence margin were the most likely to produce frequent revolts. Nghe An province, mother of revolutionaries, birthplace of Ho Chi Minh and many other revolutionary leaders, and the site of uprisings against the imperial, the French, and even the North Vietnamese regimes, was one of the most ecologically dangerous and least productive areas in Vietnam. Rainfall was the most irregular in Vietnam, typhoons hit the coast here much more frequently than elsewhere, and the soil was thin, sandy, and unproductive. Rice production in Nghe An in the 1930s was only 190 kilograms per capita, the lowest in Annam with the exception of arid and sparsely populated Phan Thiet, which was not exposed to the same typhoon risk or irregular rain as was Nghe An.[46] In Nghe An province natural conditions produced a frequent disruption of the stable economic and ecological base of the traditional Vietnamese village. In most other areas of northern and central Vietnam these disasters were much less frequent, and the political stability of the traditional village was correspondingly greater. If Nghe An illustrates that the stability of the traditional village can be disrupted by natural disaster, the Mekong delta of southern Vietnam illustrates that this stability could be destroyed by economic forces. In the Mekong delta the precarious balance of the traditional village was never firmly established, and the rapid penetration of the world economy created a new form of village organiza-

[46] Henry, *Économie Agricole*, p. 32.

tion. The economic and social organization of the villages of the Mekong not only created political instability, but also led to new forms of class conflict and class-based political organization that were largely absent in the traditional villages of central and northern Vietnam.

THE MEKONG DELTA

Many of the fundamental characteristics of the villages of the traditional areas of Vietnamese culture in northern and central Vietnam are reproduced in the villages of the Mekong delta. The council of notables, the village chief, the list of registered inhabitants, the cult of the guardian spirit, and the communal ceremonies at the *dinh* appear in Mekong delta villages just as they do in the villages of the north and center from which the settlers of the delta migrated in the eighteenth and nineteenth centuries. The economic base of the village social structure, however, is different in almost all respects from that of the traditional village, and in fact Gourou suggests that it is legitimate to examine rice culture in Cochinchina along with the modern rubber plantations, since both developed under French colonial rule in the nineteenth and twentieth centuries and reflect modern market forces.[47] Even though the economic base of the villages of the Mekong is based on wet rice cultivation just as it was in the older settled areas and the techniques of production are similar, the class structure and productive organization in the delta are very different. This is especially true in the so-called Mien Tay or new west—the former frontier areas southwest of the Hau Giang River, which diverges from the Mekong as the latter enters Vietnam from Cambodia. The provinces of the upper delta northeast of the Mekong share some elements of the village organization and economic structure of the older areas of Vietnam, while the Mien Tay is the most deeply affected by modern economic forces. Most of the detailed information about village structure, however, comes from the upper delta region accessible by road from Saigon. Khan Hau, a village in Long An province, was intensively studied by a team of researchers from the Michigan State University Viet-Nam Advisory Group and in 1962 became a demonstration village for the ill-fated strategic hamlet program.[48] The adjacent province of Dinh Tuong was the site of a study of village economics conducted by Robert Sansom.[49] There are no detailed studies of the village structure in the Mien Tay, but more general statistical information is available on the delta as a whole.

[47] Gourou, *French Indochina,* p. 332.
[48] See Lloyd W. Woodruff, *The Study of a Vietnamese Rural Community: Administrative Activity* (Michigan State University Viet-Nam Advisory Group, May 1960), James B. Hendry, *The Small World of Khan Hau* (Chicago: Aldine, 1964), and Gerald Cannon Hickey, *Village in Vietnam* (New Haven: Yale University Press, 1964), for parallel and to some extent overlapping accounts of this project.
[49] Robert Sansom, *The Economics of Insurgency in the Mekong Delta of Vietnam* (Cambridge, Mass.: M.I.T. Press, 1970).

In both the colonial and postindependence periods the southern regions of Vietnam and particularly the Mekong delta were regions of large estates worked in small units by share tenants and sharecroppers. In 1932 Yves Henry found that 95 percent of all holdings of more than 50 hectares were concentrated in Cochinchina, where 6,316 large landowners controlled 45 percent of the cultivated land. Another 28,141 medium to large landholders with between 10 and 50 hectares controlled an additional 32.5 percent, so that together less than 15 percent of the landholders controlled more than three-quarters of the cultivated area.[50] Almost all this land was divided up into small plots, typically of approximately 5 hectares in size. Gourou reports that 80 percent of the land in western and central Cochinchina was in tenancy and that three out of every four male heads of households were either tenants or landless laborers.[51] Despite land reforms carried out by the Viet Minh between 1945 and 1954 and the much less ambitious land reform initiated by Ngo Dinh Diem in 1956, these patterns of land ownership changed only slightly after the end of colonialism. In 1955 the South Vietnamese Directorate of Land Reform reported that 5,880 holders of over 50 hectares continued to control 46.57 percent of the land in the former area of Cochinchina and 28,840 holders of from 10 to 50 hectares controlled an additional 24.02 percent.[52] Just as in the colonial period, less than 15 percent of landowners continued to control almost three-quarters of the land and 2.4 percent controlled almost half. On October 22, 1956, the Diem government issued its most important land reform decree, Ordinance 57, which placed an upper limit of 100 hectares on holdings of rice and declared all lands above this limit subject to expropriation. In a pattern that was followed by successive South Vietnamese regimes, however, only a small part of this land found its way into the hands of landless laborers and tenant farmers. As late as 1967 only 681,260 hectares had actually been expropriated, and only 261,213 hectares had been redistributed to small holders.[53] Even this limited reform was of questionable value to many former tenants, since most of the land had been under their de facto control for years under the Viet Minh. Tenants were required to repay the government for the land, so that many found themselves once again in the role of tenant, with the government rather than the landlord as the rent-collecting agent. Tenancy remained a problem in the land not subject to reform, and in 1961, 62.5 percent of land in the former area of Cochinchina was still held in tenancy and only 21.9 percent of all holdings were owner operated. Since approximately 20 percent of the population were landless laborers, more than 80 percent of the Mekong delta population was without land.[54] The reform did succeed in almost doubling the amount of land in hold-

[50] Henry, *Économie Agricole*, pp. 182–183, 190–191.
[51] Gourou, *French Indochina*, p. 339.
[52] Data presented in Stanford Research Institute, *Land Reform in Vietnam: Working Papers* (Menlo Park, Calif.: Stanford Research Institute, 1968), vol. 4, part 1, annex table A2.
[53] *Ibid.*, vol. 1, part 1, app. B-11, pp. B-72–B-73.
[54] Republic of Vietnam, *Agricultural Census*, p. 27.

ings of under 5 hectares, although by 1967 these holdings controlled less than a third of all cultivated land even though they represented 85 percent of all holdings. Some very large holdings were eliminated, but holdings over 10 hectares still controlled 54.09 percent of the cultivated area in 1967.[55] The Diem reforms eliminated only the largest landowners, many of who were severely compromised by their association with the French colonial regime or were themselves French citizens. The middle-level landowners of Cochinchina who would have represented the agrarian upper class in Annam or Tonkin were left untouched by the reforms because the Diem regime depended on this stratum as the effective base of its administration in the countryside.

Although the French colonial regime established a system of free concessions for French nationals and encouraged French settlement and cultivation with preferential tax policies, most of the large landowners in Cochinchina were Vietnamese. Henry reported that only 253,400 hectares of concessions had been granted to French nationals by 1932, and an approximately similar amount was appropriated from French citizens in the Diem reform of 1957.[56] Even though French concessions in Cochinchina constituted more than 90 percent of all French concessions in Vietnam, they represented only 11 percent of the approximately 2 million hectares of rice land in cultivation during the colonial period. Most of the remaining land was granted in large tracts to Vietnamese who were strategically placed in the colonial political system. Collaborators in the French military conquest, members of the colonial council, lower-level civil servants in the colonial administration, and even French-educated professionals were the principal beneficiaries of French land policies. Peasant farmers had neither the political influence nor the knowledge of French administrative procedures necessary to compete effectively for land. Lands were auctioned off in blocks too large for most peasants to afford, information about land registration procedures and auctions was severely restricted, and claims for land titles depended more on political influence than on actual cultivation. Just as was the case in traditional areas of Vietnam, local landowners generally controlled land registration, and with the assistance of Vietnamese colonial bureaucrats could effectively prevent small holders from securing title to their lands. Many peasants migrated into the frontier areas of the delta and performed the preliminary labor of clearing the land and constructing paddies only to find that their plot had been appropriated as part of a large tract ceded to a colonial bureaucrat. Although small frontier areas remained in the Mekong delta until as late as 1930, most of the cultivated and uncultivated land had been effectively claimed by this time, and since land sales were infrequent, little or no land was available to tenants or landless laborers after 1930.

The new land-owning elite in Cochinchina was bureaucratic rather than entrepreneurial, and its position depended on the political backing of France

[55] Stanford Research Institute, *Land Reform,* vol. 4, part 2, annex table A2.
[56] Henry, *Économie Agricole,* p. 225; Stanford Research Institute, *Land Reform,* vol. 1, app. B-11, p. B-73.

rather than on the workings of free markets in land, labor, or capital. The Vietnamese elite took little interest in the actual running of their estates and usually lived in Saigon or in major delta towns such as My Tho, leaving the collection of rent to hired agents. Smaller landowners might live in a village with their tenants or in smaller provincial towns, but like the large landowners they performed an essentially extractive function and were little concerned with technological innovation or market forces. Sansom has pointed out that the landed upper class was in fact remarkably insensitive to fluctuations in the export price of rice because its revenues depended only on the costs of rent collection and even in a bad year these costs were usually far less than the revenues from the sale of rice.[57] The landlords showed little interest in marketing and sold their rice to Chinese merchants in Cholon just as did peasant small holders. The landlords had little incentive to adopt direct cultivation of their estates, since a sizeable part of their income depended on loans to tenants and low land prices and taxes did not require an efficient use of the land to extract large profits. As the population of the delta increased, the landlord's position improved, since he could rely on competition for subsistence to keep the rent of rice lands at high levels. Rents were in fact determined largely by the pressure of population on land rather than by the price of rice.

No matter how large the estate, it was usually divided up into plots of from 5 to 10 hectares and worked by tenants. The status of tenant in Vietnam in particular and Southeast Asia in general is, however, similar to that of a dependent agricultural laborer paid in kind rather than an independent entrepreneur paying a rent for particular factors of production. Few tenants had written contracts, and, even those who did had little recourse in the landlord-dominated colonial legal system. Rents in the colonial period usually represented 50 percent or more of the primary rice crop, although in some cases loans extended by the landlord for seeds, equipment, or draft animals could raise the landlord's share to 70 or 80 percent. The rent was actually a standing rent in kind rather than a share rent, since the share was computed on the normal yield of the plot and was expressed in a fixed quantity of rice. In bad years delta landlords were extremely reluctant to extend "tolerance" to their tenants by absorbing part of the losses, so that all risk was born by the tenant and a poor harvest could lead to the complete expropriation of the crop. Even during the depression, when falling rice prices made it impossible for tenants to meet their obligations to moneylenders and still retain enough rice to support their families, the landlords would not relax their demands. Landlords sought out relatively solvent tenants so they would not have to expose themselves to a plea for tolerance from a starving tenant whom they had pushed over the subsistence margin. The landlord had an effective lien against the entire rice crop, and the tenant had no freedom to dispose of the crop or to use it as the primary collateral for loans.

[57] Sansom, *Mekong Delta,* p. 33.

The landlord's claim on the crop is the fundamental explanation of the phenomenal interest rates charged in the Mekong delta. Although high interest rates and chronic indebtedness were a problem everywhere in Vietnam, nowhere did they reach a more disastrous level than in the Mekong delta. According to the French administrator Roger Sylvestre:

> There is no one who is neither borrower nor lender, the *ta dien* borrows from his landlord, the latter if the need arises, from a larger capitalist; the coolie will establish credit with his foreman, the latter with his employer, the fisherman with the fisheries contractor, the small trader with the large merchant, those with an independent calling—artisans, officials,—contract debts with a Chinese merchant or with a usurer.[58]

Interest rates on small unsecured loans in colonial Vietnam ran from 3 to 5 percent a month, although landlords were sometimes able to charge 50 to 100 percent interest for six-month loans until the next harvest. Rates on petty loans extended on a daily basis sometimes went much higher, and the rate on the so-called *vay cat co*, or throat-cutting loan, was 10 percent per day, or 3,650 percent a year.[59] These extraordinary interest rates have often been attributed to usurious lending practices on the part of Chinese and Vietnamese middlemen who, along with the landlords themselves, were the principal sources of agricultural credit. Actually the rates are not excessive considering the financial insecurity created by the landlord's demands on the peasant. Since in a bad year the landlord might claim the entire crop, the moneylender absorbed the risk that the landlord passed on to the tenant. Tenants were frequently forced into bankruptcy and would default all their obligations and flee to the frontier areas where they could not be traced by either the landlord or the moneylender. The high interest rates of the Mekong delta suggest that credit is artificially manipulated, but actually the small lender is in no position to maintain a monopolistic control over credit. Interest rates were high, but only in comparison to what they would have been if the tenants were independent landowners and consequently better credit risks. The restricted market in agricultural credit is an indirect result of landlordism, which in turn is a result of the political dominance of the landed elite.

The large land concentrations and legally inferior position of the tenant also created discontinuities in the marketing of rice. Since the landlord's agent collected the major share of the crop for transport to Saigon, most middlemen were concentrated in the Saigon suburb of Cholon, where they purchased rice in large quantities, milled it, and then sold it for export. The entry costs of this middleman role were substantially higher than if the rice had been purchased in the countryside from a dispersed population of small holders. Since most rice was sucked out of the countryside by the large landowners, there were few

[58] Quoted in Gourou, *French Indochina*, p. 334.
[59] *Ibid.*, p. 348.

opportunities for small Vietnamese traders to establish themselves at the village level. After 1945, however, when the Viet Minh and later the NLF (National Liberation Front) were able to force down rents in areas they influenced, the rice trade passed increasingly into the hands of local village entrepreneurs. The greater share of rice remaining in the hands of small producers increased opportunities for local rice milling, and more mills moved out into the countryside. The development of local markets in rice greatly reduced or even eliminated the large differential in the Saigon and delta rice prices that had formerly worked to the advantage of the landlord and the Chinese middlemen. Landlord dominance of the Mekong delta restricted the workings of the market in rice just as it had restricted the market in agricultural credit.

Landlord dominance also restricted the opportunities for technological innovation and capital investment in the tenants' plots. This effect is most striking in irrigation, which remained at the same primitive level as it had in northern and central Vietnam despite considerable incentives for artificial irrigation. Paradoxically, the ecology of the Mekong delta made irrigation both simpler and more critical than it had been in northern and central Vietnam yet delta farmers made less use of artificial irrigation than their northern counterparts. The Mekong delta is not exposed to the light rains and drizzle of the northeast monsoon and has a pronounced dry period from November to May, during which no second crop can be grown and both peasants and lands remain idle. The Mekong, however, is a considerably more tranquil river than the Red, and its floods are regular and predictable. The Tonle Sap in Cambodia acts as a hydraulic regulator, containing the flood of the Mekong and gradually releasing the water, which spreads out over the gently sloping expanse of the delta. The gradual predictable flooding of the Mekong makes it possible to grow floating rice in areas near the Cambodian border where the flood reaches its maximum. The rice is planted when the river is near its minima, and as the flood rises, the rice grows at an extremely rapid rate, always keeping its head near the surface. Since too rapid or too slow a rise will disturb the growing cycle of the plant, this rice can only be grown in areas where flooding is regular and predictable. The regularity of the Mekong flood makes it much less necessary to build huge defensive irrigation works before water can be put to use in local fields. In fact the only irrigation works necessary after the French built canals and drained the delta were small connecting channels between the canals and the Mekong's many tributaries and the fields. Even though most delta fields are within reach of this easily controlled water source, very few connecting canals were built before the 1960s. Irrigation was based entirely on rain water impounded in field dikes, and little use was made of community standing water. Irrigation in the Mekong delta was largely an individual matter, and there were no community water resources to be collectively managed or mismanaged. Disputes over irrigation did occur in the Mekong delta, but they usually involved transit rather than the redistribution of community water resources. The absence of artificial irrigation in the delta despite its apparent advantages is a result of the indirect effects of landlord dominance. Poor peasants and landless laborers who had the most to benefit from an irrigated second crop which might protect them against starvation in a year of drought were the least politically influential members of delta villages. The large landowners who controlled most of the land were not inclined to permit diversion of any of their lands for canals and pools which would not benefit them directly and might cause their tenants to demand lower rents in compensation for the lost land. Even minor improvements in local water management required the permission of the landlord, and tenants hesitated to take advantage of nearby water sources for fear that the landlord would evict them or raise the rent. Although collectively and in the long run landlords might have benefited from increased irrigation, individually and in the short run they feared lower rents and fragmented holdings. As long as the land-lords dominated the structure of the village, no collective irrigation works were possible. The presence of the landlords tended to restrict the workings of the land, commodity, and credit markets, and discouraged technical improvements which would have increased productivity.

Nevertheless, in contrast to the regions of traditional subsistence, production in the Mekong delta was oriented toward the rice export market. In the colonial period three-quarters of total delta production was exported through the Saigon market, and even the larger tenant farmers were actively engaged in the export trade. About half of the exports were accounted for by landlord sales, but 20 to 25 percent of exports were contributed by the tenants themselves, who typically sold as much as half of their share of the crop. In Khan Hau in Long An province Hendry found that three-quarters of all farmers sold at least some part of their crop during the year and only the poorest farmers did not participate in the rice trade.[60] Almost half of the farmers sold some or all of their crop immediately after the harvest, and although most farmers retained part of their harvest for their own needs, others sold the entire crop and bought lower-quality rice for their own use. Only a minority of the wealthiest farmers were able to withhold rice and sell when the price was highest, and many farm-ers looked upon their rice crop as a form of savings that they could draw on for cash needs during the entire year by periodically selling a small portion of the crop. The money was necessary to meet interest payments, taxes, and gambling debts, to purchase consumer goods, and to meet the ceremonial expenses which were part of village life in the delta as well as in the older areas of Vietnam. In contrast to the northern and central villages, however, there was an active con-sumer market in Mekong river villages, and small shopkeepers provided a wide range of consumer products from kitchen utensils and clothing to traditional Chinese medicines and betel leaves. Since most consumer goods were purchased from outside the community, there was none of the elaborate craft specialization which marked the economy of northern and central Vietnamese villages, and even weaving was a poorly developed skill. In Khan Hau there were a variety of small shops in competition with a roughly similar line of products, and there

[60] Hendry, *Khan Hau*, p. 120.

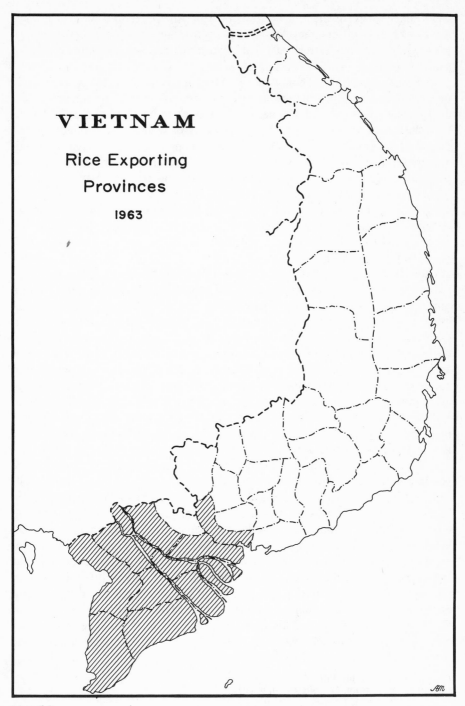

VIETNAM

Rice Exporting
Provinces

1963

MAP 5.2

309

were larger shops in the nearby town of Tan An which sold more expensive goods such as fertilizers, bicycles, and sewing machines.[61] Even essential agricultural equipment was purchased, and all transactions were strictly on a cash basis, with barter in rice extremely infrequent.

The agricultural economy of the Mekong delta was almost exclusively dependent on rice which in most areas covered 90 percent of the cultivated land and in some areas covered 100 percent. Although in northern and central Vietnam there were various secondary crops, many of which were produced in the period of the drier winter monsoon, in the Mekong delta there were no secondary crops of any importance and the absence of artificial irrigation and the pronounced dry season made cultivation of a second crop impossible. The rice monoculture and the extensive commercialization of agriculture in the Mekong delta made delta farmers acutely sensitive to fluctuations in the market price of rice. Since most farmers sold their rice immediately after the harvest, prices routinely fell by 12 to 25 percent, but the close connection between the Saigon price and world commodity market fluctuations exposed the tenant to even greater price drops. Between 1929 and 1931 the wholesale price of rice in Saigon dropped by almost 40 percent, and by 1933 it had fallen to less than a third of its 1929 high.[62] A large drop in the rice price made it difficult or impossible for the tenant to meet his usually substantial loan payments while still satisfying the landlord and the tax collector. The reserve supply of rice sold during the year to meet periodic consumer needs declined drastically in value, and the tenant might find himself unable to purchase essential agricultural equipment, clothing, or supplementary foods. The cash economy of the Mekong delta introduced an important additional element of insecurity in the lives of Vietnamese peasants, but this insecurity, unlike that created by natural disasters in northern and central Vietnam, was closely tied to the social arrangements governing the marketing of rice.

Rice exports and the commercial rice economy of the delta were made possible by both a relatively low ratio of population to rice land and a well-developed transportation network. The average amount of land per capita in Cochinchina in 1932 was more than three times greater than that available in either Tonkin or Annam, and production per capita was approximately 650 kilograms per capita in comparison with 217 kilograms in Tonkin and 233 kilograms in Annam.[63] Despite this relatively large surplus the extractions of the landlords and rice sales by the tenants themselves left only a little more rice to be consumed by the primary producer than in the traditional areas of Vietnam. Sansom estimates that actual consumption in the Mekong delta seldom exceeded the caloric minimum of 240 kilograms per day and in the middle thirties was considerably less.[64] In contrast to the traditional areas of Vietnam, however, the

[61] *Ibid.,* pp. 140–141.
[62] Sansom, *Mekong Delta,* p. 261.
[63] Henry, *Économie Agricole,* pp. 332–333.
[64] Sansom, *Mekong Delta,* p. 36.

barriers to increased consumption were economic and social rather than demographic and ecological.

In contrast to the Tonkin delta the physical infrastructure of the Mekong delta presented no significant barriers to the development of a rationalized market economy. Villages were typically laid out along the tailings left by French canal dredges and therefore paralleled the principal water transport routes of the delta. The delta road network spread out along canal embankments, and later villages usually clustered along these roadways. The nucleated structure of the traditional villages of northern and central Vietnam is not found in the delta, where improved transportation made a more dispersed village structure possible. Khan Hau, for example, is stretched out along both sides of the principal highway linking Saigon and the delta, and the nearby town of Tan An is more easily reached from some hamlets along the roadway than are other hamlets in the same village.[65] The rice markets of Cholon are within a day's journey from most points in the upper delta when security conditions permit travel. The traditional differential between the Saigon and delta rice price was not a consequence of expensive transportation, and the major transit expenses are the tolls and bribes required at army checkpoints along the principal roads. The differential in the prices is a result of discontinuities in the market created by landlord monopoly of the largest share of the rice crop. In the absence of the landlords the delta peasants would have had more direct access to world markets for their marketable surplus.

The division of the delta economy between large landowners and tenants created a distinct class line that was largely absent in the traditional villages of the north and center and created a pronounced barrier to upward mobility through individual effort. The ranked order of precedence was not as important a feature in the delta as it was in the north and center, and the fundamental determinant of status was a holding large enough to require relatively little work on the part of the owner. After 1930 land was extremely difficult to acquire at any price, and mobility into the land-owning gentry was almost impossible after that time. Lands could not be expanded at the expense of adjacent plots by hard work and chicanery; the landlords of the delta were much too powerful to allow gradual attrition of their lands by illegal means. A tenant who worked a relatively large plot of 10 hectares or more could accrue considerable political and social status, but his position was always precarious. There was no assurance that his lease would be renewed for any considerable length of time, and he was usually unable to pass on his tenancy rights to his children. As the delta population increased, competition for available tenancies became increasingly intense, and in a process Sansom refers to as "Malthusian evictions" many substantial farmers lost their plots to those with smaller families or more efficient agricultural techniques.[66] Even during the colonial period when land was relatively plentiful, tenure was unstable and indebtedness frequently forced tenants

[65] Hickey, *Village in Vietnam*, p. 1.
[66] Sansom, *Mekong Delta*, p. 25.

to flee their own village and seek new holdings in the frontier regions to the west. Most but not all large landowners, on the other hand, were able to pass on their holdings to their children. In the Mekong delta the proverbial wisdom of the older areas of Vietnam that no one stays rich or poor for three generations had limited applicability. Most landowners remained rich, and tenants fluctuated from minimal solvency to bankruptcy.

Within the class of landless laborers and tenants there was considerably greater homogeneity and considerably less internal stratification and conflict than among small holders in the traditional areas of Vietnam. Although all Mekong delta farmers attempted to secure a tenancy whenever possible, the differences between a tenant and a landless laborer were considerably less than the differences between a small landholder and a landless laborer in Tonkin. Even landless laborers were in fact somewhat better off than owners of dwarf holdings in Tonkin or Annam, and a laborer in Cochinchina earned almost as much as a small tenant. A landless laborer in Cochinchina earned almost twice as much as a typical small holder in Tonkin and 80 percent as much as a small Cochinchina tenant working 5 hectares or less.[67] The demand for labor in the Mekong delta was considerably greater than it was in either northern or central Vietnam, and it was possible to find work almost year-round by migrating across the delta with the harvest and planting seasons. This migration was facilitated by the looser village structure of the delta. The Cochinchinese laborer did not face political sanctions if he left his home village, and could easily be integrated into a new village in a frontier area. In fact this large population of floating migratory laborers represented a social control problem for the colonial regime, since the village was the basic unit in the administrative structure and the village affiliations of many delta villagers were fluid. Only the largest tenants hired labor on a year-round basis, so that conflicts over wages did not divide the economic interests of small tenants and landless laborers. In the Mekong delta tenants and landless laborers formed a huge homogeneous agricultural proletariat with no prospects of mobility into the land-owning class and a substantial range of common economic interests. Tenants could be and frequently were reduced to landless laborers, and some fortunate laborers managed to attain the status of tenants, but further upward mobility was extremely unlikely.

The small prospects of upward mobility through individual effort and the relatively more favorable position of landless laborers led to a markedly different orientation toward risk in Cochinchina. According to Gourou, "The Cochinchinese, living in a region of large estates, is not attached to the soil to the same degree; he is less stable, perhaps less of a worker, more inclined to gamble, more apt to indulge in speculations which are astonishing in their audactiy and variety." [68] Gambling was in fact one of the major social problems of the Mekong delta, and the Diem regime even passed a law outlawing it as one of the "four vices" along with alcoholism, prostitution, and opium smoking, but this law,

---

[67] Gourou, *French Indochina,* pp. 531 and 552.
[68] *Ibid.,* p. 332.

like so many other administrative decrees, had little effect on the behavior of the peasantry. Gambling was a reasonable proposition in a region where only by the most improbable circumstances could a tenant or landless laborer hope to rise to the secure status of the landed gentry. Hickey's analysis of the life histories of the residents of Khan Hau indicates that gambling may be one of the few ways other than through inheritance and marriage to attain land-owning status. Most of Hickey's case studies describe families who moved down in the social structure because of partible inheritance, debt, or dissipation. His single success story is the case of Ong Dan, who won 1 million Vietnamese dollars in the national lottery, purchased 20 hectares of good rice land, contributed 200,000 dollars to the village primary school, and settled down to enjoy the life of a respected member of the village aristocracy.[69]

The limited prospects for mobility through individual effort markedly reduced the individualism that was a dominant characteristic of peasant small holders in the traditional areas of Vietnam. Paradoxically, individualism was also reduced by the absence of substantial amounts of communal land or water in villages in the Mekong delta. In the north and center communal land and water were sources of community conflict and were viewed as the spoils of community political life. In Cochinchina, however, community lands had never been significant, and Henry reports that less than 2.5 percent of lands in Cochinchina were held communally in 1930.[70] The absence of communal lands eliminated one important source of division within the class of cultivators, and the absence of collective irrigation water eliminated a second. Since impounded rain water provided almost all irrigation water, there were no pools of community water to be fought over in droughts or allotted to villagers in order of precedence. These important sources of internal village conflict in Tonkin and Annam were largely absent in Cochinchina. The peasants of the Mekong delta could not hope to increase their own holdings either by appropriating community lands or water intended for other members of the village or by expanding their holdings at the expense of their neighbors. Although the absence of these sources of individual economic gain did not necessarily lead to increased economic or political cooperation, it did eliminate the important barriers to cooperation which existed in the villages of the north and center.

Opportunities for individual initiative were also limited by the social and physical environment of the delta, which provided weaker incentives for the investment of extravagant amounts of labor in individual holdings and led to methods of cultivation which were distinctly less intensive than those practiced in the north or center. Since a large percentage of the rice crop was consumed in rent and interest, additional labor inputs would benefit the landlord and the moneylenders as much as it would the primary producer. Additional labor applied either to more intensive cultivation or to permanent improvements would simply increase the size of the normal crop on which the landlords' rents

[69] Hickey, *Village in Vietnam*, pp. 256–257.
[70] Henry, *Économie Agricole*, p. 213.

were computed and therefore increase rents. Although the tenant was compelled to apply enough labor to insure his subsistence minimum, incentives for additional labor beyond this point were weakened by the substantial share of the crop taken by noncultivators.

Protecting the subsistence minimum was also a considerably less difficult task in the Mekong delta than it was in the deltas of the north and center. Population density was lower in the Mekong delta, the average size of a plot was larger, and less intensive cultivation was necessary to support the population. The Mekong delta was also exposed to a considerably lower risk of natural disaster than were the deltas of the north and center. Typhoons struck the delta less than a third as frequently as they struck the coasts of northern and central Vietnam, rainfall was considerably more regular, and the Mekong flood was gradual and predictable. Since the intensity of cultivation in northern and central Vietnam was in part designed to insure the subsistence minimum against these natural risks, their absence in the Mekong delta considerably weakened incentives for intensive cultivation. The pronounced dry season of the Mekong delta also restricted opportunities for the application of additional labor. Since no second crop could be cultivated, the dry season forced tenants and landless laborers to spend the period from December to May in enforced idleness or unproductive maintenance work. As a result of both social and ecological factors the total amount of labor required for a hectare of rice land in Cochinchina was only one-fifth of what was required in the regions of intensive cultivation in Tonkin.

The less intensive cultivation in the Mekong delta is apparent not only in the total amount of time invested per hectare but in the nature of the cultivation techniques themselves. In Cochinchina much greater use was made of animal traction, although the use of animals declined as population increased in the older areas of the upper delta. While in Tonkin two distinct harvests had been carried out by hand to insure that the most valuable part of the plant, the rice kernels, was harvested without loss, in Cochinchina there was only a single harvest and buffalo were used both to transport the stalk with the head attached and to thresh the harvest after it had been brought in from the fields. In Tonkin both harvesting and threshing were done entirely by hand. Plowing and harrowing were also done almost exclusively with the aid of animal traction in Cochinchina, while in Tonkin the harrowing in particular was often done by hand. In contrast to the intensive preparation of the soil practiced in Tonkin, in Cochinchina the land was often simply rolled without any preliminary tilling and in some places the rice fields underwent no preliminary preparation whatsoever. In the areas of floating rice near the Cambodian border even the transplanting step could be eliminated, and the peasant simply planted his seed and waited for the flood to rise. Because of these less intensive cultivation techniques commitment to the work ethic was considerably weaker in Cochinchina than it had been in Tonkin or Annam. Rugged individualism, frugality, and disciplined hard work were not of great value in a world in which minimal subsistence could be secured with a half year's labor and only a stroke of extraordinary luck could lead to any dramatic increase in economic status.

In comparison with Tonkin and Annam, individualistic economic competition was less intense in Cochinchina, but community solidarity was actually weaker. The solidarity of traditional communities of Tonkin and Annam was not, of course, a result of a communal economy, but rather of the tyrannical rule of the council of notables, and it was the weakness of the notables of Cochinchina which led to less cohesive villages. The absence of substantial amounts of community land and water in Cochinchina eliminated two of the notables' most powerful weapons against community nonconformity, and although the internal distribution of taxes remained under their control, the notables were never able to coerce the commitment to the village solidarity customary in Tonkin and Annam. Hickey notes that the village of Khan Hau lacked any real focal point and that neither the *dinh* nor the council house was a center of community life. Although attendance at ceremonies at the *dinh* was obligatory for male members of the community, the observances were perfunctory and lacked the intensity of religious commitment apparent in northern villages.[71] In Khan Hau villagers seemed to know little and care less about the activities of those in other hamlets, and the shrines of local religious sects drew the interest only of their adherents, not the commitment of the village as a whole. The weakness of the internal village government in the Mekong delta made it more difficult for the central government to enforce its will on the dispersed population, but it made it possible for outside ideologies to penetrate the village with ease. The notables were unable to maintain village commitment to a conservative orthodoxy, and even radical political and religious doctrines were able to find adherents in the villages of the Mekong.

The weakness of the notables did not, however, create a power vacuum in the village, since many of their functions were assumed by the large landowners or their agents. The landowner in the early period of settlement in the delta was a paternalistic figure who supervised the affairs of his tenants, provided minimal social welfare services, and arbitrated disputes and maintained security, often with the aid of a private army. As a growing population increased competition for tenancies, the delta landlords found it less necessary to provide expensive services and increasingly withdrew to the major towns, leaving the collection of their rents to hired agents who became the most hated figures in delta life. By the 1930s the connections between the landlord and the tenant had been reduced largely to the contractual obligation to pay rent, and the support of the landlords' increasingly sumptuous life style required higher rents and fewer services. Smaller landlords remained in the village and continued to compete for positions in the order of precedence and the council of notables, but the large absentee landowner was the real power in the village. Both the sanctions and the inducements available to the Mekong delta landlord, however, were more limited than

[71] Hickey, *Village in Vietnam*, p. 279.

those of the notables of northern and central Vietnam. He controlled no community economic resources to periodically distribute to villagers, and even the local administration of taxes was out of his direct control. Perhaps most importantly, he lacked the notables' most powerful inducement to conformity, the opportunity to rise in the order of precedence into the upper class of the village. The peasants of northern and central Vietnam were willing to tolerate the machinations of the notables because of the persistent hope that they too would some day profit from the same devices. No such hope existed for the tenants and landless laborers of the Mekong delta. As landlords withdrew from the delta, they increasingly came to depend on military force, and in the period of revolution beginning at the outset of World War II the landlords' withdrawal became a rout and their dependence on military power became almost total. By the beginning of the NLF offensives in the early 1960s the landlords no longer dared return to their villages and relied on government troops to collect their rents. The landlord class of the delta had originated in the military conquest of the French, and increasingly it would be external military power that made its hold on the delta peasants possible.

The large landlords and commercial agriculture of the Mekong delta created incentives for peasant political action which were usually absent in the small holder subsistence economy of the traditional Vietnamese village. The political economy of the delta created a peasantry receptive to radical political and social doctrines, encouraged collective rather than individual solutions to economic problems, and promised substantial material rewards for successful political action. In the villages of the north and center the owners of even marginal subsistence plots identified with the interests of the wealthier landowners and feared any economic and political change which might threaten their ties to the land. Since there were no opportunities for wage labor either within or outside the village, the peasant without land was reduced to the status of a pauper. The conservativism created by the small holder's tie to the land was reinforced by the threatening ecology of the northern and central deltas, which required intense effort to minimize the risks from natural disasters. In the Mekong delta the interests of wealthier landowners were clearly differentiated from those of tenants and laborers, there was no possibility for most of the population to own land, and the natural environment was distinctly less threatening. Even if crop failures or financial insecurity forced a tenant's eviction, he could either find another tenancy in a new village or work as a laborer and was not immediately reduced to abject poverty. In the north and center the optimum peasant strategy was to minimize the chance of an overwhelming loss that could lead to landlessness and poverty. In the Mekong delta on the other hand the optimum strategy was to maximize the chances of a maximum gain that might somehow lead to relief from debts, taxes, and rents even if the probability of that maximum gain was relatively small. If the gamble failed, the tenant was at worst reduced to the status of agricultural laborer, and if it succeeded, he might somehow gain secure title to land and relief from landlord exploitation. The prevalence of games of chance in the delta was one expression of this attitude toward risk, but the same economic incentive structure favored the spread of radical religious and political doctrines. Millenial religions promising economic salvation in an indefinite spiritual future found numerous adherents in the delta but had little success in the traditional villages of the north and center. Similarly, radical political ideologies promising a total restructuring of society appealed to the delta peasantry even if their objective probability of success appeared very low. The millenium might never arrive and the political utopia might be crushed by the landlords, but the delta peasant had everything to gain and very little to lose from his commitment to religious or political radicalism.

The economy of the delta not only created a receptivity to radical ideas; it also promoted the class solidarity essential for converting ideas into action. The individualistic competition for land and water which was endemic in northern and central Vietnam was markedly less intense in the Mekong delta, and stratification within the peasant population was also less pronounced. In the north and center a peasant could gradually move up in the order of precedence by expanding his holdings at the expense of his neighbor, but any improvement in the status of a delta tenant or laborer could only come at the expense of the landlord. Economic security in northern and central Vietnam depended on a lonely struggle with the natural environment, but security in the Mekong delta depended on a control of the social and economic environment which was beyond the resources of individual peasants. Only by changing the structure of land ownership, marketing, and credit could the delta peasants hope to improve their position, and such changes could be carried out over landlord resistance only through collective political action.

If such action did succeed, the potential rewards for the delta peasantry were considerably greater than they would have been in the north and center. Reducing or eliminating the political power of the landlords in the delta not only opened opportunities for land ownership but also led to lower rents, improved credit, and more equitable marketing arrangement. It was the landlords' presence which restricted agricultural development in the delta, and any group strong enough to break their power would eventually gain credit for the improved economic conditions which resulted. In the 1960s, when the NLF first began to threaten landlord control over the delta, precisely such a series of economic changes began to occur. The NLF set an upper limit of 2 hectares on holdings of rice land, one-fiftieth of the Diem 100-hectare limit, and therefore subjected more than 85 percent of the delta land to redistribution in contrast to less than a third marked for eventual distribution under the Diem reform. In areas under NLF control peasants became de facto owners of the land they worked, but even in areas outside their control the threat of NLF sanctions markedly reduced rents, and the greater the NLF control, the lower the rents.[72]

[72] Sansom demonstrates that rents in Long Binh Dien village in Dinh Tuong province declined in direct proportion to the distance from the government guardpost. Sansom, *Mekong Delta*, p. 61, fig. 3.2.

The lower rents, greater security of tenure, and larger share of the crop remaining in peasant hands created a more credit-worthy population, and interest rates declined. A new class of village entrepreneurs developed to market the surplus now in the hands of small peasant producers and the use of artificial irrigation increased, since landlords were no longer able to block peasant initiatives. Although in the long run these reforms would have transformed the agricultural proletariat of the delta into a conservative, property-owning class of commercial farmers, in the short run the NLF received the credit for dramatically increasing the peasant standard of living. No such dramatic increase in living standards would have been possible in the north and center because of the dense population, scarcity of land, and absence of any marketable surplus. Landlordism in the delta not only decreased prospects for individual economic mobility; it greatly increased the potential benefits of concerted political action.

In the Mekong delta, where the oligarchic political controls of the traditional village were weakest, the economic pressures for radical political action were greatest. The direction of this action, however, was severely limited by the structure of landlord control. The landlords depended on a politically disenfranchised and legally impotent labor force, their control of land was based on French military power rather than on their financial acumen, and their minimal concern with agricultural technology and management led to stagnating production in the face of an ever-increasing population. The landlords were unable to extend legal rights to their tenants without markedly reducing the share of the crop they could extract in rents and interest; they could not permit an extension of the franchise without jeopardizing the political hegemony which was essential to their control, and there was no expanding share of agricultural production which could be shared to diffuse a developing agrarian movement. Faced with the unyielding position of the landlord, the tenant had few options. Withholding labor was without meaning, since it would jeopardize the tenant's as well as the landlord's share of the crop, and a rent strike would be regarded either as the theft of the landlord's share of the crop or the illegal occupation of his lands. The struggle over the share of the crop and the right to the land was the basic issue in the delta, and from the landlord's point of view this struggle was an attack on the institutions of property themselves. The tenant could not withhold part of the harvest without risking immediate eviction or confiscation of the entire crop, and the landlord's political or military agents would see that his rights were enforced. To take effective political action in the Mekong delta inevitably meant, therefore, to be prepared to resist the landlord or his agents with force if necessary. Any other form of action was doomed to failure by the inability of the landlords themselves to make any economic or political concessions and by their willingness to use force to defend their rights.

The political economy of the Mekong delta therefore combined a landless agricultural proletariat with a strong incentive for political organization and an economically weak and politically rigid landed elite. These are the conditions which should be most conducive to agrarian revolution. Just as was the case in

Angola, the agrarian upper class in Vietnam depended on the political privileges of colonial rule to provide servile labor and inexpensive land concessions, and the technology of rice production, like that of coffee production, does not permit extensive industrialization. The Vietnamese landed elite was in no better position to transfer its limited skills to any other economic activity than were the *fazenda* owners of Angola, and without its lands and political protection it would rapidly lose any claims to upper-class status. Unlike the situation in Angola, however, the organization of the Vietnamese peasantry was based on class rather than tribal or national ties. In Vietnam the traditional organizational apparatus of the mandarinate and village notables benefited from colonial rule, and there were no large-scale appropriations of village land to drive the large village landowners into a nationalist coalition against the colonial power. In Angola the massive Portuguese land concessions undermined the power of the traditional chiefs through whom the Portuguese hoped to rule and threw them into a common political movement with landless laborers and displaced small holders. In Vietnam the French concessions were never extensive, and it was the Vietnamese elite in the delta and the village notables in other areas of Vietnam that benefited from French military security and French land policies. The agricultural economy of the Mekong was divided between two classes of Vietnamese, not between foreign nationals and displaced indigenous inhabitants of all classes. The revolutionary movement in Vietnam correspondingly reflects this class division rather than the racial and tribal themes of the Angolan revolt. In Vietnam a revolt against the French colonial regime invariably involved the French-created Vietnamese upper class in the delta, and this class persisted in Vietnam even after the end of French rule.

Revolutionary socialism succeeded in Vietnam not because it evoked the image of the tranquil communal village of the past, but because it provided an accurate portrait of the class-based economic exploitation of the present. The combination of large landholdings and a commercial rice economy in the Mekong delta introduced capitalism in its least productive and most exploitative form. The landlords of Vietnam were not industrial, but mercantile capitalists who used their monopoly of rice land to extract peasant surpluses through rents, interest rates, and marketing advantages. The profits of the Vietnamese export economy went primarily to middlemen and carriers, and only a small portion ever reached the primary producer. The penetration of the export economy into the Mekong delta was not accompanied by the rationalization of agricultural production, by any advances in agricultural technology, or even by the investment of private capital. The mercantile capitalism of Vietnam did not create a rural middle class or cause any overall increase in the standard of living, and it provided no opportunities for Vietnamese entrepreneurs to begin small-scale manufactures or rice-milling businesses in the countryside. The colonial capitalism of the Mekong delta created a stark two-class system in which peasant labor created the only form of wealth and landlords simply confiscated this wealth in the form of rent. The world of nineteenth-century socialism, of predatory capitalists and exploited workers reduced to subsistence wages, was an everyday experience for the peasants of the delta. Class interests were apparent to anyone in the division of the rice crop into shares for rent, interest, taxes, and subsistence, and price fluctuations caused by speculative hoarding by landlords and mill owners were felt throughout the delta and regularly worked to the disadvantage of the tenants. The NLF in particular did not concern itself with the structure of the future socialist society but was careful to focus on the redistribution of lands and on the immediate economic gains brought by the destruction of landlord influence and the departure of rent collectors from the areas they controlled. In Vietnam it was not capitalism that led to revolution, but the constrained capitalism of a landed elite that used the political advantages of colonial rule to restrict the workings of the market and protect itself against both political and economic change. Colonialism had brought the landed elite to Vietnam, but it survived the passing of colonialism, although with reduced power, and found new sources of military and political support. The growth of a market economy and landlordism were problems to some extent throughout colonial Vietnam, but they reached their peak in the Mekong delta. It was here, in both the colonial period and in an independent South Vietnam, that there existed the greatest pressures for rural social movements in general and revolutionary socialism in particular.

RURAL SOCIAL MOVEMENTS UNDER FRENCH RULE

In the period between the consolidation of French colonial power after the defeat of the last armed uprising of primary resistance in 1917 and the August 1945 revolution that brought the Viet Minh to power in Hanoi there were two major peasant uprisings directed by the Vietnamese Communist party, both of which affected wide areas of the Mekong delta. By 1930 the Communists had built a party apparatus of an estimated 1,500 members, claimed approximately 100,000 peasants affiliated through party-controlled peasant organizations, and felt strong enough to attempt a direct challenge to French colonial rule.[73] The Communist offensive began with May Day demonstrations in 1930, and when peaceful crowds were fired upon by French troops, unrest rapidly widened to include political assassinations, and violent resistance in the countryside. The strength of the revolt in the countryside was a result of a combination of natural disasters in northern Vietnam and the falling price of rice in the Mekong delta precipitated by the world depression. A period of extended drought had caused the loss of three successive harvests in Annam and brought on famine, increased landlessness, and indebtedness and an acute need for cash to meet tax bills. Nghe An was once again at the center of this natural disaster and as a result once more became the focal point of a peasant revolt—this time, however, led by

[73] John T. McAlister, Jr., *Viet Nam: The Origins of Revolution* (New York: Knopf, 1970), p. 98.

the Indochinese Communist party. The principal goal of this peasant revolt as of so many others in Nghe An in the past was relief from tax payments. On September 12, 1930, a long series of peaceful tax demonstrations at district towns culminated in a march on the provincial capital at Vinh by a crowd of 6,000 peasants. They were promptly attacked by French aircraft as they were still stretched out along the road into town and were dispersed with heavy casualties.[74] The peasant movement, however, moved into the countryside, where village notables and local landlords were attacked and driven from the rice fields and tax and village registration lists were burned. Armed soviets were established in a number of districts in Nghe An and the neighboring province of Ha Tinh, and they continued to exercise local authority until the French reestablished their control in late 1931. During 1930 the movement spread to the Mekong delta, where protests were reported over a wide area extending from what were, in terms of the 1960 administrative divisions shown in Map 5.1, the provinces of Vinh Binh, Vinh Long, and Kien Hoa at the mouth of the Mekong to the western provinces of An Giang and Kien Phong near the Cambodia border.[75] As the shaded area in Map 5.3 indicates, the revolt was concentrated in the area between the Mekong and the Hau Giang and did not spread to the provinces of the lower delta. As was the case in the north, the revolt became a peasant *jacquerie* in which landlords and local village notables were the principal targets and French colonial officials were affected only indirectly. Although the Communists did not succeed in establishing village soviets even temporarily in the delta, assassinations of landlords and village notables continued sporadically until 1933 in the original centers of the revolt.[76] In addition to the delta and the Nghe An–Ha Tinh area, a third center of the uprising developed in the sugar-growing regions of Quang Ngai province in central Annam.[77] The villagers of northern Quang Ngai retained a commitment to the Communist cause that persisted in spite of French repression, and this commitment was still apparent when troops of the Americal division moved into the Batangan Peninsula of Quang Ngai in 1968. My Lai was one of many villages of the area which retained a loyalty to the Communists dating back to the revolt of 1931. The French response to the revolt was a bloody repression in which colonial troops and the Foreign Legion were turned loose in the countryside of Annam and Cochinchina and were allowed to murder and loot with little supervision or control and without any effective resistance from the poorly armed peasants. More than 10,000 Vietnamese were killed and more than 50,000 deported during the year of repression which followed the revolt.[78] The organizational cadre of the Communist party was decimated, its peasant base in large part liquidated, and Ho Chi Minh himself was arrested in Hong Kong in 1931.

[74] *Ibid.*, p. 95.
[75] Joseph Buttinger, *Vietnam: A Dragon Embattled* (London: Pall Mall Press, 1967), p. 217.
[76] *Ibid.*
[77] Jean Chesnaux, *The Vietnamese Nation: Contribution to a History* (Sydney, Aus.: Current Books, 1966), p. 145.
[78] Buttinger, *Dragon Embattled,* p. 219.

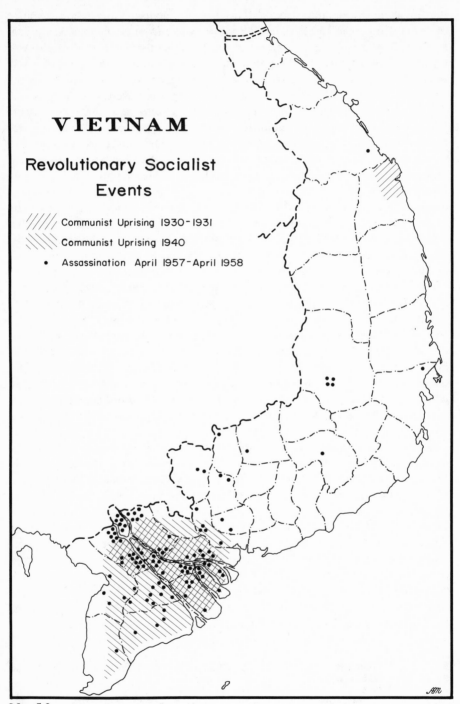

VIETNAM

Revolutionary Socialist
Events

///// Communist Uprising 1930-1931

\\\\\ Communist Uprising 1940

• Assassination April 1957-April 1958

MAP 5.3

322

The distribution of this revolt shows both the persistence of the traditional pattern of revolutionary activity in Nghe An and a new pattern of revolution in the delta areas influenced by the export economy. Tonkin, where the pattern of marginal subsistence holdings and oligarchic village control was strongest, was not involved in the revolt despite its large population and its scarcity of arable land. In Annam the principal regions of revolt were those where natural disasters were most likely to undermine the traditional structure of the village, but in Cochinchina it was the provinces of the delta which were involved in the export economy and therefore exposed to the fluctuations in the rice price which were most actively involved. Quang Ngai province is an interesting exception to the usual pattern of agrarian revolt in Vietnam, since it shares neither the ecological risks of Nghe An nor the rice export economy of the Mekong delta. Quang Ngai, however, is unique in two respects. First, in the areas where the revolt was concentrated, commercial sugar is grown interspersed with the rice crop, and second, this is the only region in colonial Vietnam where irrigation water was sold by the owners of *norias*, or water wheels, in return for a one-third share of the rice crop. The farmers of Quang Ngai faced both market forces and a need to purchase water in addition to the rents and interest payments common in other areas of Vietnam, and both of these problems were exacerbated by drought and the world depression.

In 1940 the Japanese invasion of northern Vietnam and an invasion threat from the Kingdom of Siam (later Thailand) seemed to provide another opportunity for a rebuilt Communist organization to stage a decisive revolt. The French, however, anticipated the Communist strategy and initiated mass arrests of leaders of the southern branch of the party, effectively eliminating central direction of the revolt. The revolt itself began with demonstrations in Saigon, My Tho, and Cantho to protest the arrest of Communist officials and, despite the lack of central direction, expanded to an armed insurrection centered on the Plain of Reeds in what were in 1960 the provinces of Kien Giang and Kien Phong in the delta southwest of Saigon.[79] The armed revolt temporarily succeeded in Cao Lanh in Kien Phong province, and it was here that the flag of the North Vietnamese government was first raised in Vietnam. The Plain of Reeds uprising in turn touched off a widespread peasants' revolt that extended both south of the Hau Giang into what were in 1960 the provinces of Phong Dinh, An Xuyen, and Ba Xuyen and to the east into most of the area involved in the 1930 delta revolt.[80] As the shaded area in Map 5.3 indicates, most of the delta provinces were eventually involved, but in contrast to the earlier revolt none of the provinces of Tonkin or Annam were affected. The revolt was quickly crushed by the French, who arrested more than 6,000 suspected Communists, including almost all the southern leadership.[81] The abortive delta

---

[79] Philippe Devillers, *Histoire du Vietnam de 1940 à 1952* (Paris: Editions du Seuil, 1952), p. 80.

[80] *Ibid.* See also Le-Thanh-Khoi, *Le Vietnam: Historie et Civilization* (Paris: Les Editions de Minuit, 1955), pp. 452–453, and McAlister, *Viet Nam*, map, p. 133, for other descriptions of the area of the 1940 revolt.

[81] McAlister, *Viet Nam*, p. 132.

revolt effectively destroyed the organizational structure of the Communist party in the southern region and marked the last attempt of the Communist party to stage a popular mass insurrection in the lowland areas of Vietnam.

The political and military base from which the Viet Minh launched their seizure of Hanoi in 1945 and to which they returned after they were driven from the cities by the French was not in the lowlands areas where most of the Vietnamese peasant population was concentrated, but rather in the forested highlands inhabited by a sparse population of tribal peoples.[82] Paradoxically the Vietnamese revolution was dependent on these hill tribesmen, particularly the Tho people of northern Vietnam, for political and military support even though it was carried out on behalf of the lowland Vietnamese peasant population. The Communists benefited from the Tho's desire for autonomy and hostility to French rule, and the mountainous homeland regions close to the Chinese border provided a secure military base area in which the effects of French armor and aircraft were blunted. The base area was also strategically located with respect to supplies of armaments from China, which were first purchased from Nationalist troops that occupied northern Vietnam after the French withdrawal and later supplied directly by the government of the People's Republic. When large-scale military action replaced mass insurrection as the fundamental Communist tactic, the arena shifted from the lowlands to the mountains, and this pattern would be repeated in the second phase of the Indochina war in South Vietnam. The major battles of Indochina from Dien Bien Phu to Khe San have been fought in the rugged mountains and jungle of the tribal areas of Vietnam because it is here that guerrilla troops have the greatest tactical advantage over conventional forces. The location of zones of combat in both the American and French phases of the Indochina war, however, is a poor indication of the distribution of the mass base of the Communist party. The mass insurrections of 1930 and 1940 are a better indication of the distribution of Communist support, and it is clear that the Mekong delta was the only region to be involved in both uprisings. Despite the apparent support for the Communist party among delta peasants, the delta has not been able to sustain a successful armed uprising. The excellent transportation, flat alluvial surface, and absence of jungle cover except along the coast make the delta ideal terrain for modern armies, and both French and American expeditionary forces were able to control the central delta while losing the highlands to the Communists. The inability of either the Viet Minh or the NLF to dominate the delta in periods of large-unit combat does not indicate the absence of Communist appeal, but rather the scarcity of terrain favorable to guerrilla war.

During the period of insecurity which followed the fall of France and the Japanese invasion, a millenial religious sect promising the end of colonial rule and relief from rural indebtedness also swept across the delta. The movement began to pick up momentum in precisely those areas that were later engulfed by the Plain of Reeds revolt, and after the defeat of the Communist uprising the

[82] *Ibid.*, pp. 127–128.

movement came to dominate the western delta. The founder of the movement, Huyen Phu So, was the son of the president of the council of notables in the village of Hoa Hao in what is now An Giang province, and the village provided the name of the movement. Hoa Hao village is less than 25 miles from Cao Lanh, where the North Vietnamese flag was first raised in November 1940, and the messianic preaching of So, who came to be called "the Mad Bonze," spread the Hoa Hao doctrine throughout the western delta in what were in 1960 the provinces of An Giang, Kien Giang, and Kien Phong between the Plain of Reeds and the Cambodian border at the same time as the Communists were preparing to launch the Plain of Reeds uprising in the same area.[83] The spiritual ambiguities of the teachings of the Mad Bonze permitted him considerable flexibility, and he alternatively formed political alliances with the Japanese, the Viet Minh, and the French. So offered a doctrine which promised relief from rural indebtedness not through the violent elimination of the landlords and middlemen advocated by the Communists, but through personal abstinence reminiscent of fundamentalist Protestantism. Unlike the Communist teachings So's doctrine did not expose the peasant to violent retaliation from the French because he challenged their power obliquely or not at all, and as his power grew, the Hoa Hao was able to extend military protection to its adherents. Hoa Hao doctrine eliminated both expensive ceremonial observances at the *dinh* and elaborate funerals and weddings, required no religious hierarchy, monuments, or pagodas, and forbade gambling, opium, and alcohol. The doctrine did offer obvious advantages to the indebted delta peasantry, since ceremonial expense and gambling were major sources of debt, and opium and alcohol were French monopolies and heavily taxed, but the Mad Bonze was notably silent on the secular economics of the delta rice economy. Hoa Hao leaders in fact had established a monopoly over rice milling and transport in the lower delta and engaged in speculative hoarding just as had the landlords and Chinese middlemen.[84] As the French became increasingly preoccupied with their battle against the Viet Minh, they delegated political and military power to the Hoa Hao, and by the end of the first Indochina war Hoa Hao fiefs were the effective government over much of the delta. Both the Hoa Hao and the Communists were competing for the allegiance of the same tenants and landless laborers in the same region, but the Mad Bonze had no desire to change the social structure and offered a safer if illusory solution to the economic crisis of the delta.

The weakening of French power in Cochinchina also provided political opportunities for the Cao Dai, a second religious sect whose syncretic doctrines combined the western revelations of Moses and Christ with the Eastern vision of Buddha and Lao-tse. The Cao Dai hagiography included Chinese warrior heroes and Buddhist and Christian saints and even beatified Joan of Arc, Victor

---

[83] By 1955 most of this area was administered as a Hoa Hao fief. See Bernard Fall, "The Political Religious Sects of Viet-Nam," *Pacific Affairs*, 28 (September 1955), map, p. 236.

[84] *Ibid.,* p. 249.

Hugo, and the French Admiral Duclos. The spirit of Cao Dai first revealed itself to Ngo Van Chieu, the colonial administrator of Phu Quoc Island, and the movement spread to include wealthy merchants, Vietnamese civil servants, and small landowners. If the Hoa Hao represented Buddhist Protestantism, then the Cao Dai represented Buddhist Catholicism and its hierarchical organization included nuns, priests, bishops, and even a pope at the church's holy see at Tay Ninh. In contrast to the Hoa Hao the Cao Dai maintained the elaborate cere- monies of both Catholicism and Buddhism and erected numerous temples, in- cluding a monumental but architecturally bizarre structure at Tay Ninh which combined elements of a Catholic cathedral and a Buddhist pagoda. Cao Daism was as much a state as a religion, and its administrative hierarchy included a legislative and executive branch, a specialized department of social welfare and a large and well-trained army. Although Cao Dai congregations established themselves in some parts of the delta, notably in the town of Camau in An Xuyen province and My Tho in Dinh Tuong province, most of their strength was in the transition zone between the delta and the highlands in the provinces of Tay Ninh, Binh Duong, and Phuoc Thanh.[85] Even in the delta their appeal was largely to the wealthier peasants, and unlike the Hoa Hao and the Com- munists they never achieved a mass base among the landless laborers and tenants. The political economy of the delta was receptive to doctrines promising even milleniel solutions to economic problems, but the expensive ceremonies of the Cao Dai were no improvement over contributions at the *dinh*. The delta was, however, the area in which both revolutionary socialism and millenial asceticism had their greatest success in colonial Vietnam.

THE ORIGINS OF THE WAR IN SOUTH VIETNAM

The distribution of Communist support revealed by the revolts of 1930 and 1940 and the persistence of large landholdings and tenancy in the Mekong delta after independence would seem to suggest that the delta should also have been the center of the Communist revolt which grew to become the war in Viet- nam. Even after independence the delta remained an area in which a landless agricultural proletariat had the most to gain from the expulsion of the landlords and the most to lose from the limited Diem land reform. Although exports declined during the first Indochina war, the political economy of the delta was still based on commercial agriculture, and rents and interest rates, although below their levels in the colonial period, were still major sources of economic conflict. Nevertheless there is considerable disagreement about the geographic base of support of the National Liberation Front in South Vietnam and even disagreement about the importance of land and other economic issues in the early Communist successes. In 1967 Edward Mitchell of the RAND Corporation released a formerly classified statistical study of the distribution of control by

[85] *Ibid.*, map, p. 236.

the Government of Vietnam (GVN) which reached conclusions very different from those suggested by the economy and history of the delta described above.[86] According to Mitchell:

> From the point of view of government control, the ideal province in South Vietnam would be one in which few peasants farm their own land, the distribution of landholdings is unequal, no land redistribution has taken place, large French landholdings existed in the past, population density is high and the terrain is such that accessibility is poor.[87]

With the exception of terrain all the conditions of the government's ideal province are, of course, typical of the Mekong delta, and even the terrain variable fits the delta pattern when Mitchell's rather idiosyncratic definition of "accessibility" is taken into account. Mitchell's accessibility variable groups rice paddies along with swamps, marshes, and forests as inaccessible terrain, and of course paddies constitute most of the terrain of the delta. If Mitchell's findings on the distribution of GVN control are correct, they suggest, conversely, that NLF support was weakest in the delta and therefore that the historical pattern of Communist strength in the area of what is now South Vietnam has been reversed. Since rebellious Nghe An is now part of North Vietnam, the historical centers of Communist strength are now concentrated almost entirely in the delta, and of the provinces of the central lowlands only Quang Ngai was involved in either the 1930 or the 1940 revolt. Mitchell's data suggest, however, that the provinces of the central lowlands—in which peasants farm on their own land, the distribution of land is relatively equal, little land redistribution took place under the Diem reforms, and few large French landholdings existed—should be the center of Communist support.

Mitchell's study received wide public attention and was used by advocates of increased American military intervention to bolster their argument that Communist insurgencies are a result of foreign subversion, not of internal economic grievances. The study appeared at a time when official United States thinking on Vietnam was changing from an emphasis on economic development and nation building to an overwhelming reliance on military force. Although Mitchell's study no longer has policy implications, it continues to be important in understanding the origins of the Vietnamese revolution and of agrarian revolutions generally. Mitchell himself compared the Vietnamese revolution to the French and English revolutions and claimed that all three cases indicated that the greater power of landlords and docility of peasants in areas of large estates leads them to oppose revolution and support the forces of the old regime.

---

[86] Edward J. Mitchell, "Land Tenure and Rebellion: A Statistical Analysis of Factors Affecting Government Control in South Vietnam," RAND Memorandum 5181-ARPA (Santa Monica, Calif., June 1967), published as "Inequality and Insurgency: A Statistical Study of South Vietnam," *World Politics*, 20 (April 1968), 421–438.

[87] Mitchell, "Inequality and Insurgency," pp. 437–438.

Frances FitzGerald also found support for her theories of the origins of the Vietnamese revolution in Mitchell's findings. Although she regarded Mitchell's regression analysis as "most tortuous," she insisted that his findings were "quite evident to anyone with a history book and a map." [88] To FitzGerald, politics, not economics, was the key to the Vietnamese revolution, and the decay of the traditional village, not the hunger for land, was the basis of the NLF appeal in South Vietnam. Eric Wolf also used Mitchell's findings to support the central idea in his theory of peasant revolution—that middle peasants who own at least some land are more receptive to revolutionary movements than laborers or tenants with no access to land. According to Wolf, Mitchell's findings on Vietnam are "quite consonant with conclusions which we have drawn elsewhere in this book. We have already found in other cases we have discussed—Mexico, Russia, China—that revolutionary movements among the peasantry seem to start first among the peasants who have some access to land, rather than among the poor peasants or those deprived of land altogether." [89] Since Vietnam is the critical case in Wolf's argument, the basic principle expressed by Mitchell's findings, if not the particular findings themselves, are crucial to his theory. Needless to say, if Mitchell, FitzGerald, and Wolf are right about the sources of Communist support in Vietnam, the inferences of this chapter and the contention of this book that decentralized share-cropping systems are the most receptive to revolutionary socialism stand in serious need of revision. The determinants of the distribution of Communist support in Vietnam are therefore crucial to an understanding of the causes of agrarian revolution.

This question can be addressed just as it was in the case of Peru and Angola by examining the relationship between the distribution of events reported in newspaper sources and the distribution of characteristics of the agricultural economy. Indeed Mitchell's own study is based on a map of government control published in the *Los Angeles Times*. Mitchell's measure is not, however, based on the distribution of events in the early stages of the war in the south, but on the situation at the end of 1965, when American troops had already been engaged in combat for more than six months and the war increasingly consisted of conventional engagements between American troops and large NLF units backed by North Vietnamese regulars. As was the case in past large-unit combat in Vietnam, the jungles and mountains of the central highlands favored the guerrillas, and proximity to North Vietnam and the Ho Chi Minh trail in Laos made the highlands even more favorable for the NLF. This pattern is not apparent in Mitchell's data because he chose to exclude from his analysis all central highlands provinces and included only lowland agricultural areas. Nevertheless it is still clear that the provinces of the coastal lowlands which are closest to both North Vietnam and the supply trails and base areas in Laos and the highlands are the areas of greatest NLF control. Five of the six provinces in the low-

[88] FitzGerald, *Fire in the Lake,* p. 203.
[89] Eric Wolf, *Peasant Wars of the Twentieth Century* (New York: Harper & Row, 1968), p. 202.

est quartile of GVN control in 1965, according to Mitchell's data, form an almost continuous strip along the northern coastal lowlands from Quang Tri at the demilitarized zone south to Phu Yen, and in this strip only Thua Thien falls outside the lowest quartile of control. The sixth province in the lowest quartile is Binh Duong, a transition province between the central highlands and the upper delta. It is clear that Mitchell's data reflect not the distribution of Communist support among the peasantry, but rather the tactical military advantages of favorable terrain and short supply lines. If it is the case, as FitzGerald contends, that Mitchell's data reflect the distribution of control on earlier military maps of Indochina, it is because the same terrain considerations influenced the Viet Minh.

Although by 1965 the distribution of GVN military control was not a useful indication of peasant support for the NLF, the second Indochina war began with much the same pattern of assassinations of notables and village chiefs which had marked both the 1930-31 and 1940 revolts. There were no large-scale crowd actions as there had been in both of the earlier revolts, but by 1957 and 1958 the rate of assassinations of government officials and pro-government political leaders had reached a level comparable to the earlier revolts. The distribution of events in this period would seem to provide a much better indication of the initial political base of the NLF than would military positions in 1965. Accounts of the events of early 1957 and 1958 are sparse in the sources used in the world analysis, but Bernard Fall computed the number of assassinations reported by the Saigon press from April 1957 to April 1958,[90] and this data source is therefore comparable to the primary press sources used in the case studies of Peru and Angola. Fall also estimated the area under the control of politicoreligious sects in 1955,[91] and this information provides a means both of comparing the distribution of revolutionary socialist and millenial activity in Vietnam and of assessing the validity of secondary source accounts for the Vietnamese case. Before the outbreak of the Communist insurgency the Diem regime had defeated the sects in a series of battles in 1955, and these are rural collective events according to the definitions of the world analysis. Table 5.1 compares the distributions of revolutionary socialist and millenial events reported by the *New York Times* with the number of assassinations and the area of sect control reported by Fall for the 37 mainland provinces of Vietnam according to 1960 administrative boundaries. It is clear that secondary source reports are considerably less accurate in localizing rural social movements in Vietnam than they were either in Peru or Angola. Although there are strong correlations between the distributions of both Hoa Hao ($r = .71$) and Cao Dai ($r = .71$) activity in the two sources, there is considerably less agreement about the origin of the revolutionary socialist movement ($r = .34$). In part this difference reflects the different time periods in which the revolutionary socialist

---

[90] Bernard Fall, "South Vietnam's Internal Problems," *Pacific Affairs,* 31 (September 1958), map, p. 256.
[91] Fall, "Political Religious Sects," p. 236.

TABLE 5.1   *Intercorrelations of Revolutionary Socialist and Politico-religious Sect Activity as Reported by Bernard Fall and the* New York Times

VARIABLE	(2)	(3)	(4)	(5)	(6)
1. NLF 1957–58, Fall	−.01	.83	.34	−.04	.78
2. Cao Dai, Fall		−.14	.24	.71	−.04
3. Hoa Hao, Fall			.57	−.10	.71
4. NLF 1959 *NYT*				.15	.52
5. Cao Dai, *NYT*					.06
6. Hoa Hao, *NYT*					—

events were recorded in the two sources. Although the *New York Times* began reporting Communist violence in early 1958, the initial accounts were sketchy and did not provide any information about the provincial location of the events. Only one of the ten events recorded for 1958 in the *New York Times* could be localized by province, so that it was necessary to compare events from the *New York Times* for 1959, when locations had begun to be reported, with Fall's 1957–58 events. Given the generally low level of activity in this period, however, it seems unlikely that the location of events would switch dramatically in a short time, so that the explanation of the difference probably lies in the inadequacy of the *Times* coverage. Since both the millenial movements were reported with relative accuracy, it would seem that the *Times* systematically erred in its report of Communist events rather than simply inadequately covered Vietnam. Despite the relative lack of agreement on the provincial location of NLF activity, the two sources do, however, agree on one crucial point. In contrast to the findings of Mitchell both Fall's data and the *New York Times* reports indicate that from 1957 to 1959 the NLF was overwhelmingly concentrated in the Mekong delta with very little activity reported in other areas of Vietnam. Eighty-five percent of the assassinations recorded by Fall and 81 percent of the events reported in the *New York Times* occurred in delta provinces.

The concentration of NLF activity in the delta means, of course, that it is correlated with the characteristics of the land tenure system and commercial agriculture of the rice export economy. These relationships are apparent in the correlations in Table 5.2 and in the distribution of rice exports and the distribution of assassinations shown in Maps 5.2 and 5.3 respectively. Map 5.2 shows those areas of the delta which in both 1929 and 1963 exported rice to the Saigon market, and this area includes all but one of the delta provinces (Kien Tuong). Similarly Map 5.3, showing the distribution of assassinations plotted by Fall, indicates that they are concentrated in the western delta and that there is a considerable overlap between provinces with large numbers of assassinations and provinces which exported rice.

Table 5.2 shows the pattern of interrelationships in the distribution of activity between both of the earlier communist revolts and the beginning of the current war and between the Communist events and politicoreligious sect con-

TABLE 5.2   *Intercorrelations of Revolutionary Socialist and Politico-religious Sect Activity with Rice Exports, Rice Production, and Land Tenure by Province*

VARIABLE	(1)	(2)	(3)	(4)	(5)	(6)	(7)	(8)	(9)	(10)
1. NLF 1957–58		.63	.61	.83	—	−.01	.71	.59	.57	.36
2. Com. 1930–31	.54		.36	.48	—	−.02	.66	.65	.52	.13
3. Com. 1940	.58	.28		.57	—	−.18	.88	.63	.80	.65
4. Hoa Hao	.83	.43	.52		—	−.14	.64	.48	.38	.45
5. GVN control 1965	.44	.15	.14	.42	—	—	—	—	—	—
6. Cao Dai	−.06	−.08	−.05	−.20	−.19		−.03	.01	−.02	−.16
7. Rice exporting	.69	.61	.85	.61	.10	−.11		.73	.79	.58
8. Rice production	.55	.42	.52	.42	.11	−.10	.67		.48	.43
9. Rented land	.57	.52	.81	.38	.21	−.02	.79	.48		.58
10. Transfer land	.36	.13	.65	.45	.15	−.16	.58	.43	.58	

trol.[92] The upper matrix of Table 5.2 is based on all 37 mainland Vietnamese provinces extant in 1960, while the lower matrix is based on the 26 lowland provinces included in Mitchell's analysis. It is apparent from the correlations in the triangular submatrices in the upper left corner of Table 5.2 that NLF activity in 1957–58 followed the pattern of earlier Communist movements in Vietnam. In the upper matrix showing the country as a whole assassinations in 1957–58 are correlated .63 with agrarian unrest in 1930–31 and .61 with agrarian unrest in 1940, and these relationships are not significantly weaker in the lower matrix showing the lowlands only. It is also clear from Table 5.2 that Mitchell's measure of GVN control is *positively*, not negatively, correlated with Fall's index of assassinations and insignificantly correlated with agrarian unrest in either 1930–31 or 1940. These correlations indicate that the area of maximum NLF activity shifts markedly from 1957 to 1965 and in fact reflects the pattern of a peasant-based guerrilla insurgency moving from its natural base of support in the delta to the safer military terrain of the central highlands. It is also clear from Table 5.2 that Hoa Hao activity is concentrated in the same areas as the early Communist uprisings and is strikingly correlated ($r = .83$) with assassinations in 1957–58. The areas of strength of the middle-class Cao Dai movement, on the other hand, show no significant correlations with either the Communist movements or the Hoa Hao. In 1957–58 the Hoa Hao once again appears to be in direct competition with the Communists for the allegiance of the peasantry of the western delta, and there is a large cluster of NLF activity in eastern An Giang and Kien Phong provinces (Map 5.3) in the area where the Mad Bonze first began his mission.

Table 5.2 also indicates that the pattern of Communist and Hoa Hao activity is correlated with the principal economic indicators of the delta agricultural export economy. The lower right triangular submatrices in Table 5.2 indicate that there is a close association between rice production, rice exporting,

[92] See notes 75, 77, 79, and 80 above for sources used in determining the provincial location of the 1930–31 and 1940 revolts.

rented land, and the presence of large estates subject to expropriation under the Diem land reform. Total rice production and rice exports were determined from the *Agricultural Statistics Yearbook* of the Republic of Vietnam for 1963, although a comparison with Henry's data for 1929 indicate that the areas exporting were precisely the same in 1929.[93] The area of rented land was determined from the 1960 agricultural census of Vietnam and includes the rented area of all holdings whether they are rented in whole or in part.[94] The amount of land subject to expropriation under the Diem reforms was computed from data in Mitchell's article. As the pattern of correlations in the rectangular submatrices at the upper right and lower left in Table 5.2 indicate, all these measures of the commercial rice export economy of the delta are highly correlated with Communist activity in 1930–31, 1940, and 1957–58 and with Hoa Hao control in 1955, although the single best predictor of Communist and Hoa Hao activity is simply whether or not a given province exports rice. The data in Table 5.2 clearly demonstrate that in both the current war in South Vietnam and in the Communist uprisings of the colonial period the pattern of relationships between Communist control and land tenure and commercial agriculture are precisely the opposite of those suggested by Mitchell. The ideal province from the point of view of the Communists in 1930–31, 1940, or 1957–58 was one in which few peasants farmed their own lands, large Vietnamese and French estates existed in the past, and land distribution was therefore unequal and, of course, one which exported rice.

These findings do not indicate that estate size and landlessness are in themselves determinants of revolutionary socialist movements in the countryside, since large estates and landlessness are also associated with both migratory estate and plantation systems. In Vietnam these variables are indicators of the peculiar distribution of political resources and options established by an export economy based on a decentralized tenancy system of wet rice cultivation. In Vietnam just as was the case in the world analysis, such export sectors tend to create receptivity to revolutionary socialism. In the Mekong delta of Vietnam the large estates created by French colonial policy and the corresponding landless tenant status of most of the population eliminated the conservative dedication to individual subsistence plots which had caused the peasants of traditional Vietnam to identify their interests with those of the larger landowners and avoid political or economic risks. The large estates and the absence of communal land and water in delta villages also eliminated the internal conflict that had inhibited collective organization in traditional Vietnam, and the landless status of most of the delta population reduced internal stratification in the peasant class and eliminated opportunities for upward mobility through individual effort. The ties of the market economy of the delta could only be affected by collective action,

---

[93] Republic of Vietnam, Agricultural Economics and Statistics Service, *Agricultural Statistics Yearbook* (Saigon, 1964), p. 44; Henry, *Économie Agricole*, pp. 332–333.

[94] Republic of Vietnam, *Agricultural Census*, p. 27.

and the collective goods which could be distributed by such action in the form of more land, lower rents, better irrigation, and better marketing were a valuable tool in peasant organization. When the NLF began its campaign in the countryside in 1957 and 1958, it therefore focused on the landless peasants of the Mekong delta, who were the most receptive to an ideology of class conflict, who were the most willing to take risks in pursuit of a millenial dream, and who could be won to the cause by the substantial economic benefits available in the delta and nowhere else. In the delta, therefore, the NLF found the economic conditions to create strong peasant political solidarity.

In the delta, too, the power of the traditional village notables based on their control of community land and water and on persistent peasant dreams of mobility was considerably weaker, and the decentralized sharecropping economy prevented the landlords from effectively exercising the power that the notables lacked. The landlord did not directly control irrigation water, the management of work, or the sale or processing of the crop and therefore, unlike the large landowners of a centralized sharecropping system, could not use economic sanctions directly against his tenant. The decentralized system of the delta placed all operations of the productive process under the operating control of the tenant even though the landlords were able to block effective production and claimed rights to the crop. The landlord, then, was economically superfluous and forced to rely exclusively on military power to collect his rents and protect his lands. Dependent on special colonial land concessions and a legally impotent class of laborers, without substantial prospects for applying industrial processes to agricultural production, the landlord of the delta found himself unable to yield to economic or political change without undermining his social position. In the Mekong delta the commercial rice export economy created both a peasantry strongly organized along class lines and an economically weak but politically powerful landed elite with little managerial control over its tenants. The result has been the dominance of revolutionary socialism in almost all agrarian political movements in Vietnam and the persistence of agrarian revolution in spite of more than a quarter of a century of foreign intervention and continual war.

CHAPTER 6

Conclusions

THE ANALYSIS of the effects of the social organization of export agriculture on rural social movements began with two sets of hypotheses linking variations in the principal source of income of both cultivating and noncultivating classes with their political behavior in conflict situations. In both sets of hypotheses the source of income was an exogenous independent variable not explained by other variables in the model, and the conflict behavior of the two agricultural classes was the principal dependent variable. The interaction of the conflict behavior of both classes led to a discrete form of social movement for each combination of income sources, and the four summary hypotheses of Chapter 1 (hypotheses A to D) expressed these overall relationships between combinations of income sources and types of social movements as well as indicating special conditions under which the likelihood of such movements would be increased. Each of these general hypotheses, however, was based on a long causal chain beginning with the source of income moving first to its economic consequences, then to the political behavior associated with these economic consequences, and finally to the conflict behavior of a particular agricultural class. These intervening relationships were described in hypotheses 1 to 6 of Chapter 1, which concerned the behavior of cultivators and noncultivators. In the world analysis the principal categories of agricultural organization, the commercial hacienda, the small holding, the plantation, the migratory labor estate, and the sharecropped estate represented combinations of income sources, and the relationships between these variables and the social movements measures therefore tested the general pattern of relationships expressed by the summary hypotheses A to D rather than the specific intervening causal sequences expressed by hypotheses 1 to 6. Both the cross-national analysis and the case studies, however, suggested that it was possible to evaluate hypotheses 1 to 6 by moving within the four broad categories established by the logical combinations of two income sources and two classes and examining finer variations in economic organization. Although the predictions expressed by the broad groupings of income sources and types of movements are in general supported by the world analysis, the power of prediction in both the world analysis and the case studies was improved if variations within the categories were considered. Plantation systems, for example, generally represent a combination of wages as the principal source of income for the cultivating class and capital for the noncultivating class, but the world analysis indicated that some plantation owners, notably those in sugar, tea, sisal, and bananas, were generally more dependent on industrial capital that were the owners of the tree crop plantations and that it was these industrial plantations that were most likely to lead to reformist labor movements. Such movements were considerably less common, for example, on rubber plantations, where non-cultivator behavior was more typical of the commercial hacienda than the plantation category. Although a rubber plantation required a greater investment in processing machinery than did a typical commercial hacienda, the investment was considerably smaller than that represented by a sugar refinery. This pattern of relationships is also apparent in the sugar plantations of Peru, where a strong labor movement is closely associated with manufacturing enterprises located on the plantations. Plantations in Peru are even more highly industrialized than many sugar plantations elsewhere in the world, and their labor movement was correspondingly one of the strongest recorded in the world statistical analysis. These distinctions within the plantation category do not, of course, illustrate the effects of broad income categories, but rather the workings of the hypotheses governing the behavior of noncultivating classes outlined in Chapter 1. The advanced industrialization of the sugar plantation in general and of the Peruvian sugar plantations in particular leads to economic power, relatively free labor, and increasing productivity, and according to hypotheses 1 to 3 of Chapter 1, these economic characteristics should lessen the need for political control, weaken resistance to rights for cultivators, and eliminate zero-sum economic conflict. These political characteristics in turn lead to a shift from political conflict over the means of production to economic conflict over distribution of income from production and therefore establish a pattern of noncultivator behavior conducive to a reformist labor movement.

Each combination of income sources in fact includes both the dominant enterprise type of this combination, variations on this general type, and marginal cases which resemble the dominant enterprise type in other income combinations. This is not to say, however, that the variations in social organization reflecting different sources of income are necessarily continuous. There are definite points of inflection in the organization of agriculture, and at these points one system is transformed into a qualitatively different one, as, for example, when sugar plantations in Peru completely displaced the indigenous haciendas or when the peasants of La Convención demolished the hacienda system and created a system of small holdings. These dramatic changes in agricultural organization mark the boundaries of the major categories of enterprise type, and it is not difficult to distinguish the transformation of one system into another. Frequently, of course, as the data in the world analysis indicated, such transformations will be marked by a revolutionary movement or by a major political change such as the end of colonialism. The distinction between the broad categories of enterprise type in the income source model therefore is not simply an artificial division of a continuous variable. Instead it reflects natural groupings caused by major technical and economic variables. This fact explains both the long-run stability of each class of systems and the rapid transformation to another class which can occur when this stability is disturbed by revolution or dramatic economic changes.

Although the boundaries of the major agricultural types are well defined, the distribution of forms of agricultural organization within each type forms a continuum of decreasing similarity, usually without sharp discontinuities. The differences between sugar and banana plantations, expressed in the greater capitalization and more factory-like operation of the sugar plantation, are significant but slight. Similarly the differences between the haciendas of the sierra and the coast in Peru are not qualitative differences of type, but rather differences in the degree of capitalization and productive rationality. Although such differences do not affect the placement of an economic organization in one of the four broad classes, they might be expected to have significant effects on the political behavior of both cultivating and noncultivating classes. Hypotheses 1 to 6 of Chapter 1 linking income sources and political behavior were expressed in continuous rather than discrete form, and it is therefore possible to understand variations within each cell of the four-cell model by applying the variables described in these hypotheses. Since the relative dependence on land and capital and land and wages varies within each broad category, it is possible to use the data from the world analysis and the case studies not only to see if one or the other form of payment has the predicted effects but to see if a greater or lesser degree of dependnce on one or the other of the two sources leads to a stronger or weaker predicted change. For example, according to the three hypotheses governing noncultivator behavior differences in the degree of mechanization between the coastal and sierran haciendas of Peru should lead the hacienda owners of the coast to greater economic power, to a greater use of wage labor, and to at least a gradually increasing income from agriculture. These economic characteristics lead in turn to less reliance on political controls over land, greater willingness to grant political rights to workers, and an ability to make economic concessions in negotiations. In general, of course, this description does fit the relative behavior of the two systems, although the coastal cotton estates do not show as pronounced a pattern of upper-class flexibility as do the sugar estates, which represent a wholly different and considerably more industrialized form of production. Both the quantitative analysis of interaction effects in the world analysis and the qualitative analysis of agricultural organization in the case studies considered these variations within the broad categories, and these analyses therefore provide a means of checking the utility of the hypotheses describing intervening causal linkages.

The case studies also provided an opportunity to examine factors other than income sources which might affect economic behavior and, consequently, both political behavior and social movements. Although the hypotheses state, for example, that in general payment of cultivators in land tends to lead to the avoidance of risk, to economic competition, and to structural isolation, they do not state that payment in land is the *only factor* influencing these three variables. It is entirely possible, for example, that one or more of these economic variables may be influenced by some exogenous variable other than land. If this does occur it provides an opportunity to test the hypothesized connections between the next two links in the model, those between political behavior and social movements, respectively. In Vietnam, for example, the peasants of the north and center drew their income almost entirely from land and should, according to hypothesis 4 of Chapter 1, therefore show among other things a pronounced aversion to risk and an unwillingness to permit any change that might threaten landlessness. This in turn should lead them to be unreceptive to any political doctrine involving radical change, and in normal circumstances this is in fact the case in these areas. The dangerous ecology of the region and numerous dwarf holdings divided into many small parcels increase the risk of landlessness and therefore should intensify economic behavior designed to minimize risk. This it turn should lead to even more resistance to radical doctrines than is typical of systems dependent on land as the principal source of cultivator income. The natural environment and the population density of Tonkin are both exogenous variables which like payment in land enter the causal chain at the beginning, but it is possible to trace their effects on economic behavior, political behavior, and conflict behavior, at least in qualitative terms, by the use of hypothesis 4. The case studies, then, provided an opportunity not only to examine variations in income source within major categories of economic organization but also to examine the effects of variables other than income source on the entire theoretical model. In this chapter an attempt will be made to draw together the results of the word analysis and case studies which illustrate the principles expressed in the hypotheses with which the study began.

LAND AND LAND

A combination of both cultivating and noncultivating classes drawing their principal income from land is typical of commercial hacienda systems, although this class of systems includes a considerable range of tenure types and productive organizations. Although the focus of this study has been on the export economy, it is clear that this combination of income sources is typical of most peasant subsistence communities, and the analysis of the behavior or such communities in both Peru and Vietnam indicated that the same general principles that govern the behavior of cultivators in the export economy also tend to affect subsistence cultivators. In the world analysis and the case studies a number of different kinds of economic organizations which fall within this general category have been considered, and even though they vary substantially among themselves, they share some common political and economic characteristics. In the world analysis this category included agricultural systems in which laborers resident on the landlord's land are paid in some combination of wages and usufruct rights, systems in which owners of dwarf subsistence holdings must hire out as laborers on nearby estates, and systems in which wage laborers working on estates without processing machinery are given access to individual plots to supplement their food supply. In the case studies this general category includes the agricultural export economies of the Peruvian coastal cotton haciendas, the coffee valley of La Convención, and the pastoral communities of the central sierra, but also subsistence communities outside the export economy such as the tillage agriculture sierran communities and the village economies of northern and central Vietnam. Whatever the differences among these various systems, they all involve a noncultivating class which is dependent on its control over land to extract peasant surpluses in the form of rent, labor, taxes, or profits, and by definition land revenues must be the most important component in its total income. These systems also share a cultivating class which has at least some long-term access to land which it either owns or holds in long-term usufruct, and by the definition of this category it must derive more than half of its income from this land. In all these systems the land-owning class dominates the cultivating class even if, as in the case of the indigenous communities of the Peruvian sierra, its members are nominally independent. According to hypotheses 1 to 6 of Chapter 1, upper class reliance on land rather than financial or industrial capital and lower-class dependence on land rather than wages should have a series of economic and political consequences for both classes. An upper class dependent on land should, first, be economically weak and therefore dependent on political concessions and privileges to protect its interest in the land. Second, the upper class should rely on a servile or semi-servile labor force, and the limited gains from a disciplined labor force should lead it to oppose either the granting of rights of organization or the extension of the franchise to members of the cultivating class. Third, the dependence on land should create a restricted opportunity for increasing agricultural production through mechanization and, therefore, lead to a fixed share of agricultural income that becomes the source of zero-sum conflict between landowners and cultivators. Overall, these economic and political consequences of income from land tend to generate political conflict over the control of landed property. Hypotheses 4 to 6 suggested that payment in land should have three principal consequences for the behavior of cultivators. First, it should lead to an avoidance of risk in order to minimize the possibility of a change that might lead to landlessness and a consequent fear of radical political doctrines which might benefit the landless at the expense of even small property owners. Second, payment in land should lead to individualistic economic competition in which gains can come only at the expense of other members of the cultivating class. Third, payment in land should lead to isolated production techniques which typically make it impossible for other cultivators to enforce group solidarity by threatening withdrawal of communal economic resources. Such structural ties, if they exist at all, are likely to link cultivators with the upper classes rather than with other cultivators. The hypotheses suggest that these economic and political consequences of payment in land should, under normal circumstances, lead to political passivity and an inability to mobilize around the interest of the cultivating class. Combining the behavior of both classes in this category indicates that the political control and rigidity of the upper class and the weakness of the lower class will usually combine to inhibit social movements. On the other hand it was clear that a number of circumstances, including the weakening of upper-class coercion because of national political changes or the introduction of organizational resources from outside the peasant community, could and frequently did upset this stability. In this case the behavior of the upper class tended to focus conflict on control of property and usually led the peasant to attempt to directly gain control of the land in an agrarian revolt. When such revolts succeed, however, the normal economic conditions affecting cultivators paid in land reassert themselves, and the formerly revolutionary peasantry becomes a conservative class of small commercial farmers.

These hypothesized linkages among income sources, economic behavior, political behavior, and social movements are apparent in both the world analysis and the case studies. Consider first the behavior of the land-controlling class. In Peru the haciendas of the sierra were based on a primitive agricultural technology which was identical to that used in peasant subsistence plots, and mechanization of the coastal cotton estates was limited to tractors and power-driven pumps. In the sierra in fact it was the peasants, not the estate owners, who took up coffee production for export, and the small mills and evaporating tanks used in the wet processing of coffee were not beyond the resources of even medium peasant producers. Estate wool production was, with the exception of the Cerro de Pasco holdings, extensive rather than intensive, and even at the Cerro holdings there was little agricultural mechanization. Neither the subsistence crops of the traditional haciendas nor the pastoral economy of the central sierra nor the cotton economy of the coast permitted the substantial economies of scale or extensive mechanization possible in the coastal sugar plantations. In no case did the landed upper class of the haciendas have extensive market power, control over exports, or independent financial resources, and even the relatively modern coastal cotton estates were frequently in debt to the major trading companies which controlled cotton ginning and export. The reliance of the Peruvian haciendas on land rather than financial and industrial capital made them dependent on political controls to protect rights in land, although this phenomenon was less important on the coast than in the less mechanized sierra. In the sierra the hacienda owners used their control of the police, the military, and the courts and the linguistic and political handicaps of the Indian population to expropriate Indian lands and defend their own properties against peasant retaliation. Even on the coast most of the large properties originated in the early expropriations of the Indian population, and the political impotence of the peasantry contributed to the haciendas' dominance of the cotton valleys. In the sierra the large landowners required the support of conservative military- or landlord-dominated governments, and the election of Belaúnde spelled both the decline of their political power and a rapid loss of control over their lands. The sierra *hacendados* came to be viewed as expendable by a new urban and later military elite, and the passing of their political power found them with no economic resources to use in the defense of their lands. The cotton estates, on the other hand, more mechanized and with correspondingly greater economic power, were able to use their strong position in the export economy to gain political influence in Lima and protect their estates against growing peasant pressure in the constricted cotton valleys. Of course, even Grace and Company eventually lost its lands to the growing nationalism of the military rulers, but to Grace Peruvian sugar was a detail in its worldwide operations, while the life style and social status of the *hacendados* were completely dependent on land. Thus the behavior of the Peruvian hacienda owners illustrates both that political controls are necessary to compensate for economic weakness in landed estate systems and that in such systems economic conflicts lead to political struggles to control the land. The difference between the sierra and the coastal haciendas also supports this general hypothesis, since the coastal estates' greater mechanization and greater economic influence allowed them to more readily survive the passing of landlord-dominated governments.

The haciendas of both the sierra and the coast, like landed estates generally, were dependent on at least some degree of coercion in the recruitment of their labor supply. In the sierra the coercion was direct, and laborers were threatened with eviction, confiscation of their animals, seed, and equipment, and even flogging, imprisonment, or death. The *colonos* of the central sierra and the *arrendires* of La Convención were effectively bound to the land, and ownership of the Indians of a hacienda was transferred along with ownership of its land. Even the peasants of the indigenous communities were frequently subjected to forced labor by the mestizo upper class, and many of course worked on nearby haciendas where they were exposed to the same harsh discipline as the resident laborers. The greater prosperity of the coastal haciendas provided them with the means to attract at least some free labor, although their dependence on the labor contractors indicates that workers were to some extent coerced. In some cases, however, cotton estate owners actually assisted in the registration of indigenous communities to legally bind peasants to an inadequate amount of land and therefore force them into labor on nearby cotton estates. The degree of coercion was considerably less than in the central sierran estates, but it was considerably greater than on the sugar plantations, which had dispensed with the services of labor contractors by the early 1960s. Labor relations in both the sierran and coastal haciendas were characterized by a combination of brutality and paternalism, with brutality more significant in the sierra and paternalism more important on the coast. In a social system in which the illegal planting of a coffee bush or the unauthorized use of Spanish could lead to the threat of eviction, labor organization or workers' rights were out of the question. Even in the coastal haciendas, where owners at least tolerated labor unions, they depended on personal services to undermine union power and draw laborers into the dependence that characterized the sierran laborers. These labor tactics in both areas were necessary to support the inefficiencies of centralized production of crops better suited to small holder production and to provide labor at a cost that the limited financial resources of the haciendas could tolerate. The primitive agricultural techniques of both commercial and subsistence haciendas of the sierra therefore created a demand for servile labor, which in turn led to rigid, often brutal opposition to workers' organizations. On the coast once again a more mechanized agricultural organization within the same general category of enterprise type created greater flexibility and tolerance of unionization. The labor relations of the sierra and the coast therefore illustrate both attitudes toward the work force characteristic of landed estates as a general category and the specific difference within this category caused by variations in the relative dependence on land versus industrial capital.

Finally the limited prospects for mechanization on haciendas of either the sierra or the coast led to a fixed agricultural product and required that any economic concessions to workers be taken directly from the incomes of landowners rather than from productivity gains. Once again this was a more critical problem in the sierra, where the division of the agricultural product depended almost entirely on the distribution of land and increases in peasant production could come only at the expense of hacienda lands. In the coastal cotton estates milling of cotton was outside of the control of the estate owners, and although investment in irrigation and farm equipment was possible, the limits of mechanization had been reached during the postwar modernization of the haciendas. Higher wages for laborers would therefore have meant lower incomes for landowners and eventually threatened their upper-class life style. The hacienda owners of neither the sierra nor the coast could concede anything because they had nothing to concede, although once again flexibility was greater on the coast. Thus all three of the hypotheses of Chapter 1 concerning the influence of land as the source of upper-class income are supported by the Peruvian hacienda systems. Dependence on land led to economic weakness and political vulnerability, to servile labor and resistance to worker organization, and to static production and zero-sum conflict. Both in the sierra and on the coast these political characteristics of the upper class led to political conflict over the ownership of landed property and resulted in a series of peasant land invasions. The difference between the coastal and sierran haciendas also illustrates that within the category of commercial haciendas the degree of dependence on land versus industrial capital exerts a crucial effect on both the political and the economic behavior of the agrarian upper class. The greater mechanization and commercialization of the coastal cotton estates led to a more influential land-owning class, less use of coercion in labor recruitment, and greater productivity. These economic characteristics in turn led to less political vulnerability, greater tolerance of worker organizations, and a greater ability to concede a share of agricultural income to workers. As a result conflict in coastal estates was focused not only on the question of land, which concerned the small holders and peasant communities in the valleys, but also on wages, which were the principal concern of the resident laborers of the estates. The marginal position of the cotton estate between the total dependence on land of the backward haciendas of the sierra and the fully rationalized production of the sugar plantations led to a mixed agrarian social movement. Analysis of the distribution of rural collective events in Peru indicated that in the sierra only agrarian events were reported and in the sugar valleys only labor events; only in the cotton valleys were *both* types of events reported.

The case studies also provide evidence to support the linkages among income sources, economic behavior, political behavior, and social movements expressed in the hypotheses concerning the behavior of a cultivating class drawing its principal income from the land. These tendencies are apparent both in peasant communities completely outside the market economy, like the villages of northern and central Vietnam or the traditional indigenous communities or subsistence haciendas of the Peruvian sierra, and among peasants drawn into the world market either as small commercial producers, like the coffee farmers of La Convención, or as part-time agricultural laborers, like many of the workers on Peruvian cotton estates. In all these peasant agricultural systems cultivators tend to avoid risk, compete with other cultivators, and produce in isolation from other members of the cultivating class. These economic characteristics lead in turn to political conservatism, weak organization, and weak class solidarity, and as a result political mobilization is usually low among cultivators drawing their income from the land.

In both subsistence and commercial peasant agricultural systems small plots and marginal agriculture produce a pronounced aversion to risk and resistance to political radicalism. In Peru, hacienda expropriations forced peasants out of the fertile bottom lands and up along the precipitous rocky hillsides of the Andes, and an increasing population forced many indigenous communities out of agriculture altogether and into precarious subsistence pastoralism. In Vietnam, population pressures and partible inheritance led to ever smaller plots divided into parcels of decreasing size, and a threatening environment made agriculture even more precarious. On the haciendas of Peru the *colonos* could not devote all their time to their own small plots of rocky hillside land because the *patrón* demanded labor at the same time as it was needed on the peasant subsistence plot. Although in all these systems agriculture produced little more than a bare existence, the alternatives confronting the landless were uniformly stark. The peasant who lost his lands in Peru would only add to the expanding slums of Lima or compete for the rapidly decreasing number of jobs in the mines or plantations; in Vietnam the major employers were the deadly rubber plantations. In both countries a peasant outside of his village was at a distinct political and social disadvantage, in Vietnam because of the administrative role of the village and in Peru because of the handicaps of Indian language and appearance. A small plot of land, even one too small to support the peasant and his family, was the only protection against the dangers of landlessness. The precarious subsistence agriculture and stark alternatives facing the landless in both Peru and northern and central Vietnam created a resistance to technical or political change. In Vietnam there was almost no market participation, and agricultural technology remained static for a millenium. In Peru the serfs of hacienda Vicos resisted most suggestions for improvements by the Cornell Peru Project until they saw some chance of buying the hacienda, and most sierran agriculture remained dependent on the foot plow inherited from the Incas. Even the peasants of La Convención, who speedily adopted to market production of coffee, did so only because it could be combined with their subsistence crops and grown on higher and less valuable land. Peasant conservatism in Vietnam inhibited both Communist and millenial religious doctrines in the north and center. In Peru, as Hugo Blanco was to learn to his sorrow, even the ambitious coffee farmers of La Convención were fundamentally economic conservatives and once they controlled the land were certainly not inclined to risk it in a Trotskyist revolution.

In both the Peruvian sierra and northern and central Vietnam there was a considerable range of wealth within the cultivator population and intense competition to move upward to the status of medium landowner and enjoy the perquisites of community political office. The marginal subsistence agriculture of both areas restricted any advance in wealth to what could be gained at the expense of other members of the community. The more affluent peasant leaders of the Peruvian hacienda community of Vicos controlled 10 times as much wealth in cattle and land as did the poorer members, and in Vietnam the notables not only controlled more land and were wealthy enough to loan money to poor villagers but also controlled taxes, community land, and community water. The indigenous community of Hualcan was divided into two distinct strata, and wealthier peasants held the bottom lands along the river while the poorer members of the community tried to cultivate the hillsides. In the valley of La Convención the peasant class was split between the original usufructuaries, the *arrendires*, and later arrivals who became their tenants, the *allegados*. In the cotton valleys of the coast the cultivating class included small holders, displaced tenants, and part-time laborers who also worked small plots, as well as a class of petty merchants composed of recent arrivals from the sierra, and the economic interests of these groups were not identical. These differences in wealth and economic interests led to envy, suspicion, mistrust, and chronic conflict. Deceit, fraud, and outright theft were the principal means of expanding holdings in subsistence villages, and litigation arising out of these disputes was a major drain on peasant resources. The intensity of this individualistic economic competition is perhaps most vividly illustrated by the guard huts in the fields of Hualcan and the furtive expansion of garden plot bamboo hedges in the villages of Tonkin. Even in the indigenous communities of Peru there were no community economic resources, and the communal land and water of the villages of Tonkin and Annam led to more, not less internal village conflict. In both Peru and Vietnam traditional peasant villagers dreamed of moving up the order of precedence into the ranks of the notables in Vietnam and the *varayoc* in Peru. If the incentives for individual upward mobility in peasant communities of both Peru and Vietnam were strong, the incentives for collective economic or political organization were correspondingly weak. In northern and central Vietnam the dense population and finely divided plots left little surplus land to be distributed even by a revolutionary Communist regime, and collective irrigation works were difficult to build in the turbulent hydraulic environment of the Tonkin delta. In Peru the technology of peasant subsistence production did not permit any cooperative action, and even pastoral communities outside the market economy found few incentives for collective economic action. In contrast to the situation in Vietnam, however, there was a considerable amount of surplus land controlled by the haciendas; but any attempt to put even unused hacienda lands to collective use was dangerous in the extreme. Even if some form of collective action had been feasible, it is likely that much of the increase in production would have been siphoned off by the mestizo upper class of the sierra or by the notables and tax collectors of Vietnam. As the *colonos* of hacienda Vicos discovered, communal improvements led to higher rents and collective attempts to purchase land met with overwhelming political opposition. If the rewards of collective land invasions had been greater, it is possible that even subsistence peasant communities might have participated. As it was, in both Peru and Vietnam primitive cultivation techniques limited the amount of additional production that could have been drawn from the additional land, and hence the value of this land and the rewards for collective seizures were lower than in a more productive economy. Commercial agriculture in both La Convención and the central sierra increased the value of land and the size of the economic surplus that could be used to support lawyers, organizers, and political leaders and made the collective rewards sufficiently great to offset the considerable risks of collective land seizures. In the traditional subsistence communities of both Vietnam and Peru, however, the rewards for collective action were considerably weaker and the incentives for individual competition stronger.

The isolated production techniques of the subsistence economies of both Peru and Vietnam did not lead to interdependence that might have made it possible for the community to enforce loyalty to peasant interests. Peasant work gangs were used in Peru only on the haciendas, and the behavior of these gangs was controlled by the foremen and straw bosses, not by the work group itself. The weak structural links in the political economy of the subsistence villages were largely under the control of the traditional village leaders, the hacienda administration, or both. In the indigenous communities of Peru and the villages of northern and central Vietnam the civil religious hierarchy of the notables or the *varayoc* controlled the important collective goods of the community, and they in turn were directly or indirectly responsible to outside authorities. In Vietnam the notables controlled land, water, and taxes and could force villagers into a dependent relationship by threatening withdrawal of these community resources or by calling on outside authority. In Peruvian hacienda villages the *varayoc* were under the control of the foreman and were responsible for determining when work obligations had been satisfied, who was to work in the master's house, and who would be called for obligatory unpaid labor on public works. On the haciendas of both the sierra and the coast the *patrón* controlled community welfare, and survival in times of economic crisis or illness ultimately rested on his sense of *noblesse oblige* rather than on a cohesive peasant community. The strongly interdependent work groups and worker communities of the sugar plantations of Peru were entirely absent on either the traditional or commercial haciendas. Ties ran not from one cultivator to another, but from each isolated cultivator to the village hierarchy or the hacienda administration. Community solidarity was therefore imposed from above rather than originating within the class of cultivators themselves and reflected the conservative interests of the oligarchy and the outside authorities it represented.

Thus the economy of the traditional subsistence villages of both Peru and Vietnam created avoidance of risk, individual economic competition, and structural isolation of cultivators from one another. These economic characteristics and their related political consequences should, according to the hypotheses governing the behavior of cultivators, lead to political passivity under normal circumstances. The subsistence communities of the Peruvian sierra and the villages of northern and central Vietnam where these characteristics were most pronounced were not likely to be involved in political action in general and agrarian revolts in particular. In the commercial pastoral communities of the sierra and the commercial coffee valley of La Convención, however, the market economy created greater incentives for collective organization and weaker dependence on conservative linkages to either the hacienda administration or the village hierarchy, and it was these communities which participated in the agrarian revolt of the Peruvian sierra.

The evidence of both the case studies and the world analysis suggests three general conditions under which the organizational weakness of cultivators drawing their income from the land can be overcome and social movements created. First, both the world analysis and the Peruvian case studies indicate the critical importance of strong reformist or socialist parties in the organization of an agrarian revolt. The interaction effects within the commercial hacienda category indicated that agrarian events occurred only when such a party was in control of the national government, and in Peru the election of Belaúnde Terry marked the beginning of large-scale sierran land invasions. The presence of socialist or reformist parties is critical for two reasons. First, they weaken the political power of the land-owning class and therefore markedly reduce the penalties for land seizures and other actions against the landowners. Second, they supply the organizational resources the peasants lack. The coercion on which the commercial hacienda system fundamentally rests is undermined by the reform party's efforts to recruit mass support in the countryside. It is apparent that these parties cannot shoot their own political followers even if they do not show the proper respect for the institutions of private property. The Belaúnde government, for example, declared the San Pedro de Cajas invasion an orderly occupation of lands in litigation rather than a land invasion, and the military regime that displaced Belaúnde actively encouraged the transfer of land from *hacendados* to peasants. The rural organizers and party activists of the reform party also provide the organizational resources that poor peasant economies cannot support and thereby supply the critical ingredients lacking in the competitive individualistic world of the peasant. This was perhaps most apparent in the community of San Pedro de Cajas whose close ties to the Alianza Popular Revolucionaria Americana and to Francisco Espinoza gave it access both to the Agency for International Development and to the APRA party organ *La Tribuna*. San Pedro de Cajas was a unit in a local and provincial political machine and therefore had the organizational resources that peasants of a traditional indigenous community like Hualcan so noticeably lacked.

The second general condition under which peasant mobilization can take place is the presence of economic incentives for collective organization. Since such incentives do not in general exist in a subsistence economy, they are most likely to be created by increasing market participation. This principle was apparent in both La Convención and the central sierra in Peru. The commercial pastoral communities of the sierra were organized in communal granges which provided a corporate economic structure and encouraged cooperative political action. The commercially successful grange of San Pedro de Cajas, for example, created strong incentives for gaining additional lands, and the wealth of the communal economy made it possible to finance the logistics of a land invasion including trips to Lima for press conferences and bus service to the invasion site. In La Convensión the profits from commercial coffee production made it possible for *arrendires* to hire Cuzco lawyers to represent them in disputes with hacienda owners who were nominally their owners. The peasant syndicates of La Convención could afford both a political organization and political campaigns, and their increasing political influence at the polls began to offset the political power of the *hacendados*. In La Convención the incentives for collective action were not only greater than in areas of subsistence haciendas but also greater than in other coffee-producing areas. La Convención was unique in combining small plots and wet-processed coffee, creating both an intense need for additional land and a profitable way of exploiting it. The machinery required in wet processing was too expensive to be purchased on an individual basis for each small parcel, so that cooperative mills could be used to process the crop from several such parcels. In both San Pedro de Cajas and La Convención the commercial export economy created incentives for collective economic organization which were absent in the traditional subsistence villages.

The third general condition under which peasant social movements might be expected is the disruption of peasant subsistence production. Peasant mobilization under these circumstances takes place not because the incentives for collective organization are greater, but rather because the commitment to individual subsistence plots and the structural ties to the conservative leadership have been weakened or destroyed. Such changes can occur either through natural disasters, as was the case in Nghe An, or through economic change, as was the case in the agrarian movement of both the Peruvian coast and sierra. In Nghe An floods, droughts, and typhoons destroyed the peasants' subsistence margin, increased landlessness and indebtedness, and demanded immediate countermeasures. Since the disaster of landlessness had already occurred, the peasant's prior conservatism was pointless and political radicalism became a possibility. The natural disasters of northern and central Vietnam in general and Nghe An in particular also undermined the authority of the council of notables and the central administration, which both found that the interdependent economic relations which gave them control over poor villagers were weakened by the disaster. In Peru economic changes disrupted the traditional relation between the peasants and village and hacienda authorities in two principal ways. Depending on the nature of commercial agriculture, either the peasants expanded production at the expense of the estate or the estate expanded production at the expense of the peasants. In the valley of La Convención the expansion of coffee production on the *arrendires'* plots gave them a source of income independent of the hacienda administration or the conservative village leadership. They developed new allies in the small traders and merchants who came into the valley to profit from the coffee trade, and their ties to lawyers and other urban groups in Cuzco were also strengthened by commercial considerations. The backward *hacendados* became not only oppressive but superfluous. The benefits they once begrudgingly extended to loyal workers could now be purchased on the open market with the profits from the coffee trade. Control began slipping from *hacendados* precisely at the same time that the incentives for collective organization were increasing, and they were unable to prevent the resulting peasant movement. In the cotton valley of the coast and in the indigenous communities of the central sierra the expansion of large estates engaged in commercial production threatened to undermine the fragile economic base of the peasant economy. As population increased, the competition for land and water in the cotton valleys became increasingly fierce and the modernization and expansion of the cotton estate threatened the further loss of peasant lands. If this process had been carried out with the dispatch characteristic of the sugar valleys, no small landowners would have been left to protest. In the cotton valleys the threat of the loss of even the small subsistence plots decreased the resistance to radical action which is usually associated with small landed properties. In the sierra the fumes of La Oroya and the subsequent growth of commercial cattle haciendas threatened the destruction of peasant communities and once again weakened the conservative tie to the land. Thus the commercial export economy not only increased the incentives for collective organization against the landed upper class but also disrupted the ties to individual subsistence plots and to the conservative village leadership which restrained peasant political organization.

Both the world analysis and the case studies therefore support the general principle associating income sources and social movements expressed in hypothesis A of Chapter 1 and the specific intervening causal linkages between income sources and social movements suggested by hypotheses 1 to 6. As hypothesis A suggested, the combination of both upper and lower agricultural classes drawing their income from the land characteristic of the commercial hacienda and closely related systems led to agrarian revolts in which redistribution of landed property was the principal objective and long-range political objectives were lacking. In the world analysis the commercial hacienda category was associated with land invasions in which no revolutionary socialist or nationalist parties were active and no demands were made for fundamental political transformations. In Peru the limited objectives of the agrarian revolts of both the sierra and the coast are clearly indicated by the inability of the Peruvian Communist party to influence the timing or organization of the land invasions and by the failure of Hugo Blanco's Trotskyist revolt in La Convención. Peasants of both the sierra and the coast remained committed to the established political system and in fact carried the Peruvian national flag during land invasions as a sign of their patriotism. Long-run political changes in Peru were brought about not by a peasant-based political party, but by a modernizing military elite that took advantage of the instability created by the peasant revolt. Once the objective of the land invasions had been attained, the peasants lacked the organizational resources to carry out a thorough political revolution, and in La Convención in particular they relapsed into the conservatism and political indifference characteristic of cultivators drawing their incomes from the land.

The world analysis and the case studies also provide support for the specific pattern of causal linkages suggested by the hypotheses governing the behavior of cultivators. In both analyses agrarian revolts took place only when the risk avoidance, individualistic competition, and structural isolation of cultivators could be overcome, and the strongest movements occurred when more than one of these three factors were eliminated simultaneously. In the world analysis the presence of reformist or socialist parties in control of the national government promoted agrarian revolts by providing the organizational resources to overcome the structural isolation typical of peasant cultivators. In the case studies the strongest agrarian movements took place in those areas in which the traditional economic behavior of subsistence cultivators had been most completely changed by economic, political, or ecological change. In Vietnam the dangerous ecology of Nghe An periodically threatened the conservative ties to the land and the structural relations to the conservative village notables which had restrained peasant activism. In Peru the wool export economy of the central sierra increased the economic rewards of land seizures by providing a profitable means of exploiting additional land, threatened the *comuneros'* ties to their lands through the increasing encroachments of commercial stock-raising haciendas, and increased structural interdependence through the organization of communal granges. Only when all three of these factors were present as the analysis of interaction effects demonstrated, were *comunero* movements likely to occur in the sierra. In the valley of La Convención the commercial coffee economy increased the incentives for collective organization, and the *hacendados'* attempts to reclaim coffee lands for their own use threatened the *arrendires'* control over their plots. The interdependence of the coffee producers, however, was considerably less than that of the commercial pastoralists, and after they carried out their invasions, the political consequences of the essentially isolated production technique of small holder coffee production reappeared and the movement lapsed into conservatism. Although cooperative wet processing provided some interdependence, the peasant syndicate of La Convención had no communal granges to command the loyalty of their members. On the coast hacienda encroachments did weaken the tie to the land represented by individual subsistence plots, but the subsistence small holder economy provided only weak incentives for collective organization and created no structural interdependence among cultivators. The coastal agrarian movement was therefore the weakest of the three agrarian movements in Peru. The distribution and intensity of agrarian movements in Peru, then, supports the general pattern of intervening relationships outlined in the hypotheses describing the behavior of cultivators. Events occurred in general where the theory suggested they should and did not occur where the theoretical conditions were absent.

The agrarian revolt is a product not only of organizational resources on the part of cultivators but also of political inflexibility on the part of the noncultivators. In the agrarian revolt of the sierra the economic weakness, servile labor, and low productivity of the sierra *hacendados* focused conflict on political control of the land and inhibited reformist movements. On the more mechanized commercial haciendas of the coast, however, greater economic power, freer labor, and greater productivity made possible a reformist labor movement as well as a relatively weak agrarian revolt. Thus the case studies and the world analysis provide support for the specific hypotheses concerning both cultivator and noncultivator behavior in agricultural systems in which both classes draw their income from the land.

CAPITAL AND WAGES

A combination of a noncultivating class drawing its income from industrial and financial capital and a cultivating class drawing its income principally from wages is typical of plantation systems, although once again there is a considerable range of variation within this general category. This category includes the industrialized corporate sugar plantations of the Peruvian coast, the mixed system of estate and industrialized plantations of northeast Brazil, the individually owned but industrialized sisal estates of Tanzania, and the individually owned but poorly mechanized rubber estates of colonial Malaya, Indonesia, Vietnam, or Ceylon. Despite this range of variation these systems share a range of economic characteristics that make them particularly likely to produce reformist labor movements rather than either agrarian revolts or revolutions. According to the hypotheses 1 to 6 of Chapter 1 the income sources of the cultivating and noncultivating classes should have a series of economic and political consequences for both. An upper class dependent on industrial capital should, first, be economically powerful and therefore less dependent on political concessions and privileges than an upper class dependent on land. Second, the industrial upper class should make greater use of free wage labor and therefore be less opposed to granting limited political or economic rights to workers. Third, the increasing productivity associated with mechanization should provide an increasing share of agricultural production to be used to grant benefits to workers, eliminating the zero-sum conflict situation typical of landed estates. Overall these political characteristics tend to focus conflict on the distribution of income from property rather than property itself. Similarly the payment of cultivators in wages rather than land should also have three principal consequences. First, it should eliminate the conservative tie to the land that inhibits political radicalism in small holding systems. Second, it should decrease prospects for individual mobility and increase incentives for group political action. Third, it should create structurally interdependent work groups and worker communities, increasing the strength of sanctions available to workers' organizations in enforcing loyalty to the cultivator class. These three characteristics should lead to more powerful political organizations than those found among cultivators dependent on land. In general, then, a well-organized politically powerful cultivator class confronts an economically powerful but politically flexible upper class, and the likely result according to hypothesis C of Chapter 1 is a reformist labor movement whose objectives are limited to economic issues and which lacks broader revolutionary political goals.

As was the case in the land and land category, the internal variations in plantation category can be used to examine the utility of the intervening theoretical linkages between income source and social movements expressed in the first six hypotheses of Chapter 1. The interaction effects in the world analysis of plantation systems clearly indicated that the more highly industrialized sugar, tea, rubber, and sisal plantations were considerably more likely to generate labor movements than were less industrialized tree crop plantations in rubber, plam, or copra. This distinction was also apparent in the contrast between the rubber systems of Malaya and the tea plantations of Ceylon and was also supported by the case of analysis of Peruvian sugar plantations. In fact the sugar plantations of Peru described in Chapter 3 can be taken as representative of the economic and political characteristics of the most highly

industrialized plantations in the world analysis. In Peru the production parameters for plantation sugar production were close to ideal. The flat alluvial river
deltas and continuous sunlight of the northern Peruvian coast provided perfect
growing conditions, and yields were among the highest in the world. Cane
could be harvested year-round instead of in two or three campaigns as is the
case in other sugar areas, and processing plants could therefore be kept in
constant operation. Cane could be ratooned for 10 or more years before replanting and therefore required no sudden annual labor inputs at planting. As
the world analysis of crop production parameters indicated, a continuous harvest
and expensive processing machinery are the principal determinants of efficient
centralized production. The continuous harvest of Peruvian sugar made it
possible not only to keep the sugar mills operating 24 hours a day but also
provided a steady supply of raw materials for subsidiary manufacturing enterprises. The Paramonga plantation of Grace and Company was one of the most
highly industrialized sugar installations in the world and one of the principal
industrial centers of Peru. It combined plants for the manufacture of cardboard
boxes, caustic soda, and chlorine gas as well as a large sugar refinery. All aspects
of cane cultivation and processing except harvesting were automated, and the
irrigation required in the arid coastal valleys increased capital expenditures.
Sugar cultivation generally requires more investment in capital machinery than
any other crop, and this was particularly true in the case of Peru. Peruvian
plantations more closely resemble the highly industrialized sugar plantations of
Jamaica, Cuba, or the Dominican Republic than either the less fully rationalized
hacienda-like forms of the Phillipines or northeast Brazil or the sugar plantations
of Indonesia with their mixed tenancy and industrial organization. Grace's
capital investment in its sugar plantations in 1969, at the time of their nationalization by the Peruvian military regime, amounted to some 9 million dollars.

These immense capital requirements quickly forced indigenous Peruvian
sugar estate owners into bankruptcy, and, as was the case in other sugar systems
throughout the underdeveloped world, foreign capital and foreign corporate
ownership were dominant in Peruvian sugar. Casa Grace is typical of the
largest and most influential corporations involved in the world sugar trade, and
its immense holdings include shipping and a broad range of other transportation
and manufacturing activities. The substantial capital assets of Grace and other
large sugar producers in Peru gave them immense political power and a limited
immunity to political threats. Even though Grace's holdings were nationalized
by the Peruvian military regime in 1969, it was able in 1974 to report one of
the best year's earnings in its history, and its total worldwide assets had increased more than tenfold since the middle fifties and amounted to more than
2 billion dollars. Grace's immense political influence in both Peru and the
United States allowed it to wield substantial market power in the politicized
world sugar trade. Grace could influence allocations of the United States' sugar
quota to Peru and attempt to block such allocations when its estates were
seized. Sugar even more than tea satisfies a major craving of much of the earth's

population, and sugar consumption is relatively insensitive to price fluctuations. Over a wide range of uses there are no effective substitutes, and the demise of artificial sweeteners in the Unitd States at least temporarily eliminated a possible substitute. The cartelized and politicized sugar market therefore provides considerable security for large producers, and a company like Grace can use its monopoly power in Peru and its political influence in the Unted States to protect its interests.

The plantations of Peru were also relatively invulnerable to small holders' movements, since unlike the cotton haciendas the sugar estates had managed to clear all the small holders out of their irrigated valleys and monopolized the cultivated area. Land monopolization seems in fact to be characteristic of sugar economies in a number of export sectors, including both the Caribbean littoral and the sugar islands of the Pacific. Even if the small holders had remained, however, they could not have broken up the large estates without causing a substantial loss in export earnings because of the economies of scale in sugar production. The market and land monopolies of sugar plantations thus gave them immense power, and their corporate owners were often economically invulnerable even to total nationalization. Thus the case of Peruvian plantations indicates support for the hypothesized connection between industrial capital and political influence.

The Peruvian case also supports the hypothesis linking industrial capital, free labor, and worker rights. The increasing mechanization of sugar production in Peru during the 1950s and 1960s made it possible for the plantations to close their sierra recruiting offices and rely on resident labor in the sugar valleys. Mechanization caused a substantial decline in the number of workers required, and although this created substantial unemployment, it transferred the burden of welfare services from the corporation to the state. A disciplined responsible labor force, even if organized by a populist party, was useful in maintaining the continuous flow of cane and refinery by-products necessary for the efficient operation of industrial installations like Paramonga. The plantation owners of Peru therefore were much more able to tolerate labor organization than were the owners of commercial cotton haciendas, and in contrast to the hacienda owners they received some benefits in the form of better utilization and maintenance of their expensive machinery. The greater the industrialization of the plantation, therefore, the greater its dependence on wage labor and the greater the tolerance of workers' organizations.

The increasing mechanization of the plantations and the consequent increase in worker productivity made it possible for Grace to pursue a strategy of gradually granting anticipatory wage increases to frustrate labor organizers. Even after organizers succeeded, Grace was still able to prevent radical demands for nationalization by keeping wages moving upward and as a result the sugar workers became a labor aristocracy in Peru. It was the peasant revolt in the sierra, not the protests of the sugar workers, which precipitated the military coup which led to the nationalization of the plantations. The workers in fact were ambivalent about the new government administrators and regretted the demise of the freewheeling union tactics which had been possible under the old corporate owners. The Peruvian case supports the proposition that industrial capital leads to productivity gains which make it possible to increase wages in order to diffuse worker discontent. The overall results of the Peruvian case study therefore support hypotheses 1 to 3 of Chapter 1 concerning the behavior of noncultivators and provide the intervening causal linkages necessary to understand the distinction between industrial and nonindustrial plantations in the world analysis.

The Peruvian case study also illustrates the three political and economic consequences of a cultivating class paid almost entirely in wages rather than land. First, after 1960, when the last labor recruitment offices in the sierra were closed, the workers of the Peruvian sugar plantations lost their last ties both to the land and to the Indian culture of the sierra and rapidly became fully assimilated into the Hispanicized culture of the coast. Since housing was provided by the company and sugar cane consumed any land which could have been used for subsistence plots, the workers controlled no real estate whatsoever and therefore were receptive to economic and political change.

Second, individual economic mobility was difficult if not impossible, since the narrow occupational pyramid of the sugar oasis was completely dominated by the plantation work organization and the small middle class of shopkeepers and tradesmen had been completely displaced by the company store and company managers. In addition the relative affluence of the sugar workers made it possible for them to support a labor leadership through a dues check-off system, and as a result the most talented workers competed for these positions rather than seeking status in the miniscule middle class. In contrast to the conditions of the commercial haciendas, on sugar plantations there were both strong incentives for organizer efforts and weak incentives for individual economic competition. Economic gains could only be made at the expense of the plantation administration, and any such gains required collective, not individual efforts.

Third, the interdependent work groups of the harvesting gangs and the worker plantation community itself created strong ties of functional interdependence and mutual aid among the workers. Although the plantation administration dominated welfare, education, and recreation in the oases, these services tended to decline as the population in the oases increased, and the ties between management and worker did not reflect the paternalism of the hacienda, but rather the negotiated benefits of a union contract. In addition the worker community itself exerted an important influence on worker behavior because community support was valuable and community ostracism was dangerous. In contrast to the indigenous communities of the sierra, in which Indian identity was a source of shame and a mark of political weakness, in the plantation communities it became a symbol of solidarity and opposition to the mestizo overlords. This solidarity could be enforced if need be by union disciplinary units which fought strikebreakers and maintained strike discipline. During strikes the entire community acted as a whole, with the men carefully avoiding arrest while the women protested against strikebreakers or rioted at the company store. Thus the resident wage labor force of the plantation was willing to accept political risks, was compelled to take collective rather than individual action to improve its economic situation, and could enforce a strong sense of class solidarity. These political characteristics made the sugar plantations a bastion of APRA support and one of the most important voting blocks in Peru.

Despite the class-based political organization and the radical populist rhetoric of APRA, the demands of the workers' organizations of the coastal sugar estates were limited almost entirely to wages and working conditions, and no demands were made to nationalize the plantations or to overthrow the government. Political strikes did occur, but they were in support of, not in opposition to, constitutional government. The reformist character of the sugar plantation labor movement is of course a result of the negotiating flexibility of the corporation managers. Unlike the inflexible *hacendados* of the sierra they offered the workers a surer and less dangerous route to economic gains through collective bargaining rather than through outright attacks on the institutions of property. Thus in both Peru and in the world analysis sugar plantations and other industrialized plantations were likely to generate reformist labor movements. In Peru labor events were considerably more highly correlated with the distribution of sugar production and hence with industrialized plantation organizations than they were with cotton production and hence with commercial hacienda organizations. The pattern of events in Peru therefore supports the general hypotheses linking income sources and reform labor movements and also the specific causal linkages expressed in the hypotheses concerning the behavior of cultivators and noncultivators.

If the sugar plantation is typical of the industrialized plantations most likely to lead to reformist labor movements, the exceptional cases of Malaya and other rubber systems in the world analysis are typical of plantation systems which either do not lead to reformist labor movements or do lead to other forms of movements. Nevertheless, as the analysis of the apparently deviant case of Malayan rubber indicated, these exceptions can in fact be accounted for by the specific hypotheses governing the behavior of cultivators and noncultivators. Rubber, unlike sugar, requires little or no estate processing and therefore no expensive industrial equipment, and although rubber can be harvested continuously, it actually benefits from neglect, so that peasant subsistence farmers can easily allow their trees to vegetate when the rubber price is low and harvest when it is high. Small holders are therefore formidable competitors in the world rubber market, and in both Ceylon and Indonesia as well as in Malaya they produce somewhat less than half of total exports. The rubber market is not subject to either cartelization or political control, and the competition from synthetics and fluctuations in industrial demand expose the rubber producers to market forces unknown to sugar producers. Most rubber estates are in fact individually rather than corporately owned, although there are notable exceptions such as the rubber estates of Firestone in Liberia or Michelin in Vietnam, and the small estate owners are unable to exercise significant market or political power. Their existence in fact was dependent on colonialism, and the estate owners found after independence that their survival had been of much greater importance to colonial governors than to parliamentary governments in former metropoles. Firestone and Michelin command great market power and political influence, but their methods of cultivation and processing closely resemble the smaller estates of colonial Ceylon, Malaya, or Indonesia. A substantial part of world rubber production is, however, in the hands of small estate owners who lack the market power of industrial sugar plantations and were exposed to both political uncertainty and increasing competition from small holders after the end of the colonial epoch.

Rubber plantations are also more dependent on forced labor than are sugar plantations, and this is true of both corporate and individually owned estates. Although most laborers on sugar plantations are resident for long periods, most rubber workers are sojourners hired for a fixed term of from one to three years and usually return to a peasant subsistence economy at the end of these terms. Laborers are recruited under varying degrees of compulsion and are frequently brought in from other countries or regions to undercut the price of indigenous labor. In Vietnam the peasants of overpopulated Tonkin were impressed by notables acting under the direction of Michelin labor contractors, in Liberia Firestone recruits labor through the agency of local village chiefs, and in Malaya Chinese and Tamil indentured laborers were also recruited by contractors. The ethnically distinct groups favored by rubber estates are either socially isolated or actively discriminated against by the indigenous population. The Tonkinese peasant in Cochinchina was outside his village and therefore without political rights, and the tribal laborers of Liberia work in areas dominated by Liberians with close ties to the United States. In both Ceylon and Malaya chronic racial hatreds were expressed in frequent riots against Tamils and Chinese, and after independence the role of the minority plantation population has been a major, perhaps the major, political issue. Thus rubber plantations rely on a politically disenfranchised, frequently foreign work force recruited under at least some degree of compulsion. The need for forced labor is a direct result of limited economies of scale in rubber production and intense price competition from small holders. This dependence on semiservile labor leads to opposition to any extension of political or economic rights to workers and reinforces the estate owners' reliance on political control.

Similarly, since total rubber production is limited by the physical capacity of the trees and not by the size of the investment in processing machinery and since the price of rubber fluctuates widely and has shown a steady decline since the invention of synthetic rubber, the share of agricultural profits available for wage increases has been fixed or declining throughout the postwar period. Production can be temporarily increased by strip tapping, but this process destroys the future productivity of the trees and therefore damages the principal asset of the estate owner. In contrast to sugar production, in which increased production usually leads to increasing profits, increased production in rubber estates may actually decrease future profits. As a result little money is available to grant periodic wage increases, and in fact, as was the case in Malaya, wage cuts may be necessary. These economic constraints are a direct result of the technology of rubber production and apply equally to individually owned estates and corporate plantations. In summary, then, the upper classes of rubber plantations are in general politically vulnerable, opposed to cultivator rights, and restricted to zero-sum conflict over a fixed agricultural income. Their behavior is in these respects more similar to the behavior of the owner of a commercial hacienda than to that of the corporate managers of a typical sugar plantation.

The mixed labor incentives of the rubber estate involving both coercion and wages, both part-time resident labor and part-time peasant subsistence production, create similarly marginal behavior on the part of the cultivating class. To some extent rubber workers show the three principal economic and political consequences of the payment of a working class in land rather than in wages. First, they maintain at least some ties to the land because they will usually return to a peasant or tribal village at the end of their term, and their wages may in fact be saved to buy land as was the intention of many Chinese laborers in Malaya and most Tonkinese peasants in Cochinchina. Although this tie to the land may be illusory and the laborer may not be able to save or even stay alive during his term, this weak tie to landed property makes him less susceptible to radical political doctrines than a propertyless sugar plantation laborer.

Second, both the economic competition between workers and the prospects for upward mobility in the home village undermine solidarity among the rubber estate workers and provide an important tool to be used against unions. The tribal rubber workers of Liberia or the Belgian Congo were usually recruited from a variety of tribal groups often not resident in the immediate area of the plantation, and the most likely candidates for recruitment by tribal authorities were young single men who could at least try to save money toward a bride price and perhaps gain enough influence in their home village to avoid being recruited a second time. Three years was too short a time for the Tonkinese peasant to lose his hope of returning to his home village or to forget that individualistic economic competition was the principal route to village success. The isolated foreign workers and the hostility of the indigenous population could be used by the plantation owners to undermine worker solidarity, and the reserves of indentured labor provided a ready source of strikebreakers and competitors for employment. The incentive for collective organization so evident in the sugar valleys of Peru was considerably weaker on rubber estates.

Third, rubber plantation work is not organized in the interdependent work gangs typical of sugar estates, and in fact rubber tappers frequently work in the forest by themselves or in small groups and are paid on a piece rate basis. The structural ties of the rubber estate do not link workers to one another, but rather to the labor contractor, who is responsible for their employment and, often, for their satisfactory behavior during their term of service. The Liberian tribesman on a Firestone rubber plantation is responsible to the tribal chief who impressed him, and the chief's future diplomatic relations with the company depend on the worker's performance. With such important political issues at stake and with return to his native village probable, the worker is unlikely to challenge the administration. The same relationship exists between the Tonkinese laborer and the village notable in Vietnam, and in Malaya the *kangany* was accountable for the worker's performance throughout his term and might lose money if the worker escaped or refused work. The sanctions and inducements for conformity were therefore controlled not by other workers, but by the contractor, and the pressures for working-class solidarity were correspondingly weakened.

Both the cultivating and noncultivating classes of the rubber plantation therefore share some of the economic and political characteristics of classes dependent on land rather than of classes dependent on wages and capital, respectively. Like the commercial cotton estates of the Peruvian coast the rubber estate is a marginal economic enterprise, and like the cotton haciendas its behavior shares characteristics of both plantations and landed estates. Although receptivity to radical ideologies, incentives for collective action, and class solidarity are all weaker among rubber workers than among sugar workers, all three factors are stronger than in isolated peasant communities in which incomes are drawn entirely from the land. Although the rubber workers do not show the same commitment to unionization and willingness to strike found among sugar workers, they are capable of organization, and plantation unions, some of them company dominated, are found on rubber estates. These unions, however, must negotiate with an owner whose behavior is very much like that of the owner of the hacienda, and as a result the prospects for reformist movements in rubber estates are limited. In fact the political vulnerability, hostility to workers' organization, and inability to grant wage increases characteristic of the upper class of rubber plantations are likely to politicize conflict and even lead to revolutionary action, as was the case in Malaya. Strikes are possible in rubber plantations, especially the larger corporate systems, but they frequently involve more radical demands than those of sugar plantation workers. In Vietnam, for example, the rubber workers joined the 1931 Communist insurrection, and in Indonesia the rubber workers joined a 1958 general strike demanding the nationalization of Dutch plantations. Despite the marginal position of the rubber plantation in the fourfold typology of income sources, its behavior supports the specific hypotheses governing the behavior of cultivators and noncultivaotrs. Its marginal position on each of the six economic variables affecting the political behavior of both classes leads to an intermediate form of political movement.

Under normal circumstances, however, neither the commercial hacienda nor the plantation form of agricultural organization is likely to lead to an agrarian revolution, although agrarian revolts occur in hacienda systems under some circumstances and reformist labor movements are common in industrial plantations. In agricultural systems in which both cultivators and noncultivators draw their incomes from the land, cultivators usually lack the organizational resources to mount a revolutionary movement and the political momentum to carry it on after the immediate economic objective of land to the tiller has been realized. The combination of capital and labor produces the necessary organizational resources on the part of the cultivators, but revolution is made unlikely by the flexible behavior of the noncultivating classes. Of course when both organizational resources on the part of the cultivators and inflexibility on the part of noncultivators are absent, revolution is most unlikely. This combination is typical of commercial small holding systems, and the world analysis indicated that such systems were not likely to lead to any particular form of social protest except for a relatively modest tendency for the more commercialized small holding systems to generate reformist commodity movements. This is not to say, on the other hand, that small holdings *per se* inhibit revolutionary movements, since the distribution of events with respect to small holding systems seems to be relatively random and the correlations between events of various types and the dummy small holding variable were low or insignificant, not strong and negative. The findings of the world analysis therefore provide only modest support for the relationship between small holding and commodity reform movements, and since no case study was undertaken for this category, there is no way of tracing the intervening causal pathways in detail. The results did indicate, however, that all but a small proportion of small holders involved in export production are subsistence farmers who produce the export crop as a sideline, and the absence of commodity movements in these systems may be an indication of the weakness of market ties and the relative small influence that middlemen, exporters, and other members of the noncultivating classes exert on the small holders. This tentative conclusion is supported by the relatively greater commodity event activity in the small number of more commercialized systems. The results do make clear, however, that a combination of a noncultivating class dependent on financial or commercial capital and a cultivating class drawing its income from the land is not conducive to agrarian revolution.

LAND AND WAGES

This combination of income sources for cultivating and noncultivating classes includes some forms of agricultural organization which combine the inflexible behavior of the cultivators of a landed estate with the strong cultivator organizations of the corporate plantation. When both conditions exist simultaneously, the result is likely to be an agrarian revolution in which a strong peasant-based guerrilla movement organized by a nationalist or Communist party attempts to destroy both the rural upper class and the institutions of the state and establish a new society. This general statement, however, stands in immediate need of qualification. Although this general category is the only one likely to produce agrarian revolution, not only systems within the category share the same degree of revolutionary potential and not all the revolutionary movements share the same objectives. Two principal subcategories of the land and wages combination were distinguished in Chapter 1, the migratory labor estate and the sharecropped estate, each of which tends to produce a different form of agrarian movement and each of which shows the same internal variation in agricultural organization as do the commercial hacienda and plantation categories. Once again the world analysis indicated that some systems within each of the two subcategories were more likely to produce the characteristic form of social movement than others. The world analysis indicated that revolutionary nationalist movements were likely to occur only in migratory estate systems located in colonial areas and that revolutionary socialist movements were more likely in decentralized than in centralized sharecropping systems. These general principles were also evident in the analysis of both the colonial migratory estate system of Portuguese Angola and the decentralized share-cropping export sector of the Mekong delta of Vietnam. As was the case in the summaries of the land and land and capital and wages categories, variations within the general land and wages category and within the two principal sub-categories provide a means of assessing the validity of the specific causal linkages between income sources and social movements described in hypotheses 1 to 6 of Chapter 1. It is these linking hypotheses, not the general land and wages combination, which permit precise prediction about the causes of agrarian revolution in both migratory labor estate and sharecropped estate systems.

The migratory labor estate category includes any individually owned enterprise which lacks power-driven machinery and is worked by seasonal, migratory wage laborers. This definition includes the coffee systems of Central America and southern Africa, the grape and citrus systems of the Maghreb, and sheep ranches in South Africa and Chile. With the exception of the sheep ranches, most of these systems are based on perennial tree crops with harvest periods of four months or less. Perennial crops eliminate the labor inputs associated with annual planting and therefore reduce slightly one of the principal obstacles to efficient centralized production. The perennial trees or bushes are, however, usually the most valuable capital asset of the estate and cannot be trusted to tenants who might damage them by overzealous exploitation during their tenure. The world analysis indicated that there was a negative correlation between perennial crops and sharecropping, and this system, when it is used at all with tree crops, either offers future ownership to tenants to encourage arboreal husbandry or must move frequently when trees at one location are exhausted. Since the harvest period of migratory estate tree crops is short, neither a year-round resident labor force nor expensive processing machinery can be economically maintained. In addition, crops grown on migratory estates do not in general require much processing, so that both of the two principal determinants of efficient plantation organization are absent. Migratory labor systems also tend to occur in areas where agricultural land is either too scarce or too expensive to permit the payment in usufruct rights characteristic of the commercial hacienda system. Usually, as was the case for example in Angola or Algeria, the migratory labor estates expand to include almost all the valuable land in the export sector, driving the indigenous small cultivators back into crowded reserve areas. In general, of course, the laborers themselves would no doubt prefer to live in proximity to the estates, but the incompatibility of the subsistence and export economies in most migratory estate systems makes this impossible. The commercial coffee economy of La Convención in Peru, for example, developed in a relatively sparsely settled area, and labor could be provided at least initially through additional tenancies and subtenancies, but as land became scarcer and more valuable, migratory harvest labor became necessary and an acute labor shortage developed in the valley. In many other Latin American coffee systems, on the other hand, the topography of mountain valleys provides strata successively suitable to lowland ranching, to coffee culti-vation at moderate altitudes, and to high-altitude precarious subsistence farming, and the laborers therefore live in close proximity to the estate. In migratory estate systems land values, land scarcity, and topography make this close proximity between subsistence plots and export production impossible.

The production parameters of the crops of the migratory estate economies lead to a characteristic division between a commercial export sector where labor is employed during the harvest and an economically and spatially distinct sub-sistence sector where the laborers support themselves in the off season. The migratory estate system throws the cost of subsistence back onto the peasant or tribal community from which the laborers come and thereby minimizes estate labor costs. Ordinarily, of course, such a migratory pattern would not be expected to lead to any kind of cultivator organization, let alone an agrarian revolution, since migrants are notoriously difficult to organize. Seasonal migrants picking grapes or coffee are tied to the peasant or tribal subsistence community even more closely than are the fixed-term migrants of rubber estates and therefore share many of the political and economic characteristics of workers paid in land rather than wages. In most cases the hypotheses concerning the behavior of cultivators dependent on land should apply to workers in migratory estate systems, and political passivity should be the result. The potential for revolution in migratory estate systems does not, however, depend on wage laborers alone, but on an incongruous coalition between the leadership of the traditional tribal or peasant community supplying the laborers and the laborers themselves. The traditional leadership provides the organizational resources that seasonal migrants, like subsistence peasants, typically lack. On the basis of economic interests alone, however, such a coalition would seem unlikely in the extreme. In Vietnam, for example, this coalition would involve the fixed-term migrants working on the Cochinchina rubber estates and the village notables who had impressed them into service in the first place. In Angola it would involve contract laborers and village chiefs, who often acted as the labor contractors' agents. Politics has made stranger alliances, and as the case of Angola indicated, such alliances can have considerable revolutionary potential. Nevertheless, this coalition is possible only under a narrow range of economic and ecological circumstances, and many migratory estate systems show no tendency toward revolutionary nationalism whatsoever. Traditional village authorities' willingness to throw in their lot with the poorest members of their village who have been sent to labor on estates is evident only when their own economic base of support is being eroded by the same estate system that is exploiting the poor laborers. Such a constellation of political and economic forces depends ultimately on the relationship between the two sectors, export and subsistence, which constitute the migratory estate system.

Only when the estate system is expanding at the expense of the subsistence sector and therefore both increasing overcrowding within the subsistence sector and threatening lands controlled under traditional tenure can the traditional village leaders be mobilized to resist. This overcrowding and land expropriation is likely only if the two sectors of the migratory estate system are adjacent and not spatially or economically segregated when the export sector is expanding. Just as was the case among the peasants of the sierra, the expansion of commercial estates undermines peasant conservatism and makes revolution possible. If the export and subsistence sectors are far enough apart so that expansion in one sector does not affect the other directly, there will be no social movement. Guatemala, for example, has the largest migratory labor stream as a percent of total population of any nation in the world, yet its repressed Indian majority shows no tendency toward revolutionary nationalism. Migration takes place between the mountains and plateaus of the densely populated Indian areas and the *Ladino*-dominated coffee piedmont and coast, and estate agriculture is not, therefore, a direct threat to the remote, if inadequate, peasant small holdings. Agrarian social movements in Guatemala have therefore involved either the small numbers of laborers resident on the coffee estates or fights between land-starved peasants in the mountain and high-plateau areas and have not led to an Indian uprising based on communal rather than class solidarity. If the subsistence sector comes to be too completely integrated into the export sector, on the other hand, the cultivator communities come to represent the lower class of a commercial hacienda system, and the traditional village leadership is weakened or eliminated. Most sierran Indians who came to the cotton valleys of Peru, for example, were quickly integrated into the Hispanicized culture of the coastal lower class, and the few remaining coastal Indian communities had lost much of their traditional leadership structure and Indian cultural characteristics. The communities of the central sierra were integrated into both the hacienda system and the world market and therefore formed an agricultural lower class just as did the captive communities on the haciendas themselves.

Only when there is some economic and political segregation of the two sectors, subsistence and export, but not so much as to completely eliminate land conflicts is a revolutionary nationalist movement possible. If the two sectors are completely segregated, as they are in Guatemala, there will be no threat to the leaders of the traditional village, and therefore one element of the coalition will be eliminated. If the two sectors are completely integrated, as they are in a hacienda of Peru, the traditional leadership is so completely dominated by the upper class that organization takes place along class rather than communal lines.

In the world analysis these principles were supported by the finding that only in colonial migratory estate systems did nationalist movements occur. In colonial settler economies such as those of Algeria, Kenya, or Angola the new settler class appropriated the best land, expanded its holdings at the expense of indigenous tribal groups, and recruited labor from the shrinking, over-populated indigenous reserve areas but, significantly, did not integrate these reserves politically or socially into the economy of the export sectors. Although the indigenous reserves were, of course, under at least nominal military control, the traditional tribal leaders of the Berbers, the Kikuyu, or the Bakongo continued to rule in what amounted to separate but subordinate states. They were, however, states whose economic base was under continual pressure from the labor and land demands of the export sector, and as a result tribal oligarchies that in other times and other places might have become the loyal intermediaries in a colonial administration became instead its most vigorous opponents. The indigenous reserve which provides the organizational resources that migratory seasonal workers lack is most often found in colonial systems, and it is in such systems that the incongruous nationalist revolutionary coalition is most likely to form.

The case study of Angola illustrates both the mechanisms by which such a cultivator coalition can be created and the political response which can be expected from the noncultivating class. The outbreak of a revolutionary nationalist movement depends not only on cultivator organization but also on noncultivator response, and in Angola and other colonial migratory estate systems the behavior of cultivators closely resembled the political inflexibility of the most backward commercial *hacendados* of Peru. In fact the *fazenda* owners of the Angolan coffee economy were as dependent on land rather than capital as the *hacendados* of La Convención, and their economic position was, if anything, even more precarious. In an economic system in which a major article of processing equipment is a flattened ant heap and hulling machines are transported from farm to farm in pickup trucks, the income of the cultivating class must come entirely from its control over land rather than capital. In fact the technology of estate coffee processing is only a slight improvement over the oversized wooden mortar and pestle used by indigenous African cultivators. The low grade robustas of Angola do not require the wet processing necessary for the finer arabicas of La Convención, so that investment in processing equipment may actually be less on some *fazendas* in Angola than on the larger peasant farms of Peru. The minimal processing equipment and relatively short four-month harvest of Angolan coffee production are both parameters which favor small holder, not estate production, and it was only the substantial colonial privileges of the *fazenda* owners that made them even marginally competitive. Despite the overwhelming political and social advantages of the Portuguese nationals, who controlled all aspects of the coffee trade, 50,000 African producers tenaciously clung to their trees and contributed one-quarter of all exports despite land expropriation, forced labor, and direct intimidation. Their survival is a result of the invisible prod of the market, which offset the overt coercion of the Portuguese. *Fazenda* owners faced intense price competition from small holders not only in Angola but in the Ivory Coast, Uganda, or, for that matter, La Convención.

The limited prospects for capital improvements and indeed the capital shortage in the northern coffee region of Angola led to the three patterns of economic and political behavior typical of noncultivating classes dependent on land. These patterns are also apparent in the contrast between the northern estates and the more highly capitalized mixed sugar and coffee plantations of the southern coffee zone. The northern producers were poorer and more politically vulnerable than even the *hacendados* of La Convención. In fact many of them had recently left the status of bush trader or Portuguese peasant, which would have placed them in the lower rather than the upper class of the Peruvian sierra. Even during their golden years in the middle fifties the *fazenda* owners never acquired the vast estates of the *hacendados* of La Convención or the landlords of Cochinchina and never earned the substantial incomes of the coastal *hacendados* of Peru. If they were an upper class dependent on land it was on a relatively small amount of land, and their economic alternatives were even more limited than those of members of most other landed upper classes. The landlord of Cochinchina could bask on the French Riviera after his lands had been paid for by the Republic of Vietnam, and the displaced *hacendados* of La Convención could usually rely on their highly placed relatives to ease the shock of the loss of their estates, but the *fazenda* owners of the Angolan north might be forced into the slums of Lisbon or Luanda where their position was little better than that of a landless peasant. Few could save money during the boom years, and with the fall in coffee prices most became bankrupts.

Since no *fazenda* owner controlled any substantial market power and each was forced to deal with large exporting firms just as did African producers and none had any capital assets other than his land, all were ultimately dependent on the special land concessions made possible by the colonial regime. The absence of capital was in fact so profound that petty trading activities persisted even after large-scale coffee production had begun. The northern landowner was ultimately dependent on the Native Statutes, particularly the legal distinction between the indigenous and nonindigenous populations, for the ownership of his centralized estate. Such privileged access to land would of course not survive the passing of colonial rule, and in the event of independence the coffee farmers of northern Angola could expect to fare no better and indeed, given the bitterness aroused by the guerrilla war, might fare considerably worse than the coffee *colons* of the Belgian Congo who departed *en masse* shortly after independence. Therefore the political vulnerability of the *fazenda* owner was acute and his alternatives were more restricted than those of any other landed class examined in the case studies. His desperate defense of the colonial order even at the risk of his own life was a direct result of his economic weakness and political vulnerability.

Like other landed classes the *fazenda* owners of Angola were dependent on a coerced rather than a free labor force, and as with landed classes elsewhere this reliance on force required total opposition to political or economic rights for workers. The provision of forced labor was as essential to the economic survival of the northern Angolan coffee estates as was the forced expropriation of land, and the colonial legal distinction between indigenous and nonindigenous rights made this forced labor possible. The labor relations of the northern Angolan estates depended on a minimum of inducement and a maximum of coercion, and the *chicote* and the *caderneta* were the twin symbols of this coercive system. Significantly the southern coffee estates, much more highly capitalized and mechanized than the northern estates, were distinctly less likely to use coercion in labor relations and in fact were something of a model of paternalistic plantation management in sub-Saharan Africa. This is not, of course, to say that they approached the labor relations of a highly industrialized sugar plantation, and in fact their labor relations more closely resembled those of a Peruvian sugar plantation in the *enganche* period. Nevertheless the relative use of coercion in labor management in the north and the south once again supports the general hypothesis that exclusive dependence on land rather than industrial capital leads to servile labor and complete opposition to workers' rights. CADA (Companhia Agrícola de Angola) and other large southern estates could probably survive the passing of colonial rule and still manage to recruit labor, especially if the population pressure on land in the central plateau continued to increase. No similar hope existed for the *fazenda* owners of the north, and their commitment to colonial rule had, therefore, to be correspondingly greater.

Finally, the *fazenda* owners of the north could look forward to no expanding agricultural production out of which wage increases might have been financed. Instead, of course, the collapse of the coffee boom led to a dramatic fall in revenues just at a time when wage increases would have been most useful in defusing the growing political discontent associated with the African independence movement. Whether or not wage cuts at the Primavera plantation, as Holden Roberto insisted, led to the March 1961 uprising, it is clear that wages must have decreased to compensate for falling prices. This in turn implied even more coercion and greater dependence on colonial rule. At a time when much of Africa was moving toward independence, the former peasant farmers and bush traders of northern Angola found that they needed more, not less colonialism. In the southern coffee estates, of course, crop diversification and substantial capital reserves made it possible to continue paternalistic benefits for workers and maintain wage levels even if some laborers had to be discharged. Consequently the need for additional coercion was considerably less in the south than in the north.

Thus the Angola *fazenda* owners showed all three economic characteristics which were hypothesized to be consequences of dependence on land rather than industrial capital, and they represented an extreme position on all three characteristics. Their poverty and lack of capital made them dependent on colonial land concessions, their reliance on forced labor depended on the moral and legal obligation of work under the Native Statutes, and their inefficient production techniques combined with falling prices not only made wage increases impossible but made substantial wage cuts essential. These characteristics rapidly focused all conflict on the ultimate sources of political power, which were also the source of the estate owners' economic privileges. The estate owners' intransigence would end only with the end of colonialism. The bitter, desperate resistance of the northern Angolan settlers and their brutal, ruthless slaughter of poorly armed Africans can only be understood in terms of their own extreme economic weakness and the stark economic alternatives that faced them if they lost their estates. Of all the landed estate systems examined in the case studies none produced such a marginal landed class, and none, consequently, produced such a tenacious and personal landlord defense of property. The southern Angolan estate owners, on the other hand, were considerably more able to use their economic influence in Luanda or even in Lisbon if a nationalist regime took power in Angola; their need for forced labor was much less compelling, and their ability to grant workers adequate wages and benefits was correspondingly greater. Thus the three hypotheses concerning cultivator behavior account for both the brutality of the northern estate owners during the revolt and the location of the centers of the uprisings in the northern rather than the southern coffee region.

The revolutionary coalition that first made itself felt in March of 1961 was composed of three distinct elements: the migratory laborers on the northern estates, the small Bakongo and Mbundu coffee growers of the northern region, and the Bakongo tribal and monarchic leadership. The expansion of the estate economy affected each of these groups in somewhat different ways, but in each case it created conditions conducive to a nationalist uprising against the Portuguese. Although the migratory laborers were the most directly exposed to the labor discipline of the estate and had the most to gain from the end of Portuguese forced labor, under normal circumstances they would not have been able to overcome the political weakness which resulted from their close ties to their own villages. The three hypotheses governing the behavior of cultivators indicate that the laborers' dependence on village lands for subsistence after the end of their term would tend to inhibit political organization. First, their ties to lands in traditional reserves remained strong, and work on the coffee estate was considered a disagreeable if temporary separation from their tribal lands. Second, the mixture of different tribal groups on the estates, the Portuguese policy of using arrogant pastoral tribesmen as foremen, and the ease with which laborers could be replaced created intertribal and even interpersonal competition which severely undermined class solidarity on the estates. The high turnover rate, amounting to almost two-thirds of the work force in a typical year, further undermined incentives for collective organization. Individual or small group escape attempts, not collective resistance to the foremen, were the surest way of escaping the *chicote* and the *tarefa diária*. Third, the worker relied on the immediate ties of kinship and tribe for support in a financial or medical emergency, and each small lineage or tribal group tried as best it could to reconstruct the basic elements of its home village on the estate. Furthermore ultimate safety could be found only in the home village, and the close proximity of Bakongo villages and the long trek to the Ovimbundu villages on the central plateau explain much of the difference in political orientation of the two tribal groups. The Ovimbundu, isolated in a different tribal and linguistic zone, were dependent on structural linkages with the estate management rather than ties with local villages, and their less enthusiastic response to the rebellion reflects this greater dependence on the estate management. In general there were strong impediments to even communal organization among the workers, and tribal ties made class-based organization difficult if not impossible.

In the absence of estate cultivation small African farmers would have shared the economic characteristics of cultivators drawing their income from the land and should, according to the hypotheses of Chapter 1, show an inability to mobilize politically under normal circumstances. The expansion of the Portuguese estates, however, changed the parameters affecting the normal economic behavior of cultivators holding land, and just as had been the case in Peru, estate expansion was associated with social movements of small holders. In the absence of the estates the small holders would have had a much stronger tie to the land than traditional swidden cultivators, and tribal practice recognized individual ownership over coffee trees if not over land generally. The land expropriations of the estate owners and the reluctance of the colonial administration to recognize African titles, however, dramatically reduced the strength of this tie to the land and threatened the economic existence of the small African coffee producers. Portuguese domination also prevented the small holders from retaining the full share of their agricultural production and, of course, made it impossible to buy additional lands or even to protect those already in cultivation. Thus the colonial presence created considerable incentives for African collective action to gain new coffee lands, to eliminate Portuguese middlemen, and to allow the profits of the coffee trade to pass entirely into the hands of the considerably more efficient African producers. Although both the conservative tie to the land and the individualism characteristic of small holders were reduced by the Portuguese presence and willingness to take risks and organize collectively were correspondingly increased, the third principal determinant of collective cultivator action was largely absent. Production was entirely an individual matter, and no cooperative organization like the communal ranges of Peru was available to reward loyalty and group solidarity. Even the cooperative processing possible in La Convención was not significant in northern Angola because the cheaper robusta grades did not justify the more expensive wet processing used in La Convención. The isolated production techniques of the small holders suggest, therefore, that even though collective incentives and weak ties to the land were present, only a weak cultivator movement should have been expected, certainly not one strong enough to challenge the Portuguese in open combat. In fact the principal structural linkages of the coffee farmers were to the traditional tribal leadership because the indigenous social structure provided the only legitimate recognition of their rights to their coffee groves. This leadership was in turn the instrument of the *chefe de pôsto*, the lowest link in the Portuguese administrative chain, and consequently the village structure might be expected to inhibit, not encourage small holder movements against the *fazendas*.

The traditional village chiefs and the vestigial Kongo monarchy are thus the key to the uprising in northern Angola. The chiefs had much to gain from collaboration and in Ovimbundu areas made substantial profits through recruiting laborers for the north and in both north and south frequently received modest retainers from Portuguese administrators. Nevertheless, the evidence presented in Chapter 4 makes clear that these leaders and the tribal if not monarchic UPA (União das Populações de Angola) were a critical element in the uprising of 1961 and that they provided the organizational resources that the workers and small holders lacked. The critical element in this change in orientation toward the Portuguese was of course the massive land expropriations of the central coffee districts. These expropriations not only displaced thousands of small coffee producers but also required the forced evacuation of entire villages and tribes, the resettlement of large numbers of people in reserves and temporary camps, and the separation of the tribal leadership from geographic areas which it had long controlled and from which it drew its ultimate power. Access land in the traditional areas of northern Angola was through tribal and lineage ties, and defense of that land under the loose Portuguese military occupation was often a matter of collective tribal or lineage action. The swidden cultivation of northern Angola did not lead to the intense interest in individual property characteristic of peasant villages in Peru or Vietnam because the site of cultivation was moved frequently in order to permit a long fallow period, and a general geographic area, not a particular subsistence plot, was the major source of wealth. The tribal economy of northern Angola, unlike the peasant subsistence economies of Peru and Vietnam, was a communal rather than individual economic enterprise, although as in those peasant villages the economy was controlled by an oligarchy of lineage heads and other notables. In Angola, however, this communal economy and the chiefs who controlled it were threatened by exactly the same force, the expansion of the coffee estates, which threatened the small holders with eviction and poor men with forced labor. Thus the nationalist coalition brought together men with very different dreams. The migratory laborer hoped for the end of the forced labor and his return to his village, the small holder wanted free expansion of the market and commercial success, the members of the tribal oligarchy looked forward to the restoration of their power and perhaps in their more nostalgic moments dreamed of the return of the Kongo monarchy to its former position of glory. All these dreams were blocked by the Portuguese presence, and it was the economic and political events of 1961 that transformed the dreams into violent action. The expansion of the Portuguese estates, therefore, eliminated the restraints on the political behavior of migratory laborers, small holders, and traditional leaders, all of whom to one degree or another drew their incomes from the land.

The resulting nationalist coalition, however, might not be expected to endure long beyond the passing of the Portuguese. The commercial small holders might be expected to become successful conservative commercial farmers interested in expanding their holdings at the expense of traditional tribal lands if necessary and defending them against any demands from the landless laborers. The Ovimbundu contract laborers who replaced the Bakongo after the 1961 revolt lacked the tribal ties that solidarified the nationalist coalition in the north, and in fact their close association with Portuguese estate owners during the war may someday expose them to violent retaliation from local Bakongo. The traditional chiefs' continued existence depended in part on their usefulness to the Portuguese, and although whoever comes to power in Angola will make use of their influence, a strong nationalist regime would curtail their power. Since the nationalist coalition was based on tribal and racial solidarity against the Portuguese and not on diverse economic interest of its members, the end of the colonialism is likely to signal intensified economic conflict and the end of communal solidarity.

The coffee boom of northern Angola and Portuguese colonial policies radically changed the three principal economic characteristics which the hypotheses of Chapter 1 suggested were critical for the political mobilization of cultivators, and these changes affected all three classes—the migratory laborers, the small holders, and the chiefs. First, in all three cases land concessions undermined the economic base of the traditional village, cutting off the laborers from their base of support, the small holders from their coffee groves, and the chiefs from their principal political resource. Second, the colonial land and labor politics provided substantial incentives for collective organization because the migratory laborers could gain their freedom, the small farmers could profit from the export trade, and the chiefs could regain their power only if the Portuguese political privileges were ended. Third, the thin Portuguese skein of military outposts and the recency of the Portuguese conquest permitted a communal swidden economy to exist until the beginning of the coffee boom, providing the laborers, the small holders, and the chiefs with a degree of economic and political interdependence which was seldom found in individualistic peasant communities. It was this formidable combination of economic and political characteristics which ended the years of silence in the north. The statistical analysis of Angola clearly indicated that the uprising was most intense in areas where the demand for contract labor was greatest and land expropriations were most extensive. Thus both the qualitative analysis of the political economy of northern Angola and the quantitative distribution of events support the hypotheses concerning the behavior of cultivators. The fact that the events occurred in the northern rather than the southern coffee area and the analysis of the political economy of the two coffee systems also support the three hypotheses concerning the behavior of noncultivators. Finally the fact that the revolt was nationalist rather than socialist and revolutionary rather than reformist supports the summary hypothesis D of Chapter 1.

The sharecropping system, like the migratory labor estate, involves a combination of a cultivating class deriving its income from the land and a noncultivating class paid in a share of the crop rather than in rights to land. This system is most common in annual crops which require minimal processing, and most of these crops could be efficiently produced by small holders. This system is most common in the rice economy of South and Southeast Asia and in the cotton economy of the Middle East, although it is used with food crops in both Southern Europe and the Middle East. In all cases, however, small holders are strong competitors since annual plantings restrict centralized production. On economic grounds alone, then, sharecropping systems establish strong pressures for small holding systems, and as the world analysis indicated, this is the most likely outcome of a revolutionary transformation of these systems.

The sharecropping category like the migratory estate category includes systems in which a well-organized cultivator class confronts an economically weak and politically rigid noncultivating class, and it is in these systems that revolution is possible. Unlike the migratory estate systems, however, sharecropping typically divides the indigenous land-owning class and cultivating classes, preventing the natonalist coalition which is possible in some migratory systems but making possible class-based organizations which are extremely unlikely in migratory systems. Thus hypothesis D of Chapter 1 suggested that revolutionary socialism rather than revolutionary nationalism should occur in some systems in the general sharecropping category. Once again, however, it is important to recall that the world analysis indicated that only a subgroup of all sharecropping systems, those in which production is carried on in decentralized tenant plots, is likely to lead to revolutionary socialism. Centralized sharecropping is no more likely to produce revolutionary socialism than is the commercial hacienda, and many centralized sharecropping systems closely resemble the hacienda organization. Of the two principal sharecropping crops, rice is invariably decentralized while cotton is usually centralized even where sharecropping is practiced. Thus rice sharecropping in particular and decentralized sharecropping in general are most likely to lead to agrarian revolution based on a socialist ideology demanding not only the restructuring of the rural class system but also the reorganization of the state itself.

The case study of Vietnam provided support for the finding of the world analysis that decentralized rice sharecropping systems are likely to lead to revolutionary socialism, but it also demonstrated that this association is a result of the intervening processes outlined in hypotheses 1 to 6 concerning the behavior of noncultivators and cultivators. The behavior of the landlords of Cochinchina displayed the three principal characteristics of a noncultivating class dependent on land. First, the landlords controlled no capital assets other than land and took no active role in agricultural production, leaving the details of cultivation entirely to the tenant. Their control over delta land was not a result of their strong capital position, but rather of their close ties to the colonial administration. As a result they were dependent on a series of military protectors, from the Foreign Legion to the ARVN (Army of the Republic of Vietnam) to the American Marines, for their continued existence as a class. Without such protection, of course, the lands of the Mekong would long since have passed into the hands of the cultivating class.

Second, the landlords were dependent on the land scarcity which they had helped to create to maintain high rents and demanded a legally impotent labor force which could not question the terms of tenancy or protest capricious evictions or excessive interest charges. The landlords of Cochinchina even discouraged migration from colonial Tonkin because they feared that the more independent northerners might be less compliant tenants than southerners accustomed to landlord dominance. Small landowners who settled in frontier areas often found their lands confiscated from beneath them and the landlord-village notable coalition made it possible for the landlords to maintain an adequate supply of low-cost labor for their estates. The Diem reforms and the more vigorous actions of the NLF placed greater rights in the hands of tenants and immediately led to a decrease in landlord incomes. A disenfranchised colonial population was therefore an ideal source of low-cost labor.

Although prospects for mechanization in the delta rice economy were not extensive, the landlords' presence inhibited any technological change that might have been possible. Their land monopoly and the resulting high rents limited tenant incentives for permanent improvements, produced exorbitant interest rates, blocked irrigation projects, and hindered marketing and processing. All these restraints on increased productivity, of course, worked in one way or another to the advantage of the landlord. Permanent improvements were unnecessary or dangerous since the landlord could increase his income by increasing rents, irrigation projects might cut away valuable parts of his land, exorbitant interest rates increased his profits through money lending, and market discontinuities made it possible for him to profit from rice hoarding and speculation. Not only was there no share of increasing agricultural production to be used to defuse a gathering agrarian movement; on the contrary, every possible effort was made to confiscate as much tenant rice as possible even if it meant bankruptcy or starvation for the tenant. Even during hard times the land-lord would not decrease these demands on the crop.

Thus the landlords of the Mekong were economically weak and dependent on outside military and political power, required a legally impotent labor force produced by a landlord-dominated political system, and discouraged any productivity gains which might have increased the share of agricultural production going to the tenants. Like the *hacendados* of the Peruvian sierra or the *fazenda* owners of Angola, the landlords of the Mekong combined economic and political characteristics which should lead to political conflict over economic issues and force laborers to either violent opposition or inaction.

The tenants and landless laborers of the Mekong delta shared the economic and political characteristics of cultivators paid in wages rather than those paid in land and therefore, unlike the peasants of northern and central Vietnam or the Peruvian sierra, might be expected to show the strong cultivator organizations typical of laborers on industrial plantations rather than the weak organizations typical of peasant small holders. Each of the three major economic characteristics which, according to the hypotheses 4 to 6 of Chapter 1, should increase the possibilities for collective political organization were apparent in the Mekong delta. First, the closed land market and the dominance of large land-holdings eliminated peasant small holdings, and even tenancies were precarious and could be lost through Malthusian evictions or chronic indebtedness. Frequent turnovers were in fact typical of the delta tenancies, and former tenants could either flee debts and rents to new villages in the west or find work as landless laborers. Their orientation toward risk was therefore completely different from that of northern or central small holders, and political as well as economic speculation was one of the dominant features of delta life. Millenial dreams or political utopias could always find adherents in the unstable economic environment of the Mekong delta.

Second, individual mobility into the land-owning class was a practical impossibility, and stratification within the cultivator class was less pronounced than in most peasant communities. Since even a large tenant could be reduced to a landless laborer and would not in general be able to pass his holdings on to his sons, the individualistic competition for even the smallest piece of land characteristic of peasant communities in both northern and central Vietnam and in the Peruvian sierra was entirely absent in the delta. Nor were there any large amounts of community land or water to reward factional village conflict or to be stolen by enterprising individuals. If the incentives for individual economic action were weak, the incentives for collective action were correspondingly stronger. The Mekong delta produced substantial profits from the rice export trade, but the social arrangements controlling land ownership and marketing insured that only a small percentage of the crop ever reached the tenants. High interest rates, restrictions on irrigation, and marketing discontinuities could all be eliminated by driving out the landlords and rent collectors, and of course the demise of the landlords would provide the tenants with clear title to the land they worked and a claim to the entire rice crop and most of the profits of the export economy. NLF successes in the Mekong delta during the early phases of the war in Vietnam were a result of availability of these collective goods and the NLF's ability to deliver them to the peasants.

Third, the loosely structured villages of the Mekong were not controlled by the conservative oligarchies of the traditional villages of the Vietnamese north or center or the Peruvian sierra, which had used their control over community resources to establish petty despotism subservient to outside authority. The notables of the villages of the Mekong controlled no communal land or water to be granted or withheld to reward conformity to the village oligarchy, and they were unable to generate the religious enthusiasm at the *dinh* characteristic of the older areas of Vietnam. The landlords, who represented the ultimate source of power in the village, were remote from day-to-day running of village affairs and lacked the graduated sanctions available to the notables of northern and central Vietnam or the *varayoc* of Peru. Since the landlords provided few services, their principal tie to the village was through their rent-collecting agents, and increasingly, as resistance to these agents increased, this tie came to depend on military force. The absence of structural linkages between tenants and landlords is most clearly illustrated by the landlords' reliance on ARVN troops and provincial officials to collect their rents during the postwar period. With little managerial control over their tenants, with marketing and credit in the hands of middlemen, with no welfare services to offer, the landlords held only military control over their tenants. Like the peasants of La Convención, the sharecroppers of the Mekong delta could purchase from small merchants goods and services provided by landowners in more paternalistic centralized estate systems, and the landlords of the Mekong delta, like those of La Convención, became socially as well as economically superfluous.

The development of the rice export economy of the Mekong delta and the political dominance of the large estates completely altered the conditions of peasant cultivation; it broke conservative linkages to the land, increased incentives for economic organization while decreasing prospects for individual mobility, and removed the structural linkages to the landed class that inhibited peasant organization in many commercial hacienda systems. The tenants and landless laborers of the Mekong were an agricultural proletariat with the political characteristics associated with the proletariat of an industrial plantation. Unlike the plantation workers, however, they confronted not an economically powerful upper class capable of compromise, but an economically backward and politically unyielding class of mercantile capitalists who derived their profits from their land monopoly and their consequent ability to manipulate marketing and interest rates to their advantage. The result was an agrarian revolution, and in both colonial Vietnam and at the beginning of the second Indochina war the Mekong delta was the base of Communist support in Vietnam. The analysis of the political economy of the delta and the distribution of revolutionary socialist events in Vietnam support both the general association between decentralized sharecropping systems and revolutionary socialism and the specific intervening causal linkages which make this association possible.

Centralized sharecropping systems, on the other hand, do not show the potential for revolutionary socialism typical of wet rice sharecropping systems like Vietnam even though in some respects the systems are similar. Cotton estates, which represent the single largest class of centralized sharecropping systems, are more similar in some respects to commercial hacienda systems than to decentralized sharecropping systems. The world analysis, for example, indicated that although rice and other grains are almost invariably produced in the small units of decentralized sharecropping or small holding systems, cotton is often produced on centralized commercial haciendas as well as in sharecropping and small holding systems. In fact as market penetration increases, cotton production is likely to move from sharecropping to wage labor, while in areas of high market penetration rice cultivation tends toward greater, not lesser rates of tenancy. Cotton slightly favors centralized production because of the bulk reduction advantages of local ginning and because it cannot be consumed for subsistence but must be marketed usually for export. Estate owners, who own ginning machines and have economic and social ties with exporters, are therefore in a slightly stronger market position than are landlords in rice sharecropping systems. Since cotton is an annual, the advantage of centralized production is slight and small holdings are actually more efficient producers in most circumstances. Nevertheless, as the example of the coastal cotton haciendas of Peru indicated, a favorable political situation can lead to rationalized centralized cotton production. When this happens, however, it usually leads to the replacement of sharecroppers by laborers as, for example, when the Peruvian *yanaconaje* were evicted from the Peruvian cotton valleys after World War II. Sharecropping in cotton estates is therefore usually associated with low market penetration and relatively low land values. If land is valuable and particularly if it is irrigated, greater profits can be had through efficient centralized production than through sharecropping, which tends to discourage permanent improvements and turns over at least part of the land to the tenant.

Thus the typical sharecropped cotton estate, such as those of the cotton valleys of Peru before 1940, shares many of the characteristics of the commercial hacienda in which a class of laborers is fixed to the land, enjoys some rights to cultivate subsistence crops, and is under the paternalistic control of the hacienda owner. The owners of such sharecropped cotton estates, like the landlords of a rice sharecropping system, have very little capital other than land and consequently, like the rice landlords, are dependent on political influence, opposed to cultivator rights, and restricted to zero-sum economic conflict. If they did acquire additional capital, they would transform the sharecropped estate into a commercial hacienda and eliminate the sharecroppers. The difference between the behavior of the two sharecropping systems is not, therefore, a result of differences in the behavior of the upper class, but rather of differences in the economic and political behavior of the sharecroppers themselves. On at least two of the three economic variables affecting cultivator behavior, the cotton sharecroppers resemble a class drawing its income from the land, and the rice sharecroppers resemble a cultivator class drawing its income from wages.

First, tenancies in most rice sharecropping systems are unstable because of the economic vulnerability of the small tenant farmer and the landlord's interest in higher rents rather than greater production. In cotton systems sharecroppers may remain on the estate for years or generations if they provide loyal service in the fields. The less rationalized production and the paternalistic management of the cotton estate maintain a loyal dependent labor force and will insure that the landlord's crops will be brought in at harvest and estate production will be maximized, given the limits of capitalization and management skill. The position of a *yanaconaje* on a Peruvian cotton estate before World War II was almost identical to that of a *colono* of the sierra, and it was only after these tenants were evicted during the transition to the commercial haciendas of the postwar period that they showed any signs of collective protest. Conservative ties to the land and subsequent resistance to radical politics are much stronger factors on sharecropped cotton estates than in decentralized rice sharecropping systems.

In both cotton and rice sharecropping systems the prospects for individual mobility into the land-owning class are minimal, and the incentives for collective action are not dissimilar. Both cotton and rice sharecroppers would gain control over productive commercial land if the landlords could be eliminated, and both would profit through effective collective action at the landlords' expense. Internal stratification within the tenant class may actually be greater in dispersed tenancy systems, so that this variable cannot account for the observed difference in the behavior of the two systems. The amount of competition for tenancy is also approximately equal, although the greater turnover in the decentralized systems may lead to slightly more intense competition. Differences between the two systems cannot therefore be explained by differences in economic incentives for competition or cooperation.

The most important difference between cotton and rice sharecroppers, however, is the relative strength of their structural linkages to the landlord class. On the centralized cotton estate the distribution of work, the management of irrigation water, the processing of the crop, the provision of small loans, and even the sale of consumer goods are all under the control of the estate owner. In addition the estate owner may provide small personal favors to his workers, such as assisting in their daughters' weddings or providing burial plots for their dead. These economic and social ties to the landlord were apparent in the cotton haciendas of Peru even after the transformation to wage labor and were even more pronounced in the prewar period. The economic controls of the hacienda store and the estate management provide a valuable political tool to enforce loyalty by closely observing and punishing worker nonconformity.

Even in the postwar period Peruvian cotton estate workers could be whipped into town before their master for carelessly diverting irrigation water. The surveillance possible in a centralized estate makes it possible to detect worker organization at the earliest possible moment, and the numerous linkages between worker and management make it possible to reward or punish even small changes in behavior.

In decentralized rice tenancy systems such as Vietnam, of course, no such close surveillance is possible or even considered necessary by the landlords. The tenant is responsible for day-to-day management of work, he can sell his own share of the crop to middlemen just as does the landlord, irrigation management is his own responsibility, he can borrow money from middlemen or other tenants as well as from the landlord, and he can purchase goods and services from small merchants rather than from the company store. Thus the structural linkages to the landlord and the possibilities for landlord control, as was clear in the Mekong delta of Vietnam, are considerably weaker in decentralized rice systems than they are in centralized cotton estates, and it is this fact that explains the vastly greater radicalism of cultivators in decentralized rice sharecropping systems.

Of all the major types of agricultural organization considered in this analysis only the decentralized sharecropping systems show this potential for class-based agrarian revolution. In agricultural systems in which both the cultivating and noncultivating classes draw their income from the land the cultivators are in general not capable of the strong political organization necessary to challenge the politically inflexible landed upper class. Only when outside organization in the form of a socialist or reformist party is provided or when the economic base of the peasant community is destroyed by estate expansion are social movements likely in such systems, and even in these cases the result is usually a short-lived agrarian revolt, not an agrarian revolution. Industrial plantation systems create economic conditions conducive to strong cultivator organizations, but the economic power and flexibility of the corporate plantation owners divert this political energy into reformist channels. In small holding systems cultivator political organizations are weak and upper-lass economic power is strong, and only weak reformist movements are likely. The politically inflexible landed class of the migratory labor estate tends to generate political conflict over the control of property and the state, but migratory laborers are difficult to organize, and only under the peculiar circumstances of settler estate expansion in colonial systems can they be mobilized in an agrarian revolution. Even in this case, however, the revolutionary coalition tends to reflect the interests of the traditional tribal groups which provided the organizational resources and the movement's goals are tribal or racial rather than economic. Only in sharecropping systems is an inflexible upper class combined with a cultivator class strongly organized along class lines, and only in decentralized systems is the cultivator class able to overcome the political controls of the noncultivators. The decentralized sharecropping system therefore combines the characteristics of both cultivators and noncultivators most conducive to agrarian revolution, leads to solidarity based on class, and increases the appeal of revolutionary socialism as the dominant ideology of cultivator movements.

It is in decentralized sharecropping systems like that of Vietnam that the social organization of export agriculture creates both incentives for class-based cultivator organizations and bitter landlord resistance to cultivator rights. These incentives were sufficient in the case of Vietnam to provide new generations of recruits for an indigenous revolutionary movement despite Draconian counter-measures and massive casualties. The export economy of the Mekong delta created the strong class-based revolutionary movement that both French and American expeditionary forces have struggled to control for more than a quarter of a century. The landlords of Cochinchina remain to haunt the military governors of South Vietnam, and the application of overwhelming military power has had surprisingly little effect on the economic conditions in rural areas which provided the driving force of the revolution in the south. External military power, first under the French and later under the Americans, has provided the means of prolonging the life of an unstable economic system dominated by a preindustrial landlord class. Without this foreign intervention the revolutionary effects of the world export economy would have long since transformed the social structure of rural Vietnam and removed both the in-centives for peasant organization and the unyielding landlords. Instead, Amer-ican intervention has insured for a time that both the landlord class and the incentives for agrarian revolution will remain intact. As a result the outcome of the long American effort in Vietnam was not a revolution defeated but a revolution postponed.

APPENDIX 1 *World Population of Agricultural Export Sectors*

Country	Crop	Country	Crop
EUROPE		**CENTRAL AND SOUTH AMERICA**	
Finland	Dairy	Brazil	Coffee
Greece	Tobacco	Brazil	Cotton
Greece	Grapes	Brazil	Sugar
Ireland	Cattle	Brazil	Cocoa
Italy	Vegetables	Chile	Sheep
Italy	Grapes	Chile	Vegetables
Italy	Citrus	Colombia	Coffee
Italy	Apples	Costa Rica	Coffee
Italy	Rice	Costa Rica	Bananas
Italy	Wheat	Cuba	Sugar
Portugal	Grapes	Dominican Republic	Sugar
Portugal	Vegetables	Dominican Republic	Coffee
Spain	Citrus	Dominican Republic	Cocoa
Spain	Vegetables	Ecuador	Bananas
		Guatemala	Coffee
		Guatemala	Cotton
MIDDLE EAST AND NORTH AFRICA		Haiti	Coffee
		Haiti	Sisal
Algeria	Grapes	Honduras	Bananas
Iran	Cotton	Honduras	Coffee
Iraq	Dates	Jamaica	Sugar
Iraq	Barley	Jamaica	Bananas
Lebanon	Vegetables	Mexico	Cotton
Lebanon	Temperate fruits	Mexico	Coffee
Libya	Groundnuts	Nicaragua	Cotton
Morocco	Citrus	Nicaragua	Coffee
Morocco	Vegetables	Panama	Bananas
Syria	Cotton	Paraguay	Cattle
Sudan	Cotton	Peru	Cotton
Tunisia	Olives	Peru	Sugar
Tunisia	Grapes	Peru	Coffee
Turkey	Tobacco	El Salvador	Coffee
Turkey	Cotton	El Salvador	Cotton
Turkey	Eating nuts	Venezuela	Coffee
U.A.R.	Cotton	Venezuela	Cocoa

Country	Crop	Country	Crop
	SUB-SAHARAN AFRICA		SOUTH AND SOUTHEAST ASIA
Angola	Coffee	Burma	Rice
Burundi	Coffee	Cambodia	Rice
Cameroon	Cocoa	Cambodia	Rubber
Cameroon	Coffee	Ceylon (Sri Lanka)	Tea
C.A.R.	Cotton	Ceylon (Sri Lanka)	Rubber
C.A.R.	Coffee	China (Rep.)	Sugar
Congo (Zaire)	Palm	China (Rep.)	Rice
Congo (Zaire)	Coffee	India	Tea
Congo (Zaire)	Rubber	India	Cotton
Congo (Zaire)	Cotton	India	Spices
Ghana	Cocoa	India	Tobacco
Guinea	Coffee	India	Sugar
Guinea	Bananas	India	Coffee
Ivory Coast	Coffee	India	Groundnuts
Kenya	Coffee	Indonesia	Rubber
Kenya	Tea	Indonesia	Palm
Liberia	Rubber	Indonesia	Copra
Malagasy Rep.	Coffee	Indonesia	Tea
Malawi	Tobacco	Indonesia	Tobacco
Malawi	Tea	Indonesia	Coffee
Mozambique	Cotton	Indonesia	Spices
Nigeria	Groundnuts	Indonesia	Sugar
Nigeria	Cocoa	Korea (Rep.)	Rice
Rhodesia	Tobacco	Malaysia	Rubber
Rwanda	Coffee	Pakistan	Jute
Senegal	Groundnuts	Pakistan	Rice
Somalia	Bananas	Pakistan	Tea
South Africa	Sheep	Pakistan	Cotton
Tanzania	Sisal	Philippines	Copra
Tanzania	Coffee	Philippines	Sugar
Tanzania	Cotton	Thailand	Rice
Togo	Coffee	Thailand	Rubber
Uganda	Coffee	Vietnam (Rep.)	Rubber
Uganda	Cotton	Vietnam (Rep.)	Rice
Zambia	Tobacco		

APPENDIX 2 *Agricultural Codes*

Columns		Code
1–3		Country
	001	Finland
	002	Greece
	003	Ireland
	004	Italy
	005	Portugal
	006	Spain
	101	Costa Rica
	102	Cuba
	103	Dominican Republic
	104	El Salvador
	105	Guatemala
	106	Haiti
	107	Honduras
	108	Jamaica
	109	Mexico
	110	Nicaragua
	111	Panama
	201	Bolivia
	202	Brazil
	203	Chile
	204	Colombia
	205	Ecuador
	206	Paraguay
	207	Peru
	208	Venezuela
	301	Afghanistan
	302	Burma
	303	Cambodia
	304	Ceylon (Sri Lanka)
	305	Taiwan
	306	India
	307	Indonesia
	308	Iran
	309	Iraq
	310	Jordan
	311	South Korea
	312	Lebanon
	313	Malaysia

379

Columns	Code
1–3	

314	Nepal
315	Pakistan
316	Philippines
317	Saudi Arabia
318	Southern Yemen
319	Syria
320	Thailand
321	Turkey
322	South Vietnam
323	Yemen
401	Algeria
402	Angola
403	Burundi
404	Cameroon
405	Central African Republic
406	Chad
407	Congo (Zaire)
408	Dahomey
409	Ethiopia
410	Ghana
411	Guinea
412	Ivory Coast
413	Kenya
414	Liberia
415	Libya
416	Madagascar
417	Malawi
418	Mali
419	Mauritania
420	Morocco
421	Mozambique
422	Niger
423	Nigeria
424	Southern Rhodesia
425	Rwanda
426	Senegal
427	Sierra Leone
428	Somalia
429	South Africa
430	Sudan
431	Tanzania
432	Togo
433	Tunisia
434	United Arab Republic (Egypt)
435	Uganda
436	Upper Volta
437	Zambia

Columns	Code
4–5	Crop
01	Cattle
02	Dairy
03	Other livestock

Columns 4–5		*Code*
	04	Wheat
	05	Rice
	06	Barley
	07	Other grains
	08	Maize
	09	Citrus fruits
	10	Bananas
	11	Grapes
	12	Temperate fruits
	13	Eating nuts
	14	Vegetables
	15	Sugar
	16	Coffee
	17	Cocoa
	18	Tea and mate
	19	Spices
	20	Tobacco
	21	Groundnuts
	22	Copra, coconuts
	23	Palm
	24	Other oil nuts
	25	Cotton
	26	Rubber
	27	Silk
	28	Sisal
	29	Other fibers
	30	Olives
	50	Subsistence

6

System number: If more than one enterprise type is involved in the production of the crop specified in columns 4–5 during the 1948–1970 period, number systems chronologically and code each separately. Otherwise always 1.

7

Card number (1).

8–9

Last two digits of first year of period in which this system was observed.

10

If columns 8–9 are coded 48, code 9. Otherwise explain initial date of observation specified in column 8–9.

1   New export crop introduced at this date.
2   Changing economic or production parameters (e.g., mechanization) bring about change in enterprise type.
3   Redistributive land reform: redistribution of more than 20 percent of land in this crop to individual or cooperative owners. If land reform has occurred, begin observation of new system created by reform after it is clear that reform will not be stopped or reversed and the new system is firmly established. In no case should this interval be less than four years.

Columns	*Code*
	4 Nationalization or collectivization.
	5 Insufficient information before this date.
	6 Other (specify).

11–12   Last two digits of last year of period in which this system was observed.

13   If columns 11–12 are coded 70, code 9; otherwise explain reason for ending observation in year specified in columns 11–12.

1   Crop abandoned as no longer economically or ecologically practical (loss of markets, blights).
2   Changing economic or production parameters bring about change in enterprise type (e.g., mechanization).
3   Redistributive land reform: redistribution of more than 20 percent of the land in this crop to individual or cooperative owners. Beginning of *effective* reform terminates period of observation.
4   Nationalization or collectivization.
5   Insufficient information.
6   Other (specify).

14–15   Period of observation. Columns 11–12 − columns 8–9 + 1 (1970–1948 + 1 = 23).

16   Unproductive period: number of years between planting and first harvest.

1   One year or less (annuals).
2   Two to four years.
3   Five to nine years.
4   Ten years or more.

17   Productive lifetime: number of years crop bears before replanting.

1   One year or less (annuals).
2   Two to four years.
3   Five to nine years.
4   Ten years or more.

18–19   Harvest period: Number of months per year in which harvesting takes place. If there are two campaigns, add them together.

20   Is primary processing carried out within the enterprise?

0   No.
1   Yes—manually operated machinery.
2   Yes—specialized power driven machinery, e.g., gins, mills, centrifuges.

21–22   Median percent agricultural exports contributed by this crop, 1948–1968.

Columns	*Code*
23–38	Agricultural enterprise: a personal or corporate entity with the right to control the use of a given parcel of land and to dispose of the crop produced on that land, subject only to specific contractual obligations with any other party who may have an interest in the land. (Note: In share-cropping and manorial systems all the land of a single owner is treated as a single enterprise.)

23–24   Ownership: indicates effective authority over land for at least 20 years. A 20-year lease or a benefice from a defunct sovereign will be considered ownership for purposes of this code.

10 Individual or family ownership or control by an incorporated family estate in which a single family controls 75 percent or more of the stock.
11 Foreign individuals and families, including settlers and colonists.
12 Indigenous individuals and families.

20 Tribe, lineage, extended family, or other form of precommercial communal ownership.

30 Commercial corporation.
31 Commercial corporation, domestic control.
32 Commercial corporation, foreign control.

40 Government body.
41 Local or municipal government.
42 State, provincial, or department government.
43 National government.

50 Cooperative, communal, or *ejidal* ownership (those actually working the land share in the ownership).

25   Residence of owners.

1 Resident.
2 Rural nonresident.
3 Urban nonresident.

26–27   Operation: operator must control productive use of land and have all residual rights to crop. He may or may not perform labor or supervise the recruitment of labor himself. The administrators and agents of absentee landlords are considered to be the effective operators.

10 Owners and part owners.
11 Cash renters.
12 Standing or share renters.

20 Administrator residence unknown.
21 Resident administrator.
22 Nonresident administrator (agent).

Columns	*Code*
28	Tenant middlemen: an intermediary class which neither performs managerial functions described in columns 26–27 nor carries out the largest proportion of the physical work of cultivation described in columns 29–30. Tenant middlemen share in the profits of crop lands under their control and are responsible for labor recruitment and supervision. They may not determine the crop to be grown and have limited rights to its disposal. The tenancy may be held on cash, standing, or share rental terms. Salaried overseers are not tenant middlemen and should be included as part of the administrative staff coded in columns 26–27.

0　Tenant middlemen absent.
1　Tenant middlemen present.

29–30　　Labor: mechanism by which physical work is performed on operating unit. Code the principal source of income for the class of workers performing the greatest number of hours of work per year.

10　Operator, unpaid family labor, and one or two "hired hands."

20　Usufructuaries: rights to yield from a subsistence plot in exchange for labor on domain lands, personal services to the landowner, or payment of a share of the *subsistence* crop.
21　Usufructuaries: cash crop produced on domain lands.
22　Usufructuaries: cash crop produced on subsistence plot. In this case the usufruct rights must be paid for in labor dues or in a share of the *subsistence* crop. If share of a cash crop is paid system should be classified under "30　Cropper" below.

30　Cropper: precise terms unknown.
31　Share tenant: a cropper who provides his own implements and traction power and is paid a share of the crop.
32　Sharecropper: a cropper who provides only his own labor.

40　Wage laborers: paid in cash, rations, or shelter.
41　Wage laborers: resident.
42　Wage laborers: fixed-term migrants.
43　Wage laborers: seasonal or harvest migrants.
44　Wage laborers: short-range migrants commuting on a daily basis from nearby subsistence plots.

31–32　　Country–crop system work force: the total number of economically active individuals, paid and unpaid, actually providing labor in the fields in a given system.

Columns

Code

This information is obtained in one of two ways:

1. Wherever possible, by direct estimates given in agricultural source materials. These will generally be available for systems which pay wages and therefore generate records (e.g., plantations and migratory estates).

2. When necessary (especially in systems in which labor is unpaid or paid in usufruct rights, e.g., small holdings, sharecropping, and haciendas), by multiplying the number of units (enterprises or holdings) by the average number of economically active individuals per unit. The former figure is generally available from agricultural source materials as the number of operators, farms, etc. The latter figure is estimated by taking the family unit, nuclear or extended, as the basis for calculating the number of individuals in each of the following categories and summing:

> Operator (plus heads of associated nuclear families, if any).
> Wife of operator, if she works in the fields.
> Children of operator, if they work in the fields (assume 2.5 economically active children for each nuclear family).
> Hired hands, if any (estimate number from agricultural source materials).

Code this information in scientific notation to one significant figure.

33

Enterprise work force: the modal number of economically active individuals, paid and unpaid, employed in the fields of an enterprise. When the country–crop system includes enterprises which vary enough in size that they cannot be placed within a single one of the categories below, select the single category which is responsible for the largest share of the total production (if not available, use bulk or acreage).

1 1–5.
2 6–20.
3 21–100.
4 101–500.
5 501–1000.
6 1000–5000.
7 5000 and more.

34

Sharecropping dispersal code: Code whether the various sharecropping holdings of a single owner, which together constitute an enterprise, are consolidated or dispersed. Holdings are considered consolidated when they are contiguous or when there is other evidence of daily contact

Columns	Code
	among individuals working different holdings, such as common use of implements or capital goods provided by the landlord.

1   Consolidated.
2   Dispersed.
9   Not applicable.

| 35 | Market participation of labor force described in columns 29–30. |

1   Produces cash crop as a supplement to primary subsistence production.

2   Combination of market production and subsistence activities.

3   Primarily dependent on market.

| 36–38 | Ethnic stratification: In the next three columns indicate the racial, religious, or nationality characteristics of the enterprise work force. A group is ethnically distinct if racial, religious, or national differences are widely recognized and if intermarriage with other groups is largely or wholly absent. |

0   No ethnic stratification—work force does not come from an ethnically distinct group.

1   The work force is ethnically distinct from the landowners but not from indigenous subsistence farmers.

2   The work force is ethnically distinct in comparison to both the landowners and the indigenous peasant population.

3   Both owners and workers are a distinct ethnic group in comparison with subsistence farmers.

| 36 | Race: assumed biological differences. |

| 37 | Religion: major religious groupings, e.g., Christian, Hindu. |

| 38 | Nationality. |

| 40–80 | Provinces which define crop system. Two-column fields; attach alphabetical list of provinces to code sheet. |

CARD 2

Columns	Code
1–6	Repeat codes in columns 1–6 of card 1.
7	Card number (2).

Columns	*Code*
8–39	Province codes (continued from card 1, columns 38–79).
40–79	Code any additional provinces which are not part of the crop system but which provide migratory laborers in large numbers. Use these fields only if columns 31–32 in card 1 have been coded 42 or 43 (migratory labor). If migratory labor is recruited from within provinces specified in the crop system field, do not use this code.

APPENDIX 3 *Social Movement Codes*

Rural social movement: a linked series of noninstitutional collective events engaged in by cultivators who constitute a solidary group.

Cultivators: a clear majority of the personnel in any event must be recruited from the class of rural residents who perform the physical work of cultivation. Thus references to peasants, agricultural laborers, rural strikes, land seizures, destruction of crops by mass action, peasant unions, and plantation strikes are automatically included. Explicit references to other occupational groups—students, miners, government workers—mean the event is not agrarian. If no specific information is included on the occupational composition of the participants, include any rural event (i.e., those occurring outside cities of more than 2,500 population). References to entire countries or entire regions should not be included unless there is other evidence of participation by cultivators.

Exclude the following:

1. Foreign invasions unless they are part of a general uprising of the rural population.
2. Institutional populations—military barracks, prisons, concentration camps, asylums.
3. Military and police mutinies and revolts even if they occur in rural areas.
4. Owner and administrator actions (unless owners are also cultivators). Actions by tenant middlemen should be included.
5. Movements of regional secession which include members of land-owning and land-working classes on both sides, e.g., the Katanga secession in the Congo.
6. Blanquist, or guerrilla *foco*, movements unless there is clear evidence that all or most of their fighting force is former cultivators (peasants, plantation workers, etc.). In movements of this type a small group of urban intellectuals, students, or workers retreat to the countryside to wage guerrilla war against the government. They frequently hope to convert the peasantry to their cause through "armed propaganda" and, at a minimum, expect the peasants to provide food, shelter, and protection from police intelligence. The guerillas frequently claim peasant support or sympathy, but these events should not be included unless the evidence for peasant support is unambiguous. Guevara's Bolivia expedition of 1967 is an example of the kind of movement which should not be included.

Noninstitutional: event either is illegal or occurs outside the established normative framework.

1. Any evidence of violence, destruction of property, personal injury, illegal seizure of persons or property.

388

2. Strikes—usually a marginal case. Include all strikes, illegal and legal.
3. Any collective action which involves violence on the part of social control forces.
4. Mass rallies, demonstrations, marches, and other mass actions even if they do not lead to violence. Exclude regularly scheduled patriotic, sports, or religious events unless they lead to violence. Rallies sponsored by legitimate parties are a marginal case. They should be included if they are not a part of the regular activities of the party—e.g., annual conventions would be excluded, marches on such a convention by a dissident faction would be included.

Collective: more than 10 persons or indirect evidence by use of words such as "crowd," "rally," "march," "demonstration," "mass action," "uprising," "revolt," "revolution," "riot," "strike," etc., or by references to the acts of collectives such as guerrilla bands, union locals, or military patrols.

Event: An event is any collective act or series of actions which occurs on the same or successive days in the same crop system or in the same or contiguous provinces. Thus if cultivators from two different crop systems engage in a simultaneous co-ordinated action (e.g., sugar plantation workers strike in sympathy with a strike by cotton sharecroppers), each action is a separate event. If two crop systems are contiguous, the crop criterion takes precedence over the contiguity criterion.

Events may be divided conceptually into *phases.* An event extending over several days may change its tactics or targets or even its organizational level sufficiently to alter the coding category originally assigned. For example, a peaceful strike which has continued for a week may turn into a riot when strikebreakers appear on the scene. Since the action is continuous, these actions constitute a single event. Each phase, however, should be described separately on the code sheet, and each should be numbered successively.

Linked: Events which share any of the following characteristics are said to be linked and form the constituent units of a movement.

1. Concerted actions of formations: A sugar workers' strike is called to support a series of peasant land invasions.

2. Overlap in personnel: 10 percent of the participants in the smaller of the two events or evidence of the same leadership. A peasant league which, two months before, organized a series of land invasions leads a march on a government building.

3. Provision of material assistance: A covert terrorist group receives arms and financial support from a nationalist party which is conducting a series of marches and rallies.

4. Overt imitation: repetition of identical actions with evidence that one formation knew of the activities of the other. Land invasions in one province spread to several other provinces over a period of weeks.

5. Overt response by demands, slogans, ritual acts. Peasants engaging in a series of different kinds of actions spread over several weeks are reported to have shouted "Land or death" or "Free Hugo Blanco" during each action.

Each event should be coded separately and assigned a number indicating its chronological position in the movement sequence. Movements should also be assigned sequence numbers beginning with the first movement observed in the 1948–1970 period (single events may constitute movements for purposes of assigning sequence numbers). Thus each collective action will have a total of three sequence numbers. Each phase of the spatially and temporally continuous actions which make up an event will have an identification number. In most cases there will be only one pnase, and hence this number will usually be 1. A series of events distinct in time, space, or crop system may be linked together to form a movement by criteria 1–5 above. Each event should be numbered successively for any given movement. Finally, movements themselves must be numbered to indicate that two or more series of events are not closely tied to one another. In general it is unlikely that more than three or four movements will be observed in any one country during the 1948–1970 period.

Solidary groups: The collective must share some belief that the fortunes of its members are interdependent, i.e., some common consciousness that actions taken for or against any member of the collective are actions which potentially affect all its members. Therefore exclude panics, mass movements of refugees, crazes, and other acts which do not involve any sense of common identity.

CODING INSTRUCTIONS

1. Agrarian events can frequently be identified from items in newspaper or press summary indexes. If the index item is ambiguous, the actual article or report must be looked up and the final evaluation based on a full reading. If, for example, an index item refers to a "general strike," the article must be consulted to determine whether agrarian workers are mentioned explicitly. If the article still makes no mention of agriculturalists, then no event would be coded.

2. Events and newspaper articles are not identical. A single event may be reported in more than one article, or a number of events may be summarized in a single article. It may be possible to infer factual information from other articles reporting on the same country. An article on tea estate workers may mention that there are 500,000 tea workers in the country. Other articles reporting on different events may simply state that "all the tea workers" or "most of the tea workers" have gone on strike. The information from the earlier article may be used to infer the number of participants for the later events. Similarly, if an organization title is mentioned in one article with no explanation and another article on a separate event in the same movement gives a detailed description of the organization, then the latter article can be used to supplement information in the former. Nevertheless, it is important to keep in mind that you are attempting to describe a single event or phase of an event when you are coding. While you should read all the articles in a given country before beginning to code, you should concentrate on the particular characteristics of each event.

3. In general, the estimates and opinions on factual matters of commentators in news sources should be used in preference to similar information from supporters or opponents of the movement. Thus if General X claims that an incident is Communist inspired but the commentator indicates that there is little factual support for the general's view, the commentator's opinion should be coded. Direct statements of movement leaders about their ideology or objectives, on the other hand, should be used in preference to the opinions of commentators about the same matters.

4. If more than one collective composed of cultivators is engaged in a given action and they are not in different crop systems or separated spatially, then the collective that *initiated* the action is the one to be coded. If a group of Muslim

peasants attacks a group of Communist peasants, for example, the codes would apply to the Muslims, not the Communists, even if the Communists fight back. If the Communists retaliate in a separate event and attack the Muslims, then of course the Communists' actions would be coded.

5. Summary articles: Newspaper articles sometimes summarize a series of events occurring over several weeks or months in one or two articles. These summary articles must be broken down into their constituent events before they can be coded even if this requires creating "dummy" events to approximate the actual number of events reported in the summary. Coding categories for the duration of an event, the number of participants, the number of casualties, etc., should be applied to individual events, not to summary articles as a whole. The duration of an event, then, is a measure of the duration of a single action, *not* the length of the time period covered by the summary article. Total numbers of participants or casualties reported in a summary article refer to the sum of all events occurring in the period covered by the article. Thus an estimate of the number of participants or casualties must be made when coding a specific event. This estimate may be made either by taking an average for each event or, when information permits, by estimating the relative contribution of each event to the total based on its inferred magnitude. In the analysis of event data the duration of an event and the number of participants are important measures of a social movement's capacity to mobilize its supporters for action. The use of totals from summary articles therefore defeats the purpose of collecting this information.

   The precise strategy for coding a summary article depends on the amount of information provided:

   a. If several events are described in some detail, then each should be coded separately and summary information should either be ignored or distributed over the reported events in accord with their inferred magnitude. This procedure may result in some loss of information, but it is always preferable to code actual event descriptions.

   b. If one or two typical events are described but the article indicates that substantial numbers of additional events of the same type have occurred in the past few weeks or months, "dummy" events should be constructed to indicate that the described event is one of several such events. If, for example, an article reports that several land invasions have occurred in the past few weeks and describes one of them in some detail, you should first code this one event about which you do have information. Next you should fill out identical sets of cards for two or three additional "dummy" events to indicate that there were several events. Remember the information to be used is that of the typical event, not simply summary statistics for the entire period covered in the article.

   c. If the article simply states that "unrest" or "agitation" occurred in the period summarized and no further information is given about the type of event, then no attempt should be made to code detailed information about duration, number of participants, etc., even if information is provided in summary statistics for the period covered by the article. Remember you are attempting to code this information for an actual event, not an artificial time period created by the newspaper reporters.

6. Category and subcategory codes. Two-column codes concerned with qualitative characteristics of an event (e.g., columns 40–41, "administrative apparatus") are organized by category and subcategory codes. A general category code is indicated by a 0 in the second column of a two-column code. A 40 code in

columns 40–41, for example, indicates that the administrative apparatus directing this particular event is some kind of labor union but no more specific information about the union's organization is available. Codes 41, 42, 43, 44, and 45 are subcategories of the general category "labor unions," and each represents a particular level of union organization. If, for example, specific information was available that a banana workers' union called the strike, column 40–41 would be coded 43, which indicates that a union spanning all the workers in a particular crop is involved. It would not simply be coded 40, which would indicate that no additional information was available about the kind of union organization. All two-digit codes ending in 0 are general category codes and should not be used when more specific information is available.

CARD 1

Columns   *Code*
1–3   Country: see Appendix 2, "Agricultural Codes."

4–5   Movement number: Movements should be numbered consecutively beginning with the first movement observed in the 1948–1970 period. The ordinal position of a movement is determined by the date of its first event. The movement with the earliest initial event will be assigned the number 1, the movement with the next earliest initial event will be assigned the number 2, and so on until all movements are numbered.

6–8   Event number: Number all events in each movement consecutively beginning with the earliest and continuing until a number has been assigned to every event in that movement.

9   Phase number: consecutive within each event.

10   Card number (1).

11–12   Year: last two digits of the year in which this event or phase occurred.
         99   Insufficient information.

13–14   Month: number the month in which this event occurred (January = 01).
         99   Insufficient information.

15–16   Day: day of the month on which the event or phase begins. In general this will be a day or two before the date of the newspaper article, but it may be even earlier in summary articles.
         99   Insufficient information.

17–18   Number of provinces affected: number of provinces in which event activity is reported to have actually occurred. Include only those provinces which contain substantial proportions of the active participants in this event. Do not include provinces with marginal proportions of total number of participants. For all-country or all-region events count only those provinces in which the actions of cultivators are reported.
         99   Insufficient information.

19–48   Provinces affected: list province numbers (see alphabethical list in "Agricultural Organization" file for this country) of provinces counted in columns 17–18. Each province number should be listed as a two-digit number, and province numbers should be listed in successive two-column

Columns	*Code*

fields beginning in columns 19 and 20. This field is to be used for the actual provincial location of an event, not the source of an event's support.

Blank field   Insufficient information.

49–76   Provincial base of support: The provincial base of a movement is that geographic area in which the participants in the event normally carry on their agricultural activities. Some events may occur in provinces which are different from those in which this base area is located. This may occur, for example, when a group of peasants travels to a national capital to protest a government policy or when a guerrilla unit retreats to the mountains or when a group of mountain tribesmen raids a lowlands village. In such situations the actual location of the event should be coded in columns 19–48 but the actual base area should be described in this field if it is different. If the location of the event falls in the base area, then this field should be left blank. If, however, the provincial area in which the event occurs includes even a *single province* outside the base area, the base area provinces must be listed in this field. List the two-digit province numbers for the base area in successive two-column fields.

Blank field   Insufficient information or inappropriate (base area includes all provinces in which event activity is reported).

CARD 2

Columns	*Code*

1–9   Repeat 1–9, card 1.

10   Card number (2).

11–13   Duration of event in days.

14–16   Numbers of participants to two significant figures in scientific notation. In columns 14–15 indicate the integer values and in column 16 the order of magnitude. Thus five participants $= 5.0 \times 10$ would be coded 500 in columns 14–16; 550 participants $= 5.5 \times 10^2$ would be coded 552; and $550,000 = 5.5 \times 10^5$ would be coded 555. Missing data should be indicated by 999. Estimated values should be used where more detailed information is not available, and missing data codes should be used only as a last resort.

17–19   Number injured (total suffered and inflicted by collective). Same format as columns 14–16. When no injuries are reported, it should be assumed that none have occurred. Zero injuries should be coded 000.

20–22   Number killed: Repeat code for columns 17–19.

23   Identity of casualties.

    0   No casualties.
    1   Initiators.
    2   Victims.
    3   Social control forces.
    4   Initiators, victims.

5   Initiators, control forces.
6   Victims, control forces.
7   All three.
8   Others.

24   Property damage (after Gurr).
0   None or negligible: a few windows broken, rocks thrown at police headquarters, crop trampled in process of land invasion.
1   Slight: burning or looting of a few peasant dwellings, easily repaired damage to agricultural machinery, damage, but not destruction of, manor houses or other large buildings, killing a few cattle, or burning crops on a few small fields or holdings.
2   Moderate: damage to a large number of peasant dwellings or to an entire village, destruction of agricultural machinery on a few estates, substantial but not irreparable damage to expensive processing machinery, destruction of a few manor houses or other substantial buildings, destroying the crops or herds of an extensive holding or of a number of moderate-sized holdings.
3   Extensive: destruction of a number of peasant villages or equivalent number of dwellings, large-scale destruction of agricultural machinery, total destruction of processing machinery on plantations over a wide area, burning of manor houses or other buildings over large areas, destruction of cattle and crops throughout wide area.
4   Massive: total devastation of peasant villages in a wide area, virtual elimination of machinery buildings and standing crops throughout a crop system or similar large area.

25   Role of social control forces (after Gurr).
0   Not committed, committed after end of action.
1   Victims: no opportunity for defensive action, e.g., bombing of a military barracks.
2   Present but passive.
3   Defensive action: action to defend control forces or threatened property or persons, restraining demonstrators, protecting minority group members from crowds, reinforcing a police or military unit.
4   Moderate repressive action: limited selective use of force. Breaking up riots by selective arrests, tear gas and waterhoses, and active patrolling of riot areas. Include reports that police "dispersed" a crowd.
5   Extreme repressive action: social control forces use most or all means at their disposal. Indiscriminate beatings of rioters, mass arrests or executions, repeated firing into crowds, and full-scale military operations against rebels.
6   Provocative action: control forces initiate action by assaults on non-violent demonstrators or strikers. Crowds rioting in response to attempted arrests, uprisings when troops attempt to impose control in areas formally not under government authority.

26   Nature of control forces.
1   Police, including secret and irregular forces.
2   Military: regular army, national guard.

27–29   Number of arrests: Repeat code for columns 17–19.

ORGANIZATION

Columns	Code
30	Occupational group of collective: occupational group of a plurality of the participants or of the most vocal or forceful participants. Code the actual occupation even if the action is not one in which occupation functions as a basis of solidarity, e.g., a religious or racial riot involving groups of peasants.

    1   Operator commercial farm.
    2   Peasants, including peasant subsistence farmers, usufructuaries, and peasants producing for market.
    3   Sharecroppers and share tenants.
    4   Wage laborers, seasonal, fixed term, or migratory.
    5   Combinations of above with no one clearly predominating (use this code only as a last resort).
    6   Rural participants but no occupation group can be determined.

31–32   Crop worked by cultivators coded in 30. See Appendix 2, "Agricultural Codes," for crop.

33–34   Basis of group solidarity: shared social characteristic recognized by participants as basis for collective action. Find the least inclusive group that unites the participants.

    10   Simultaneous response to shared economic or social conditions with little or no sense of common identity.

    20   Communal ties.
    21   Neighborhood, community, kinship.
    22   Tribal.
    23   Racial.
    24   Religious.
    25   Language.
    26   Nationality.

    30   Class ties—bourgeoisie.
    31   All those drawing sustenance directly from the land identity formed around class of peasants. Note that peasants may frequently be united by communal ties or only by coacting. Be sure there is some recognition of class status of peasant.
    32   Owner operators, defined by relationship to land and to commercial markets, e.g., coffee growers' association.

    40   Class ties—proletarian.
    41   Workers in a particular enterprise.
    42   Workers in a particular region.
    43   Workers in a particular crop.
    44   Agricultural workers.
    45   Working class in general.

35–36   Organization of acting collective: the structure of the unit actually carrying out the collective act.

    10   Crowds: loose aggregates acting to achieve individual objectives without leadership and with only implicit coordination.

20   Mass formations: disciplined aggregates with clear leadership, frequently with advanced planning, e.g., marches, strikes.

30   Military organizations (armed collectives).
31   Irregular bands without formal military organization.
32   Paramilitary political groups—guerrillas organized around a party cell or cadre.
33   Irregular forces organized along conventional military lines—distinct officer group.
34   Regular military organization—uniformed soldiers under a military chain of command.

37–39   If coded 3 in column 35 only. Otherwise code 999.

37   Is the current provincial location of this military unit a result of a movement away from its original source of support in response to military exigencies?
0   No.
1   Yes.
9   Not ascertained or not applicable.

38   Is the current position of this unit a result of proximity to border sanctuaries?
Repeat 37.

39   Is the current location of this unit primarily a result of mountains, forest, or jungle used for military protection?
Repeat 37.
Comment: If yes to 32, 33, or 34, describe movements and indicate provinces where you feel the actual base of support of this movement is or was located. Attach to code sheet.

40–41   Administrative apparatus controlling unit described in 35–36 above. An organization will be considered to control a collective if:
a.   Spokesmen for the organization announce in advance their intentions to deploy the collective.
b.   Leading participants in the acting collective are also members of the organization.
c.   The participants identify themselves through slogans or public statements as a unit of the organization.
Vague references to outside agitators, particularly Communists, should not be accepted as evidence of organizational control without additional evidence.

10   No overall coordination or direction.

20   Communal groups.
21   Church organizations and affiliates.
22   Religious sects or cults.
23   Family, lineage tribe or neighborhood organizations.
24   Clubs or societies emphasizing ethnic solidarity.
25   Organized criminal groups including bandits.
26   Peasant unions, leagues, and groups organized around peasant communities.

Columns		*Code*
	30	Market-oriented commercial associations.
	31	Common local market, credit facilities, or local processing machinery provide basis for organization.
	32	Crop system as a whole.
	33	Farmers and other commercial operators generally.

	40	Labor unions.
	41	Enterprise level.
	42	Locality.
	43	Crop system.
	44	Farm workers' union, not crop specific.
	45	Industrial union spanning both farm workers and other worker groups.

	50	Political parties.
	51	Legal, contest elections, provincial representation or less.
	52	Same, but representation in national assembly or parliament.
	53	Illegal, underground parties, local or provincial level.
	54	Illegal, underground and above provincial level.

60   Alternate governments: Political organizations which claim sovereignty and have any of the following characteristics:
a.   Collect taxes.
b.   Administer areas.
c.   Are recognized by at least one foreign state.
This code does not include traditional areas which provide shelter for insurgent movements but are not themselves organized for collective action.

TACTICS

Codes in this section refer to the actions of the collectives described in columns 35–36 above. Concentrate on actual behavior of collective. Long-range objectives are coded later under ideology.

42–43   Primary tactical objective.

Threats

10   Displays—attempts to marshal large numbers in order to demonstrate the potential political influence of the movement.
11   Marches.
12   Rallies.
13   Seizures of buildings, public places for symbolic effect.

42–43   20   Mass economic action—large numbers organized with the specific goal of threatening or inflicting economic damage on an enterprise, individual, market, or consumer sector.
21   Strikes, plant seizures, sit-ins in processing plants.
22   Boycotts.
23   Crop destruction (when designed to raise price of produce).
24   Rent strikes.

Coercive acts

30   Diffuse coercive acts.
31   Land seizures with no attempt to destroy land-owning class.
32   Attacks on persons of landowners and managers or burning of manor houses (*jacquerie*).
33   Destruction of agricultural machinery.
34   Pogroms—attacks on an opposing communal group if object is the destruction or expulsion of some part of its membership.
35   Riots—disorganized property destruction or attacks on persons not elsewhere specified.
36   Combat with police and national security forces without intent to destroy opposing unit, not elsewhere specified.

40   Focused coercive acts.
41   Banditry—instrumental use of force to achieve private gain.
42   Terrorism—systematic use of force against selected individuals or groups with the intent to intimidate the group generally.
43   Sabotage—selective property destruction.
44   Warfare—attacks on government or police units or installations with the intent of limiting or destroying the fighting power of the unit.

44–45   Primary target: object, individual, or social group that demands are made on, that actions are directed against, or that is regarded by demonstrators as directly responsible for the conditions making their actions necessary.

00   Diffuse targets.

10   Strikebreakers, collaborators, and others threatening to break solidarity of acting collective.

20   Extraterrestrial beings.

30   Inanimate objects, machinery, land (e.g. attempts to eliminate machine competition by eliminating machines).

40   Race, religious, linguistic, or other communal groups.
41   Settlers and *colons* (regarded as illegitimate because they are outsiders).

50   Social classes
51   Landlords, middlemen, and administrators
52   Upper classes generally.
54   Capitalists or imperialists.

60   Government agencies and organizations.
61   Local.
62   National autochthonous.
63   National colonialist (including metropolitan government).
64   Foreign governments.

70   Nongovernmental political parties and groups.

80   Police and internal security forces.
81   Police.
82   Courts, judiciary.
83   Regular army, national guard.

Columns	Code

46–48　In these columns code the demands of the acting collective. The demands may be communal (column 46), economic (column 47), or political (column 48) or some combination of these categories, but a demand should be coded only if it is clear that it is central concern of most participants in the event or phase. Demands may be inferred from public statements, slogans, names of movements, or written platforms. They may also be inferred from general background of the movement or from the actions of participants. Remember to code only demands which are significant in this particular event or phase.

46　Communal concerns.
0　None evident.
1　Millenial and religious demands—return to piety, preservation of tribal virtues, expectations of miraculous events.
2　Primitive rebels—return of the good landlords, belief in Robin Hood figures.
3　Populist concerns with the sanctity of rural life and traditions, including restoration of peasant land tenure forms.
4　Reactionary demands for the abolition of new forms of machinery or new agricultural techniques.
5　Attribution of evil to another racial, religious, linguistic or other communal group and concern for its expulsion or elimination.
6　Demands for civil liberties or an end to oppression of ethnic groups.
7　Demands for the expulsion or destruction of a land-holding group on the grounds that it is not indigenous, e.g., *colons*, settlers.
8　Nationalist demands—national purification or autonomy expulsion of foreigners including colonial regimes.

47　Economic concerns.
0　None evident
1　Food scarcity and prices, starvation central concern.
2　Concern with greater access to land, land to the tiller.
3　Control over free market—socialized credit, elimination of middlemen, cooperative control of processing facilities.
4　Higher wages, shorter hours, better working conditions.
5　Rights to organize for economic goals.
6　Socialization of land and processing machinery including nationalization of plantations and establishment of collective farms.
7　Nationalization of entire economy or of substantial parts of the industrial, agricultural, and financial sectors.

48　Political concerns.
0　None evident.
1　Change in particular policy or program.
2　Change in leaders or administrative personnel.
3　Change in ruling party, defeat of rival political group.
4　Changes in legislation, legal order.
5　Fundamental constitutional changes including suspension of civil rights or extralegal replacement of a regime.
6　Change in the political community—fundamental change in the ideology legitimating the political system, including the termination of colonialism or the establishment of socialism or communism.

Columns	*Code*
49–50	Party affiliation of participants: If the participants display any attachment to an organized political party or faction, the dominant ideology of that party or faction should be coded here. Party affiliation should be coded even if the party organization itself does not directly control the actions of participants. Party affiliation may be inferred from any of the following:

1. The party organization is the administrative apparatus (columns 40–41) for this event.
2. The party it not itself the administrative apparatus for the event, but it is organizationally connected with that administrative apparatus. The actual administrative apparatus may be a subunit of the political party or it may form a coalition with the party for political purposes. The Peruvian sugar workers' union, for example, is closely associated with the APRA party organization. If the sugar workers' union calls a strike, the union would be the effective administrative apparatus, but the APRA party ideology would be coded as the political affiliation of the strikers.
3. Political leaders affiliated with a particular party either call the action, address a crowd of supporters, or are the focal point of the action. A group of Baganda tribesmen demonstrating for the return of their king, the Kabaka, would be considered to be associated with the king's political faction. Peruvian peasants who attack a jail and demand the freedom of Hugo Blanco would be considered to be affiliated with Blanco's Trotskyist party.
4. A newspaper article makes direct reference to the participants as supporters of a particular party or faction. In an account of a Mexican land invasion the *New York Times* notes that the participants are supporters of General Miguel Henriquez Guzman the leader of the *Henriquista* movement.
5. The participants indicate by their demands, slogans, or banners that they support a particular party. Indonesian squatters who moved onto Sumatra tobacco estates shouting "Long live Stalin" would be considered supporters of the Communist party.

CAUTION: Do not code Communist party affiliation on the basis of statements by opponents of the party or of government officials. Most rebels are called Communists at one time or another whether or not they are affiliated with an actual Communist party. The government of Cameroon persistently referred to rebel guerrillas as Communists despite the absence of any ideology beyond the desire for greater tribal autonomy. In such cases such statements should be ignored. Code Communist party affiliation only if participants, their spokesmen, or their leaders claim such affiliation, the party organization itself includes "Communist" in its formal title, or the newspaper report presents considerable evidence that Communists are actually involved.

Code the dominant ideology of the party with which participants in this event are affiliated. The party ideology should be inferred as much as possible from the party's actual demands, the actions of its supporters, and especially its public statements. The formal party name may give some idea of the party ideology, but as the German "National Socialists" indicate, such titles can be deceptive. If no other information is available, however, code the party title rather than insufficient information.

Columns	*Code*
00	No party affiliation: indicates political apathy or absence of any ties to political parties or factions.

10 Revolutionary socialist: parties advocating the revolutionary overthrow of the state and complete government control of the economy. Communist parties.
11 Communist, Moscow.
12 Communist, Peking.
13 Trotskyist.
14 Other Communist.

20 Democratic socialist: parties advocating partial or complete government control of the economy but advocating electoral politics and a democratic polity.

30 Democratic reformist: parties advocating increased welfare activities, rights of labor organizations, and mild redistributive measures all to be attained through democratic elections. APRA party in Peru, FRAP in Chile.

40 Nationalist socialist: parties advocating partial or complete government control of the economy but stressing the peculiar national characteristics of this intervention. Tanzanian TANU party.
41 African socialist.
42 Arab socialist.
43 Other.

50 Religious socialist: parties combining advocacy of government control of some economic activities with support for a particular traditional religious ideology.

60 Religious: all other nonsocialist religious parties. (Note that this code indicates that participants are affiliated with a particular religious party and are *not* simply adherents of the religion.)
61 Parties of established religious groups—Christian, Muslim, Hindu.
62 Parties of religious sects and cults and radical variants of major religious groups.

70 Nationalist and communalist parties.
71 Anticolonial or Anti-imperial nationalist parties.
72 Secessionist or separatist nationalist parties.
73 Parties advocating regional, tribal, or other ethnic group autonomy but not actual secession.

80 Conservative or Fascist parties.

90 Other party ideology (specify).
99 Insufficient information.

CARD 3

Columns	*Code*
1–9	Repeat columns 1–9 of card 1.
10	Card number (3).

Columns	*Code*
11–80	Sources in which this event is mentioned. Fifteen-column fields listing sources in order of importance. First column of each field identifies source. Remaining columns specify article according to format indicated.

    1   *Times, New York*: year (2), month (2), day (2), page (3), column (1).

    2   *Times*, London: year (2), month (2), day (2), page (3), column (1).

    3   *Le Monde*: year (2), month (2), day (2), page (3), column (1).

    4   *Hispanic American Report*: year (2), month (2), volume (2), number (2), page (4).

    5   *Latin American Newsletter.*

    6   *Asian Recorder*: page (4).

    7   *Africa Digest.*

    8   *Africa Report.*

    9   *Africa Diary.*

If all information is not relevant for any single source, leave remaining columns in field blank.

APPENDIX 4   *Cross-National Bibliography*

EUROPE

Finland

Bacon, Walter. *Finland.* London: Robert Hale, 1970.

Bukdahl, Jørgen, et al., eds. *Scandinavia Past and Present: Five Modern Democracies.* Odense, Denmark: Arnkrone, 1959.

Haatanen, Pekka. *Suomen Maalaisköyhälistö. Tutkimusten ja Kaunokirjallisuuden Valossa.* English summary. Helsinki: Werner Söderström, 1968.

Hall, Wendy. *The Finns and Their Country.* London: Marx Parrish, 1967.

Kallas, Hillar, and Sylvie Nickels. *Finland: Creation and Construction.* London: Allen & Unwin, 1968.

Mead, W. R. *An Economic Geography of the Scandinavian States and Finland.* London: University of London Press, 1958.

O'Dell, Andrew. *The Scandinavian World.* London: Longmans, Green, 1957.

Platt, Raye R., ed. *Finland and Its Geography.* New York: Duell, Sloan & Pearce, 1955.

Royal Institute of International Affairs. *The Scandinavian States and Finland: A Political and Economic Survey.* London, 1951.

Somme, Axel, ed. *A Geography of Norden: Denmark-Finland-Iceland-Norway-Sweden.* Oslo: J. W. Cappelens Forlag, 1960.

Greece

France, Institut National de la Statistique et des Études Économiques. *La Grèce: Mémentos Économiques.* Paris: Presses Universitaires de France, 1952.

Kingdom of Greece, Center of Planning and Economic Research. *Draft of the Five Year Economic Development Plan for Greece (1966–1970).* Athens, 1965.

Kingdom of Greece, Ministry of Coordination, National Statistical Service of Greece. *Agricultural Statistics of Greece 1968.* Athens, 1970.

Kingdom of Greece, National Statistical Service of Greece. *Statistical Yearbook of Greece 1968.* Athens, n.d.

Kingdom of Greece, National Statistical Service of Greece, Statistical Service of the Ministry of Agriculture. *Agricultural Statistics of Greece 1962,* vols. 1–2. Athens, 1964.

McNeil, William H. *Greece: American Aid in Action 1947–56.* New York: The Twentieth Century Fund, 1957.

Negreponti-Delivanis, Maria. *Le Développement de la Grèce du Nord depuis 1912.* Thessalonica, 1962.

403

Thompson, Kenneth. *Farm Fragmentation in Greece: The Problem and Its Setting.* Athens: Center of Economic Research, Research Monograph Series, 1963.

Ireland

Arensberg, Conrad M. *The Irish Countryman: An Anthropological Study.* Gloucester, Mass.: Peter Smith Publisher, 1959.

Chaline, Claude. *Le Royaume-Uni et la République d'Irlande.* Paris: Presses Universitaires de France, 1966.

Dury, G. H. *The British Isles: A Systematic and Regional Geography.* London: Heinemann, 1965.

Figgis, Allen, ed. *Encyclopaedia of Ireland.* New York: McGraw-Hill, 1968.

Newman, Jeremiah, ed. *The Limerick Rural Survey: 1958–1964.* Tipperary, Ireland: Muintir Na Tire Rural Publications, 1964.

Rees, Henry. *The British Isles: A Regional Geography.* London: George G. Harrap, 1966.

Steers, J. A., ed. *Feld Studies in the British Isles.* London: Nelson, 1965.

Wreford, Watson J., ed. with J. B. Sissons. *The British Isles: A Systematic Geography.* London: Nelson, 1964.

Italy

Antonietti, Alessandro. *Operatori di Mercato e Canali di Distribuzione dei Prodotti Ortoflorofrutticoli.* Palermo: Conferenza Nazionale per l'Ortoflorofrutticoltura, 1967.

Barberis, Corrado. "Men, Farms, and Product in Italian Agriculture." *Review of the Economic Conditions in Italy,* vol. 25, no. 5, Rome: Banco di Roma, 1971, pp. 398–419.

Barbero, Guiseppe. *L'Evoluzione dell'Agricoltura Meridionale nel Decenio 1950–1960.* Bari: Editori Laterza, 1962.

Burke, J. Henry. *A Study of the Citrus Industry of Italy.* U.S. Department of Agriculture, Foreign Agricultural Report no. 59. October 1951.

Giorgi, Giacomo. *The "Metayage" in the Province of Perugia.* 2nd ed. Perugia: Tipografia Perugina, 1947.

Italy, Cassa per il Mezzogiorno. *Strutture e Mercati dell'Agricoltura Meridionale: 1. Cotone-Agrumi.* Rome, 1960.

Italy, Cassa per il Mezzogiorno. *Strutture e Mercati dell'Agricoltura Meridionale: 2. Prodotti Ortofrutticoli.* Rome, 1960.

Italy, Istituto Centrale di Statistica. *Annuario di Statistica Agraria,* vols. 13–14. Rome, 1966 and 1967.

Italy, Istituto Centrale di Statistica. *Annuario di Statistiche del Lavoro e dell' Emigrazione,* vol. 9. Rome, 1969.

Italy, Istituto Centrale di Statistica. *Annuario di Statistiche Provinciali,* vol. 7. Rome, 1968.

Italy, Istituto Centrale di Statistica. *I° Censimento General dell'Agricoltura, 1961,* vol. 6. Rome, 1968.

Italy, Istituto Nazionale di Economia Agraria. *Carta dei Tipi d'Impresa nell'Agricoltura Italiana.* Rome, 1958.

Italy, Istituto Nazionale di Economia Agraria. *Risultati Economici di Aziende Agrarie, 1962.* Sicily, 1962.

Lupori, Nello. *L'Agricoltura e lo Sviluppo Economico del Mezzogiorno.* Rome: Realta Editrice, 1962.

Medici, Guiseppe. *Italian Agriculture and Its Problems*. Champaign, Ill: Bartlett Foundation, 1945.

Medici, Guiseppe. *Italy: Agricultural Aspects*. Bologna: Edizioni Agricole, 1952.

Medici, Guiseppe. *Land Property and Land Tenure in Italy*. Bologna: Edizioni Agricole, 1952.

Meo, Guiseppe de. *Evoluzione e Prospettive delle Forze di Lavoro in Italia: Annali di Statistica, Anno 99*, vol. 23. Rome: Istituto Centrale di Statistica, 1970.

Rossi-Doria, Manlio. *Dieci Anni di Politica Agraria nel Mezzogiorno*. Bari: Editori Laterza, 1968.

United Nations, Food and Agriculture Organization. *World Crops Harvest Calendar*. Rome, 1959.

United Nations, Organization for Economic Cooperation and Development. *Production of Fruit and Vegetables in OECD Member Countries: Present Situation and 1970 Prospects, Italy*. Paris, 1966.

U.S. Department of Agriculture, Foreign Agricultural Service. *The Deciduous Fruit Industry in Italy*. Washington, April 1959.

U.S. Department of Agriculture, Office of Foreign Agricultural Relations. *The Citrus Industry at Sorrento. Italy, 1950*. Foreign Agricultural Circular FCF 6–51. Washington, May 7, 1951.

Portugal

Amorim Girao, A de. *Geografia de Portugal*. Porto: Portucalense Editoria, 1951.

Birot, Pierre. *Le Portugal: Étude de Géographie Régionale*. Paris: Librairie Armand Colin, 1950.

Descamps, Paul. *Le Portugal: La Vie Sociale Actuelle*. Paris: Librairie de Paris–Firmin-Didot, 1945.

Pintado, Xavier V. *Structure and Growth of the Portuguese Economy*. Geneva: European Free Trade Association, 1964.

Sergio, Antonio. *Introduçao Geografico-Sociologica: A Historia de Portugal*. Lisbon: Grafica Santelmo, 1948.

Teran, Manuel de. *Geografía de España y Portugal*. Barcelona: Montaner y Simon, 1955.

Vilá Valentí, J. *La Péninsule Ibérique*. Paris: Presses Universitaires de France, 1968.

Way, Ruth. *A Geography of Spain and Portugal*. London: Methuen & Co., Ltd., 1962.

Spain

Burke, J. Henry. *A Study of the Citrus Industry of Spain, 1950*. U.S. Department of Agriculture, Office of Foreign Agricultural Relations, Foreign Agriculture Report no. 56. November 1950.

International Bank for Reconstruction and Development. *The Economic Development of Spain*. Baltimore: Johns Hopkins Press, 1963.

International Bank for Reconstruction and Development and the Food and Agriculture Organization. *The Development of Agriculture in Spain*. Washington, November 1966.

Krause, Elfriede. *Spain: Changes in Agricultural Production and Trade*, U.S. Department of Agriculture, Foreign Agricultural Service FAS-M56, 1959.

Spain, Instituto Nacional de Estadística. *Primer Censo Agrario de España, Año 1962*. Madrid, 1964.

Spain, Ministerio de Agricultura. *Anuario Estadístico de la Producción Agrícola: Campana 1963–1964*. n.d.

CENTRAL AND SOUTH AMERICA

Brazil

Brazil, Instituto Brasileiro de Estatística. *Anuário Estatístico do Brasil: 1969.* Rio de Janeiro, 1968.
Cacau Actualidades, vols. 1–5 (1964–1968).
Comité Interamericano de Desenvolvimento Agrícola. *Posse e Uso da Terra e Desenvolvimento Socio-econômico do Sector Agrícola: Brasil.* Washington: Pan American Union, 1966.
Dean, W. "The Planter as Entrepreneur: The Case of São Paulo." *Hispanic American Historical Review* 46 (May 1966), 138–52.
Hutchinson, Harry William. *Village and Plantation Life in North-Eastern Brazil.* Seattle: University of Washington Press, 1957.
Inter-American Cacao Center. *Cacao.* Turrialba, Costa Rica: Inter-American Institute of Agricultural Sciences, 1963.
James, P. E. "The Coffee Lands of Southeastern Brazil." *Geographical Review* 22 (April 1932), 225–44.
James, P. E. "Observations on the Physical Geography of Northeast Brazil." *Annals of the Association of American Geographers* 43 (March 1953), 98–126.
James, P. E. "Trends in Brazilian Agricultural Development." *Geographical Review* 43 (July 1953), 301–328.
King, Winfield C. *Brazil's Coffee Industry.* U.S. Department of Agriculture, Foreign Agricultural Service FAS M-131, March 1962.
Porter, Horace. *Cotton in Brazil,* U.S. Department of Agriculture, Foreign Agricultural Service FAS M-156, April 1964.
Stevens, R. L., and P. R. Brandão. "Diversification of the Economy of the Cacao Coast of Bahia (Brazil)," *Economic Geography.* 37 (July 1961) 231–253.
U.S. Department of Agriculture, Foreign Agricultural Service. *Brazilian Cotton: Trends and Prospects.* FAS M-187, 1967.
Valverde, O. "A Fazenda de Café Escravocrata, no Brazil." *Revista Brasileira de Geografia,* no. 1 (January–March 1967), 37–82.

Chile

Barraclough, Solon. *Notas Sobre Tenencia de la Tierra en América Latina.* Santiago: Instituto de Capacitación e Investigación en Reforma Agraria, 1968.
Chile, Dirección de Estadística y Censos. *Agricultura e Industrias Agropecuarias 1959–1960.* 1962.
Chile, Ministerio de Agricultura, Dirección de Agricultura y Pesca. *La Agricultura Chilena 1956–1960.* Santiago, 1963.
Chile, Oficina de Planificación Nacional. *Distribución de Ingreso y Cuentas de Producción, 1960–1968.* Santiago, 1968.
Comité Interamericano para el Desarrollo Agrícola. *Tenencia de la Tierra y Desarrollo Socio-económico del Sector Agrícola: Chile.* Washington: Pan American Union, 1965.
Inter-American Committee for Agricultural Development. *Inventory Basic to the Planning of Agricultural Development in Latin America: Chile.* Washington: Pan American Union, 1964.
McBride, G. M. *Chile, Land and Society.* Research Series, no. 19. New York: American Geographical Society, 1936.

Rockefeller Foundation. *Chilean Agricultural Program.* Director's Annual Report August 1958–July 1959. New York, n.d.

Colombia

Adams, Dale. "Landownership Patterns in Colombia," *Inter-American Economic Affairs.* 17 (Winter 1964), 77–86.

Colombia, Departmento Administrativo Nacional de Estadística. *Directorio Nacional de Explotaciones Agropecuarias (Censo Agropecuaria) 1960.* Bogotá, 1962–1964.

Colombia, Dirección Nacional de Estadística. *Anuario General de Estadística 1959.* Bogotá, n.d.

Colombia, Secretaria de Agricultura de Antioquia, Sección de Comunicaciones. *Servicios Rurales en Antioquia.* Medellín, September 1968.

Comité Interamericano para el Desarrollo Agrícola. *Tenencia de la Tierra y Desarrollo Socio-Económico del Sector Agrícola: Colombia.* Washington: Pan American Union, 1966.

Fundación para el Progreso de Colombia. *La Industria Cafetera en la Agricultura Colombiana.* Bogotá: Banco Cafetero, 1962.

Hirschman, Albert. *Journeys toward Progress: Studies of Economic Policy-Making in Latin America.* New York: The Twentieth Century Fund, 1963.

International Bank for Reconstruction and Development. *The Coffee Economy of Colombia.* Economcis Department Working Paper no. 15. Washington, 1968.

Machado, Alberto. *Curso Práctico para Cafeteros.* Chincina, Colombia: Federación Nacional de Cafeteros de Colombia, 1949.

Stafford, F. "Significación de los Antioqueños en el Desarrollo Económico Colombiano," *Anuario Colombiano de Historia Social y de la Cultura,* 1967, 49–69.

Smith, T. L. *Colombia: Social Structure and the Process of Development.* Gainesville, Fla.: University of Florida Press, 1967.

Costa Rica

Biesanz, John, and Mairs Biesanz. *Costa Rican Life.* New York: Columbia University Press, 1944.

Blutstein, Howard I., et al. *Area Handbook for Costa Rica.* Washington D.C.; Government Printing Office, 1970.

Goldrich, Daniel. *Sons of the Establishment: Elite Youth in Panama and Costa Rica.* Chicago: Rand McNally, 1966.

Jones, Clarence Fielden, and Gordon Darkenwald. *Economic Geography,* revised. New York: Macmillan, 1954.

Jones, Clarence F., and Paul Morrison. "Evolution of the Banana Industry in Costa Rica." *Economic Geography* 28 (January 1952), 1–17.

León, Jorge. "Land Utilization in Costa Rica," *Geographical Review* 38 (July 1948), 444–56.

Loomis, Charles P, et al., eds. *Turrialba: Social Systems and the Introduction of Change.* Glencoe, Ill.: Free Press, 1953.

May, Stacy, et al., *Costa Rica: A Study in Economic Development.* New York: The Twentieth Century Fund, 1952.

May, Stacy and Galo Plaza. *The United Fruit Company in Latin America.* Washington: National Planning Association, 1958.

Nunley, R. E. *The Distribution of Population in Costa Rica.* Washington: National Research Council, 1960.

Peterson, Lyall E. *Agricultural Development Prospects in Costa Rica.* Washington: Inter-American Development Commission, 1947.

Powell, Jane Swift. *Agriculture in Costa Rica.* Washington: Pan American Union, 1943.

Universidad de Costa Rica. *Estudio del Sector Agropecuario: El Desarrollo Económico de Costa Rica.* San José, 1959.

Wagner, P. L. "Nicoya: A Cultural Geography." *University of California Publications in Geography* 12 (April 1958), 195–250.

West, Robert C., and John Augelli. *Middle America: Its Lands and Peoples.* Englewood Cliffs, N.J.: Prentice-Hall, 1966.

Cuba

Dyer, D. R. "Sugar Regions of Cuba," *Economic Geography* 32 (April 1956), 177–184.

Guerra y Sanchez, Ramiro. *Sugar and Society in the Caribbean: An Economic History of Cuban Agriculture.* New Haven: Yale University Press, 1964.

Nelson, Lowry. *Rural Cuba.* Minneapolis: University of Minnesota Press, 1950.

Ortiz, Fernando. *Cuban Counterpoint: Tobacco and Sugar.* New York: Knopf, 1947.

Seers, Dudley, ed. *Cuba: The Economic and Social Revolution.* Chapel Hill: University of North Carolina Press, 1964.

Truslow, F. A. *Report on Cuba.* Baltimore: Johns Hopkins Press, 1951.

Dominican Republic

Augelli, J. P. "Agricultural Colonization in the Dominican Republic," *Economic Geography.* 38 (January 1962), 15–27.

Dyer, D. R. "Distribution of Population on Hispaniola." *Economic Geography* 30 (October 1954), 337–46.

Inter-American Committee for Agricultural Development. *Dominican Republic.* Washington Pan American Union, 1964.

Logan, R. W. *Haiti and the Dominican Republic.* London: Royal Institute of International Affairs, 1963.

Moscoso Puello, F. E. *Cañas y Bueyes.* Santo Domingo, Dominican Republic: Editorial La Nación, 1935.

Secretaria Estado Industria Comercio Banco. "La Historia Azucarera y Su Evolución en la República Dominicana," *Revista Secretaria Estado Industria Comercio Banco,* 42 (1955), 59–86.

West, Robert C., and John Augelli. *Middle America: Its Lands and Peoples.* Englewood Cliffs, N.J.: Prentice-Hall, 1966.

Ecuador

Bottomley, A. "Agricultural Employment Policy in Developing Countries: The Case of Ecuador," *Inter-American Economic Affairs.* 99 (Spring 1966), 53–79.

Comité Interamericano del Desarrollo Agrícola. *Tenencia de la Tierra y Desarrollo Socio-Económico de Sector Agrícola: Ecuador.* Washington: Pan American Union, 1965.

Ecuador, Dirección General de Agricultura y Bosques. *Servicio Cooperativo Inter-Americano de Agricultura Ecuador,* no. 8. Quito, January 1959.

Ecuador, Programa de Desarrollo Agropecuario. *Metas y Proyecciones.* Quito, 1964.

May, Stacy, and Galo Plaza. *The United Fruit Company in Latin America.* Washington: National Planning Association, 1958.

Miller, E. V. "Agricultural Ecuador." *Geographical Review* 49 (April 1959), 183–207.

Parsons, J. J. "Bananas in Ecuador." *Economic Geography* 33 (July 1957), 201–216.

Guatemala

Adams, R. N. *Crucifixion by Power: Essays on Guatemalan National Social Structure, 1944–1966.* Austin: University of Texas Press, 1970.

Adams, R. N. *Guatemala.* Cultural Surveys of Panama, Nicaragua, Guatemala, El Salvador, Honduras. Pan American Sanitary Bureau, Scientific Publication no. 33. Washington: World Health Organization, 1957.

Comité Interamericano del Desarrollo Agrícola. *Tenencia de la Tierra y Desarrollo Socio-Económico del Sector Agrícola: Guatemala.* Washington: Pan American Union, 1965.

Dombrowski, John et al. *Area Handbook for Guatemala.* Washington: Government Printing Office, 1970.

Higbee, E. "The Agricultural Regions of Guatemala." *Geographical Review* 37 (April 1947), 177–201.

Hill, George W., and Manuel Gollas. *The Minifundia Economy and Society of the Guatemalan Highland Indian.* Land Tenure Center, Research Paper no. 30. Madison: University of Wisconsin, 1968.

Horst, O. H. "The Spectre of Death in a Guatemalan Highland Community." *Geographical Review* 57 (April 1967), 151–167.

Hoyt, Elizabeth E. "The Indian Laborer on Guatemalan Coffee Fincas," *Inter-American Economic Affairs.* 9 (Summer 1955), 33–46.

Jimenez, Julio M. "A Critique of the Policies and Attitudes Affecting Cotton Agriculture in Guatemala through a Study of Its Development." M.A. thesis, University of Texas, 1967.

McBride, G. M., and M. A. McBride. "Highland Guatemala and Its Maya Communities." *Geographical Review* 32 (April 1942), 252–268.

McBryde, F. W. *Cultural and Historical Geography of Southwest Guatemala.* Institute of Social Anthropology Publication no. 4. Washington: The Smithsonian Institution, 1947.

Mosk, Sanford A. "The Coffee Economy of Guatemala, 1850–1918: Development and Signs of Instability." *Inter-American Economic Affairs* 9 (Winter 1955), 16–20.

Pacheco Herrarte, Mariano. *Agriculture in Guatemala.* American Agricultural Series. Washington: Pan American Union, 1944.

Pearson, Neal J. "Guatemala: The Peasant Union Movement, 1944–1954," in Henry A. Landsburger, ed. *Latin American Peasant Movements.* Ithaca, N.Y.: Cornell University Press, 1969.

Schmid, Lester. *The Middle-sized Farm in Guatemala.* Land Tenure Center, Research Paper no. 38. Madison: University of Wisconsin, 1969.

Schmid, Lester. *El Papel de la Mano de Obra Migratoria en el Desarrollo Económico de Guatemala.* Madison: University of Wisconsin, 1968.

Schmid, Lester. "The Productivity of Agricultural Labor in Export Crops in Guatemala: Its Relation to Wages and Living Conditions." *Inter-American Economic Affairs* 22 (Autumn 1968), 33–45.

Tax, Sol. *Penny Capitalism: A Guatemalan Indian Economy.* Institute of Social Anthropology Publication no. 16. Washington: The Smithsonian Institution, 1953.

Whetten, N. L. *Guatemala: The Land and the People.* New Haven: Yale University Press, 1961.

Haiti

de Young, M. *Man and Land in the Haitian Economy.* Latin American Monograph, no. 3. Gainesville: University of Florida Press, 1958.

Holly, Mare Aurele. *Agriculture in Haiti.* New York: Vantage Press, 1955.

Inter-American Committee for Agricultural Development. *Haiti.* Washington: Pan American Union, 1963.

Moral, P. "La Culture du Café en Haiti." *Les Cahiers d'Outre-Mer* 8 (July–Sept. 1955), 233–256.

Moral, P. *L'Économie Haitienne.* Port-au-Prince: Imprimerie de l'État, 1959.

Moral, P. "La Maison Rurale en Haiti." *Les Cahiers d'Outre-Mer* 10 (April-June 1957), 117–130.

Moral, P. *Le Paysan Haitien: Étude sur la Vie Rurale en Haiti.* Paris: G. P. Maisonnueve et Larose, 1961.

Street, J. M. *Historical and Economic Geography of the Southwest Peninsula of Haiti.* Office of Naval Research Technical Report. Berkeley: University of California, 1960.

West, Robert C., and John Augelli. *Middle America: Its Lands and Peoples.* Englewood Cliffs, N.J.: Prentice-Hall, 1966.

Wood, U. A. *Northern Haiti: Land Use and Settlement.* Toronto: University of Toronto Press, 1963.

Honduras

Adams, Richard N. *Honduras.* Cultural Surveys of Panama, Nicaragua, Guatemala, El Salvador, Honduras. Pan American Sanitary Bureau, Scientific Publication no. 33. Washington: World Health Organization, 1957.

Checci, V., et al., eds. *Honduras:* A Problem in Economic Development. New York: The Twentieth Century Fund, 1959.

Coghill, J. P. *Economic and Commercial Conditions in Honduras.* London: H. M. Stationery Office, 1954.

May, Stacy, and Galo Plaza. *The United Fruit Company in Latin America.* Washington: National Planning Association, 1958.

Parsons, J. J. "The Miskito Pine Savanna of Nicaragua and Honduras," *Annals of the Association of American Geographers,* 45 (March 1955), 36–63.

Squier, E. G. *Honduras: Descriptive, Historical and Statistical.* London: Trübner and Co., 1870.

Stockley, G. E. *Honduras: Economic and Commercial Conditions in Honduras.* London: H. M. Stationery Office, 1951.

Tower, F. J. *Basic Data on the Economy of Honduras.* Washington: U.S. Bureau of International Programs, 1961.

United Nations. *El Desarrollo Económico de Honduras.* Mexico City, 1960.

Villanueva, Benjamin. *The Role of Institutional Innovations: International Economic Development of Honduras.* Land Tenure Center, Research Paper no. 34. Madison: University of Wisconsin, 1968.

Jamaica

Abbott, George. "The West Indian Sugar Industry with Some Long-Term Projections of Supply." *Social and Economic Studies* 13 (March 1964), 1–37.

Blant, J. M., et al. "A Study of Cultural Determinants of Soil Erosion and Conservation in the Blue Mountains of Jamaica." *Social and Economic Studies* 8 (December 1959), 403–420.

Carley, M. M. *Jamaica: The Old and the New.* London: Allen & Unwin, 1963.

Cumper, G. E., ed. *The Economy of the West Indies.* Kingston: University College of the West Indies, 1960.

Cumper, G. E. "Labour Demand and Supply in the Jamaican Sugar Industry, 1830–1950." *Social and Economic Studies* 2 (March 1954), 37–86.

Cumper, G. E. "A Modern Jamaican Sugar Estate." *Social and Economic Studies* 3(2) (1954).

Cumper, G. E. "Population Movements in Jamaica: 1830–1950." *Social and Economic Studies* 5 (September 1956), 261–280.

Cumper, G. E. *Social Structure of Jamaica.* Caribbean Affairs 1. Kingston: University College of the West Indies, 1949.

Edwards, D. *Report on an Economic Study of Small Farming in Jamaica.* Mona, Jamaica: University College of the West Indies, 1961.

Hall, Douglas. *Free Jamaica, 1838–1865: An Economic History.* New Haven: Yale University Press, 1959.

Jamaica, Department of Statistics. *Sample Surveys of Agriculture 1954 and 1958.* Kingston, 1960.

Jamaica, Department of Statistics. *Survey of Agriculture, 1961–62.* Kingston, 1966.

McFarlane, Dennis. "The Future of the Banana Industry in the West Indies." *Social and Economic Studies* 13 (March 1964), 38–93.

McMorris, C. S. *Small Farm Financing in Jamaica.* Kingston: University College of the West Indies, 1957.

Roberts, G. W. *The Population of Jamaica: An Analysis of Its Structure and Growth.* London: Cambridge University Press, 1957.

Thomas, C. V. "Coffee Production in Jamaica." *Social and Economic Studies* 13 (March 1964), 188–217.

West, Robert C., and John Augelli. *Middle America: Its Lands and Peoples.* Englewood Cliffs, N.J.: Prentice-Hall, 1966.

Mexico

Barloro, Frank D., Jr., and Grady Crowe. *Mexican Cotton Production: Problems and Potentials.* U.S. Department of Agriculture, FAS Report no. 98. Washington, 1957.

Blanco, Gonzalo. *Agriculture in Mexico.* American Agriculture Series. Washington: Pan American Union, 1950.

Chardon, R. *Geographic Aspects of Plantation Agriculture in Yucatán.* Washington: National Academy of Sciences–National Research Council, 1961.

Dozier, C. L. "Mexico's Transformed Northwest: The Yaqui, Mayo, and Fuerte Examples." *Geographical Review* 53 (October 1963), 548–571.

"El Futuro del Algodón," *Agro-síntesis*, no. 4 (May 1971), 12–14.

Inter-American Committee for Agricultural Development. *Mexico.* Washington: Pan American Union, 1964.

McDowell H. G. "Cotton in Mexico." *Journal of Geography* 63 (February 1964), 67–72.

Scott, Robert E. "Budget Making in Mexico." *Inter-American Economic Affairs* 9 (Autumn 1955), 3–20.

Venezian, Eduardo L., and William Gamble. *The Agricultural Development of Mexico: Its Structure and Growth since 1950.* New York: Praeger, 1969.

Whetten, N. L. *Rural Mexico.* Chicago: University of Chicago Press, 1948.

Wilkie, Raymond. *San Miguel: A Mexican Collective Ejido.* Stanford, Calif.: Stanford University Press, 1971.

Nicaragua

Adams, Richard N. *Nicaragua.* Cultural Surveys of Panama, Nicaragua, Guatemala, El Salvador, Honduras. Pan American Sanitary Bureau, Scientific Publication no. 33. Washington: World Health Organization, 1957.

International Bank for Reconstruction and Development. *The Economic Development of Nicaragua.* Baltimore: Johns Hopkins Press, 1953.
International Labour Organization. *Social Consequences of Technological Development in Plantations.* Geneva: International Labour Office, 1970.
Rippy, J. Fred. "State Department Operations: The Rama Road." *Inter-American Economic Affairs* 9 (Summer 1955), 17–32.
Ryan, John Morris, et al. *Area Handbook for Nicaragua.* Washington: Government Printing Office, 1970.
Taylor, B. W. *Ecological Land Use Surveys in Nicaragua.* Managua: Instituto de Fomento Nacional, 1959–1961.
West, Robert C., and John Augelli. *Middle America: Its Lands and Peoples.* Englewood Cliffs, N.J.: Prentice-Hall, 1966.
Winters, D. H. "The Agricultural Economy of Nicaragua." *Journal of Inter-American Studies* 6 (October 1964), 501–517.
Zelaya, José M. *Agriculture in Nicaragua.* Washington: Pan American Union, 1945.

Panama

Adams, Richard N. *Panama.* Cultural Surveys of Panama, Nicaragua, Guatemala, El Salvador, Honduras. Washington: World Health Organization, Pan American Sanitary Bureau, Scientific Publication no. 33, 1957.
Fuson, R. H. "House Types of Central Panama." *Annals of the Association of American Geographers* 54 (June 1964), 190–208.
Guzmán, Louis E. *Farming and Farmlands in Panama.* Department of Geography Research Paper no. 44. Chicago: University of Chicago Press, 1956.
Inter-American Committee for Agricultural Development. *Panama.* Washington: Pan American Union, 1965.
May, Stacy, and Galo Plaza. *The United Fruit Company in Latin America.* Washington: National Planning Association, 1958.
Rubio, A., and L. Guzmán. "Regiones Geográficas Panameñas." *Revista Geográfica* 24 (Jan.–June 1959), 53–66.

Paraguay

Comité Interamericano para el Desarrollo Agrícola. *Inventario de Información Básica para el Desarrollo Agrícola en Latinoamérica: Paraguay.* Washington: Pan American Union, 1963.
Paraguay, Ministerio de Financia. Dirección de Estadística y Censos. *Censo Nacional de Población y Vivienda.* Asunción, 1950.
Paraguay, Ministerio de Hacienda. *Boletín Estadístico del Paraguay.* Asunción, December 1962.
Patty, Gordon. *Agriculture and Trade of Paraguay.* U.S. Department of Agriculture. Economic Research Service, ERS-Foreign 6. June 1961.
Pendle, George. *Paraguay.* New York: Oxford University Press, 1967.
United States, Institute of Inter-American Affairs. *Agricultural Progress in Paraguay.* Washington, 1949.

Peru

Burgess, E. W., and F. H. Harbison. *Casa Grace in Peru.* Washington: National Planning Association, 1954.
Claure, Carlos Martínez. *La Producción de Café en el Perú.* Lima: privately published, 1967.

Comité Interamericano de Desarrollo Agrícola. *Perú: Tenencia de la Tierra y Desarrollo Socio-económico del Sector Agrícola*. Washington: Pan American Union, 1966.

Craig, Wesley W. *From Hacienda to Community: An Analysis of Solidarity and Social Change in Peru*. Latin American Studies Program, Dissertation Series, no. 6. Ithaca, N.Y.: Cornell University, September 1967.

Delavaud, Claude Collin. *Les Régions Côtieres du Pérou Septentrional*. Lima: Institut Français d'Études Andines, 1968.

Ford, Thomas P. *Man and Land in Peru*. Gainesville: University of Florida Press, 1955.

Hammel, E. A. *Power in Ica*. Boston: Little, Brown, 1969.

Matos Mar, José. "Las Haciendas en el Valle de Chancay." in *Les Problèmes Agraires des Amériques Latines*, Paris: Centre National de la Recherche Scientifique, 1967. pp. 317–353.

Miller, Solomon, "The Hacienda and the Plantation in Northern Peru." Ph.D. dissertation, Columbia University, 1964.

Perú, Convenio de Cooperación Técnica. *1963: Estadística Agraria*. Lima, 1964.

Perú, Dirección Nacional de Estadística y Censos. *Primer Censo Nacional Agropecuario*. Lima, 1963.

Porter, Horace G. *The Cotton Industry in Peru*. U.S. Department of Agriculture, Foreign Agricultural Service FAS M-121. September 1961.

El Salvador

Adams, Robert N. *El Salvador*. Cultural Surveys of Panama, Nicarague, Guatemala, El Salvador, Honduras. Pan American Sanitary Bureau, Scientific Publication no. 33. Washington: World Health Organization, 1957.

Choussy, Felix. *Economia Agrícola Salvadoreña*. San Salvador: Biblioteca Universitaria, 1950.

El Salvador, Ministerio de Economia. *El Desarrollo Económico de El Salvador 1948–1957*. San Salvador, 1960.

Loenholdt, Fritz. *The Agricultural Economy of El Salvador*. San Salvador: Mimico, 1953.

West, Robert C., and John Augelli. *Middle America: Its Lands and Peoples*. Englewood Cliffs, N.J.: Prentice-Hall, 1966.

Venezuela

International Bank for Reconstruction and Development. *The Economic Development of Venezuela*. Baltimore: Johns Hopkins Press, 1961.

Venezuela, Dirección General de Estadística y Censos Nacionales. *Anuario Estadístico de Venezuela 1957–1963*. Caracas, 1964.

Venezuela, Dirección General de Estadística y Censos Nacionales. *III Censo Agropecuario 1961: Resumen Parte A y B*. Caracas, 1967.

Venezuela, Dirección de Planificación Agropecuaria. *Atlas Agrícola de Venezuela*. Caracas, 1960.

Venezuela, Ministerio de Agricultura y Cría. *Estados Aragua y Carabobo*. Caracas, 1946.

Venezuela, Ministerio de Agricultura y Cría. *Informe sobre Superficie, Producción, Rendimiento, Importación y Exportación de Productos Agropecuarios 1945–1961*. Caracas, December 1962.

Venezuela, Ministerio de Agricultura y Cría. *Programa Nacional de Extensión*. Caracas, 1963–1968.

NORTH AFRICA AND THE MIDDLE EAST

Algeria

Ageron, Charles-Robert. *Histoire de l'Algérie Contemporaine.* Paris: Presses Universitaires de France, 1970.

Amin, Samir. *L'Économie du Maghreb: La Colonisation et la Décolonisation.* Paris: Éditions de Minuit, 1966.

Hance, William A. *The Geography of Modern Africa.* New York: Columbia University Press, 1964.

Tiano, André. *Le Maghreb entre les Mythes: l'Économie Nord-Africaine depuis l'Indépendance.* Paris: Presses Universitaires de France, 1967.

Tidafi, Tami. *L'Agriculture Algérienne: Conditions et Perspectives d'un Développement Réel.* Paris: Maspero, 1969.

United States Army. *Area Handbook for Algeria.* Washington: Government Printing Office, 1965.

Wolf, Eric R. *Peasant Wars of the Twentieth Century.* New York: Harper & Row, 1969.

Iran

Baldwin, George, B. *Planning and Development in Iran.* Baltimore: Johns Hopkins Press, 1967.

Bémont, Frédy. *L'Iran devant le Progrès.* Paris: Presses Universitaires de France, 1964.

Ginsburg, Norton (ed.). *The Pattern of Asia.* Englewood Cliffs, N.J.: Prentice-Hall, 1958.

Jacobs, Norman. "Economic Rationality and Social Development: An Iranian Case Study." *Studies in Comparative International Development* 2 (1966), 137–142.

Johnson, V. Webster. "Agriculture in the Economic Development of Iran." *Land Economics.* 36 (November 1960), 313–321.

Khatibi, Nosratollah. "Land Reform in Economic Development with Special Reference to the Experience of Iran." In *Man, Food and Agriculture in the Middle-East,* pp. 203–216. Edited by Thomas S. Stickley et al. Beirut: The American University of Beirut, 1969.

United States Army. *Area Handbook for Iran.* Washington: Government Printing Office, 1964.

Warriner, Doreen. *Land Reform in Principle and Practice.* Oxford: Clarendon Press, 1969.

Iraq

Ahmed, Mohammed. "Technological Changes and Agricultural Production in Iraq. In *Man, Food and Agriculture in the Middle-East,* pp. 177–202. Edited by Thomas S. Stickley et al. Beirut: The American University of Beirut, 1969.

Al Barazi, Nuri. *The Geography of Agriculture in Irrigated Areas of the Middle Euphrates Valley.* Bagdad: Al-Aani Press, 1961–1963.

Fisher, W. B. *The Middle East: A Physical, Social and Regional Geography.* New York: Dutton, 1952.

Ginsburg, Norton (ed.). *The Pattern of Asia.* Englewood Cliffs, N.J.: Prentice-Hall, 1958.

Harris, George L. *Iraq: It's People, Its Society, Its Culture.* New Haven: Human Relations Area Files Press, 1958.

Meyer, A. J. *Middle Eastern Capitalism.* Cambridge: Harvard University Press, 1959.

Smith, Harvey, et al. *Area Handbook for Iraq.* Washington: Government Printing Office, 1969.

Warriner, Doreen. *Land Reform and Development in the Middle East.* London: Oxford University Press, 1962.

Warriner, Doreen. *Land Reform in Principle and Practice.* Oxford: Clarendon Press, 1969.

Lebanon

Abu-Izzeddin, Halim Said. *Lebanon and Its Provinces.* Beirut: Khayats, 1963.

Binder, Leonard. *Politics in Lebanon.* New York: Wiley, 1966.

Ginsburg, Norton (ed.). *The Pattern of Asia.* Englewood Cliffs, N.J.: Prentice-Hall, 1958.

Khalidy, Ramzi. "Current Status and Future Outlook of Major Lebanese Fruit Crops." In *Man, Food and Agriculture in the Middle-East,* pp. 527–534. Edited by Thomas S. Stickley et al. Beirut: The American University of Beirut, 1969.

Longrigg, Stephen H. *The Middle-East: A Social Geography.* London: Gerald Duckworth & Co., 1963.

Meyer, A. J. *Middle Eastern Capitalism.* Cambridge: Harvard University Press, 1959.

Peretz, Don. *The Middle-East Today.* New York: Holt, Rinehart, 1963.

Smith, Harvey, et al. *Area Handbook for Lebanon.* Washington: Government Printing Office, 1969.

Libya

Church, Harrison R. J., et al. *Africa and the Islands.* London: Longmans, Green, 1964.

Hance, William A. *The Geography of Modern Africa.* New York: Columbia University Press, 1964.

Higgins, Benjamin H. *The Economic and Social Development of Libya.* New York: United Nations, 1953.

Owen, Roger. *Libya: A Brief Political and Economic Survey.* London: Oxford University Press, 1961.

Stanford Research Institute. *Area Handbook for Libya.* Washington: Government Printing Office, 1969.

United Kingdom of Libya, Ministry of Agriculture. *1960 Census of Agriculture.* Tripoli, 1962.

Morocco

Amin, Samir. *L'Économie du Maghreb.* Paris: Éditions de Minuit, 1966.

Ashford, Douglas E. *Political Change in Morocco.* Princeton, N.J.: Princeton University Press, 1961

France, Centre National du Commerce Extérieur. *Le Marché Marocain.* Paris, 1961.

Gallisot, René *Le Patronat Européen au Maroc: Action Sociale, Action Politique.* Rabat: Éditions Techniques Nord-Africaines, 1964.

Morocco, Division de la Coordination Économique et du Plan. *Plan Quinquennal 1968–1972.* Rabat, n.d.

Morocco, Economic Coordination and Planning Division. *Three Year Plan: 1965–1967*. Rabat, 1965.

Morocco, Service Central des Statistiques. *Résultats de l' Enquête à Objectifs Multiples, 1961–1963*. Rabat, 1964.

Mountjoy, Alan B., and Cliffard Embleton. *Africa: A New Geographical Survey*. New York: Praeger, 1967.

Quarterly Economic Review of Algeria, Morocco, Tunisia. London: The Economist Intelligence Unit, July, 1965.

United States Army. *Area Handbook for Morocco*. Washington: Government Printing Office, 1965.

Syria

Bureau des Documentations Syriennes et Arabes. *Étude sur la Syrie Économique*. Damascus, 1958.

El-Ricaby, Akram. "Land Tenure in Syria." In *Conference on World Land Tenure Problems*, pp. 84–94. Edited by Kenneth H. Parsons et al. Madison: University of Wisconsin Press, 1956.

Hansen, Bent. *Economic Development in Syria*. Santa Monica, Calif.: Rand Corporation, 1969.

Longrigg, Stephen H. *The Middle-East: a Social Geography*. London: Gerald Duckworth, 1963.

Meyer, A. J. *Middle Eastern Capitalism*. Cambridge: Harvard University Press, 1959.

Office Arabe de Presse et de Documentation. *Rapport 1966–1967 sur l'Économie Syrienne*. Damascus: Antoine Guiné, 1967.

United Nations, Economic and Social Office in Beirut. "Plan Formulation and Development Prospectives in Syria." In *Studies on Selected Development Problems in Various Countries in the Middle East*. New York, 1969.

United States Army. *Area Handbook for Syria*. Washington: Government Printing Office, 1965.

Warriner, Doreen. *Land Reform and Development in the Middle East*. London: Oxford University Press, 1962.

Sudan

Barbour, Kenneth M. *The Republic of the Sudan: A Regional Geography*. London: University of London Press, 1961.

Cookson, John, et al. *Area Handbook for the Republic of the Sudan*. Washington: Government Printing Office, 1964.

Gaitskell, Arthur. *Gezira: A Story of Development in the Sudan*. London: Faber & Faber, 1961.

McLoughlin, Peter F. M. "Economic Development and the Heritage of Slavery in the Sudan Republic." *Africa* 32 (October 1962), 355–391.

Tothill, John. *Agriculture in the Sudan*. London: Oxford University Press, 1948.

Tunisia

Amin, Samir. *L'Économie du Maghreb*. Paris: Éditions de Minuit, 1966.

Despois, Jean. *La Tunisie Orientale: Sahel et Basse Steppe*. Paris: Publications de la Faculté des Lettres d'Alger, 1940.

Despois, Jean. *La Tunisie: ses Régions*. Paris: Armand Colin, 1961.

Despois, Jean, and René Raynal *Géographie de l'Afrique du Nord-Ouest.* Paris: Payot, 1967.
Poncet, Jean. *Paysages et Problèmes Ruraux en Tunisie.* Paris: Presses Universitaires de France, 1962.
Reese, Howard, et al. *Area Handbook for Tunisia.* Washington: Government Printing Office, 1970.
Sebag, Paul. *La Tunisie: Essai de Monographie.* Paris: Éditions Sociales, 1951.
Tiano, André. *Le Maghreb et ses Mythes: L'Économie Nord-Africaine depuis l'Indépendance.* Paris: Presses Universitaires de France, 1967.

Turkey

Government of Turkey. *1950 Agricultural Census Results.* Ankara, 1956.
Government of Turkey, State Institute of Statistics. *Statistical Yearbook of Turkey, 1968.* Ankara, 1969.
Roberts, Thomas, et al. *Area Handbook for the Republic of Turkey.* Washington: Government Printing Office, 1969.

United Arab Republic

Issawi, Charles. *Egypt in Revolution: An Economic Analysis.* London: Oxford University Press, 1963.
Mead, Donald. *Growth and Structural Change in the Egyptian Economy.* Homewood, Ill.: Richard D. Irwin, 1967.
Oxford Regional Economic Atlas: The Middle East and North Africa. London: Oxford University Press, 1960.
el-Sarki, Mohamed Youssef. *La Monoculture du Coton en Egypte et le Développement Économique.* Geneva: Droz, 1964.
U.S. Department of Agriculture, Economic Research Service. *Agricultural Development in the Nile Basin.* Foreign Agricultural Economic Report no. 48. Washington, 1968.
U.S. Department of Agriculture, Economic Research Service. *The Agricultural Economy of the United Arab Republic (Egypt).* Foreign Agricultural Economic Report no. 21. Washington, 1964.
Warriner, Doreen. *Land Reform and Development in the Middle East.* London: Oxford University Press, 1962.

SOUTH AND SOUTHEAST ASIA

Burma

Bixler, Norma. *Burma: A Profile.* New York: Praeger, 1971.
Cook, B. C. A. *Economic and Commercial Conditions in Burma.* London: Overseas Economic Surveys, 1957.
Henderson, John, et al. *Area Handbook for Burma.* Washington: Government Printing Office, 1971.
Tinker, Hugh. *The Union of Burma.* London: Oxford University Press, 1957.
Trager, Frank N. *Building a Welfare State in Burma.* New York: Institute of Pacific Relations, 1958.
Walinsky, Louis J. *Economic Development in Burma 1951–1960.* New York: The Twentieth Century Fund, 1962.

Union of Burma, Central Statistical and Economics Department. *Census of Agriculture*. Rangoon, 1955.
Union of Burma, Central Statistical and Economics Department. *Statistical Yearbook 1963*. Rangoon, 1964.
Union of Burma, Ministry of National Planning. *Economic Survey of Burma*. Rangoon, 1964.

Cambodia

American University. *Area Handbook for Cambodia*. Washington: Government Printing Office, 1968.
Cambodia, Direction de la Statistique et des Études Économiques. *Annuaire Statistique du Cambodge*. Pnompenh, 1966.
Nuttonson, M. Y. *The Physical Environment and Agriculture of Vietnam, Laos and Cambodia*. Washington: American Institute of Crop Ecology, 1963.
Steinberg, David J., et al. *Cambodia: Its People, Its Society, Its Culture*. New Haven, Conn.: Human Relations Area Files Press, 1959.

Ceylon (Sri Lanka)

Ceylon, Department of Census and Statistics. *Census of Agriculture, 1952*, vols. 1–2. Colombo, 1956.
Ceylon, Department of Census and Statistics. *Census of Agriculture, 1962*. Vols. 1–3. Colombo, 1965.
Ceylon, Rubber Control Department. *Administration Report of the Rubber Controller for 1968*. Colombo, 1969.
Huttman, John Peter. "Land Tenure, Political Institutions, and Agricultural Production in Ceylon." M.A. thesis, University of California, Berkeley, n.d.
International Bank for Reconstruction and Development. *The Economic Development of Ceylon*. Baltimore: Johns Hopkins Press, 1953.
Sarkar, N. K. *The Demography of Ceylon*. Colombo, 1957.

China (Republic)

China, Ministry of Economic Affairs. *The Sugar Industry in Taiwan, Republic of China*. Taipei, 1958.
China, Ministry of Economic Affairs. *Taiwan Sugar*. Taipei, 1955.
Committee for Economic Development. *Economic Development Issues: Greece, Israel, Taiwan, Thailand*. New York, 1968.
Ginsburg, Norton F. *Economic Resources and Development of Formosa*. New York: Institute of Pacific Relations, 1953.
Hsieh, Chiao-min. *Taiwan: A Geography in Perspective*. London: Butterworth, 1964.
Jacoby, Neil H. *U.S. Aid to Taiwan*. New York: Praeger, 1966.
Jen-Hu, Chang. *Agricultural Geography of Taiwan*. Taipei: China Agricultural Service, 1953.
Klein, Sidney. *The Pattern of Land Tenure Reform in East Asia*. New York: Bookman, 1958.
Nuttonson, M. Y. *The Physical Environment and Agriculture of Central and South China, Hong Kong and Taiwan*. Washington: American Institute of Crop Ecology, 1963.
Riggs, Fred W. *Formosa under Chinese Nationalist Rule*. New York: Macmillan, 1952.

Rhynsburger, Willert. *Area and Resources Survey: Taiwan*. Taipei: U.S. Security Mission to China, 1956.

Shen, T. H. *Agricultural Development on Taiwan since World War II*. Ithaca, N.Y.: Comstock, 1964.

India

Binani, G. D. and T. V. Rao, eds. *India at a Glance*. Calcutta: Orient Longmans, 1953.

Harler, C. R., *The Culture and Marketing of Tea*, 3d ed. London: Oxford University Press, 1964.

Hirsh, Leon V. *Marketing in an Underdeveloped Economy: The North Indian Sugar Industry*. Englewood Cliffs, N.J.: Prentice-Hall, 1961.

India, Bureau of Labour. *Agricultural Labour in India: Report on the Second Enquiry*, vol. 1. Delhi, 1960.

India, Central Statistical Organization. Department of Statistics. *Monthly Statistics of the Production of Selected Industries of India*. Calcutta, October 1958–May 1971.

India, Central Tobacco Committee. *Indian Tobacco: A Monograph*. Madras, 1960.

India, Council of Scientific and Industrial Research. *The Wealth of India: A Dictionary of Indian Raw Materials and Industrial Products*. Delhi, 1948.

India, Central Tobacco Committee. *Indian Tobacco Statistics, 1939–1959*. Madras, 1960.

India, Directorate of Economics and Statistics, Ministry of Agriculture. *Agricultural Situation in India*. Delhi, 1971.

India, Directorate of Economics and Statistics, Ministry of Food and Agriculture. *Abstract of Agricultural Statistics, India, 1957*. Delhi, 1959.

India, Directorate of Economics and Statistics, Ministry of Food and Agriculture. *Economic Survey of Indian Agriculture, 1959–60*. Delhi, 1961.

India, Directorate of Economics and Statistics, Ministry of Food and Agriculture. *Indian Agricultural Atlas*, 2d ed. Delhi, 1958.

India, Directorate of Economics and Statistics, Ministry of Food, Agriculture, Community Development and Co-operation. *Economic Survey of Indian Agriculture 1967–68*. Delhi, 1970.

India, Directorate of Economics and Statistics, Ministry of Food, Agriculture, Community Development and Co-operation. *Indian Agriculture in Brief*, 9th ed. Delhi, 1968.

India, Ministry of Agriculture. *Brochure on the Marketing of Groundnuts in India*. Delhi, 1950.

India, Ministry of Food and Agriculture. *Atlas on Marketing Aspects of Commercial Crops*. Delhi, 1957.

India. Ministry of Information and Broadcasting, Publications Division. *Facts about India*. Faridabad, 1967.

India. Ministry of Information and Broadcasting, Publications Division. *India: A Reference Annual, 1964*, Delhi, 1964.

India Ministry of Labour and Employment. *Report of the Central Wage Board for the Sugar Industry, 1960*. Delhi, 1961.

India. *Report of the Plantation Inquiry Commission, 1956: Part I. Tea*. Delhi, 1956.

India. *Report on the Plantation Inquiry Commission. 1956: Part II. Coffee*. Delhi, 1956.

Mujumdar, N. A. *Some Problems of Underemployment: An Analytical Study of Underemployment in the Agricultural Sector*. Bombay: Popular Book Depot, 1961.

420   *Agrarian Revolution*

Nanjundayya, C., et al. *Cotton in India: A Monograph*, vol. 3. Bombay: India Central Cotton Committee, 1960.
Narayanaswamy Naidu, B. V., and S. Hariharan. *Groundnut: Marketing and Other Allied Problems.* Annamalainagar: Annamalai University, 1941.
Patel, Surendra J. *Agricultural Labourers in Modern India and Pakistan.* Bombay: Current Book House, 1952.
Ramamurti, B. *Agricultural Labour: How They Work and Live.* Delhi, 1954.
Rege, D. V. *Report on an Enquiry into Conditions of Labour in Plantations in India.* Delhi, 1948.
Sikka, S. M., et al. *Cotton in India: A Monograph*, vol. 6. Bombay: Indian Central Cotton Committee, 1960.
United Nations, Food and Agriculture Organization, Committee on Commodities. *A Review of Recent Developments in Pepper Production and Marketing Problems.* CCP: 69/19. July 25, 1969.
U.S. Department of Agriculture. *World Pepper Report: Part I. India and Ceylon.* Foreign Agricultural Circular FTEA 4–55. Washington, Aug. 12, 1955.

Indonesia

American University. *Area Handbook for Indonesia.* Washington: Government Printing Office, 1964.
"The Cultivation of Pepper in Indonesia." *The Economic Review of Indonesia*, 6 (October–November 1952), 112–115.
Grant, Bruce. *Indonesia.* Melbourne: Wilke and Co., 1964.
Indonesia, Central Bureau of Statistics. *Statistical Pocketbook of Indonesia, 1964–1967.* Djakarta: Biro Pusat Statistik, 1968.
Indonesia: Review of Commercial Conditions. London: H.M. Stationery Office, 1952.
McVey, Ruth T., ed. *Indonesia.* New Haven: Yale University Southeast Asia Studies, 1963.
Morgan, William. *Economic Survey of the Tea Plantation Industry.* Brussels: The International Federation of Plantation, Agricultural and Allied Workers, 1960.
R.M. "The Price Level of Rubber from Indonesia." *The Economic Review of Indonesia*, 6 (October–November 1952), 102–104.
United Nations, Food and Agriculture Organization. *World Crop Harvest Calendar.* Rome, 1959.
U.S. Department of Commerce. *Investment in Indonesia: Basic Information for United States Businessmen.* Washington: Government Printing Office, 1956.

Korea (Republic)

Clare, Kenneth, et al. *Area Handbook for the Republic of Korea.* Washington: Government Printing Office, 1969.
Clyde, Paul H., and Burton F. Beers. *The Far East: A History of the Western Impact and the Eastern Response.* Englewood Cliffs, N.J.: Prentice-Hall, 1966.
Cole, David S., and Princeton N. Lyman. *Korean Development: The Interplay of Politics and Economics.* Cambridge: Harvard University Press, 1971.
Klein, Sidney. *The Pattern of Land Tenure Reform in East Asia.* New York: Bookman, 1958.
Korean Reconstruction Bank. *Report on Mining and Manufacturing Survey 1967.* Seoul: Eung Suh Park, 1968.
Lee, Hoon K. *Land Utilization and Rural Economy in Korea.* Shanghai: Kelly and Welsh, 1936.

McCune, Shannon. *Korea's Heritage: A Regional and Social Geography.* Tokyo: Tuttle Co., 1956.
Reeve, W. D. *The Republic of Korea: A Political and Economic Study.* London: Oxford University Press, 1963.
Republic of Korea, Bureau of Statistics. *Korea Statistical Yearbook.* Seoul, 1965.
United Nations Korean Reconstruction Agency. *Rehabilitation and Development of Agriculture, Forestry, and Fisheries in South Korea.* New York: Columbia University Press, 1954.

Malaysia

Edgar, A. T. *Manual of Rubber Planting (Malaya).* Kuala Lumpur: The Incorporated Society of Planters, 1958.
Federation of Malaya. *Annual Report of the Department of Agriculture, 1959, 1960, 1961, 1962, 1963.* Kuala Lumpur, n.d.
Federation of Malaya. *Census of Agriculture, 1960: Preliminary Report Number Twelve: Farm Labour.* Kuala Lumpur, 1962.
Gamba, Charles. *Labour Law in Malaya.* Singapore: Donald Moore, 1957.
Ginsburg, Norton, and Chester Roberts, Jr. *Malaya.* Seattle: University of Washington Press, 1958.
Gullick, J. M. *Malaysia.* New York: Praeger, 1969.
Ooi, Jin-Bee. *Land, People and Economy in Malaya.* London: Longmans, Green, 1963.
Purcell, Victor. *Malaysia.* London: Thames and Hudson, 1965.
Robequain, Charles. *Malaya, Indonesia, Borneo, and the Philippines.* London: Longmans, Green, 1958.
Silcock, T. H. *The Economy of Malaya: An Essay in Colonial Political Economy.* Singapore: Eastern Universities Press, 1960.
Wilson, Joan. *The Singapore Rubber Market.* Singapore: Eastern Universities Press, 1958.

Pakistan

Abbas, S. A. *Supply and Demand of Selected Agricultural Products in Pakistan 1961–1975.* London: Oxford University Press, 1967.
Andrus, Russel J., and Azizali F. Mohammed. *The Economy of Pakistan.* Stanford, Calif.: Stanford University Press, 1958.
Ghosh, Kali Sharan. *Economic Resources of India and Pakistan.* Calcutta: Basu Publishing Co., 1956.
Human Relations Area Files. *The Economy of Pakistan,* vols. 1–2. New Haven, Conn., 1956.
Khan, M. H. *The Role of Agriculture in Economic Development: A Case Study of Pakistan.* Wageningen: Center for Agricultural Publications and Documentation, 1966.
Nyrop, Richard, et al., *Area Handbook for Pakistan.* Washington: Government Printing Office, 1971.
Pakistan, Agricultural Census Organization. *1960 Census of Agriculture,* vols. 1–2. Karachi, 1962.
Pakistan, Ministry of Agriculture and Works, *Agricultural Statistics of Pakistan.* Karachi, 1970.
Pakistan, Ministry of Agriculture and Works, *Yearbook of Agricultural Statistics: 1968.* Karachi, 1969.

Peach, W. N., M. Uzair, and G. W. Rucker. *Basic Data of the Economy of Pakistan.* Karachi: Oxford University Press, 1959.

Platt, Raye R. (ed). *Pakistan: A Compendium.* New York: American Geographical Society, 1961.

West Pakistan, Department of Agriculture. *West Pakistan Agricultural Statistics.* Series no. 1—Crops. 1967.

Philippines

Arenato, Salvador. "Philippine Economic Problems, Progress and Programmes." In *Economic Problems of Underdeveloped Countries in Asia*, pp. 194–213. Edited by B. K. Madan. New York: Russel & Russel, 1967.

Chaffee, Frederick, et. al. *Area Handbook for the Philippines.* Washington: Government Printing Office, 1969.

Cutshall, Alden. *The Philippines: Nation of Islands.* Princeton, N.J.: Van Nostrand, 1964.

Dalisay, Amando. *Development of Economic Policy in Philippines Agriculture.* Manila: Phoenix Publishing House. 1959.

Dobby, E. H. D. *Southeast Asia.* London: University of London Press, 1966.

Espiritu, Socorro C., and Chester L. Hunt, *Social Foundations of Community Development.* Manila: R. M. Garcia, 1964.

Estrella, Conrado F. *The Democratic Answer to the Philippine Agrarian Problem.* Manila: Solidaridad, 1969.

Galang, Zoilo, ed. *Encyclopedia of the Philippines*, vols. 6–7 .Manila: Exequiel Floro, 1952.

Ginsburg, Norton, ed. *The Pattern of Asia.* Englewood Cliffs, N.J.: Prentice-Hall, 1958.

Jacoby, Erich H. *Agrarian Unrest in Southeast Asia.* Bombay: Asia Publishing House, 1961.

Kurihara, Kenneth. *Labor in the Philippines Economy.* Stanford, Calif.: Stanford University Press, 1945.

Philippine Sugar Industry. *The Sugar News Press.* Manila, 1964.

Philippines, Bureau of the Census and Statistics. *Census of the Philippines: Report by Province.* Manila, 1960.

Piguing, Rafael. *The Philippine Sugar Industry.* East Lansing, Mich.: Michigan State College of Agriculture, 1935.

Runes, Ildefonso. *General Standards of Living and Wages of Workers in the Philippine Sugar Industry.* Manila: Philippine Council, 1939.

Takahashi, Akira. *Land and Peasants in Central Luzon.* Tokyo: Institute of Developing Economies, 1969.

Tiongson, Fabian A. *Improved Merchandising of Selected Farm Products.* Quezon City: University of the Philippines, Community Development Research Council, 1964.

Thailand

Blanchard, Wendell, with Henry C. Ahalt, et al. *Thailand: Its People, Its Society, Its Culture.* New Haven: Human Relations Area Files Press, 1957.

Judd, Laurence. *Dry Rice Agriculture in Northern Thailand.* Data Paper no. 52. Ithaca, N.Y.: Cornell University Press, 1964.

Nuttonson, M. Y. *The Physical Environment and Agriculture of Thailand.* Washington: American Institute of Crop Ecology, 1963.

Silcock, T. H. *The Economic Development of Thai Agriculture.* Ithaca, N.Y.: Cornell University Press, 1970.

Sriplung, Somnuk, *Potentials in the Economic Development of Thailand's Agriculture.* Bangkok: Ministry of Agriculture, n.d.

Thailand, Ministry of Agriculture. *Agriculture in Thailand.* Bangkok, 1957.

Thailand, Ministry of Agriculture. *Report on Economic Survey of Rice Farmers in Nakorn Pathom Province.* Bangkok, 1957.

Thailand, Ministry of Agriculture. *Thailand and Her Agricultural Problems.* Bangkok, 1950.

Thailand, National Statistical Office. *Census of Agriculture, 1963.* Bangkok: Office of the Prime Minister, n.d.

Vietnam (Republic)

American University. *Area Handbook for the Republic of Viet-Nam.* Washington: Government Printing Office, 1964.

Hammer, Ellen. *Vietnam Yesterday and Today.* New York: Holt, Rinehart, 1966.

Lê-Châu. *La Révolution Paysanne du Sud Viet Nam.* Paris: Maspero, 1966.

Nighswonger, William A. *Rural Pacification in Vietnam.* New York: Praeger, 1966.

Nuttonson, M. Y. *The Physical Environment and Agriculture of Vietnam, Laos and Cambodia.* Washington: American Institute for Crop Ecology, 1963.

Republic of Viet-Nam, National Institute of Statistics. *Economic Situation in Viet-Nam.* Saigon, 1967.

République du Viet-Nam. Institut National de la Statistique. *Annuaire Statistique du Viet-Nam.* Saigon, 1962.

Règublique du Viet-Nam. Institut National de la Statistique. *Évolution Économique du Viet-Nam en 1960.* Saigon, 1961.

Sansom, Robert L. *The Economics of Insurgency in the Mekong Delta of Vietnam.* Cambridge: M.I.T. Press, 1970.

Thái-công-Tung. *Natural Environment and Land Use in South Vietnam.* Saigon: Ministry of Agriculture, 1967.

Van-Hao, Nguyen. *Les Problèmes de la Nouvelle Agriculture Vietnamienne.* Geneva: Droz, 1963.

Van Vinh, Nguyen. *Les Réformes Agraires au Vietnam.* Louvain: Librairie Universitaire, 1961.

SUB-SAHARAN AFRICA

Angola

Angola, Direcçao dos Servicos de Economica e Estatística Geral. Anuário Estatístico: Luanda, 1960.

Angola, Instituto de Investigação Agronomica de Angola. *Relatorio de 1965.* Nova Lisboã, Angola, 1965.

Dongen, Irene S. van. "Coffee Trade, Coffee Regions and Coffee Ports in Angola." *Economic Geography.* 37 (October 1961), 320–346.

Dos Santos Thomas, Alfonso. *Angola, Coração do Imperio.* Lisbon: Republica Portuguesa, 1945.

Duffy, James. *A Question of Slavery.* Cambridge: Harvard University Press, 1967.

Ehnmanrk, Anders, and P. Wastberg, *Angola and Mozambique: The Case against Portugal.* London: Pall Mall, 1963.

Gonzaga, Norberto. *Angola: A Brief Survey.* Lisbon: Centro de Informação e Turismo de Angola, 1967.
Great Britain, Commercial Relations and Exports Department. *Portuguese West Africa, Angola.* London: H.M. Stationery Office, 1949.
Phillips, John. *Agriculture and Ecology in Africa.* New York: Praeger, 1959.
Urquhart, Alvin W. *Patterns of Settlement and Subsistence in Southwestern Angola.* Washington: National Academy of Sciences, 1963.

Cameroon

Fordham, Paul. *The Geography of African Affairs.* Baltimore: Penguin Books, 1965.
Gardinier, David E. *Cameroon: United Nations Challenge to French Policy.* London: Oxford University Press, 1963.
Legum, Colin, and John Drysdale. *Africa Contemporary Record: Annual Survey and Documents 1969–1970.* Exeter, England: Africa Research Ltd., 1969.
Lembezat. B. *Cameroun.* Paris: Nouvelles Éditions Latines, 1964.
République Fédérale du Cameroun. *Cameroun 1966: Bilan de Cinq Années d'Indépendance.* 1966.

Central African Republic

Church, Harrison R. J., et al. *Africa and the Islands.* London: Longmans, Green, 1964.
International Monetary Fund. *Surveys of African Economies,* vol. 1. Washington, 1968.
Mortimer, Edward. *France and the Africans 1944/60.* London: Faber & Faber, 1969.
Thompson, V., and R. Adloff. *The Emerging States of French Equatorial Africa.* Stanford, Calif.: Stanford University Press, 1969.
United States, Agency for International Development. *A.I.D. Economic Data Book: Africa.* Washington, 1968.

Congo (Zaire)

Belgium, Belgian Congo and Ruanda-Urundi Information Office. *Belgian Congo,* vols. 1 and 3. Brussels, 1961.
Belgium Ministère des Affaires Africaines. *La Situation Économique du Congo Belge et du Ruanda-Urundi en 1969.* Brussels, 1960.
Belgium, Ministère des Affaires Africaines. *Volume Jubilaire 1910–1960 du Bulletin Agricole du Congo Belge et du Ruanda-Urundi.* Brussels, 1961.
Bouvier, Paule. *L'Accession du Congo Belge a l'Indépendance: Essai d'Analyse Sociologique.* Brussels: Université Libre de Bruxelles, 1965.
Carter, Gwendolen M. *Five African States: Responses to Diversity.* Ithaca, N.Y.: Cornell University Press, 1963.
Drachoussoff. V. "Agricultural Change in the Belgian Congo: 1945–1960." *Food Research Institute Studies* 5 (May–Aug. 1965), 137–201.
Fédération des Associations Provinciales des Entreprises du Congo. *The Congolese Economy on the Eve of Independence.* Brussels: Federation of Congolese Enterprises, 1960.
Hathcock, James. *A Study in Agricultural Conditions in the Belgian Congo and Ruanda-Urundi.* Paris: Office of the United States, Special Representative in Europe, 1952.
Institut National pour l'Étude Agronomique du Congo Belge. *Normes de Main-d'oeuvre pour les Travaux Agricoles au Congo Belge.* Brussels, 1958.

Institut de Recherches Économiques et Sociales. *Cahiers Économiques et Sociaux Kinshasa.* Université Lovanium, 1969.

Joye, Pierre, and Rosine Lewin. *Les Trusts au Congo.* Brussels. Sociéte Populaire d'Éditions, 1961.

Lemarchand, René. *Political Awakening in the Belgian Congo.* Berkeley: University of California Press, 1964.

McDonald, Gordon, et al. *Area Handbook for the Democratic Republic of the Congo (Congo Kinshasa).* Washington: Government Printing Office, 1971.

Merlier, Michel. *Le Congo de la Colonisation Belge à l'Indépendance.* Paris: Maspero, 1962.

Miracle, Marvin P. *Agriculture in the Congo Basin.* Madison: University of Wisconsin Press, 1967.

République Démocratique du Congo, Bureau du President, Bilan, *1965–1970.* Kinshasa, 1970.

U.S. Department of Agriculture, Foreign Agricultural Service. *The Agriculturau Economy of the Belgian Congo and Ruanda-Urundi.* FAS M-88. Washington: Government Printing Office, 1960.

Young, Crawford. *Politics in the Congo: Decolonization and Independence.* Princeton, N.J.: Princeton University Press, 1965.

Ghana

Boateng, E. A. *A Geography of Ghana.* London: Cambridge University Press, 1954.

Hill, Polly. *The Gold Coast Cocoa Farmer: A Preliminary Survey.* London: Oxford University Press, 1957.

Hill, Polly. *The Migrant Cocoa Farmers of Southern Ghana.* London: Cambridge University Press, 1963.

Hill, Polly. *Studies in Rural Capitalism in West Africa.* London: Cambridge University Press, 1970.

Killick, Tony. "Cocoa." In *A Study of Contemporary Ghana.* Vol. 1, pp. 236–249. Edited by Walter Birmingham et al. London: Allen & Unwin, 1966.

La Anyane, Seth. *Ghana Agriculture: Its Economic Development from Early Times to the Middle of the Twentieth Century.* London: Oxford University Press, 1963.

Wills, J. Brian, ed. *Agriculture and Land Use in Ghana.* London: Oxford University Press, 1962.

Guinea

Adloff, Richard. *West Africa: The French-speaking Nations.* New York: Holt, Rinehart, 1964.

Ameillon, B. *La Guinée: Bilan d'une Indépendance.* Paris: Maspero, 1964.

American University. *Area Handbook for Guinea.* Washington: Government Printing Office, 1961.

Church, Harrison R. J. *Africa and the Islands.* London: Longmans, Green, 1964.

Church, Harrison R. J. *Environment and Policies in West Africa.* New York: Van Nostrand, 1963.

Church, Harrison R. J. *West Africa.* London: Longmans, Green, 1968.

Gigon, Fernand. *Guinée, État-Pilote.* Paris: Plon, 1959.

Ord, H. W., and I. Livingstone. *An Introduction to West African Economics.* London: Heinemann, 1969.

Mortimer, Edward. *France and the Africans 1944–1960.* London: Faber & Faber, 1960.

Woddis, Jack. *L'Avenir de l'Afrique.* Paris: Maspero, 1964.

Ivory Coast

Adloff, Richard. *West Africa: The French-speaking Nations Yesterday and Today.* New York: Holt, Rinehart, 1964.
American University. *Area Handbook for the Ivory Coast.* Washington: Government Printing Office, 1962.
Holas, Bohumil. *Changements Sociaux en Côte d'Ivoire.* Paris: Presses Universitaires de France, 1961.
Holas, Bohumil. *La Côte d'Ivoire: Passé, Présent, Perspectives.* Paris: P. Geuthner, 1965.
Ivory Coast, Direction de la Statistique et des Études Économiques et Démographiques. *Les Comptes Économiques de la Côte d'Ivoire 1958 et 1960.* Abidjan, 1961.
Jakande, L. K. *West Africa Annual.* Lagos: Academy Press, 1967.
Oboli, H. O. N. *An Outline Geography of West Africa.* London: George G. Harrap, 1967.

Kenya

Barnett, Donald, and Karari Njama. *Mau Mau from Within.* New York: Modern Reader Paperbacks, 1966.
International Bank for Reconstruction and Development. *The Economic Development of Kenya.* Baltimore: Johns Hopkins Press, 1963.
International Monetary Fund. *Surveys of African Economies.* Vol. II. Washington, 1969.
Kenya. *Development Plan, 1965/1966 to 1969/1970.* Nairobi, 1966.
Kenya, Ministry of Finance and Economic Planning, Economics and Statistics Division. *Agricultural Census, 1963.* Nairobi, 1964.
Kenya, Statistics Division. *Economic Survey, 1968.* Nairobi. 1969.
O'Connor, A. M. *An Economic Geography of East Africa.* London: G. Bell & Sons, 1966.
Ominde, S. H. *Land and Population Movements in Kenya.* London: Heinemann, 1968.
Sorenson, M. P. K. *Land Reform in the Kikuyu Country: A Study in Government Policy.* London: Oxford University Press, 1968.

Liberia

Clower, Robert, et al. *Growth without Development: An Economic Survey of Liberia.* Evanston, Ill.: Northwestern University Press, 1966.
Liebenow, J. *Liberia: The Evolution of Privilege.* Ithaca, N.Y.: Cornell University Press, 1969.
McLaughlin, Russell U. *Foreign Investment and Development in Libia.* New York: Praeger, 1966.
Taylor, Wayne C. *The Firestone Operations in Liberia.* Washington: National Planning Association, 1956.

Malagasy Republic

Gendarme, René. *L'Économie de Madagascar: Diagnostic et Perspectives de Développement.* Paris: Cujas, 1963.
Malagasy, Commissariat Général au Plan. *Économie Malagache: Évolution 1950–1960.* Tananarive, 1962.

Malagasy, Institut National de la Statistique et de la Recherche Économique. *Inventaire Socio-économique de Madagascar 1960–65.* Tananarive, 1966.
Malagasy, Institut National de la Statistique et des Études Économiques. *Enquête Agricole.* Tananarive, 1966.
Stratton, Arthur. *The Great Red Island.* New York: Scribner's, 1964.

Malawi

Brelsford, W. V. *Handbook to the Federation of Rhodesia and Nyasaland.* London: Cassell, 1960.
Debenham, Frank. *Nyasaland: The Land of the Lake.* London: H.M. Stationery Office, 1955.
Hornby, A. J. W. *Tobacco Culture, Nyasaland Protectorate.* U.S. Department of Agriculture, Agronomic Series Bulletin 1. Washington, 1926.
Nyasaland, Department of Agriculture. *An Outline of Agrarian Problems and Policy in Nyasaland.* Zomba, 1955.
Nyasaland Protectorate. *Report of a Commission Appointed to Enquire into the Tobacco Industry of Nyasaland.* Zomba, 1939.
Pike, John G. *Malawi: A Political and Economic History.* London: Pall Mall, 1968.
Rhodesia and Nyasaland, Ministry of Economic Affairs. *Report on an Economic Survey of Nyasaland, 1958–59.* Zomba, n.d.
Rhodesia and Nyasaland. *Report of the Select Committee Appointed on the 8th February, 1957, to Consider the Effects of Non-African Agriculture Being Included in the Concurrent Legislative List.* Zomba, n.d.

Mozambique

Azevedo, Ário Lobo. *O Clima de Moçambique e Agricultura.* Lisbon: Papelaria Fernandez Livraria, 1947.
Duffy, James. *A Question of Slavery.* Cambridge: Harvard University Press, 1967.
Ehnmark, Anders, and P. Wästberg. *Angola and Mozambique: The Case against Portugal.* London: Pall Mall, 1963.
Great Britain, Commercial Relations and Exports Department. *Portuguese East Africa, Moçambique.* London: H.M. Stationery Office, 1955.
Phillips, John, *Agriculture and Ecology in Africa.* New York: Praeger, 1959.
Spence, C. F. *Moçambique.* Cape Town: Howard Timmins, 1963.
U.S. Department of Agriculture, Economic Research Service. *The Africa and West Asia Agricultural Service.* ERS–Foreign 117. Washington, 1965.

Nigeria

Buchanan, K. M. and C. J. Pugh. *Land and People in Nigeria.* London: University of London Press, 1966.
Forde, Daryll, and Richenda Scott. *The Native Economies of Nigeria.* London: Faber & Faber, 1946.
Galletti, R. et al. *Nigerian Cocoa Farmers: An Economic Survey of Yoruba Cocoa Farming Families.* London: Oxford University Press, 1958.
Hill, Polly. *Studies in Rural Capitalism in West Africa.* London: Cambridge University Press, 1970.
Oluwasanmi, H. A. *Agriculture and Nigerian Economic Development.* Ibadan: Oxford University Press, 1966.

Southern Rhodesia

Brelsford, W. V. *Handbook to the Federation of Rhodesia and Nyasaland.* London: Cassell, 1960.
Bull, Theodore (ed.). *Rhodesian Perspective.* London: Michael Joseph, 1967.
Rhodesia. *The Development of the Economic Resources of Southern Rhodesia with Particular Reference to the Role of African Agriculture: Report of the Advisory Committee,* by John Phillips et al. 1963.
Rhodesia, Ministry of Finance. *Economic Survey of Rhodesia.* Salisbury, April 1971.
Rhodesia, Ministry of Information. *Farming in Rhodesia.* Salisbury, 1965.
Rhodesia. *Agriculture in Rhodesia: Supplement to Rhodesian Property and Finance.* Salisbury, 1964.
Sadie, J. L. *Planning for the Economic Development of Rhodesia.* Salisbury, 1967.
Stansby, I. "Farm Management: A Business Approach to Farming." *Rhodesia Agricultural Journal* 63 (March–April 1966), 35–40.

Rwanda–Burundi

Association Européene de Sociétés d'Études pour le Développement. *Étude Globale du Développement du Ruanda et du Burundi.* Arnhem, 1961.
Belgium, Monsieur le Ministre des Colonies. *Rapport sur l'Administration Belge du Ruanda-Urundi pendant l'Annee 1954.* Brussels Imprimerie Fr. Van Muysewinkel, 1955.
Le Marchand, René. *Rwanda and Burundi.* New York: Praeger, 1970.
Leurquin, Philippe. *Le Niveau de Vie des Populations Rurales du Ruanda-Urundi.* Leopoldville: Publications de l'Université Louvanium, 1960.
Maquet, Jacques. "La Participation de la Classe Paysanne au Mouvement d'Indepdance du Rwanda." *Cahiers d'Études Africaines,* no. 16, 1964, pp. 552–568.
Nyrop, Richard, et al. *Area Handbook for Rwanda.* Washington: Government Printing Office, 1969.

Senegal

American University, *Area Handbook for Senegal.* Washington: Government Printing Office, 1963.
Church, R. J. Harrison. *West Africa: A Study of the Environment and of Man's Use of It.* London: Longmans, Green, 1966.
Pélissier, Paul. *Les Paysans du Sénégal.* Sain-Yrieux: Imprimerie Fabrègue, 1966.

Somalia

International Bank for Reconstruction and Development. *The Economy of the Trust Territory of Somaliland.* Washington, 1957.
International Monetary Fund. *Surveys of African Economies,* vol. 2. Washington, 1969.
Kaplan, Irving, et al. *Area Handbook for Somalia.* Washington: Government Printing Office, 1969.
United Nations, Food and Agriculture Organization. *Marketing of Bananas: Report to the Government of Somalia.* 1967.

South Africa

Andrews, H. T. et al. (eds.). *South Africa in the Sixties.* Cape Town: The South Africa Foundation, 1962.

Cole, Monica. *South Africa.* London: Methuen, 1961.

Hanekom, A. J. *The South African Wool Industry.* Pretoria: The South African Wool Board, 1960.

Horwitz, Ralph. *The Political Economy of South Africa.* London: Weidenfeld and Nicolson, 1967.

Houghton, D. H. *The South African Economy.* Cape Town: Oxford University Press, 1964.

Hurwitz, Nathan, and Owen Williams. *The Economic Framework of South Africa.* Pietermaritzburg: Shuter and Shooter, 1962.

Sachs, E. S. *The Choice before South Africa.* London: Turnstile Press, 1952.

Van Huyssteen, J. F. "The Sheep and Wool Industry in South Africa." *Agrekon: Quarterly Journal on Agricultural Economics* 1 (April 1962), 28–34.

Tanzania

Fuggles-Couchman, N. R. *Agricultural Change in Tanganyika: 1945–1960.* Stanford, Calif.: Ford Research Institute, 1964.

Guillebaud, C. W. *An Economic Survey of the Sisal Industry of Tanganyika.* Welwyn, England: The Tanganyika Sisal Growers Association, 1958.

Ruthenberg, Hans. *Agricultural Development in Tanganyika.* Berlin: Institut für Wirtschaftsforschung, 1964.

U.S. Department of Agriculture, Foreign Agricultural Service. *Cotton in Tanzania.* FAS M-219. Washington, 1970.

U.S. Department of Agriculture, Foreign Regional Analysis Division. *The Agricultural Economy of Tanganyika.* ERS-Foreign 92. Washington, n.d.

Togo

Cornevin, Robert. *Le Togo.* Paris: Presses Universitaires de France, 1967.

Jakande, L. K. *West Africa Annual.* Lagos: Academy Press, 1967.

Oboli, H. O. N. *An Outline Geography of West Africa.* London: George C. Harrap, 1967.

Togo, Service de la Statistique Générale et de la Comptabilité Économique National. *Annuaire Rétrospectif du Commerce Special du Togo, 1937–1964.* Lomé, 1965.

Uganda

International Bank for Reconstruction and Development. *The Economic Development of Uganda.* Baltimore: Johns Hopkins Press, 1962.

O'Connor, A. M. *An Economic Geography of East Africa.* London: G. Bell & Sons, 1966.

Richards, Audrey I. *Economic Development and Tribal Change.* Cambridge, England: Heffer & Sons, 1954.

Uganda, Department of Lands and Surveys. *Atlas of Uganda.* Kampala: Government Printer, 1962.

Uganda, Ministry of Agriculture and Co-operatives. *Report on the Uganda Census of Agriculture,* vol. 3. Entebbe, 1966.

Uganda Protectorate. Commission of Inquiry into the Coffee Industry. *Report.* Entebbe, 1957.

Wrigley, C. C. *Crops and Wealth in Uganda: A Short Agrarian History.* Kampala: East African Institute of Social Research, 1959.

Zambia

Baldwin, Robert E. *Economic Development and Export Growth: A Study of Northern Rhodesia, 1920–1960.* Berkeley: University of California Press, 1960.

Brelsford, W. V. *Handbook to the Federation of Rhodesia and Nyasaland.* London: Cassell, 1960.

Hall, Richard. *Zambia.* New York: Praeger, 1965.

Northern Rhodesia, Department of Agriculture. *Annual Report for the Year 1955.* Lusaka, 1956.

Republic of Zambia. Central Statistical Office. *Agricultural and Pastoral Production Statistics, 1966.* Lusaka, 1967.

Republic of Zambia, Ministry of Finance. *Economic Report, 1966.* Lusaka, 1966.

Republic of Zambia, Ministry of Labour. *Annual Report of the Department of Labour for the Year 1966.* Lusaka, 1967.

Republic of Zambia, Zambia Information Services. *A Handbook to the Republic of Zambia.* Lusaka, 1965.

INDEX

Mussolini believed that in numbers lay the key to national, economic, political and military strength. Between 1925 and 1943 the Italian Fascist regime sought to translate that belief into policy, and embarked upon a 'demographic battle' to increase the Italian population. Using a combination of propaganda, incentives and penalties, the Fascists waged campaigns to increase the birth rate and decrease infant mortality, to establish demographic colonies in Italy, Libya, and Ethiopia, and to prevent emigration and urbanization. Ultimately they became concerned about demographic 'quality' and introduced laws against miscegenation with Africans and marriage with Jews.

Dictating demography is a detailed examination of that policy. Based on archival, legislative and journalistic sources, it also shows how the Fascists used statistics to mould public opinion and to form policy, and demonstrates the ways in which population theory at the time both reflected and informed official positions. Carl Ipsen argues that Mussolini's demographic policy can tell us something about the contradictory nature of Fascism itself – at once modern and anti-modern, revolutionary and reactionary – and describes the Fascist efforts to mould the Italian population as a telling example of the failed attempt to create a totalitarian Fascist utopia.

Dictating demography

Cambridge Studies in Population, Economy and Society in Past Time 28

Series Editors

ROGER SCHOFIELD
ESRC Cambridge Group for the History of Population and Social Structure

RICHARD SMITH
ESRC Cambridge Group for the History of Population and Social Structure

JAN DE VRIES
University of California at Berkeley

PAUL JOHNSON
London School of Economics and Political Science

Recent work in social, economic and demographic history has revealed much that was previously obscure about societal stability and change in the past. It has also suggested that crossing the conventional boundaries between these branches of history can be very rewarding.

This series exemplifies the value of interdisciplinary work of this kind, and includes books on topics such as family, kinship and neighbourhood; welfare provision and social control; work and leisure; migration; urban growth; and legal structures and procedures, as well as more familiar matters. It demonstrates that, for example, anthropology and economics have become as close intellelectual neighbours to history as have political philosophy or biography.

For a full list of titles in the series, please see end of book

Dictating Demography

The problem of population in Fascist Italy

CARL IPSEN

Indiana University

CAMBRIDGE
UNIVERSITY PRESS

304.60945
I64d

Published by the press Syndicate of the University of Cambridge
The Pitt Building, Trumpington Street, Cambridge CB2 1RP
40 West 20th Street, New York, NY 10011-4211, USA
10 Stamford Road, Oakleigh, Melbourne 3166, Australia

First published 1996

Printed in Great Britain at the University Press, Cambridge

A catalogue record for this book is available from the British Library

Library of Congress cataloguing in publication data
Ipsen, Carl.
Dictating demography : the problem of population in fascist Italy
/ Carl Ipsen.
p.   cm. – (Cambridge studies in population, economy, and
society in past time: 28)
Includes bibliographical references (p.   ).
ISBN 0 521 55452 7 (hc)
1. Italy – Population – History.   2. Italy – Population policy –
History.   3. Italy – History – 1922–1945.   I. Title.   II. Series.
HB3599.I67   1996
304.6′0945′0904–dc20   95–48989 CIP

ISBN 0 521 55452 7 hardback

AL

Contents

vii

Figures

Tables

Acknowledgments

The present work was researched and written during a period of several years most of which I spent in Rome. I have a number of organizations to thank for this opportunity. As a doctoral candidate at the University of California at Berkeley I received the University of California at Berkeley Italian–American Award, a Fulbright grant, a National Institute of Health Traineeship (thanks to the then called Graduate Group in Demography), the Allan Sharlin Memorial Award (Institute of International Studies), the Berkeley Science Historians Award and a Humanities Graduate Research Grant. Recalling that period I would also like to thank my doctoral committee: Jan de Vries, Richard A. Webster, Ronald Lee and John Lesch. I completed the rewriting of the book while a guest, as visiting professor, of the National Institute of Population Research in Rome (Italian National Research Council) and its director Antonio Golini. Final revisions were made as an assistant professor at Indiana University. Thanks to all of them.

Any errors of fact or interpretation are of course mine, but I would like to thank especially those friends and colleagues who devoted time and concentration to any of various drafts and who gave me valuable advice. First I would like to thank those who read and commented on the entire text in one form or several: Massimo Livi Bacci at Florence (who also shared with me his personal library and recollections of his father), Victoria De Grazia at Columbia, Jay Winter at Cambridge, an anonymous reader at Cambridge University Press, Alexander Nützenadel (then at the German Historical Institute in Rome), Alexander De Grand (North Carolina State), and my father David C. Ipsen. Others who have read various sections and made useful observations include: Jeff Bale (fellow, Columbia), Ruth Ben Ghiat (Fordham), Mario Biagioli (Harvard), Bernardo Colombo (Padua), Carlo Corsini (Florence), Nora Federici (Rome), Luigi Goglia (Padua), Maria Guercio

(Ministry of Cultural Affairs), Annunziata Nobile (Naples) and Claudio Pogliano (Trieste). Some final touches were achieved thanks to the discussions I had with graduate students in my Fascist Italy seminar at Indiana University.

I would also like to thank the directors and employees of the various institutes where I conducted my research and the offices that gave me technical (and in some cases financial) assistance. The first category includes the Central State Archive (Rome), the Historical Archive of the Ministry of Foreign Affairs (Rome), the Central Archive of the Central Statistics Institute (Rome), the Allessandrina Library (Rome), the Library of the Chamber of Deputies (Rome), the library of the business faculty (*economia e commercio,* Florence), the Library of Modern and Contemporary History (Rome), and the National Central Libraries of Florence and Rome. The second category instead includes the Commission for Cultural Exchange between Italy and the US in Rome (Fulbright Commission, director Carlo Chiarrenza), the Office for the History of Science and Technology at Berkeley (director then John Heilbron), the National Institute for Population Research (Rome), and the Department of West European Studies at Indiana University (director Peter Bondanella). Finally I thank Cynthia De Nardi who came along for the ride and to whom I dedicate this book.

Table for lira conversion to 1990 US dollars

	10 lire	1,000 lire	1,000,000 lire
1861–70	42.16	4,216	4,216,000
1871	39.09	3,909	3,909,000
1872–4	33.03	3,303	3,303,000
1875–81	35.38	3,538	3,538,000
1882	37.54	3,754	3,754,000
1883–1906	38.18	3,818	3,818,000
1907–14	34.67	3,467	3,467,000
1915	31.71	3,171	3,171,000
1916	25.34	2,534	2,534,000
1917	17.91	1,791	1,791,000
1918–19	12.75	1,275	1,275,000
1920	9.63	963	963,300
1921–4	8.13	813	813,000
1925–7	6.94	694	694,500
1928–30	7.75	775	775,500
1931–3	9.07	907	906,500
1934–6	9.71	971	970,800
1937–8	8.11	811	810,500
1939	7.48	748	747,900
1940	6.40	640	640,200
1941	5.53	553	553,400
1942	4.79	479	479,100
1943	2.85	285	285,500

Note:
This table is constructed using the "coefficients by which to multiply lira values for the years (1861–1990) in order to translate them into 1990 lire" as based on the cost of living (ISTAT, *Annuario statistico 1991*, p. 543) and

the 1990 period average of 1,198 lire per US$ (IMF 1992, p. 290). The periods were chosen so that within each the smallest of the abovementioned annual coefficients was no less less than 90% of the largest.

Abbreviations

AOI	Africa orientale italiana (Italian East Africa = Ethiopia, Eritrea, Somalia)
ATI	Azienda tabacchi italiana (Italian Tobacco Company)
CGE	Commissariato generale dell'emigrazione (General Emigration Commission)
CISP	Comitato italiano per lo studio dei problemi della popolazione (Italian Committee for the Study of Population Problems)
CORI	Commissione permanente per il rimpatrio degli italiani all'estero (Permanent Commision for the Repatriation of Italians Abroad)
CMC	Commissariato per le migrazioni e la colonizzazione (Commission for Migration and Colonization)
CPMI	Comitato permanente per le migrazioni interne (Permanent Committee on Internal Migration)
CSS	Consiglio superiore di statistica (Statistics Council)
Demorazza	Direzione generale della demografia e della razza (General Directory of Demography and Race)
DGIE	Direzione generale degli italiani all'estero (General Directorship of Italians Abroad)
DIRSTAT	Direzione generale della statistica (General Directorship of Statistics)
ECC	Ente per la colonizzazione della Cirenaica (Organization for the Colonization of Cyrenaica)
ECIE	Ente per la colonizzazione per gli italiani all'estero (Organization for the Colonization of Italians Repatriating from Abroad)
ECL	Ente per la colonizzazione della Libia (Organization for the Colonization of Lybia)

EFC	Ente ferrarese di colonizzazione (Colonization Association of Ferrara)
FNFL	Fondazione nazionale figli del littorio (National Children of the Lictor Foundation)
INFPS	Istituto nazionale fascista per la previdenza sociale (National Fascist Social Security Institute)
INS	Istituto nazionale di statistica (National Statistics Institute)
ISTAT	Istituto centrale di statistica del Regno d'Italia (Central Statistics Institute of the Kingdom of Italy)
MAE	Ministero degli affari esteri (Ministry of Foreign Affairs)
MEN	Ministero per l'economia nazionale (Ministry of National Economy)
MVSN	Milizia volontaria per la sicurezza nazionale (Fascist militia)
ONC	Opera nazionale combattenti (National Veterans Organization)
ONMI	Opera nazionale per la protezione della maternità e dell'infanzia (National Organization for the Protection of Motherhood and Infancy)
PCM	Presidenza del consiglio dei ministri (Office of the Prime Minister)
PNF	Partito nazionale fascista (National Fascist Party)
RSI	Repubblica sociale italiana (Italian Social Republic)
SBS	Società anonima bonifiche sarde (Sardinian Land Reclamation Co.)
UCD	Ufficio centrale demografico (Central Demographic Office)
UFFN	Unione fascista per le famiglie numerose (Fascist Union of Large Families)

Introduction

Between the two world wars, the decrease in European fertility became a major concern of politicians, intellectuals, and others who viewed it as both cause and symptom of a general "decline of the West." The frightening specter of overpopulation raised by Malthus over a century before had lost its menace as European economic, political, military, and cultural hegemony seemed threatened by lowering birth rates, and European racial integrity also appeared at risk. It was a situation which finds parallels today.

Fear of denatalism – the decline of birth rate – fueled interest in demography, the new science of population. Political leaders and social scientists wanted to know not only the size of national populations, but also the rate of growth (or shrinkage) in the present and future. More (and more intimate) data were demanded of individual Europeans, and statistical institutes were created or enlarged to better gather and process these data.

The founding of national statistics institutes, however, served to assess the nature and scope of the problem, not to provide remedies. Remedies were suggested instead by politicians and clerics, by demographers and physicians, and by various self-appointed authorities who called for policies to combat fertility decline, policies ranging from paternalistic measures to encourage childbearing by easing the burdens of stay-at-home mothering to police measures aimed at the repression of birth control and abortion.

Fertility decline – and so also alarm over the phenomenon – had the longest history in France. Nonetheless, the first broadly conceived population policy came from Italy, a relative newcomer to denatalism. Italy owed this precociousness to the establishment of a Fascist dictatorship: Mussolini's vision of a new Fascist civilization was expansive and required demographic growth as well as political and ideological indoctrination. In a Fascist corporate economy, not only labor but also labor supply would come under the purview of the state.

The demographic policy was a fundamental aspect of the overall Italian Fascist program. It was linked to economic policy insofar as labor force size affected production. It was central to Fascist social policy and contained the Fascist attitude – at times ambiguous – toward the family and, implicitly, women. And it would become crucial to Fascist foreign policy as Italy sought to expand both politically and demographically in the 1930s and 1940s. Finally, Fascist racial policy also found its justification in the already well-established population policy. For the student of Fascist Italy, the "demographic battle" aids understanding of both Fascist ideology and Fascist policy-making. It was, moreover, an important if particular expression of the general European between-the-wars concern about the population question.

Fascist population policy has been little studied. This neglect may in part be due to a resistance to accept or take seriously the Fascist logic that linked anti-urbanism, land reclamation projects, and pronatalism – the encouragement of fertility – as parts of a populationist whole. And, in retrospect the constant harping of generally bombastic politicians exhorting the population to "make babies" tends to be classified with the more ridiculous aspects of Fascist rule. The fact remains, however, that Fascists and non-Fascists alike considered the demographic problem to be among the most pressing affecting Italian society; the "problem of problems" it would be called. And similar alarm signals were going up throughout Europe.

Various aspects of the demographic policy have been treated separately, though little attempt has been made to tie them together,[1] and references to the policy in general works on Italian Fascism tend to be fleeting. Renzo De Felice, for example, describes it as perhaps the most absurd aspect of Fascist ruralism (1974, p. 147), absurd in that demographic goals (increased fertility, arrested urbanization) were generally directly opposed to the prevailing trends; elsewhere, however, he does note the policy's importance both to Mussolini's achievement of "consensus" and also to the general effort to create a new Fascist civilization (1968, p. 379; 1981, pp. 290–300). Ernst Nolte, on the other hand,

---

[1] These are cited below in the relevant places; for another general discussion, see Nobile 1990b. Since I completed the bulk of the present work, a couple of other relevant publications have come out, signaling perhaps a re-evaluation of the importance of the policy. Cecilia Dau Novelli (1994) has written on Fascist family policy and is especially good on the relationship between the Church and Fascism in this regard. David Horn (1994) instead places several aspects of the population policy in the context of the current literature on discourses of the body.

describes the demographic problem as that which most occupied Mussolini for a number of years, without however pursuing the nature or significance of this interest (1965, pp. 224–5). In fact, the demographic policy falls somewhere in between absurdity and Mussolini's greatest concern.

Demography in Italy was dictated in two ways. First, population policy sought to dictate the demographic behavior of the Italian population, calling for higher fertility and migration to certain destinations as part of a battle against urbanization (the transfer of population from country to city). Second, official populationism – the favoring of demographic increase – meant that certain views could not be advocated: neo-Malthusianism (support of birth control), Anglo-American eugenics (sterilization and nuptiality restrictions), and the favoring of emigration, for example.

In the pages that follow, I shall consider both of these ways. First, by way of background, I discuss some general questions of Fascist historiography, the European political and demographic context against which Fascist policy was enunciated, and the nature of the population question in the Liberal period that preceded Fascism. Then I turn to the legislative and institutional development of the various elements of Fascist demographic policy and the way in which these elements fit into a theoretically, if not always practically, coherent framework. Chapter 2 considers the period during which the policy was enunciated and the relevant institutions created, from the end of 1924 to 1929 (more or less the period between Mussolini's resolution of the Matteotti crisis and the Lateran Treaty). Chapters 3 and 4 consider the more mature implementation of the policy divided generally into spatial and qualitative/quantitative measures. Spatial measures are those dealing with the geographical movement of population (migration); quantitative measures are those aimed specifically at population growth (maximum fertility and minimum mortality) and qualitative measures those aimed at the health or racial makeup of the population (infant and maternal care and racism). These chapters consider primarily the period between the Lateran Treaty and Italy's entry into World War II (1929–40) – a period of consolidation during which Mussolini sought to create a new, vigorous, and prolific Fascist Italy – but also examine the fate of the policy in wartime.

A significant – and, I will argue, "modern" – aspect of the policy was its dependence on statistical data. Italian official statistics was given special emphasis in the period in response to Fascist needs, and statistics were used in new ways to inform both policy and public opinion. Furthermore, Italian demography in the period provides an interesting

example of the interaction between politics and science. It was a symbiotic relationship from which both – at least in the short run – benefitted;
and demography proves to be, as one would expect of a policy science,
particularly sensitive to political context. The final chapter then considers the reinvigoration of official Italian statistics as well as population
theory in the period. I explore the ways in which official policy influenced the gathering and publication of demographic statistics and also
the work done by economists, statisticians, and others on demographic
questions.

One more word on organization. I have taken a combined chronological and topical approach. A straight chronological treatment would, I
fear, be confusing and might cause the thread of one policy or another to
be easily lost. On the other hand, I do not want to present the various
sections (pronatalism, internal colonization, racism etc.) as discrete
units. Instead, they were all parts of an Italian Fascist populationist
whole, and it is the global nature of the policy that I want ultimately to
emphasize. A couple of those readers thanked in the Acknowledgments
have suggested that my discussion of Italian statistics and demography
– perhaps the least familiar material presented – might have come
earlier. I did consider and even try out this inversion, but I feel that
putting, for example, Gini before Mussolini overemphasizes the influence that statistical data or population theories had on policy. The
former did indeed help create the general climate of demographic
concern, even panic, but as I hope becomes clear the influence of policy
on scientific activity was, if anything, greater than the reverse.[2]

---

[2] This work is being published in Italian by Il Mulino (Bologna). Several changes have
been made for the English edition. All translations from the Italian are my own unless
otherwise noted.

1

The background: Fascism, European population policy, European demography, and the problem of population in Liberal Italy

Fascism

Over the last two centuries, state intervention in private life has greatly increased. In Western Europe this process peaked in the interwar period when Fascist regimes attempted "total" control of both the political system and society as a whole.[1] The "Fascistization" of society was a crucial element in the hoped-for (by some) creation of a new Fascist civilization and ultimately a "new European order." To achieve these goals, national populations had to be mobilized: politically, economically, militarily, but also demographically.

A general though uncoordinated European anti-parliamentary movement of the first half of the twentieth century, Fascism combined radical Nationalism and Revolutionary Syndicalism to synthesize a new sort of right-wing revolutionary movement. It was a movement marked by contradictions – modern and anti-modern, revolutionary and reactionary – and these contradictions came to the fore when the movement became regime and so was forced to make compromises with traditional conservative forces.[2]

Fascism grew out of World War I and it was only a few years after the end of that conflict that Fascists first came to power: in Italy in 1922. They did so with the intention of replacing liberal parliamentary democracy, which they accused of being cumbersome and ineffective, with a new and more dynamic Fascist style of rule. They did not, however, bring with them either a well-enunciated ideology or a

---

[1] See Lesthaeghe 1992, p. 3 for a similar claim.
[2] On the general phenomenon of European Fascism and its nature, see Collotti 1989; De Felice 1977; De Grand 1995; Mosse 1979; Nolte 1965 (and also his comments on paradoxes in Nolte 1979); Payne 1980; Sternhell 1994 and also his earlier works (1972, 1978, 1984); Weber 1964. There is of course a vast literature on the topic.

long-term political plan. These elements emerged only partially and with time as the regime eliminated or replaced some liberal institutions and preserved others in the pursuit of its goals. One of these emerging goals was the regulation of Italian fertility and migration for combined productive, military, and imperial purposes.

Inspired by a Spenglerian vision of the decline of the West – an important symptom of which was the downward trend of European birth rates – Mussolini sought to create a new and heroic Fascist man in place of the decadent Liberal, *laissez-faire*, and bourgeois individual produced by finance and capital and infected with urban values and petty consumerist aspirations. Fascism would foster a new civilization based on the traditional rural values of family and hard work, but also on a general commitment to the state and to Fascism which required the sacrifice of individual aspirations to the higher interests of the nation.[3]

Though it traces ideological origins back to the nineteenth century (see again Sternhell 1994), Fascism did emerge out of the war and this bore heavily on its nature. It was born of struggle, combat, and sacrifice, experiences that would continue to form its outlook. In a sense, Fascism sought to continue the war experience in peacetime and struck a chord with those who felt betrayed by the outcome of the war and by Italy's "mutilated victory" and apparently pointless sacrifice, those who were repelled by a return to the dull routine and limited horizons of peacetime. Fascism instead offered continued struggle and sacrifice, but also the realization of some indefinite and future Fascist utopia, a utopia to be ushered in by the new Fascist man whose prototype was of course Mussolini (and like Mussolini, the new Fascist man would be a prolific father).[4] The various Fascist battles, including the "battle for grain" and more important for our purposes the "demographic battle", were expressions of this Fascist transference of the war to a domestic and peacetime front.

In spite of Fascism's undoubted emphasis on men, it ignored neither women nor children in its attempt to create a Fascist society. It was in fact because of its pronatalism that Fascism was forced to pay special attention to women (both mothers and prospective mothers) and infant children. More generally the demographic battle was aimed at the

---

[3] On the Fascist *nuova civiltà,* see especially Mariani 1976, pp. 73–86; Collotti 1989, pp. 55–7; De Felice 1981, pp. 254–330. I briefly discuss the importance of Oswald Spengler to Mussolini's thought in chapter 2 below.

[4] See Mosse 1979, especially p. 26. Mussolini had five children. Like Mussolini the new man might also have several mistresses. By contrast, the Nazi movement in Germany was stricter regarding sexual morality and the Nazi new man more closely reflected the traditional bourgeois values of paternity *and* fidelity. See Mosse 1985, pp. 153–80, especially p. 156.

Italian family, especially its migration and procreational choices. The family was, some claimed, the basis of Fascism itself (e.g. Solmi 1934), and the entire demographic policy can be interpreted as an attempt to mobilize (and also control) the family for the purpose of creating a prolific, productive and expanding population.

The role of the family, and also of women, in Fascism is problematic. In her work on the socialization of youth in Fascist Italy, Tracy Koon identifies the family as the primary agent of political socialization in totalitarian systems (1985, p. xv), a claim supported by the intense interest the regime took in the family and the promotion of a particular traditional (and probably mythical) family type. Max Horkheimer instead asserted, not long after the fall of Nazi-Fascism, that totalitarian regimes, in spite of any homage paid, were basically antagonistic to the family, as the family constituted an alternative source of authority to the regime.[5] Whether in collaboration or competition, the family became in any case an important object of social control.

The difficult place of women in Fascism stems from this dichotomy as well and is also relevant to the present study. Women, as the bearers of children, ultimately held the key to the success or failure of the demographic battle. In the belief that a "traditional" female role was conducive to large families, women were encouraged to be model wives and mothers. Public need invaded private space as state authority attempted to dictate what were normally personal or family decisions, and so a situation was created in which public and private could easily come into conflict. In the more obviously public realm, some women (a minority) were called upon to play a more visible role in the battle as volunteer workers in the infant and maternal care movement. They were to participate in the modern state in order to reaffirm and support the traditional role of their sex.[6]

Our look at the problem of population in Fascist Italy forces us to confront a number of thorny problems regarding the nature of Fascism itself.[7] I have already referred to the contradictory nature of, especially, Fascism in power, and those contradictions are reflected in the historiographical debate, as depending upon where one looks one is inclined to

---

[5] Moreover, Horkheimer attributes the success of these regimes in part to the decline of the family which leads the individual to search for a "super-father" in the dictatorial leader; see Horkheimer 1949.

[6] On the question of women and Fascism, see chapter 4 below and works there cited, in particular de Grazia 1992.

[7] Without entering here into the debate over the question of "generic" Fascism, the various comments in this section should be understood as applying to European Fascisms in general. On this question, see the works cited in note 2 above and also Michaelis 1989.

identify one aspect or another as characteristic of Fascism. For example, was Fascism a revolutionary movement as many Fascists claimed or instead a backward-looking and reactionary one? Did Fascism embrace or even embody forces of modernism, or was it fundamentally opposed to them? Was the Fascist will imposed by a brutal minority upon a silent and suffering majority, or did the regime succeed in achieving some real degree of national consensus? And was Fascism in either its aims or its achievements totalitarian? Each of these questions addresses broad issues and difficult problems of definition. Let me discuss each briefly and in relation to the present work.

The Fascists themselves invoked their own modernism, describing for example programs of land reclamation and improved infant care as modern. But before we can evaluate these claims and the general modern or anti-modern nature of the Fascist regime, we need to consider what we mean by modern or modernity. We might start by describing modernity as that which distinguishes the new from the old and that which anticipates the future. Modernism then is the championing of this modernity and is fundamentally opposed to traditionalism.[8] For our purposes, though, a working and pragmatic definition may be more useful than a theoretical one. The fundamentally modern aspects of nineteenth and twentieth-century European society have been economic development and industrial growth (and the associated technologies). These are, for example, the steps most eagerly emulated by non-Western states and societies seeking to modernize. The Fascist regime encouraged economic and industrial growth and Italian industry was certainly modernized in the Fascist period.[9] At times, though, these trends ran counter to Fascist programs and ideology, as for example in the perceived link between industrial urbanism and declining fertility (a recurring theme in the pages that follow). Other "modern" characteristics have of course accompanied the industrial and economic growth of twentieth-century society. Several of these are especially relevant for our purposes. They include the political mobilization of the mass of society, the expansion of social services, increased state intervention in private life, development of an American-style consumerist culture, and female emancipation. The extent to which the Fascist regime favored or opposed these processes

---

[8] The sort of socioeconomic modernism described here is of course to be distinguished from cultural modernist movements, to which Fascism did trace certain origins but which at times opposed economic modernization. On Italian cultural modernism, see Adamson 1993 including pp. 7–10 for a definition of this modernism.

[9] For comments on Fascism and modern technology, see Hughes and Kolinsky 1976; Mosse 1979, p. 24; Sternhell 1994, pp. 6–7; Payne 1980, p. 82 (n.).

tells us much about Fascist modernism or anti-modernism and the degree to which Fascism succeeded or failed to modernize Italian society.[10]

In any setting, modernization is a mixed blessing. From the British industrial revolution to Stalinist five-year plans to the Chinese Great Leap Forward, recent history abounds in examples of the frequent brutality of modernity, and Fascism of course contributed to this list as well. With regard to Italian population policy (certainly not among the most brutal Fascist creations), consider the hardships endured by those brought to colonize the reclaimed malarial swamplands of Latium and western Sardinia, or the continued lack of rural birthing assistance in spite of maternal "protection." Modernization need not be a positive thing, particularly not the "perverse reactionary corporative modernization" of Italian Fascism.[11]

The need to garner *massive* support for the regime and involve large sectors of the population in political activity (a "modern" political characteristic) translated into the Fascist attempt to engineer "consensus." For unlike traditional authoritarian regimes, Fascism to succeed needed the active support and participation of Italian citizens, not simply their quiet obedience.[12] The question of consensus has been much debated since De Felice advanced the claim in the mid-1970s that Fascism did indeed enjoy widespread support, especially in the early to mid-1930s. Some have claimed, in particular Nicola Tranfaglia, that one cannot speak of consensus in a context like the Italian Fascist one where the expression of anything else – of opposition – was suppressed. Koon, instead, smooths over this conflict when she describes the organization of consensus and the repression of dissent as "two sides of the same coin."[13]

Clearly, Fascism did not survive over twenty years simply on violence and terror. Mosse's description of its being "built on a fragile consensus" comes closest to the mark (Mosse 1979, p. 3; see also De Grand 1995, pp. 75–8). For Fascism did at times enjoy broad support among the Italian population, particularly at the moments of its greatest

---

[10] For general and more theoretical discussions of modernism and anti-modernism in German and Italian Fascism, see Dorn Brose 1987; see also Mason 1987 and works there cited.

[11] The association of modernity and brutality is Ortega y Gasset's. The characterization of Italian Fascist modernization cited here is from Preti 1987. For another discussion of modernism and family policy see Dau Novelli 1994, especially chapter. 6. Thanks to Andy Evans for helping me to better understand what I mean by modern.

[12] See Lyttelton 1973, p. 149 for a similar observation.

[13] On the question of consensus, see Collotti 1989, pp. 53–5; De Felice 1968, pp. 369–81; 1974, pp. 3–322; 1981, pp. 156–253; Koon 1985, p. xvii; Tranfaglia 1989, pp. 59–75.

successes in foreign policy (and foreign conquest). This consensus was pursued via propaganda, policy, and new and old institutions intended to organize Italian society under Fascist authority: the youth and after-work groups, for example, and also the veterans' organization which the Fascists coopted and gave the task of managing much of the demographic colonization both in Italy and in Africa. Various Fascist policies – including demographic policies such as colonization and maternal and infant care – served a propagandistic and consensus-building purpose by projecting the image that Fascism was finally doing something for working-class Italians, and the support gained by this impression may have obscured the limitations of the policies. To the disappointment of Mussolini and others, however, when it came time to test the depth of this consensus in opposing both the internal enemy, by means of racial policy, and the external one, in war, the Italian population showed itself insufficiently committed to the Fascist vision and the fragility of the Fascist consensus became all too apparent.[14]

The need for consensus was part of the Fascist attempt to establish a "totalitarian" as opposed to simply authoritarian regime and society. Stanley Payne describes a totalitarian system as one "that attempts to exercise total control over all significant aspects of all major national institutions from the economy to the armed forces to the judicial system, the churches, and culture" (Payne 1980, pp. 95–6). Although the Fascist one-party state did wield exclusive political control, important institutions nonetheless remained independent, in particular the Church, the military (ultimately loyal to the monarchy), and industry. This is not to say, however, that Fascism did not aspire to total control; it did. Moreover, totalitarianism is more than an institutional concept. Totalitarian regimes, including the Fascist, seek to extend control to society at large and to many realms of individual behavior. Through policies and Fascist organizations, Mussolini intended to weave a web of social control which would impinge upon not only the individual's politics, but also his or her economic, social, and cultural activity.

Totalitarianism can of course never be total. Some areas will always escape control. And the fact that the Fascist regime did not succeed in creating a totalitarian system does not mean that the concept is not useful to its study. For the Fascists – starting with Mussolini – did aspire to create just such a system, and the Fascist utopia was clearly totalitarian. With regard to population policy the *intent* there too was totalitarian: to dictate fundamental individual choices in the areas of

---

[14] For a similar observation see De Grand 1995, p. 76; on the *dopolavoro*, see de Grazia 1981; on the youth groups, Koon 1985.

migration, fertility, and nuptiality in the service of the nation and Fascism.[15]

Mosse and others identify Marxism and Fascism as the two European revolutionary movements of our century.[16] At the same time Fascism was in many ways reactionary, traditionalist, and conservative. Mussolini's background (in Syndicalism and Radical Socialism) was certainly revolutionary. His move to Fascism marked a break with important elements of this background, but continuity with others. He brought along, for example, the Sorelian ideas of myth and violence and joined them to the anti-parliamentary radical Nationalist right. The Fascist revolution would be one of the nation rather than of class. In addition, Fascism drew early inspiration from Futurism, a cultural-artistic movement that emphasized speed, modern technology and a rejection of traditional bourgeois society and values, and from the poet-adventurer Gabriele D'Annunzio. Often seen as precursors of Fascism, D'Annunzio and a group of war veterans in 1919 seized (for Italy) the contested Adriatic city of Fiume where they set up a short-lived and socially radical dictatorship.[17]

The revolutionary nature of this Fascism of the first hour was, however, much qualified in practice. In order to widen his base of support and come to power, Mussolini made compromises with traditional agricultural and industrial interests as well as with the existing Liberal power structure and opted for an essentially conservative solution. In particular, he seized power not by revolutionary means but by basically legal ones.[18]

Still, these conservative forces did not succeed in taming Fascism as they had hoped, and the revolutionary nature of Fascism was not entirely suppressed. Politically, the Fascists managed over the space of a few years to replace or coopt the ruling elite, and economically Fascism

[15] It is probably clear that my use of "totalitarian" in chapter titles represents a variation on Aquarone's *Organizzazione dello Stato totalitario* (1965); The totalitarian debate is a (another) long one. Some would exempt Italian Fascism from the category while saving the label for Nazi Germany and Stalinist USSR, but again I would maintain that such a distinction is based more on success than intention. Others reject the label altogether. Although coined by the Fascists (or their early detractors), the historiographical debate probably began with Arendt's classic study (1951); on totalitarianism, and its limits, in Fascist Italy, see Aquarone 1965, especially pp. 290–311; Collotti 1989, pp. 29–31, 50; De Grand 1995, p. 2; Mosse 1979, pp. 1–5; Payne 1980, pp. 73–6, 95–6; Tranfaglia 1989, pp. 95–116.

[16] On the revolutionary nature of Fascism, see Mosse 1979, pp. 1–11; Payne 1980, pp. 3–21; Weber 1964, p. 78.

[17] For the *Manifesto-programma del Partito politico futurista*, see De Felice 1965, pp. 738–41; On D'Annunzio and Fiume, see De Felice 1978, pp. 227–54; Ledeen 1977. The radical nature of these programs, however, already found little echo in the 1921 *Programma del PNF*, see De Felice 1966, pp. 756–63.

[18] On the Fascist seizure of power, see Lyttelton 1973.

advocated a revolutionary "third way" between capitalism and Marxism. The Fascist corporative experiment was, however, largely frustrated as industrial interests continued to exercise important influence both on and within the regime. More relevant to the present work are the culturally and socially revolutionary aspects of Fascism: the emphasis on (virile and prolific) youth and on the continuation of the wartime experience, the hoped-for quasi-military mobilization of society. Fascist youth were taught to have faith in the new religion of the state, to believe, obey, fight, and also procreate. The Fascist irrational appeal to myths and symbols was revolutionary as well. In particular, once achieved, the Fascist revolution would usher in a utopian Italy in which the various battles, demographic included, had been won. Ironically, this new revolutionary society was based on profoundly traditional values and morality (the non-emancipation of women, rejection of divorce, glorification of the large rural family).

Ultimately the Italian Fascist revolution failed. Mussolini neither achieved a profound consensus, nor created a new civilization, nor erected a totalitarian regime; and these are all facets of his fundamental failure, of his inability to Fascistize Italian society. The Fascists did manage to mobilize large demonstrations of support for the regime and lead the nation to war, but there were more intimate areas where Fascist totalitarianism never reached. In a telling and relevant example, Mussolini succeeded in convincing Italian women to donate their wedding rings to the Fascist cause, but not their procreational potential.

Population, policy, and statistics in late modern Europe

The Italian Fascist population policy coincided with a general European preoccupation with population problems; it emerged from a particular psychological and demographic context which, combined with the political innovation of Fascism, in large part explains its existence. Declining and differential fertility in late nineteenth century Europe had turned the tide against Malthusian concern over the possibility of overpopulation and famine and inspired instead fears of depopulation and racial decline. Both pronatalist and eugenic movements emerged as a result and exercised varying degrees of influence over national policies regarding fertility, maternity, infant care, and migration. Many came to view depopulation as a threat to national industrial and military strength, and as a result the early twentieth century saw a general push for welfare and pronatalist legislation. At the same time the publications of national statistics institutes came under ever-greater scrutiny in order to better understand the European demographic reality.

European demography

The most salient aspect of European demography in the nineteenth and early twentieth centuries was rapid population growth compared to previous periods and other parts of the world (see figures 1.1, 1.2). The population of Europe, about 200 million at the time of the Congress of Vienna, had grown to over 500 million by World War II, and the combined population of Europeans and neo-Europeans by that time was about 700 million.[19] Growth, however, was not shared evenly. Germany and European Russia grew in this period by over 200% and England and Wales by almost 300%. France grew much more slowly, increasing by only about one-third (and Ireland actually suffered a period of decline). Italy's growth was considerable, about 150%. To keep track of this growth, national governments began taking regular censuses (usually every ten years) in the early nineteenth century.[20]

European population growth took place because of mortality decline, especially during infancy and childhood. The immediate cause of this decline was a reduction in the lethalness of epidemic and infectious diseases. How Europe succeeded in checking the fatality of disease is still debated, but it certainly involved a combination of sociological and economic factors. The social elements of mortality decline included improved infant care, general social organization, and personal hygiene; and the economic development of the nineteenth century led to higher standards of living and so better protection from the elements and from pathogens.[21]

Mortality and fertility levels began to be measured during this period of "demographic transition." The longest tradition of national population registry is that of Sweden, whose records suggest that mortality began to decline around the turn of the nineteenth century. Records from other countries generally show decline already initiated at the time when registration began (usually about the time of the first census or a little after). This latter trend holds for Italy, where the crude death rate was considerably above that of northern and western Europe at the time of unification (1861), but which dropped rapidly and reached comparable levels by the 1930s (see figure 1.3). Infant mortality (IMR) declined still more steeply than general mortality (see figure 1.4). Initial divergence of national rates again narrows to a smaller range by the 1930s, though the Italian IMR declined more slowly than did those of

---

[19] Neo-Europe is Crosby's term for those lands outside of Europe settled primarily by population of European extraction. See Crosby 1986.

[20] On the history of census taking, see Dupâquier and Dupâquier 1985.

[21] Livi Bacci 1992, pp. 106–13. The more intuitive explanations of improved medical care and better nutrition do not stand up to scrutiny; see Livi Bacci 1991; McKeown 1976; Razzell 1974.

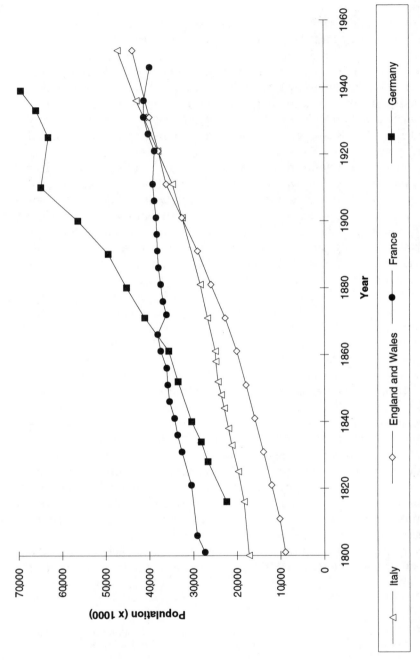

Figure 1.1 Population of major European countries (except Russia) at censuses, 1800–1950
Source: Mitchell 1981 (see this work for notes on boundary changes etc.)

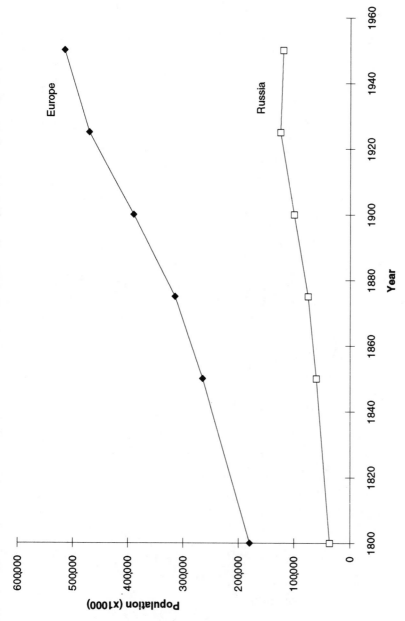

Figure 1.2 Population of Europe (including Russia) and European Russia, 1800–1950
Source: McEvedy and Jones 1978

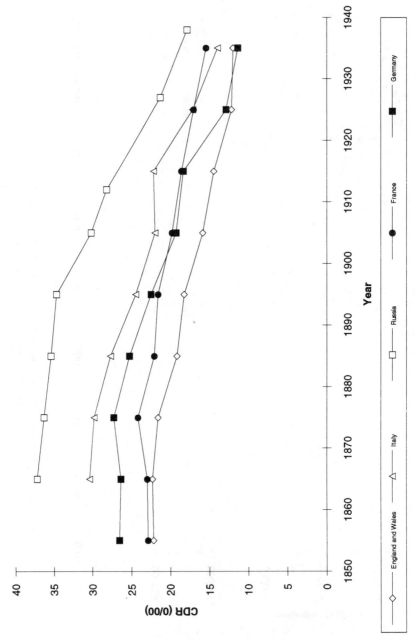

Figure 1.3 Crude death rates for major European countries, *c.* 1855–1940
Source: Mitchell 1981

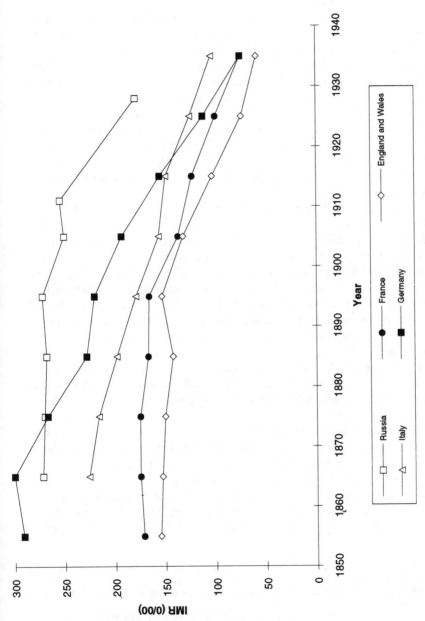

Figure 1.4 Infant mortality rates in major European countries, *c.* 1850–1935
Source: Mitchell 1981

other western European nations, a point of some embarrassment for Italian governments.

The potential European population growth resulting from mortality decline was attenuated by two opposing forces: a parallel decline in fertility and overseas emigration. Historical studies suggest that for the long stretch of history prior to about 1650, births and deaths balanced one another fairly closely (except for the occasional catastrophe). Indeed, had a situation of disequilibrium existed for any considerable period of time, it would have led to either explosive growth or else extinction. In most European countries mortality decline preceded the decline of fertility with the result that population grew as described above (see figure 1.5). The relatively slow growth of France, instead, was due to a precocious fertility decline which nearly kept pace with the decline of mortality.

French fertility decline seems to have been well established by about 1830, a phenomenon variously explained as resulting from the Napoleonic property laws and from a widespread perception of the incompatibility of repeated childbearing with individual or familial socioeconomic improvement (Spengler 1979 [1938]). For most of the rest of Europe, decline set in during the decades around 1900. Italian fertility remained at pre-transition levels until about World War I, after which it joined in the general downward trend (see figure 1.6).[22] Debate over the causes of fertility decline came to dominate theoretical discussions of population, though as with mortality, explanation of the historical transition of fertility behavior is not entirely resolved. Fertility limitation was first practiced by certain select and generally elite groups; and its spread to the general population is explained variously in social and economic terms.[23]

The other major force affecting European population growth in this period was migration. Total gross emigration from Europe has been estimated at over 60 million for the period 1650–1945, and most of this exodus took place in the nineteenth and early twentieth centuries. The earlier phase of emigration came primarily from the United Kingdom, Germany, Scandinavia, and Ireland. Beginning in the latter decades of the nineteenth century, a new phase of European emigration began

[22] The Princeton European Fertility Project threshold of a 10% decline in marital fertility (I_g) was reached in France in 1827. By comparison, Germany reached that point in 1888, England and Wales in 1892, Sweden in 1902, and Italy in 1913 (Coale and Watkins 1986, p. 38).

[23] On European fertility decline, see Coale and Watkins 1986, and, for Italy, Livi Bacci 1977; for further consideration of this decline in its social, economic and political context, see Gillis, Tilly and Levine 1992 and Teitelbaum and Winter 1985.

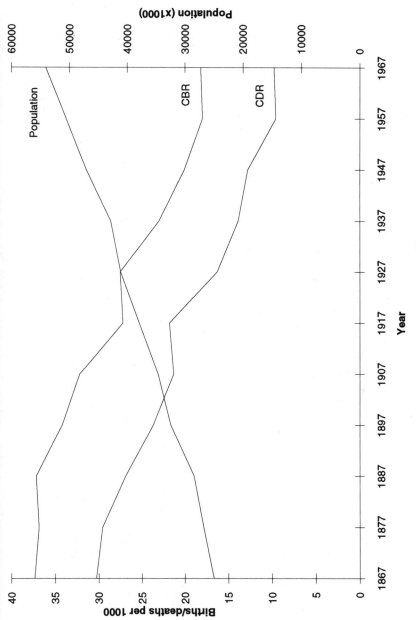

Figure 1.5 Italian demographic transition
Sources: Livi Bacci 1977, Mitchell 1981

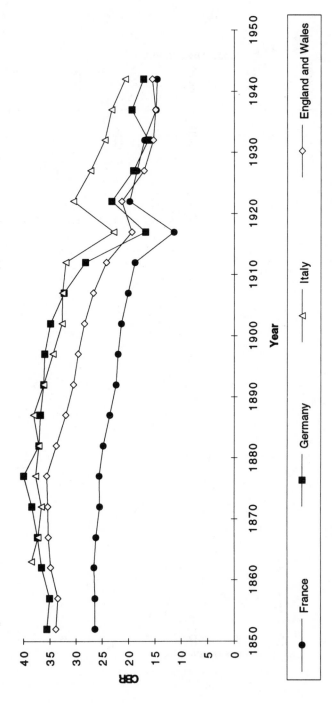

Figure 1.6 Crude birth rates for major European countries, 1850–1940
Source: Mitchell 1981

which peaked just before World War I. The leaders of this second phase were the Italians (see figures 1.7, 1.8), and Italy became historically the single greatest national exporter of population, a fact which significantly influenced the foreign policy of Italian governments (see figure 1.9).

A third factor checking European population growth was war; the demographic losses of World War I in particular contributed to fears of depopulation and racial degeneration in the main belligerent countries. Using Jay Winter's estimates, war-related deaths among the adult population amounted to about 2 million in Germany, 1.75 million in France, and a bit over half a million in Britain (Winter 1988b). Large as these numbers are (as high as 200% of "normal" mortality), emigration might deplete population at nearly the same rate. Net Italian emigration, for example, for the years 1909–13 (an admittedly exceptional period) amounted to nearly a million.[24]

In addition to migration overseas, European population in this period was also characterized by considerable movement within Europe and within individual countries, in particular from rural areas to the cities. Much of modern population increase occurred in the cities, and the process of urbanization was a necessary companion to industrialization. Associated with urbanization, or rural to urban migration, was the general phenomenon of urbanism, or the increasingly urban quality of life, a development encouraged by improved communication, increased literacy, and economic development. Italian cities did not generally match those of the other major powers in size; they did, however, share in the dramatic growth of the period. Between 1800 and 1940, for example, the populations of Rome and Milan increased about tenfold (see figure 1.10).

In the face of continued mortality and fertility decline, massive emigration, and urbanization, various European states debated population problems and took measures to combat them. In this context, the Fascist attempt at demographic manipulation stood out as an especially broad attempt to combat the spontaneous movement of population; it was one aspect of a general effort to reshape Italian society both economically and ideologically.

Population policy
European governments began investing in human capital – in programs of education, social welfare, and the like – in the early decades of the

---

[24] By contrast, Italy was in fact unique in gaining population during World War I due to repatriation.

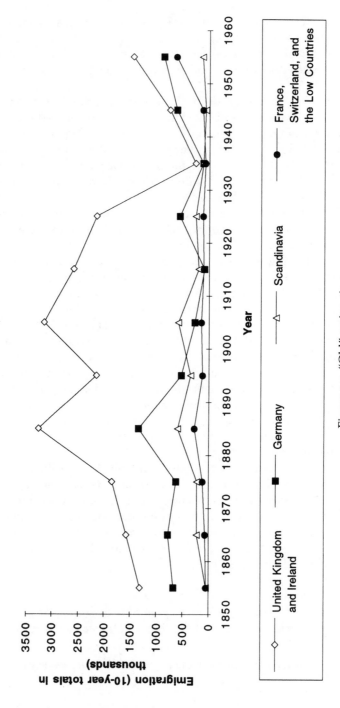

Figure 1.7 "Old" emigration
Source: Mitchell 1981 (based on Kirk 1946)

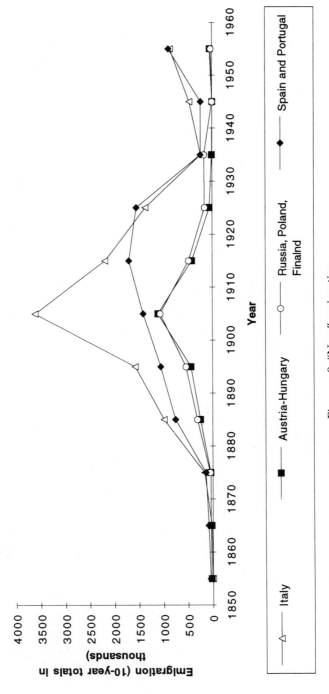

Figure 1.8 "New" emigration
Source: Mitchell 1981 (based on Kirk 1946)

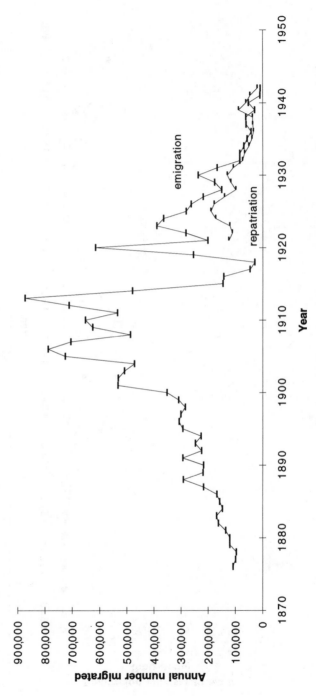

Figure 1.9 Italian emigration and repatriation, 1876–1942

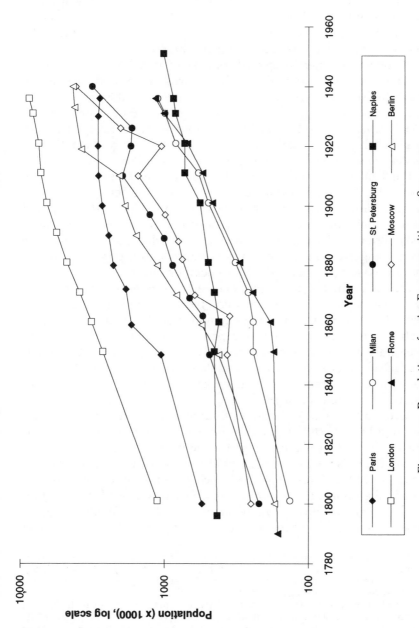

Figure 1.10 Population of major European cities, c. 1800–1940

Source: Mitchell 1981 (Mitchell gives 1920/1 population of St. Petersburg as 722,000 which I take to be 1,722,000)

nineteenth century, and in the context of fertility decline calls for improved social hygiene became ever more insistent toward that century's end. High levels of infant mortality, for example, especially among the illegitimate, came to be viewed as both an economic and a demographic loss to the nation. Eugenic, pronatalist, and family measures, however, generally met with opposition from both Conservatives and Liberals on the grounds that health was the responsibility of the individual and that the state should not intervene in the private sphere of the family. This opposition was gradually overcome as programs of social welfare were introduced on the grounds that the state must take responsibility for the health of the family and so future generations, a process generally championed by progressives and Socialists.

The demographic shock of World War I intensified these efforts as the liberal state became less so in the social realm. In the democracies of the French Third Republic and Weimar Germany, though, the proposed demographic measures rarely advanced beyond the planning stage, and in Britain resistance to state intervention in this realm was for a time even stronger. Only in Sweden was a comprehensive population policy introduced in a pre-World War II democratic context.

Various of the late nineteenth and early twentieth-century calls for social engineering did eventually find fertile terrain in the Fascist contexts of interwar Italy and Germany, and later also France, where promotion of (selective) population expansion was unfettered by concern over individual liberties or belief in the necessary privacy of the family. The debate and development of population policies in other European national contexts provide a useful background for our consideration of similar phenomena in Italy.[25]

As described above, European fertility decline on a national scale began in France. Widespread concern over the phenomenon followed French defeat at the hands of the Prussians in 1870, a defeat attributed in part to France's relative demographic weakness. In the period leading up to World War I, however, the French government took no effective part in the populationist movement which was instead furthered by private organizations.[26] Family allowances (or a family wage or child allowances) had been introduced in France in 1840. They spread

---

[25] For some of the general points alluded to here regarding population policy and the fear of population decline, see Lees 1992; Teitelbaum and Winter 1985; Weindling 1989; Winter 1988a; 1992. On European population policies up to 1940, see Glass 1940 and the works cited in the following paragraphs.

[26] In particular Jacques Bertillon's National Alliance for the Growth of the French Population founded in 1896. On French population policy, see Glass 1940, pp. 99–218; Hecht 1991; Dupâquier 1988, vol. IV, pp. 181–93; McDougall 1983; McLaren 1983; Prost 1988; Spengler 1979 (1938).

gradually and were encouraged by the Catholic Church in Pope Leo XIII's 1891 encyclical *De rerum novarum*. Infant protection organizations had also been created in Paris as early as 1866 and various measures were taken to regulate wetnursing and provide aid to needy mothers. Maternity leave, however, was not introduced until 1913, following three decades of parliamentary debate. The 1870–1914 period was also characterized by the encouragement of immigration and calls for colonization, in part as an incentive to fertility (colonial populations were traditionally characterized by lower ages at marriage and notably larger families than those of their parent countries).

The demographic losses of World War I inspired the founding of new French pronatalist organizations and of a government body specifically concerned with the problem of fertility, as well as a series of demographic measures. In particular, the Blue Horizon parliament (a reference to the horizon blue uniforms worn by the many officers elected to the assembly) of 1919–24 passed a new anti-abortion law, banned the advertisement of contraceptives, created a Mothers' Day, and introduced child allowances for a restricted low-income group. Nonetheless, child allowances, which had become fairly widespread during the war, were generally left to the initiative of the employer (private and public) until 1932 when they were made obligatory. Tax rebates based on marital status and parity were introduced in 1917 as well as tax increases for unmarried and childless men. In addition, during World War I France introduced immigrant recruitment and regulation.

In spite of this flurry of activity (and many more proposals which languished in parliament), French population policy in the interwar period was generally considered non-substantial and ineffective. However, in 1938 family allowances were substantially increased, and a comprehensive policy, the *Code de la famille*, was introduced in July 1939. This legislation passed shortly after the German occupation of Bohemia and Moravia and so was aided by an already war-time climate of national solidarity and emergency.[27] Drawn up by the newly formed High Committee for Population, the new code extended the coverage of family allowances and introduced marriage loans for young rural couples who agreed to remain agriculturally employed for at least ten years following their wedding. The couple's debt was gradually reduced with the birth of each child until, on the birth of the fifth, the balance was canceled. The *Code de la famille* also provided aid for needy

[27] The *Code de la famille* was for example supported by the French Communists (in opposition), a position made possible by the Soviet adoption of a populationist stance in the 1930s; see Winter 1988a. The *Code de la famille* is *Décret-loi du 29 Juillet 1939 relatif à la famille et à la natalité françaises.*

parents, increased penalties for abortion and for the advertising and sale of contraceptives, banned the sale of abortifacients, and stipulated instruction in all schools regarding the demographic problem from statistical, moral, and family points of view. Subsequently, the Vichy regime increased family allowances, passed a severe abortion law, and introduced a parity-determined allowance (which was several times larger than the family wage) for families in which there was only one wage earner. The latter was an undisguised attempt to discourage women from taking salaried work.

British denatalist concern dates instead from about the 1880s, a decade or so after France, and the French example of fertility decline (and military defeat) contributed to its arousal.[28] The British example, however, differs from the French in that the major source of worry was not so much fertility decline as "differential" fertility. The observation that Britain's great families (presumed guarantors of the nation's best hereditary stock) were reproducing at a slower rate than the lower classes led the father of eugenics, Francis Galton, and his followers to advocate incentives to middle and upper-class fertility and disincentives to proletarian breeding. The Boer War of 1899–1902 and the apparently poor quality of British recruits heightened concern over racial decline and led to a 1904 study of physical deterioration. Demographic measures introduced during the period of Liberal government between 1906 and 1914 included a parity-based income tax allowance in 1909 (considered eugenic, since only the relatively well-off paid income tax), a fertility-of-marriage survey in conjunction with the 1911 census, a state maternity benefit in 1911, the creation of child welfare centers, and a National Birth Rate Commission created in 1913. World War I was considered particularly dysgenic in Britain, destroying the flower of the nation's youth, or what little there was of it judging from signs of degeneracy, and 1918 saw passage of the Maternal and Child Welfare Act and the creation of a second National Birth Rate Commission.

Alongside growing fear of depopulation, the neo-Malthusian or birth-control movement was important in Britain, supported in part by eugenicists who hoped to convince the lower classes to adopt contraceptive practices. Acceptance was widespread, and in 1930 both the government and the Church of England endorsed birth control. The 1930s, however, saw increased concern over declining fertility. In 1933, for example, a law to control the advertisement and sale of

---

[28] On British demographic policy, demographic concerns and eugenics, see Kevles 1986; Soloway 1990.

contraceptives was proposed but defeated, and in 1937, the Population (Statistics) Bill was passed in spite of criticisms that the data collection it called for represented an incursion into family life. Repeated calls for official inquiries into the population problem and for pronatalist measures were resisted by the government in what persists today as a decided reluctance to invade the family sphere. Indeed, the interwar years witnessed repeated calls for family allowances, marriage loans, and compulsory sterilization for eugenic reasons, none of which, however, were legislated.

In Germany as well, concern over fertility decline combined with eugenic fears of racial deterioration.[29] In keeping with the later onset of fertility decline in that country, visions of Malthusian overpopulation gave way to those of demographic, military, and industrial decline a bit later than in France or Britain, around the turn of the century. In response to declining fertility, the issue of children's health and infant mortality came to the fore. Infant hospitals were already being founded in the 1890s, and in 1904 a Society to Combat Infant Mortality was created. Subsequently, child welfare clinics were established throughout Prussia and other infant hospitals and protection agencies created in what has been described as a covert population policy. In the same period calls were made for more systematic population registration and, following a 1911 meeting of the Prussian Medical Advisory Committee, the Ministry of the Interior carried out a survey soliciting local opinions throughout the country on the causes of fertility decline. (This was the same year in which the British Fertility of Marriage survey was carried out.) The majority of respondents blamed the voluntary limitation of fertility. In 1913 an abortion study was carried out as well. Conservative and Socialist forces, however, disagreed over demographic policy and many proposed measures were not enacted in the prewar period, for example midwifery reform (certification, minimum wage, and territorial distribution) and maternity benefits. Maternity benefits *were* granted to soldiers' wives during the war and in general a more decisive move in the direction of population policy and social welfare was taken in wartime, including the creation in 1915 of a Society for Population Policy and repeated meetings of the Inter-Ministerial Committee on the Birth Rate.

The postwar Weimar government was openly pronatalist, but legislation proved difficult to implement; in addition, Weimar welfare programs were threatened by economic depression. Midwifery reform was

---

[29] On German population policy including Nazi sterilization policy, see Bock 1983, Glass 1940, pp. 269–313; Proctor 1988; Weindling 1989.

attempted in 1924 but was a failure; a Reich League for Child Rich Families as well as a Reich Committee for Population Questions (1929) were created but calls for family allowances went unheeded; while proposals for a bachelor tax (after the Italian model) were instead acted upon in 1930. On a eugenic note, proposals were made for premarital health certificates and for a sterilization law; again both remained proposals.

The coming to power of the National Socialists of course changed the German political situation entirely as democratic obstacles to policy initiatives disappeared and the Nazis introduced a pronatalist and also eugenic policy. The fertility of healthy Aryan Germans was to be encouraged while the unfit would be sterilized (and eventually also killed in the euthanasia programs). In 1933, marriage loans were introduced for young couples providing the new wife gave up her salaried work; one-quarter of the loan was canceled with each birth (these loans provided the model for the French loans of 1939 mentioned above). Also in 1933, the Law to Prevent Hereditarily Sick Offspring was enacted, a eugenically inspired forced sterilization law. Laws against contraceptives and, especially, abortion were made harsher (except for degenerate parents), and in 1935 physicians and midwives were required to report all miscarriages to the authorities so that suspicious cases could be investigated. The year 1935 also saw special grants for large families and the Nuremberg law which forbade healthy Germans from marrying either the hereditarily ill or Jews. Nazi population policy was not of course limited to fertility-related measures. Programs for massive resettlement of Germans in the East were planned, together with the expulsion of Poles, Slavs, and Jews; and the holocaust too must be considered one of the principal aspects of Hitler's plan for redrawing the demographic map of Europe.

Following the Nazi seizure of power, the German birth rate did increase,[30] and many attributed this rise to the pronatalist measures, in particular the marriage loans. The birth rate increase, however, took place in the context of economic recovery, and it has been suggested that it was this recovery combined with abortion suppression that explains the increase rather than the response of women to Hitler's call for larger families (Bock 1983).

The only democracy to introduce a comprehensive population policy in the interwar period was Sweden. The fact that Sweden had one of the lowest birth rates in the period is not sufficient to explain this

---

[30] From a low of 14.7 per 1,000 in 1933, the German crude birth rate rose to 20.4, a 39% increase, by 1939.

development.[31] Following publication of Alva and Gunnar Myrdal's book on the population question in 1934 (Myrdal and Myrdal 1934), fertility became the most important Swedish political topic of the day – described as literally a question of the life of the Swedish people – and the so-called Mothers and Babies parliament of 1935 appointed a population committee which laid the bases of subsequent Swedish policy; that parliament also called for a special census to assess the demographic situation. Swedish measures included home-furnishing loans for newlyweds, free school meals in high unemployment areas, the extension of maternity insurance coverage, and increased parity-based income tax exemptions. In addition, birth-control clinics were opened and abortion laws relaxed. In contrast to French, German, or Italian policies, Sweden's included neither restrictive measures regarding birth control nor disincentives to female salaried employment. Subsequently, Alva Myrdal attributed Sweden's success in creating a policy to encourage and facilitate voluntary parenthood to the relative absence there of political and sociocultural obstacles found elsewhere. These obstacles included: French clerical and conservative opposition to birth control; German nationalist and expansionist goals; British individualism, economic stagnation, unemployment, and lack of vision; and the deep economic depression, relatively high birth rate, and immigration of the United States (Myrdal 1945).

The rise of statistics
An important tool of population policies were the demographic data generated by official statistics institutes and analyzed by scholars interested in the population question.[32] For European nations seeking to establish their identity, population statistics took on special importance. The Liberal Italian statistician Angelo Messedaglia expressed a commonly held view when he described population (together with territory) as one of "the two fundamental elements of every national state, of every civil society" (Messedaglia 1879, p. 234). Statistics had indeed been born of the study of the state and so its inhabitants; and the primary tasks of national statistics offices were the taking of censuses and the keeping of population registers.

Ted Porter identifies the science of statistics as having grown out of the "quantitative empirical social science" of the nineteenth century

---

[31] For Swedish interwar policy, see Glass 1940, pp. 314–43; Myrdal 1945.
[32] "Statistics" has at least two (related) meanings. One, the mathematical analysis of uncertainty, will not be considered in the present work (for the history of mathematical statistics, see Stigler 1986 as well as Daston 1988 and Hacking 1975); the other, statistics as a data gathering function of national governments, will be.

"statists" who compiled aggregate data of *national* interest: "society... had to be understood before the aims of the state could be put into effect" (Porter 1986, p. 17). Both Porter and also Stuart Woolf attribute the development of institutional statistics to nineteenth-century liberal and reform movements. Porter writes that "statistics was for the most part a liberal enterprise, pursued by business and professional men who favored a narrower definition of the state" (Porter 1986, p. 17). With regard to nineteenth-century Britain, Woolf observes that "the state needed to have knowledge in order to act," and on the subject of Italian unification that: "the need to discover an unknown nation through its description and the assumption that the information could be rendered operational through numerical comparisons underlay the expectations placed in statistics" (Woolf 1989, p. 602). There is a contradiction here in that liberalism generally posited limited economic and social intervention, which are among the primary purposes of official statistics gathering. Nonetheless, official statistics, and in particular Italian official statistics, did develop in the context of nineteenth-century liberalism.[33]

Official interest in population and its quantitative measurement extended to academe as well, and the same period which saw the general adoption of census taking and population registration also saw the development of the science of demography. The population question had garnered intellectual attention after the publication of Malthus' *Essay*, and throughout the nineteenth and twentieth centuries the debate over the significance, and desirability, of various demographic trends has continued. Moreover, the contributions of scholars were necessary in order both to establish the criteria of data gathering and to interpret those data. The work of demographers (and others interested in the population question) came to influence but still more to reflect the general political aspects of the population debate.

The development of demography as a science paralleled the increasing interest taken by national governments, politicians, and scholars in population questions and population statistics. The expansion of the role of the state in economic development and public assistance in the nineteenth century required more precise knowledge of the populations which these programs were designed to employ and serve; and the step from knowledge of population – and in particular of the demographic indices of mortality, fertility, nuptiality, and migration – to an attempt to influence these indices is conceptually a short one.

---

[33] Both Woolf and Marie-Noëlle Bourguet (Bourguet 1988) do, however, also discuss the importance of the statistical enterprise in Napoleonic France.

The problem of population in Liberal Italy[34]

The twenty years of Fascist rule in Italy followed sixty of "liberal" governments which tried, ultimately unsuccessfully, to establish a parliamentary democracy in the newly unified country. Politically, the liberal period provided important precedents in emigration policy, African colonization, foundling care, and maternity leave; and the increasing importance attached to statistics reflected a concern with the demographic aspects of national identity and power.

Population problems

While the fear of fertility decline and of racial degeneration already dominated population discussions in other countries prior to World War I, the Italian debate in that period centered on emigration and the possibility of overseas colonization.[35] In the period of the *Destra storica* (Historic right, 1861–76), emigration was virtually unanimously condemned by agricultural interests (who saw their traditional source of cheap labor threatened), while other groups, the shipping industry for example, favored "free" emigration as it increased Italian transport of both population and goods. The coming to power of Agostino Depretis and the left in 1876 did not signal an important shift on emigration, though the agricultural crisis of the late 1870s did lead to attrition of the anti-emigration camp as some agriculturalists saw in emigration a means to attenuate social unrest and strikes.

Italian colonial history is closely tied to the history of Italian emigration. Among both the advocates and opponents of emigration, a number favored the creation of an Italian colony for the migrating masses, while others countered that "free" or economic colonies already existed in the various receiving countries. Among the left especially, it was claimed that colonization was needed at home in the uncultivated areas of Italy, not overseas (Manzotti 1962, pp. 108–9).

Italian colonization began in 1882 when Aseb (Assab), a town on the Red Sea occupied privately by Italian interests in 1870, became an official Italian colony; in 1885 the Italian military established itself to the north in Mitsiwa (Massaua) as well.[36] Pasquale Mancini, foreign minister under Depretis and engineer of this expedition, cited "the

---

[34] For a more detailed discussion of the topics treated in this section, see Ipsen 1992a, pp. 1–65; 1992b. On Liberal Italy, see Bosworth 1979; Seton-Watson 1967.

[35] On the emigration debate and legislation in Liberal Italy, see Manzotti 1962. For general discussions of Italian emigration in the period, see Ciuffoletti and Degl'Innocenti 1978, I; Coletti 1912; Foerster 1919; Sori 1979.

[36] On the first phase of Italian colonialism in Ethiopia, see Battaglia 1958.

economic and political profit of any colonial initiative" (Battaglia 1958, p. 179), a sentiment which found favor among Italy's ruling classes, and especially the aristocracy. The Republican-Socialist parliamentarian and statistician Napoleone Colajanni instead attacked Italy's new colonial policy as anti-democratic and a product of the psychological infection of the social body. He rejected the suggestion that Italy was overpopulated and that an African colony might serve as an alternative destination for Italian emigrants (Colajanni 1891).

Procolonialist sentiments got the upper hand, particularly during Crispi's tenures as prime minister (1887–91, 1893–6); under him the Italian Red Sea colony, which Crispi himself named Eritrea, was expanded and a demographic justification invoked: "Our aim in Eritrea is the institution of a colony that can gather up the immense emigration that goes to other lands and so is drawn away from the dominion and the laws of Italy."[37]

On a small scale, demographic colonization in Eritrea was carried out by the Tuscan conservative Leopoldo Franchetti. With government funds and the support of Crispi he set up experimental farms, and in 1893 established a small colony of ten carefully selected families of Italian peasants (Franchetti 1894). Three years later, however, the Ethiopians under Menelik routed the Italian forces in the Battle of Adwa (Adua). As a result, Crispi fell from power, and the experiment in demographic colonization ended. After Adwa, Italians temporarily lost their appetite for colonial expansion, and an 1896 peace treaty with the Ethiopians stabilized the modest borders of the Italian colony of Eritrea. Further efforts to settle Italians there were abandoned.

The economic problems which were at the root of Italian emigration did not of course go away after Crispi's failed attempt at military expansion. Emigration continued to increase in the late 1890s and especially in the first decade of the twentieth century. The Liberal line of free or spontaneous emigration replaced imperialist plans and the "safety valve" of emigration continued to function, though not as well as some hoped (Ciuffoletti and Degl'Innocenti 1978, I, pp. 306–19).

In addition to seeking "Italian" outlets for emigration, Liberal governments also attempted to regulate the ever-growing stream of expatriating Italian nationals and to protect these emigrants from some of the many abuses they suffered. Liberal emigration legislation consisted of two much-debated laws (of 1889 and 1901). Neither was particularly effective, nor do they appear to have had much influence on the general exodus of the Italian population.

---

[37] Crispi (1890) as reported in Battaglia 1958, p. 429.

The 1901 law did create a Commissariato generale dell'emigrazione (General Emigration Commission – CGE) to monitor and control emigration. The CGE was intended primarily as a tutelary institution, though its role as an agent of emigration control increased with time. In addition to protecting emigrants from unscrupulous enrolment agents, the CGE became responsible during World War I for issuing the authorization form (*nulla osta*) necessary for obtaining a passport and so emigrating; it was a measure intended to control emigration and in particular prevent the departure of military age males (R.d. 18 February 1915, n.147; R.d. 2 May 1915, n.635; D.l. 16 April 1916, n.339). After the war, this legislation was slowly dismantled. Roberto De Michelis, head of the CGE from 1919 until the elimination of the position in 1927, advocated maintenance of the CGE *nulla osta* in spite of the fact that emigration, and so the necessary paperwork, was increasing dramatically. When the Fascists came to power, restrictions on emigration of military age males – the group most likely to emigrate – had been partially relaxed, but the *nulla osta* remained (R.d. 7 August 1919, n.1362; R.d. 30 November 1919, n.2377; R.d.-l. 27 June 1920, n.1008).

The post-Adwa silence on colonialism was not to endure as Crispian-style nationalism slowly revived in the decade or so following that disaster. Led spiritually by Gabriele D'Annunzio and politically by Enrico Corradini, who founded the Associazione nazionalista italiana (Italian Nationalist Association) in December 1910, the new breed of Italian Nationalist emphasized the need for Italy to take its place among the great powers and exploit the nation's one abundant resource, labor. Nationalist agitation as well as general pressure from the right and the economic crisis induced Prime Minister Giovanni Giolitti to undertake the colonization of Libya, hailed by many as a "national" destination for Italian emigration. In October 1911, Italian marines landed at Tripoli and the poet Giovanni Pascoli announced that "the great proletariat has stirred" (Valeri 1962, p. 343). Approval was, of course, not unanimous. Some of the strongest opposition came from then Socialist Benito Mussolini who countered that there were still many Italian "Tripolis" in need of colonization. Contemporary with the Italian attack, Mussolini was arrested and sentenced to several months imprisonment on charges of instigation to violence and damaging railroad, telephone, and telegraph lines (De Felice 1965, pp. 103–11).

Conquest did not come quickly. A peace treaty was signed in October 1912, when Italy had succeeded in securing only the coastal areas. Nonetheless, thousands of southern Italians applied for passports to go to Tripoli (Seton-Watson 1967, p. 370). Franchetti went to Libya in search of land for southern peasants, and Nitti, then minister of agriculture, sent a commission to explore the new colony's resources (p. 380). But the demographic colonization of Libya was slow in getting underway. According to Salvemini, the Libyan enterprise had not only failed to provide a destination for Italians forced to emigrate, it had also led to still greater transoceanic emigration due to the negative effect of the colonial war on the Italian economy (Salvemini 1963, p. 291). Hampered by Arab uprisings and the distraction of war, Libyan settlement would only begin in earnest in 1935.

Except for the emigration measures mentioned above, it is artificial to speak of Italian population policy in the Liberal period. Nonetheless, the Fascist policy that eventually emerged in response to denatalist fears was based on important Liberal precedents, including both foundling care and maternity leave and insurance. Because of relatively high fertility, unreliable contraception, the costs of childrearing and the social stigma attached to illegitimacy, infant abandonment was still an important social issue in nineteenth and early twentieth-century Europe. Italy's approach to this problem resembled that of other Catholic countries, especially France. Abandoned infants were cared for in foundling homes until they could, if possible, be farmed out to hired wetnurses, usually in the countryside. To allow anonymous abandonment while avoiding exposure, foundling homes introduced turning boxes where an infant could be deposited and an attendant alerted. Foundling homes might also administer an attached birthing hospital where unwed pregnant women could come to bear their children anonymously and then abandon them. A fee was charged for this service or, alternatively, poor mothers were obliged to provide wetnursing services (though not for their own children) for a few months. At the end of this period, the mothers left and the children were considered of unknown parentage.

Foundling homes were generally overcrowded, and mortality there was frighteningly high. During the Liberal period, foundling home reform was pursued and most of the turning boxes closed: the first was closed in 1867, and from a high of almost 1,200, their number was reduced to about 300, almost all in the south, by the turn of the century. They still numbered about 200 when finally banned by a Fascist decree in 1923. In general, closure of the turning box meant that infants would only be accepted where the mother's unmarried (or in some cases poor) status could be determined. This elimination of maternal anonymity came in tandem with an apparent change of attitude about unwed mothers. Where previously these women had been encouraged to abandon their children, more and more foundling homes encouraged "affiliation" and the nursing of illegitimate children by their own mothers; nursing subsidies to unwed mothers, for example, were awarded. These reforms became widespread throughout the north and center after the turn of the century and seem to have been a success, as abandonment decreased and affiliation increased; contrary to some expectations, no evidence of increased infanticide, public exposure, or criminal abortion was detected. Reform was less successful in the south, where the condemnation of illegitimacy was stronger; in Naples, for example, reform had to be generally abandoned (though the turning box was closed in 1875).

In part due to regional differences of this sort, national legislation on foundling care came late to Italy. Beginning in 1876, various laws were proposed, one inspired by the shocking report that out of 856 infants accepted at the Neapolitan foundling home in 1895, only 3 survived to the following year. Still, on a national level nothing more was done and reform did not come until 1923.[38]

Just as Liberal statistics revealed high levels of infant mortality (especially among foundlings), so did it measure a high (though declining) level of work force participation among Italian women of childbearing ages. Indeed, sections of Italian industry and agriculture depended almost entirely on cheap female labor. Protection of these women came slowly and in a limited fashion. In 1902, certain jobs were prohibited for women and a four-week post partum leave was legislated for industrial workers; its enforcement seems to have been lax, certainly in part because the mother received no compensation during this leave. Maternity insurance was introduced eight years later (1910) and was paid for by a fund to which female workers and their employers were obliged to contribute. This Liberal *cassa di maternità* provided the basis for similar Fascist measures later on.[39]

Official statistics

In the period of the *Risorgimento* (1815–71), statistics offered the unifiers of Italy a means to present the social, political, and economic disparities of the peninsula under a cloak of uniformity. In monographs and scientific meetings, Italy was treated as a statistical, if not political, whole, and some regional governments came to consider statistics as

---

[38] On abandonment in Liberal Italy, see Bononi 1897; Gorni 1974; Hunecke 1989; Pomata 1980; Raseri 1894; for the period 1900–22, see also *Rivista di beneficenza sociale* and *Difesa sociale*.

[39] The laws referred to are L. 19 June 1902, n. 242; L. 17 July 1910, n. 520; see Ballestrero 1979, pp. 11–56 for a discussion of this legislation.

subversive of the existing pre-unification order.[40] Following unification (1861), this view was put into practice, and statistics were called upon to cement together a heterogeneous society and make the new nation known to itself.[41]

As a validation of nationhood, the new Italian kingdom undertook to count its population almost before the smoke had cleared from the battlefields. The prologue to the (December) 1861 census described it as: "one of the first and most important administrative acts which responded to the new needs of the reconstituted and unified kingdom and at the same time one of the most undeniable manifestations of the force and spread of the national and unitary ideal."[42] The census was carried out by Italy's new statistics "directory", the Direzione generale della statistica (DIRSTAT). DIRSTAT would also be responsible for compiling and publishing population registry data on births, deaths, marriages, and changes of residence for all the nation's administrative units.[43] These data appeared in various volumes which, together with a yearbook covering all of the institute's statistical activities, were intended to appear annually. The census was scheduled for every ten years.

The first concern of DIRSTAT had been to describe the newly unified nation, demographically and otherwise. As attention shifted to Italy's pressing economic and social problems, new areas of investigation were added to its responsibilities. One of these was emigration. Previously left to private hands (Carpi 1874), DIRSTAT took over collection and publication of emigration statistics in 1876, and ultimately emigration became the demographic index of greatest official and scientific interest, a fact explained by the already noted scale of the phenomenon: total emigrants, about 100,000 per year in 1876, tripled by 1899 and tripled again by 1913, when almost 900,000 Italians sought work abroad. World War I brought emigration to a virtual halt, but the exodus began again immediately afterward, though it was impeded by receiving country immigration restrictions, particularly those of the US (see figure 1.9).

Death, too, attracted considerable interest, and the development of actuarial science provided an additional incentive for mortality

---

[40] Woolf describes the *Risorgimento* as a period when statistics were used by patriots as a political weapon (1989, p. 602). For a general discussion of *Risorgimento* statistics from both political and social perspectives, see in particular the work of Patriarca (Patriarca 1996, one chapter of which appears in an earlier version as Patriarca 1989).

[41] On Italian Liberal statistics, see Corsini 1985 and 1989; Leti 1989; Moretto 1991; Pravato 1990; Romanelli 1980 (as well as the final chapters of Patriarca 1996).

[42] DIRSTAT, *Censimento* 1861, p. v; see also Keyfitz's contribution to Alonso and Starr 1987, especially pp. 238–9, for a general statement in this regard.

[43] See Moretto 1991; *Annali di statistica*, I, 1 (1871).

research.[44] DIRSTAT publications in fact reveal progressively increasing sophistication in the representation of mortality and improving quality of data. By contrast, fertility received considerably less attention in the Liberal period. Colajanni, for example, commented that fertility measures were not well studied, and the general stability of fertility during the Liberal period explains in part this relative lack of official interest (Colajanni 1904, p. 213).

In spite of initial enthusiasm, both popular and official indifference long plagued the efforts of Italian government statisticians. The institute was not well funded, and suspicion regarding the purposes of data gathering would long hamper its efforts, especially in the south. Following a relative "golden age" in the 1870s and 1880s, the DIRSTAT budget in fact declined, and the institute's publications decreased in size and frequency. Under the premiership of Crispi, the 1891 census (it would have been the fourth) was simply canceled. However, not all areas of demographic investigation suffered from the general climate of economic crisis in those years. Population data on Italy's African possessions, for example, had been included in the statistical yearbook from 1884, and in 1893 (again under Crispi and just after the canceled national census) a colonial census of both indigenous and European populations was in fact carried out.

The new century saw something of a revival of Italian statistics, thanks to a budget increase and to the efforts of Ministers Luigi Luzzatti and Francesco Severio Nitti. It was short lived, and World War I interrupted attempts at statistical reform, though DIRSTAT did continue to function. In the war's aftermath, the institute extended its data gathering to those Italian-speaking regions that had remained part of Austria-Hungary following Italian unification and which would, following dissolution of that empire, presumably become part of Italy. In the words of DIRSTAT's director:

When hostilities ceased as a result of our glorious victory, those provinces acquired the right to be included along with the others as important territorial components of the Kingdom. Although this right has not yet received official recognition in those treaties which should establish the new European order, delaying as a result the completion of national unification – which was both the dream of our ancestors and the ideal which inflamed the heroism of our soldiers – nonetheless we could not ignore the conquests assured Italy by the very conditions of the armistice. Hence our desire to present in these pages for the first time the name of those lands which must soon be joined indissolubly to Italy. (*Annuario di statistica*, 2,7 [1917–18], p. vi)

---

[44] See, e.g., Rameri's contributions to *Annali di statistica* first and second series; and also Beneduce 1907–8, p. 675; Rameri 1898.

Just as the *Risorgimento* statisticians had established the statistical bases of Italy before the nation had been united, so their successors statistically annexed the expected new regions. At the peace conference, Italy did not receive all the territory and population she expected (and had already counted). This disappointment was the source of her so-called "mutilated victory" and the later irredentist demands of Nationalists and Fascists.

In the turmoil of postwar Italy, subsequent attempts at statistical reorganization came to naught. Then in 1926, following the Fascist consolidation of power, the *Istituto centrale di statistica del Regno d'Italia* (Central Statistics Institute of the Kingdom of Italy – ISTAT) inaugurated a new era in Italian statistics. This development will be taken up in chapter 2.

Demographic theory
The official statistics of Liberal Italy naturally reflected the vicissitudes of governmental and economic situations. That attention should be concentrated on the areas of emigration and mortality rather than, for example, fertility – a situation which would change dramatically – was both a reaction to the dynamics of population and a response to political priorities. The political discussion of population problems in the period also bore on academic circles, where the new science of demography was emerging as a discipline; and economists, sociologists, statisticians, and others debated the theoretical aspects of population movement.

As a scientific discipline, demography came into existence in the mid to late nineteenth century. In Italy, the first university courses dedicated to demography were offered in the 1880s, and Italian demography texts began to appear at the turn of the century.[45] In the last decades of the nineteenth century one finds Italian references to demography as an autonomous discipline, though it was sometimes considered to be a subdiscipline of either political economy or applied statistics. In the introduction to his 1877 statistics course Messedaglia divided the science of population into two parts: the statistics and the economy of population. The first considered population itself, the second the relation between population and the means of subsistence (Messedaglia 1879). Isidoro Blumerù, one of a number of foreigners who came to work and study at DIRSTAT, described demography as the most exact and the most important part of statistics, as a sort of

---

[45] Although Messedaglia taught a course in demography and statistics in 1877, the first Italian chair dedicated solely to demography was only created in 1961. On the evolution of demography in Italian higher education see Nobile 1987 and 1989.

anatomy and physiology of the social body and as the basis of all social sciences (Blumerù 1885).

The demography texts of Rodolfo Benini (1901) and Colajanni (1904) were the first of their kind in Italy (but see Nobile 1987). Benini divided demography into "qualitative" and "quantitative" theories of population and devoted most of his work to the qualitative, which sought to measure the physical and mental characteristics that enhanced or diminished societal cohesion. On an individual level, he calculated an index of attraction between couples, the factors of which included age, marital status, place of birth, nationality, level of culture, profession, and religion. Benini's work rested on the assumption that, just as the family was the basic organizational unit of society, so familial cohesion was the basis of societal cohesion.

While Benini's qualitative theory dealt with the statistical treatment of individual characteristics, the quantitative theory considered the demographic "movement" of society as a whole – fertility, nuptiality, mortality, and migration – a less original if more "modern" approach. By contrast, Colajanni's text conformed to what today seems more conventional demographic organization. He rejected Benini's qualitative/quantitative theories in favor of his own division of demography into statistics, theory, and policy. Colajanni organized his text according to the "status" (anatomy) and "movement" (physiology) of population.

The appearance of the texts of Benini and Colajanni, following Messedaglia's earlier treatment, signaled the emergence of demography as an academic discipline in Italy, and the debate over its nature and scope revealed a science in the process of identifying itself. The application of statistics to population was, however, only one aspect of the discipline. The other consisted of socioeconomic and political analysis.

Long after his death in 1834, Thomas Malthus continued to dominate the European population debate. Although his famous *Essay*, first published in 1798, did identify a universal truth of population dynamics, namely the eventual impossibility of sustaining an ever-growing population in a fixed territory, it was also significantly a product of its time. European per capita food consumption probably reached an historic minimum around the turn of the nineteenth century, and the frequency of famine in the eighteenth century made tragic overpopulation seem a real possibility. The flood of Irish immigrants entering England strengthened this impression, as would the potato famine of 1845–6.[46] Malthus' theory was both simple and convincing: population

---

[46] On the "century of famine" centered on about 1800, see Montanari 1994, pp. 129–51; on European nutritional levels, see Livi Bacci 1991, pp. 79–110.

potentially grows at a faster rate than does agricultural production and this potential can be checked in two ways: by the "positive" checks of famine and disease or the "preventive" check of moral restraint, in particular the postponement of marriage. Malthus was later incorrectly associated with other forms of restraint which he actually condemned, and the European birth control movement came to be known as neo-Malthusianism. The irony of Malthus' theory is that it was penned at just that moment when European agriculture and industry began to reap the fruits of those non-organic energy sources and technological innovations that would free European population from the Malthusian trap. Nonetheless, hunger did not disappear, and Malthusian views persist to this day.

The Italian debate over Malthusianism experienced a revival in the period 1880–1900 (Isenburg 1977, pp. 41–2). There were two reasons for this: it was in this period that Italian emigration began to grow at an alarming rate (Manzotti 1962, p. 66) – and many interpreted this movement as a reaction to Malthusian population pressure – and it was also around 1880 that reasonably good demographic data became available in Italy, a factor which had a stimulating effect on all areas of population study.[47]

Messedaglia, Benini, and Colajanni all addressed the population question as framed by Malthus, though perhaps the most thoughtful and extensive Italian discussion of population theory in the period was that of the Socialist Achille Loria. Loria conceded that the combination of population growth and diminishing returns from agriculture could theoretically create a Malthusian situation. He denied, however, the necessity of this. According to Loria, Malthus had erred in asserting that the geometric and arithmetic ratios were the result of physiological and natural laws. The well-known phenomenon of differential fertility, or the inverse relationship between fertility and wealth, revealed that human reproduction was governed by economic considerations rather than physiological law, and the fact that agricultural production had increased more than population in recent decades reflected the importance of the intensity of land cultivation. Loria followed the standard Socialist line in claiming that Malthusian overpopulation was indeed a function of the present economic system. He accused Marx, however, of erring in the belief that overpopulation might be a uniquely capitalist problem. Loria gave population pressure a central role in all economic systems, describing it as "the great economic impetus, the prodigious

---

[47] On the Italian Malthusian debate in this period see Isenburg 1977, as well as Lanaro 1979, pp. 56–7; Nobile 1989, p. 67; Wanrooij 1990, pp. 72–80.

demiurge of social transformations, the providential ferment of human progress" (Loria 1909, pp. 40–1). He proposed a "dynamic population theory" which emphasized the important relationship between population density and systems of agriculture and industry. The present-day economy was Malthusian insofar as it encouraged non-intensive use of the land and high fertility among the poor (Loria 1882, 1897, 1909).[48]

Various authors, including Loria, identified in the theories of Darwin the generalization of Malthusian ideas. With Darwin, the grim inevitability of the Malthusian positive checks became instead the motive force of progress and evolution for all species. It was, however, the evolutionary theory of Herbert Spencer which most influenced the Italian discussion of population theory. According to Spencer, population pressure acted as a stimulus to intelligence and the progress of civilization. Physiologically, this progress is associated with increasing cranial capacity in man (confirmed by the more voluminous skull of the highly evolved Englishman as compared to those of other races, particularly uncivilized ones) and an associated decreasing ability to procreate; in evolutionary terms, the more intelligent and less fertile are more likely to survive (high fertility being on average a disadvantage in modern society). Spencer offered a biological/evolutionary explanation for fertility decline, as opposed to one based on social or economic factors (Spencer 1972, pp. 33–7) (and this distinction would be important to subsequent discussion of population theory in the Fascist period).

In his 1894 *Population and the Social System* (dedicated to Loria), Francesco Nitti, while ascribing greater importance to economic factors, did find resolution of the problem of population in the biological doctrine of Spencer. Nitti claimed that *laissez-faire* economics led to inequalities in the distribution of wealth and to high fertility. On the other hand, a fairer distribution of wealth would lead to Spencerian "individualization" and so fecundity decline and population equilibrium. In an unusual political twist, Spencer, the champion of *laissez-faire* capitalism, was here enlisted by Nitti in support of economic equalization and the redistribution of wealth (Nitti 1894).

French theories also influenced the Italian population debate. According to Arsène Dumont's theory of "social capillarity" – intended to explain French fertility decline – individual socioeconomic advance leads to voluntary fertility control as repeated childrearing is incompatible with economic wellbeing. Social capillarity characterized open democratic societies because it was in these that social mobility was

---

[48] On the general topic of Socialism and the population question, see Pogliano 1985.

possible (Dumont 1890). Nitti, following the suggestion that social capillarity was a problem in need of resolution, claimed that Dumont's message was *socializzate!* Socialism would remove income disparities and so social capillarity, with the result that French fertility would be restored to respectable levels (Nitti 1894, p. 99). Loria's analysis was virtually the reverse. He instead concluded from the French example that a predominance of small proprietors and also good wages – certainly both signs of a more equal distribution of wealth – led to fertility control.[49] Also with reference to Dumont's theory, Colajanni argued that the combination of social equality and economic inequality led to social capillarity and so fewer births. Unlike Dumont or Nitti, however, he concluded: "And this is a good thing" (Colajanni 1904, p. 263).

The Malthusian debate in Italy should presumably have been put to rest by one chapter of Benini's *Principii* (1901) bearing the immodest title of "The correct interpretation of the Malthusian problem and its solution." Benini claimed that the Malthusian assumption of a direct relationship between population movement and the means of subsistence ignored the mitigating factors, for humans, of custom and imitation. A segment of any human population, he claimed, was capable of intelligent and voluntary changes of habit, the rest of simple imitation. As such, the social change taking place among urban elites and resulting in fertility decline was likely to spread to the rest of the population and so eliminate the Malthusian threat. Benini's assessment was prescient, but the question was far from put to rest as it was just this spread of fertility decline which Fascist policy would later seek to combat.

Just as the Italian discussion of population in the late nineteenth century was rarely, if ever, characterized by unqualified Malthusianism, so were unreserved populationist views, or cries of demographic panic, equally infrequent. Italian population theorists were of course aware of French fertility decline and the attendant general concern, but their attitude seems to have been more that of interested observers than potential participants. This attitude would change, and an early indication was a 1911 article by Giorgio Mortara who attributed reduced natality to the primarily urban phenomenon of the voluntary limitation of childbearing. According to Mortara, given the inefficiency of legislative measures to boost fertility, it was the mission of the true Nationalist to educate the population on the collective need for the maintenance of growth (Mortara 1911).

Neither neo-Malthusianism (birth control) nor eugenics found much

[49] In 1927, Mussolini too would identify small property holdings as a denatalist force; see below.

support in Italy. Those who made reference to such practices tended to condemn them as immoral or disgusting. Loria, for example, opposed artificial practices aimed at limiting births, preferring, if necessary, Malthusian moral restraint (Loria 1909, p. 47). Primarily an Anglo-American and Northern European phenomenon, a degree of neo-Malthusian propaganda did enter Italy by way of translation. One of these was done by Mussolini in his Socialist days (Mussolini, XXXIII, p. 258). Ideas on the need for the qualitative improvement of population (eugenics) were also a primarily transalpine and transoceanic innovation. The work of Francis Galton and his successors on the need for selective human breeding did raise a degree of interest in Italy, and scholars of note, including Loria and Corrado Gini, took part in the international debate over eugenics. As in other European states, fears were raised about the potentially dysgenic effects of World War I and the possibility of racial deterioration. Still, in fundamental ways the Italian discussion did not resemble the "mainline" eugenics advocated elsewhere. Isolated and few were the voices favoring a negative eugenic program of sterilization or limitation of procreative/marital freedom.[50]

In general, the relatively lower fertility of the upper classes – deplored by eugenicists – was viewed with less concern in "proletarian" Italy than, for example, in imperial Britain. The economist Vilfredo Pareto, for example, saw in it a potential benefit. According to Pareto's theory of the circulation of elites, there is in any society a Gaussian distribution of ability which does not coincide precisely with the distribution of wealth and power. As a result of intense competition in the middle and low income groups, superior elements emerge in a process of natural selection aided by relatively high mortality and form a new elite, replacing the decadent elements of the old. The decline of the existing elite is moreover accelerated by the universally low fertility of the upper classes (Pareto 1964 [1896], pp. 244–50).

Corrado Gini (who would be the leading Italian demographer of the Fascist period) incorporated the ideas of Pareto in the early formulation of his cyclical theory of population. According to Gini, recent work on evolution theory – that of Hugo de Vries[51] – had shown natural selection to be relatively less important than the positive or negative influence of environment. This basically Lamarckian view, acquired by Gini early in his career, would continue to color his later work, as well as that of many

[50] These arguments are taken up again in chapter 5; see also Pogliano 1984, pp. 61–77; for Anglo-American "mainline" eugenics see Kevles 1986 and Soloway 1990.
[51] It is interesting to note that Loria, with whom Gini collaborated was also converted to the devriesian theory of evolution at this time (see Loria 1912).

other Italian demographers. Gini's theory, like Pareto's on the circulation of elites, worked from the common observation of differential fertility. Differential fertility was not a cause for concern, according to Gini, but rather an important factor of "social exchange" according to which the best elements of the large and fertile lower classes rise in an "upward current" and enter the upper classes. He concluded: "the slower growth of the upper classes will not lead to the deterioration of the human race, but it will impede its rapid evolution" (Gini 1909, p. 82). Over the following decades, Gini would considerably elaborate these ideas, ideas which, moreover, did find a small degree of acceptance elsewhere in Europe.[52]

The attention of Italian population theorists in this period naturally focused on emigration. Advocates of free emigration likened it to a "safety valve,"[53] relieving Italian population pressure. Hoped-for benefits included reduced unemployment, increased wages, improvements of (especially southern) agriculture, increased exports, and an increased volume of shipping, but most of all remittances from Italians working abroad, estimated as high as 2.4% of the gross national product.[54]

Alternatively, emigration was viewed as a national loss. Countering the benefits of remittances was the financial loss associated with each emigration. According to the "money value of man" argument, each individual represents an investment by the state in terms of education and upbringing, an investment which can only be repaid if the individual remains in Italy during his or her productive (i.e. wage-earning or working) years. And though emigration never exceeded natural increase, as was repeatedly pointed out (and high levels of repatriation made this possibility remoter still), the possibility of

---

[52] Gini cites Fahlbeck 1903, p. 173 for the idea of social exchange. See Gini 1912, p. 25. The idea, however, seems not to be new as the concepts of upward current and social exchange (not so-called) are found in Messedaglia 1858. Similar ideas were voiced in Britain in the pre-World War I period: see Soloway 1990, p. 18. I discuss Gini and his cyclical theory at greater length in chapter 5.

[53] This phrase is generally attributed to Sonnino, although it appears to have been used before him. See Ciuffoletti and Degl'Innocenti 1978, I, pp. 79, 116. See also, e.g., Colajanni 1904, p. 438.

[54] For the various emigration arguments, see, in addition to Manzotti 1962, Beneduce 1904; Di San Giuliano 1905, p. 93; Montemartini 1907, p. 68. On remittances, see Beneduce 1904; Colajanni 1904, p. 44; Coletti 1912, pp. 241–3; Montemartini 1907, pp. 68–70. Mortara (1921, p. 3) estimated 1909–13 annual remittances at 1,030 million lire; according to ISTAT 1976, the annual *totale prodotto lordo interno* (GDP) was 14,605 million lire for the period 1901–10 and 42,655 million for 1911–20. The latter figure is probably too high for 1909–13 so Mortara's estimate might well represent a percentage of GDP well above that suggested here. See also Ciuffoletti and Degl'Innocenti 1978, I, pp. 456–65 and Sori 1979, pp. 119–27.

depopulation was also cited as an argument against emigration.[55] Other arguments against emigration cited the depletion of the labor force, the weakening of the military, and the fact that uncultivated land remained in Italy that could be exploited by those departing (Manzotti 1962, p. 79). Francesco Coletti, a professor of statistics, political economy, and demography, listed among the negative consequences of emigration the break up and, for the south, the reduction in size of the already small family, but claimed that arguments about the increased immorality of women or weakening of the military were exaggerated (Coletti 1912, pp. 229–32). Luigi Villari, later among the early propagandists of Fascism, complained of the harmful influence of the United States, claiming that in return for the export of healthy workers Italy received alcoholic tubercolitic repatriates (Villari 1909, p. 309). Villari's position was a bit extreme, but many were rightly concerned for the welfare of Italian emigrants whose suffering was well known.[56]

Others of course took a subtler line somewhere between the advocacy and the condemnation of emigration. Luigi Bodio, head of DIRSTAT and later the CGE, found it sad that so many thousands left Italy each year, but not so sad as if they should stay: "Let them go. Both those who leave and those who stay behind will be better off" (Bodio 1892, p. 145). He claimed that emigration was for Italy a necessity and described migration as the social equivalent of oceanic or atmospheric currents seeking equilibrium (p. 109). Crispi shared Bodio's view, seeing emigration as essentially "a harsh and sad necessity."[57] Gini, while identifying emigration as one sign of national decadence, nonetheless questioned the wisdom of emigration control, as those more vital sections of the population that emigrate might represent the population's rebirth in new lands. Gini also believed that emigration exercised a negative effect on the morality (and fertility) of the Italian population in general because of the decadent habits imported by returning emigrants (Gini 1912, pp. 102–6, 119–39).

The most developed treatment of emigration in the period was that of Coletti. Coletti rejected the various proposed "laws" of emigration which linked it to a certain level of population density or growth, fertility, illiteracy, or to particular economic or climatic conditions. Instead he

---

[55] See Bodio 1892, p. 110; Coletti 1912, pp. 81, 225; Nitti 1888, pp. 14–19. This observation held on a national level. Between 1901 and 1910, however, the population of Basilicata did decline by about 1% and that of Abruzzi and Molise by almost 4%. See Sori 1979, p. 190.
[56] On the plight of the Italian emigrant see Ciuffoletti and Degl'Innocenti 1978, I, pp. 199–256, 341–52.   [57] At least according to Nitti (1888, p. 45).

claimed that it depended on the collective psychology of the population group from which the emigrants came. Coletti's analysis was based on an essentially utilitarian "theory of need," according to which the actions of an individual are motivated by the desire to remove pain or maintain pleasure. Emigration, then, is the product of a general awareness of the actual or eventual suffering associated with remaining, and a recognition that emigrating entails less suffering than not emigrating. Coletti identified unification as having opened the horizons of many Italians to the possibility of emigration. By introducing the psychological element, Coletti was able to cope with the inevitable exceptions that accompany a theory based exclusively on demographic or economic variables. His theory, for example, accounted for increasing emigration in a socioeconomically static situation. He attributed such an increase to the possibility and desirability of emigrating becoming more and more a part of the collective psychology with each additional departure (Coletti 1912).

The Italian discussion of population theory revealed a science in the process of defining itself. In addition, it used the primary strands of the general European discussion, with differing emphases and points of originality. Attempts were made to resolve the long standing Malthusian debate; a more sophisticated, economic approach was applied to population theories, and full-blown theories of emigration and the evolution of populations were enunciated, incorporating biological and psychological considerations.

As compared to France, Britain, or Germany, Liberal Italy lagged a bit behind in demographic developments and in population policy. The statistical investigation of the Italian population was initiated in this period, however, and insofar as we can equate knowledge and power, demographic study implies a degree of power over population status and movement, which is to say over population itself, still among the central (and most difficult to control) of the resources of any state. Two questions face those who consider the acquisition of this knowledge. If the aim is indeed control, are such investigations legitimate in a liberal-democratic state? And are they worth the investment?

The subsequent period would witness many changes: in the institutional organization of Italian statistics, in the patterns of demographic movement and the priorities of demographic study (fertility would dominate both), in the theoretical considerations of population, and in the population policy of the Italian government which, under Fascism, would move from implicit to explicit attempts at demographic control.

Any doubts regarding the legitimacy of government attempts at demographic intervention would be cast off and the only limits to policy would be those imposed by knowledge of the factors influencing population movement, the resistance of that movement to attempts at manipulation, and budget.

2

The organization of totalitarian demography

When the Fascists came to power in 1922, the statistics institute was in a state of neglect; emigration was considerable, though not as high as it had been; and fertility decline was beginning to be a source of concern, though not yet in government circles. Lacking a preconceived program regarding population questions, Mussolini's government inherited the limited policies and institutions of its Liberal predecessors and only gradually came to revise them.

In the first few years of Fascist rule, questions of power and holding on to it generally took precedence over social policy,[1] and it was only in the period between the resolution of the Matteotti crisis in January 1925 (generally regarded as signalling creation of the dictatorship) and the signing of the Lateran treaty in February 1929 (reconciliation with the Church and definitive consolidation of power) that Fascist policy moved from vague to more certain and authoritarian positions. In this, population policy was no exception.

It was, in fact, in the period 1925–9 that Mussolini adopted what had been the traditional Nationalist line on emigration and in general developed the populationist stance that would characterize the rest of the *ventennio*. The first emigration, anti-urban, and pronatalist measures date from this period as do the Fascist internal migration, infant and maternal care, and statistics institutes. In this chapter then I consider the creation of the policy's ideological, legislative, and institutional infrastructure, all basically in place (and untested) by 1929. In subsequent chapters I shall return to each of these areas and their developments in the mature years of Fascist rule during which the policy underwent revision, expansion, and attempted reinvigoration.

As it developed, the Fascist population policy emerged as an attempt

---

[1] School reform was an exception; see Koon 1985, pp. 33–59.

to protect the traditional Italian family, threatened – or so it seemed – by the departure of fathers or potential fathers, a trend to fewer births, continued demographic waste in the form of infant deaths, and the spread of urban values. In its ambition, if not its realization, it was one of the largest scale programs of population management ever attempted. Only subsequent years would reveal the limitations of this "totalitarian" plan.

Migration

Prior to the rise of Fascism, emigration had been the demographic variable which generated the greatest official concern, and after 1922 opinions continued to vary between the "safety valve" and Nationalist positions. According to the former, emigration relieved population pressure and so lowered unemployment and social tension; according to the latter, the departure of Italian workers represented the loss of Italy's greatest resource: while Italian workers populated the colonies of others, Italian imperialism was frustrated.[2]

At the time of the March on Rome (the Fascist seizure of power on 28 October 1922), opinion inclined to the pro-emigration view. Post-war unemployment had created considerable unrest, unrest which had aided the Fascist rise to power and which many attributed to population pressure made worse by the recent US immigration restrictions (Ipsen 1990). In response, the Liberal Treasury Minister Giuseppe Paratore had presented a report to the Presidenza del consiglio dei ministri (Office of the Prime Minister – PCM), one month before Mussolini came to power in which he emphasized the inability of Italy to feed her 40 million inhabitants[3] and proposed emigration as the only truly practical solution to the problem of unemployment (ACS PCM 1922 f.2.9.2732; Nazzaro 1972).

In this same period, Stefano Jacini, a parliamentary deputy and member of the Partito popolare (the Catholic party), was conducting a survey on emigration for the Opera Bonomelli, a charitable Catholic organization concerned with emigration of which he was general director.[4] The results of this survey, published in the Bonomelli's journal, give a good indication of contemporary educated opinion on the emigration question. Those questioned covered a large political and professional

---

[2] On emigration policy in Fascist Italy, see Cannistraro and Rosoli 1979, pp. 9–48; Ciuffoletti and Degl'Innocenti 1978, II; Nobile 1974; Sori 1979.

[3] The 1922 population of Italy is estimated at 38,370,000.

[4] The survey was distributed three days prior to the March on Rome. On the *Opera Bonomelli*, see Cannistraro and Rosoli 1979.

spectrum including Socialists, Fascists, Liberals, and *popolari*; professors, physicians, lawyers, industrialists, and others. Few advocated repression of emigration and many thought it should be encouraged. The most repeated recommendation, suggested by the questionnaire, was the odd-sounding "regulated freedom." Almost none of those questioned advocated the acquisition of foreign lands by Italy, favoring instead the traditional emigration of Italians to Europe, America, and the Mediterranean. Jacini sent a copy of the survey to Mussolini in April 1923. Previously – in early November 1922 – Jacini had communicated to Mussolini, via the minister of the colonies, Luigi Federzoni, his belief that the emigration process needed to be freed of excessive bureaucratization (ACS PCM 1923 f.2.8.1810). This was a concern shared by Paratore and many of those questioned in the Bonomelli survey, and the bureaucratization Jacini referred to was that imposed by the Commissariato generale dell'emigrazione (General Emigration Commission – CGE) which had been created by the 1901 emigration law (see chapter 1).

In Mussolini's first address to the Camera dei deputati (Chamber of Deputies) as prime minister,[5] he made a brief reference to the emigration problem: "Our emigration policy must be freed of excessive paternalism" (Atti C. disc. 16 November 1922, p. 8393). Two days later the CGE budget was discussed in the *Camera*.[6] Jacini took the opportunity to criticize the apparent attempt to create a state monopoly of emigration, treating the phenomenon as a safety valve which could be opened and closed at will. Achille Pellizzari, also a *popolare*, called for elimination of the CGE, a call for the moment unheeded. Mussolini announced that he

---

[5] The parliament of the Kingdom of Italy consisted of two houses, the Camera dei deputati, the members of which were elected, and the Senato, the members of which were appointed for life. The king chose a member of the *Camera* to form a government and so become *presidente del consiglio dei ministri* (or prime minister). The prime minister in turn chose his ministers from among the members of the *Camera*. The result of the March on Rome was to force Victor Emmanuel to appoint Mussolini prime minister, a position which he held until July 1943.

[6] The CGE budget came in large part from a tax imposed on each ticket sold by the shipping lines which transported Italian emigrants. Below is a list of the CGE post-war total expenditures in current prices (lire):

1919–20	6,888,997[a]	1923–24	11,762,298[b]
1920–21	10,774,413[a]	1924–25	12,283,350[c]
1921–22	8,186,815[a]	1925–26	12,318,550[c]
1922–23	10,724,846[a]	1926–27	16,105,050[c]

[a] confirmed expenses, CGE 1924–5, III, p. 18.
[b] confirmed expenses, MAE AS: CGE Gab. 20.
[c] anticipated expenses, MAE AS: CGE Gab. 20.

had not yet decided the CGE's fate, but in any case would work to reconcile the various demographic needs of the nation (Atti C. disc. 18 November 1922, p. 8507).

These needs, according to Fascists and others at the time, were primarily more opportunities for emigration. Legislation was quickly implemented to both speed up the passport process – law required (unsuccessfully) that they be issued twenty-four hours after application – and further relax wartime restrictions (R.d. 21 January 1923, n.228; R.d. 18 March 1923, n.590). Emigration restrictions for military age males were actually liberalized relative to the prewar era. In this same period, the autonomy of the CGE was reduced as it became part of the Ministero degli affari esteri (Ministry of Foreign Affairs – MAE) (D.l. 18 January 1923, n.227), a move in keeping with the Fascist position that the emigration problem was "keenly political" and an important aspect of foreign policy. As a result, emigration matters came more closely under the supervision of then minister of foreign affairs, Mussolini.

Early statements within the government of what would eventually become Fascist emigration policy came from the Nationalists, who merged with the PNF in 1923 and generally disapproved of free emigration. Inaugurating a congress on economic and commercial expansion abroad held in Trieste in November 1923, Alfredo Rocco, subsequently minister of justice, gave a speech which echoed Nationalist sentiments expressed at least since the Libyan War and also sounded much like those delivered by Mussolini three-and-one-half years later:

Expansion is for us a necessity. Our land is limited and relatively poor while we have a scarcity of capital and an exuberant population . . . Spontaneously, instinctively, the nation has found a solution to this problem . . . the route of exile: it has resolved the problem of expansion by means of emigration.

But frankly many, too many, in Italy view with pleasure and approval this solution to our national problem . . .

Whether its balance be positive or negative, the phenomenon of emigration today is a serious one . . . The fertility of the Italian population is considerable, but cannot long resist a bleeding of this sort. Remember: our true and greatest wealth is population, because in numbers is the greatest strength of all races. The most numerous peoples are not simply those militarily most important – because in numbers is the essential element of military strength – but economically every man has a value and represents capital. To lose millions of Italians means to lose billions of lire. Up until now our high fertility has allowed us to endure this open wound in the flank of the nation. It has even allowed us to enjoy population increase in spite of emigration, an increase, however, which in the years before the war was fairly limited. And even though the birth rate remains high, the tendency in Italy is also one of decline.[7]

[7] *Bollettino dell'emigrazione* (November 1923), pp. 821–2.

At this same conference the economist Livio Livi discussed the economic and demographic consequences of US immigration restriction:

We can ask whether these restrictions, as far as our country is concerned, constitute a permanent and ever more serious danger. Probably not: regarding the problem of surplus workers, Italy has passed the most critical point. Whether the checks to emigration are maintained or even intensified, the pressure cannot be greater than that of the past two years during which the economic infrastructure has shown itself resistant.[8]

So while the Fascist government did not pursue an anti-emigration policy until several years later, elements encouraging such a policy already existed within the ruling hierarchy and some economists thought that reduced emigration might be economically sustainable. The Trieste conference, however, generally supported the existing pro-emigration policy and urged the creation of a national institute to aid enterprises employing Italians abroad. This institute came into existence the following month and Mussolini identified it as a means of Italian expansion.[9]

This new institute would presumably complement the efforts of the two-decades-old CGE which under De Michelis generally pursued a policy of *valorizzazione* (utilization or exploitation). Ideally *valorizzazione* worked to the benefit of both the state and the emigrant. Its primary tool was the work contract negotiated by the CGE with foreign governments and companies. A feasible program during the war, when France for example badly needed workers, this sort of arrangement was generally less attractive to foreign employers than the standard free market arrangement, and the number of Italian workers so employed was moderate compared to the number who emigrated spontaneously.[10]

A more general aspect of *valorizzazione* consisted of the CGE's constant study of the international labor market, with the intention of encouraging or discouraging, as the situation suggested, Italian migration to specific areas. This action was facilitated by the fact that Italian passports – a special category for emigrants had been introduced in 1921 – were issued for specific destinations and were valid for only one

---

[8] *Bollettino dell'emigrazione* (November 1923), p. 829. Indeed 1923 saw the greatest decline in real wages of the entire Fascist period; see Lyttelton 1973, p. 232 and works there cited. On the economic history of Fascist Italy, see Ciocca and Toniolo 1976; Clough 1964, pp. 211–59.

[9] Istituto nazionale di credito per il lavoro italiano all'estero, R.d.-l. 15 December 1923, n.3148. For Mussolini's statement, see *Bollettino dell'emigrazione* (February 1924), pp.134–5. On the Trieste conference, see also "Per l'espansione dell'Italia all'estero," *Economia* (December 1923), pp. 319–44.

[10] For 1926, for example, the *Bollettino dell'emigrazione* (January 1927, p. 39) reported 55,000 contracted emigrants as compared to well over 200,000 non-contracted ones.

Table 2.1 *Total (gross) Italian immigration to the*
US, 1900–1930

1900	100,135	1916	33,625
1901	135,996	1917	34,596
1902	178,375	1918	5,250
1903	230,622	1919	1,884
1904	193,296	1920	95,145
1905	221,479	1921	222,260
1906	273,120	1922	40,319
1907	285,731	1923	46,674
1908	128,503	1924	56,246
1909	183,218	1925	6,203
1910	215,537	1926	8,253
1911	182,882	1927	17,297
1912	157,134	1928	17,728
1913	265,542	1929	18,008
1914	283,738	1930	22,327
1915	49,688		

Source: Livi Bacci 1961, pp. 7–8.

year.[11] In the post-war period De Michelis regularly issued circulars instructing prefects to withhold passports for destination countries where either economic conditions were known to be poor or immigration restrictions had been imposed and the unprepared migrant was likely to be turned away.

Italian efforts to encourage or "valorize" emigration were, however, frustrated by outside forces. The most important of these, and indeed the single most significant factor in the history of interwar Italian emigration was the introduction of national immigration quotas by the United States. Calculated as a small percentage of the total population of each national group present in the US at an earlier census date, the first quota, legislated in 1921, established an annual limit of 42,057 Italian immigrants, less than 20% of the actual level (see table 2.1). Quotas were reduced and made permanent in 1924 (when the Italian quota became 3,845). Both De Michelis and Mussolini carefully

---

[11] According to the 1901 norms for their issuance, passports cost 10.02 lire for those well off, 2.02 lire for those not and were free for the destitute. They were valid for three years (R.d. 31 January 1901, n.36). According to the 1919 legislation, passports for emigrants carried a special stamp of the CGE and cost 2 lire, rather than the standard25 lire (R.d.-l. 13 November 1919, n.2205, art.15). In 1920, in response to the increased demand, the CGE began issuing a special red passport for emigrants. The price was unchanged. It was valid for one year (CGE circ. 30 April 1921, n.20 in *Bollettino dell'emigrazione* [April 1921], pp. 287–92).

monitored the US developments as almost daily communications were received from both the CGE representative in Washington and the Italian ambassador regarding the proposed legislation, legislation which passed in spite of official Italian protest (Nazzaro 1972; Nobile 1974; MAE AS: CGE Gab. bb.23, 25). In the absence of the US quota, the Fascist position on emigration might have been different. The decision to suppress Italian emigration, however, came only in 1927, long after the introduction of US legislation, though not long after Mussolini had firmly seized control of the state.

Because it led to an increase in clandestine emigration, the US quota complicated the monitoring of Italian emigration (Atti C. disc. 10 February 1923, pp. 1597*–9*). Partially in response to problems of this sort, the CGE employed a squad of emigration inspectors and provincial emigration delegates.[12] Their function was one of surveillance, control, and protection. Although the effectiveness of the agents was criticized by De Michelis himself, there were occasional references in the CGE Bulletin to successes in repressing clandestine emigration and it seems to have been the police function that was emphasized.[13] As further evidence of official support for *valorizzazione*, both De Michelis and Mussolini affirmed in circulars to prefects and the provincial delegates that emigration was an issue too delicate and important to be left in private hands.[14]

Emigration *valorizzazione* (and expansion) continued to characterize official discussion over the following years during which regulated emigration was encouraged, and the CGE Bulletin referred regularly to the success of Mussolini's policy at increasing Italian emigration. De Michelis described the policy as one aimed at expatriating the largest number possible of individuals not employable at home, taking into account of course the potential for absorption of workers abroad.[15] Fascist national list candidates campaigning for the election of 6 April 1924 naturally referred to the government's expansive pro-emigration policy.[16] In late May of that same year, following the Fascist electoral victory, the Italian government sponsored an international migration conference. If the conference – as seems likely – had been partially inspired by the hope of relaxing receiving country restrictions, these

---

[12] R.d. 19 July 1923, n.1686; R.d. 6 December 1923, n.2825; R.d.-l. 1 May 1924, n.767. As of April 1924, there were one central inspector, four regional inspectors and thirty-three provincial delegates (*Bollettino dell'emigrazione* (May 1924), pp. 459–62).

[13] *Bollettino dell'emigrazione* (December 1926), pp. 1621–4; (July–August 1924), p. 578.

[14] *Bollettino dell'emigrazione* (March 1924), p. 275; (November 1924), pp. 989–90; (January 1925), pp. 128–9.

[15] *Bollettino dell'emigrazione* (January 1924), pp. 35–40; (November 1925), pp. 1136–9; (January 1926), pp. 30–41.   [16] *Bollettino dell'emigrazione* (April 1924), pp. 303–6.

hopes were dashed as it was during the conference that the US Congress passed the second quota act.[17]

In the newly elected legislature, dominated by a two-thirds majority of the Fascist national list, a changing emphasis on emigration emerged only slowly. In an address to the Senate, Alberto De Stefani, minister of the treasury, warned of the need to reduce the dangerous disproportion between Italy's demographic and economic power made worse by restrictions and work force saturation in receiving countries.[18] In the lower house the theme of demographic imperialism – virtually absent, for example, from the Bonomelli survey of one and one-half years earlier – began to re-emerge while a degree of Socialist opposition to government policy endured (Atti C. disc. 4 June 1924, pp. 128–9 (Pedrazzi); 11 June 1924, p. 272 [Lazzari]). During the Matteotti crisis (which followed the April elections), Mussolini continued to emphasize the need to find new outlets for emigration in the face of Italy's inevitable demographic expansion (Mussolini, vol. XXI, pp. 97–8 [4 October 1924]).

In the parliamentary discussions of the Foreign Affairs Ministry budget, both Giovanni Gentile, then minister of public education, and Mussolini himself addressed this theme. Gentile identified the demographic problem as "the primary and most difficult of our national problems," while Mussolini stated that there were two solutions to the problem: one internal, a greater exploitation of national resources, and one external, emigration. While he held little hope that US immigration restrictions would be relaxed, he did envision continuing and increased migration to South America (Atti C. disc. 13 November 1924, pp. 420–1; S. disc. 11 December 1924, pp. 570–1). This expectation had been recently encouraged by the soon to become minister of public works, Giovanni Giuriati, who, returning from a special mission to South America, announced in a Palazzo Venezia address to Mussolini, the king, De Michelis, and others that there existed an intense demand for workers in the various republics he had visited.[19]

Mussolini's reference to an internal solution for the demographic problem presaged one of the principal directions that his population policy would subsequently take, namely, the encouragement of internal migration to those areas of Italy that were relatively under-populated and so presented opportunities for agricultural expansion

---

[17] The conference was held in Rome on 15–31 May 1924. The Johnson bill was approved by the US Senate and Congress on 15 May and became law on 26 May.

[18] Atti S. disc. 27 June 1924, pp. 142–3; see also De Stefani 1921.

[19] The meeting occurred on 17 November 1924. See *Bollettino dell'emigrazione* (November 1924), pp. 908–12.

and intensification. Shortly after Mussolini's parliamentary address, the 82-year-old *garabaldino*[20] Edoardo Pantano proposed creating a National Institute for Internal Colonization. In spite of the appeals made by Senator Pantano to both Mussolini and Giuriati over the next couple of years, his project, opposed by the latter, never became law. Giuriati objected to the degree of state intervention and expense called for in Pantano's proposal (50 million lire per year), claiming that the existing law on land redistribution together with private initiative was a more appropriate way to deal with the problem. Nonetheless, Fascist internal migration policy as it would subsequently develop resembled the Pantano proposal on many counts. The unrealized law called for internal migration programs as a way to attenuate emigration, and called also for the state to purchase uncultivated land, establish colonial villages, settle agricultural families, provide the necessary loans and so on. War veterans were to be preferred as colonists, and the project included special provisions for Sicily and Sardinia. Subsequent internal colonization programs of the Opera nazionale combattenti (National Veterans Organization – ONC) and other semi-private (but government funded) organizations might well have cited Pantano's plan as their model.[21]

The ONC had been created in 1917 in order to manage land distribution and so help war veterans obtain small property holdings (D.l. 10 December 1917, n.1970). It was intended to fulfill the call for "land for the peasants" but also to control the unauthorized land occupation that took place in the immediate post-war years. Although well funded, the ONC initially accomplished little, and Mussolini ordered investigation by a special commission. The commission's report made recommendations in line with both the Pantano and later CPMI (see below) proposals, namely the creation of small property holdings, development in the south, and anti-urban measures. Without eliminating the ONC, the Fascist regime did succeed in co-opting its program and took over its pro-peasant and pro-veteran mandate.[22]

More modest than the Pantano proposal, a Comitato permanente per le migrazioni interne (Permanent Committee on Internal Migration – CPMI) was created in early 1926 as part of the Ministry of Public Works, but dependent upon the head of government. Its task was primarily to

---

[20] A *garibaldino* was one who fought with Garabaldi in the wars for Italian unification and so enjoyed the status of a national hero.

[21] Atti S. D.l. N.98, 98-A (20 January 1925) also published as Pantano 1925; S. disc. 20 January 1925, pp. 946–72; ACS PCM 1934–6 b.1762 f. 1.1.23.3299 sf.2-C. On internal migration in this period, see also Corsini 1983; Di Rienzo 1965; Sori 1979, pp. 441–73; Treves 1976; Vitali 1974. [22] On the ONC see Mariani 1976, especially pp. 16–39.

study the problems of internal migration, but also to coordinate the transfer of unemployed workers from the north to the south and islands where they were needed for public works, in particular the *bonifiche* (land reclamation projects), and eventually to fill positions created by the attendant growth. It did not, however, have the power or the means to pursue its own programs of migration and colonization. The shift in emphasis from external to internal migration found spatial expression in Rome, where the CPMI used the offices of the CGE. The CPMI also included De Michelis.[23]

For a period, official policy included the encouragement of both internal and external migration. In his report on the 1926–7 MAE budget, the Liberal Democrat Andrea Torre[24] called for a more balanced distribution of the work force in Italy and also lauded the CGE for transforming Italian emigration during the past twenty-five years from a "breathless and haphazard rush" into "an organized and disciplined exodus" (Atti C. D.l. N.684-bis [31 January 1926], pp. 21–3). Responding to Torre's report, Orazio Pedrazzi once again raised the question of Italian imperialism and expansion in the Mediterranean (Atti C. disc. 19 May 1926, pp. 5814–18). In the Senate discussion, Mussolini betrayed a changing attitude when he referred to emigration as "a sad but endurable necessity," and added that: "emigration is indeed nothing less than the pauperization of the people and the nation itself" (Atti S. disc. 28 May 1926, p. 5893). He repeated this theme in a meeting with De Michelis in late 1926, announcing, nonetheless, that emigration would continue and might even increase and so the services of the CGE would continue to be needed.[25]

In tandem with the shift of focus in Fascist discussions from external to internal migration, the advocacy of demographic expansion in the Italian possessions, especially Tripolitania (western Libya), became more frequent. Mussolini visited Libya in April 1926 and called for increased agricultural colonialism (Mussolini, vol. XXII, pp. 117–18 [15 April 1926]). His appeal was seconded by Federzoni who, both in private communication to *il duce* and in the Senate, claimed that hundreds of thousands of Italian workers might be profitably employed on Italy's "fourth shore" and called for a program of public works and *bonifiche* to encourage Italian migration to Libya. Federzoni also proposed the transfer of Italians from Tunisia to Libya in an attempt to avert the

---

[23] L. 24 December 1925, n.2299; R.d. 4 March 1926, n.440(735); *Bollettino dell'emigrazione* (March 1926), pp. 213–22.

[24] Torre, initially hostile to Fascism, gradually became reconciled with the regime and in 1929 was appointed senator.

[25] *Bollettino dell'emigrazione* (November 1926), pp. 1433–4.

feared "denationalization" of this latter population[26] (Atti S. disc. 17 March 1927, p. 7023; C. disc. 21 May 1928, pp. 8989–90; ACS SPD-ris. b.23.224). However, Federzoni also claimed, again in the Senate, that the lands under the Italian flag were insufficient to absorb Italy's demographic exuberance (Atti S. disc. 4 April 1927, p. 7420).

Emigration was once again the object of parliamentary discussion in relation to the 1927–8 MAE budget (Atti C. disc. 30–31 March 1927, pp. 7364–92, 7408–30), a budget which, presented in December 1926, still included the CGE. Familiar themes were repeated as Gentile reiterated Mussolini's identification of emigration as the external solution for the demographic problem, but asked how long Italy would continue to give to other nations this "wonderful wealth." Great peoples and great nations, he claimed, feel the need to expand beyond their borders and colonize new lands of their own. Criticism of the CGE was renewed by Carlo Delcroix, president of the National Association of Disabled Veterans and by this time a fervent supporter of Mussolini, who launched an attack against "the sultanate of via Buoncompagni" – street address of the CGE. As emigration was a "keenly political" problem, it should be under the direct control of the appropriate ministry, not an autonomous *Commissariato* whose ballooning budget was out of all proportion to the importance of its activities. Indeed, Delcroix thought these activities basically mistaken and ineffective as the search for new outlets for emigration appeared to be fruitless. He called for the transfer of responsibility for emigration to a general directorship of the MAE, and for the establishment of emigration policy on new Fascist foundations: currents of Italian population should only be directed where they could benefit Italy and never where they might aid a potential enemy. At the conclusion of his address, Delcroix received a standing ovation and an embrace from the head of government.

Mussolini himself did not speak on this occasion.[27] In his place, Dino Grandi, undersecretary for foreign affairs, ended the discussion. Grandi seconded Delcroix's condemnation of the CGE as a basically Liberal and so outdated institution which "jarringly contradicts the principles of Fascism." With the authorization of Mussolini, he announced that the CGE would undergo substantial modification. Reciting arguments which would be repeated continually during the following years, he asked:

---

[26] The Italian population in (French) Tunisia was estimated at 97,000 in mid-1927 (MAE 1928, p. LXII).

[27] He did during the discussions of the MAE budgets for both the previous and following years.

Why must our race[28] continue to serve as a sort of human nursery, destined to feed the more or less organic unity of demographically impoverished nations? Why must our mothers continue to bear children who will serve as soldiers of other nations? . . . Fascism does not intend to encourage an emigration which will diminish the strength of the race and of the state. Meanwhile let us strengthen and enlarge our economy and internal production. (Atti C. disc. 30–31 March 1927, pp. 7428, 7430)

One month later the CGE was replaced by a Direzione generale degli italiani all'estero (General Directorship of Italians Abroad – DGIE) within the MAE (R.d.-l. 28 April 1927, n.628).[29]

The suppression of the CGE signalled the advent of unqualified Fascist populationism, a policy initiated by various measures to control emigration. According to an article of the November 1926 unified text of laws for public security, itself a significant step toward authoritarian dictatorship, all passports held by Italians in Italy had been made invalid. Although this was primarily a police action intended to impede the expatriation of politically dangerous elements, it had an effect on regular emigration as well, causing confusion, delay and clogging at exit points. It also provided a clean slate for subsequent emigration repression.[30]

New guidelines on passport issuance did not come until June 1927. One week after Mussolini's Ascension Day speech (see below), *il duce* issued a circular to prefects calling for "the utmost severity and restrictiveness in issuing passports," invoking the familiar money value of man argument according to which emigration represented an economic loss to the nation.[31] Subsequent circulars issued by Mussolini and Grandi further restricted passport issuance and established new regulations to go into effect in September. Passports would only be issued to those who could demonstrate a work contract or a summons from a no more than third degree relative. The restrictions with regard to both the contracts and the summons were further tightened on several occasions.[32]

---

[28] On the use of the term race in the period, see chapter 4, pp. 185–6 below.

[29] Subsequently the CGE's separate fund was incorporated into the national budget and the Consiglio permanente dell'emigrazione was suppressed (R.d. 18 June 1927, n.1036[1303]; R.d. 23 October 1927, n.2146(2457)).

[30] T.U. 6 November 1926, n.1848(2132), art.231; see Aquarone 1965, pp. 97–9; MAE AS: CGE b.84.800.

[31] Circ. 3 June 1927, n.63 in *Bollettino dell'emigrazione* (June 1927), pp. 829–30. In addition to the relevant discussion in chapter 1 above, see Gini's use of this argument in Jacini 1923, p. 3.

[32] Circulars 13 June 1927, n.67-bis, 20 June 1927, nn.75–77, 16 July 1927, n.97 in *Bollettino dell'emigrazione* (June 1927), pp. 933–4; (July 1927), pp. 951–7; (August 1927), pp. 1155–8; Circulars 3 November 1927, n.148, 2 November 1927, n.149 in *Bollettino dell'emigrazione* (November 1927), p. 1737; circ. 18 July 1928, n.65 in *Bollettino del MAE* (July 1928), pp. 578–9.

The measures to prohibit unauthorized emigration and restrict the acquisition of passports were subsequently brought together and made more severe in the 1930 new penal norms for emigration. These raised fines and penalties for aiding or engaging in clandestine emigration. They also sought to repress the distribution of false reports on emigration and the speculation of bureaucrats selling emigration authorization (R.d. 24 July 1930, n.1278(1607); Atti S. D.l. N.356 [19 February 1930]). This legislation concluded the Fascist transition from emigration encouragement to tolerance to repression.

Traditional emigration was to disappear both in fact and in name. With the demise of the CGE, "emigration" no longer figured in the roster of institutional appellations, and Mussolini described *emigrante* as "a term which is disappearing from Italian terminology" (Atti S. disc. 5 June 1928, p. 10722). The emigrant passport was in fact eliminated and the fee increased from 2 to 80 lire (though not for repatriation) (R.d. 21 June 1928 n.1710[2107] and n.1730[2137]). Those who went abroad for work were subsequently described as *"lavoratori* (workers)." In contrast to its predecessor CGE, the new DGIE would concentrate not on those Italians still leaving the country, but on the estimated over 9 million already abroad.[33] In order to maintain a national spirit among Italian expatriates, they were encouraged to make return visits to the old country for so-called baths of Italian-ness.

Several small measures were taken in this regard. The CGE had been financed in part by a tax levied on each emigrant transferred by ship and in 1926 the charge was applied to the return voyage of the "emigrant" as well. In 1929 this latter repatriation tax was eliminated in order to facilitate both return migration and also return visits by Italians who continued to live abroad. For visiting Italians the (re)expatriation tax was also eliminated (R.d.-l. 13 November 1919, n.2205, art.26; R.d. 30 September 1929, n.1801(2114); R.d.-l. 28 July 1929, n.1929, n.1363(1990); Atti C. D.l. N.385 [28 November 1929]).

Emigrants had long enjoyed considerable fare reductions (up to 75%) for both their departing and return voyages on Italian trains (to or from ports or the frontier) (R.d. 29 December 1901, n.561). With the elimination of the category "emigrant" these fares were no longer applicable. A 70% train fare reduction was reintroduced in 1929 but, as with the sea passage tax exemption, it applied only to the *repatriation of lavoratori.* A

---

[33] According to MAE 1928, p. LXIV, total Italians abroad in mid-1927 numbered 9,168,367. For statements of the new emigration policy see circ. 26 October 1927, n.144 in MAE 1934; circ. 26 July 1928, n.70 in *Bollettino del MAE* (July 1928), pp. 584–5; *Bollettino del MAE* (August 1928), pp. 617–20.

train fare reduction (50%) was also introduced for Italians residing abroad and visiting Italy.[34]

The new passport fees of 1928 also awarded repatriation while penalizing departure. Subsequently, however, this policy experienced something of a setback, as the 80 lire passport fee was recognized as exorbitant and in September 1930 a special fee of 20 lire was introduced for *lavoratori* "while still firmly maintaining the principle of a single passport, equal for all and not distinguishing between workers and the well off" (Atti C. D.l. N.923 [21 April 1931]; R.d. 26 February 1931, n.315). Also at this time, a 100 lire fee was applied to passports for overseas destinations, money that was to go to the FNFL (see ch. 3); so the 20 lire must only have applied to European or Mediterranean-destination passports (R.d.-l. 26 February 1931, n.300; Atti C. D.l. N.920 [12 April 1931]). Several years later the repatriation fee exemption was eliminated for all but those returning to do military service. It was thought that this money might better be spent to aid Italians abroad.[35]

In this same period, the various sub-committees of the CPMI compiled new norms for internal migration and their reports on the possibilities for agricultural and demographic colonization in Italy, reports which inspired Mussolini's oft-repeated command on ruralism: "we must ruralize Italy even if it costs billions and takes half a century" (R.d. 28 November 1928, n.2874(3316); ACS PCM 1934–36 b.1762 f.1.1.23.3299.2-A). This legislation outlined an ambitious program including worker housing, transport, and lodging for state projects, and subsidies to charitable organizations and private concerns aiding or undertaking internal colonization. The funds were to come from the Ministry of Public Works. A telling indication of the new direction in policy, there appeared in the last issue of the *Bollettino dell'emigrazione*[36] a notice about the first experiment in internal colonization: 150 rural Venetians[37] were to be sent to Sardinia.[38]

Mild reservations about the new migration policy were expressed in the Senate where praise for the attempt to create jobs was tempered by the observation, later borne out, that the scale of internal migration programs could not match either traditional emigration or existing

[34] Dec. Min. 8 October 1929 in *Gazzetta ufficiale* n. 9 (13 January 1930); Dec. Min. 29 December 1931 in *Gazzetta ufficiale* n. 250 (27 October 1932).
[35] R.d.-l. 4 December 1933, n.1734; DGIE circ. n. 2 in *Bollettino del MAE* n. 1, 1934, pp. 163–4.
[36] It was subsequently incorporated into the *Bollettino del Ministero degli affari esteri*.
[37] Venetian is unfortunately an ambiguous term. In the present work I make no reference to the inhabitants of the city of Venice (*veneziani*) and Venetian always refers to those of the region of Venetia (*veneti*).
[38] *Bollettino dell'emigrazione* (November 1927), pp. 1928–9; see also *Bollettino del MAE* (April 1928), p. 415 and chapter 3, pp. 107–9 below.

unemployment (Atti S. Disc. 13 December 1927, pp. 9482–5). Certain categories of migration were in fact still allowed, including temporary emigration for those with a work contract lasting no more than three years and taking with them no accompanying family members, and also intellectual, professional, and commercial emigration. The latter were perceived as furthering the economic and cultural expansion of Italy.

In addition to the virtual prohibition of emigration and the encouragement of internal migration from areas presumed overpopulated to those where population seemed scarce, the Fascist attempt to manage spatial population movement included the discouragement of migration to cities. Although Fascism owed an important debt to urban ideas and support, the regime came with time to reject this legacy. Initial encouragement of urban growth was soon abandoned as the cities came to be viewed as centers of bourgeois decadence, opportunism, and low fertility: "We must take measures . . . to arrest the flow of population into the cities . . . Fertility is nullified in the major centers which in turn render less fecund the countryside as the countryside tends to imitate the unhealthy city" (Atti S. D.l. N.1804-A [8 December 1928]). Fascist modernization was to be pursued in a non-urban environment. Mussolini had adopted an anti-urban stance abruptly as part of the demographic policy in May 1927, and anti-urban legislation empowering prefects to take measures to limit city growth was introduced in December 1928.[39] The resultant measures were uncoordinated and generally ineffective, and in spite of the rhetorical importance of anti-urbanism, national legislation would not be introduced until 1939 (see chapter 3 below).

To sum up, between 1922 and 1930, Italian emigration policy underwent a dramatic change. Initially adopting the institutional framework inherited from previous Liberal governments, Mussolini (and De Michelis) promoted emigration, relaxed wartime regulations, and pursued new outlets. For a time the post-war silence on imperial expansion endured as well. Nationalist opposition to emigration and support of colonization/imperialism, however, gained momentum, and the suppression of the CGE in 1927 was the institutional expression of a revised evaluation of emigration. In a sense, Mussolini swung from one side to the other of Italy's decades-old emigration debate: from the "safety valve" position that favored emigration, to the traditional Nationalist position that opposed the export of Italian workers and advocated Italian overseas colonization. It was a move he would repeat with regard to fertility policy. It was also in keeping with the

[39] R.d. 24 December 1928, n.2961(72); see Treves 1976, pp. 65–85.

populationist stance he developed in these years and was part of a general attempt to control population mobility, inspired by the belief that the nation as a whole would gain from the correct spatial management of the workforce. Suppression of emigration, then, was to be accompanied by planned internal migrations, anti-urbanism, and the demographic colonization of Italian possessions.

The timing of the shift was also a function of the internal political situation. Certainly from the time of the absorption of the Nationalists into the Fascist party (March 1923), elements in favor of such a policy had held important positions in the government, and while the policy change must be seen as a reaction to international immigration restrictions, the US had introduced the first quota act in 1921 and the second and definitive one in 1924, years before the Fascist suppression of emigration. The new emigration policy came on the heels – and as an integral part – of the general move toward totalitarian social control initiated in January 1925. The attempt to regulate all the aspects of national production entailed control of the work-force's mobility as well. Recovery from the immediate post-war depression and Fascist successes at controlling unions made this action less disruptive than it might have been otherwise, and, given that the international situation had severely limited emigration anyway, the policy was not likely to inspire serious opposition from Italian economic interests. In this, Fascist migration policy was part of a broader program to control the economy, and society, in general.

The demographic battle

Numero come forza

Mussolini in his Socialist days had been a supporter of birth control, and his switch to pronatalism paralleled that on emigration. A similar switch, occasioned by World War I demographic losses, was made by many European Socialists, including those who did not follow Mussolini in the "slide to the right" (see Winter 1988a, p. 136). For Mussolini, and Fascism in general, it further confirmed the abandonment of early positions which linked the movement to revolutionary Socialism. By the time of his May 1927 Ascension Day Speech, Mussolini's transition was complete, and that speech together with his 1928 article "*Numero come forza*" (Strength in Numbers) constitute the fundamental documents for understanding his populationism. Nationalists in Mussolini's government, like Rocco, had expressed similar sentiments from at least 1923 (see above), and *il duce* himself had revealed an interest in Italy's demographic strength from at least

1925.[40] Still, it was with the 1927 speech that Mussolini forced "the nation to confront itself" and the problem of fertility decline (Mussolini, vol. XXII, pp. 360–90).

In the speech, delivered in his capacity as minister of the interior, Mussolini discussed the demographic problem as an aspect of public (or racial) health. He criticized as suicidal previous Liberal indifference to the problem, given that demographic strength constituted the basis of a nation's political, economic, and moral strength. He equated declining fertility with moral decadence and cited statistics that demonstrated Italy's decline. Mussolini blamed two basic causes for this decline: industrial urbanism, as borne out by the low fertility of Italy's most industrial cities (Turin, Milan, Genoa); and small property holdings, which gave rise to the fear that having several children would lead to the eventual division of an already small holding. This was a surprising statement as it contrasts dramatically with much subsequent demographic policy, in particular the programs for internal and African colonization which were intended precisely to create small property holders. Predictably, this position disappeared from subsequent Fascist rhetoric.[41] As a first step, Mussolini urged: "We must care for the race beginning with motherhood and infancy." The Opera nazionale per la protezione della maternità e dell'infanzia (National Organization for the Protection of Motherhood and Infancy – ONMI) had recently been created to this end; in future it would be financed by a new bachelor tax, a tax which also served to give the nation a "demographic jolt."

"Numero come forza" is a still more interesting piece. It was published in Mussolini's newspaper, Il Popolo d'Italia, and also served as a preface to the Italian translation of Richard Korherr's Geburtenrückgang.[42] Korherr's book also sported a preface by Oswald Spengler, author of the influential Decline of the West. According to Spengler,

---

[40] Mussolini's 1925 statistics gathering is discussed below; his earlier references to Italy's prolific population and opposition to neo-Malthusian doctrines, while a hint of things to come, do not signal his adoption of strongly populationist views. See Mussolini 1934, pp. 47, 295 for his comments in 1924.

[41] A classic example of the Malthusian preventive check, this factor had been invoked to explain French fertility decline, by Le Play among others; see Spengler 1979 (1938). Il duce's comments may have generated a degree of interest in academic circles. In an article appearing only months after the Ascension Day speech, Livi analyzed the relation between fertility and size of property holding, concluding that while up to a certain point (especially in northern Italy) family size and size of holding correlated positively, it was difficult if not impossible to determine if this was due to economic considerations and intentional family limitation (Livi 1927a; see also C. Alessandri in Maternità ed infanzia [February 1929], pp. 167–71; Annali di statistica 6, 16 [1932], pp. 1–58; Ballestrero 1979, p. 91, n. 12).

[42] Or "Birth Decline", the Italian title was Regresso delle nascite, morte dei popoli (Korherr 1928); the first German edition appeared in 1927.

Mussolini was the sole European leader of the period who responded to his call for a "Caesar" to battle the decadent forces of democracy and capitalism and so stave off the decline of Western civilization. Moreover, Spengler considered fertility to be a political force and Italy's *only* weapon. In the Liberal period population had also been described as Italy's sole resource, wasted in emigration and – so it seemed – finally mobilized in the taking of Libya. In the post World War I period, fertility differentials between nations had grown and Italy emerged as procreationally the greatest European power (save Russia). Mussolini shared the Spenglerian view of a declining West and believed that a demographically and politically expanding Fascist Italy might lead the way to its resurgence.

Korherr followed Spengler in his praise of *il duce* and also expressed anti-democratic sentiments as well as the view that fertility decline represented the fundamental threat to the West, particularly given the continued prolificity of the non-white races. He attributed this decline to the "extinction of religious sentiment" (linked to urbanism). The remedy lay in a spiritual transformation led by a strong ruler and a strong church, and aided by appropriate policies including the suppression of birth control, public assistance to mothers and children, and reversal of the process of female emancipation. The role of Spengler and Korherr, the latter a Catholic and future SS functionary, in Mussolini's political development represents an early and significant precedent to the Germanization (and Nazification) of Italian Fascism that would follow.[43]

Taking the lead from Spengler and Korherr, Mussolini in his own article raised the specter of the submergence of the white race by the more prolific black and yellow races. He cited the pathological growth of the cities – namely, their rapid increase in spite of low fertility thanks to the attraction of rural population – as a general European affliction, reviewed the Italian demographic situation, and questioned the effectiveness of pronatalist measures, concluding that they might work if introduced before fertility decline is too far advanced. He closed with an appeal to Fascist families:

And so my discourse is directed squarely at Fascists and Fascist families. This challenge is the purest touchstone against which the conscience of Fascist generations will be measured. We must determine whether or not the spirit of

---

[43] See Korherr 1928; Spengler 1926; for Korherr's Nazi activities, see Höhne 1970, pp. 433–4. Spengler's work first appeared in German, a language Mussolini read, in 1918. The revised two-volume work came out in 1922–3. Within two or three years the latter version was translated into French, Spanish, and English (but not it appears Italian). De Felice believes that Mussolini did not encounter Spengler's work until 1925; see De Felice 1974, pp. 38–44.

Fascist Italy is irreparably infected with hedonistic, bourgeois, and philistine values. The birth rate is not simply an index of the progressive power of the nation; it is not simply, as Spengler suggests, "Italy's only weapon"; it is also that which will distinguish the Fascist people from the other peoples of Europe as an index of vitality and the will to pass on this vitality over the centuries. If we do not succeed in reversing this trend, all that the Fascist revolution has accomplished and will accomplish in the future will be perfectly useless, as at a certain point in time fields, schools, barracks, ships, and workshops will be empty.

In this passage Mussolini reveals the centrality of the demographic problem to his vision of a new Fascist civilization, and also identifies the family – its Fascistization and acceptance of the large family ideal – as the key to Fascist population policy. In subsequent years this same motivation – preservation and reinvigoration of the Fascist revolution – inspired a more ambitious demographic policy and ultimately more extreme attempts (racism and war) to Fascistize Italian society (Mussolini, vol. XXIII, pp. 209–16, see also Mariani 1976, pp. 73–86).

Infant and maternal care
In the Ascension Day speech Mussolini identified ONMI as a fundamental aspect of the demographic policy. The genesis of ONMI, however, reveals little in the way of populationist intent and was in part an outgrowth of the earlier debate over foundling care, an area which would become one of the institute's primary responsibilities.

The long-called-for reform of Italian foundling homes (see chapter 1 above) finally came in 1923. The turning boxes, reportedly still numbering about 200, were banned, and maternal anonymity, long compromised in practice, was formally eliminated as the reception of illegitimate offspring was only allowed by direct consignment. In addition, unwed mothers were encouraged to nurse and affiliate their children; incentives included nursing payments and also legitimation prizes (prizes for officially recognizing one's illegitimate children). Local governments continued to be responsible for funding and managing foundling homes, and the legislation was criticized on this count and also for its leniency. One Sicilian critic claimed that the social stigma of illegitimacy was still too great for the encouragement of nursing by unwed mothers to be effective; he recommended instead that it be enforced.[44]

The problem of illegitimacy and foundlings was closely linked to that of Italy's high infant mortality rate (IMR), as this rate continued to be much higher for abandoned children. In the face of these high rates (see table 2.2), calls were raised for the creation in Italy of an institution for the protection of infancy after the model of those in other European

---

[44] R.d. 16 December 1923, n.2900; see also Foà 1922; Modigliano 1923; La Rosa 1923.

Table 2.2 *Italian infant mortality (deaths of infants under one year old per 1,000 live births)*

1913	138	1919	129	1925	119
1914	130	1920	127	1926	127
1915	148	1921	131	1927	120
1916	166	1922	128	1928	120
1917	159	1923	129	1929	125
1918	196	1924	126	1930	106

Source: Mitchell 1978, p. 141.

countries, especially Belgium where an *Oeuvre Nationale pour l'Enfance* had been created in 1903. Ernesto Salvia, a senator of the constitutional left, championed this cause in the months prior to the March on Rome, and as a result a Royal Commission, including Salvia, was appointed to draw up relevant legislation. Following the Fascist takeover, the Commission was reconstituted (still including Salvia) and its recommendations served as the basis for the ONMI legislation of 1925.[45]

Salvia's initial proposal had come during discussion of the Interior Ministry budget and this would continue to be a forum for the discussion of maternal and infant care. Following the Matteotti murder, Mussolini resigned from this ministry and appointed Federzoni in his place as part of an effort to regain national confidence.[46] The next budget discussion took place just as the crisis was reaching a peak (November–December 1924), and so the topic dominating discussion was political violence, normalization, and the question of whether laws would be respected and enforced (Atti C. disc. 18–25 November 1924; S. disc. 3–9 December 1924); it was "a rather warm session." Still, the need for infant protection was discussed, particularly by physician/deputies in the Fascist camp, and Federzoni, after an announcement in the press, officially presented the ONMI legislation on 8 December.[47]

Neither the law's presentation nor its discussion reveal much concern with fertility levels or population growth, though Umberto Gabbi did refer to "these young lives which must make up the armed forces of our defence" (Atti C. disc. 19 November 1924, p. 611). Federzoni stated that

---

[45] On the pre-history of ONMI see Atti S. disc. 9 June 1922, pp. 2409–11; Dalmazzo 1923; de Grazia 1992, pp. 234–5; Salvia 1922.

[46] Federzoni's ministries were: Colonies: 31 October 1922–17 June 1924, Interior 17 June 1924 – 6 November 1926, Colonies 6 November 1926–18 November 1928. His stint as minister of the interior represents the only period during the Fascist regime that Mussolini did not occupy that post.

[47] Atti S. D.l. N.79 (8 December 1924); see also *Il Messaggero*, 19 November 1924.

his legislation "represents one of the most urgent needs of the nation, an essential element of defence, of survival and of progress . . . the problem of infancy . . . is today a consummately political problem, of eugenics, demography and social hygiene, of moral, cultural and economic progress" (Atti S. D.l. N.79 [8 December 1924], p. 1). For both orators the primary concern remained the high rate of infant mortality.[48] While reduction of the IMR would eventually become an important goal of Italian pronatalism, the ONMI legislation originally responded not so much to a populationist impulse, but rather to a combination of embarrassment over Italy's international IMR ranking, a need to demonstrate that the processes of government were functioning, and perhaps also charity.

ONMI came into existence a year later in December 1925.[49] In addition to the IMR issue, several eugenically minded physician/parliamentarians, including Gabbi and Ettore Marchiafava, claimed at the time that ONMI would serve the purpose of "racial" improvement. According to Gabbi, "this law . . . realizes perfectly the biological conception which we must have of Fascism . . . it may represent for us in the future . . . a new human sanction for the protection of our race" (Atti C. disc. 25–26 November 1925, p. 4623). A biological conception of Fascism, as Gabbi called it, is less frequently encountered in Italy than it would be later in Nazi Germany, and negative eugenics of the sort practiced in the US, Germany. and elsewhere (including sterilization and marital certificate programs) would not be advocated by Italian Fascists; such practices would have created unresolvable conflicts with the Church. Nonetheless, some sorts of biological management were acceptable as will become clear in the theoretical discussion below (see chapter 5).[50]

Apparently, the first statement of the populationist aspect of the legislation came from the Deputy Luigi Macotta:[51]

the bill presented . . . aims to resolve . . . several of the most complex and serious questions connected with the infancy problem.
It is a complex and serious problem whose solution responds not only to a moral duty and a sentiment of social responsibility, but also and especially to a great

---

[48] Federzoni cited illegitimate and legitimate rates of 304 and 151 o/oo (Atti S. D.l. N.79 [8 December 1924], p. 4), considerably higher than the 1923–4 levels cited in table 2.2.

[49] L. 10 December 1925, n.2277 (27 of 1926); the ONMI bill was to take effect 7 May 1926, shortly before the beginning of the fiscal year (1 July). Norms for ONMI are included in R.d. 15 April 1926, n.718 (1020). Some of these were to take effect by 5 June 1926, the others on 5 November.

[50] Atti S. D.l. N.79-A (20 May 1925); S. disc. 9–10 June 1925; C. D.l. N.568, 568-A; C. disc. 25–26 November 1925; for Italian eugenics, see chapter 5, pp. 247–8 and works there cited.   [51] Macotta had been elected on the Fascist sponsored national list of 1924.

national interest. For to protect, aid and properly bring up infants is to impede demographic decline and the attendant reduction of the productive energy of the nation, to improve the race physically and morally, to prepare the strong youth of tomorrow, a generation physically, spiritually and intellectually healthy ...
Stated in this way the problem of infancy is consummately political and constitutes one of the cornerstones of the program of the national government. (Atti C. disc. 25 November 1925, pp. 4595–6)

Macotta here expresses concern over both quantitative and qualitative demographic decline.

The ONMI legislation – debated in a period when the Fascist hold on power was far from certain – did meet with some opposition. Antonio Pestalozza, who had founded a group of ex-*popolari* friendly to Fascism, asked how many women might actually profit from the legislation given the limited resources of Italian hospitals (Atti S. disc. 9 June 1925, pp. 3369–72); while Eugenio Morelli, a physician elected on the Fascist list, also questioned how the costs would be met and accused the measures of responding to urban rather than to more pressing rural needs (Atti C. disc. 26 November 1925, pp. 4608–11).

Federzoni had claimed that ONMI would require no new expenses, as it would be funded primarily by the budget item for charitable institutions. This item had been repeatedly criticized as inadequate,[52] and ONMI was to absorb over half (8 million) of its 15 million lire, a situation which even the legislation's proponents recognized as potentially devastating (Atti S. disc. 10 June 1925, pp. 2435–6). Over the next two years, charitable works received increases to 17.6 and then 22.6 million lire (Atti C. D.l. N.687 [18 December 1925]; Atti C. D.l. N.1172 [14 December 1926]); though the budget for all other institutions covered was effectively reduced just the same.[53]

The 1926–27 budget was the last over which any sort of debate took place. Gabbi spoke again, identifying the two major threats to maternity and infancy as alcoholism and syphilis, and reiterated his eugenicist views by advocating personal health cards and premarital medical exams to protect against morbid hereditary dispositions. He also called for stricter policing of abortion, above all by physicians, and concluded on a populationist note: "We must absolutely see to the respect of that *crescite et multeplicamini* which today impresses itself upon us with the

[52] Atti C. disc. 19 November 1924, p. 611; S. disc. 6 December 1924, p. 434; C. disc. 10 March 1925, pp. 2513–4; during discussion of the 1925–6 Ministry of the Interior budget, the deputy Barbiellini-Amadei described the situation for charitable works as disastrous (Atti C. disc. 10 March 1925, p. 2436).
[53] Fascist economy of this sort did not extend to all fronts, as that part of the budget dedicated to public security increased by over 180 million lire.

rebirth of our colonizing tendencies" (Atti C. disc. 1 May 1926, pp. 5500–3).

A physician of a different stripe was the Communist Fabrizio Maffi who criticized Gabbi, ONMI, and the regime:

You have approved the law for the protection of women and children. But laws are not enough, just as the votes of your assemblies are not enough, nor the pro-eugenic speeches of the honorable Gabbi . . . The situation of pregnant women, of young apprentices, the situation of nursing babies has nothing in common with your laws, because basic day to day needs come between laws and reality. (Atti C. disc. 1 May 1926, p. 5507)

Maffi also praised the liberal abortion laws in the Soviet Union. As a result of the exceptional decrees in November, he was relieved of his parliamentary duties, arrested, and sentenced to internal exile in a remote part of Italy.

Thanks to Mussolini's bachelor tax (see below), starting with fiscal year 1928–9 ONMI received its own (and much increased) budget line of 30 million lire (C. D.l. N.1840 [30 January 1928]). ONMI's total budget was considerably larger and included private and public contributions solicited personally by Mussolini; it hovered around 80 million lire (ACS PCM 1926 f.1.6.1.1909; 1928–30 f.6.1.3200; Atti C. D.l. N.15-A and 15-A-bis [25 May 1929], p. 12). Still, this seems to have been insufficient. In the Senate, Francesco Pullè calculated that to be effective ONMI would require a budget of 137 million lire (Atti S. disc. 30 May 1928, pp. 10318–20), and ONMI estimates put the figure at approximately 160 million, double the amount available (ACS PCM 1927 f.1.6.1.4637). These large sums were needed to cover ONMI's expanded duties as it had taken over responsibility for the administration of provincial orphan and foundling services (R.d.-l. 8 May 1927, n.798(1102); Atti C. D.l. N.1540; S. D.l. N.1424; L. 6 December 1928, n.2838[3298]). The institutional and hygienic problems associated with illegitimacy and abandonment had of course been among the primary ones ONMI had been created to combat.

Underfunding was only one of the obstacles that ONMI would encounter in its efforts to modernize infant and maternal care; its success was also compromised by conflicting and unrealistic goals. ONMI was handicapped from the start, for example, by its dependence on the "voluntary" participation of physicians, foundling homes, and other institutions involved in infant or maternal care. Moreover, it embodied an inherent conflict as it was intended to serve both tutelary and police functions.[54] In addition to generally monitoring infant and

[54] See Caravaggi 1976 for a similar characterization of ONMI.

maternal care, ONMI was also expected to assist in the repression of contraception and abortion.

Pronatalist measures
The police role of ONMI brings us to the more explicitly pronatalist aspects of the Fascist population policy. Although considerably revised in the 1930s, the basic elements were all put in place in the couple of years following the Ascension Day speech. These included the "positive" measure of rewarding procreation (at first only large families) and the "negative" measures of penalizing bachelors and prosecuting (where possible) procurers and suppliers of abortions and also advocates of birth control practices and traffickers in contraceptive devices.

As Mussolini announced in the Ascension Day speech, the ONMI budget increase was to be paid by a new tax on all unmarried men between the ages of 25 and 65, the bachelor tax. It went into effect on 1 January 1927, and Mussolini predicted that it would bring in 40 to 50 million lire.[55] Income tax discrimination against single or childless men had been introduced in France during World War I, but measures of this sort (like parity-based tax exemptions) were generally intended to partially compensate for the unequal financial burden shouldered by parents. Mussolini instead presented the Fascist bachelor tax as a means to increase fertility, a "demographic jolt" he called it. The Fascist example would be emulated a few years later in Weimar Germany.

The other negative aspects of the early demographic policy were punitive rather than fiscal, namely reinforcement of anti-abortion laws and new regulations to control contraception. The widespread use of contraception at the time was well known and frequently cited as a major cause of fertility decline. As early as 1908, Giorgio Mortara had noted the apparently frequent recourse to birth control among urban

---

[55] R.d.-l. 19 December 1926, n.2132(2426) and norms: R.d. 13 February 1927, n.124 (349). This tax included a fixed rate determined by age and a variable one determined by income. The initial fixed rates were:

25–35 years of age	L.35
35–50 "	L.50
50–65 "	L.25

In 1931, by which time the tax had doubled, variable rates ranged from 0.5–5% of income, for example 15 lire on a 3000 lire income, 4,350 lire on a 174,000 lire income, 50,000 lire on a 1,000,000 lire income (Boidi 1931). For Mussolini's statement, see Atti C. disc. 26 May 1927, p. 7619. During the first six months of its implementation the tax brought in 21 million lire according to the Ministry of Finance. In addition to ONMI numerous other organizations hoped to benefit from these funds. See ACS PCM 1928–30 f.9.2.1237.

residents, and by 1935 Pietro Battara guessed that there were virtually *no* couples in the cities who did not use some method of contraception (Mortara 1908, pp. 144–7; Battara 1935b, p. 67). The question of method, however, presented a problem for lawmakers who hoped to control reproductive practices. Mortara and others guessed that *coitus inter-ruptus* – a practice of course unaffected by laws controlling birth control "devices" – was the most common method used.[56]

Abortion too was perceived to be widespread and generally socially acceptable, and prosecution for the crime was rare. In the words of Guglielmo Tagliacarne: "As we well know, social morality forgives and often even encourages recourse to abortion in order to avoid having too many children" (Tagliacarne 1925, p. 415). Tagliacarne reported official statistics revealing about 50 prosecutions a year for abortion. Others questioned the usefulness of the (1889) anti-abortion law which found so little support in society.[57]

Measures against contraception and abortion were taken nonetheless. In the context of the ONMI legislation, Federzoni in fact called for the suppression of both abortion and neo-Malthusian propaganda.[58] These measures were included in the important 1926 public-safety law (already referred to in regard to passport cancellation). The sale, display, advertisement, transportation or distribution of publications, plastic objects, or other devices that might aid in either preventing conception or interrupting pregnancy were declared offensive to morality and public decency and so prohibited (T.U. 6 November 1926, n.1848, art. 112, 113, 115). The new penal code of 1930 recategorized these offences as "crimes against the race (*stirpe*)" rather than against morality or the individual and introduced stiffer penalties for abortion (two to five years, for example, for both aborter and consenting abortee) and also penalties for contraceptive propaganda. Penalties were increased for members of the health profession, who would if convicted be banned from that profession, while penalties were reduced if the abortion was performed in order to save one's honor.[59]

---

[56] Mortara 1908, p. 146; Palmieri 1935, pp. 180-1; post-World War II studies have con-firmed these earlier evaluations, see Bonarini 1994. For the debate over the causes of fertility decline, see chapter 5 below.

[57] Tagliacarne 1925; Pellegrini 1925; Carrara 1925; see also Passerini 1984, pp. 181–223 for first hand reports of abortion and contraception practices.

[58] Atti S. disc. 9 June 1925, p. 3373; see also Atti C. disc. 1 May 1926, pp. 5516–17.

[59] See art. 545–55 of the 1930 Penal Code, the so-called Codice Rocco; on the evolution of Italian abortion legislation and its enforcement in the Fascist period, see Detragiache 1980. It is interesting to note that the anti-contraception measures resembled a similar French law introduced in 1920 by a conservative and pronatalist parliament. Measures of this sort were clearly not limited to authoritarian settings. On the French law, see McLaren 1983, pp. 169–83.

The police role of the medical profession (and so ONMI) came with the modifications to the public security law (in 1927). These stipulated that midwives refer any irregularities in labor and childbirth immediately to a physician and that physicians report all miscarriages to the provincial physician in order to detect and punish instances of induced miscarriage, a measure which received Catholic praise.[60] Prosecutions for abortion did increase – 669 in 1930 for example as compared to 87 in 1922 – but their number was still far shy of the actual number of induced abortions, estimated as variously as 15–20% of all pregnancies and 80,000 per year.[61]

The foundations of Italian Fascist pronatalist legislation were completed with the 1928 pronatalist law, which consisted primarily of a tax exemption granted to large families (L. 14 June 1928, n.1312[1736]). While the bachelor tax had sought penalize the drones of society, this new tax represented a positive reward and encouragement of fertility, though its application was limited: to qualify, state employees needed to have seven living dependent children while non-state employees needed ten. It represented the first of a series of such measures.

Fascism and the Church
Mussolini's Socialist background included a good dose of anti-clericalism. As *il duce* of Fascism and head of the Italian government, he generally sought – not always successfully – to repress his hostility toward the Church and present instead a pious and cooperative facade. This policy of cooperation culminated in the Lateran Treaty of 1929 which settled the sixty-year-old "Roman question" and established Italy as a Roman Catholic confessional state. Mussolini hoped as a result (another goal inherited from the Nationalists) to make Catholicism serve national (and so Fascist) interests. And while he did gain in prestige and in other ways from reconciliation with the Holy See, the Church continued to be one of the main power centers that remained outside of Fascist control and so presented an ultimately insuperable obstacle to the Fascist totalitarian program.

[60] L. 23 June 1927, n.1070. Detragiache, however, suggests that both legislators and judges may have interpreted this law as serving a primarily statistical purpose; see Detragiache 1980, p. 711, n. 68; for the standard interpretation of the law, see Spallanzani 1934, p. 187. For Catholic comment, see, for example, *Rivista internazionale di scienze sociali* (May 1927), p. 76.

[61] Spallanzani 1934 gives some annual figures for abortion prosecutions. For estimates of total abortions, see Battara 1935b, p. 68; Marconcini 1935, p. 309, Ravicini 1930 and other sources cited in these works. Post-war studies again suggest that these estimates may not have been far from the mark; see Bonarini 1994. On the questionability of abortion statistics in this period, see Detragiache 1980, pp. 701–14.

One of the major points on which Catholics and Fascists (and so of course Catholic-Fascists) agreed was the profamily demographic policy, generally applauded in Catholic circles.[62] The Church had for decades advocated a family policy, and specifically a family wage, as a measure to ease the lot of worker families (and so lessen the allure of Socialism);[63] and it had of course traditionally presided over the creation of families, namely marriage (as well as the other demographic events of birth and death). Marriage was an important point of contention as the Liberal Italian state had not recognized the legitimacy of Catholic marriage, an anomalous situation resolved by the Lateran Treaty.

One year after the treaty, Pius XI issued an encyclical on chaste marriage (*Casti connubii*) which constituted a general defense of Christian marriage and the family. Partially in reaction to the recent approval of neo-Malthusian measures by Anglican bishops at the Lambeth conference, Pius attacked birth control practices, induced abortion, divorce, the emancipation of women, eugenic sterilization (and of course sterilization in general), and eugenic attempts to prevent marriage and childbearing by certain individuals. In addition he cited the Lateran treaty as a model for Church–State relations.[64]

Some Catholics were particularly enthusiastic. Giovanni Cazzani, the bishop of Cremona, praised Fascist population policy and described Mussolini as "the skipper who has given a masterstroke to the sails." Religion offered the most efficient remedy for fertility decline, Cazzani claimed, but he nonetheless welcomed the collaboration of the state:

The head of government can rest assured that the Church, which has always exercised its moral strength in opposition to all propaganda, doctrine, and practices contrary to the sanctity and fertility of conjugal love, will in future fulfill its mission with even greater effectiveness now that it is seconded by the measures of the state. (Cazzani 1929, p. 128)

One aspect of this collaboration was the promotion of Fascist population policy from the pulpit. In 1928, for example, Cardinal Tosi, the archbishop of Milan, read a pastoral letter on the topic of large families in which he made positive references to Mussolini's Ascension Day speech and to the newly introduced pronatalist policy; Mussolini sent thanks

---

[62] Webster 1960, p. 155 notes that "the population policy of Fascism . . . harmonized with the morality of the Church," and according to Ballestrero 1979, p. 62: "the most enthusiastic support and unconditional approval of the demographic battle must have been that of the Church and Catholic circles." For a discussion of the Church, Fascism, and family/demographic policy, see Dau Novelli 1994. There were of course points of Fascist-Catholic contention as well, especially Catholic Action and the fate of the youth groups; see Koon 1985, pp. 116–42.

[63] See, for example, Leo XIII's 1891 *De rerum novarum*.

[64] Pius XI 1939; see especially paragraphs 52–75, 88–90.

by telegram.[65] The archbishop's example was certainly emulated at lower levels of Church hierarchy.

In general, however, the Church attitude was more careful. An article on Catholic opposition to extramarital sex and contraception, for example, concluded "that the religious attitude regarding the fertility problem is entirely separate from the political attitude, insofar as the concept of a greater number of births as a means to greater national strength is an end in itself and of no relevance to religious morality" (Chiarelli 1934, p. 105). This statement does not suggest any opposition between Catholic and Fascist aims, but rather that their motivations in seeking a similar end differed. It is an argument which might allow the Church to maintain a degree of autonomy while promoting a pronatalist program.[66]

Discussions of the Interior Ministry budget generally included references to the essential demographic questions, the role of ONMI in caring for and improving the quality of the race, and the "brilliant intuition" demonstrated by *il duce* in linking ONMI support to the bachelor tax (Atti C. D.l. N.1840-A[10 March 1928]; C. disc. 16–17 March 1928; S. D.l. N.1473-A[10 May 1928]; S. disc. 30 May 1928). The deputy, Alberto Geremicca, who had expressed basically populationist views prior to the rise of Fascism, called attention in 1928 to "the problem posited by *il Duce* as the basis of national strength, the demographic phenomenon," and generally summed up the new demographic policy:

Encouragements to fertility, the bachelor tax, the organization for assistance to maternity and infancy are all measures which converge from different directions toward the goal . . . Previously we spoke of emigration in a completely different way than we do today. I myself . . . dealt at length with the question of whether emigration was a good or an evil . . . concluding that it was an evil, but necessary given the conditions of the nation at that time; but the new conception has completely banished any doubt on the subject.

And prolificity is a good because only the prolific peoples are strong . . . As for mortality, which is an element of growth, the Fascist government has not avoided the difficult task of reducing it . . . But . . . it is infant mortality which should concern us . . . And it is to the problem of infant mortality that we must call all our forces and attention . . .[67]

By 1929 the Fascist demographic program had been enunciated in all its important aspects: discouragement of migration abroad and to the cities, encouragement of certain internal migration and migration to the

---

[65] See Tosi 1928; *Rivista internazionale di scienze sociali* (April–May 1928), pp. 367–8 or Gemelli 1928a.
[66] Catholic opinions are further discussed in relation to the fertility decline debate in chapter 5 below.   [67] Atti C. disc. 16 March 1928; see also Geremicca 1918.

colonies, positive and negative pronatalist measures, and protection of motherhood and infancy. In order to monitor and manage Italian migration, fertility, and mortality, the regime needed knowledge of Italian demographic behavior and so good statistics.

Statistics

In *The Politics of Numbers*, Alonso and Starr write: "Official statistics do not merely hold a mirror to reality. They reflect presuppositions and theories about the nature of society. They are products of social, political, and economic interests that are often in conflict with each other" (Alonso and Starr 1987, p. 1). In Fascist Italy, where official statistics probably excited greater governmental attention than in any other period, these sorts of interests were particularly evident. Under Mussolini, the state statistics institution was completely reorganized and much better funded, and among the statistics collected, demographic held pride of place, as it was only by understanding the current Italian demographic realities that the Fascists could hope to manipulate them.

Fascist statistics do not necessarily fit the models developed for other countries and regimes. Starr, for example, goes on to link statistics gathering to democracy and capitalism (Alonso and Starr 1987, pp. 7–57, esp. 20–2), an observation which does find a degree of confirmation in the Anglo-Saxon world. However, statistical inquiry is not incompatible with a Fascist and corporativist state (nor for that matter with a traditional monarchy). Indeed, it can be argued (as Starr concedes) that a controlled economy requires more statistical information than one based on a freer market economy. Nor is there any indication that the Fascists had a more difficult time prying information from a reluctant population than did their Liberal predecessors or republican followers. Italian statistics in fact improved dramatically in the Fascist period. And while this development owes much to increased funding, improved methods, and better training of personnel, it may also be that a combination of consensus and fear made the otherwise suspicious and reluctant Italian population more forthcoming with the requested information.

Starr also associates the free dissemination of information and the imposition of statistical blackouts with, respectively, "open" and "closed" societies. And while the Italian Fascist state, presumably closed, did impose statistical blackouts (in particular, regarding economic statistics during wartime), a huge quantity of demographic statistics was disseminated and even popularized in an effort to propagandize the demographic programs of the regime.[68] Decidedly modern in this respect, Mussolini used statistics to inform both policy and public opinion.

In his 1 May 1926 address to the *Camera*, Gabbi complained of the lack of available statistics on the diseases threatening maternity and infancy, but added: "when I heard of the emergence of a statistics institute I rejoiced, truly rejoiced, because now we shall have certain data for a problem which needs a certain solution" (Atti C. disc. 1 May 1926, p. 5500). The institute to which Gabbi referred was the Istituto centrale di statistica del Regno d'Italia (Central Statistics Institute of the Kingdom of Italy – ISTAT) which, inaugurated in July 1926, would represent the revival of Italian statistics.

At the time of the March on Rome the quantity and quality of Italian official statistics were perhaps at their lowest point. The statistics office had an annual budget of 50,000 lire and a staff of thirty-five and was in the process of being passed from ministry to ministry. Indicative of the general state of statistical neglect, Rodolfo Benini protested, in March 1922, the inexplicable delays in work on the 1921 census and threatened to resign from his post as president of the Consiglio superiore di statistica (Statistics Council – CSS) – the committee of experts and politicians that oversaw first DIRSTAT and then ISTAT – if the long hoped-for reform of Italian statistics did not come to pass.[69]

Reform had been repeatedly called for by the CSS. The DIRSTAT director, Alberto Aschieri, had drafted a proposal in early 1922 which called for the centralization of statistical services, at the time divided among various ministries, and the transfer of the statistical office from dependence on a ministry to direct dependence on the PCM.[70] In the social turmoil of post-war Italy, however, statistical reform was a less than burning issue, and a general national indifference to the problem was noted by the CSS.[71] In its first meeting after the March on Rome, Benini renewed his call for "the need to remedy the semi-anarchic state in which the statistical services currently find themselves." To the relevant minister, who was present, he insisted "on the absolute necessity for the constitution of a great observatory of the life of the nation, so as to meet the needs of legislators and scholars."[72]

The new administration seems to have heeded Benini's appeal. In June 1923 the statistics office was reorganized and elevated to a *Direzione generale* (which had been its status from 1878 to 1917) as part of

---

[68] Failures, however, were also conceded; in 1937, for example, in preparation for the second and more ambitious phase of Fascist demographic policy.
[69] *Annali di statistica* 6,6, p. 21.   [70] *Annali di statistica* 5, 11, pp. 20–1; 6, 6, pp. 119–24.
[71] *Annali di statistica* 5, 11, pp. 89–90.   [72] *Annali di statistica* 6, 6, p. 35.

the newly formed Ministry of Industry, Commerce and Labor (later MEN).[73] In December, legislation was passed raising the statistics budget to 600,000 lire (R.d. 2 December 1923, n.2673). The fate of this money, however, is a little mysterious. For while it appeared in the projected 1924–25 MEN budget (Atti C. D.l. N.14-bis [30 May 1924]), the hoped for new personnel were not hired, a fact lamented by both the CSS and the MEN.[74] One explanation seems to be that salaries were too low to attract qualified people (350 lire) (Atti S. D.l. N.470-A [11 June 1926]). In any case, by the time of its demise the Direzione generale di statistica numbered twenty-seven employees. According to a later publication, its budget was still 50,000 lire (ISTAT 1936, p. 31).

The law creating ISTAT was presented in March 1926 by Mussolini who took a personal interest in the legislation (Atti C. D.l. N.808 [25 March 1926]; ACS PCM 1940–3 f.1.1.16.1.27000-1 sf.1). The new institution was organized more or less along the lines of the Aschieri recommendations. It was attached to no ministry but dependent upon the PCM. Ultimately all statistical services would be centralized in it, but this would be a gradual process. ISTAT would take over the quarters of the defunct *Direzione generale* and also those employees who chose to make the transfer. Its initial annual budget was 2 million lire. The CSS, which would continue to direct statistical activities, was also reorganized (L. 9 July 1926, n.1162[1470]). Its new president – and so the acting president of ISTAT, though the position was not formally created until 1929 – was the statistician/demographer Corrado Gini. Benini was chosen to fill one of the other professorial positions on the council. Initially he declined the invitation, but after repeated urging from the office of the PCM and following instructions from Mussolini himself, he accepted (ACS PCM 1940–3 f.1.1.16.3.1 N.27000–3 sf.1). It would not have reflected well on the regime if Italy's senior statistician (b.1862) declined to take part in the new initiative.

Gini, the man chosen to oversee Italy's new statistical enterprise, had already achieved a degree of prominence prior to the Fascist seizure of power. In the years leading up to World War I he began his university career and enunciated a population theory which he would elaborate in the following decades and which would prove congenial to Fascism (see below). Gini had been a Nationalist and already in the years leading up to World War I his populationist views regarding the threats posed by emigration and declining fertility had caught the attention of both

---

[73] R.d. 14 June 1923, n.1560. Several months later this became the Ministry of National Economy (MEN) (R.d. 6 September 1923, n.2125).

[74] ACS PCM 1926 f.1.1.1.4116; *Annali di statistica* 6, 6, pp. 76–7 (9–11 November 1925).

Enrico Corradini (head of the Italian Nationalist Association) and Alfredo Rocco (later Mussolini's minister of justice). During and after the war, he acted as an adviser to the Italian government and also to the League of Nations on the problem of primary resources. He was probably brought to Mussolini's attention by Rocco or other prominent Nationalists in Mussolini's government, and, several months before being chosen to head ISTAT, he had addressed the Fascist Grand Council and been well received.[75] Gini would develop close ties to the regime and ultimately heralded the new international order to be ushered in by Nazi-Fascist victory in World War II.[76]

The *Camera* ISTAT legislation report outlined how the planned reinvigoration of Italian statistics would serve the regime's population management program: "Post-war Italy must resolve its specific problems also by the clear application of the statistical method. The general problem of the conquest of wealth requires statistical calculations . . . of the possible exploitation of over-population, of the regulation of internal migration, of the prevention of emigration . . . " (Atti C. D.l. N.808 [25 March 1926], p. 3). In the report to the Senate, Pietro Sitta, a member of the new CSS, described the projected institution as a true national observatory: "For a modern state, statistics are truly the pulse . . . upon which nations constantly keep a finger in order to understand who they are and what they are worth" (Atti S. D.l. N.470-A [11 June 1926]).

ISTAT was inaugurated with a ceremony at Palazzo Chigi, seat of the MAE, in which Mussolini, and of course Gini, took part. In a speech on the past and future of Italian statistics, the new president described the institute's various responsibilities:

But perhaps the most important task of the research office will be to study the trends of demographic change . . . The forecasting of future demographic trends in the various regions . . . assumes in Italy a special importance, both because of the extreme population pressure and also because of large regional differences in population growth, which is generally high, but which is declining alarmingly . . . in the provinces nearest France. Furthermore, the exploitation of hydraulic sources of energy, the *bonifiche* and the division of large areas of land . . . are likely to call forth great movements of population.

Obviously the study of these trends must be the guide for all programs of internal colonization.[77]

---

[75] As a member of the commission of eighteen, Gini addressed the GCF on parliamentary reform, advocating representation for the corporations in the Senate. His recommendations were approved by the Grand Council, but never acted upon (ACS SPD-ris. b.27 f.3-C); see also Aquarone 1965, pp. 53–60.

[76] On Gini's early Nationalist connections, see Federici 1941, pp. 240-1; on his general political leanings, see Lanaro 1979, pp. 44–51; for his anti-emigration views, see Jacini 1923, p. 3; his World War II statements are discussed in chapter 5 below.

[77] *Annali di statistica* 6, 2, pp. 17–18.

Mussolini also took part in the first meeting of the new CSS. On that occasion *il duce* described ISTAT as one of the most important creations of the Fascist regime (a phrase often repeated): "The Central Statistics Institute will be, by means of the dry but suggestive eloquence of figures, an instrument for government action in the present and future."[78] Mussolini, Gini, Sitta and others all shared the idea that statistics gathering was a necessary and important tool of government, and demographic statistics of course provided the basic information necessary for any attempt to control demographic behavior.

In order to revive Italy's faltering statistical service, Gini was given free rein to bring together at ISTAT noted statisticians from throughout the peninsula. He chose, for example, Livio Livi, then at the University of Trieste, to head ISTAT's research office and, in order to facilitate this move, had a position created for Livi in the political science department at the University of Rome. Gini was not, however, successful in keeping this group together and seems to have been something of a autocrat at ISTAT. Complaints made about his conduct and disagreements with ISTAT employees at all levels reveal that he was probably better at managing statistics than people (ACS SPD-ord. 208.492, 208.453, 208.454). Symptomatic of this state of affairs, Livi left ISTAT in June 1928 after arguing with Gini.[79]

Gini's problems outside of ISTAT were, if anything, greater than those within. He interpreted literally the legislation according to which Italian statistics be both autonomous and centralized, and perceived his position as equivalent to that of a government minister who had only to answer to the head of government (to whom ISTAT was directly responsible). Gini's "excessive" behavior, which included the enlistment of ministry personnel without consulting the appropriate minister and the proposal of laws (province of the ministers and head of government), led him into conflicts with at least the ministers of the interior, public works, national economy, foreign affairs, and finance (ACS PCM 1940–3 b.2674 f.1.1.16.3.5.27000–5; b.2675 f.1.1.16.3.27000-10). It was with the last Ministry, led from July 1928 until July 1932 by Antonio Mosconi, that Gini would have the most serious differences.

Parallel to the new status for statistics within the government framework, the discipline of statistics also received a new place in the Italian educational system. New "statistical schools" were to be created at the universities as part of either the political science or law faculties, and a

---

[78] *Annali di statistica* 6, 2, p. 23.
[79] Ugo Giusti and Guglielmo Tagliacarne were also early defections (or casualties).

state statistical exam was instituted.[80] To encourage the study of statistics, special student grants were also offered. The statistics exam could be taken only by those holding either a diploma from the statistical schools or else a university degree which included work in statistics. The exam subsequently became a prerequisite for employment in statistical offices and so ISTAT.[81]

Mussolini himself devoted considerable attention to ISTAT, choosing its president, proposing the new headquarters, and following closely its activities (ACS PCM 1940–3 b.2669 f.1.1.16.1.27000-1 sf.4; ISTAT 1936, pp. 37–9). His interest in statistics, and specifically demographic statistics, dates from at least summer 1925 when he initiated a series of censuses by circular. On three different occasions he requested from prefects estimates of the populations of major cities, provinces, and provincial capitals on specific dates. The last of these was sent out in January 1926, several months before the ISTAT legislation was introduced. *Il duce's* personal attempt at data gathering corresponded closely with the revival of Italian statistics.

Mussolini was the direct and ultimate authority over ISTAT, and during his tenure as ISTAT president Gini went regularly (usually twice a month) to Palazzo Venezia for personal audiences with *il duce* in order to receive instructions and report on the institute's activities. This procedure was apparently unusual and resulted in a protest within the PCM offices, due in part to resentment over Gini's minister-like free access to the head of government (ACS SPD-ord. f.509.560/II). The relation between the two men, both of whom were difficult, seems to have been cordial. Gini sent his personnel recommendations to Mussolini and the latter forwarded Gini newspaper clippings and occasionally even corrected statistical publications which he seems to have read carefully. In fact, Mussolini personally reviewed the proofs of the monthly statistical bulletin two days prior to publication, a practice which continued through July 1943 (SPD-ord. f.509.560/I,II,III,IV[1]; PCM 1928–30 f.1.1.16.1306).

Shortly after ISTAT's creation, for example, Gini forwarded to Mussolini a brief general treatise on modern statistics in which he referred to demographic growth as "the first and most vital premise of all national greatness" (ACS PCM 1926 f.1.1.16.4642). Two days later the CSS inauguration attended by Mussolini took place, and Gini referred to an ISTAT study of those regions where the ratio of births to marriages

[80] R.d.-l. 17 November 1927, n.2372(2662); Dec. Capo Gov. 13 February 1931 in *Gazzetta ufficiale*, n. 70 (1931).
[81] R.d.-l. 24 March 1930, n.436; see also *Annali di statistica* 6, 1 (1931).

was insufficient to maintain a stationary population.[82] Mussolini may, in fact, have been following Gini's lead in his similar Ascension Day analysis of regional fertility five months later.[83] Mussolini did receive the data for the Ascension Day speech directly from Gini, including, for example (in March) a table of regional crude birth rates in descending order which *il duce* used in the May speech. Again in March, Gini wrote to Mussolini in response to a query regarding the population legislation of the Roman Emperor Augustus. Gini forwarded an excerpt from Bertillon's *Dépopulation de la France*, according to which (contrary to Tacitus) the laws had been effective, and also an article by Gini himself according to which they had not. Mussolini chose to ignore Gini's position in this case and cited only Bertillon's optimistic view of pronatalist legislation. Finally, in May, Gini sent *il duce* the 1926 birth and death totals for six major Italian cities, and these too Mussolini cited in his speech.[84]

Given Mussolini's reliance on Gini for demographic statistics and the frequent contacts between the two, Gini undoubtedly had the opportunity to encourage *il duce's* populationist views, and the two must have found much to agree upon. Gini stated as much in an attempted 1928 letter of resignation, further evidence of the storminess of Gini's career at ISTAT; he referred to their similar points of view: "I believe that at present my efforts could be more profitably employed, both with regard to public usefulness and personal satisfaction, in the area of population problems . . . an area in which I have had the honor to see my ideas shared by yourself" (ACS PCM 1940–3 b.2661 f.1.1.16.1.27000–1 sf.4). Gini's attitudes regarding emigration and fertility decline were pre-Fascist and account in part for the favor he found with first the Nationalists and then Mussolini. *Il duce* was developing similar attitudes in 1926, attitudes which Gini likely helped to form, though Gini was by no means the only populationist voice that had access to Mussolini. For example, he was reading both Korherr and Spengler at the time.

After the Ascension Day speech *il duce's* interest in demographic statistics increased if anything. In various circulars he insisted that

[82] *Annali di statistica* 6, 2, pp. 32–4.

[83] *Il duce*, however, chose to cite the more familiar population totals and crude birth rates in his speech as more appropriate to a wider audience. Mussolini's desire that demographic statistics be generally intelligible is further revealed in his response to a request from ISTAT that he choose between four possible methods of taking into account the military in population figures, Mussolini wrote: "Use the method which is the clearest and the most intelligible to a large public" (ACS PCM 1928–30 b.1106, f.1.1.16.1306).

[84] With minor variations, as Mussolini also had figures from the Ministry of the Interior (ACS SPD Autografi del Duce, sc.4, f.5.1.3, all. 9).

population figures appear in all daily and weekly newspapers and also requested prefects to send him local items of demographic interest. Just as he had previously conducted an independent census by circular, so in 1928 he conducted his demographic policy, citing the relevant figures to those prefects unfortunate enough to administer a low fertility province and urging them to remedy the situation. One example of many (to the prefect of Como):

From the municipal bulletin which has been sent to me I note that between the last census and today the population of Como has declined by 27 stop if all the provinces of Italy were to follow this brilliant example the Italian race would have its days numbered stop tell the *Podestà* to do something for large families stop Como needs it (ACS SPD-ord. f.509.560/I)

Mussolini's enduring interest in statistics reveals several general aspects of his style of rule. Statistical data responded well to his considerable intellectual curiosity and journalist's desire to gather facts. In addition, Mussolini recognized the generally reluctant nature of the Italian population and in particular its reluctance to provide information. He saw in official statistics a means to combat this streak of suspicious egoism and obtain data necessary to the totalitarian control of society. Mussolini also saw in statistics and their popularization a means to better form a *national* consciousness, as did the *Risorgimento* statisticians described in the previous chapter. *Il duce*'s statistical enterprise was an early and relatively mild example of subsequent efforts to change the Italian character, efforts that would culminate in a racial policy and a disastrous war.

The activities of ISTAT in this period revealed a special concentration on problems of fertility and a particular synchronicity with the actions of Mussolini. Prior to the latter's direct appeal and prior to the Ascension Day speech, ISTAT had created, according to *il duce*'s instructions, an archive for provincial publications on fertility. In the same period that low fertility province prefects were receiving goading circulars from the head of government, they received from Gini a request for their opinion on the cause of this situation, whether they thought it advantageous that the decline be arrested and what measures they might propose (and Gini and Mussolini were likely working from the same list).[85] In late 1929 and early 1930 Gini once again canvassed prefects, this time asking for details on local measures taken to encourage population growth. This information would be used in compiling a

[85] It is interesting to note that this same approach had been taken in an attempt to understand Prussian fertility decline in 1911 (by the Interior Ministry); see Weindling 1989, pp. 263–6.

study to appear in an upcoming volume on the accomplishments of Fascism (Gini 1930a).

In another example, contemporary with Mussolini's call for increased population growth a study of large families was initiated by ISTAT, and *il duce* emphasized to the prefects his personal interest in the project.[86] Gini reported a preliminary estimate to Mussolini in February 1928 according to which the number of families having seven or more children and headed by public and private office workers or laborers and "low personnel" employed by the state was approximately 35,000 (ACS SPD-ord. f.599.560/II). Legislation allowing tax exemptions for state workers with seven or more children came in June.[87]

The centralization of statistical services, part of ISTAT's original mandate, was a difficult process. In order to speed it up, a modification of the 1926 law creating ISTAT was proposed and circulated among the members of the government in mid-1928. The modifications included an increase in budget and personnel, affirmation of ISTAT's authority over all government statistical work, the gradual transfer of all statistics gathering to ISTAT (from the various ministries, many of which kept their own statistics), and the creation of commissions of experts to which the ISTAT president could call government employees from all sectors. Most ministers it seems voiced objections to this proposed law, but the strongest were those of Mosconi who wrote repeatedly to the PCM objecting to the proposed modifications, even after having received a communication from Mussolini asking for his support of the plan. Gini, in his tactless way, suggested that Mosconi's views be ignored. It was to be expected that the finance minister would object to the proposed budget increase from 2 to 3 million lire. In fact, as part of general belt tightening, Finance had previously reduced the initial ISTAT budget by 10%.[88] Thanks to *il*

---

[86] A circular clarifying procedures is dated 27 August 1927; data was gathered for 30 June 1928; ISTAT AC C.40, N.21 (21 February 1927, 18 February, 15 April, 6 June 1928).

[87] L. 14 June 1928, n.1312(1736); R.d. 10 August 1928, n.1944(2362).

[88] The 1929–30 Finance budget (*bilancio di previsione*) lists 1.8 million lire, down from the original 2 million, scheduled for ISTAT. As funds were also received from other sources, the total budget was considerably larger and that for 1929–30 seems in fact to have been the largest ever:

1926–27	L.3,180,530
1927–28	L.4,369,158.60
1928–29	L.3,896,459.57
1929–30	L.5,668,160.25

(Bilancio di competenza per i soli servizi ordinari. Parte ordinario. Entrate effettive. ISTAT 1936, p. 152). The above figures, however, only represent the "ordinary" part of the budget and so do not include "extraordinary" items like censuses which explains their being much smaller than those included in table 5.1.

duce's support, the various objections were overcome and the modifications became law in mid-1929.[89] Needless to say, passage of the law did not eliminate animosity between ISTAT and the government ministries:[90] Gini himself referred to this sort of friction in an address to the CSS in late 1929,[91] and his opinion that the relation of the head of government to ISTAT was identical to that of the minister to his ministry would bring him into conflict with the office of the PCM as well.[92] Nor did the law settle the question of statistics centralization. ISTAT was from its inception responsible for the collection of demographic statistics (except migration). It took over responsibility for agricultural and forestry statistics in early 1927 (R.d. 2 June 1927, n.1035[1314]) and for migration statistics in early 1929 (ISTAT 1936, p. 89). Nonetheless, various important areas of statistics gathering and evaluation still remained outside the purview of ISTAT at the end of the Fascist period.[93]

By 1929 opposition to Fascism in the *Camera* had been eliminated. It was also at this point that the legislative and institutional framework for the monitoring and control of Italian population movement was in place. Admittedly, much of the Fascist pronatalist legislation would come later but the basic direction of the policy, one guided by populationist and totalitarian principles, was established. The various aspects of the *politica demografica* were nicely summarized in 1929 by the deputy and soon to become CSS member Gaetano Zingali:[94]

Deputies, I see and summarize Mussolini's population policy in these terms: there is a very important and necessary goal, namely the quantitative increase and the qualitative improvement of the population; and there are means which also represent other points of the policy and which lead to and are perfectly in tune with this goal: the condemnation of bachelorhood and the measures favoring fertility, the condemnation of barren and low fertility marriages and the measures taken to stimulate high fertility, the care of the physical health of the population and the measures taken to achieve a decline in mortality.
 All this in the area of the so-called natural movement of the population.

---

[89] ACS PCM 1940–3 b.2669 f.1.1.16.1.27000-1 sf.4; R.d.-l. 27 May 1929, n.1285(1930). In the midst of these negotiations Gini submitted the letter of resignation referred to above.
[90] In a petty example, the Ministry of Finance refused to lend ISTAT a journal from its library on the grounds that the 1929 law stated that ISTAT was to receive the free loan of *books* from all state libraries (ACS PCM 1940–3 b.2669 f.1.1.16.27000-1 sf.5).
[91] *Annali di statistica* 6, 7 (1930), p. 34.
[92] *Annali di statistica* 6, 26 (1931). Gini had political supporters as well of course. See the laudatory words of the Senator Paolo Fortunati who described Gini as "one of the most authoritative advocates of the regime's demographic policy" (Fortunati 1932, pp. 75–8).
[93] See in particular D'Autilia 1992 on this question and the interesting case of agricultural statistics.
[94] Zingali became a member of the CSS on 2 August 1929. He was also professor of statistics and economics at Catania.

Outside of that area, but always within the demographic arena, are other factors which can aid in the achievement of this goal: namely a restrictive, and in any case prudent, emigration policy and a strict control of internal migration. With regard to this last point, it goes without saying: battle against urbanization and encouragement of ruralization.

I shall examine singly and quickly each of these points, but not without first affirming in a general way, that this famous demographic quintet – nuptiality, fertility, mortality, emigration, and internal migration – has been examined and disciplined by *il duce* in such a harmonious and unequivocal way as to answer in all ways the goal to which I have referred.

He then proceeded to discuss, with statistical accompaniment, this famous quintet and concluded his speech, dedicated entirely to the *politica demografica*, with laudatory words for ISTAT and its president, proposing that

we consider how great and important are the official statistics which carry throughout the world, to the delight of friends and the envy of enemies, proof of the impressive progress accomplished by Fascist Italy where not only men, but also statistical data, have become dynamic, almost as if following with the same insistent rhythm the course of these glorious times.[95]

Zingali's stirring comments summarized the various aspects of the Fascist *politica demografica*, an effort to manipulate population movement on all fronts, and emphasized the important role played by statistics.

In the face of immigration quotas and declining fertility, the Fascist regime, contemporary with the stabilization of power, adopted a populationist and expansionist position with regard to questions of both spatial and quantitative population movement. This position found expression in institutions and programs which discouraged migration abroad and to the cities, seeking instead to direct these currents to new rural population centers within Italy and eventually also in the Italian colonies, and others aimed at lowering Italian infant mortality and propping up sagging fertility. By 1929 the basic elements of this multifaceted demographic policy, probably the most ambitious pursued by any government up to that date, were in place.

Some of the more contradictory aspects of the policy must have been apparent from the outset: for example, the suppression of both emigration abroad and urbanization when, in fact, the emigration stop stimulated migration to the cities as an alternative escape from rural unemployment; and clearly the scale of planned organized migrations

---

[95] Atti C. disc. 5 June 1929, pp. 693–9; similar comments were made on this occasion by Castellino who linked together pronatalism, land reclamation, emigration, and African colonization; see ibid., p. 654.

could not hope to approach that of previous spontaneous emigration. Also, some, including for example Gini, questioned the utility of pronatalist measures. Still, it was thought to be worth a try (and considerable expense), and certainly the ambition to manipulate society demographically was in keeping with the general Fascist social experiment aimed at creating both a totalitarian web of control and popular consensus for government programs.

3

The realization of totalitarian demography I:
Spatial population management

Conventionally, the resolution of the Matteotti crisis and the signing of the Lateran treaty circumscribe that period of Fascist rule during which Mussolini consolidated power and assembled the institutional elements necessary for the "totalitarian" control of society. In chapter 2 I have traced one aspect of this process: the evolution of the Fascist program of population management. This program would continue to evolve in the decade that followed: a brief interim of emigration liberalization would follow the economic crisis of 1929; efforts to encourage fertility and certain types of internal and colonial migration would be renewed; and Fascist racism would be introduced. Nonetheless, the 1930s were, for the Fascist regime in general and population policy in particular, more a period of realization – or non-realization – than organization. It was the period in which Fascism sought to bind the population to the regime, to inject the masses with a "totalitarian spirit" and create, by means of a martial and Fascist culture, a new Italian consciousness in reaction against the decadent and bourgeois nature of the previous Liberal society.[1] Fundamental to the Fascist vision of a new civilization was the demographic aspect, and following the creation of the various institutions described in chapter 2, the regime launched a multipronged attempt to mold society spatially, quantitatively and qualitatively. These efforts were audacious in their aspirations but modest in their accomplishments.

In this chapter I shall look at the Fascist programs of spatial population management, namely plans for internal and African colonization and the battle against urbanization. The complementary (and at times overlapping) quantitative and qualitative measures – infant protection, pronatalism and racism – are dealt with in chapter 4.

---

[1] See Collotti 1989, pp. 55–6 for a similar characterization of the decade 1929–39.

Emigration

Perhaps the most notable aspect of the official discussion of emigration subsequent to the establishment of the Fascist anti-emigration policy was its absence. Previously the primary demographic variable of governmental (and academic) interest, after mid-1930 the question of Italian migration to non-Italian destinations became a virtual non-issue. To some degree this silence had a quantitative justification in that the number of Italians leaving, and returning to, Italy fell much below the pre and early postwar levels (see figure 1.9). Still, these natural or spontaneous movements of population always remained more significant than the much discussed regime-sponsored migrations to the Italian colonies (and a parallel situation existed regarding spontaneous versus official internal migrations). The suppression of emigration effectively eliminated the forum for its discussion.

Symptomatic of this switch, the *Bollettino dell'emigrazione* (*Emigration Bulletin*), organ of the Commissariato generale dell'emigrazione (General Emigration Commission – CGE), ceased publication after December 1927 and was absorbed into the *Bulletin of the Foreign Affairs Ministry*. The latter continued to discuss emigration questions – in particular announcements of the new policy – through 1928 and into 1929, after which references were few and often limited to reporting the latest government fixing of third-class fares for sea passage, a surviving relic of the 1901 legislation to protect emigrants. Similarly, the ISTAT *Notiziario demografico* (*Demographic Bulletin*), initiated in 1928, included only a paucity of information on the traditional currents of Italian population directed to (and from) Europe and the Americas. This situation would endure for almost a decade.

From the logic of Mussolini's populationist rhetoric, one might have expected a concerted effort to encourage repatriation. However, neither the Direzione generale degli italiani all'estero (General Directorship of Italians Abroad – DGIE) nor the associated Fondazione nazionale figli del littorio (National Children of the Lictor Foundation – FNFL) – founded in January 1929 "with the aim of providing material and spiritual aid to the children of Italians abroad" – seem to have made notable efforts to lure Italians home.[2] Given the economic situation of the period this lack is not surprising. Repatriation only became an important issue after the Ethiopian war of 1935–6 (see below).

The general emphasis of Fascist policy regarding Italians abroad in

---

[2] The statutes of the *figli del littorio* include no reference to repatriation (R.d.-l. 28 January 1929, n.192).

the early 1930s was not so much on repatriation, but on the maintenance of a spirit of *italianità* (Italian-ness), and so fidelity to the regime, by means of newspapers, schools, "Italian houses," and the Fasci all'estero (Fascist groups abroad). The activities of the DGIE and the FNFL and the program for the 1930 Congress of Italians abroad[3] all emphasized the function of assistance and the encouragement of touristic visits to the homeland. The expenses of the Ministero degli affari esteri (Ministry of Foreign Affairs – MAE) reveal this trend as well. In 1930 what remained of the emigration fund (about 3 million lire) was dedicated to the assistance of Italians abroad, and another 15 million was added. The 1932–33 budget reveals 12 million for the "defense of *italianità* abroad."[4] The money dedicated annually to repatriation (3–7 million) seems primarily to have served the indigent (R.d.-l. 18 July 1931; Atti C. D.l. N.1201 [29 January 1932], line 39).

In spite of the official position, a degree of unpublicized interest in emigration endured, at least so long as the economic situation kept unemployment high. In 1932 for example – in the midst of the economic crisis – the DGIE seems to have been more concerned with expatriation than repatriation as it reported to the PCM every few days on the international labor situation and possible destinations for Italian workers abroad. Needless to say, opportunities were few. This is the same sort of monitoring that the CGE had conducted before its suppression in the interest of emigration "valorization" (ACS PCM 1931–3 b.1590 f.7.1.1.6822–1-B).

Official indifference to emigration was revealed in the collection and publication of emigration statistics as well. After the suppression of the CGE, responsibility for these statistics passed to the DGIE, whose performance was spotty at best, and then in 1929 to ISTAT, but financial difficulties – and here we can read priorities – prevented prompt publication. As a result, the emigration statistics volume for 1926–7 was only published in 1933 and for 1928–33 in 1934 after which they appeared annually.[5] When they finally did appear, the emigration statistics were accompanied by a discussion of the new policy and the way in which the latter had altered the data presented: "The migration policy introduced by the Fascist government at the beginning of the

---

[3] Described in DGIE circ. n.13 in *Bollettino del MAE* n. 3 1930, pp. 187–90.
[4] Atti C. D.l. N.489 (5 March 1930); C. D.l. N.655 (10 October 1930); C. D.l. N.1201 (29 January 1932). In addition, approximately 30 million a year was spent on Italian schools abroad in this period.
[5] Both DGIE and ISTAT data on emigration did appear in the ISTAT *Bollettino mensile di statistica* from 1927. Migration statistics for the years 1926–37 were published by ISTAT in the series *Statistica delle migrazioni da e per l'estero*. For 1938 and after they formed one section of the series *Movimento della popolazione e cause di morte nell'anno . . .*

second half of 1927 as a consequence of its demographic policy has modified, from 1928, both the methods and criteria for the gathering and elaboration for migration statistics."[6] There were several changes. First of all, the sources of data were changed. As a supplement to passport registers, passports had themselves since 1921 included detachable coupons which were removed at entry and exit points and forwarded to the agency responsible for gathering the statistical data. In 1931, when ISTAT officially took over emigration statistics these coupons became the primary source of statistical data for continental and North African emigration. For transoceanic emigration, ships' registers were used.

As the category of emigrant was replaced by that of the *lavoratore*, a new conception of what constituted emigration was also needed. Emigrants had been defined, according to the 1919 legislation as: "every citizen who emigrates in order to engage in manual labor or small trade" together with their family members. *Lavoratori*, on the other hand, were "all persons, of any profession, who emigrate for work" and again their family members. Non-*lavoratori* were those who emigrated for any other reason: business, amusement, medical care.[7] The statistical recognition of this latter sort of "emigration" was in keeping with the Fascist contention that intellectual, professional, commercial and technical emigration represented "an affirmation of national prestige, a sure increase for Italian trade and an efficient propaganda tool for Italian ideas, culture and industry."[8]

According to ISTAT, the new worker/non-worker criterion rendered emigration statistics from 1928 not comparable with those kept before. Still, if we make the conventional shift to *lavoratore* emigration in 1928 we see the expected steady decline in emigration except for 1929–30, years of economic crisis (see figure 1.9).[9] The 1930 increase was due in part to a brief period (September–November) during which Mussolini ordered that emigration be authorized (and so passports issued) for northern and some of central Italy. According to *il duce* this measure served to correct the mistaken idea of those who believed the economic situation was better abroad than in Italy (Mussolini, vol. xxiv, p. 313 [13 December 1930]). Ercole Sori suggests instead that the issuance of

---

[6] ISTAT, *Migrazioni 1928–30*, p. 1*.   [7] ISTAT, *Movimento 1938*, p. 133.
[8] ISTAT, *Migrazioni 1928–30*, p. 3*.
[9] The data used for figure 1.9 after 1928 refer to the expatriation and repatriation of *lavoratori*. These are essentially the same as the figures reported in ISTAT volumes of historical statistics; see ISTAT 1968. The annual "total" emigration figures for 1928–39 ranged from 70% to 193% larger than the *lavoratori* totals (see ISTAT statistics of the period or else Ipsen 1992b, pp. 143–5, 444).

passports was inspired by the desire to export social unrest caused by high unemployment in the areas targeted.[10]

Although non-*lavoratore* emigration was not only allowed, but officially encouraged, it too declined after 1929, remaining fairly stable for the years 1932–8, during which it averaged over two-and-a-half times the *lavoratore* emigration. One wonders how many of those leaving as non-*lavoratori* were not in fact looking for better economic opportunities abroad. The initiation of hostilities in Europe naturally depressed the levels of both sorts of emigration, and, as had been the case twenty-five years before, the outbreak of war turned the migratory deficit to a surplus.

Fascist policy did not prohibit the temporary (less than three years) migration of workers abroad, provided that a contract be previously negotiated. Except under unusual circumstances, however, this sort of arrangement held little attraction for foreign employers. The CGE had previously encouraged such emigration, but only met with success during World War I. Similarly, it was only as a result of special agreements reached subsequent to the creation of the Rome–Berlin axis that organized temporary emigration was accomplished on a significant scale. Questions of emigration and repatriation would in fact only come to the fore in the post Ethiopia climate as international tensions mounted and Italy cleaved ever closer to Nazi Germany (see pp. 135–43 below). More central to the Fascist plans for spatial population management were instead the programs of demographic colonization in Italy and in Italy's African possessions.

Internal migration

There were two fundamental and distinct aspects of the Fascist policy regarding internal migration: encouragement of officially supervised migrations, and discouragement of the natural tendency to migrate from rural to urban areas. To a degree these represented the positive and negative sides of the same political coin in that they both responded to Mussolini's command to "ruralize" Italy. They were also both presented as pronatalist measures. The cities were held responsible for the diffusion of family limitation practices, while the new Fascist settlements in Italy (and also in Africa) were to be models of high rural fertility.

The government-sponsored migrations were presented as a means to

---

[10] Sori's suggestion seems likely, although he cites the Turin demonstrations of 24–26 November as the culmination of the unemployment crisis, while the passport orders came in mid-August (Sori 1979, p. 436).

correct population disequilibria and exploit previously unused lands, while the anti-urban measures were intended to halt a significant flow of population. The urbanization process in Italy had been accelerating since at least the turn of the century, and after a lull during World War I, the trend continued into, and throughout, the Fascist period, in spite of government measures and Fascist rhetoric. As compared to this spontaneous migration to the cities, the numbers involved in state-sponsored internal migrations were small. Still, with regard to both the logic and the realizations of the Fascist population policy, the internal migration programs were of central importance and left a more lasting and tangible impact than any other aspect.

The Fascist program to manage internal migration and colonization depended primarily upon the related institutions of the Commissariato per le migrazioni e la colonizzazione (Commission for Migration and Colonization – CMC) and government employment offices; while other organizations carried out the actual work projects and colonizations, these two institutions provided the framework within which the various population transfers took place. Transfers were of two types: the temporary importation of (male) workers for the execution of public works (including *bonifiche*) in areas where local labor may have been lacking (although it is difficult to determine whether the workers primarily filled a labor deficit in the area of immigration or else attenuated a politically difficult labor surplus in the area of emigration), and the permanent transfer of tenant farming families (*famiglie coloniche*) for the settlement and development of the new *bonifiche*.

As part of the general corporativist scheme aimed at regulating the Italian economy, a network of employment offices was created in 1928.[11] According to the initial legislation, unemployed workers could register free of charge with these offices and employers could only hire an unemployed worker if he were so registered. Both employer and worker were required to report new employment to the relevant office and employees were also required to report all lay-offs, firing, and resignations (R.d. 15 April 1928, n.996[1436])

The employment offices, part of the Ministry of Corporations, were created to take an active role in the management of the Italian work force. The CPMI, created two years previously as part of the Ministry of Public Works, was also involved and initially had the strictly theoretical task of studying the problem of (and possibilities for) internal migra-

---

[11] These were the Fascist replacements of the formerly Socialist-controlled Giunte provinciali per il collocamento e la disoccupazione, eliminated five years earlier (R.d. 4 February 1923, n.249). See also Sori 1979, p. 455.

tion, especially as it related to the south and the islands. Beginning in 1928, however, the CPMI passed from a theoretical to a practical role. It was expected to propose and evaluate plans for internal migration, and also to take part in these programs, providing transport and lodging for workers needed for "urgent" public works (R.d. 28 November 1928, n.2874).

The activities of the CPMI in this period created a degree of conflict. Its attachment to the Ministry of Public Works was in keeping with its function of supplying labor for public works projects; however, it also provided the workers and eventually colonizing families for the *boni-fiche*, and the *bonifiche*, originally also under the aegis of Public Works, had been transferred to Agriculture and Forests (R.d. 27 September 1929, n.1729). The Agriculture minister, Giacomo Acerbo, asserted that he should have responsibility for the demographic colonization of the *bonifiche* as well and that the CPMI should be transferred to Agriculture. Neither di Crollalanza, minister of public works, nor Bottai, minister of corporations (which directed the employment offices), agreed.

The transfer of the CPMI to either Agriculture or to the PCM was advocated by the Fascist deputy and journalist Davide Fossa. Calling for this move in the *Camera*, Fossa also addressed the general topic of internal migration, describing it as the solution to agricultural unemployment, which he blamed on disproportionate regional popula-tion density that ranged from 258 persons per square kilometer in Lombardy to 35 in Sardinia. According to Fossa:

We are few and poorly distributed. Births must increase so that we may always have a positive demographic balance; population must be distributed in a just way which responds to the vital needs of our people . . . We must prepare the environment and cultivable lands, build houses . . . and reclaim new lands to be colonized by families of day laborers who will become settlers . . . In this way the *bonifica integrale* will not simply be a public works program, but a vast social and political undertaking which will expand the territory and the productive poten-tial of the nation. (Atti C. disc. 9 April 1930, pp. 2342–6)

The CPMI conflict was resolved by its transfer to the PCM as a *commis-sariato* (the CMC) in 1931; the new CMC closely resembled the institute originally proposed by Pantano in 1925 (see chapter 2, p. 58 above).[12] More than simply the resolution of an intragovernmental conflict, this transfer coincided with an elevation in status for internal migration pro-

---

[12] ACS PCM 1940–3 b.2765 f.1.1.23.3299.1; R.d. 26 June 1930, n.870(1176); Dec. Capo gov. 3 August 1930 in *Gazzetta ufficiale* n. 157 (1930); L. 9 April 1931, n.358(630). Nevertheless Acerbo would again propose the transfer of responsibility for internal migration to his ministry in July 1932 (ACS PCM 1931–3 b.1375 f.1.1.2.6282).

jects, as revealed by a budget increase and the personal interest of *il duce*.[13] Both in name and degree of autonomy, internal migration had come to occupy the institutional niche of external migration some years before. The 1931 norms for internal colonization, which created the CMC, called for coordination between the internal migration commissioner and the minister of colonies regarding the possibility of transferring Italian workers to the colonies and between the commissioner and the minister of corporations for domestic colonization. Appointed to the new position of *commissario* was the *sansepolcrista*[14] Luigi Razza, who during his tenure as head of the CMC would work closely with Mussolini, meeting with him weekly (ACS SPD-ord. f.106.414 sf.3).

The *Camera* report on norms for the new CMC emphasized the institution's role in the Fascist economic program and also, of course, the overall demographic policy:

> By resolving the internal colonization problem with the establishment of migratory currents and the formation of new rural centers, our nation will achieve the increase desired by the regime . . . In this way Fascism will have pointed to a new way and resolved two of the most complex and vital problems of the modern life of the collective: that of unemployment and that of the creation of new centers of life. (Atti C. D.l. N.692 [15 November 1930], pp. 2–3)

The Finance committee appointed to examine the CMC norms described the *commissariato* as representing "in the corporativist order of the regime, the general command of the army of workers," but expressed doubts about its ability, given limited resources, to accomplish the various tasks assigned, which included moral, sanitary, and economic assistance; medical check-ups to select workers and families; the providing of lodging; and financial awards to colonists (Atti C. D.l. N.692-A [3 December 1930]).

Nonetheless, these norms became law in early 1931 and included the following directive: "The Commission for Migration and Internal Colonization will, together with the Ministry of Corporations, see to the enrollment and rational distribution of available workers in order to achieve their most advantageous employment in the entire Kingdom . . . " (L. 9 April 1931, n. 358 (630), art. 2). The previous emphasis on migration to southern and insular Italy had been abandoned, in part

---

[13] The Ministry of Public Works budgets (*bilanci di previsione*), for the years 1927–31 dedicate 2–300,000 lire annually to the CPMI. The CMC budget on the other hand was over 1 million for 1930-1, increased to 2.5 million by 1932–3 and to almost 7 million in 1933–4 (Razza 1933, ACS PCM 1940–3 b.2765 f.1.1.23.3299.6). See the much cited circular of Mussolini to the prefects of 20 July 1930 (ACS PCM 1940–3 b.2765 f.1.1.23.3299.3).

[14] *Sansepolcrista* refers to one who was present at the creation of the Fascist movement in Piazza San Sepolcro in Milan on 23 March 1919.

because the CPMI had encountered difficulties in transferring workers from north to south (ACS PCM 1928–30 f.8.1.8974[10195]), but also in response to a recent resolution of the Fascist Grand Council which singled out population pressure in the Po Valley as a problem in need of a solution.[15]

The CMC legislation stipulated that both the minister of corporations (via the employment offices) and the provincial prefects were to provide the CMC with monthly reports on the number of workers and families either needed for work or available for emigration. The CMC could also require that a certain number of workers from other provinces be used for any projects receiving government funds, and could intervene in the negotiation of collective work contracts.[16] Once established, the CMC maintained its general form throughout most of the Fascist period. Its powers were expanded in 1933 when it was authorized to send workers and families migrating without CMC authorization back to their places of origin.[17] In 1935 Razza became minister of public works and was succeeded as *commissario* by Sergio Nannini who was in turn replaced by Giuseppe Lombrassa in late 1939. During its existence the CMC established offices in Italy, in Albania, and in the Italian colonies.

The definition of internal migration is more difficult than that of migration abroad. Leaving aside the emigrant/*lavoratore* distinction, the physical action of international emigration, at least, is fairly well defined and involves crossing a national border. For internal migration, one has also to define what sort of travel constitutes migration: outside the *comune*, the province, the region?[18] Like emigration abroad, internal migration presents the problem of establishing criteria (border crossed, distance traveled, length of stay) on which to base statistics.

The CPMI/CMC began the compilation and publication of internal migration statistics in 1927.[19] As stated from the outset, the aim of the

[15] See PNF 1938, pp. 443–5; *Il Popolo d'Italia* 26 March 1930; ACS SPD-ris. b.30 f.242.8(A).

[16] On the evolution of the CPMI/CMC during these years, see Razza's address to the *Camera* in Atti C. disc. 6 May 1931, pp. 4525–30. On the evolution of the CMC and employment offices, see Loschiavo 1936.

[17] Dec. Capo Governo 22 July 1933 in *Gazzetta ufficiale* n. 184 (1933). See also Sori 1979, p. 472.

[18] We are left in any case, as Sori puts it, with "very unsatisfactory categories" (Sori 1979, p. 441).

[19] The internal migration statistics volumes went through a number of transitions. The original title (1927 volume, published 1928) was *Le migrazioni interne in Italia*. It was changed for 1935 to *Le migrazioni nel Regno e nelle colonie* and then to *Le migrazioni nel Regno e nell'Africa Italiana* (1936–9). The author changed too with the changes of the migration office: Ministero dei Lavori Pubblici – Comitato permanente per le migrazioni interne (1927–8); PCM – CPMI (1929); PCM – Commissariato per le migrazioni e la colonizzazione interna (1930–4); and PCM – Commissariato per le migrazioni e la colonizzazione (1935–9). I have abbreviated the Commissariato throughout as CMC.

CPMI was to measure "the temporary and periodic currents of agricultural and industrial workers directed from one part of the kingdom to another."[20] The principal source of data was a form filled out in the application for railway fare reductions available to those traveling for the purpose of temporary employment in groups of five or more.[21] Evidently this source did not provide information on workers traveling in small groups[22] nor on those not traveling by train. Subsequently a second source was found in data supplied by the employment offices. A general distinction was made between industrial and agricultural migration and the latter constituted the majority, approximately 80% of the total intercommunal migration for the period 1928–9 for example.[23] The initial emphasis on temporary migration was in keeping with the fact that the CPMI was a part of the Ministry of Public Works and so primarily concerned with population movement related to public works projects.

On creation of the CMC and as attention turned to colonization, tables on "relocated families" were added to its statistical publication (from 1931). Presumably these were only the families for whom the CMC arranged migration and as such the data was collected directly by the CMC. After the creation of the Italian empire in 1936, the CMC volumes came to include data on migration to the Italian colonies in Africa as well. The sources for the latter included lists compiled by the employment offices of departing workers, permits issued by the CMC to companies transferring workers to the colonies, and the CMC forms filled out at the ports of exit.

The CMC publications provide an example of non-ISTAT statistics and so ran counter to the centralizing intent of that institution. In fact, it appears that for the first few years these volumes were not even sent, as required by law, to ISTAT for review, a situation which resulted in a protest by Gini who found so many errors in the work that he recommended that all calculations be redone and a new volume issued. Mussolini agreed that in future the *Commissario* would send a draft to the statistics institute.[24]

---

[20] CPMI, *Migrazioni interne 1927—gennaio 1928*, p. 3.
[21] This was initially the same reduction offered to emigrants travelling abroad (R.d. 29 December 1901, n.562 [concessione X]). Subsequently, with the changes regarding the latter, a separate reduction was established for internal migration (Dec. Min. 29 December 1931 in *Gazzetta ufficiale*, n. 250 [27 October 1932] [concessione XI]).
[22] Though as the minimum reduction offered was 50%, it might also have profitably been used by those traveling in groups of three or four.
[23] The statistics published included perhaps an excessively fine breakdown by type of work; for example: migration in 1931 for the digging of licorice root distributed according to the worker's province of emigration and immigration.
[24] ACS PCM 1931–3 b.1524 f.3.2.6.3033; *Annali di statistica* 6, 27 (1932), pp. 21–35.

Another potential source of data for measuring internal migration were the population registers, established in Italian *comuni* in 1862, though apparently only useful for measuring internal migration from 1902 following new regulations (Di Rienzo 1965, p. 671; R.d. 21 September 1901, n.445). In addition to permanent records for every resident family and individual, the *comune* also recorded births, marriages, deaths, enrollments (immigrations), and cancellations (emigrations). All residents were required to inform the registry office of their movements and, in particular, when changing *comune* to cancel with the old and register with the new. This system was perfected and presumably made reliable in 1929 (Di Rienzo 1965, p. 671; R.d. 2 December 1929, n.2132[2812]). The 1929 legislation gave the recently created ISTAT authority to issue instructions to the *comuni* on the keeping of registers and also required the *comuni* to forward annual population registry data to ISTAT. In spite of the availability of this source, ISTAT did not begin the regular publication of internal migration statistics until after World War II;[25] they were finally compiled in the 1960s (Di Rienzo 1965). They do not of course include the migration of those who did not officially change residency; in particular they do not include clandestine migration to cities after 1939. Table 3.1 gives these figures for 1922–43 and also the CMC figures for internal migration.[26] The two series are based on entirely different conceptions of internal migration. The CMC figures were intended primarily to measure temporary internal migration for which residency was presumably not changed; while the ISTAT figures attempt to measure semi-permanent migration (between *comuni*). Of the CMC figures only those for relocated families (see table 3.2) relate to permanent migration and these numbers are small, never more than about 1% of the residence changes in a year. The CMC definition of internal migration gave only a limited idea of the actual movement of population. In order to obtain a clearer picture of the volume of internal population migration during the *ventennio*, one should perhaps sum the ISTAT and CMC figures in table 3.1. As noted above, only the CMC series gained currency at the time. Testimony to this state of affairs is the entry on migratory currents in the *Enciclopedia italiana* (published in 1934)[27] which misleadingly reports the CMC figures as if they constituted the entire volume of internal migration.

---

[25] ISTAT, *Annuario di statistiche demografiche 1955*; ISTAT, *Annuario statistico 1961*. The *Bollettino mensile di statistica* did, however, include total registrations and cancellations, without distinguishing between internal and international migration, from 1930. One could have compared these figures to those for emigration abroad and so estimated internal migration; for a rare attempt, see *Notiziario demografico* (10 April 1938), pp. 68–9.
[26] The ISTAT figures are the same included in both Treves 1976 and Corsini 1983.
[27] See the entry *migratorie, correnti*.

Table 3.1 *Internal migration*

Year	Population registers (ISTAT)			CMC	
	Entries (1)	Cancellations (2)	* (3)	Totals (4)	Inter-regional (5)
1922	542,143	528,996	14.9		
1923	681,535	613,833	17.3		
1924	775,592	703,911	19.4		
1925	846,015	759,260	21.2		
1926	963,594	855,912	24.2		
1927	1,025,184	898,655	25.3		
1928	999,687	873,720	24.4	227,939	
1929	1,011,617	941,276	24.4	345,966	166,988
1930	1,112,421	1,077,739	27.1	352,595	159,472
1931	1,051,947	1,074,479	25.2	313,068	132,463
1932	1,119,678	1,092,827	27.1	344,593	134,641
1933	1,211,136	1,148,858	29.3	373,132	
1934	1,296,180	1,268,961	30.3	272,180	110,231
1935	1,384,392	1,362,685	32.3	293,775	107,318
1936	1,004,164	1,004,884	23.2	343,492	129,016
1937	1,486,868	1,486,983	34.2	404,334	139,503
1938	1,406,542	1,419,401	32.2	400,826	156,255
1939	1,331,768	1,332,462	30.2		
1940	1,347,893	1,348,323	30.8		
1941	1,106,284	1,106,050	24.3		
1942	1,156,681	1,156,569	25.3		
1943	799,779	799,779	17.3		

Note:
* Entries per 1,000 inhabitants
Sources: Di Rienzo 1965 (1–3); CMC, *Le migrazioni interne* (4–5).

Table 3.2 *Migration for internal colonization*

Year	Relocated families	Total members
1930	266	1,870
1931	841	5,650
1932	1,371	11,309
1933	1,547	12,350
1934	1,456	12,057
1935	1,285	9,343
1936	1,320	9,922
1937	1,522	10,099
1938	1,241	7,981

Source: CMC, *Le migrazioni interne.*

Dictating demography

Table 3.3 *Primary regions of inter-regional temporary emigration as a percentage (>10) of total inter-regional migration*

	1929	1930	1931	1932	1934	1935	1936	1937	1938
Lombardy		10.5	10.0	11.5	13.3	12.1	11.2	10.7	12.2
Venetia	16.4	15.5	13.1	17.1	15.9	15.9	14.7	15.1	13.8
Em.-Rom.	19.4	24.1	27.4	27.4	30.0	31.6	29.8	28.7	26.9
Apulia	22.5	17.0	19.1	12.0			19.0	19.2	17.8

Source: CMC, *Le migrazioni interne.*

Internal migration was a category of population movement which ISTAT chose not to deal with in the interwar period. It is difficult to imagine that this was simply an oversight, nor is it conceivable that ISTAT (especially under Gini) was reluctant to intrude in CMC territory. Permanent internal migration seems to have interested the regime only when directed to the *bonifiche*. The remainder (and majority) of internal migration reveals a considerable process of Italian urbanization under way, a clear sign of the failure of Fascist rural policy and so apparently a statistic to be ignored.

As mentioned above, the CMC was able to stipulate that a certain number of workers employed in state-subsidized projects come from outside provinces; yet while the internal migration statistics included the categories of *bonifiche*, road work etc., it is not possible to deduce from these how many of those migrating for employment in public works were actually selected or transferred by the CMC (after 1931). As such it is difficult to evaluate the way in which the *Commissariato* used its powers to defuse population pressure.

We can, however, look at the overall figures and see if workers followed the hoped-for channels. It is possible to extract from the CMC figures, for most years, series for inter-regional migration, and inter-regional migration seems a more definitive way to relieve population pressure than migration between provinces (or *comuni*) of the same region. A look at these (see tables 3.3 and 3.4) shows that the major sources of temporary emigrants were Lombardy, Venetia, Emilia-Romagna, and Apulia; for a few years (1929–32) Abruzzi-Molise also provided a significant contribution given its small population. The primary destinations for inter-regional migration were Piedmont, Latium, and Basilicata. The Piedmont migration consisted almost entirely of workers directed to the provinces of Vercelli and Novara for the cultivation and harvest of rice. Most of these came from Emilia-Romagna, but significant numbers also from Venetia and

Table 3.4 *Primary regions of inter-regional temporary immigration as a percentage (>10) of total inter-regional migration*

	1929	1930	1931	1932	1934	1935	1936	1937	1938
Piedmont	29.8	32.4	30.9	29.8	33.8	37.9	35.0	35.7	35.9
Lombardy						10.7		10.5	
Latium	21.1	19.3	17.3	28.0	31.0	13.2	11.3		
Basilicata	15.6	12.6	15.4				16.5	17.8	17.4

Source: CMC, *Le migrazioni interne.*

Lombardy.[28] A smaller current of workers went to Turin for industrial work. In Basilicata, temporary immigration consisted primarily of Apulians coming to work the wheat fields.[29] Most of the Latium migration was agricultural, though not accounted for by a single crop or activity. In addition, Latium attracted many workers to the *bonifica* of the Pontine marshes, Roman public works, and construction of Mussolini's planned universal exposition (EUR 42).[30] The choice of inter-regional migration, it should be noted, overlooks significant local population movements, especially within Piedmont and Sicily.

The subsequently compiled ISTAT figures do not show greatly different patterns for this period (see table 3.5): net migration into

[28] Interregional migration *to* Lombardy was also mostly for working the rice fields. This is the migration depicted in De Sanctis' classic film *Riso amaro*.

[29] A 1929 CPMI publication identified Basilicata as a target for *bonificazione* and colonization: "This pamphlet seeks to demonstrate that even the poorest of our regions is able to carry out the demographic policy of the regime" (Azimonti 1929, p. 7). Little, however, was realized in this regard.

[30] For data on the nature and direction of temporary internal migration see the CMC, *Migrazioni interne* volumes. The Esposizione Universale di Roma was scheduled to open in 1942, but was interrupted by the war. A random choice among the CMC weekly reports on internal migration reveals the following numbers for 29 August 1939 for migrant workers employed in the following regions:

6,643	Agro Pontino
4,520	EUR
2,397	Latium hydraulic works
2,039	the Rome subway
969	Fertilia (EFC – Sardinia)
14,759	Carbonia (Sardinia)
331	Bolzano (Alto-Adige)
2,053	Pomezia (Latium)

(ACS PCM 1934–6 b.1761 f.1.1.23.3299 sf.2-A). The fact that Sardinia does not appear among the primary destinations for migration in table 3.5 (which does not include 1939) is due to the fact that most of the Carbonia migration was *intra*regional. Nor does it appear that agricultural migration was included in these reports.

Table 3.5: *Net internal migration based on*
population registers

	1931–5	1936–40
Piedmont	+27,143	+41,185
Liguria	+54,051	+41,456
Lombardy	+30,301	+56,422
Trentino-A.A.	−1,584	+18,990
Venetia	−85,605	−120,614
Friuli-Ven.G.	−31,656	−20,655
Emilia-Rom.	−23,004	−33,984
Marches	−20,944	−23,332
Tuscany	+3,898	−1,241
Umbria	−4,690	−2,156
Latium	+159,279	+111,225
Campania	+20,092	+5,712
Abruzzi-Mol.	−11,405	−16,688
Apulia	−7,565	−17,357
Basilicata	−627	−6,491
Calabria	+2,352	−21,554
Sicily	−3,835	−31,626
Sardinia	+9,316	+5,770

Source: Di Rienzo 1965.

Piedmont, Liguria, Lombardy, and especially Latium; net migration out of Venetia, Emilia-Romagna, Trentino-Alto Adige, the Marches, and Abruzzi-Molise. Basilicata, although a primary destination for temporary migration, shows net emigration on the basis of population registers.

With regard to the areas identified by the Fascist Grand Council as suffering particular population pressure, Venetia and Emilia-Romagna accounted for about 40% of all CMC-recorded temporary inter-regional emigration, which amounted to about 1% of their combined regional populations per year.[31] They were also regions of net emigration as read from population registers: in a ten-year period Emilia-Romagna's population decline due to migration was about 1.7%, that of Venetia about 5.8% (see table 3.5), though these declines were more than compensated for by natural increase.

---

[31] Very few of these were Emilia-Romagna to Venetia or vice versa.

Our ability to evaluate CMC activity with regard to internal migration and colonization[32] is a bit different, as the CMC was directly involved in the selection and transfer of the colonizing families and reported their numbers (see table 3.2). The Fascist program of internal colonization differed from other aspects of the overall population policy in that, unlike the pronatalist measures, its effects were generally measurable, and unlike colonization in Africa, its demographic (and geographic) impact still manifests itself today.

Internal colonization consisted primarily of the creation and inhabitation of new population centers in those previously insalubrious and sparsely populated areas that became the *bonifiche*. Not all *bonifiche*, however, were also destinations for the long-distance relocation of families. Often the "colonization" of reclaimed land was carried out by local elements, as was generally the case in the *bonifiche* of the Ferrarese, the Latifondo siciliano and the Tavoliere di Puglia. In other cases, considerable numbers of families were brought long distances to settle the newly agricultural lands, as in western Sardinia and the Agro Pontino (south of Rome).

While the CMC publications do provide us with the total numbers of families (and members) relocated, they are unfortunately not consistent in reporting the origin and destination of these migrants.[33] Nonetheless, we can derive some insight from the information that is given (see tables 3.6 and 3.7). As expected, the majority of internal colonists came from Venetia and in particular the provinces of Padua and Rovigo. While in 1931 Venetian migration of this sort was directed about equally to Cagliari and Rome, by 1932 Rome (which included the Agro Pontino) predominated by a considerable margin. Indeed Rome[34] was easily the major destination for internal colonization from all parts of Italy. The large percentage of migration directed to Tuscany in 1930–31 consisted of Paduans migrating to colonize the *bonifiche* in Grosseto; total colonization in those years, however, was still very low (see table 3.2). After Venetia, the regions of Lombardy, Emilia-Romagna and the Marches all

---

[32] In the literature of the era, the term colonization has a broad meaning, not always demographic (for example a *bonifica* in Africa might well be referred to as colonization whether or not it is to be populated by Italian settlers) and, when demographic, not always referring to the movement of population from other areas (one might "colonize" using the local population). I shall use internal colonization to refer to those cases where new population centers were established as a result of the importation of colonists.

[33] Over the years there are tables for: internal colonization by province of origin and destination; *lavoratori* migrated for internal colonization and agricultural contracts by province and then region; and migration of families by region. Only the latter (1935 and 1938) corresponds to the numbers in the series for relocated families.

[34] Later tables only give regional breakdowns but for Latium we can essentially understand Rome until the creation of the new province Littoria in 1934.

Table 3.6 *Primary regions of inter-regional emigration for internal colonization as a % of total*

	1930	1931	1932	1935	1938
Lombardy	21.1	14.6	4.1	12.3	7.2
Venetia	61.3	63.7	82.9	29.5	45.3
Em.-Rom.	9.0	8.5	2.2	29.2	12.0
Marches	4.9	10.5	5.3	12.8	12.2

Source: CMC, *Le migrazioni interne.*

Table 3.7 *Primary regions of inter-regional immigration for internal colonization as a % of total*

	1930	1931	1932	1935	1938
Tuscany	18.9	31.5	3.6	3.5	3.0
Latium	19.0	34.0	86.4	39.1	40.7
Sardinia	60.7	23.4	3.4	7.9	9.3

Source: CMC, *Le migrazioni interne.*

shared about equally in inter-regional emigration for the purpose of col-onization.[35] The Lombards and Marchigiani went primarily to Latium, while the Emiliani also went in notable numbers to Lombardy and Sardinia. There was also considerable internal colonization in Emilia by Emiliani and in Lombardy by Lombards.

Demographic colonization of the *bonifiche* was carried out by various private, semi-private and public organizations. There was, however, a general formula that applied in most cases. The organization received from the government a concession of land to be reclaimed. If necessary, land was expropriated from the previous owners and compensation offered.[36] The government extended special credit terms to the coloniz-ing agency which might also receive financial subsidies. In conjunction with the CMC, both the workers for the initial phase of *bonificazione* and the families for eventual settlement were selected, examined, brought to

[35] Though their populations were very different. According to the 1931 census: Lombardy (5.6 million), Emilia-Romagna (3.3 million), the Marches (1.2 million).

[36] Though it appears that this compensation may have been minimal given that it was on a number of occasions refused. See, for example, R.d. 9 August 1935 in *Gazzetta ufficiale* n. 192; R.d. 17 January 1938 in *Gazzetta ufficiale* n. 46; R.d. 7 June 1938 and R.d. 21 June 1938 in *Gazzetta ufficiale* n. 165.

the site, and housed. The arrangement with the colonist was one of several variations on a lease-purchase contract according to which the colonist received his land, home, necessary tools, seed and often a fixed wage for the first several years. He would then work off his debt with the final goal of ownership, usually planned for fifteen to thirty years after the start of the contract. The colonist too might be eligible for government loans and also for financial prizes.

The first of the "Fascist" internal colonizations pre-dated the creation of the CMC and even the March on Rome. It was carried out by the Società anonima bonifiche sarde (Sardinian Land Reclamation Co. – SBS) on the gulf of Oristano in western Sardinia.[37] The SBS obtained concessions in this area shortly after World War I. The plan was to drain the malarial swamps of a part of the Campidano plain including Terralba and direct water for irrigation from the Tirso river, which was being dammed to produce electrical power. The first group of colonists arrived in 1928[38] and came from the Polesine (province of Rovigo), an agricultural area of the Po delta characterized by high fertility and high rates of emigration.[39] Official interest in the project was high and Mussolini himself wired the prefect of Cagliari (on 19 February 1928) to announce the arrival of these colonists. This first group was followed by sporadic additions generally from Venetia, Emilia-Romagna and Lombardy.[40] The village "Mussolini" was inaugurated by the king on the Fascist new year, 28 October 1928. It achieved the status of *comune* as Mussolinia in December 1930 (after the war it would become Arborèa). It appears that the CPMI was not directly involved in these initial migrations (Atti C. disc. 6 May 1931, pp. 4527–8).

The first colonists had a difficult time, victims of both environment and their contracts. Fossa traveled to Sardinia in 1930; having observed the situation, he met with the SBS and received, it seems, satisfaction on a number of the colonists' complaints. Nonetheless, he reported to *il duce* a notable level of discontent and the desire of many to return home. It seems that after the fiscal year 1928–29 all colonists had closed their accounts with a debit. News of the general dissatisfaction of the colonists seems to have made its way back home as, again according to Fossa, the project was regarded with diffidence in the town of Forlì (Emilia-Romagna). In marked contrast to Fossa's observations, the

---

[37] For what follows, see Di Felice n.d.; ACS SPD-ord. 197.095; and subsequent citations.

[38] Per Di Felice, one family did arrive in 1927.

[39] The Polesine was an important source of emigrants for all the Fascist programs of internal and African colonization. Enrico Casalini, codirector of *Economia* with Livio Livi, described it as "the best basis for Italy's demographic growth" (Casalini 1928, p. 45). See also the entry "Polesine" in *Enciclopedia italiana* and Cavaglieri 1902.

[40] On 22 May 1930, for example, Mussolini was informed that ten families from Predappio, his hometown, would be going.

Table 3.8 *Mussolinia*

Year	families	members	
1924		4 or 5 shepherds[a]	
1926*		c. 500[a]	
1929	61	557	(gross immigration of colonists)[b]
1929	91	788[c]	
1931(?)	200(?)	2,050	(stable population)[d]
1 June 1931(?)	460	2,700	(fixed inhabitants – Acerbo to Mussolini)[e]
Nov. 1934	174	1,892[e]	
1936		c. 4,000[f]	
1938	243	2,649[b]	
1941		4,286[g]	
1942		2,690	(SBS census – 366 absent for military service)[b]

Notes:
*(sic) but must be 1928
[a] Report of the Ministry of Agriculture (ACS:PCM 1928–30 b.1283, f. 8.3.10235)
[b] Di Felice n.d
[c] Martinelli and Nuti 1981
[d] *Conquista della terra* (May 1931)
[e] ACS-ord. 197.095
[f] Alivìa 1938
[g] Casini 1941

Ministry of Agriculture carried out a study of Mussolinia at exactly this same period, issuing a favorable report regarding its success and the treatment of the colonists (ACS PCM 1928–30 b.1283 f.8.3.10235). In spite of a degree of defection and the difficulties encountered by both colonists and the SBS, the project continued. Initially a private venture, Mussolinia ran into difficulties during the subsequent economic crisis and had to be salvaged by government intervention.

We can attempt to follow the demographic growth of Mussolinia by gathering together from various sources references to the number of inhabitants. These figures are of varying degrees of reliability, but at least give an idea of the scale of the project (see table 3.8). It would appear that the population grew until 1931, after which financial diffi- culties halted further colonization and a large number of those already settled left. Early growth is revealed by the jump from 90 to 200 to 460 colonizing families between January 1930 and June 1931 (and CMC figures show 703 migrations to the province of Cagliari for internal colonization in 1930, mostly Lombards and Venetians (CMC 1930, p. 194)). The colony continued to grow, most notably in the years 1935–37,[41] after which colonization efforts in general turned from Italy to Africa. As to composition, of the January 1930 tenant-farming population, most were from the north (78%) and of these most were Venetians. There was also a significant contingent from Sicily.[42]

Mussolinia was the first of the new Fascist cities,[43] though it should be remembered that these "cities" were specifically intended as *non*-urban population centers. On a small scale, the settlement of Mussolinia by colonists enrolled from an entirely different region of Italy began to realize the Fascist program of demographic management. The subsequent colonization of the Agro Pontino would do so in a grander fashion.

The reclamation and colonization of the Agro Pontino was carried out by the Opera nazionale combattenti (National Veterans Organization – ONC) in conjunction with the CMC.[44] The swamps along the

---

[41] Di Felice n.d. refers to new expeditions of colonists in 1936. CMC figures for migration to Sardinia for internal colonization and agricultural contracts are consistent, showing a jump in 1936:

1933	144
1934	149
1935	316
1936	575
1937	391
1938	92 (includes intraregional migration).

[42] Mussolinia colonists (1930):

	families	number
Polesani (all Rovigo?)	30	255
Vicentini	11	89
Veneziani	16	179
(Venetia total)	(57)	(523)
Friulani	8	74
Mantovani	2	20
Maremanni	2	13
Siciliani	12	108
Sardi	9	52
Total	90	790

(ACS PCM 1928–30 b.1283 f.8.3.10235. See also Di Felice n.d. on 1927–9 population breakdown).

[43] On the Fascist new cities (or towns) see Ghirardo 1989; Mariani 1976; Martinelli and Nuti 1981; Millon 1978; Ruinas 1939.

[44] On the Agro Pontino see the ONC journal *La conquista della terra* which chronicles month to month progress (in the expected glorifying manner), esp. Nannini 1935, 1937. See also Ghirardo 1989, pp. 40–81; Mariani 1976; Martinelli and Nuti 1981, pp. 17–42.

Tyrrhenian coast of Latium, where the sparse population had to deal with the constant threat of malaria, had long been a target for land reclamation projects. Legislation for reclamation of the Agro Romano (west of Rome) was instituted in 1878 (L. 11 December 1878, n.4642), and work began ten years later. By the time of the Fascist rise to power, a degree of land reclamation had been accomplished in Ostia, Isola Sacra, and the Maccarese, though demographically the impact was not great: the population of Ostia was about 1,000 and of the rural Agro Romano about 800.[45] A precedent for internal migration of Po Valley peasants was established here, and Mussolini himself made reference in the *Camera* to the 600 immigrants from Romagna who had died in the *bonifica* of Ostia.[46]

The Agro Pontino, down the coast from the Agro Romano, provided the regime new and multiple opportunities: here the Fascists could demonstrate their ability to act decisively where Liberal governments had faltered; only a short drive from the capital, it would be a showplace for the Fascist pro-rural policy; and it would provide an outlet for population pressure in the northeast far greater than that in Sardinia.[47]

The ONC would ultimately be involved in carrying out *bonifiche* throughout Italy and also in Africa, but the Agro Pontino was its most publicized project. Canals were dug, swamps drained, irrigation systems introduced, and families – preference given to veterans – installed in individual farms. The contract offered the colonists was again drawn up jointly by the ONC and the CMC. In contrast to Mussolinia, the possibility of urban crowding was to be entirely avoided by settling the families in ONC houses scattered through the countryside (and attached to the farms). Numbers of these are still visible today. The new cities were intended more as administrative than population centers.

The ONC received the Agro Pontino concession in August 1931.[48] To the strains of the Fascist hymn *Giovinezza*, the first workers (1,327

---

[45] On the pre-Fascist *bonificazione* of the Agro Romano see Viana 1921.

[46] Atti C. disc. 9 April 1930, p. 2346. For other precedents see *"Migratorie, correnti"* in the *Enciclopedia italiana*.

[47] The attraction of a purely Fascist *bonifica* seems to have been overwhelming, as the contemporary progress in the Agro Romano was minimal in spite of new concessions. The ONC reported the 1936 population of the Maccarese as 8,000 (*Conquista della terra* [February 1936], pp. 5–6). In June 1937, the new director of the latter *bonifica*, Senator Boncompagni, described it to Mussolini as an expensive failure and estimated the population at about 5,000 (ACS PCM 1940–3 b.2268 f.3.1.1.1906). This figure was essentially unchanged by August 1941 when the Maccarese population amounted to 4,398 plus 746 absent conscripts.   [48] R.d. 28 August 1931 in *Gazzetta ufficiale* n. 224 (1931).

Tuscans)[49] arrived in early November at the already existing town of Cisterna (ACS PCM 1934–6 b.1762 f.1.1.23.3299.2-A). These workers, hired for the initial work of *bonificazione* and so classified as temporary migrants, were selected and transported by the CMC. By the end of November their number had swollen to 10,000 and would grow to as many as 25,000. This vast work force had to be housed (for which purpose dormitories were built) and fed by the CMC, a situation that created "serious difficulties" (ACS PCM 1940–1 f.1.1.23.3229 sf.10). Five years later, in December 1936, the CMC announced the closure of workers' dormitories due to greatly reduced numbers.[50] However, these dormitories seem still to have been operating the following year and workers were still employed in the Agro Pontino at the end of 1941, when Lombrassa reported that much still needed to be done (ACS PCM 1940–1 f.1.1.23.3229 sf.10; SPD-ord. 106.414).

The first families (100) arrived in October 1932. These, all Venetians, had been selected by the CMC from a large number of applicants. By the end of 1932 there were 350 families in place. Mussolini visited the Agro Pontino *bonifica* in April 1932 and again in December of that year to inaugurate the new town of Littoria (now Latina). The colonists of this model settlement received considerable official attention including multiple visits from *il duce* (who also distributed colonist prizes), other Fascist hierarchs, and Italian royalty. Mussolini threshing grain with the Agro Pontino peasants is perhaps the classic image of the Fascist "battle for wheat." Subsequently, four other ONC cities were inaugurated here: Sabaudia (1934), Pontinia (1935), Aprilia (1937) and Pomezia[51] (1939). In 1934 the Agro Pontino was promoted to provincial status (as Littoria). Aprilia differed from the earlier cities in that it was to be populated not by colonists brought from the north, but by the natural increase of those already settled in the Agro Pontino.

The demographic growth of the Agro Pontino is reconstructed in table 3.9, which shows rapid growth between the initiation of the project and 1935. Apparently the 60,000 present in 1935 were approximately

---

[49] It is interesting to note in this regard Razza's promise to the prefect of Pistoia (Tuscany) that unemployed woodcutters from the latter's province would be hired for the Agro Pontino project. Local pressure of this sort characterized the official projects for colonization in Africa as well (ACS PCM 1931–3 b.1589 f.7.1.1.2689). With regard to the initial group of workers for the Agro Pontino project, however, the CMC volume reports only seven workers migrating from Pistoia to Rome for *bonifica* work in 1931 (CMC, *Migrazioni interne* 1931, pp. 418–27).

[50] Note the decline in internal migration to Latium after 1934 in table 3.4.

[51] Pomezia is more properly considered part of the Agro Romano and was not part of the Littoria province. It was in part settled by Romagnoli left homeless after floods in their own region (at least forty families) and also by a community of 600 "Italians" coming from Romania where they had established a colony seventy years before (*Conquista della terra* (July 1939), p. 40; [October 1939], p. 47; [July 1940]).

Table 3.9 *Agro Pontino*

Cumulative total of colonial families arrived[a]			Population		
Year	Families	Members	Date	Total	
1932	623	5,165	Nov. 1932	<350[b]	
1933	1,343	11,402	30 Oct. 1932	2,013	(stable)[c]
1934	1,936	16,653	30 Nov. 1932	6,308	(stable)[c]
1935	2,215	19,048		17,800	(total)[c]
			Oct. 1933	15,000	(stable)[c]
1941 population by locality[h]			18 Mar. 1935	60,292[d]	
			Nov. 1937	>2,500	families[e]
			1938	60,000[f]	
Littoria	19,500		1941	60,000[g]	
Pontinia	4,000				
Aprilia	1,500				
Sabaudia	5,000				
Province	30,000				

Notes:
[a] *Conquista della terra* (Dec. 1935).
[b] *Ibid.* (July 1932).
[c] Alvaro 1935
[d] ACS: PCM b. 1762, f. 1.1.23.3299, sf.2-A
[e] *Conquista della terra* (Nov. 1937).
[f] *Ibid.* (Nov. 1938).
[g] *Ibid.* (Nov. 1941).
[h] *Bonifica e colonizzazione* (June 1942)

two-thirds temporary workers, which would explain the decline revealed in 1941, a decline probably accelerated by mobilization. The other 1941 figure of 60,000 is probably an inaccurate declaration by then president of the ONC, di Crollalanza, citing the previous maximum rather than the current population.[52] The colonists were primarily

[52] CMC figures reveal a marked decline in interregional migration to Latium for land reclamation in 1936 and internal colonization and agricultural contracts in 1938:

	land reclamation and hydraulic works	internal colonization and agricultural contracts	
1934	6,164	7,021	
1935	1,496	2,433	
1936	261	1,875	
1937	71	1,594	
1938		218	(may include intraregional migration).

Venetians, and their presence is still evident today. In numerical terms this was the grandest of the Fascist efforts at population management and for order of magnitude would only be approached by the later efforts to demographically colonize Libya on a large scale.[53] Nonetheless, the relocation of 30,000 individuals in a five-year period did not come close to matching contemporary spontaneous migration. Even given the difficulties of migration abroad in this period, more Italians left the country in search of work in a single year than were settled in the entire Agro Pontino project.

The Agro Pontino *bonifica* and colonization were throughout an ONC project. In fact, the president of the ONC, Orsolini-Cencelli, was also the first *podestà* (mayor) of both Littoria and Sabaudia. The CMC cooperated in colonist selection, contract negotiation, transportation, and housing of the temporary workers. In total, the undertaking was estimated to have cost 549 million lire. In 1941 the lease-purchase contracts were terminated and the property transferred to the colonists. Owners in name, they nonetheless retained debt obligations.[54]

The Agro Pontino in particular and Fascist *bonifiche* and public works in general served an important propaganda purpose both at home and abroad. The transformation of landless laborers into tenant farmers and ultimately small property owners could be presented as fulfillment of the World War I promises of land for peasants. And though the numbers involved were not large enough to noticeably affect Italian unemployment nor to alter the class structure of Italian society, still the Fascists did give the impression of embarking on a revolutionary project, a project in keeping with both the Fascist creation of a new civilization and revolt against urban society. The fact that Agro Pontino colonists tended to be chosen from among those deemed least desirable by the sending provinces and that the project was plagued by imperfect land reclamation (and so disease), theft among the colonists, and even strikes was hidden behind a barrage of positive publicity, publicity that extended to the foreign press as well.[55] Salvemini pointed out that no foreigner of any importance visiting Rome for more than three days could avoid the obligatory tour of the Agro Pontino in the company of some Fascist hierarch (Salvemini 1974, vol. III, pp. 242–3). In fact, for the inauguration of Aprilia, which took place not long after the creation of the Rome–Berlin axis, Mussolini was accompanied by German Reichsminister Hess.

More modest in scale than the Agro Pontino, or even Mussolinia, but

---

[53] But see remarks on Altoatesini migration below in this chapter.
[54] "Epilogo dell'impresa pontina," *Conquista della terra* (November 1941).
[55] On discontent and hardship among the colonists, see Ghirardo 1989, pp. 49–55.

interesting for certain unique and common aspects it had with these, was the colonization of Fertilia, near Alghero, in northwestern Sardinia. Fertilia was colonized by the Ente ferrarese di colonizzazione (Colonization Association of Ferrara – EFC). The province of Ferrara is located in Emilia, across the Po from the Polesine province of Rovigo (which is in Venetia). Ferrara resembled the neighboring Venetian provinces in its agricultural and high density population (primarily landless laborers) and historically high rates of natural population growth and emigration. Although important *bonifiche* were carried out in the province of Ferrara itself, it nonetheless remained one of the high pressure areas identified for programs of internal emigration.

In July 1933 Mussolini instructed that the CMC take whatever measures were necessary to relocate Ferrarese families in the less densely populated areas of Italy, and this meant primarily Sardinia.[56] In October he called for the creation of the EFC under the supervision of the CMC,[57] an *Ente* to be financed by "voluntary" contributions from the professional associations of Ferrara. For the purpose of colonization the EFC received three penal colonies in the Nurra region of Sardinia to which would be added various expropriations (R.d.-l. 30 November 1933, n.1719). Prisoners were still present and so colonization would have to await their removal. One of these colonies, Cuguttu, became Fertilia. As in the Agro Pontino, this "city" was planned as an administrative center while the colonists' dwellings would be dispersed in the *bonifica*. The "occupation" of Fertilia was begun in 1934 and the city inaugurated in March 1936. The initial plan was for 110 farms of which 40 were occupied by 1938, apparently by families averaging over 10 members each! (Alivìa 1938, pp. 28–30) *Bonifica e colonizzazione* reported that the average population during the first three years was 600 (with 29 marriages and 56 births),[58] but these may have included laborers brought in to complete the *bonifica* work begun by the prisoners. The same journal announced that in January 1939, 109 colonial houses were inaugurated (the initial quota?) and that 100 more were planned.[59] The permanent population cannot have been much more than 1,000 at this time and it is doubtful that much work was carried out from 1940 to the end of the war.

The scale of Fertilia was small. As in the case of the Agro Pontino, the stated aim was the relief of population pressure and the transformation

---

[56] Dec. Capo Gov. 22 July 1933 in *Gazzetta ufficiale* n. 184.
[57] Dec. Capo Gov. 7 October 1933 in *Gazzetta ufficiale* n. 255. Its president was Mario Ascione (Dec. Capo Gov. 11 November 1933 in *Gazzetta ufficiale* n. 267).
[58] *Bonifica e colonizzazione* (November 1939), p. 349.
[59] *Bonifica e colonizzazione* (January 1940), pp. 60-1.

of landless laborers into property owners. Here again a lease-purchase arrangement was used. This effort differed from the other two examples cited, however, in the specificity of the area targeted for emigration, and it was a model emulated on a regional level for the colonization of Ethiopia. It also represented a still more direct involvement of the CMC, and so the state, in colonization efforts, indicative of the general transition from private to public colonization, a trend again still more evident in Africa.

As a whole, the Fascist *bonifiche* represented a huge investment,[60] of which, however, only a part went to the inter-regional migration and colonization projects described above. Other *bonifiche* involved the movement and employment of population within the region in question: Emiliani in Ferrara, Apulians in the Tavoliere di Puglia, Sardinians for the new mining town of Carbonia, and so on. But out of this larger project, the creation of new population centers using groups transplanted from other regions represented the most significant, and enduring, aspect of Italian demographic management.

It was recognized at the time that these projects constituted a novel demographic experiment. From a eugenic point of view, the population of, especially, the Agro Pontino represented a unique example of a group selected for its propensity for hard work and high fertility. In the words of CMC *Commissario* Nannini: "clearly Littoria represents the first large scale selection of population, an experiment which has not failed to raise the interest of scholars of eugenics" (Nannini 1935, p. 95). Nannini was likely referring to interest expressed by the noted physiologist Nicola Pende (on whom more below) who described the regime's internal colonies as true human nurseries from which would spring "a race of Italians selected and tested for productivity and fertility" (Pende 1933, p. 241). The expectations of Nannini and Pende were rewarded as Littoria repeatedly led the list of provincial birth rates[61] and the 1936 census reported that Littoria had enjoyed the highest intercensus crude growth rate.[62]

The new cities of the Agro Pontino and western Sardinia still exist and have enjoyed varying degrees of demographic growth (see table 3.10), and the Venetian dialect can still be heard there. The ruralist aspects of the projects have, however, not been entirely realized. Aprilia and Pomezia are essentially suburbs of Rome, characterized by high-rise apartment buildings; Latina is a bustling and pleasant small city; while

---

[60] Martinelli and Nuti 1981, p. 24 report that 7 billion lire was spent in 14 years.
[61] In this it was of course aided by a significant advantage in age structure, i.e. a disproportionate number of individuals of childbearing age. See *Notiziario demografico* (16 June 1931); Alessandri 1936.   [62] ISTAT, *Censimento 1936*, vol.III, pt.1, p. 19*.

Table 3.10 *Population figures, 1981*

Aprilia	37,045
Latina	92,674
Pontinia	10,912
Sabaudia	12,430
Latina (prov.)	427,432
Pomezia(Roma)	29,801
Fertilia	1,494
Arboréa	3,387

Source: 1981 census, resident population

Sabaudia, due to its fortunate location, has become a chic beach resort. Pontinia maintains much of its original character, as its position off the main transport arteries seems to have limited growth, and not much more than the original rationalist center exists. Arborèa has grown and is an active agricultural center. In this it perhaps most closely realizes the intentions of its founders. Fertilia is little more than an appendix to Alghero.

The internal migration, *bonifiche*, and colonization programs reveal the contradictory nature of Fascist internal migration policy in general. Following the externally imposed restriction on migration abroad, the regime sought to suppress the internal currents of migration and the general urbanization process which the former situation encouraged. And while the land reclamation efforts perhaps lowered unemployment among laborers and farm workers, they also eliminated pasture and so deprived animal herders of their livelihood. Nor was much done about the contemporary depopulation of the mountains and forests.[63] One deputy, in a general discussion of the *bonifiche* and internal colonization programs, described this problem as "the sad reverse of a beautiful medallion" (Atti C. disc. 9 April 1932, p. 6212 [Sertoli]).

The CMC data show that during the years of the *Commissariato's* maximum internal colonizing efforts (1932–8), it was transferring slightly more than 10,000 individuals a year to new homes, primarily in the *bonifiche*. From the point of view of selection, medical exams and care, transportation, and housing, this was not a small number. In the nine years for which data were published, the CMC reportedly

---

[63] See Treves 1976, pp. 110–26; Scarzanella 1977, p. 178. A multi-volume report on the depopulation of the mountains was compiled (and edited by Ugo Giusti), see *Istituto nazionale di economia agraria* 1932–8.

managed the internal colonization of about 82,000 Italians. Still, this represented less than 10% of the "spontaneous" migration in a *single* year as revealed by the postwar ISTAT population register calculations. The Fascist ideal of government "valorization" and control of internal population movement was far from total.

In 1938 it was calculated that natural increase in Venetia alone would create a population surplus of 24,000 rural families (160,000 individuals) in the following ten years. Of these, 10–11,000 could presumably be absorbed as a result of *bonifiche* and more intensive cultivation within the region. But the excess population from this one region was greater than had been managed by internal migration programs in the previous decade. Clearly another outlet was needed. The author of the above calculations was not alone in proposing the newly conquered Italian Empire in Africa for this purpose (De Polzer 1938).

Anti-urbanism

The repressive side of the internal migration policy was anti-urbanism. Urbanization was part of the general demographic transition and industrialization process that Italy underwent in the interwar period, as many Italians went to the cities to find work, better social services, and greater opportunities for diversion and profit. Political and scientific authorities at the time generally agreed on the negative effects of urban life on the health, morality, and fertility of the Italian population (but see chapter 5, pp. 240–2 below), and, complementing the Fascist efforts to encourage migration to favored destinations, the regime attempted to prevent population flow into the cities.

The association of urbanization with fertility decline was not a Fascist discovery. Low birth rates characterized cities throughout Europe, and this fact had been widely noted before World War I.[64] The devirilizing effects of urban life were much studied, and cited, during the Fascist *ventennio*, and it was noted that neo-Malthusian (or birth control) practices spread along the major axes of communication which had the cites as their hubs; for Italy the point of entry was the French border (Livi 1940a). ISTAT figures consistently revealed lower birth rates in the large cities and provincial capitals than in the surrounding countryside.[65]

Rural and urban fertility levels present another problem of definition. No single criterion of urbanism or rurality was adopted in the period,

---

[64] For Italy, see Mortara 1911.
[65] See ISTAT, *Movimento* after 1926 and also *Notiziario demografico* (1 May 1931), pp. 264–5; (16 February 1932), pp. 90–3.

and even if "urban" (or "industrial")[66] fertility were always lower than "rural," which it was not, the lack of a standard definition makes it difficult to gauge how either was changing with time. And though rural fertility figures were normally higher than urban, by changing either the measure of fertility or the definition of rurality the correlation might change, and on at least one occasion an ISTAT study revealed that for the four large regions of Italy, the highest fertility was not always found in the most rural areas, nor the lowest in the most industrial.[67] Nonetheless, ISTAT studies did reveal increasing urbanization throughout the *ventennio*, and a slowing down of its rate in the period 1939–42.[68] Though during this latter period, the 1939 law against urbanization certainly created an artificial picture of stagnation as many migrating illegally to the cities did not officially change residence.[69]

In spite of problems of definition, there was general consensus on the negative effect of urbanization on fertility.[70] The initial 1928 legislation called for by Mussolini in the Ascension Day speech empowered prefects to take measures to limit urban growth (L. 24 December 1928, n.2961 [n.72 of 1929]), and ISTAT subsequently canvassed provincial, *comune*, business, and trade union representatives in order to assess the kind of actions being taken. These included both propagandistic and police measures: the expulsion from cities of unemployed non-residents, imposition of a time period within which new arrivals had either to find work or leave, and the prohibition of hiring non-residents. In a couple of cases, programs to improve rural housing were introduced, but positive measures of this sort were the exception rather than the rule. In all, sixty-two (of ninety-two) provinces took some action. Some prefects claimed that the problem did not exist in their province.[71]

The creation of the CMC in 1931 and joint CMC/employment office control of internal migration created a potential instrument for the control of migration to the cities, but no measures were taken at a national level until 1939, when legislation was introduced prohibiting changes of residence to cities (*comuni capoluoghi*) of over 25,000 inhabi-

---

[66] Mussolini had conflated the two in his Ascension Day speech when he identified "industrial urbanism" as the denatalist force to be combatted. See chapter 2, pp. 65–6 above.

[67] *Notiziario demografico* (10 April 1938). Compare to ibid. (10 December 1937), (1 April 1931). See also the Giusti and Livi studies discussed in chapter 5, pp. 240–2.

[68] *Notiziario demografico* (1 December 1942), p. 66.

[69] On the nature of Italian urbanization (for the period 1870–1927) and the problems of its measurement, see Mariani 1976, pp. 44–52.

[70] See, for example, Molinari 1937; above *Notiziario demografico* citations (notes 65–8); and also Atti C. disc. 6 June 1929, pp. 720–2; S. disc. 13 May 1937, p. 2907; C. disc. 26 April 1940, pp. 572–4.   [71] *Annali di statistica* 6, 32, pp. 55–61.

tants, or else of notable industrial importance, unless stable employment was arranged beforehand.[72] In addition, authorization was
required from either the CMC or employment offices, and those leaving
their own *comune* for temporary employment were required to return
home within thirty days of the end of employment or else face police
"repatriation" and a fine. This law was intended to lower urban
unemployment and prevent the depopulation of the countryside. It was
further hoped that official channels of internal and African migration
could divert those pouring into the cities, though, as we have seen
above, these channels turned out to be at least an order of magnitude
shy of the task. Several more pragmatic legislators did in fact express
concern about the plight of the rural unemployed or the worker who
depended on seasonal migratory employment (Atti C. D.l. N.220 [15
May 1939]; C. disc. 25 May 1939, pp. 40–1; S. disc. 1 June 1939, pp. 22–4).

Many went to the cities anyway, risking deportation and fines in
hopes of finding work. Although it is impossible to say what the levels
of migration to the cities would have been in the absence of the 1939 law,
it seems that the anti-urban measures were not particularly effective.
Nor were statisticians unaware of this: a 1942 Demorazza publication
identified the general trend of population movement – in spite of internal and African colonization and anti-urban legislation – as agglomera-
tion in the cities of the north and center,[73] and Treves has even described
Fascist anti-urbanism as extraneous to the demographic history of Italy
(Treves 1976, p. 101). Nonetheless, anti-urbanism served a political
purpose. It helped to prevent the creation of large and potentially
revolutionary urban mobs by threatening many workers (both
employed and unemployed) with repatriation to their home *comuni*
should they draw attention to themselves. It was also consistent with
Mussolini's general revolt against urban culture, a significant aspect of
his attempt to create a new Fascist civilization based on the "rural"
masses.[74]

Colonization in Africa

The program of demographic colonization carried out by the Fascist
regime in Libya and Italian East Africa resembled in many ways that
of the *bonifiche* and internal colonization within Italy. The colonial

---

[72] L. 6 July 1939, n.1092; see also Preti 1987, pp. 27–31.
[73] Demorazza 1942. This organization is discussed in chapter 4.
[74] Sori 1979, pp. 471–3; Treves 1976, pp. 97–101. Sori also points out that this law continued
to serve such a purpose until its suppression in 1961. See also Mariani 1976, pp. 73–86
on the ideological importance of anti-urbanism.

governments acquired land (by the creation of public domain) which was then granted to the colonizing organizations. The state provided special credit, subsidies, and prizes for the purpose of semi-private reclamation and colonizing, and eventually took over all aspects of the project embarking on a costly program of state colonization. Organizations involved in the process included the CMC, INFPS, ONC, and others created specifically for African colonization. As with internal migration programs, population pressure reduction and increased industrial and agricultural production were among the stated aims of the transfer of workers and families to Africa; these colonies too would help to absorb that part of Italy's natural population increase that had traditionally migrated to other countries. Again land was to be given to the peasants, and again the regime employed its considerable propaganda resources to publicize the program and promote consensus among the population.

There were also differences. The motivation for African colonization was naturally more complex than that for the projects within Italy. The creation of population centers in Africa was part of an attempt to expand the Italian sphere of influence by affirming, with bodies, the Italian presence there; it was an important aspect of foreign policy. And according to the traditional colonialist logic, it was hoped that demographic colonization would lead to the creation of significant markets for Italian goods. The actual process of colonization was also complicated by the presence of indigenous and potentially hostile population, and both the creation of public domain for agricultural settlement and coexistence with the local inhabitants presented difficulties not encountered in Italy.[75] African and internal migration also differed in that the migrants who went to Libya and Ethiopia, contrary to expectations, did not ultimately remain there.

As described above (see chapter 1, pp. 33–6 above), the limited Liberal efforts at government-sponsored colonization in Eritrea had been a failure. Subsequently, and until the taking of Ethiopia, the Italian possessions in the Horn of Africa (Eritrea and Italian Somaliland) were repeatedly referred to as unsuitable for demographic colonization. Libya, on the other hand, was perceived as a pos-

---

[75] Though people were also displaced by land reclamation in Italy (in the Agro Pontino for example). The question of the impact of Italian demographic colonialism on the local population in Libya was not entirely ignored by the Fascists; see, for example, Balbo 1938. It was repeatedly stated, for example, that the *indemaniamento* there was in keeping with Islamic law, and the colonial government also created "colonies" for the indigenous populations, which entailed programs of *bonifiche* and the construction of colonial homes and rural centers, though the investment was minimal. See Segré 1978, pp. 61–9, 172–9.

sible destination for Italian workers, but efforts were for the most part left to private initiative prior to the enunciation of the Fascist population policy.

African colonization during the *ventennio* passed through several phases. Contemporary to the March on Rome, the new *Governatore* of Tripolitania (western Libya), Giuseppe Volpi, embarked on a program of *indemaniamento* (state acquisition of property) that was continued by his successor Emilio De Bono, and large concessions were granted to those considered capable (that is having sufficient means) of cultivating the land. This policy was later lamented when – as with internal colonization – the purpose of the Libyan *bonifiche* was identified as the creation of small landowners. After 1928 (under *Governatore* Pietro Badoglio), colonization remained a generally private enterprise, but concessions carried with them the requirement that Italian colonists be employed and settled there. With the final pacification of Cyrenaica (eastern Libya) in 1932, a semi-official colonizing organization was created, whose activities were subsequently extended to Tripolitania as the government became more directly involved in colonization. The Ethiopian War imposed a temporary lull in colonization efforts, but after the proclamation of Empire (May 1936), they were initiated in Ethiopia and renewed in Libya. The Libyan efforts culminated in the "intensive demographic colonization" of 1938–9 after which World War II intervened, and the eventual loss of Italy's colonies led to the return of most of those who had migrated there.[76]

The Fascist policy encouraging the demographic colonization of Libya was initiated, not surprisingly, in 1928, more or less contemporarily with the imposition of emigration restrictions and the assumption of an active role for the regulation of internal migration by the CPMI. The Libyan program called for the identification of areas reserved for colonization. Individuals (preferably veterans) and organizations receiving concessions were obliged to settle Italian peasant families. The colonial governments were to undertake the necessary public works, while those developing the concessions would receive subsidies for the work of reclamation. Prizes for the eventual colonial families were also legislated and special lines of credit were established for agricultural development in Tripolitania.[77]

[76] For the colonization of Libya see Nobile 1990a; Papini 1933–4; Segré 1978; Vöchting 1940. For Ethiopia see Del Boca 1982; Ghirardo 1989, pp. 88–106; Larebo 1994.

[77] R.d. 7 June 1928, n.1695(2122); R.d. 29 July 1928, n.2433(2901); Dec. Min. 30 July 1928 in *Gazzetta ufficiale* n. 182. A 50 million lire line of credit was established in 1928 (R.d.-l. 26 February 1928, n.614[1066]) and renewed in 1931 (R.d.-l. 18 June 1931, n.1011).

The colonial legislation seems not, however, to have created a great deal of excitement in parliament and discussion of the 1929–30 Ministry of Colonies budget was a far cry from Luigi Federzoni's procolonialist rhetoric of some years before (see chapter 2, pp. 59–60 above). Various references were made to demographic colonization, but De Bono, at the time undersecretary of state for colonies, emphasized the difficulty of convincing potential colonizers to invest in or move to Libya. He called for increased colonial propaganda, but did not include demographic colonization among the principal points of the government program (Atti C. disc. 5 June 1929, pp. 664–72, S. disc. 14 June 1929, pp. 651–60). During the following two years the general tenor of this discussion was one of restraint in the face of the high cost of colonization and general economic crisis.

Again in 1928, Mussolini reviewed an Istituto coloniale fascista (Fascist Colonial Institute) report authored by the noted colonialist Armando Maugini and outlining a plan for the promotion of demographic colonization in Libya. *Il duce* passed this report on to various ministers all of whom expressed reservations about the cost of the proposal and the negative repercussions of eventual cut-backs on enrolled colonists if the proposal were adopted and then found to be unaffordable.[78] Apparently this project was shelved. The CMC instead took over responsibility for the selection of colonists and in 1930 established an office in Tripoli. Just as it had been instructed to work together with the Minister of Corporations on internal migration, so it was instructed to coordinate with the Minister of Colonies regarding migration to Africa (R.d.-l. 26 May 1930, n.870).

Fascist-sponsored demographic colonization in Africa began in Tripolitania. One of the early, and longest-lasting, colonies was founded by the Azienda tabacchi italiana (Italian Tobacco Company – ATI) which received a concession in Tigrinna in order to grow tobacco for the State Monopoly. The original plan called for 500 tenant-farming families, and colonization began in the second half of 1931. An enthusiastic report to the PCM in 1933 described the ATI colony as flourishing, the colonists – mostly Abruzzesi – in excellent health, and the babies abundant (ACS PCM 1931–3 b.1703 f.14.4.8950). By the end of that year 230 families were in place (Atti S. D.l. N. 1843-A [30 December 1933]). These grew to 260 (1,600 individuals) one year later and about 300 in

---

[78] ACS PCM 1928–30 b.1353 f.17.1.5062. The Maugini report estimated that the cost of installing 250 colonial families (1250 individuals), including the necessary *bonifica*, would be 25 million lire. On Maugini, see Segré 1978.

1936.[79] The ATI contract required that the colonists devote one-half of their cultivation to tobacco which the company guaranteed to purchase. As usual the cost of transportation and the initial expenses of settlement were borne by the company and charged to the colonists' accounts. Transfer of land ownership was projected for thirty years later.

Contemporary to the ATI project, a colonial experiment was carried out by the Fascist militia (Milizia volontaria per la sicurezza nazionale – MVSN) with the sponsorship of *Governatore* Badoglio. This was to be a military colonization, which seems to have meant harsher conditions and less in the way of financial compensation for the work of setting up the colony. It was to be started up by the militiamen only; the families would join later. Begun in March 1931 with 30 heads of household, it eventually grew to 100 but was a failure, apparently due to poor management (Papini 1933–4, p. 36; Atti S. D.l. N. 1843-A, pp. 16–23; Vöchting 1940, pp. 179–81).

The following year, in reaction to high levels of unemployment, the Provincial Council of Corporative Economy of Ravenna (Emilia-Romagna) requested two large concessions in the highlands of Cyrenaica for colonization; in Ravenna alone 30,000 workers were in need of "a normal and tranquilizing economic employment." The Council's report, dated 16 February 1932, also suggested that this solution could be generally applied to the Valpadana, given the extent of cultivable land in Cyrenaica. This suggestion seems to have been heeded, as shortly afterwards, and following a Fascist Grand Council meeting that called for resolution of the Po Valley population problem, the Ravenna initiative was coopted by the Ministry of Colonies and the CMC. On 13 April a meeting was held by the Minister (De Bono) which included among others Maugini and CMC head Razza, and an Ente per la colonizzazione della Cirenaica (Organization for the Colonization of Cyrenaica – ECC) was proposed. This *Ente* would be in charge of designating land for cultivation and colonization. Colonists would be chosen by the CMC and

---

[79] Atti C. D.l. N. 442-A (29 January 1935), though Atti S. D.l N. 543-A (8 May 1935) gives 1934 figures of 320 and 2500. Segré (1978) reports these numbers:

	families	members
1931	22	166
1936	299	1,794
1937 (census)	271	1,548

Vöchting (1940, pp. 179–81) reports 290 families in March 1939. This concession continued to function after the war.

transported at its expense. They were to enter into a variation on the standard lease-purchase contract. The initial government contribution to the ECC would be 50 million lire, and other semi-official and private organizations were also solicited for contributions. Plans called for the transfer of a first group of colonists by the following autumn. Curiously, this initiative was emphatically *not* to be considered one of state colonization as the *Ente* would have the status of a private recipient of a concession. Razza actively promoted the project over the objections of several ministers. De Bono announced the new program in the Senate in May and the ECC came into existence shortly afterward. Its initial budget had been reduced to 38 million over five years. On the recommendation of De Bono, Razza was made president of the ECC.[80] In spite of the stated non-government nature of the ECC, it was nonetheless under the *vigilanza* of the CMC. The structure of the ECC would be duplicated by the EFC (created sixteen months later and also presided by Razza) which colonized Fertilia (see pp. 114–16 above), more evidence that the regime viewed internal and Libyan colonization as two aspects of the same problem.

The sudden interest in Cyrenaica as a destination for Italian colonists derived from the colony's recent pacification. Since the initial conquest in 1911, the Italian occupation of Cyrenaica had been confined to the coastal regions. The drive to occupy the highlands was initiated in 1923 but brought to a conclusion only in January 1932 when Badoglio announced that the rebellion was "completely and definitely crushed" (Rochat 1973, pp. 98–104). The Ravenna proposal came on the heels of this announcement.

The displacement of the local population seems to have been less of a problem in Cyrenaica than in Tripolitania. In Cyrenaica, war, internment, and exile had severely reduced both the Arab resistance and population.[81] De Bono's plan for the initiation of ECC colonization in autumn 1932 was slightly delayed, but the first small group of colonists left Italy for Cyrenaica in April 1933. These were followed by other and larger groups of generally southern Italians. By the end of 1934 the ECC had settled 326 families (2,340 individuals) in various locations.[82] The

---

[80] ACS PCM 1934–6 b.2039 f.17.1.842; Atti S. disc. 13 May 1932, p. 5002; R.d.-l. 11 June 1932, n.696; Dec. Capo Gov. 13 August 1932 in *Gazzetta ufficiale*, n.191.

[81] Rochat (1973, p. 101) estimates 60,000 deaths and 20,000 exiles, leaving a 1936 population of 142,000.

[82] Atti C. D.l. N. 442-A (22 February 1935), pp. 18–19. According to the budget report here cited the April 1933 group consisted of six families. Vöchting 1940, p. 184 on the other hand states that the heads of families were sent first, followed in October by their families. The latter seems to be the case as Razza wrote in a 14 October 1933 memorandum to Mussolini that the emigration of families (twelve) to Cyrenaica had begun "today" (ACS PCM 1934–6 b.2039 f.17.1.842 sf.8).

predominance of southern Italians among the Libyan colonists – in spite of the Ravenna initiative – is not a surprise given the proximity of the colony and the fact that spontaneous emigration (especially from Sicily) had traditionally found an outlet in Northern Africa (especially Tunisia). The emphasis on southern migration was included among the fundamental precepts of the ECC and distinguished for a time African colonization from the internal programs like the Agro Pontino (Atti C. D.l. N.442-A [22 February 1935], C. disc. 6 May 1935, p. 1333). In 1935, for example, almost 40% of the colonists settled in Libya were from Sicily, followed by Venetia (13%), Campania (8%) and Emilia (8%).

The Ministry of Colonies budget discussions reflected the increase in colonial activity. During the years 1932–5 reference was frequently made to the activities of the ECC and the need to establish Italian small landowners in Libya. Italy's right, as a great power, to colonize was invoked as well, though the repeated protestations of her demographic need are not entirely consistent with statements that population pressure was no longer an issue in Italy provided that population be properly distributed by internal migration. This inconsistency was noted at the time by Salvemini who wrote: "A government which boasts about both its repression of emigration and encouragement of population growth does not have the right to invoke this growth as a justification to demand colonies, colonies which in any case will not absorb emigration."[83]

In early 1934, *Commissario* Razza returned from a tour of Libya and reported glowingly to *il duce* on the achievements of the ECC colonists, numbers of whom he had awarded with colonial prizes. He also relayed the desire of the newly appointed *governatore* of Tripolitania and Cyrenaica, Italo Balbo, that the ECC activities be extended to Tripolitania as well.[84] Various ministers expressed reservations about this plan. Minister of Colonies De Bono was concerned that political problems might arise with regard to the native population as a result of the expropriations made necessary by this plan. Razza continued to push the program and prevailed (ACS PCM 1934–6 b.2039 f.17.1.842 sf.9; R.d-l. 11 October 1934, n.2038). The new legislation, unlike that originally creating the ECC, required that colonists be chosen from among the ranks of the PNF, MVSN, and veterans. The Ente per la colonizzazione della Tripolitania e la Cirenaica (which soon became the Ente

---

[83] Salvemini 1974, II, p. 423; though of course it was invoked and frequently, and not only by Fascists. For similar Catholic claims, see Webster 1960, pp. 123–4.

[84] The two colonies had been assigned to a single *governatore* under Badoglio (R.d.-l. 24 January 1929, n.99[524]) and were formally joined under Balbo (R.d.-l. 3 December 1934, n.2012).

Dictating demography

Table 3.11 *Families relocated in Tripolitania – annual totals (Libya after 1932)*

Year	Families	Individuals	Year	Families	Individuals
1921	6		1931	167	1,102
1922	8		1932	192	1,328
1923	11		1933	416	3,586
1924	17		1934	452	3,675
1925	8		1935	163	1,281
1926	20		1936	122	959
1927	55		1937	197	1,556
1928	48		1938	1,902	15,518
1929	74		(1938	1,775	14,633)
1930	169	1,227	1939	1,453	10,802

Sources: 1930–8: CMC, *Le migrazioni interne*. The figures for 1921–9 come from Atti C. D.l. N. 1588-A (2 Mar. 1933 – Pace), p. 28. The latter series also includes 1930–2. The 1930–1 figures agree with the CMC figures; for 1932 it reports 188 families. The last two lines of the table (1938–9) come from the ISTAT, *Movimento* volumes for those years.

per la colonizzazione della Libia (Organization for the Colonization of Libya – ECL) [R.d. 26 September 1935, n.2283]) received a new and slightly increased budget of 5 million lire per year for five years (R.d.-l. 18 March 1935, n.432). However, what might have been an intensification of colonizing efforts in Libya was postponed as the Italian interest in Africa moved southeast.

Just as for internal migrations, the CMC collected and published statistics for migration to the colonies. Table 3.11 combines the CMC figures (1930–8) with those from two other sources for the number of families transferred annually to Tripolitania and then Libya. If these were indeed the families transferred to government granted concessions for the purpose of colonization – as is suggested – then it would appear that the 1928 legislation and the activities of the CMC resulted in about a tripling of migration for the years 1930–2 relative to 1927–9. These numbers tripled again in 1933–4 when government efforts increased and the colonization of Cyrenaica began. They declined during and after the Ethiopian War. The years 1938–9 saw "intensive demographic colonization" and a dramatic increase in numbers. Except during this last phase, the scale of organized Italian colonization in Libya was always small.

The figures for European population in Libya reveal another picture (see table 3.12). The Italian population in Libya numbered about 45,000

Table 3.12 *Population of Italian Africa (European except where indicated otherwise)*

Year	Libya	AOI
1921 census	27,163	4,439
1931 census		
Italian	44,600	5,819
indigenous	654,716	1,687,935
1936 census		
Italian	66,525	
Libyan	750,851	
31 Dec. 1937	78,721[a]	
31 Dec. 1938	95,176[a]	
1 July 1939		132,182[a]
31 Dec. 1939	118,718[a]	147,132[a]
1 Mar. 1940		151,567[a]
30 Apr. 1940	128,264[a]	
1947	49,536[b]	

Sources: ISTAT, *Censimenti;* [a] *Bollettino statistico dell'Africa Italiana* (AOI figures are for fifteen principal centers of population); [b] Segré 1978, p. 199.

in 1931 and so the tenant-farming families counted by the CMC and migrated since 1921 must have accounted for less than 10% of this total.[85] By 1936, however, the Italian population had increased by over 20,000; and the total number of individuals in the 1931–5 tenant-farming families were 10,972, so a good portion of European population increase in Libya during this period can be attributed to organized migration.

Along with ISTAT and the CMC, the MAI also published (or announced) figures on the Italian presence in the colonies. As Libya was an Italian possession (and eventually a part of the kingdom), the movement of workers there was not considered emigration to a foreign country, nor did the CMC publish data on this in some sense "internal" migration. The ministry did publish figures on migration to Libya for

[85] The cumulative sum of colonial families up to and including 1931 (from table 3.11) is 583. Assuming that the average family size for 1930–1 (6.93) applies generally, the population of colonial families would have numbered 4,041, 9.06% of the total Italian population in Libya, or 14.18% of that in Tripolitania where the families were settled. This admittedly hazardous estimate assumes incorrectly no return migration. Parliamentary figures, on the other hand, estimate a colonist population of about 5,000 in 1931. See table 3.13 and text below.

Table 3.13 *Colonial families present in Libya as reported in parliamentary reports on the Ministry of Colonies budget and Segré 1978*

Year	Families	Members
1924[a]	863	
1925	1,125	
1926	1,400	
1927	2,024	
1928	2,620	
1930[b]	734	2,814
1931[c,f]	1,082	5,385
1933[d]	1,592	8,052
1937[e]	2,700	11,400
1940[f]		39,000
1941		8,426
1942		4,163
1947		15,000
1960	1,272	5,100 (not incl. private colonization)
1964	120	

Notes:
NB: Tripolitania only 1924–30, 1947–64; Cyrenaica only 1941–2
Sources:
[a] 1924–28: Atti S. disc. 14 June 1929, p. 655 (De Bono).
[b] Atti S. D.l. N. 771-A, p. 11 (Schanzer – 14 Mar. 1931).
[c] Atti S. D.l. N. 1179-A, p. 13 (Schanzer – 26 Apr. 1932).
[d] Atti S. D.l. N. 1843-A, pp. 17,20 (Schanzer – 30 Dec. 1933).
[e] Atti S. D.l. N. 2168-A, p. 18 (Sirianni – 28 Mar. 1938).
[f] 1931, 1940–64: Segré 1978, pp. 97, 188, 195, 199, 206, 209.

the purpose of work and these are apparently CMC-sponsored temporary migrations.[86]

In addition to the total population figures published in the MAI bulletin (table 3.12), the ministry also generally announced the number of Italian colonial families in Libya on the occasion of the parliamentary budget discussion (table 3.13). These figures do not necessarily correspond with the CMC statistics and the two organizations might have disagreed over what constituted a colonial family (for example a CMC-sponsored tenant-farming family or simply a family emigrated to Libya). The MAI figures reveal steady increase until 1937 after which they were no longer reported. Other estimates suggest that this number continued to climb until 1940, after which it declined.

[86] See *Rassegna economica* 1937 or Ipsen 1992a, p. 451.

Libya, of course, was not the only African destination for Italian colonists. On the evening of 5 May 1936 the Deputy Giorgio Maria San Giorgi, speaking in the *Camera*, was interrupted by the announcement of a general assembly of the Italian people. The entire Chamber left Palazzo Montecitorio, marched down the Via del Corso, and gathered in Piazza Venezia to hear Mussolini announce victory in Ethiopia. The next day San Giorgi recommenced his speech, immediately identifying Ethiopia as a demographic colony, and echoing sentiments that might have been expressed by an Italian pro-colonialist of the pre World War I era: "for years we have colonized not just the lands of the Mediterranean, but also lands across the oceans for the benefit of other peoples; our workers have built the cities and bridges and roads and founded the communities which have brought prosperity to entire nations."[87] Mussolini himself, in an August 1936 address to the people of the high fertility region of Basilicata, linked the creation of empire to Italy's demographic needs: "it is the prolific peoples, those who proudly and willfully propagate their race on the face of the earth, virile peoples in the strictest sense of the word, who have a right to empire" (Mussolini, vol. xxviii, pp. 29–30).

The colonization of Ethiopia began in some sense even before victory, as thousands of workers accompanied Italian troops and undertook the public works which characterized the brief existence of the empire. CMC figures reveal an intense movement of workers beginning in October 1935, the month when hostilities broke out (see table 3.14). The CMC reported monthly to the PCM on this movement and the peak of activity seems to have been reached in March 1937 when over 124,000 Italian workers were present in Italian East Africa (AOI = Ethiopia, Eritrea, Somalia) (ACS PCM 1934–6 b.1762 f.1.1.23.3299 sf.2-A). As with domestic public works projects, those in AOI provided a means to defuse population pressure and reduce unemployment and social tension in critical provinces. The CMC presumably selected the workers, but there was considerable pressure on the part of the provincial prefects to choose workers from their provinces.[88] The hastiness of these selections made in the heat of conflict occasionally resulted in confusion. In December 1935, for example, prefects were notified that of a recent batch of 4,000 workers sent to Mits'iwa (Massaua), only 300 were of the category requested. In keeping with the desire to foster large families, Razza's replacement as *commissario*, Sergio Nannini, made special provisions for prolific

---

[87] Atti C. disc. 6 May 1936, p. 2597. See also p. 2596 and 5 May 1936, p. 2592.
[88] The ACS files cited below include requests from Bari, Forlì, Mantua, and Vercelli.

Table 3.14 *Migration of workers to Italian East Africa*

	Workers migrated	Workers repatriated	Workers deceased	Workers present
Oct.–Nov. 1935	61,807	11,288	247	50,272
1936	102,548	45,647	571	106,602
1937	27,694	84,426	709	49,161
1938	7,333	51,338	649	4,507
Jan.–June 1939	2,098	15,302	192	2,217

by region

	Total 1935–June 1939	*	Total repatriated
Piedmont	6,432	18.4	6,459
Liguria	4,137	28.2	3,262
Lombardy	20,902	36.4	20,313
Ven.-Trident.	1,475	21.4	1,853
Venetia	41,000	97.2	38,177
Friuli-Ven.G.	4,354	43.5	4,018
Emilia-Rom.	31,809	96.9	26,075
Tuscany	9,896	33.8	10,137
Marches	4,606	36.9	4,342
Umbria	1,043	14.6	1,111
Latium	8,896	32.9	8,007
Abruzzi-Mol.	5,210	33.7	8,207
Campania	13,443	36.9	15,936
Apulia	11,126	42.6	14,523
Basilicata	1,400	26.3	2,472
Calabria	8,874	51.6	10,761
Sicily	25,521	64.9	27,835
Sardinia	1,556	15.2	4,513
Italy	201,480	47.5	208,001

Note:
*per 10,000 inhabitants (1936 census)
Source: CMC, *Le migrazioni interne.*

fathers.[89] Needless to say the export of labor to Africa did not solve the unemployment problem at home. After the departure of 480 Forlivesi, the prefect of Forlì called for more of the same, as he estimated the unemployed in his province at 11,000. The drastic cut-back in the

---

[89] Razza had abandoned the CMC post in order to fill that of minister of public works. He died, however, shortly afterward in a plane crash in Egypt (7 August 1935). An ECL settlement in Cyrenaica was named after him.

number of workers transported to the empire after 1936 obviously frustrated hopes of this sort. Probably inspired by economic consider-ations, the curtailment of this program seems to have stranded many already scheduled to leave (ACS PCM 1940-1 b.2765 f.1.1.23.3299 sff.14–16; SPD-ord. 106.414 sf.2). As with internal migration, Venetia and Emilia-Romagna were the major sources of temporary migration to the empire, though significant numbers of Sicilians and Lombards also migrated. In no region did less that 1 person in 1,000 go to the empire for work and the national average was close to 1 in 200.[90]

The war in Ethiopia temporarily diverted attention away from demo-graphic colonization in general (see tables 3.2 and 3.11). Subsequent to the creation of the empire, however, new plans for the transfer of colo-nizing families to both Libya and AOI were introduced. Some, like Giovanni Volpe, editor of *Bonifica e colonizzazione*, drew the standard parallel between African and internal colonization (Volpe 1937), while others, including Fossa, held out the hope that Ethiopia might represent a "true" demographic colony, namely one to which emigrants flowed spontaneously without the need for state intervention (and investment) of the sort undertaken in Libya (Fossa 1937).

Nonetheless, the Libyan example was followed in its basic outline, and colonization of the Ethiopian highlands was to be carried out by organizations receiving the usual concessions and subsidies, and preferably using Ethiopian War veterans as colonists (R.d.-l. 19 December 1936, n.2467). Among these organizations was the ONC, which had colonized the Agro Pontino but had until this point been left out of African colonization. In March 1937 ONC president di Crollalanza reported enthusiastically on the colonization possibilities in Ethiopia and the ONC project already underway there.[91] Demobilized soldiers were enrolled to set up the colony and their families brought over subsequently. Two sites were chosen near Adis Abeba and plans were to settle 1,000 familes on each within five years (Larebo 1994, p. 86). The first families (56) arrived in March 1939 and a smaller contin-gent followed. Later that year they were reported as numbering 2,000 individuals, but these probably included workers. A more reliable figure for the same period is 92 families and 451 persons.[92] In spite of the

[90] This calculation assumes no repeat migration.
[91] Crollalanza 1937; The ONC was only officially authorized to undertake such activities in October (R.d.-l. 14 October 1937, n.1897).
[92] *Rassegna economica* (March 1939), p. 260; *Bonifica e colonizzazione* (March 1939), pp. 38–9; (May 1939), pp. 44–5; Crollalanza 1939; Atti S. D.l. N.678-A (2 May 1940), p. 34. Larebo 1994, p. 132 reports contingents of 56 families (293 members) in March and 28 families (95 members) in May which if they joined a similar number of household heads would total 416 individuals (84 families).

ONC plans, these colonies would remain about this size for the next two years until their abandonment in the face of Italian defeat and Ethiopian independence.[93]

The example of the EFC (and the ATI) was repeated in Ethiopia by the creation of several regional colonizing organizations.[94] These would reproduce, in a sense, Italian localities in Africa (for example, Bari d'Etiopia). Three of these organizations were created: for Romagna, Apulia, and Venetia – all traditional regions of emigration – though only the first two actually transferred colonists (R.d.-l. 6 December 1937, nn.2300, 2314, 2325). In spite of the notable Sicilian presence in Libya, that region was not included in this original group. Each organization received a 50 million lire budget and was assigned a particular area in Ethiopia. Colonists were to be enrolled in the Fascist militia and the model was more or less that of both the failed MVSN "military" colonization in Libya and the contemporary ONC efforts in Ethiopia: first the heads of families (preferably Ethiopia veterans) would migrate and establish the colony, and only later would the families follow. Colonists of course were chosen by the CMC. The first group of 400 Romagnoli (from Forlì) was scheduled to depart on 28 October 1937 (again the Fascist New Year). The Apulian and Venetian contingents would follow at exactly two-year intervals. The overall plan called for 1,000 families in six years.[95]

The ONC journal, *Conquista della terra*, reported in December 1937 that the 400 Romagnoli had left on schedule and that grain was being harvested in the ONC colony. This work must have been carried out either by the demobilized troops or else by indigenous labor as in spite of the above report (apparently a product of hasty printing), the colonists had not yet departed. The same journal reported, first in February and then again in April, that the departure of this contingent was imminent. Instead it seems that the first true colonists to go to Ethiopia were a group of 105 Apulians who departed on 17 January 1938.[96] The Romagnoli – a smaller group than planned, including only 50 settlers – departed shortly afterward, in late March.[97] *Bonifica e colonizzazione* reported 200 heads of families in the colony in late 1939 (November 1939), but, according to Larebo, by the end of 1940 there

---

[93] See Larebo 1994, pp. 82–137 on the ONC colonies.
[94] On regional colonization see Larebo 1994, pp. 138–76.
[95] *Conquista della terra* (August 1937), p. 36; *Bonifica e colonizzazione* (September 1937); (October 1937), pp. 1091–4.
[96] *Rassegna economica* (March 1939), p. 260; *Conquista della terra* (December 1937), p. 32; (February 1938), pp. 55–6; (April 1938), p. 39; *Bonifica e colonizzazione* (October 1938).
[97] They numbered 124 in all including administrators and wage labor (*Rassegna economica* [March 1939], p. 260).

Table 3.15 *Families transferred to Italian East Africa*

	Families	Members
1937	145	967
1938	597	1,560
1940	854	(total present)

Source: CMC, *Le migrazioni interne; Razza e civiltà* (May–June 1940)

were less than 100 settlers and no joined families. The Apulian colony does seem to have grown to about 200 individuals including 14 joined families.[98] Two other non-regional organizations also carried out limited colonization in Ethiopia, settling a total of 55 families.[99] As had been the case with internal colonization programs in Italy, the African projects were beset by numerous problems including inappropriate selection of colonists and defection; squabbling and crime among those who stayed; colonist mistreatment and hardship; and generally disappointing agricultural results (Larebo 1994, pp. 114–34, 172–4).

The CMC sought to monitor these colonizing efforts and reported the figures given in table 3.15. The last CMC and Demorazza published data report a June 1939 worker population in AOI of just over 2,000 (table 3.14) and a 1940 colonist population of 854 families (table 3.15). Applying the 1937–38 average family size (3.4), the latter population would amount to just under 3,000[100] for a grand total of 5,000. Clearly the CMC numbers refer to only a fraction of the Italian population in AOI as the MAI estimates July 1939 population at over 130,000 (table 3.12). Again, parallel to the situation regarding migrations within Italy, the CMC appears to have applied a restricted concept of migration, namely officially enrolled temporary workers and tenant-farming families, the two categories which best responded to the demographic policies of the regime. The significant numbers of colonists in the more traditional sense – government bureaucrats and officials, traders, pro-

---

[98] Larebo 1994, pp. 169–70; *Bonifica e colonizzazione* (November 1939) reports 114 colonists in 15 families.

[99] These were the *Ente di Colonizzazione De Rege* and the *Comprensorio del Consorzio Agricola di Gimma*; see Larebo 1994, pp. 170–2.

[100] This figure is considerably larger that the total obtained by summing Larebo's figures for ONC, regional, EDR, and CAG colonists in 1940–1 (1994, pp. 134, 159, 163, 169–70, 171–2). This operation yields a total of about 820 individuals plus 55 families of indeterminate size, or about 1,000 peasants.

fessionals, shopkeepers, and others who inhabited the cities of AOI (not to mention the military) – were left out of the CMC count. The ministry estimates reveal significant concentrations of population in cities – Adis Abeba, Asmera, and Mogadishu accounted for about 70% of the total – and suggest that the Italian presence in AOI was increasing up to 1940.

In 1938 the Fascist population policy intensified on several fronts – anti-urbanism, pronatalism, and colonization – as part of the ultimate and futile attempt to mold a new Fascist civilization. The new coloniz-ing efforts, however, focused on Libya, not Ethiopia. The pre-existing infrastructure and bureaucratic apparatus, as well as Libya's vicinity to Italy and the presence there of many Italians, probably made this an obvious choice. Presented as necessary for the security of the colony, the regime embarked upon a program of intensive demographic coloniza-tion according to which 3,500 rural families would be transferred to Italy's "fourth shore." This program, championed by *Governatore* Balbo, involved the concession of vast territories to the ECL and to the Istituto nazionale fascista per la previdenza sociale (National Fascist Social Security Institute – INFPS). The contracts were to be slightly different: shortened or eliminated periods of tenancy replaced by longer periods of debt. Colonists were required to be members of the PNF and prefer-ence was given to large families. The initial legislation established a budget of 500 million lire over a five-year period – well above previous expenditures – to be used for the usual transportation, loans, subsidies, prizes, etc.[101]

The first mass migration was scheduled to begin (as usual) on the Fascist New Year (28 October) 1938. Mussolini himself boarded a naval vessel in Gaeta (Campania) to review the departing fleet on the festive occasion.[102] The departing army of peasants consisted of about 1,800 families. Apparently due to a penchant for round numbers, *il duce* and others repeatedly overstated the size of this group as 20,000 persons, though it numbered closer to 15,000 (see table 3.11).[103] According to ISTAT and CMC figures, almost 40% of the migrants came from the provinces of Rovigo, Padua, and Venice. Together, Venetia and Emilia-Romagna accounted for 75%, followed by Sicily (6%), Abruzzi, and

---

[101] R.d.-l. 17 May 1938, n.701; Atti C. D.l. N.2435 (13 September 1938); S. D.l. N.2428-A (19 December 1938); S. disc. 21 December 1938, pp. 4639–40; Volpe 1937. The ECL budget had previously been increased to 15 million per year (R.d.-l. 18 February 1937, n.56) and a new line of agricultural credit (400 million lire) established (R.d.-l. 12 August 1937, n.1692).

[102] Actually 31 October. For details on preparation for this mass migration, directed by Balbo, see Segré 1978, pp. 126–9.

[103] See, for example, Mussolini's salutary telegram to Balbo in Libya (ACS PCM 1937–9 b.2567 f.17.4.6001).

Apulia (5% each). As had been the case earlier with internal migration programs, the needs of the depressed south – the object of the initial proposal – were sacrificed in favor of the politically volatile Po Valley.

The 1939 Libyan colonization legislation betrayed a heightened sense of urgency relative to 1938. The budget for colonization (450 million lire) was spread out over only three years (while the 1938 program was shortened by one year and 100 million lire) (R.d.-l. 13 February 1939, n.284). The 1939 batch of colonists was also smaller, about 10,000 persons. "Intensive" colonization was to be completed by the migration of about 500 more families, but this last phase never took place.[104] Intensive demographic colonization seems to have cost about 1 billion lire and in general demographic colonization came to occupy a considerable portion of the Ministry of Colonies budget, 15% for example of the projected 1940–41 budget. The 25,000 colonists transferred to Libya in 1938–39 brought the total number of Italian tenant farming family members to about 35,000, perhaps 30% of the Italian population in Libya.[105]

In some sense, intensive Libyan colonization replaced the outlet of the Agro Pontino, virtually saturated by 1938; and while the volume of migration to these locations may not have been sufficient to alleviate unemployment, the simple fact that these programs existed served an important function by maintaining a degree of popular consensus for the regime. On another propagandistic note, Fascists were also able to cite, just as they could for the Agro Pontino, the high birth rates of the Libyan colonies.[106] War and the eventual occupation of the Italian colonies, however, led to the repatriation of most of the Libyan and AOI colonists, and their numbers swelled that current of repatriation from Europe caused by international tension and eventually conflict.

Emigration and repatriation in Imperial Italy

The period following victory in Ethiopia saw a more complicated migration pattern emerge. In addition to internal and Libyan programs, there were also plans for the new colony. In addition, repatriation became an ever more important issue; government-sponsored temporary migration of workers to Germany began in the context of the Nazi–Fascist alliance; and, again in this latter context, attempted

---

[104] L. 13 May 1940, n.673 which stipulated that 180 million lire and 70 million lire be added to the 1941–2 and 1942–3 MAI budgets for this purpose. Atti S. D.l. N.678-A (21 May 1940).
[105] For a discussion and budget figures, see Ipsen 1992a, pp. 206–7, 454; see also Nobile 1990c.   [106] See *Razza e civiltà* (April 1940); Segré 1978, pp. 168–9.

resolution of the Alto Adige problem led to the emigration of tens of thousands of German-speaking Italians.

After the hiatus caused by economic crisis and then war, the question of repatriation received renewed official attention following creation of the Italian Empire. Apparently the excitement caused in Italy by this event spilled over into the foreign communities and encouraged some expatriates to return home. To manage this aspect of population movement the MAE proposed the creation of a suitable institution in late 1938:

On 17 November . . . at the Ministry of Foreign Affairs . . . a "Commissione permanente per il rimpatrio degli italiani all'estero" (Permanent Commision for the Repatriation of Italians Abroad – CORI) was created; its purpose will be to coordinate and facilitate the many currents of Italians who have, especially since conquest of the Empire, expressed the desire to return home.[107]

It is hard to gauge the degree to which return migration to Italy after the conclusion of the war in Ethiopia was a result of imperial fervor. Certainly it was in this period that Mussolini's popularity at home reached a peak and the official statistics show a mild increase in the level of repatriation for several years after 1936 (though the migratory deficit increased, see figure 1.9). The levels of repatriation had been declining from an all-time (recorded) high in 1930 and reached a relative minimum in 1936. However, economic factors are at least as significant as political in explaining this trend. The repatriates of 1930 certainly included many, especially from the United States, who were unable to find work abroad and preferred to be unemployed at home. As the economic crisis declined, so did repatriation. During the Ethiopian war and the League of Nations sanctions, repatriation and the spatial movement of population in general (except for troop movement) was relatively low. Subsequently, a degree of economic recovery,[108] combined with both the pull of a new and grander Italy, but also the push of hostility toward Italy (and so Italians) as Mussolini's position moved closer to that of Hitler, reversed the trend.

The new repatriation commission, CORI, was created in early 1939 (R.d.-l. 5 January 1939, n.306). Its norms called for payment of repatriation travel expenses, customs exemptions, ensured employment, and a *"duce"* prize for the returning emigrants.[109] Repatriates were to be selected from among those applying on the basis of moral, physical and

[107] *Bollettino del MAE* (November 1938), p. 1182.
[108] On the Italian economy in this period see again Clough 1964, p. 257–9; Ciocca and Toniolo 1976.
[109] The latter amounted to 1,000 lire for the head of the family, 500 for his wife, and 250 for each child.

political considerations. Large families were in particular to be favored (ACS PCM 1940-1 b.2938 f.2.7.7.141.1–2). The repatriates were not necessarily sent to their traditional homes, as these were generally the areas that had in the past suffered from the greatest demographic pressure, but were instead to be directed to less densely populated areas where their labor could be used to develop the more backward regions of the peninsula. In this the activities of CORI were perfectly in keeping with the general Fascist concept of population management, particularly as revealed in the area of internal migration. As the minister of foreign affairs, and so president of CORI, Galeazzo Ciano put it: "The purpose of the commission has been . . . to select and rationally distribute repatriated Italians in those areas and occupations where they are most needed and so also where they will find the most favorable living conditions."[110] He also commented that the number of Italians requesting repatriation was far greater than CORI could manage. Repatriates were guaranteed the same professional status that they had enjoyed abroad and exempted from the Fascist Party membership card requirement for obtaining government jobs; predictably, the plan to find work for their rising number ran into "notable obstacles" (ACS PCM 1940–1 b.2938 f.2.7.7141.1–2; L. 25 June 1940, n.1066).

In spite of CORI's initial link to the creation of the empire, the majority of Italians repatriating at the time did so as a result of imminent hostility in Europe. The *Camera* discussion of the CORI legislation took place in April 1939, shortly after Hitler had annexed Bohemia and Moravia, and the law's proposer estimated current levels of repatriation at about 3,500 per month coming primarily from France and French possessions. As partial retribution for the hardships suffered in abandoning property and economic activities abroad, it was proposed that these political refugees, "first victims of international Jewry," be awarded the confiscated property of Italian Jews. This proposal was, however, considered impractical (Atti C. disc. 25 April 1939, pp. 2–3).

In this same period (from 1938) and counteracting to some extent the unemployment caused by repatriation, Italy began supplying Germany with tens of thousands of workers for German industry and agriculture (see table 3.16). Virtually all of these came from northern Italy, in particular from the traditional emigration regions of Emilia-Romagna and Venetia.[111] Judging from police records and intercepted letters sent

---

[110] *Bollettino del MAE* (April 1940), p. 243.
[111] See also Confederazione fascista dei lavoratori dell'agricoltura 1939; which organization apparently managed this migration. It is interesting to note, however, that some of the workers sent to Germany came from the safety-valve province of Littoria (ACS SPD-ord. 106.414 sf.3).

Table 3.16 *Industrial and agricultural workers
migrating to Germany for temporary work as a
result of special agreements*

Year	Expatriates	Repatriates
1938	38,294	
1939	43,334	
1940	94,872	62,204
1941	232,902	223,430

Source: ISTAT 1968.

home by these workers, their experience was not a happy one. Complaints included poor and insufficient food, filthy living conditions, low pay, poor treatment by Italian and German foremen alike, and extortion by the former. Many seem to have left their posts without authorization and others did not return as planned after scheduled leaves in Italy. One can only imagine what repatriation must have been like for those still in Germany in 1943. One worker wrote of the bombing of his factory which killed many of his co-workers as well as destroying his personal belongings (including passport) and wages (ACS Min. Int. PS 1942 bb.3/b, 3/c; 1943 b.22 ctg. c1).

One of the most unusual emigrations from Italy in the period and the single instance of large-scale forced migration under the Italian Fascist government[112] also took place in the context of Nazi–Fascist cooperation. In the South Tyrol (Alto Adige), there lived a significant German-speaking population that consisted primarily of those individuals, and their offspring, who had become Italian citizens following World War I, when the Italian–Austrian border was shifted northward.[113] With the coming to power of the Nazis in Austria (in 1938), this group became politically more and more of a problem for the Italian Fascists, whose hopes for their assimilation proved futile. In 1939 an agreement was reached according to which the German-speaking inhabitants of Trentino–Alto Adige could choose between Italian and German citizenship. The decision had to be made by 31 December 1939, and those choosing German citizenship had to leave by 31 December 1942. The choice to emigrate was optional except for a group of about 10,000 former Austrian (now German) citizens who were required to leave.

[112] The transfer of Jews to death camps outside of Italy is discussed below (see chapter 4) and took place under Mussolini's Nazi-sponsored *Repubblica sociale*; after July 1943 the legitimate government of Italy was headed by Pietro Badoglio.

[113] On the Alto Adige problem, see Cajoli 1958; De Felice 1973; Toscano 1967.

This latter group was, from the Italian point of view, the politically most undesirable. The total number of ethnic Germans in Trentino–Alto Adige seems to have been about 267,000, of which about 200,000 chose German citizenship.[114] Of these, about 78,000 migrated to the Reich. The Alto Adige migration was more in keeping with Nazi racial policy, which envisioned a Greater Germany including all ethnic Germans, than with the Italian variety, which generally tolerated non Italians as long as they were "Aryan" and not anti-Fascist. It also went against the general Fascist emigration policy. Still, it served a political purpose by eliminating a possible source of opposition to the national government. In demographic terms, the South Tyrolian population was considerably larger than the Italian Jewish population and their migration was on a scale similar to that of the entire Agro Pontino project.

After the September 1943 armistice between Badoglio's Italian government and the allies, Alto Adige, although ostensibly a part of the *Repubblica sociale* was administered by the Germans and many of those who had previously emigrated returned. The Alto Adige question remained a serious point of conflict between the postwar governments of Austria and Italy, and the fate of those who had chosen German citizenship was only decided in early 1948 when a law allowed them to reacquire Italian citizenship. At the time, over 44,000 South Tyrolians were still in Austria. Almost all of these, encouraged by the Austrian government, reacquired Italian citizenship and returned to Alto Adige. The total number of those reopting for Italian citizenship was 201,305.[115]

World War II dramatically changed the volume and nature of Italian migration. The flow of workers to and from Ethiopia had already ebbed and the government-sponsored programs for demographic colonization there, barely initiated, came to a halt. The intensive demographic colonization of Libya continued after the initial declarations of war, but the latter phases were interrupted by Italian intervention (May 1940). Subsequently, the occupation of the Italian possessions in Africa led to large-scale repatriation. Meanwhile, the major work on the Agro

---

[114] Included in these figures are small numbers of ethnic Germans in the provinces of Belluno (Venetia) and Udine (Friuli). Toscano 1967 cites a 10 January 1940 official communication which reports 185,085 out of 266,985 choosing German citizenship. Cajoli 1958 cites 1942–3 statistics according to which 205,000 chose German citizenship. De Felice 1973 cites the same figures as Toscano and also the contemporary German figure, which he thinks more accurate, of 201,775 choosing German citizenship.

[115] See Toscano 1967, esp. pp. 456–62. Toscano compares this figure with the 1939 Italian figure and ascribes the difference to marriage and natural increase. It is, however, a figure very nearly the same as that preferred by De Felice (see previous note). The citizenship question was only finally resolved in 1953.

Pontino had been completed, and while a degree of internal migration must have continued for other projects, including the numerous *boni-fiche* still underway, the war certainly slowed these currents as well. Repatriation of Italian *lavoratori* from abroad, on the other hand, more than doubled in 1939, turning the migratory deficit to a surplus and surely swelling the ranks of the unemployed. The latter problem was attenuated somewhat by the increasing volume of temporary migration to Germany (see table 3.16) and by mobilization.

The decline of migration and colonization in Italy and the colonies potentially reduced the importance of the CMC. Countering this possibility, *Commissario* Lombrassa proposed to Mussolini (in February 1940) that the CMC function of coordinating the national distribution of the work force would take on special significance in a militarized economy (ACS PCM 1940–1 b.2632 f.1.1.10.1000.6.3). He pointed out, again to *il duce* (in October 1940), that CORI, created to manage a selective and relatively small program of repatriation, was not equipped to deal with the massive influx caused by the war. The CMC, on the other hand, had always dealt with population movements on this scale. He proposed a program of labor intensive public works (of the sort not requiring steel and concrete needed for war industries) to deal with the problem. The transfer of CORI to the CMC and the expansion of repatriation assistance encountered several objections. The minister of finance asked where the funds would come from, and strong protest came from the Minister of Italian Africa, Attilio Teruzzi, who objected to the extension of the CMC's sphere of influence to the colonies. Lombrassa pushed his point of view and, supported by Mussolini, prevailed (L. 11 May 1941, n.703; ACS PCM 1940–1 b.2938 f.2.7.1831).

The new CMC responsibilities duplicated to some extent those of the recently constituted Ente per la Colonizzazione per gli italiani all'estero (Organization for the Colonization of Italians Repatriating from Abroad – ECIE). The latter organization, jointly responsible to the Ministries of Italian Africa and Foreign Affairs, seems to have been specifically created with the intention of settling repatriates in the empire (AOI), where areas for this colonization had already been chosen (L. 25 August 1940, n.1415; Atti C. D.l. N.1008 [26 July 1940]). Even before it had legally come into existence, Teruzzi announced that the work of the ECIE would be delayed until after the war. Subsequent to the definitive occupation of both Italian East Africa and Cyrenaica, the ECIE sphere of activity was expanded to all Italian possessions and protectorates, perhaps with an eye to the newly conquered areas of Yugoslavia (L. 14 December 1942, n.1754). It is not likely that much was ever accomplished in this regard.

Contemporary with his bid to absorb CORI, Lombrassa called for a more "totalitarian" and unified discipline of migration to be undertaken by the CMC, a proposal which Mussolini approved. Legislation, however, was held up by the Minister of Corporations, Renato Ricci (ACS PCM 1940-3 b.2765 f.1.1.23.3299 sf.1-G). Lombrassa seems to have initiated his program nonetheless. A mid-1941 CMC circular announced that all aspects of the organized migration to Germany – selection, transfer, care – were to become the province of the CMC, as was migration to all foreign countries (ACS PCM 1940-1 b.2938 f.2.7.1831 sf.4). The legislation proposed by Lombrassa would have put the CMC in control of all movement of workers outside of their province of residence, whether within Italy, to the colonies, or to foreign countries (Atti C. D.l. N.1541 [12 September 1941]). Much of the domestic migration referred to came under the authority of the Ministry of Corporations employment offices and Ricci insisted that the law include the stipulation that the *Commissario* consult him on these questions. Lombrassa disagreed and seems to have obtained Mussolini's approval. At the same time, he also proposed that the position of the *Commissario* in the hierarchy of the regime be elevated (ACS PCM 1940-3 b.2765 f.1.1.23.3299 sff.1-G, 1-H). *Il duce*, however, must have had a change of heart, as Lombrassa's power play was frustrated by subsequent transfer of the CMC to the Ministry of Corporations, and Lombrassa became Ricci's undersecretary of state for migration and colonization (D.l. 27 February 1942, n.316).

The Fascist program for demographic colonization in Africa was, of course, halted by the allied occupation of the Italian colonies. Already by December 1940 the British had taken Cyrenaica, though three months later the Italo-German forces under Rommel reconquered most of the colony. In May of 1941 the Italian empire fell as the British occupied Eritrea, Somalia, and Ethiopia. Cyrenaica fell again in November 1942 and Tripoli was captured in January 1943. By May 1943 the Anglo-American forces had conquered all of northern Africa.

Shortly after the fall of Italian Ethiopia, the Italian and British governments entered into negotiations (via first the Americans and then the Swiss) regarding the repatriation of Italian women, children, the wounded, and the old. June and December communications to the PCM referred to a program for the repatriation of 110,000 Italians. Another document, from July, estimated the civilian population of the ex-empire as 184,000 of which 60,000 were to be repatriated (ACS PCM 1940-3 b.3145 f.1.4.2.2124 sf.14). The last MAI estimate of the Italian population in AOI (for March 1940 – see table 3.12) falls between these figures.[116] A

---

[116] Another estimate puts the Italian population at 200,000 at the time of the declaration of war (*Enciclopedia italiana* appendice II, "Africa Orientale Italiana").

program of repatriation from the now ex-AOI was undertaken and three voyages made to Berbera (Somalia) by way of Gibraltar and the Cape of Good Hope between March 1942 and August 1943. According to a participant, the first of these (four ships) reportedly left Somalia with 9190 passengers, while the second and third voyages seem to have been smaller, perhaps two ships each (Vecchi 1963). Another report suggests that from the last voyage 4,916 passengers disembarked in Taranto (ACS PCM 1940–3 b.3145 f.1.4.2.2124 sf.14). The historian Del Boca, on the other hand, refers to plans for the evacuation of 60,000 women, children, and old persons and puts the total evacuated in the three voyages at 28,000, still far short of the total reported population (Del Boca 1982, pp. 556–66). Many it seems languished in detention camps in British Africa till the end of the war (Larebo 1994, p. 136). In May 1943 Teruzzi referred in the Senate – with a seemingly mixed sense of desperation and irony – to the approximately 20,000 Italians returned from AOI, and to the 60–70,000 remaining "who reaffirm the right of Italy to possess those lands made fertile by our blood and our labor" (Atti S. disc. 12 May 1943, p. 2071). By the time of the last of these voyages, Mussolini had fallen from power and the allies had taken Sicily.

The Italian population in Libya seems to have peaked in 1940 (see table 3.12). In late 1942 the desert war led to the destruction and evacuation of Italian colonial settlements in Cyrenaica; and many of those fleeing went to Tripolitania. In Tripolitania, the colonial settlements actually continued to function during the war and after, first under British occupation and then Libyan rule (Segré 1978, pp. 187–201). Nonetheless, there was considerable repatriation to Italy; the 1947 Italian population of Libya, in spite of a certain number of individuals who returned to the ex-colony after the war, was less than half that of 1940. This remaining nucleus gradually declined in anticipation of Libyan hostility, a fear realized in 1970 when Moammar al-Qaddafi expelled those who remained.

As Italy progressively lost its colonies, the activities of the MAI, of course, declined (except in the area of repatriation), a fact noted in the budget discussions. Nonetheless, a degree of colonial activity was maintained until the end. In May 1942, while Allied and Axis troops battled in Cyrenaica, several dozen tenant-farming families in Tripolitania received title to their property. Fossa described this remarkable and absurd event in the *Camera*:

yesterday we learned that on the anniversary of the Empire, 45 tenant-farming families in Libya will become proprietors of the farms they helped reclaim from the desert. So while war rages, even in Libya we accomplish the goals of our social policy. We recall the departure of the colonists for Libya and today, in spite of the war, witness the first accomplishments of the program established at that time. The peasants received title to their property just as has taken place in Italy, in Littoria, and just as will take place in Italian East Africa with the Organizations for the Colonization of Ethiopian Apulia and Romagna.[117]

In this same discussion Fossa referred to the need to maintain the MAI budget given the important work of repatriation from AOI and Libya.

A still more curious example of the momentum of Fascist colonial activity: on the morning of 24 July 1943, only hours before attending the meeting of the GCF at which he would vote to restore political and military authority to the king and so end Mussolini's reign, Federzoni presided over a Senate discussion of legislation involving some technical revisions to the earlier laws on intensive demographic colonization in the now wholly occupied Libya (Atti S. disc. 24 July 1943).

The CMC wartime activities testify to the importance of colonization plans to the overall Fascist vision. Indeed demographic expansion was among the Italian war aims, not just in Africa but also, for example, in the newly conquered areas of Yugoslavia, a parallel to the grander Nazi plans for the demographic transformation of Europe. Nonetheless, except for migration to the German Reich and repatriation, the Fascists did not manage notable population flows nor appreciably further their demographic plans during the war, and we can take the following November 1940 estimate as including most of the CMC-sponsored migration: "Within Italy and to the Empire, Libya, Albania, the Aegean possessions, and Germany, 732,117 workers have been transferred; and in this way labor market disequilibria have been countered and often eliminated" (ACS PCM 1940–3 b.2765 f.1.1.23.3299 sf.2). If none of these workers were repeat migrants, but some certainly were, then approximately 1.5% of the Italian population would have taken part in a CMC sponsored migration in the period considered. Still, the scale of CMC migration does not seem to have been sufficient to correct the labor market disequilibria referred to. The total number of workers monitored by the CMC in ten years amounted to about 60% of the spontaneous migration which occurred in a *single* year during that same period; and the latter movement, which took place in spite of the ineffectual anti-urban policy, was primarily a response to these same disequilibria.

The spatial management of population was meant to accomplish several ends: keep the full measure of Italian natural population growth for Italy, eliminate population disequilibria (and so social unrest) as

---

[117] Atti C. disc. 5 May 1942, p. 917. Siniscalchi 1943, p. 12 gives the number of families as fifty-six.

revealed by high rates of unemployment, and ruralize the Italian population. It responded to traditional Nationalist anti-emigration and procolonial sentiments and also represented a revolutionary experiment in population selection and management. Ideally, the new colonies would be worked by diligent and prolific families committed to the Fascist vision. And in the context of corporativism, internal and African migration were aspects of the planned eventual total control of the Italian work force, while both emigration restriction and colonization fit into the Fascist expansionist/populationist stance.

This chapter has grouped together the measures aimed at controlling population migration; chapter 4 considers those designed to influence vital rates. This division finds a basis in the nature of the phenomena considered and the ways in which the regime could intervene. In the area of migration, the regime was able to act directly through various institutions to channel population movement. Management of the more delicate areas of mortality, nuptiality, and especially fertility, on the other hand, limited the regime to less direct methods.

4

The realization of totalitarian demography II: Quantitative and qualitative population management

Institutionally, the Fascist regime depended on the midwifing and medical professions in its programs of infant and maternal care. On an individual level, the general quantitative population policy depended specifically upon women, and ironically it was Fascism, with its emphasis on virility and the male domination of society, that first sought to engage women on a large scale in the life of the Italian nation. We can even speak of a Fascist women's policy whose essential points were: the discouragement of female wage-earning activity outside the home in the interest of lowering male unemployment, the more or less private entrusting of women with responsibility for Italian demographic expansion, and the more or less public call for female volunteerism in the area of infant and maternal care. These tasks constituted women's role in the national struggle, and Mussolini himself made the analogy when he stated that "war is to men what motherhood is to women" (Mussolini, vol. xxvi, p. 259 [26 May 1934]).

This policy can be construed as a simple attempt to reaffirm the traditional female role of child bearer and carer. The institutional aspect, however, as well as the appeal to a higher collective good were novel and constituted an invasion of the private sphere which carried with it various implications. The Fascist regime sought to mobilize the female masses both as prolific mothers and as volunteer social workers, and this mobilization seems to have led to a degree of political consciousness-raising. For the call to demographic action required either compliance or refusal, and this refusal, apparently widespread, might also be interpreted as a form of resistance.

The population policy can also be described as Fascist family policy, and the new Italian woman was in fact expected to maintain allegiance to both the state and her family. This situation created what Victoria de Grazia has called "oppositional familism", as the interests of the state

145

and family did not necessarily coincide, particularly in the area of fertility (de Grazia 1992, pp. 112–15). In addition, while the reproductive
burden fell primarily on women, the complicity of their husbands was
of course needed as well; and the attempt to return women to the home
meant that men were expected to go to the factory, workshop, or office
and support a family on a single income. Women were to be wives,
mothers, and nurturers, men to be husbands, fathers, and breadwinners
(and neither of these of course are roles that suit all members of either
sex). If we take a broad view of Fascist demographic policy, it appears to
be aimed at controlling the family, both its dimensions *and* movements,
while at the same time earning its support of the Fascist vision.[1]

After the introduction of Fascist pronatalism, alarm over declining
Italian fertility was the order of the day as provincial and national
birth totals were published in every sort of newspaper and magazine;
and probably in no other period or country did the term "demography" achieve such currency.[2] Still, for a number of years the most
notable innovations of populationism in Italy were propagandistic.
Only after the conquest of Ethiopia (1936) did the attempt to encourage couples to marry and procreate receive a substantial financial
injection in the form of increased marriage and fertility prizes, marriage loans, and family subsidies. These measures came partially in
reaction to the apparent demographic accomplishments of the Nazi
government in Germany, but also as a manifestation of a new imperial
Italy. The revival of Italy's population policy in 1937 – which included
"intensive demographic colonization" in Libya, new incentives to
fertility, and also racism – represented the demographic aspect of the
regime's ultimate attempt to create a new Fascist consciousness and
civilization.

In the pages that follow I consider the evolution of measures to
protect motherhood and infancy and to promote the (prolific) family,
and also the institutional linking of demography and race. I have
already mentioned the theoretical connection between fertility or
population growth and internal/African migration. Italian racism, in
part a reaction to the movement of population to the Empire, itself
generated new migratory currents, both spontaneous and planned as
well as new areas of statistical research.

---

[1] On the relationship between Fascism and women and Fascism and the family, see
Ballestrero 1979; Caldwell 1985; Dau Novelli 1994; de Grand 1976; de Grazia 1992;
Passerini 1984; Santarelli 1976; Saraceno 1979–80 and 1992.

[2] This point is made by Treves (1976, p. vii); on the appearance of demographic policy in
school texts, see Koon 1985, p. 77.

Table 4.1 *ONMI budget (in millions)*

Year	Ministry budget	Amount spent
1926		1,470,561
1927		33,004,000
1928	30	79,990,000
1929	30	102,664,647
1930	65	121,299,000
1931	65	110,456,000
1932	65	114,352,000
1933	65	137,956,000
1934	100	157,919,000
1935	100	120,337,000
1936	100	126,893,000
1937	108	129,031,000
1938	108	133,198,000
1939	108	133,340,000
1940	108	132,735,000
1941	150	265,026,000
1942	150	381,303,000
1943	150	

Sources: Previsione bilancio del Ministero
dell'Interno (Atti C. D.l.); *Maternità ed infanzia*;
ISTAT, *Annuario statistico*. Other figures reported by
ONMI and ISTAT differ from those reported here;
see Ipsen 1992a, p. 455.

The protection of motherhood and infancy

Opera nazionale per la protezione della maternità e dell'infanzia
In the Ascension Day Speech, Mussolini identified ONMI as initiating
Fascist pronatalism, and subsequently it would also be identified as the
first step of Fascist racist policy. Both of these characterizations were
made retrospectively, however, and the genesis of ONMI reveals little in
the way of pronatalism and really no racism. Still, ONMI's status as the
forerunner of both quantitative and qualitative population policy
makes it an appropriate topic with which to begin this chapter. During
the central years of the Fascist *ventennio*, ONMI became increasingly
important as its budget grew to almost twenty times the original 8
million lire (and its actual expenses were higher still – see table 4.1), and
mother and infant care came to occupy a significant portion of the
Ministry of the Interior budget (14.5% in 1935 for example). What
follows is a look at the legislative and organizational history of ONMI

on a national level, and glimpses at best of local operations can be caught. Better understanding of the local functioning of ONMI would require individual provincial or communal studies.

ONMI was inspired by a conception of assistance that its proponents claimed was particularly Fascist. Rather than the humanitarian concept of charity which responded to individual misfortune indiscriminately, ONMI would be guided by a principle of assistance for the purpose of collective good. Referring to the law creating ONMI, the organization's first *commissario*, Gian Alberto Blanc, instructed the presidents of ONMI's provincial federations that: "Its main purpose . . . is to promote . . . , in the higher interest of the state, the physical and moral development of present and future generations . . . assistance provided by ONMI is only justified for those individuals who, given the necessary care, will as a result benefit the nation by becoming useful and productive members of society."[3] Representatives of ONMI repeatedly emphasized this distinction in order to better establish the status of the organization as a *bona fide* instrument of demographic policy, as opposed to simply a charitable institution, and so heighten ONMI's legitimacy. ONMI was also portrayed as providing – in the form of a healthier population – the qualitative aspect of the policy which Anglo-Saxon eugenicists accused it of lacking. Needless to say, the sort of justification required in the above passage of Blanc is difficult to establish and he later would complain of its non-fulfillment (Blanc 1930, 1931; Pietra 1936; Valagussa 1928b).

ONMI was to supervise, and when necessary provide, care for needy mothers and abandoned children. It was specifically entrusted with providing assistance for mothers who recognized and nursed their illegitimate children, as this was seen as a particularly effective way to combat infant mortality;[4] and the general encouragement of adequate nursing (by mothers, not wet-nurses) was a cardinal point of ONMI's program. The organization was also responsible for training personnel specialized in child and infant care, personnel who in turn were expected to operate on a local level spreading the desired practices among mothers and prospective mothers (Blanc 1931). In addition to its assistance role, ONMI was also expected to serve a police function, checking that the various institutions and individuals under its supervision were carrying out their functions according to the directives of the regime and reporting the cases where they were not.

The creation of ONMI in 1925 and the organization's special interest

[3] Circ. 20 February 1928 in *Maternità ed infanzia* (February 1928), p. 99.
[4] Circ. 5 May 1928 in *Maternità ed infanzia* (May 1928), pp. 391–3.

in providing assistance for illegitimate children and their mothers legislated in 1927 (R.d.-l. 8 May 1927, n.798) led to some unexpected results. ONMI was not intended to replace existing institutions, but to provide assistance where it was lacking. Although the 1927 law specifically placed the responsibility for maternal and infant care with the provinces "under the directives and control of ONMI," many local governments seem to have perceived instead that ONMI was taking over these tasks entirely. In 1932 the parliamentary deputy and physician Giuseppe Giardina lamented the fact that in the years since the passage of the 1927 law, provincial support for abandoned children, established in 1923, had disappeared in all but sixteen (of ninety-two) provinces (Atti C. disc. 9 April 1932, p. 6183). In some provinces this sort of assistance was the only sort being provided by the ONMI federation. In general it was that activity which consumed the largest portion of the ONMI budget, 55% in 1931 according to Senator Pestalozza, and this percentage threatened to grow larger still (Atti S. disc. 21 March 1931, pp. 3454–6; S. disc. 23 May 1932, pp. 5315–17). In order to contain these expenses, the provincial federations were assigned specific sums for foundling care.[5]

The heavy – and seemingly insupportable – burden of foundling and orphan care distracted ONMI from its fundamental task of encouraging the maternal nursing of infants (Valagussa 1928a). Primary targets of this latter task were mothers of illegitimate children and this emphasis created its own problems. In early 1929, for example, the ONMI administration complained to the presidents of the provincial federations that the norms for the care of illegitimate children were not being followed, while others objected that these norms seemed to reward illicit unions. "Fortunate is she who bears her child before marrying" was a phrase being heard in towns and villages according to Deputy Morelli (Atti C. disc. 26 February 1931, p. 4006; C. disc 3 March 1931, p. 4036). Catholic opinion seems to have generally approved of the creation of ONMI, but criticized the implicit approval of out-of-wedlock childbearing.[6]

Shortly after replacing Blanc as ONMI president (in December 1931), Sileno Fabbri[7] advanced certain criticisms regarding ONMI's first five years, complaining of the problems of inadequate funding, general lack

---

[5] Circ. 1 February 1929 in *Maternità ed infanzia* (February 1929), pp. 115–16; circ. 7 July 1932 in *Maternità ed infanzia* (July 1932), pp. 711–12.

[6] See, for example, Dalmazzo 1930, Rafaelli 1926. On the illegitimacy controversy, see also de Grazia 1992, pp. 61–4 and, for similar views expressed in the Liberal period, Wanrooij 1990, p.145. Similar polices encountered similar problems in France (Lees 1992, p. 317; Donzelot 1977, p. 33) and Nazi Germany (Mosse 1985, pp. 160–1).

[7] Fabbri was a lawyer and pre-March on Rome Fascist; see Lyttelton 1973, p. 217.

of training, defects in the original 1925 law and the "immoral" situation created by the 1927 legislation which he claimed resulted in some women preferring not to marry (Fabbri 1932a). Contemporary with Fabbri's criticism, a call for ONMI reform was raised in the *Camera* (Atti C. disc. 8 April 1932, pp. 6180–5).

Reform came with two 1933 laws; one reorganized ONMI and redefined its responsibilities, the other defined responsibility for abandoned and illegitimate children.[8] The latter specified that the provinces and *comuni* were wholly responsible for this area of public assistance except for the particular case of the illegitimate child recognized and nursed by his or her own mother. In the latter situation, ONMI would reimburse the local governments for one-third of expenses. This law effectively restored to the local governments those responsibilities which ONMI, in the absence of adequate care, had been progressively assuming. While this legislation did receive the usual Fascist praise, concern was nonetheless expressed regarding the ability of the province and *comune* to meet the attendant expenses (L. 13 April 1933, n.312; Atti C. D.l. N.1661-A [11 March 1933], pp. 2–3; S. disc. 5–6 April 1933, pp. 6337, 6349–50). With regard to the payments made to unwed mothers who nursed their own children, the 1927 law instituting these payments was significantly *not* incorporated into the ONMI 1934 *testo unico* (R.d. 24 December 1934, n.2316); nor however did the 1934 law specifically eliminate these awards, and so the issue seems to have been side-stepped.

The lightening of ONMI's load was considered necessary to enable the organization to pursue its other activities: providing child-bearing and rearing education, promoting maternal nursing, and providing pre- and postnatal care when needed. According to the original 1925 legislation, hospitals, maternal clinics, and similar institutions were obliged to provide care and hospitalization for needy mothers, expectant mothers, and children. ONMI was to reimburse expenses in some cases, but often the institutions themselves were required to bear the burden.[9] The obligation of the hospital only held, however, if there were places available and, in fact, still in 1942 ONMI officials complained that the required care was rarely provided.[10]

ONMI represented a rare and significant example of Fascist solicitation of female participation in the regime's activities, and in

---

[8] L. 13 April 1933, n.298 (compare to R.d.-l. 21 October 1926, n.1904); L. 13 April 1933, n.312; the various ONMI laws were combined in a 1934 *testo unico*: R.d. 24 December 1934, n.2316.   [9] Circ. 20 February 1928 in *Maternità ed infanzia* (February 1928), p. 102.
[10] Circ. 20 January 1942 in *Maternità ed infanzia* (atti ufficiali) (January–February 1942), pp. 7–9.

keeping with the general belief that social work was an appropriate female activity, its central council initially included two women. In 1926 the council was expanded to accommodate representatives of several groups including the Fascist Party (Partito nazionale fascista – PNF) and the Fascist women's groups (*fasci femminili*). The 1933 reform cut the council by two-thirds and no longer specified that women be included. Fascist and female representatives were also included on the provincial and communal committees, as were local priests; and physicians were represented at all levels of the ONMI hierarchy.

The changing make-up of the ONMI councils and committees reveals who were the actors in Fascist infant and maternal assistance. In some sense a pre-Fascist project, ONMI was Fascistized in 1926 with the introduction of male and female representatives of the PNF, and while the role of women would remain important, they apparently became, in 1933, dispensable at the highest levels. The year 1933 also saw a stricter regimentation of ONMI within the government hierarchy (under the Interior Ministry and its local representatives), perhaps diminishing the role of the party. Priests and physicians, two groups which traditionally assisted the population during demographic rites of passage (birth, marriage, death), were of course present, but the former only at the lowest level of the ONMI structure. A notable omission, no provision was made for the representation of midwives who continued to assist the majority of Italian births.

Subsequent to these reforms, Mussolini himself, as minister of the interior, penned a circular to the new heads of the ONMI provincial federations citing the standard trio of objectives: "strengthen family ties, increase fertility, and reduce infant and maternal mortality." To Fabbri he wrote that it was time to go to work (ACS PCM 1931–3 f.1.6.2.9084).

ONMI was further reorganized in response to the Gran consiglio del fascismo's (Fascist Grand Council – GCF) 1937 directives on demographic policy (of which more below) and representatives of two new demographic institutions – the Ufficio centrale demografico (Central demographic office – UCD) and the Unione fascista per le famiglie numerose (Fascist Union of Large Families – UFFN) – were included (R.d.-l. 5 September 1938, n.2008; Atti C. disc. 8 March 1938, p. 4447). A new position of provincial inspector (responsible to the prefects and so the minister of the interior) was created to check that ONMI was functioning properly on a local level. Its creation seems to have increased the organization's police function and added another layer as inspectors policed ONMI which in turn policed local maternity and infant-care institutions.[11] The authority of ONMI over institutions providing infant and maternal care was further expanded in 1941 when a law was passed making it possible for ONMI's local organizations to take over their administration (L. 19 July 1941, n.936).

Although eliminated from ONMI's central council in 1933, the Fascist women's groups were nonetheless expected to continue to take part in ONMI's activities on a local level. Both Blanc and later Fabbri had over the years instructed the provincial federations to maintain close ties with the *fasci femminili* and emphasized the important role that these women should play in ONMI's activities, and Fabbri claimed that their work was as essential to ONMI as that of physicians.[12] From the regime's point of view this seems to have been one of the principal functions of the women's groups. Nonetheless, their role remained relatively informal until January 1937 when Clara Franceschini and Itta Stelluti Scala Frascara were appointed PNF "*ispettrici*" (inspectresses).[13] In May 1940, Franceschini was given the responsibility of coordinating, together with ONMI president Frantoni,[14] the activities of the *fasci femminili* and ONMI. The (volunteer) position of *visitatrice* (visitor -f.) was formally recognized and the *visitatrici* were assigned special uniforms. Nonetheless, about one year later Frantoni still had cause to complain of non-cooperation on the part of the provincial ONMI federations. In early 1942, Mussolini gave symbolic support to the ONMI/*fasci femminili* collaboration by receiving Frantoni and Franceschini together.[15]

ONMI was expected, through its communal committees and female Fascist volunteers, to exercise a positive influence on the sanitary habits and personal care of mothers, potential mothers, and their children. The ONMI functionaries, however, were not generally directly involved in the most critical moment for the prevention of infant and maternal mortality, namely childbirth. In order to act in this area, ONMI had to enlist the aid of and better train midwives and physicians, who for the most part were not directly responsible to ONMI.

In 1929 it was estimated that 95% of all Italian births were attended exclusively by a midwife. Clearly this was a primary area for the

---

[11] Circ. 28 May 1941 in *Maternità ed infanzia* (May–August 1941), pp. 188–9; circ. 5 December 1941 in *Bollettino del Ministero dell'interno* (January–February 1942), pp. 27–8.

[12] Fabbri 1932b; 1936b; *Maternità ed infanzia* (April 1929), pp. 331–3; (June 1932), pp. 625–6.

[13] See de Grazia 1992, p. 268; not to be confused with the above-mentioned ONMI provincial *ispettori*.

[14] In the Spring of 1940 Frantoni replaced Bergamaschi who had replaced Fabbri in July 1937.

[15] PNF foglio di disposizione n.139 (18 May 1940) in *Maternità ed infanzia* (May–August 1941), p. 190; ibid. pp. 185–7; (January–March 1942), pp. 3–5; *Bollettino del Ministero dell'interno* nn. 23–24, 1941, p. 507.

attention of ONMI. The author of the above estimate, writing in the ONMI journal, called for better education of midwives and legislation placing them under the direct supervision of public health officials (Perondi 1929). Calls for better obstetric and childcare training for midwives and provincial doctors (*medici condotti*) were heard repeatedly and resulted in the introduction by ONMI of (separate) one-month courses for both in 1932.[16] Unfortunately, these courses did not resolve the problem, and several years later Deputy Francesco Pentimalli criticized – especially rural – physicians for more often than not violating the most basic rules of childrearing. He called for the introduction of appropriate university courses, presumably as part of the standard medical curriculum.[17]

Further obstacles to ONMI's program to improve maternal and infant care in Italy included the general lack of cooperation between physicians and midwives, whose spheres of activity of course overlapped. For though the provincial doctor occupied a higher social station than did the midwife, his was not a lucrative position and any healing done by the midwife must have been viewed as a professional and economic threat. The frequent disinclination of physicians to concern themselves with the non-clinical aspects of childrearing was also criticized (Perondi 1929, Laurinisch 1936). In order to better define the activities of the midwife and prevent her from trespassing into the province of the physician, particularly pathology, instructions were issued in 1930 regarding the practice of midwifery. These included hygienic guidelines, a list of allowed and prohibited operations, and numerous references to instances when a physician had to be called.[18]

Subsequently, midwifery was professionalized and its practitioners required to obtain a certificate from an obstetric school.[19] These schools were reorganized in 1936 according to legislation which also established a minimum wage for midwives (R.d. 5 March 1935, n.184; R.d.-l. 15 October 1936, n.2128). In the *Camera*, undersecretary of state for the interior, Guido Buffarini Guidi,[20] lauded these measures which elevated the midwife "to an economic and educational level in keeping with the importance and dignity of her activity." He added that she must become "ONMI's assistant" (Atti C. disc. 8 March 1938, p. 4446). On the other

[16] Gaifami 1929; *Maternità ed infanzia* (April 1932), pp. 313–16.
[17] Atti C. disc. 11 March 1937, p. 3268. Pentimalli was a professor of pathology.
[18] Dec. Min. 17 May 1930 in *Gazzetta ufficiale* 26 May 1930, n.123.
[19] While some obstetric schools did exist previously their introduction as an appendix to university obstetrico-gynecological clinics seems to date from 1927. See R.d. 12 August 1927, n.1634.
[20] Buffarini Guidi held this position from 8 May 1933 to 6 February 1943.

hand, in a circular to the provincial prefects he noted that many of the places in the obstetric courses remained unfilled and that many midwives continued to receive less than the minimum salary.[21] Apparently the attempt to organize this traditional occupation in a bureaucratic/professional structure did not meet with immediate success.[22]

In 1940 the midwife's responsibilities were expanded to include not just childbirth but also monitoring of the mother and child until the latter reached the age of three (R.d. 26 May 1940, n.1364). This law, like the ministerial decree of 1930, defined the limits of the midwife's functions and specified in which cases she was obliged to call in a physician or alert the appropriate authorities.

In order to rally physicians to the cause of maternal and infant care, and so to the demographic battle, ONMI and government figures made repeated appeals.[23] Mussolini himself in an address to physicians included the encouragement of fertility (and so the avoidance of population aging) in the category of preventive medicine (Mussolini, vol. xxv, p. 60 [22 November 1931]), while Paolo Orano described the gynecologist (m.) as "the front line pediatrician, called upon to preserve the fruits of virtuous fertility" (Orano 1938, p. 334). Buffarini Guidi appealed to all the physicians of Italy to help in lowering the levels of infant mortality (Atti C. disc. 25 March 1936, p. 2475).

Certain high-visibility physicians like the Deputy Nicolò Castellino[24] pledged their support: "We Italians, especially we Italian physicians, are with all our hearts behind the regime in this mission for the redemption and resurrection of the Italian stock" (Atti C. disc. 11 January 1934, p. 9477). Nonetheless, it seems that humbler physicians were somewhat less committed, and in 1943 the Ministry of the Interior was still complaining about the lack of necessary cooperation between doctors and ONMI.[25] Resistance on the part of physicians to follow ONMI directives may in large part have been due to the fact that they were not paid for the services which the organization asked of them.[26]

---

[21] *Bollettino del Ministero dell'interno* nn.5–6, 1937, pp. 136–9.

[22] Agitation for the reform of midwifery seems to have been a general European phenomenon. Reforms were introduced in Germany, for example, in 1924, but were generally a failure; see Weindling 1989, pp. 194–6, 360-1.

[23] *Maternità ed infanzia* (August 1929), p. 884; Atti S. disc. 17 March 1930, pp. 2051–2; Micheli 1930a; Laurinisch 1936.

[24] Castellino, originally a Nationalist, took part in the March on Rome. For a time he served as the *delegato straordinario* of the ONMI Federation of Naples. See Canestrelli and Fatica 1978.

[25] Circ. 22 January 1943 in *Bollettino del Ministero dell'interno* nn. 5–6, 1943, p. 101.

[26] A campaign launched by several medical journals in favor of compensation for this work was criticized in *Maternità ed infanzia* (June 1934), pp. 17–18.

In keeping with other aspects of Fascist demographic policy, maternal and infant care was to be ruralized, which entailed the location of orphanages in the "healthier" countryside and concentration on the improvement of the relevant health services available in rural areas. As early as 1929, ONMI president Blanc instructed the provincial federations to undertake ruralization and it was a theme often repeated.[27] One champion of institutional ruralization was Castellino who argued that by establishing orphanages and other infant and maternal care institutes outside of the urban centers, one would not only save money, but "accustom the children to country life" and so presumably encourage them to choose a rural occupation (Atti C. disc. 13 March 1935, pp. 945–6). Unfortunately the rural environment was not as healthy as frequently claimed. Castellino himself recognized that rural mortality was higher than urban and – in 1934 – increasing. He attributed this problem to relatively inferior health care and the ongoing economic transformation of the countryside.[28] The higher rates of rural mortality held for infants as well, and so it seems that in spite of the directives to ruralize, the shortcomings of ONMI were particularly pronounced in the countryside (Atti S. 28 March 1936, p. 2072; Buffa 1937).

Central to ONMI's activities after the 1933 reform was creation of the Case della madre e del bambino (Homes for mothers and children). These were to be staffed by medical personnel and provide maternal and infant care, consultation, and propaganda both in the institute itself and in the mothers' own homes. In the words of Fabbri they would "constitute a complete and rational organism, responding to all the needs of a vast program for the prevention of female mortality . . . " (Fabbri 1934). The Case della madre e del bambino continued to be founded throughout the *ventennio*; the intention was that there ultimately be one in every *comune*.[29] Their creation was regularly announced in the ONMI journal, and while this list is not complete, one gets the impression that most of the *Case* were located in the center and north of Italy. This impression is confirmed by the ISTAT 1943 review of the regime's demographic measures, which reported 162 *Case* at the end of 1939, of which 81 were in the north, 43 in the center, 31 in the south and 7 on the islands. ONMI institutions in general followed this pattern and were more frequent in low fertility areas than in high (see table 4.2). Notably, the regions where ONMI was least developed were those where infant mortality was traditionally highest (see figure 4.1 and

[27] Circ. 1 February 1929 in *Maternità ed infanzia* (February 1929), pp.115–16.
[28] Atti C. disc. 11 January 1934, p. 9478; on urban–rural differences, see also Micheli 1930b.
[29] Circ. 23 June 1941 in *Maternità ed infanzia* (November–December 1941), pp. 287–91; there were 7,339 *comuni* in 1941.

Table 4.2 *Regional frequency of ONMI institutions on 31 December 1939: (a) per population aged 0–9 (1936 census, resident population) and (b) per annual number of live births (1938–9 average)*

	(a)	(b)
	per thousand	
Piedmont	2.2	19.9
Liguria	1.3	12.0
Lombardy	1.4	11.4
Ven. Trid.	0.7	6.2
Venetia	0.8	7.5
Ven. G.-Zara	1.2	9.8
Emilia-Romagna	1.1	10.4
Tuscany	1.3	12.2
Marches	1.4	12.5
Umbria	1.1	9.7
Latium	1.4	11.1
Abruzzi-Molise	1.2	10.6
Campania	0.6	5.1
Apulia	0.6	4.6
Basilicata	0.9	6.8
Calabria	0.9	7.3
Sicily	1.0	7.7
Sardinia	1.0	7.8
Italy	1.1	9.3

Total: Case per la madre e il bambino

North	81
Center	43
South	31
Islands	7

Source: Annali di statistica 7, 7.

below).[30] On the other hand, ONMI notices reported 36 *Case* in Sardinia in mid-1941 and 31 in Sicily by that year's end. This development was in keeping with ONMI's program for intense regional efforts directed at the islands (see below). It is not, however, clear whether all of the above numbered institutions were at the time actually operating or still in the planning phase.[31]

[30] *Annali di statistica* 7, 7, pp. 107–15.
[31] *Maternità ed infanzia* (May–August 1941), pp. 147–51; (May–June 1942), pp. 87–92.

ONMI was also responsible for organizing the annual *Giornata della madre e del fanciullo* (Day of the mother and child). This was initiated in 1933 and held on Christmas Eve. Proximity to the Christian birthday was obviously chosen in order to associate Fascist policy with that more traditional celebration of natality and lend it a degree of religious legitimation. Festivities included the showing of ONMI films, the awarding of fertility prizes, celebrations in churches, and the inauguration of ONMI institutions. In Rome, Mussolini received ninety-two prolific couples, one from each province, and presented each with a financial award.[32] The day was of course preceded by ample advertisement in newspapers, journals, and posters and included a radio address by the ONMI president.[33] In 1935 the *Giornata della madre e del fanciullo* was preceded by a *Giornata della fede* (Day of the wedding ring or Day of faith)[34] on which, in response to the League of Nations sanctions imposed against Italy for the invasion of Ethiopia and encouraged by an exhortation of *il duce*, tens of thousands of women exchanged their gold wedding bands for rings of tin in order to aid the national cause. Fabbri recalled these two celebrations one year later: "Today the Italian mother, suffused with Fascist feeling and spirit, offers with proud dignity both her gold and her children to the *patria*" (Fabbri 1936a).

The official discussion of ONMI in parliament and in the organization's journal was replete with references to the expansion and perfection of services and to the general success of the battle to lower childbirth-related mortality. Nonetheless, revealing criticisms did occasionally appear, and it seems that in spite of the considerable financial and propagandistic investment made by the regime, ONMI did not always meet expectations. In the ONMI literature this sort of criticism generally appeared shortly after the appointment of a new president, as in the 1932 comments of Fabbri noted above. In 1937 Fabbri was in turn replaced by Carlo Bergamaschi and shortly afterward there appeared in the ONMI journal a discussion of the "problems of motherhood and infancy." Its author lamented that despite the fact that ONMI was

---

[32] In 1933 only the mothers came. Subsequently they were accompanied by their husbands. The initial criterion of most prolific in the province had, for the sake of rotation, to be substituted with others. As a result professional distinctions were introduced – one year agricultural couples, one year commercial, industrial etc. – determined by membership in the appropriate Fascist union. The prize for many years was 5,000 lire. The total distributed by the national government and ONMI in prizes on the *Giornata* was about 16 million lire in 1935 and 1937 and this may have been a peak. For more on fertility prizes, see below.

[33] *Maternità ed infanzia* (January 1934), pp. 1–3 (and any subsequent January); ACS: PCM 1934–6, b.2001, f.14.2.5361.

[34] 18 December 1935, the same day that Mussolini inaugurated Pontinia.

designed to provide social and moral care and play a supervisory role with regard to basic obstetric and pediatric care, in many, especially rural, areas these services were altogether lacking:

In truth, this state of affairs often compromises the mission of ONMI, which assumes the existence and proper functioning of other institutions of obstetric and pediatric care. Unfortunately, for large groups of women and children, especially in rural areas, the latter service is almost entirely lacking or insufficient. As a result, high levels of pregnancy-related mortality, especially from puerperal fever, persist as well as the frequency of premature births, stunted development of newborns, and, finally, miscarriages which continue to represent a high percentage of conceptions (about 10%). ONMI comes up short exactly where its work is most needed and most important: in the agricultural areas. (Buffa 1937, p. 4)

During discussion of the 1936–37 Ministry of the Interior budget, Buffarini Guidi, while not critical, did admit that ONMI was not perfect and that it was still in the experimental phase (Atti C. disc. 25 March 1936, p. 2476). Five years later in the same forum, the Senator Alberto Martin-Franklin noted that in some provinces the benefits received were not proportional to the large investment made in ONMI. Buffarini Guidi conceded that this criticism might be accurate and outlined a new approach that ONMI would take, concentrating on specific regions. The considerable budget increase of that year, for example, was to be employed entirely in Sardinia.[35] The following year Martin-Franklin commented that he now understood that ONMI was functioning much better, and splendidly in Rome (Atti S. disc. 21 May 1942, p. 755). Nonetheless, there were indications that several of the basic organizational aspects of ONMI remained unachieved at the end of the Fascist period. In addition to the various shortcomings cited above, Ministry of the Interior circulars reveal that in 1941 norms regulating the relationship between ONMI and other institutes providing maternal and infant care remained essentially unapplied, and that in 1942 some *podestà* had still not assumed the role of head of the ONMI *comune* committee assigned to them in 1933.[36] A 1941 memo to Mussolini stated that twelve (of ninety-two) provinces lacked foundling homes altogether and that in only 5 provinces were the subsidies to mothers nursing their own illegitimate children "adequate" (ACS Min. Int., Gabinetto ONMI, b. 1).

---

[35] Atti S. disc. 17 April 1941, pp. 853, 864; on ONMI's activities in Sardinia see *Maternità ed infanzia* May–August 1941, pp. 147–51 which includes a map showing the thirty-six *Case della madre e del fanciullo* referred to above.

[36] Circ. 25 September 1941 in *Bollettino del Ministero dell'interno* nn. 31–2, 1941, pp. 681–5; circ. 18 May 1942 in ibid. nn. 23–4, 1942, pp. 683–4.

It is difficult to imagine that the hundreds of millions of lire spent by ONMI did not serve to improve infant and maternal care in Italy. Certainly there were well-meaning physicians, midwives, *visitatrici*, and other ONMI volunteers who were able to provide assistance and raise levels of general hygiene. Still, in many ways the overall program seems to have fallen far short of its goals; the unintended decline of local public assistance in anticipation of its replacement by ONMI was certainly an early backfire. Nor does it seem that ONMI ever succeeded during the *ventennio* in effectively coordinating the various institutions coming under its jurisdiction. Probably religious charitable organizations viewed ONMI's activities as an unwanted incursion into their own spheres.[37] Many institutes for children (orphan, tubercular, etc.) *were* established in the countryside, but the attempt to improve rural health care and so lessen the rural/urban infant mortality gap seems to have been largely unsuccessful. In a secretly overheard phone conversation, transcribed and kept in *il duce*'s personal files, the speaker complained that "in many small towns health services are lacking and women give birth with the help of God alone" (ACS SPD-ris. b.32 f.15, inserto A).

In spite of the general command to ruralize, ONMI was most successful in the cities. Milan's federation (under Fabbri) was an early model example and Rome was later cited as having particularly good services.[38] And just as ONMI penetrated only slowly into rural areas, so did it spread slowly to the south and the islands: until the plans for expansion in Sardinia and Sicily in the early 1940s, most services were concentrated in the center and north. Nor did the investments in ONMI have a noticeable effect on infant mortality levels (see below). As seems to have been the general pattern with Fascist public health programs, assistance went not to those areas where it was most needed, but to those where it served the greatest political or propagandistic purpose.[39] Fascism was certainly not unique in this respect, but there is an interesting parallel with the demographic colonization programs that were initially intended to help the south but ended up focussing on the Po Valley. Finally, the call to physicians, midwives, and Fascist women for voluntary help for ONMI – in keeping with the Fascist theme of individual sacrifice – certainly did not get the hoped-for response. ONMI was not, however, considered a total failure nor entirely compromised by its

[37] For a parallel example involving assistance to Italian emigrants see Cannistraro and Rosoli 1979.
[38] Though Milan, for example, had long been characterized by health services well above the Italian average; see Buttafuoco 1985; Hunecke 1989.
[39] See, for example, Preti 1984, esp. pp. 999–1000.

association with Fascist demographic and racist policy, and it continued to function into the 1970s.[40]

Work and pregnancy
Parallel to the efforts made to provide care for needy infants and mothers, a series of measures was taken to ease the financial burden and ensure adequate periods of pre- and postnatal rest for working mothers. The intention was to attenuate the perceived harmful effect that work, especially industrial work, had on childbirth. The threat presented by the working mother was both qualitative (eugenic) and quantitative as excessive exertion by the pregnant woman resulted, so it was believed, in underweight and sickly children and in higher levels of infant mortality.[41] Measures taken to aid working women, however, found an ambiguous place in a regime generally hostile to female employment (though resigned to its necessity).[42]

As discussed in chapter 1, pp. 36–7, pregnancy leave for female industrial workers and the creation of a maternity fund both predated the Fascist seizure of power. These were combined into a 1923 *testo unico* (T.U. 24 September 1923, n.2157), but the first innovations in the Fascist period regarding maternal leave and insurance came in 1929 when general coverage was extended to commercial as well as industrial firms and the period of enforced pregnancy leave lengthened to one month before and one month after birth.[43] Agricultural workers were still notably left out, although the two-month leave (without the maternity fund) had been required for rice workers since 1907.[44] The pregnant woman's job was guaranteed and birth-related illness might result in an up to three month extension of leave. As with the earlier legislation, employers were required to allow women breaks for nursing and larger firms were instructed to provide rooms for this purpose.

The 1929 law resolved an earlier debate by establishing that absence from work due to pregnancy constituted involuntary unemployment, and so the temporarily out-of-work mother also qualified for

[40] ONMI was abolished, amid scandal and accusations that the Italian IMR was among the highest in Europe, at the end of 1975 (Atti C. D.l. N.3137 [26 February 1971]; L. 23 December 1975, n.698).
[41] See, for example, the series of articles by Cesare Alessandri in *Maternità ed infanzia* (1928, 1929, 1930a, 1930b, 1931) and also Gaifami 1936.
[42] See also de Grazia 1992, pp. 173–81 on this topic.
[43] (R.d.-l. 13 May 1929, n.850); The maternity fund payment was increased from 100 to 150 lire for a live birth and remained 100 lire for a stillbirth or miscarriage; the fund was administered by INFPS; see also norms for 1929 law: R.d. 28 August 1930, n.1358(1687). For a general discussion of Italian legislation regarding female workers, see Ballestrero 1979, esp. pp. 57–108 on the Fascist period.
[44] L. 16 June 1907, n.337, art. 16 incorporated into T.U. 1 August 1907, n.636 (art. 82).

unemployment insurance payments.[45] With regard to the nursing halls called for in the legislation, the ONMI vice commissar commented in 1928 that, in spite of previous non-compliance, it was now the case that in those factories where married women could work, there were the required halls (Valagussa 1928a).

The reworked pregnancy-leave legislation was presented as part of the Fascist protection of motherhood and so "one of the fundamental aspects of the demographic program" (Atti C. D.l. N.190 (9 June 1929)). Several years later Giardina commented that the previous Liberal legislation had been inadequate because it had been conceded under worker pressure and inefficient because "it was not inspired by a powerful ideal: the defense of the stock, that light which radiates from the memorable Ascension Day speech" (C. disc. 9 April 1932, p. 6181). As was the case with ONMI, the legislation in favor of working mothers was not presented as responding to a simple need for assistance, but rather to a Fascist ideal of racial or national or demographic expansion.

In a general discussion of the high levels of maternal and infant mortality and of the fact that many of these deaths could be prevented, the physician Emilio Alfieri appealed for the extension of maternity leave and insurance to those categories of workers not covered by the 1929 law (Alfieri 1930). This extension came in two phases. In 1934 all women working for an employer[46] were included, with several notable exceptions, including domestics, public employees (who had other arrangements),[47] and agricultural workers. Enforced leave was expanded to one month prior and six weeks after birth (and optional leave to a total of three months plus one month for illness), and the payment per live birth was raised to 300 lire.[48] In 1936 maternity insurance was introduced for several categories of agricultural workers, namely wage earners and members of tenant-farming families, though payments were considerably lower: 75 lire for a stillbirth and 100 lire for

---

[45] Atti C. D.l. N.190 (9 June 1929). The unemployment fund resembled in design the maternity fund and paid at this time, including a 0.50 lire maternity supplement, 1.75 lire – 4.25 lire per day.   [46] "donne alla dipendenza di datori di lavoro."

[47] A 1924 law established a one month pregnancy leave at half pay for stateworkers and also extended the maternity fund legislation cited above to include them (R.d. 31 December 1924, n.2262 [157 of 1925]). In 1937, the 1934 law cited here was extended to stateworkers (R.d.-l. 21 August 1937, n.1542). The combined legislation suggests that their situation was the most enviable as they received both the maternity fund payment (300 lire from 1937) and half wages.

[48] R.d.-l. 22 March 1934, n.654. The 0.50 lire per day maternity supplement was eliminated. However, even given a four-month absence, this loss would still amount to considerably less than the above 150 lire increase for a live birth. Those absent due to stillbirths, on the other hand, would receive less from day one.

a live birth. The law's presentation explained that higher rural fertility made a lower payment necessary. No provision was made for pregnancy leave and unlike the earlier legislation, that for agricultural workers was presented not so much as insurance against lost wages but rather as a fertility prize insuring the possibility of postpartum repose. Agricultural workers also did not enjoy unemployment insurance (R.d.-l. 7 August 1936, n.1502; Atti C. D.l. N.1325 [28 August 1936] and 1325-A [20 November 1936]). In 1939, maternity insurance was expanded again, this time to include domestic workers, and was combined with nuptiality insurance (of which more below). Payments for live births were adjusted so that they increased with successive births.[49]

The Liberal/Fascist maternity legislation described above differs from modern social programs in that the assistance was paid for not by a general fund but primarily by contributions from those who might eventually benefit from the assistance, namely female workers aged 15–50. The employer too was required to contribute for each female worker, but increasing the cost of female labor had the effect of either making it less desirable or else depressing wages in order to compensate for the added expense. As a result one can imagine that the contribution was effectively paid by the workers and so this was essentially a mandatory private insurance for working women, sponsored by the government in the interest of demographic expansion.

While the Fascist regime did recognize the desirability of provisions for working mothers, the efforts in this area should be understood in the context of the general Fascist hostility to women in the work place. The female ideal was, of course, that of the prolific mother who stayed at home to care for her children and husband. Nonetheless, it was usually recognized that barring women from work would cause serious economic problems for many families and potential families – and so depress nuptiality and fertility – and also for many businesses which depended upon (generally cheap) female labor.

The ambiguousness of the Fascist stance on women and work is

---

[49] R.d.-l. 14 April 1939, n.636. The new payments were the following:

	Office workers (*impiegati*) and laborers (except agricultural)	Agricultural workers
First child	300	150
Second and third child	350	175
Fourth and following children	400	200

nicely revealed by an incident involving female telephone workers.[50] In April 1926 the Minister of Communications established that female workers could only keep their jobs so long as they were single, a move in keeping with the idea that married women should remain at home. A similar regulation was established for postal and telegraph workers that same year according to which only unmarried women could be hired and marriage would result in termination of the contract.[51] These regulations were followed and a group of married women was fired by the STIPEL telephone company in Milan. Unable to resolve their problem locally they wrote collectively to Mussolini asking that he intervene on their behalf:

> Losing our jobs we shall also lose those necessities of life which enable us to raise our children. Did we err in legalizing a sacred tie and showing ourselves obedient to your directives, *Duce*, by procreating and preparing for the nation new young reserves? By firing wives, united to their men by the authority of the State and the Church, STIPEL shows itself to favor free unions . . .

This letter was written in October 1928. In that same month Mussolini wrote to the prefect of Milan telling him that a measure of this sort: "is or would be contrary to the general demographic directives of the regime." Several days later *il duce* received assurance from STIPEL that the Ministry's regulation would not be applied; he also received a note of thanks from the re-hired workers. It seems that Mussolini had not been aware that the original instructions had come from his own government; in December he wrote to the communications minister, Costanzo Ciano:

> Dear Ciano,
> This idiotic article 14 of the telephone, telegraph etc. regulations must be eliminated. It was created when Italian fertility seemed overflowing. Instead it is mortality that overflows (see the terrifying statistics from Turin in yesterday's *Gazzetta del Popolo*).

The regulation regarding telephone workers was quickly changed and that for postal and telegraph workers about one year later.[52]

For a time, the official attitude regarding female employment, as communicated via ONMI, seems to have been that it was a tolerable evil. A

---

[50] The documents relating to this incident are found in ACS PCM 1928–30 f.13.1.4653.

[51] R.d. 15 August 1926, n.1733(2029). Although postal, telegraph and telephone services all came under the jurisdiction of the Ministry of Communications, the latter seems to have enjoyed a degree of autonomy from the former two. In the correspondence discussed below reference is made to article 14 of regulations issued by the ministry. These may have taken the form of a ministerial decree and are distinct, but obviously similar to this law.

[52] R.d. 13 January 1930, n.34(241); for laudatory words regarding the resolution of this situation, see di Robilant 1929.

similarly pragmatic view was expressed by the Fascist hierarch Giuseppe Bottai[53] who in a 1933 article reviewed the issue of the protection of motherhood and infancy. According to Bottai, the Italian female work force was relatively small and did include a certain number of married women having children. In order to prevent cases of miscarriage and stillbirth induced by the poor hygiene of the industrial environment, he called for improved prenatal care and general "defense" of motherhood, citing the actions already taken by the regime including enforced pregnancy leave and maternity insurance. Recognizing not only the inevitability but the necessity of women working, Bottai saw the protection of the working mother as an important aspect of "the demographic policy of the Regime aimed at numerical increase and at the same time continual qualitative improvement" (Bottai 1933).

Others took a dimmer view of the phenomenon and called for the gradual elimination of women from offices and factories (and schools).[54] And a degree of Fascist tolerance of working women should not mask the fact that many positions were officially reserved for men (and certainly many others unofficially) and that women's wages were generally low. Various measures excluding women from state employment, particularly as secondary-school teachers, had been introduced from 1923, and more drastic measures were taken in 1938 as part of the second wave of *politica demografica*. According to these, no public or private office[55] could employ more than 10% women. Exceptions were made for some categories, like primary-school teachers. Both demographic and economic justifications were advanced as women working in offices were distracted from their primary, familial activity and also accused of contributing to male unemployment.[56]

In spite of official hostility to female employment, the 1936 census revealed that approximately one-third of all women over the age of 10 "participated in the economic life of the nation," that is, described themselves as engaging in an activity that was not that of a housewife. The primary categories in which these women worked were agriculture (46.3%), industry (26.3%), and domestic work (11.1%).[57] Nor, it seems,

[53] No longer minister of corporations, Bottai was, at the time he published the article cited here, president of INFPS.

[54] See, e.g., De Marzio 1936, whose suggestions were countered by the Countess di Robilant who called them anti-Fascist and accused their author of wanting ignorant mothers (1936).

[55] The law refers to *impieghi* and so presumably non-manual labor (R.d.-l. 5 September 1938, n. 1514).

[56] R.d.-l. 5 September 1938, n.1514, Atti C. D.l. N.2624, S. D.l. N.2669-A. See also Loffredo 1938.   [57] *Notiziario demografico* (10 January 1936), pp. 3–4.

was the younger generation, who passed its youth entirely under Fascist rule, likely to alter this pattern. A 1938 survey of Roman teenage girls revealed that few were interested in housework or raising large families.[58]

Infant and maternal mortality

In October 1928 ONMI vice commissar Francesco Valagussa wrote that a decade hence the government would demand a "settling of accounts," asking simple questions like: how much has infant mortality declined since ONMI became operational?[59] Indeed, a brief look at the fluctuations of the infant mortality rate is the simplest (and admittedly crudest) way to evaluate the realizations of maternal and infant policy.

Infant mortality was a frequent topic of ONMI and parliamentary discussion. It inspired a collaborative investigation by ONMI and ISTAT and another by the Ministry of the Interior.[60] Infant mortality was generally understood to be higher in the countryside than in the city and higher among the lower classes than the upper.[61] Pronatalists not surprisingly explained the association of high levels of fertility and infant mortality – Basilicata for example had the highest regional rates of both – in terms of social class. Repeated childbearing did not increase the risk of infant mortality, but those mothers who had many children generally came from lower income, and so higher risk, groups.[62]

Until the mid-1930s frequent reference was made in parliament and elsewhere to declining infant mortality, an achievement attributed to the efforts of the regime, and so ONMI.[63] Comparisons were frequently made between pre-war levels, or even those of the early 1920s, and those of the early 1930s. ISTAT, for example cited a 19% decline between 1924–5 and 1934–5.[64] Nonetheless, there remained considerable room for improvement and Italian rates continued to compare poorly with those of other western nations. In 1934, for example, Italian infant mortality was at a pre-World War II low – 99 deaths aged 0–1 per 1,000 births – while other European rates for that year were 40 (the Netherlands), 57 (England and Wales), 72 (France), 99 (Germany), 109 (Spain), and 192 (Romania) (Mitchell 1981).

[58] Spolverini 1938; see also de Grazia 1992, pp. 119–20.
[59] Valagussa 1928a, p. 822 and again 1930, p. 279.
[60] *Notiziario demografico* (1 April 1931), pp. 200–3; *Bollettino del Ministero dell'interno* nn. 15–16, 1936, pp. 300-1.   [61] Ibid. and Carelli 1929.
[62] See, e.g., Savorgnan in *Civiltà fascista* (February 1939), also cited in *Maternità ed infanzia* (May–June 1939), pp. 242–3.
[63] See, e.g., Atti C. disc. 13 March 1935, pp. 965–6; C. D.l. N.985-A (20 January 1936), p.19; C. disc. 25 March 1936, p. 2475–6.
[64] *Notiziario demografico* (10 November 1936), p. 203.

To the consternation of many, infant mortality rose in 1937–8, though not dramatically. Buffarini Guidi claimed that it was out of place to dramatize the situation as it would hopefully be temporary and any number of accidental causes might be responsible; most often cited were the Ethiopian war – though levels did not increase during the conflict – and the economic crisis – which of course had begun years prior. It was also asked what might have happened (that is, how severe might these increases have been) had it not been for the government measures (Atti C. disc. 26 April 1940, pp. 571–2; Frontoni 1942). In March 1937, on the occasion of the Fascist Grand Council directives on demographic policy and in a rare spirit of self-criticism, Fabbri noted the unfortunate coincidence of the post-1933 ONMI budget increase and a minor increase in stillbirths, infant mortality, and mortality for the ages 0–5.[65]

A look at figure 4.1 confirms Fabbri's remarks. Infant mortality did indeed decline from 1928 to 1934, but if one considers the period 1930–40, namely the years during which ONMI was well funded and in its fullest operation prior to the turmoil of world war, then the infant mortality curve is essentially flat. A look at the regional curves reveals still more of the picture. Northern rates were generally below average and central rates always were. Liguria had consistently the lowest rate, occasionally matched by Tuscany, while the other large regions of the north and center, with one exception, had similar curves. Lombardy stands out in the north as its infant mortality rate was high in the 1920s but fell to about average by 1939 (the peripheral northern regions enjoyed similar declines). As noted above, Lombardy was the one high infant mortality region where the ONMI presence was considerable. In contrast to northern and central rates, those of the more rural south were all above the national average (except for Calabria in a few years) and in the cases of Apulia and especially Basilicata well above average. Compared to the north and center, southern infant mortality declined less in the beginning of the period considered[66] and increased more at the end during the war. As for the islands, Sicily had a high rate, like the south, while Sardinia was about average. It is curious, then, that ONMI should target this latter island for its first intensive regional program. Provincial rates of course varied even more, and ISTAT reported 1936 rates of 165 in Bergamo (Lombardy) and 48 in Livorno

---

[65] Fabbri 1937. Fabbri also took this occasion to remark that frankly the nation had not responded to *il duce*'s call for demographic expansion. Fabbri left ONMI several months later.

[66] For example, ISTAT reports for the period 1924–5 to 1934–5 a 34% decline for Liguria while rates declined by only 7% in Basilicata and Calabria (and 4% in Sicily). *Notiziario demografico* (10 November 1936), p. 203.

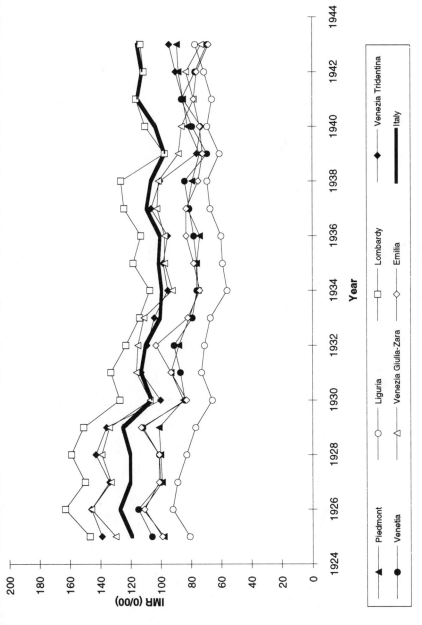

Figure 4.1a Italian IMR (north)
Source: ISTAT, Movimento

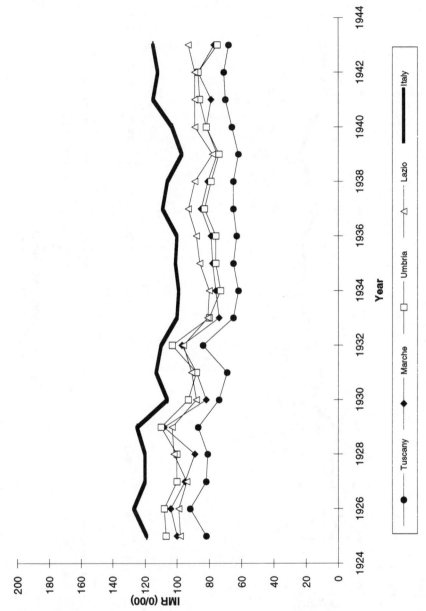

Figure 4.1b Italian IMR (center)
Source: ISTAT, Movimento

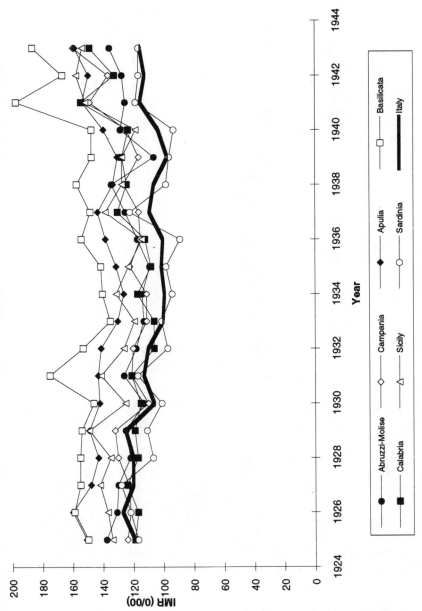

Figure 4.1c Italian IMR (south and islands)
Source: ISTAT, Movimento

Table 4.3 *Total stillbirths and in relation to live births*

	Total	per 1,000 live births
1921	53,778	45.9
1922	52,951	44.9
1923	50,768	43.8
1924	48,794	41.6
1925	48,117	41.6
1926	43,932	38.6
1927	41,899	36.9
1928	39,730	35.7
1929	38,239	35.5
1930	39,886	35.2
1931	36,411	34.3
1932	34,881	34.0
1933	35,292	34.2
1934	34,373	33.5
1935	33,849	32.8
1936	32,229	32.4
1937	32,586	31.8
1938	34,205	31.9
1939	33,655	31.3
1940	32,195	29.8
1941	27,758	28.8
1942	26,772	28.1
1943	25,892	28.5

Source: ISTAT 1968

(Tuscany).[67] The progress – or lack of it – of the infant mortality rate paralleled closely that of the overall crude death rate (see figures 1.3 and 1.4).[68]

Stillbirth rates did decline steadily through the *ventennio* (see table 4.3). These, however, are problematic rates as various factors encouraged their misreporting. Apparently physicians, and presumably also midwives, were reluctant to attribute infant mortality to complications encountered during birth and so preferred to classify such cases as stillbirths. Similarly, because of the delay allowed in filing the birth certificate, those who died in the first hours or days might be declared born dead (one form instead of two). In both cases stillbirth rates would be

[67] *Notiziario demografico* (10 June 1937), p. 103.
[68] For a contemporary discussion of regional (and provincial) IMR which essentially identifies the same trends described here, see Forni 1940.

increased and infant mortality slightly decreased (De Bernardinis, Micheli, and Gaifami 1930; Gaifami 1929). However, a probably more significant cause for misreporting were the different levels of maternity insurance payments for still and live births and the introduction of fertility prizes, which were only awarded for live births (see p. 176+n. below). This factor would have the reverse effect of encouraging a report of a live birth and subsequent infant death and so lower stillbirth rates.[69] It is difficult to gauge how these various factors might have affected the overall progress of the relevant rates. One would, however, expect the latter phenomenon to become more acute after the 1937 demographic resolution and attendant increases in prizes, etc. In fact, infant mortality increased in 1937 and the stillbirth rate decreased.

In 1930 Alfieri estimated that of the 3,000 women per year who died in childbirth, one-third could be saved (Alfieri 1930). The problem of mortality resulting from complications relating to pregnancy and child-birth, however, received relatively little attention as compared to that of infant deaths. The total number of these deaths are of course influenced by the changing size of the population at risk, namely pregnant women. Fertility was declining in this period, but population increasing, and as a result, the total number of births per year declined less (in some years it increased) than the fertility rate, however calculated. Maternal deaths related to pregnancy and childbirth as a function of total births proceeded erratically in the period peaking four times between 1921 and 1935, after which they declined (see table 4.4), a decline in a period when neither infant nor overall mortality was improving. The minimal improvement in maternal mortality between 1900–4 and 1935–9 was noted in the Demorazza journal,[70] though it is something of a surprise that more was not made of the 1936–42 improvement. Higher rates of maternal mortality in large population centers were attributed to the "influx of diseased groups" seeking better health care in the cities; only by improving rural care, it was claimed, could infant and maternal mortality be successfully combatted. By 1941 total pregnancy and child-birth related deaths were, as Alfieri had hoped in 1931, below 2,000.

ONMI represented Fascist Italy's emulation of other European nations that created institutes for the "protection" of infants and mothers. It was part of an attempt to modernize Italy by improving puerperal practices and care and by lowering the IMR to northern and

---

[69] See, for example, Atti C. disc. 8 May 1942, p. 997. A 1934 ISTAT circular instead assumes that the reported 1933 IMR rates are "much below the true rates" (ISTAT AC cassetta 21, 3 April 1934).

[70] D'Elia 1942 reports deaths due to pregnancy per total births rates for the years 1887–1939. His rates are fairly consistent with those in table 4.4.

Dictating demography

Table 4.4 *Maternal mortality (total deaths due to chidbirth related illnesses and in relation to total births)*

Year	Total deaths	Deaths/1,000 births
1921	2,887	2.46
1922	2,810	2.38
1923	2,979	2.57
1924	3,632	3.10
1925	3,111	2.69
1926	2,795	2.45
1927	2,893	2.55
1928	3,032	2.73
1929	2,991	2.78
1930	2,976	2.63
1931	2,854	2.69
1932	2,951	2.88
1933	2,846	2.77
1934	2,708	2.64
1935	3,017	2.93
1936	2,883	2.90
1937	2,725	2.66
1938	2,515	2.35
1939	2,385	2.22
1940	2,297	2.13
1941	1,824	1.89
1942	1,630	1.71
1943	1,570	1.73

Note:
1924 and following represent new borders
Sources: ISTAT, *Annuario statistico*; ISTAT 1968;
ISTAT, *Cause di morte*

western European levels. To repeat Preti's phrase though, it was "perverse" modernization given the Fascist criterion of collective good to be applied in offering assistance. Moreover, the battle to lower the IMR was unsuccessful in many regions, and these failures can be attributed to the reliance of the ONMI apparatus on a medical infrastructure that was lacking in many parts of the country.[71] ONMI did, however, serve to spread the impression that Fascism was providing

---

[71] See again Preti 1987, pp. 106–7 for this characterization of Fascist modernization. As ONMI aid was needs-tested, there was a stigma of poverty attached to those who used the services offered as well, see Triolo 1989, p. 134.

aid to those in need and so contributed to the image – still invoked today by the right in Italy – that Fascism for all its errors did improve general Italian welfare and initiated modern social services. Nor did the post-war Italian Republic immediately eliminate the institution it inherited and ONMI continued to operate during a period when the infant mortality rate declined to less than a quarter of its pre-war low.[72]

Pronatalism

In spite of the considerable amount of Fascist rhetoric devoted to pronatalism, it was nonetheless an aspect of the overall *politica demografica* which developed slowly. Between the 1927 Ascension Day speech and the GCF meeting of March 1937 (see below), a number of measures were introduced, but unlike migration, colonization, and mother and infant care, no particular institution was created to deal with the problem of raising Italian fertility in that period (though to some extent all of the institutions mentioned in the preceding pages – CMC, ECL, EFC, INFPS, ONC, ONMI, PCM, PNF etc. – were expected to exercise a positive influence on fertility). This lack is certainly related to the difficulty of the problem faced. The cause of fertility decline was far from agreed upon and, even if it were, it was not clear how it should be combatted. Procreation was an area even more intimate than childbirth and one in which the regime could not intervene directly.[73]

The demographic call to arms in the Ascension Day speech created a considerable echo in the Fascist press and parliamentary discussion, generally in the form of optimistic praise for Mussolini's policy. For himself, *il duce* reserved a pessimistic attitude. During Zingali's 1929 address to the *Camera*, for example, Mussolini repeatedly interrupted the speaker's encouraging statements about the effect of the government's new policy on fertility decline – "1929 marks the demographic collapse of the nation, the demographic collapse I say!" – so that Zingali was forced to alter his approach and adopt a more critical tone.[74]

---

[72] 1934: 99, 1975: 22 (Mitchell 1981).
[73] The ambitious Nicola Pende did propose the creation of clinics to combat pathological and physiological causes of sterility. Pende cited a sterility figure of 10% of all women, but did not suggest that this was a primary cause of denatalism (Pende 1934b).
[74] Atti C. disc. 5 June 1929, p. 696; for Zingali's comments see pp. 87–8; for subsequent continued optimism, see, for example, Atti C. disc. 3 March 1931, p. 4031.

Fertility decline was a topic to which Mussolini returned from time to time. In a 1934 article entitled "Is the white race dying?" he affirmed that since his original warning "the fatal decline has continued" and that cries of alarm were now being heard all over the world.[75] ISTAT of course monitored this decline for Italy. In 1931 the institute was able to report that monthly birth totals since March 1930 had generally been higher than those of 1928–9, perhaps a first sign of response to demographic policy. On the other hand, 35% of all *comuni* experienced a decline in population between the 1911 and 1921 censuses and the overall trend was one of decline.[76]

Although demographic pessimism was generally the province of Mussolini, some Fascist parliamentarians did acquire their leader's penchant for demographic statistics. Buffarini Guidi, for example, during his long tenure as undersecretary for the interior made frequent use of statistical material in his annual discussions of the ministry budget. These discussions came to include a separate demographic section replete with references to birth, death, and marriage rates. As another example, Senator Valagussa ascribed fertility decline to "an effective decline of the vitality of the race" as a result of which "since 1934 our nation has been threatened by the nightmare of one of the greatest disasters of the future." Among the causes of this decline, he cited an increase of social diseases (VD, TB, alcoholism) and, more importantly, a conscious choice made to have fewer children, the latter linked to economic factors and urbanism (all of these observations reflect the "expert" debate over these problems described below in chapter 5, pp. 228–37). He naturally approved of the government's response to the problem, namely legislation to combat the decline, a general program of ruralism (including internal migration), and maternal and infant care.[77]

Pronatalist and pronuptialist measures taken in the period 1927–36 included both reinforcement of the initial legislation and the introduction of new incentives. The tax on bachelors, which took effect on 1 January 1927 and was doubled in 1928, followed more or less the increases of the ONMI budget. It was increased by another 50% in 1934

[75] Mussolini, vol. XXVI, pp. 312–15. Curiously Mussolini here repeatedly refers to his 1926 speech and eight years of *politica demografica*, while the Ascension Day speech took place in 1927.
[76] *Notiziario demografico* (16 January 1931), pp. 32–3 for birth totals. Total births were in fact higher in 1930 than in either of the two previous years. *Notiziario demografico* (16 February 1929), pp. 4–7 for *comune* population decline; migration was, however, a more significant factor in these cases than fertility decline.
[77] Atti S. disc. 22 March 1935, pp. 673–6; as noted above, Valagussa was a vice commissar of ONMI. He was a physician and became a senator in 1934.

and again by a small amount in 1936.[78] Beginning in 1936 the bachelor tax was also applied in the Italian colonies (R.d. 9 July 1936, n.1561). In 1934 ISTAT compared the bachelor tax roles over the previous years, noting that the number of bachelors had increased slightly and the crude marriage rate had declined: "in conclusion, it is not yet possible to evaluate what influence the tax has had on the demographic state of the population and in particular on nuptiality."[79]

As mentioned in chapter 2, ISTAT carried out a study of large families contemporary with the 1928 law granting tax exemptions to this group. In order to qualify for benefits, stateworkers had to have at least seven dependent children (under 21, except in special cases), while non-state-worker families had to number at least ten dependent children. ISTAT counted approximately 1.5 million families in Italy having seven or more children and estimated that the number of families in the seven plus stateworker category was about 30,000; while the total number of families having 10 or more children (dependant or not) was a bit over 100,000. The Deputy Alberto Verdi pointed out, however, that average birth intervals were such that the period during which the non-state-worker families could benefit from the tax exemption, namely between the birth of the tenth child and the arrival to majority of the first, might well be six months or a year. In fact, for 1931 only just over 31,000 families received the exemption (2% of the families having seven or more children and about equal to the stateworker total).[80] The tax exemptions for very large families were followed up by a measure of more general application, namely a law according to which income tax was graduated according to family size (R.d.-l. 29 July 1933, n.1027).

In addition to the tax imposed upon them, bachelors were discriminated against in the workplace. According to 1929 "measures for demographic increase," the fact of being unmarried could not be the basis for preferential treatment in state employment. This measure presumably applied to women as well as men and so represented a

---

[78] R.d.-l. 24 September 1928, n.2296; R.d.-l. 14 April 1934, n.562; R.d.-l. 6 February 1936, n.265. The 1936 modifications also changed the age ranges for the levels of taxation with the result that those between the ages of 50 and 55 experienced an over 100% increase. The 1936 annual fixed rates were:

25–30 years of age	L.115
30–55 "	L.155
55–65 "	L. 85

To these were added the variable rate determined by income, increased by a little over three times the original rate. See chapter 2, n. 55.

[79] *Annali di statistica* 6, 32 (1934), pp. 50–2.

[80] *Annali di statistica* 6, 32 (1934), pp. 1–36; Atti C. disc. 21 March 1930, p. 1890.

complete turnaround from the earlier regulations regarding postal and telegraph workers (see pp. 162–3). Hiring and promotional preference was to be given to the married and especially the married with children. These measures also stipulated that similar preference be given regarding administrative concessions and access to *case popolari* (subsidized housing). Zingali presented the law as a response to Italy's low nuptiality.[81] Subsequent legislation and a circular of Mussolini further strengthened the bias in favor of married workers, but only for state employees.[82]

Two other fundamental features of the pronatalist policy were introduced several years later: fertility and nuptiality prizes and family subsidies. The awarding of prizes began in 1933 with the introduction of the *giornata della madre e del fanciullo* (see above p. 157). ISTAT reported that 1933 *giornata* awards, many of which were given by ONMI, amounted to 2.9 million lire for fertility (12,839 prizes) and 4.2 million lire for nuptiality (10,522 prizes). To the latter the institute attributed an increase in the marriage rate.[83] In 1936 Mussolini formalized demographic prizes for stateworkers. Marriage prizes varied according to rank and had an upper age limit between 30 and 32 years. Fertility prizes were to be awarded for each birth and varied according to the order of the birth. Multiple births received higher awards.[84] Funds to finance these awards (42 million lire) had already been legislated and were increased by another 29.5 million the following year.[85] The regime also introduced train fare reductions for honeymoon trips from 1932.[86]

Family subsidies (or a family wage) for industrial workers were introduced in conjunction with a reduced work week. A 1934 accord established that industrial workers would be limited to 40 hours employment (and wages proportionately reduced) in order to reduce unemployment (the leftover workload would presumably be picked up

---

[81] L. 6 June 1929, n.1024; Atti C. D.l. N.167-A, p. 1. In 1935 legislation was also passed to encourage local efforts to provide housing for large families: L. 13 June 1935, n.1183.

[82] PCM circ. 7 January 1933 in *Annali di statistica* 6, 32 (1934), p. 64; R.d.-l. 5 July 1934, n.1176; Atti S. D.l. N.221, 221-A (29 November 1934).

[83] *Annali di statistica* 6, 32 (1934), pp. 65–6. Both total marriages and marriages per 1,000 inhabitants did increase a little in 1933–4.

[84] Dec. Capo Governo 7 April 1936 in *Annali di statistica* 7, 7 (1943), pp. 143–5. Marriage prizes ranged from 1,500 to 5,000 lire, fertility prizes from 400 to 3,000 lire for single births and 1,000 to 9,000 lire for multiple births. As already noted, no prize was awarded for a stillbirth. *Il duce* could also award non-stateworkers at his own discretion.

[85] R.d.-l. 6 February 1936, n.236; R.d.-l. 18 February 1936, n.156. This money appeared among the *spese straordinarie* for the PCM (Ministry of Finance budget).

[86] And also for significant anniversary trips. Dec. Min. 21 September 1934 in *Gazzetta ufficiale* n. 267 (1934); Dec. Min. 14 May 1935 in *Gazzetta ufficiale* n. 158 (1935).

by newly employed workers). In order to ease the burden of reduced wages for families, a National Fund for Family Subsidies to Industrial Workers was created. This functioned much as did the maternity fund. All workers had to contribute 1% of their wages, a figure matched by the employer, and payments were made to those having dependent children under the age of 14. Like the maternity fund, it was administered by INFPS.[87] A provision for family subsidies had frequently been included in collective contracts for specific firms (especially banks and public utilities),[88] but the above measure represented the first instance of family subsidies created for an entire category of workers. Initially the 1934 subsidies were only to go to those working 40 hours or less per week. Subsequently this restriction was relaxed.[89]

Prizes, exemptions, and other measures to prop up the birth rate were carried out on a local level as well. In the region of Abruzzi-Molise, for example, a demographic competition was initiated in 1929: whichever *comune* registered the highest level of fertility and the lowest of mortality – as determined by ISTAT – would be awarded an Ascension Day cup, though a degree of confusion resulted because these two extremes were not met in the same *comune*. Similar competitions were held in Campania, Sicily and Piedmont.[90] Mussolini himself monitored local efforts, writing directly to the responsible parties when he felt the policy was not being followed. To the prefect of Milan he inquired about reports that landlords discriminated in favor of renters without children, and, on a hypocritical note, he instructed the various ministers that the continued restriction of certain state jobs to unmarried and childless men be less well advertised (ACS PCM 1928–30 b.1225 f.3.2.11.6738; PCM 1931–3 b.1430 f.1.3.1.9910).

In spite of the "shadows" of its decline, Italian demographic potential was nonetheless cited as justification for imperial expansion. The *Camera* report on the Interior Ministry budget for 1936–7, presented during the Ethiopian war, claimed that this potential confirmed Italy's

---

[87] *Contratti collettivi di lavoro* (supplement to *Bollettino ufficiale del Ministero delle corporazioni*) f.109 (15 December 1934), allegati nn.598–9.

[88] See ibid. 1929 and following years.

[89] R.d.-l. 21 August 1936, n.1632; Atti C. D.l. N.1491 (30 November 1936). The latter legislation lists a weekly payment of 4 lire per child. See also de Grazia 1992, pp. 85–7 on family wages. It is interesting to note that it was precisely in 1934 that a measure was introduced in France prohibiting the introduction of a family wage in order to cut wages, perhaps a reaction to the Italian example; see Spengler 1979 (1938), p. 243, and also Glass 1940, pp. 440–1 on the possible occasion of this practice in France as early as 1922.

[90] *Notiziario demografico* (1 July 1929); ibid. (1 September 1929); *Annali di statistica* 6, 7 (1930), p. 27; 6, 32 (1934), pp. 45–6; ISTAT carried out a survey of these local efforts which it later cataloged; see *Notiziario demografico* (16 September 1932); *Annali di statistica* 6, 32 (1934), pp. 45–9.

"right, indeed her undeniable need for colonial expansion" (Atti C. D.l. N.985-A [20 January 1936], p. 19). The following year, empire established, one reads in the same forum: "the development of our demographic strength must not stop, our population . . . must . . . continue to provide the nation with the children which it needs" (Atti C. D.l. N.1556-A [4 March 1937], p. 2). And the 1937 renewal of the *politica demografica* was in part a response to the fear that Italy might not be able to live up demographically to its new imperial status.[91]

It was during the first days of March 1937 that the Gran Consiglio del Fascismo approved the resolution which would inform the renewal of the *politica demografica* and its implementation during the remaining years of Fascist rule. Mussolini had previously announced the failure of Fascist demographic policy up to that point. At the GCF meeting he asked, in relation to Italian fertility decline, who would in future protect and people the empire.[92] Briefly, the resolution called for:

1 employment preference for fathers of large families
2 a policy of family salaries (subsidies)
3 a strengthening of existing measures favoring large families
4 the institution of family loans
5 the creation of a national association of large families
6 the redrawing of provincial and *comune* lines according to the 1941 census and in order to eliminate those (demographically) aging *comuni* not in need of public institutions, and
7 the creation of a central institution for the coordination and advancement of the demographic policy

The regime realized all of these points to some degree, with the exception of item 6, made impossible by cancellation of the 1941 census (though various *comuni* had been both created and eliminated over the years, presumably for demographic reasons). The resolution concluded: "The Fascist Grand Council . . . solemnly reminds all Fascists that the demographic problem, being the problem of life and its continuation, is in reality the problem of problems, as without life there is neither youth nor military strength nor economic expansion nor a secure future for the nation."[93] *Il duce* apparently intended to apply the new measures to

[91] See, for example, Mussolini's August 1936 exhortation to the peasants of Basilicata cited in chapter 3, p. 129 above.
[92] ACS SPD-ris. b.32 f.15 inserto A; *Popolo d'Italia* article cited in De Felice 1981, p. 294 and Nobile 1990b, p. 26.
[93] PNF 1938, pp. 622–3 or any newspaper, for example *Corriere della Sera* 4 March 1937. In a curious parallel, the population question had been described in Sweden two years before this as a "question of the life of the Swedish people"; see Myrdal 1945, p. 158.

Table 4.5 *Gran Consiglio del Fascismo fertility*
(1937)

	married (m) or single (s)	Children
Acerbo	m	–
Angelini	m	–
Alfieri	m	3
Balbo	m	3
Bottai	m	3
Ciano Costanzo	m	2
Ciano Galeazzo	m	2
Buffarini	m	3 (?)
Cianetti	m	–
De Bono	m	–
De Stefani	m	3
De Vecchi	m	3
Farinacci	m	2 (?)
Federzoni	m	3
Grandi	m	3
Lantini	m	4
Marconi	m	4
Marinelli	m	2
Muzzarini	m	2
Rossoni	s	1
Russo	m	1
Solmi	m	–
Starace	m	2
Thaon di Ravel	m	3
Tringali	m	2
Volpi	m	2
Gardini	s	–
Serena	m	2
Zangara	s	–

Note:
"TFR" (author's calculation) 55 ÷ 29 = 1.90
(ACS SPD-ris. b.32, f.15)

Fascist hierarchs as well. Included in his personal files for the 1937 meeting is a list of GCF members, their marital status and number of children (see table 4.5). The GCF (perhaps uncompleted) total fertility rate was a disappointing 1.9 (my calculation), well below replacement.

The 1937 resolution was also inspired by apparent Nazi successes in the area of demographic policy. As early as 1935, the German and Italian governments were exchanging notes on the problem of low fertility and the PCM files include a detailed report on German demographic policy (apparently prepared by ISTAT for Mussolini).[94]

ISTAT described the GCF resolution as the transition from assistance to family policy (*politica della famiglia*);[95] in parliament, Alfredo Felici called for direct intervention with regard to fertility: "In order that the demographic campaign be successful, man and woman must be persuasively led to the goal of reproduction in the highest sense of the word" (Atti S. disc. 13 May 1937, p. 2904). And the positive nature of the new program – emphasis on incentives rather than penalties – was generally applauded. Ricci, for example, found the bachelor tax perfectly just and a useful source of income for the state, but ineffective with regard to encouraging nuptiality.[96]

Shortly after the GCF resolution, the UCD was created as part of the Ministry of the Interior. In addition to its general task of policy coordination and encouragement, the UCD was also to serve a research function, studying the ways in which the policy might be pursued; in addition, it took over from the PCM administration of fertility and nuptiality prizes. The funds for these were transferred to the Interior budget and considerably increased.[97]

The other institution called for by the GCF was the UFFN. This Union was to include all those families with at least seven living children and anyone else who made a substantial contribution (10,000 lire for individuals, twice that for organizations). Its purpose was primarily propagandistic: to promote the demographic policy and aid large families in obtaining those benefits available to them. Its initial budget was 500,000 lire (R.d.-l. 3 June 1937, n.805; R.d. 22 November 1937, n.2032). Each province (and also some *comuni*) was to have its own chapter of the UFFN.[98]

---

[94] ACS PCM 1934–6 b.2038 f.15.2.5057; see also *Notiziario demografico* (10 March 1935), p. 118.   [95] *Annali di statistica* 7, 7 (1943), p. 5.

[96] See Ricci's detailed and statistically literate discussion of past and present demography and demographic policy: Atti S. disc. 13 May 1937, pp. 2904–10; comments he makes in this passage suggest that he may have been a bachelor himself. See also Atti C. D.l. N.2113-A (24 January 1938), pp. 21–3 and C. disc. 8 March 1938, pp. 4447–8 (Buffarini Guidi).

[97] R.d. 7 June 1937, n.1128; R.d.-l. 12 August 1937, n.1492. As mentioned above the original 42 million lire had been increased by 29.5, but only for 1936–37. Subsequently various additions were made in 1937–38 amounting to 138 million. R.d.-l. 28 June 1937, n.943, art.10; R.d.-l. 17 January 1938, n.18, art.1; R.d.-l. 3 March 1938, n.142, art.15; R.d.-l. 10 May 1938, n.571, art.5.

[98] Initiated at 11 a.m. on 6 February 1938 in the presence of the prefect and a representative of the clergy (circ. 16 January 1938 [UCD] in *Bollettino del Ministero dell'interno* nn. 5–6, 1938, pp. 195–7).

In addition to these institutional developments, new measures were taken and existing ones strengthened. The most important of the new measures was the creation of marriage loans after the model of those already existing, and apparently having a positive effect on fertility, in Nazi Germany.[99] These were to be offered by the provincial administrations and coordinated by INFPS. They ranged from 1,000 to 3,000 lire and were available only to couples under 26 years of age (both partners) having a combined income of under 12,000 lire. Repayment was to begin six months after the wedding unless the woman should become pregnant. On the birth of the first child, 10% of the loan was canceled and the initiation of payments put off for one year. Subsequent pregnancies and births resulted in similar postponements of debt and its progressive cancellation: additional 20, 30, and 40% cancellations for the second, third, and fourth child. One could thus avoid payments entirely by having four live children – there was no provision for stillbirths or miscarriages – in a period no longer than six and one half years. As noted above in chapter 1, p. 27, France would follow the example of Germany and Italy by introducing similar loans in 1939.

The same legislation that introduced the marriage loans also doubled the 1933 family income-tax reductions mentioned above, expanded the bachelor tax to certain military categories previously exempt, and introduced various other fiscal measures in favor of families.[100] Another new measure introduced in 1937 was a fifteen-day marriage leave for public and private office workers (R.d.-l. 24 June 1937, n.1334).

The marriage loan program seems to have gotten off to a rough start, as the local committees were slow to organize and the criteria used to administer the loans were not standardized.[101] This is not surprising if one recalls the fears previously expressed regarding the ability of local administrations to bear the burden of foundling care. Here was another expense imposed upon them, apparently without any reimbursement from the national government (which only paid administrative costs). These were interest-free loans and ideally not to be paid back. One can imagine, as well, a possible conflict between the provincial or communal UFFN chapter (and UCD propaganda), encouraging young couples

[99] See Ricci's comments on German marriage loans (Atti S. disc. 13 May 1937, p. 2910).
[100] R.d.-l. 21 August 1937, n.1542. Income tax reductions applied to families with five or more children. This law also included norms regarding pregnancy and childbirth for stateworkers discussed above, on p. 161, n.47. On loans see also circ. 25 August 1937 (UCD) in *Bollettino del Ministero dell'interno* nn. 27–28, 1937, pp. 928–34 and circ. 14 October 1937 in ibid. nn. 33–34, 1937, pp. 1176–7. The latter asks prefects to estimate, based on nuptial statistics, what their costs will be for a three-year period.
[101] Circ. 23 November 1937 (UCD) in *Bollettino del Ministero dell'interno* nn. 1–2, 1938, pp. 34–8.

to marry and take advantage of the available loans, and the prefect whose budget will suffer from providing them.[102]

The first item of the GCF resolution required that greater preference be given to the heads of families for employment. As a result, the previous legislation regarding hiring and promotion for state employment was strengthened in several instances.[103] *Podestà* (mayors), for example, were now required to be either married or widowed with children (R.d.-l. 28 April 1938, n.482). The second item called for a policy of family salaries. As mentioned above, various businesses already awarded these and family subsidies were required for industrial workers from 1934. In 1937 a program of this sort was generally required for wage earners in all sectors (including agriculture), except for stateworkers who already had a similar arrangement. Again a fund was to be created with contributions from both workers and employers and administered by INFPS (R.d.-l. 17 June 1937, n.1048). In 1939 family subsidies were also instituted in Libya (R.d. 10 July 1939, n.2251).

Also in 1939, maternity insurance was replaced with a general nuptiality and maternity insurance. All workers now paid into a fund which awarded both marriage (up to age 26, except for male office workers for whom the limit was 30) and childbirth (or miscarriage after the third month).[104]

On a propagandistic note, a *giornata demografica* (demographic holiday) was introduced in late 1939, a complement to (and to some degree repetition of) the *giornata della madre e del fanciullo*. It would take place on 3 March, anniversary of the 1937 GCF meeting. On this day the UFFN awarded its new medal of honor to mothers and fathers of large families.[105]

The combination of incentives and propaganda initiated in March 1937 was rewarded by mild increases in marital and birth rates, a situation attributed of course to Fascist efforts.[106] ISTAT subsequently identified a possible initiation of the demographic turnaround in the period 1933–4 due to improving economic conditions, interrupted by the

---

[102] But see original legislation R.d.-l. 21 August 1937, n.1542, art.12 on funding.

[103] R.d.-l. 21 September 1938, n.1587 and revisions: R.d.-l. 25 February 1939, n.335. New norms were again issued in 1939: R.d.-l. 27 March 1939, n.1223.

[104] Marriage payments varied according to sex and occupation in the way expected: from 400 lire for female agricultural workers to 1,000 lire for male office workers. Childbirth payments varied by order of birth and occupation from 150 lire to 400 lire. R.d.-l. 14 April 1939, n.636. For a contemporary discussion of maternity and nuptiality insurance, see De Tuddo 1940.

[105] *Notiziario demografico* (10 July 1939), p. 129; L. 22 May 1939, n.917. For a conflict between ONMI and the Ministry of War over these medals, see ACS PCM 1940–1 b.3111 f.12.5.1402.   [106] See, for example, Atti C. D.l. N.2022 (30 November 1937).

Table 4.6 *Crude martital and birth rates (per 1,000 inhabitants)*

Year	CMR	CBR	Year	CMR	CBR
1922	9.6		1933	6.9	23.8
1923	8.7		1934	7.4	23.5
1924	7.9		1935	6.7	23.4
1925	7.6		1936	7.4	22.4
1926	7.5	27.7	1937	8.7	22.9
1927	7.6	27.5	1938	7.5	23.8
1928	7.1	26.7	1939	7.3	23.6
1929	7.1	25.6	1940	7.1	23.5
1930	7.4	26.7	1941	6.1	20.9
1931	6.7	24.9	1942	6.4	20.5
1932	6.4	23.8	1943	4.8	19.9

Source: ISTAT 1968

Ethiopian war, and another upturn in 1937–8 due to the new demographic policy, in turn interrupted by European war. A decline in the number of men paying the bachelor tax was also cited as evidence of the success of the policy (Nina 1941). In fact, total births did increase in the period 1937–40 and the crude birth rate, which declined steadily from 1920 to 1937 (except 1930) was higher in the period 1938–40 than in the several years preceding (see table 4.6). The Deputy Pompei raised hopes even for urban fertility, citing 1938 rates for Turin, Milan, and Bologna that were higher than those for 1926.[107] The marital rate also declined from 1920, increasing slightly in 1930 and 1933–4. In 1937 it increased considerably, matching the 1923 rate – an increase largely attributable to post-Ethiopia demobilization – and then declined (see table 4.6); the 1937 increase contributed to the contemporary fertility increase as many newlywed couples had their first child within a year or two of marriage (Pacilio 1941–2). The demographically disruptive effects of economic crisis, Ethiopian conquest, and European war make it difficult to assess the effect of the 1937 measures, but the fact that 1930, 1934 and 1938–9 marriage rates (years during which these factors were relatively less acute) are all about equal suggests minimal response. ISTAT's De Berardinis, however, claimed that the policy did stave off the expected (due to unfavorable age distribution) marital rate decline in 1938 (De Bernardinis 1940).

The attempt to mold demographic behavior intensified during the

---

[107] Atti C. disc. 10 May 1939, p.164. Pompei's 1938 figures are, however, higher than those reported by ISTAT, though his point that 1938 CBR exceeded that of 1926 still holds.

war. The large family tax exemptions were extended to all families having seven-plus dependent children (up to age 28), and the heads of UFFN families (five-plus children) were assigned quotas for employment: 10% of all state jobs and 5% of private (R.d. 20 March 1940, n.224; L. 20 March 1940, n.233). In addition, UFFN families were given preference for the assignment of land for colonization and provided with special loans for the purpose (L. 29 May 1940, n.877). The requirements regarding the preferential hiring and promotion of married people, on the other hand, seem to have caused a degree of difficulty in wartime and were suspended for some categories of public workers.[108] Restrictions on female employment also became impracticable. Demographic prizes, maternal/nuptial insurance, and family subsidies, on the other hand, all continued during the war and were in some cases increased (L. 6 August 1940, n.1278; R.d.-l. 20 March 1941, n.122; R.d. 21 October 1941, n.1277).

Nonetheless, birth and marriage rates both declined – as one would expect – during the war. Declines were not so dramatic as they had been during World War I, but this was true for other countries as well. In any case, this attenuated decline was generally attributed to the demographic policy, and it was claimed that without such a policy the decline would have been much more serious.[109]

In retrospect, Fascist pronatalism seems to have done little to stave off declining Italian birth rates, and this ineffectiveness reflects both the nature of fertility decline – a phenomenon which has profoundly altered the demography of all developed countries in the twentieth-century – and also Fascism's inability to extend its influence to the more intimate areas of social behavior. In an isolated but telling example, the anthropologists Schneider and Schneider found that in the Sicilian village of their study one couple seems to have raised a large family for ostensibly patriotic reasons in the Fascist period, and for this behavior they were generally ridiculed (Schneider and Schneider 1984, p. 258).

Demography and race

Racism plays an important role in a discussion of population problems under Fascism for at least two reasons: one, racist policy impinged upon the principal demographic variables (nuptiality, fertility, migration, and

---

[108] R.d.-l. 7 April 1941, n.321; R.d.-l. 24 August 1942, n. 1092; circ. 1 December 1942 in *Bollettino del Ministero dell'interno* nn. 3–4, pp. 57–8.

[109] See, for example, Atti C. D.l. N.1765-A (14 March 1942), p. 12; *Notiziario demografico* (1 December 1942), pp. 63–6.

mortality) and two, racism was identified at the time as part of the greater *politica demografica* and also linked to it institutionally. Nicola Pende described the racial policy as "quantitative and qualitative demographic policy, land, woman, family and food policy all wrapped into one" (Pende 1939, p. 32). And Giuseppe Bottai, one of the more energetic proponents of racist policy, wrote the following as minister of national education:

After having considered the *quantitative* aspect of the problem and laid out the plan for the demographic battle, it was natural, logical and necessary that the policy of *il DUCE* also take up the *qualitative* aspect of the same problem now that, following creation of the Empire, the Italian race has come in contact with other races and so must be protected from all dangers of blood contamination. (ACS Min. Int. – Demorazza b.4 f.15)

Starting in 1938, Italian Fascists like Bottai regularly linked race to biological ideas like "blood contamination". Before that year, however, the term race (*razza*) occurred with some frequency in their pronouncements (and in those of the Nationalists before them) but usually in a different sense.[110] One needs to be careful in evaluating these earlier usages and should not immediately associate the word with a biological conception. Indeed for most Italians, prior at least to 1938, race was a cultural or social category defined by language and geography, by a shared culture, perhaps by a vague spiritual or moral ideal. This concept differed markedly from Nazi ideas about biological races. In many cases, Italian *razza* was more or less interchangeable with nation, *stirpe* (stock), or people. It is then not surprising to find statements from 1925 describing the ONMI legislation as protecting or improving the race (see chapter 2, pp. 70–1 above). Indeed, later, after a biological racist policy was introduced in 1938, early statements of this sort were dredged up as proof that Fascism had always (and so prior to the possibility of Nazi influence) been racist.[111] In another example, a section of the 1930 legal code was entitled crimes against the *stirpe* , and these included contraception and abortion. Again, however, the idea was not so much that of a biological race but of the body of the nation. The new code recast these crimes as offenses not against morality but against this body which Fascism proposed to protect and see expand by means of its demographic policy.

    This is not to say that there were not racists, biological ideas of race, nor for that matter anti-Semites in Italy in the 1920s and early 1930s. Of

---

[110] See, for example, Rocco's statement reproduced in chapter 2, p. 53 above. On Italian racism and anti-Semitism, see also Bernardini 1977.

[111] See, for example, Bergamaschi 1938, 1940.

course there were. In particular, anti-Semitism had a centuries-old history in Catholic circles, especially among the Jesuits.[112] Moreover, the reconciliation of the Fascist state and the Vatican in 1929 marked a change in status for the Italian Jews, as Fascist recognition of Roman Catholicism as the state religion officially demoted Judaism (and any other faith) to an inferior status. Catholic anti-Semitism was, however, explicitly non-biological as Jews represented so many souls to be saved by conversion to the true faith. The late nineteenth and early twentieth-century Nationalist anti-Semitism was instead less flexible. Jews were by nature internationalist wanderers and could never recognize the nation as truly their own. Fascist ant-Semitism would derive from this tradition.

And Italians did of course share the general European conceptions of racial difference, in particular between white and black, but their exposure to non-whites was so limited prior to the conquest of Ethiopia that the issue received little attention.[113] Finally, *razza* and its equivalents were at times used in a specifically biological sense prior to 1938. Gini, for example, had a biological conception not just of race but of the nation, and Pende too viewed the Italian race as a biological product of limited interbreeding. Gini's more theoretical considerations are discussed below (see chapter 5, pp. 249–51), but Pende's work included specific policy recommendations and so deserves a word here as well.

Pende was an exponent of the science of constitutionalism or orthogenesis, indeed might claim to be its creator. He believed that by monitoring individual growth anthropometrically, pathologically, socially etc., one could adjust environment and nutrition to ensure individual and ultimately racial improvement. An orthogenetic approach would ensure, he claimed, the production of "concrete and realistic men" and "intelligent mothers" (Pende 1938, pp. 223–31): "The science of orthogenesis is that which seeks to form healthy and well-balanced individuals of the sort desired by our regime" (Pende 1940b, p. 257). Pende's was an Italian variant on eugenics.

From at least the early 1920s, Pende had advocated the creation of institutes for individual biological and psychological monitoring and the introduction of personal health cards (Pende 1923). The health card proposal was supported in parliament by the physician Umberto Gabbi

---

[112] See Webster 1960, pp. 119–28 on Jesuit anti-Semitism and the common ground found by them and Fascist anti-Semites.

[113] And one might also make the argument that the pre-imperial lack of racial consciousness reasserted itself after World War II, a sort of racial amnesia from which Italy has only awaked abruptly and uncomfortably since the heavy influx of "extra-European" immigrants began in the 1980s.

(see chapter 2, p. 71), but questioned by Federzoni. In an unusual instance of Fascist reluctance to invade the private sphere, Federzoni noted that such a measure would authorize "the state . . . to pursue dangerous inquiries into the jealously guarded intimacy of the family" (Atti C. disc. 26 November 1925, p. 4618). He nonetheless recognized the "immense utility" of a health card measure, and indeed a personal booklet recording anthropometric, health, and fitness data (as well as intellectual and political observations) was introduced in 1936 for all males between age 11 and military service.[114] In 1934 Pende also proposed the establishment throughout Italy of a network of orthogenetic clinics after the model of that he had created as director of the University of Genova medical clinic (Vinci 1939b, pp. 141–6). This network was never created, but in 1938, just prior to the racist manifesto, the government approved construction of an Istituto di bonifica umana ed ortogenesi della razza (Institute of Human Improvement and Racial Orthogenesis) at a cost of 10 million lire. This institute, meant to be part of the canceled 1942 Esposizione Universale di Roma, was to be directed by Pende and was scheduled to begin operating in late 1940.[115] Pende's efforts to improve and protect the Italian race were not limited to his orthogenetic programs. He was in fact the most prominent signatory of the July 1938 *Manifesto degli scienziati razzisti* (Manifesto of Racist Scientists) which marked the beginning of the anti-Jewish campaign in Italy.[116]

The racist manifesto is rightly remembered as one of the ugliest moments of pre-war Fascism. Still, it was by no means a complete surprise as Italians already had pursued a racist policy for a couple of years in Ethiopia.[117] As the Bottai passage reproduced at the beginning of this section reveals, the new empire raised both the hope that Ethiopia would attract Italian workers and colonists and the fear that increased contacts between whites and blacks would lead to the creation of a mixed-race population. The greatest perceived danger was the establishment of stable relationships between Italian men and African women, a practice encouraged by Italian male fantasies regarding the "Black Venus" that awaited them in Italian Africa. Moreover, there was

---

[114] The *libretto personale* was introduced with R.d.-l. 26 March 1936, n.608; see also Atti C. D.l. N.1190-A (7 May 1936); Pende 1933, pp. 81–3, 1939, pp. 15ff. For another example of constitutionalist-inspired legislation, see Atti C. D.l. N.1303, 1303-A (9 April 1932) regarding the reporting of all deformed infants to ONMI for possible treatment.

[115] R.d.-l. 12 May 1938, n.1123; Atti S. disc. 15 May 1940, pp. 563–4; ACS PCM 1940–1 b.2509 f.14.2.6770.

[116] On Pende's theoretical arguments supporting racial legislation, see chapter 5, pp. 249–50 below.

[117] On racial legislation and racism in the colonies, see also Goglia 1988.

a tradition among the East African Christian cultures of Eritrea and Ethiopia according to which a man could hire a wife (from her family) for up to a year. Prior to the Ethiopian war, it had apparently been much practiced by Italian colonists in Eritrea. However, as long as the white population of Italian East Africa (AOI) had been small, the problem of *madamismo* or concubinage had been limited and dealt with by simple pressure from the police or local authorities. The conquest of Ethiopia and the influx of tens of thousands of Italian workers changed this situation and required stronger measures. In April 1937, precisely at the peak of the Italian presence in AOI, a law was introduced which prohibited any Italian citizen from maintaining "a relationship of a marriage-like nature with a subject of Italian East Africa." Punishment was one to five years' imprisonment and only applied to the Italian citizen; the law did not prohibit casual sexual contact between Italian men and black women.[118]

In 1939, after racist legislation had been introduced in Italy as well, the above law was incorporated into a larger one including measures prohibiting whites from frequenting public places reserved for natives[119] and requiring investigations of all mulattos born of conceptions that presumably occurred after the introduction of the 1937 legislation. Again sexual contact was tolerated, but not procreation (R.d.-l. 29 June 1939, n.1004).

In spite of suggestions that the article on marriage-like relations be strengthened, particularly with regard to the possibility of sexual contacts between black men and white women, the wording remained essentially that of 1937. This latter fear derived from the increasing female presence in AOI and in particular from the presence of white prostitutes whose importation had been "necessitated" by the large population of Italian males there. Several senators, however, gave reassurances that these women were only accepting white customers (Atti C. D.l. N.105 [15 April 1939]; C. disc. 20 April 1939, pp. 2–6, 15 June 1939, p. 27; S. disc. 26 June 1939, pp. 6–7).

The underlying assumption of the legislation regarding white–black sexual relations – namely that by eliminating concubinage but tolerating casual or occasional sexual contacts, the creation of a mixed-race population might be avoided – was fairly optimistic. Nonetheless, Teruzzi (then minister of Italian Africa) announced in 1940 that the

---

[118] R.d.-l. 19 April 1937, n.880; Atti C. D.l. N.2031 (30 November 1937), N.2031-A (7 December 1937); S. D.l. N.1978-A (15 December 1937). For praise and a discussion of the need for this law, see Sangiorgi 1937.

[119] This sort of *apartheid* had existed previously in the form of *Governatore* decrees. See, for example, decreto 1 July 1937, n.12723 in *Bollettino ufficiale della Somalia*, n. 14.

frequency of mulatto births had declined significantly as a result of these laws. For Eritrea, for example, he cited a drop from thirty such births per month to four. With regard to the possibility of mulatto births to white women he responded: "our laws cannot even allow for such a possibility, which runs counter to all our moral principles" (Atti C. disc. 22 April 1940, pp. 44–7).

The actual enforcement of the laws on black–white sexual contacts, as revealed in reports from the AOI courts constitutes an interesting chapter on its own.[120] Repeated sexual contacts with the same woman were at times tolerated providing that they did not go on for too long and were not characterized by those traits considered to be marriage-like. The latter included of course the desire to marry or have children with the woman, but also the sharing of the same bed. One case lists as a damning fact the presence of the native woman in the white man's bed when he is not there, while in another the fact of the man having only a small bed – not large enough to accommodate two people as a permanent sleeping arrangement – aided in his acquittal. Other frequently cited details are the taking of meals together and at the same table, the bestowal of gifts, and the request by the white man that the black woman remain faithful to him (except in one case where such a request seemed to be inspired purely by the desire to avoid disease). The details of these cases reveal the difficulties encountered in attempting to distinguish between sexual contacts "which simply respond to a physiological need" and those involving a degree of affection and permanence.

While the Italian racist laws would in general apply to Libya, those specifically designed for Italian East Africa were not repeated in Italy's other major colony.[121] Apparently the need was not felt for special controls on Arab–Italian sexual contact and potential procreation. Segré even notes that Arab men were free to use the same brothels as Europeans.[122] In addition to the fact that Mediterranean Arabs were perhaps perceived as less different racially than sub-Saharan Africans,

---

[120] These reports are published in the Demorazza journal *Razza e civiltà*; see July–September 1940, October 1940.

[121] The 1936 law clearly refers to the "subjects of Italian East Africa." The 1939 version, on the other hand, refers to "natives of Italian Africa." Some Libyans had been considered citizens (but not on a par with Italian citizens), as opposed to subjects, since 1911. Whether or not they were considered natives is presumably unimportant as just before the introduction of the 1939 law northern Libya had become part of the Italian kingdom and this presumably distinguished it from Italian Africa (Eritrea, Ethiopia, Somalia) (R.d.-l. 9 January 1939, n.70). See also Segré 1978, pp. 122–6.

[122] Segré 1978, p. 125. Segré's text surprisingly suggests that he is referring to the period after the racial manifesto. However, the race of the prostitutes is not specified and several of his citations date from several years before this event.

there were at least two reasons for the lack of special legislation: one, the greater presence of Italian women in Libya as opposed to AOI, and two, the above mentioned tradition of short-term contractual marriage in East Africa had no counterpart in Libya.[123] Further evidence that Libyan women were not considered a serious threat to Italian racial integrity was revealed in a 1940 discussion of the Nationalist Senator Maurizio Maraviglia, who overlooked the Arabs entirely, describing the Jews as the only racial group within the kingdom which could "pose a threat of pollution and endanger the ethnic homogeneity of the Italian race" (Atti S. D.l. N.675-A [4 May 1940], p. 6). A further factor in the apparent lack of Arab/Italian sexual contact was the Muslim tradition of segregating women from male society and so, one can conclude, especially from European male society.

The idea that an Italian race existed and needed to be protected from extraneous elements first found official expression in the racist manifesto which appeared in Italian newspapers on 14 July 1938 and was signed by, in addition to Pende, ISTAT president Franco Savorgnan and others. According to this document, there existed a pure Italian race which bore no relation to other Mediterranean races, in particular the Semitic and Hamitic races. By the definitions of the day the latter two groups included most of the inhabitants of AOI and Libya and also Italian Jews. The manifesto called for the maintenance of racial purity and insisted that (procreational) unions only be established with other "European" races. The racial question was discussed by the GCF in October which resolved that marriage between Italians and members of the Hamitic, Semitic, or other non-Aryan races would be prohibited. This directive became law the following month.[124]

There was of course more to Italian racist policy than nuptiality restrictions, but it is these which are most relevant to the current discussion. Marriage was prohibited between Italian non-Jewish citizens and Jews, the latter defined as anyone having at least one Jewish parent, unless the other parent were "Italian" and the person in question practiced a religion other than Judaism as of 1 October 1938. The law regarding "Italian"-Jewish contact referred only to marriage, not sexual intercourse or procreation. The production of mixed-race children would, however, later be considered a crime against the race in the

---

[123] Thanks to Luigi Goglia for having explained these differences to me. See Goglia 1988, esp. pp. 1234–5.

[124] For a discussion of the genesis of these documents (including copies of the documents themselves) see De Felice 1988, pp. 275–84, 555–7, 567–80. The law in question is R.d.-l. 17 November 1938, n.1728.

Repubblica sociale.[125] The 1939 "Measures for the defence of the Italian race" also prohibited marriage between state employees and foreigners of any race or religion. In one example, the son of ISTAT president Savorgnan hoped to marry a woman he had met while serving at an eastern European embassy. In spite of the attempts of his father to intervene with the minister of the interior, the request was turned down.

Unlike the earlier pro-natalist measures, the racist aspects of the *politica demografica* were not completely amenable to the Vatican. Marriage, of course, was an area over which the Church maintained a degree of authority and this new legislation was seen as an incursion. The central problem was that the 1938 law prohibited the marriage of Catholics and converted Jews. Vatican protests, however, seem to have amounted to little (De Felice 1988, pp. 292–8).

Shortly after publication of the racist manifesto, the UCD was transformed into the Direzione generale della demografia e della razza (General directorship of demography and race – Demorazza),[126] a clear indication of the Fascist association of demographic and racist policies. In addition to responsibility for studying the demographic problem, assessing the policy, and awarding prizes, Demorazza would also investigate how to deal with the racial problem. Its Consiglio superiore included, among others, the presidents of ISTAT, ONMI, and UFFN. In an effort to further integrate demographic and racist policy, it was even proposed that the Demorazza and ONMI budgets be combined (Atti S. disc. 27 May 1939, p. 135; C. D.l. N.6-A [25 March 1939], p. 5).

The link between ISTAT and Demorazza is significant, as one of Demorazza's first tasks was to undertake a census of all Italian Jews. The census was carried out in August 1938 and – a sign of its urgency – resulted in the cancellation of an already begun industrial census. Needless to say, it was complicated by the need to determine who exactly was a Jew and by the reluctance of subjects to be counted for what could only be ominous purposes. Undated province by province results filed together with the August 1938 census instructions give a total of 53,416 Jews "present," 14,063 "absent" (presumably from their *comune* of residence), and a not quite consistent total of 67,509. The largest concentrations were in Rome (15,201), Trieste (7,640), Milan (5,524) and Turin (4,908). A Demorazza report marked 1938 and entitled "First results of the Jewish census" gives a count-in-progress of 55,657

---

[125] Mixed race meant children produced by a person of "Italian blood" and a person of "foreign blood." The latter category included Jews, but not Aryan Europeans who were considered of "blood similar to Italian." See a copy of this law in De Felice 1988, pp. 620–1, esp. art. 9.

[126] Still as part of the Ministry of the Interior. R.d. 5 September 1938, n.1531.

and a projected total of 65,817.[127] As with general population statistics, the Jewish census was complemented by population registry data and the 1938 racist law instructed Jews to register their status with registry offices. In addition to undoubted reluctance to comply with the initial instructions, many Jews leaving Italy did not alert the local authorities, a fact bemoaned by the Demorazza general director. The census seems to have been carried out again in June 1941 and a report to Mussolini in October of that year estimated 39,000 Italian Jews present in Italy and about 8,000 foreign Jews. If these numbers are consistent with the 1938 figures, about 20,000 Jews had left Italy in the two years between the first census (only one month after the racist manifesto) and Italy's entry into the war.[128]

Though a nefarious example, the creation of Demorazza and the Jewish census have much in common with the other Italian statistical initiatives mentioned in this and previous chapters, from post-Unification DIRSTAT to post-March on Rome ISTAT to the CMC study of internal migration. Here again demographic statistics were enlisted to identify and control population. However, the intention was not in this case to establish the unity of the population, but to identify one of its parts as "other," and not to manipulate this group as a tool of national military or economic expansion, but rather to specifically exclude it from these spheres. Moreover, it was really only by identifying the "non-Italian" groups in this way that a racial identity could be assigned to the heterogeneous Italian population. In this same vein, prior to the racist manifesto the Italian Anthropology and Ethnology Society (headquartered in Florence) had proposed in December 1937 a census of all individuals belonging to races of color in the kingdom, Libya, and Italy's Aegean possessions in order that racial mixing, and so decadence, be avoided.[129] This complementary effort to quantify the "non-Italian" elements within the Italian sphere of influence was, however, not carried out.

The Jewish census served in general to identify and quantify the scope of the Jewish "problem." It does not appear that the census was ever published, but copies of both the census results and also a list of Jews resident in Italy were requested (and presumably received) by pro-

---

[127] Another total given in this file is 70,826 (see citation below).

[128] This also assumes that the c. 5,000 "discriminations" – the exemption of an individual from Jewish status because of past, generally Fascist, merits – awarded by October 1938 were included in the 39,000 figure (ACS Min. Int. Demorazza b.3; b.4, f.20; b.13, ff.43–44; b.14).

[129] The work of the anthropologist (and signatory of the racist manifesto) Lidio Cipriani was cited in support of the need for such a census (ACS Min. Int. Demorazza b.13 f.43; Cipriani 1937).

fessional associations (in order to enforce economic segregation), by the PNF and, via ISTAT, by the German Institut zum Studium der Judenfrage (Institute for Study of the Jewish Question) which was preparing (and subsequently published) a world census of Jews. Contemporary to the national Jewish census, Demorazza also canvassed all government offices to determine which state employees were Jewish and so to be dismissed.

Demorazza continued to pursue its demographic activities as well. Nuptiality and fertility prizes continued to be awarded – provided the applicants were racial "Italians" – both prior to Mussolini's fall from power in July 1943 and then again under the *Repubblica Sociale* at least until June 1944 (ACS Min. Int. Demorazza b.13, f.45). Demorazza also published a journal entitled *Razza e civiltà* from March 1940. In addition to the expected assortment of articles on the characteristics of the Italian race, anti-Semitism, the problem of inter-racial breeding etc., the editor of *Razza e civiltà* apparently sought to maintain a degree of scientific legitimacy by the inclusion in each issue of one non-racist article of demographic/scientific merit, for example the fertility work carried out by Livi and Giusti (see below).

The Italian racist policy had, of course, social and economic aspects as well as demographic. Nonetheless, it was presented as a complement to the *politica demografica* both rhetorically and institutionally, and the racist policy did affect several demographic variables. The problem of inter-racial fertility was attacked explicitly in the Empire and indirectly in the Kingdom by prohibiting marriage between Aryan Italians and Jews or Arabs. Racist policy also led to the spontaneous emigration of Jews (and one might also include the organized emigration of ethnically German South Tyrolians to the enlarged German Reich – see chapter 3, pp. 138–9 above). In its tragic conclusion Italian racism resulted in increased mortality as, under the Nazis and the *Repubblica Sociale*, over 8,000 Jews were shipped to death camps; less than 1,000 returned.[130]

Prior to the conquest of Ethiopia and alliance with Nazi Germany, Italy, except for a few groups of Catholic and Nationalist anti-Semites, had been relatively immune to racist thinking, a situation due in large part to a lack of contact with other races and the low visibility of Italy's small Jewish population. Nor were indigenous fears of Italian racial decline present: "Proletarian" Italy was predictably less sensitive to the implications of social differentials in fertility than was class-conscious Britain, and the biological concerns which fueled Nazi programs of

---

[130] Toscano 1986, pp. 29–30 gives the following figures: 8,369 deported of whom 980 returned.

sterilization and euthanasia were generally absent from the Italian discourse on population. Nonetheless, the German influence over Italian population policy was considerable. Beginning with Mussolini's interest in Korherr's book on race suicide, and followed by the Italian adoption of pronatalist measures modelled after those implemented by the Nazis, this influence culminated in the voluntary imposition by Mussolini of racist laws, or rather their extension from Black Africans to Italian Jews (and Arabs), laws which De Felice has identified as above all an attempt by Mussolini to *transform* the Italians and turn a "race of slaves" into a "race of masters" (De Felice 1988, pp. 257–8) The Defelicean analysis fits the racist policy squarely into a demographic policy aimed at molding Italian society into a new Fascist civilization. So while the racist policy served to forge closer ties with the Nazi ally, it also fitted into well-established Italian Fascist programs.

In these two chapters on the realization of totalitarian demography I have attempted to describe the institutional and legislative framework within which demographic policy was pursued. I have had occasion to cite demographic statistics: numbers migrated, infant mortality rates, birth rates, etc. However, I have not yet readdressed that point raised in chapter 2, namely the role that the gathering of statistics played in the overall policy. In chapter 5 I shall consider the development of the Istituto Centrale di Statistica after its initial establishment and also the way in which official demographic statistics reflected policy. Finally I shall return to a topic abandoned since chapter 1, namely the theory of population, a presumably less official sphere where the priorities of the regime were nonetheless much in evidence.

5

The measurement of totalitarian demography

The creation of a new Italian statistics institute in 1926 bore witness to the enhanced status and importance Mussolini and the Fascist regime assigned to the collection of "arid figures." And the increased official attention and scrutiny devoted to statistics meant that they reflected official needs and priorities even more than they had in the Liberal period (see chapter 1, pp. 37–40 above). In this chapter I shall consider the way in which demographic policy manifested itself in the activities and publications of ISTAT, and also in the theoretical work of demographers. As practitioners of a decidedly political science, many demographers had formal ties to the government via ISTAT, UCD, and other institutions, and also in their capacity as university professors.[1]

Population statistics

Chapter 2, pp. 78–87, above describes the creation of ISTAT and the relation of this institution and its president to the enunciation of demographic policy. Throughout the *ventennio*, ISTAT would be the primary source of demographic data for the government and for professional demographers pursuing and monitoring that policy. By means of censuses, the compilation of population registry data, and special surveys, ISTAT was expected to provide both a measure of the efficacy of demographic policy and an indication of the areas most needing attention. Greater official interest and support during the Fascist period translated into a significant improvement in the quality of Italian statistics, and examination of statistical emphases and lacunae as well as a series of

---

[1] Italian universities are almost exclusively state run, and university professors (as state employees) were obliged to pledge an oath to Fascism in 1931.

changing definitions and methods of data gathering reveal that Fascist statistical interest and population policy strongly influenced the gathering and presentation of that statistical data.

The initial period during which Gini was president of ISTAT stretched from the institute's creation in July 1926 to Gini's resignation in February 1932. It was a period characterized by increases in staff and budget, by the revival of statistical publications and the elimination of the previous long delays, by the establishment of ISTAT in new headquarters (on via Cesare Balbo where it still exists today), by the 1931 census, and by the 1931 International Congress for the Study of Population held in Rome.

The activities of ISTAT during the Gini period have been described partially in the previous chapters: the study of large families and the creation of an archive of material on local pronatalist measures for example.[2] The fundamental tasks facing the new institute, however, were to improve local data-gathering by the population registry offices and carry out the population censuses. These two sources provided the basic information about the Italian demographic situation – fertility, infant mortality, urbanization, demographic expansion in Africa – and so measures of the effectiveness of Fascist population policy.

New regulations for the keeping of communal population registers were introduced in 1929. The population registry offices were responsible for maintaining a roll of resident population[3] and for the collection of birth, death, marriage, and some migration statistics; local sloppiness, combined with intentional misreporting, had in the past compromised Italian demographic statistics, especially in the south and Sicily. According to the new regulations, the *comune* was not to issue any documents to individuals not properly registered and there were penalties for not reporting the required information (for example a birth or a change of residence) (R.d. 2 December 1929, n.2132[2812]). Local gathering of statistics, however, remained in the hands of local authorities and not ISTAT, and problems in data gathering, responsibility of the *podestà* (mayor), had to be referred to the minister of the interior, further contributing to ISTAT/ministry conflicts.

In addition to processing population registry data, the other major activity of ISTAT was the periodic population census, a fact borne out by the Institute's budget which ballooned around the census years (see

---

[2] For an official version of ISTAT activities in this period see ISTAT 1936; ISTAT (Fracassi) 1961, pp. 141–59; ISTAT 1977; *Annali di statistica* 8, 5–8 (1957–9).

[3] As in most European countries, Italians are required to register their "residence," established at birth, with the local government each time they move.

Table 5.1 *ISTAT budget (total expenses)*

1930–31	19,270,859
1931–32	13,648,386
1932–33	15,485,505
1933–34	6,719,315
1934–35	8,297,828
1935–36	23,281,174
1936–37	15,959,685
1937–38	17,349,870
1938–39	14,745,969
1939–40	12,872,548
1940–41	12,582,900

Sources: ACS PCM b.2672 f.1.1.16.3.3.27000–4; b.2673 f.1.1.16.313.27000–56; b.2684 f.1.1.16.6.27000–24; b.2685 f.1.1.16.6.27000–24. Many of these figures are confirmed in the CSS Atti reproduced in various issues of the *Annali di statistica*.

table 5.1).[4] According to *Il Censimento*, a single issue publication of census propaganda,[5] the 1931 census:

will allow discernment if not of the full development at least of the first tangible effects of the forward-looking demographic policy initiated by *il duce* and the national Fascist government and intended to hamper or attenuate emigration abroad, increase fertility, and make possible by ever greater land reclamation projects, the breaking up of large properties, and the better distribution of population in the most productive rural areas.

In preparation for the 1931 census, Gini wrote to Mussolini about the sorry state of local statistical offices and the need to hire competent personnel (preferably those who had successfully taken the state statistics exam). Gini proposed that ISTAT be given the power to nominate special commissions for potential problem *comuni*, those with a history of poor data collection and reporting. Such a measure would in some sense establish the authority of ISTAT over local *podestà* and prefects, and the Ministry of the Interior predictably objected to it. Gini responded that if he were not permitted these commissions, ISTAT could not take responsibility for eventual inaccuracies in the census. The Interior Ministry in turn described Gini's disclaimer as a threat "inconsistent with Fascist doctrine." The census norms as they were published in February 1931 called

---

[4] The 1931 census required 20 million lire over three years, and that of 1936 18 million over a similar period (R.d.-l. 30 October 1930, n.1417[1748]), art. 4; L. 27 May 1935, n.984).

[5] Reproduced in ISTAT, *Censimento 1931*, vol. I, following p. 273.

for the creation of both communal and provincial census commissions (responsible to the Interior Ministry) to which ISTAT was given the option of appointing special members. It is doubtful, however, that the Institute actually succeeded in doing so as subsequent correspondence reveals Gini still insisting on ISTAT's right to appoint special commissions and Mussolini siding instead with the Ministry (his own) (ACS PCM 1940–3 b.2687 f.1.1.16.7.27000–28 sff.A, 3; b.2688 f.1.1.16.7.27000–28 sf.9).

The census was scheduled for 21 April, the birthday of Rome. In the future they were to be conducted on this date every fifth (rather than every tenth) year, as the regime felt the need for more up-to-date demographic data, now that these data had become an important target of Fascist policy (R.d.-l. 6 November 1930, n.1503). In March and April, Mussolini himself addressed several circulars to the prefects urging them to follow carefully the census operations and report back to him; he would personally take note of those provinces where there were irregularities. He also warned against the temptation to inflate population figures in light of Fascist populationism and the fact that *comune* and provincial borders and economic benefits were to depend upon census results (ACS SPD-ord. 509.560/III sf.4 ssf.1; ISTAT AC cassetta 40 [1931]).

Provincial and communal census commissions were to prevent abuses and to encourage the population to correctly fill out the census forms. Precensus measures included publication of the above-cited newspaper (*Il Censimento*) explaining the purpose of the census, census announcements in the newsreels of the Istituto LUCE (state film institute) and on the radio, lessons in schools, and promotion by various professional organizations.[6]

Nonetheless, there were inaccuracies, and ISTAT did a considerable amount of post-census data verification by means of travelling inspectors (eleven in all).[7] In the Sicilian *comune* of Catania, for example, the census had to be completely redone. Archival documents (of June 1932) mention the falsification of census forms there (duplications, forms for the dead or emigrated) and so a presumably inflated total, though the population totals listed suggest that the second census gave a total slightly *above* (by about 1%) the original.[8] The Catanesi may indeed have outsmarted ISTAT as an anonymous letter written in October stated that some of the citizens of Catania, alarmed over demographic decline, had requested the second census which they then falsified in order to show more respectable growth (ACS SPD-ord. b.1172 f.509.560/III sf.4 ssf.2).

[6] On the carrying out of the census see ISTAT, *Censimento 1931*, vol. I and *Annali di statistica* 6, 27 (1932).
[7] See ISTAT, *Censimento 1931*, vol. IV, p. *1 on resulting census adjustments.
[8] Inspections in other Sicilian *comuni*, on the other hand, revealed *over*statements by as much as 15% (Caltanisetta, Trapani).

In any case, the Catania irregularities led to the dismissal of both the *podestà* and prefect (ACS PCM 1931–3 b.1373 f.1.1.1.2977).

Gini of course claimed afterward that had his proposal that ISTAT be involved directly in gathering census data been accepted, these problems might have been avoided.[9] In fact, the census results differed from the calculated population (based on intercensus vital rates and migration), though this discrepancy could equally well be attributed to inaccuracy in the 1921 census, in the keeping of population registers, or in the 1931 census. Some did claim that the 1931 census was a disaster, in part because of numerous questions respondents feared would be used for tax purposes.[10]

The definitive 1931 census population totals, by *comune*, were published almost exactly one year after the census was taken, having first been reviewed by *il duce* (R.d. 16 April 1932, n.324). They revealed a total present population of 41.177 million and so a 1921–31 annual growth rate about double that of the period 1911–21; though comparison was complicated by the earlier period having included massive emigration, the mortality and fertility losses of World War I, and a border change.[11] As compared to population projections made by Gini and published in 1930, the 1931 census total was more than 1 million short of his worst-case projection (constant mortality and declining fertility), though it should be recalled that these projections were made in the context of Mussolini's 1927 Ascension Day statement that Italy must enter the second half of the century with no fewer than 60 million inhabitants.[12]

---

[9] *Annali di statistica* 6, 27 (1932) pp. 21 ff.

[10] ACS SPD-ord. b.1172 f.509.560/III sf.4 ssf.2; according to a letter in this *busta*, the discrepancy between calculated and counted population was 830,000 or about 2%. The 1930 *Annuario statistico*, however, reports a calculated present population of 41,173,000 for 31 December 1928 almost equal to the census total of 41,177,000; the latter figure however includes another twenty-eight months of growth.

[11] For various numbers and growth rates see Livi Bacci 1977 and ISTAT 1968. Some provinces did show a slowdown of growth in the period 1921–31, Padua for example: see ISTAT, *Censimento 1931*, vol. III, f. Padova.

[12] Gini's projections were the following ($\times$ 1,000):

	a	b	c
1931	44,266	42,893	43,372
1941	50,408	45,957	47,707
1951	56,154	47,979	51,603
1961	62,963	49,711	55,571

a CDR and CBR constant; *b* CDR constant, CBR declines; *c* CDR and CBR decline *Notiziario demografico* (16 April 1930).
He considered projection c the most plausible. The 1951 census counted a resident population of 47.5 million. For Mussolini's statement see the Ascension Day speech (Mussolini, vol. XXII, p. 364).

Nonetheless, it was pointed out, the Italian rate of growth exceeded that of all other European countries save Poland and the USSR (ISTAT, *Censimento 1931*, vol. IV, p. *14).

The census included a question on occupation, the categories of which were altered in 1931 as compared to the previous census in order to reflect the new corporativist organization of the economy (ibid., vol. I, p. 7). With regard to general categories, the 1931 population was almost 50% agricultural, a few percentage points less than in 1921 (ibid. vol. IV, p. *30).

The average age of the Italian population had been increasing gradually from 1901, a sign of fertility decline. The highest average age was not surprisingly that of the low-fertility region of Piedmont, while the youngest province was Calabria; and the north was in general older than the south. Nonetheless, the Italian population was considerably younger than that of France or England (ibid., pp. *43–*64). On the other hand, rates of bachelorhood and spinsterhood were generally higher in Italy than in the rest of Europe, but lower in 1931 than at any of the previous census dates. The latter rate was lowest in low-population *comuni* and increased with their increasing size, in line more or less with Fascist accusations regarding urban sterility (ibid., pp. *65*–*75).

Given official concern about the problem, it is surprising that the census did not include an explicit measure of urbanism, though the definition of what is urban is problematic.[13] Population of provincial capitals was suggested as an approximate measure (ISTAT, *Censimento 1931*, vol.I, p. 25), though the problem was not so much urban growth *per se*, but migration to the cities (urbanization). One can distinguish this sort of growth by analyzing data on place of birth. The latter revealed that only about 50% of the population of the largest *comuni* (over 500,000 inhabitants) had been born in those same *comuni*, while the figure for small *comuni* (up to 50,000 inhabitants) was about 75%. In 1931 more than 25% of the population of the large *comuni* consisted of those born in other regions, while in 1901 this figure had been 14.5%. All of these figures revealed that a large and growing portion of the population of the largest cities had migrated from more sparsely populated areas. The smaller provincial capitals also exercised great attraction, especially in the south and islands. Furthermore, place-of-birth information revealed a general migratory movement from south to north as well as considerable migration out

---

[13] On the problems of assessing Italian urbanism in this period, see again Mariani 1976, pp. 44–52.

of Venetia, Emilia, and Apulia and into Latium, Lombardy, and Liguria (ibid. vol. IV, pp. *76–*88). Information on sex ratios may also provide information on internal migration: that of Sardinia, which had become more masculine since 1921, was attributed to worker migration for the *bonifiche*.[14]

The 1931 census measured both the so-called census family (or all those living in a single household) and also natural families (cohabiting related persons only), and both sorts of family had declined in size between 1921 and 1931.[15] Family size in relation to occupation of the family head and region was also recorded. In the north the largest families were agricultural and family size declined gradually through the categories of industrial and other laborers, office workers, and professionals; while in the south, the largest families were (contrary to the standard claim) industrial, followed usually by merchant and then agricultural. On average families were larger in the south and smaller in the north, though on a regional level the most consistently large were those of Venetia (and the most consistently small those of Piedmont);[16] appropriately, the large agricultural families of Venetia were an important component in Fascist demographic programs.[17]

Further information on Italian fertility was provided by a special survey on the fertility of Italian married women, conducted as part of the census and inspired by concern over denatalism.[18] The results of this study were published only in 1936 (ISTAT, *Censimento 1931*, vol. VI); some of these are included in table 5.2, namely the average number of children born per ever-married woman by region, large area and for the five largest *comuni*. These numbers do not represent completed fertility, but instead the average number of children for married women of all

[14] ISTAT, *Censimento 1931*, vol. I, p. 34. The male/female ratio in Sardinia had increased from 992:1000 to 1002:1000. Taking into account these ratios and 1921 and 1931 populations, and assuming that non-*bonifiche* population growth resulted in equal male and female growth, then the change in ratio would require about 4,500 male workers for the bonifiche. CMC figures are incomplete but show a total net migration to Sardinia for the years 1928, 1929 and 1931 of just over 3,000.

[15] The census families (members present on census date) were on average smaller than the natural families (which included temporarily absent members). The former dropped from 4.4 to 4.2, the latter from 4.5 to 4.3 in the period 1921–31 (ISTAT, *Censimento 1931*, vol. IV, pp. *27–*29).

[16] ISTAT, *Censimento 1931* vol. IV, pp. *30–*32. The highest overall rate was that of agricultural Venetians (6.7); the lowest, professional Piedmontese or Lucanians (1.9).

[17] See, however, Saraceno 1979–80, p. 189 on the difficulty in deriving information on family structure from census data in this period.

[18] ISTAT, *Censimento 1931*, vol. I, p. 14; a similar study had been carried out in Britain in 1911, and the Italian study would seem to be modelled after this predecessor. See Soloway 1990, pp. 9–10.

Table 5.2 *Female fertility, 1931 (average number of children born to ever-married women)*

Piedmont	3.27	Rome	3.13
Liguria	3.19	Milan	2.69
Lombardy	3.90	Naples	4.22
Ven. Trid.	4.16	Turin	2.26
Venetia	4.65	Genoa	2.83
V.G.-Zara	4.04		
Emilia	4.07	North	3.91
Tuscany	3.50	Center	3.72
Marches	4.08	South	4.61
Umbria	3.89	Islands	4.52
Latium	3.77		
Abr.-Mol.	4.20	Italy	4.11
Campania	4.61		
Apulia	4.99		
Basilicata	4.69		
Calabria	4.40		
Sicily	4.52		
Sardinia	4.52		

Source: ISTAT, *Censimento 1931*, vol. vi: "Indagine sulla fecondità della donna."

Table 5.3 *Total fertility rate and average number of children per marriage*

	TFR	CPM
1930	3.507	3.61
1931	3.324	3.38
1932	3.169	3.29
1933	3.150	3.33
1934	3.104	3.30
1935	3.085	3.29
1936	2.966	3.19
1937	3.030	3.23
1938	3.162	3.28
1939	3.166	3.31
1940	3.172	3.31
1941	3.828	2.99
1942	2.775	3.01
1943	2.685	2.98

Source: Livi Bacci and Santini 1969.

ages.[19] The fertility study gave results consistent with the census figures for natural family size (i.e. the latter rates are larger by about two – the parents). Again the highest regional rate was in Venetia, while the lowest was in Liguria (and Piedmont was not far ahead). Rates in general were higher in the south and the islands and lower in the north and the center. More married women had two children than any other number, but again this was not completed fertility. Data for women past the age of childbearing revealed signs of sustained fertility decline: those over 60 averaged 6 children; those between 50 and 59 averaged 4; and those 40–49 averaged only 3. Data on married fertility by profession of husband revealed the highest rates for agricultural families in all the large areas, then declining rates through the categories of industrial and other laborers, office workers, and professionals (ISTAT, *Censimento 1931*, vol. VI). The results of this fertility survey held no surprises. Still, they may have reinforced the gravity of the problem. They were published just before the March 1937 GCF meeting and so can be added to those other, admittedly grander, ingredients that explain the reinvigoration of Fascist demographic policy at that time.

As noted in chapter 4, anthropologists like Cipriani shared in the conviction that better demographic knowledge of Italy's subject peoples in Africa was needed, a conviction in keeping with the general belief that this sort of knowledge represented not simply a measure of colonial possession, but also a form of regimentation or control of the individuals counted. And Gini included the need to improve, or simply establish, colonial statistics among the initial tasks of ISTAT (ACS PCM 1940–3 b.2674 f.1.1.16.3.5.27000–6). Nonetheless, and in spite of the creation of an ISTAT commission for colonial statistics (presided by Livi), knowledge/power of this sort did not make great strides in Italian Africa. In addition to the problems of expense and the demo/geographical scale of the project, several other factors impeded the progress of colonial statistics.

A pre-Fascist census of the so-called metropolitan (= European) population of the Italian colonies had been carried out in 1921, though the first copy of the results was only received by Mussolini in December 1930 (ACS PCM 1940–3 b.2688 f.1.1.16.7.27000–28 sf.6). The more ambitious 1931 census included the counting of both the indigenous and European populations in Italian Africa, though minister of colonies De

[19] The national average (4.11) from the fertility survey, based on information taken from married women of all ages, is predictably higher than the average number of children per marriage for 1931, based on information taken from the (younger) group of women who actually gave birth in 1931, calculated by Livi Bacci and Santini (3.38, see table 5.3) (Livi Bacci and Santini 1969).

Bono initially suggested the indigenous census be postponed and then, once it had begun, objected that his ministry could not afford to carry it out. As a result it was almost canceled, but at Gini's urging Mussolini agreed that work should continue (ACS PCM 1940–3 b.2687 f.1.1.16.7.27000–28 sf.1; b.2688 f.1.1.16.7.27000–28 sf.6). Data gathering went on throughout 1931 and the results were published in 1935 (see table 3.12).

War in Ethiopia forced abandonment of plans for a 1936 census of Italian East Africa (AOI). In 1939 the Ministero dell'Africa italiana (Ministry of Italian Africa – MAI) did carry out a census there, but without the assistance or even knowledge of ISTAT.[20] The fact that the MAI was collecting and publishing its own statistics without so much as consulting ISTAT may indicate a degree of friction between the two government agencies and explain why only in 1940, in spite of repeated references in CSS discussions over the years, were negotiations between the two concluded for the creation of statistical offices in Libya and AOI.[21] In 1941 a census of the entire Italian Kingdom, Empire, and possessions (including Libya, AOI, Albania etc.) was planned, but never carried out, again because of the disruption of war.

In 1931 it was still early to assess the effectiveness of the Fascist population policy. Nonetheless, the census of that year, and attached fertility survey, did serve to measure the scale of the problem with regard to population age, family size, numbers of unmarried, percentage of the population engaged in agriculture (perhaps the best indication of the degree of ruralism), and the level of urbanization as revealed by place of birth. Subsequent comparison of the 1931 and 1936 censuses could be expected to yield more conclusive indications of policy effectiveness. The problems of the "rapid" census of 1936 will be discussed below.

The other major undertaking of the Gini period at ISTAT was the Rome Population Congress of September 1931.[22] In 1927, the American birth control crusader Margaret Sanger had organized a World Population Conference in Geneva. The conference was held in September (only months after the Ascension Day speech) and dealt with a wide range of population problems; it was attended by population

---

[20] When ISTAT president Savorgnan learned of the census, he asked Mussolini whether the MAI figure (10 million) should be used in the ISTAT bulletin, to which the latter replied affirmatively. The previous ISTAT estimate of indigenous AOI population had been 7.6 million (SPD-ord. b.1171 f.509.560/II sf.4).

[21] *Annali di statistica* 6, 33 (1934), pp. 39–41; 6, 35 (1936), pp. 2–3; 6, 38 (1937), p. 2; 7, 2 (1938), rel. pres.; 7, 4 (1939), p. 3; 7, 5 (1940), p. 22; 7, 7 (1943), p. 259.

[22] The congress was not organized directly by ISTAT, but by CISP (also presided by Gini); several ISTAT studies were presented there.

experts from many nations, including Gini.[23] In Italian journals, the 1927 conference was presented as a propagandistic ploy on the part of neo-Malthusian colonial powers who would have liked to see lower birth rates among non-colonialists like Italy. Adversaries of this position, and especially Catholic adversaries, claimed to have frustrated the attempt of Sanger and her ilk (Boldrini 1927, Rugiu 1933). In fact, Sanger was dismayed by the populationism of (in particular) the Italians and subsequently took no part in organizing the International Union for the Scientific Study of Population Problems (IUSSP) which grew out of the 1927 conference and was founded the following year. The inclusion of "scientific" in the title was an explicit effort to avoid political questions (like birth control). The original organization of this union (which still exists today) consisted of national committees. That for Italy was Gini's Comitato italiano per lo studio dei problemi della popolazione (Italian Committee for the Study of Population Problems – CISP). Plans for the creation of CISP date from at least February 1928; it was described as a direct response to the neo-Malthusian organization of the Geneva congress. CISP was to be supported by donations from both government and private agencies, including, for example, ISTAT (100,000 lire); as a result of a circular signed by Mussolini soliciting funds, the committee seems to have been well endowed (ACS PCM 1940–3 b.2674 f.1.1.16.3.5.27000–7 sff.1–2). The first IUSSP congress was scheduled for June 1931 in Rome. As a result of a disagreement among American organizers and concern over Gini's Fascist sympathies, it was moved to London. Gini and CISP withdrew in protest from the IUSSP, presumably over questions of demographic policy, and went ahead with plans for their own conference, soliciting and receiving many international contributions.[24] The Rome congress took place in September and may well have been more successful than the London conference of the previous June; the proceedings were published in ten volumes (Gini 1934c). Although Mussolini did not, as planned, address this gathering, he did edit Gini's opening speech, instructing the latter to remove a passage praising Malthus (ACS SPD-ord. b.1172 f.509.560/III sf.2).

Several months after the congress (in early 1932), Gini left ISTAT and returned to his academic pursuits, a move that has been described as a dismissal by Mussolini, the inevitable outcome of an encounter between

---

[23] On the 1927 conference and IUSSP history see IUSSP 1985.

[24] ACS PCM 1940–3 b.2674 f.1.1.16.3.5.27000–7 sf.3. An interesting parallel to the CISP/IUSSP split occurred with regard to the International Eugenics Federation from which the Italian representatives (headed by Gini) also withdrew in this period. An alternative Latin Federation of Eugenics Societies was created of which Gini was president (ACS PCM 1937–9 b.2515 f.14.3.654.1).

two "authoritarian personalities" (Leti 1989, p. 39). Contributing to their disagreement were both details of statistical procedure and the history of friction between ISTAT and the various ministries. Gini remained president of CISP, though the committee suffered a setback (also in 1932) as many contributors suspended or reduced their support (with the tacit approval of Mussolini), deeming CISP overfunded (ACS PCM 1940–3 b.2674 f.1.1.16.3.5.27000–7 sf.2). Later, in 1936, Gini founded (and chaired) the new faculty of statistical, demographic, and actuarial sciences at La Sapienza (University of Rome), and so held the most influential Italian academic position in the field of statistics and demography. He continued to represent Italy at international conferences.[25]

Gini also continued to object to Italian participation in the IUSSP and in 1935 attempted – via the Ministry of National Education on which CISP and its parent National Research Council depended – to block Livio Livi's assumption of the IUSSP vice presidency. Letters from the IUSSP secretary, stating that the union was apolitical and did not endorse neo-Malthusianism, and from Franco Savorgnan, who succeeded Gini as ISTAT president and attended the 1935 IUSSP meeting in Berlin, seem to have overridden these objections.

As mentioned in chapter 2, Livi had left ISTAT after arguing with Gini in 1928. Subsequently, he returned to his native Florence where he took a position at the university. On leaving ISTAT, Livi also left the CSS, which he rejoined in 1933; his letter to the head of government requesting reinstatement is dated 17 February 1932, three weeks after Gini submitted his resignation from both ISTAT and the CSS. Livi was also among the candidates to replace Gini as ISTAT president.[26]

Because of Gini's opposition, CISP ceased, from 1931, to represent Italy in the IUSSP. In 1937, contemporary with the Fascist Grand Council's resolution on population, a Comitato di consulenza per gli studi sulla popolazione (Advisory Committee for Population Study) was founded with Livi as president. This committee, which became the Società italiana di demografia e statistica (Italian Society of Demography and Statistics), was meant to both fill the role of CISP in the IUSSP and establish an intellectual common ground for demographers and statisticians. In still another institutional development, Guglielmo Tagliacarne had proposed the creation of an Italian statistics society in 1935, and Gini, with whom Tagliacarne carried on an intellectual dispute (see below), was among those who opposed it. It was created nonetheless in

---

[25] Scholars were required to receive government approval in order to attend these.
[26] ACS PCM 1940–3 b.2670 f.1.1.16.3.1.27000–3 sf.5; b.2672 f.1.1.16.3.2.27000–9; b.2678 f.1.1.16.4b.27000 sf.95.

1939, and Gini apparently relented as he accepted membership and became its second president (1941–5) (Leti 1989; Leti and Gastaldi 1989).

Savorgnan took over the ISTAT presidency in February 1932 and held that office until October 1943. A less combative personality than Gini, he seems to have been a better bureaucrat – if an inferior statistician – and the Savorgnan period was not marked by the continual conflict of Gini's. Nonetheless, it cannot be said that his tenure was uneventful. These years included completion of the 1931 census; the abbreviated 1936 census; cancellation of the 1941 census; cancellation of much statistical publication during League of Nations sanctions and the war in Ethiopia; the racist manifesto (of which Savorgnan was a signatory) and Jewish censuses; the establishment of official statistics in Italian East Africa, Albania, and territories occupied during the European war; and the fall of Fascism in July 1943.

A few months after Savorgnan took over ISTAT, Mussolini wrote asking how it was possible that provisional results of the German census of 16 June could already be published by 4 July, just nineteen days later. For the Italian census of April 1931 *il duce* may have seen the first results by August, but these had to be revised and, as mentioned above, were only published in April 1932, one year after the census. Savorgnan explained to Mussolini the German system of postcards forwarded from each province to the Central Statistics Office, and it may in part have been out of desire to emulate German efficiency that Mussolini determined to conduct an abbreviated and rapid census in 1936. At the end of 1933 he was already alerting prefects to verify that their population registers were in order in preparation for the 1936 census, and in March 1936 he wrote:

The next census will be characterized by a new and different organization of regional supervision and revision, as well as by a new and different central scheme of data processing which will notably shorten the overall process and speed up the availability of the results so as to give to this project the value of timeliness which in large part constitutes its reason for existence.[27]

Il duce insisted that the 1936 census form be *semplicissimo* and edited it himself, eliminating the questions on place of birth, education (not in 1931 census either), and fertility of married women.[28]

---

[27] ACS SPD-ord. b.1171 f.509.560/II sf.2, b.1172 f.509.560/III sf4.2; ISTAT, *Censimento 1936*, vol. I, p. 21.
[28] Archival files include two letters of Mussolini instructing that he be shown the forms before publication and a sample form accompanied by ISTAT memo. The colored-pencil editing of the form is that typical of Mussolini; the categories eliminated are essentially those suggested in the ISTAT memo (a memo in response to Mussolini's demand for simplicity?) (ACS SPD-ord. b.1172 f.509.560/III sf.4 sff.3–4.).

The shortened interval between censuses attests to the need felt for up-to-date statistics in the planned Fascist corporate economy. In the words of the statistician/demographer Felice Vinci:

In light of the general advent of controlled and regulated economies and of state and municipal monopolies, securities, and other financial activities, more frequent agricultural, industrial and commercial censuses, as well as constant studies of trade, prices, and salaries etc., have become necessary. Above all, however, we need complete, detailed, dependable, and up-to-date population measures. (Vinci 1936, p. 375)

Vinci praised generally the panopticon nature of Fascist statistics and in particular their extension to the Italian Empire (Vinci 1936; also Vinci 1939b, pp. 159–69).

As for 1931, the 1936 census was accompanied by considerable advertisement, including radio announcements, a commemorative postage stamp, two short films, and posters. The films, produced by the Istituto LUCE in spite of difficulties of funding (only resolved by Mussolini instructing ISTAT to pay), grew out of a proposal made by Livi in the CSS and furthered by the journal *Barometro Economico*, which sponsored a contest for the screenplays. This journal also designed the census posters.[29] In addition, the Ministry for Press and Propaganda distributed several pages of slogans to be used in census promotion, for example Mussolini's "The destiny of nations is tied to their demographic power," the anonymous "Like the North Star, population figures guide the helmsman who steers the ship toward the future," or "How many individuals will Italy find to devote their energies along the roads of Empire? The census of 21 April will tell us" (ISTAT, *Censimento 1936*, vol. I, part 1, pp. 213–16).

The census was again scheduled for 21 April (R.d.-l. 9 August 1935, n.1639) and the procedure was similar to that of 1931. It would be carried out by local authorities, and census inspectors were to be chosen by the prefects, though ISTAT was also given a vague directive to carry out inspections, using its own functionaries, both at the *comune* and provincial levels (R.d.-l. 9 August 1935, n.1639; R.d. 27 February 1936, n.374). Preparations (and the census itself) coincided with the war in Ethiopia (October 1935–May 1936), a situation which led the Ministry of the Interior (probably Undersecretary of State Buffarini Guidi) to propose postponement. This proposal was rejected by Mussolini (who was in fact the minister). Mobilization complicated the census, and a "special population" was used – a combination of present population

---

[29] *Barometro Economico* n. 77 (1935–6); ACS PCM 1940–3 b.2689 f.1.1.16.7.27000–55 sf.5, b.2693 f.1.1.16.8.27000–73.

plus population absent in AOI – for the calculation of various demographic rates.[30] In addition, the planned census of AOI had to be canceled and the colonial census restricted to Libya and Italy's other small possessions (ACS PCM 1940–3 b.2689 f.1.1.16.7.27000–55 sf.1; R.d.-l. 5 March 1936, n.478; Atti C. D.l. N.1175 (4 April 1936)). In reaction to war and the League of Nations sanctions, Mussolini also ordered the publication of many statistics to be canceled. These were, however, economic and financial statistics; demographic publications were unaffected. The census was carried out according to schedule and, according to Savorgnan, irregularities were limited to a few Sicilian provinces (as a result of which ten *podestà* were dismissed). ISTAT seems to have played a greater role on the local level in 1936 than in 1931, employing twenty-three principal inspectors (plus assistants) (R.d.-l 28 October 1935, n.1844; ACS PCM 1940–3 b.2692 f.1.1.16.8.27000–68 sf.1A, b.2689 f.1.1.16.7.27000–55 sf.8; ISTAT, *Censimento 1936*, vol. III, p. 5*).

The published census results subsequently claimed that provisional figures were telegrammed from the *comuni* to ISTAT (with Teutonic speed) on 5 May, presented to Mussolini on 9 May, and then distributed to the press. In fact, Mussolini's newspaper, *Il Popolo d'Italia*, reported the total present population of Italy as counted by the census on 22 May. Archival documents suggest that Savorgnan sent Mussolini the first provisional *comune* population totals on 3 July (a little more than two months after the census) and that *il duce* approved publication of these results that same month. ISTAT seems not to have published results prior to 24 July (ACS PCM 1940–3 b.2689 f.1.1.16.7.27000–55 sf.7; ACS SPD-ord. b.1171 f.509.560/II sf.3; ISTAT, *Censimento 1936*, vol. III, pp. 6*–7*).

The "special" population totaled 42,918,726 and comparison with the 1931 figure revealed an annual growth rate of 0.83%. Natural growth (derived from fertility and mortality rates) was highest in the Po Valley provinces (Treviso, Vicenza, Padua, Venice, Rovigo) and high fertility provinces were generally also net exporters of population (with the exceptions of Littoria and Taranto which had high levels of both fertility and internal immigration). The high internal-immigration provinces were in the northwest and centerwest (plus Cagliari) (ISTAT, *Censimento 1936*, vol. III, p. 19*).

The war of course made comparison of the 1931 and 1936 population totals difficult. In many cases, however, non-comparability was inher-

---

[30] Rochat and Massobrio cite an Italian military presence in Africa of 330,000 troops in May–June 1936 plus 100,000 workers. Enlistment in Italy increased the troop total to 1 million (Rochat and Massobrio 1978, p. 250).

ent in the 1936 census itself. To start with, the elimination of the question on place of birth prevented comparison of data which bore directly on demographic policy, insofar as these data revealed the scale of urbanization and general population mobility. Nonetheless, the 1936 census does reveal that *comuni* having populations over 100,000 had grown at twice the national rate since 1931.[31] In addition to the lack of place-of-birth data, the categories adopted for the 1936 census are often not comparable with those of 1931. The questions on occupation, for example, were changed, rendering comparison between the "active" agricultural population of 1931 (47.7%) and the "productive" agricultural population of 1936 (48.7%) meaningless (ISTAT, *Censimento 1931*, vol. IV, pp. *114–*115; *1936*, vol. IV, p. 11). The 1936 census does give figures on average family size (4.3), but this is the resident census family (household members whose residence is registered at that address on the census date) and so comparable with neither the natural family (relatives) nor the census family (household members present on the census date) of 1931 (ISTAT, *Censimento 1936*, vol. III, p. 40*).

The 1936 census reveals an increase in average age, and, except in the south, the rectangular based age pyramids (similar numbers of people in each one-year age group for the younger ages in spite of mortality) are characteristic of populations with a history of fertility decline. After almost ten years of pronatalism, the 0–5 and 5–10 year old layers of the pyramid showed no response to the policy.[32] The percentage of population unmarried remained high relative to other European countries, but had decreased slightly from 1931 to 1936 (from 36.8 to 35.6% of those over 15). This population, however, had aged and so was more likely to be married (ISTAT, *Censimento 1936*, vol. III, pp. 90*–95*).

Responding to the directive of *il duce*, the 1936 census was less complete and more rapid than that of 1931. The fact of the general non-comparability of the two censuses may in part be explained by the change in ISTAT president and a different conception of what information the census could most usefully provide. It may also be attributable to an official desire not to advertise the processes of urbanization, industrialization, and fertility decline taking place in Italy. Generally, Mussolini was inclined to emphasize the gravity of the demographic situation, as he would again in relaunching the demographic campaign in March 1937 (about the time when the census volumes began to

---

[31] ISTAT, *Censimento 1936*, vol. III, p. 29*. For subsequent study of 1931–6 urbanization, see Vacchini 1941, pp. 35–7.
[32] ISTAT, *Censimento 1936* vol. III, pp. 74*–83*, Appendix table 2. The width of the 0–1 layer relative to those above it in the latter reveals not an increase in births, but the fact that infant mortality remained fairly high.

appear). Still, it seems that in this case he was less willing to do so, as it demonstrated the inefficacy of the regime's pronatalist and anti-urban measures.

In addition to taking a personal interest in the census, *il duce* made frequent use of ISTAT throughout the *ventennio*. As mentioned in chapter 2, for example, he regularly reviewed ISTAT publications, especially the monthly statistical bulletin, right through to his final months in power. In December 1932, he attended the first CSS meeting over which Savorgnan presided. Mussolini himself reviewed and approved the new president's address and at the meeting reaffirmed his support for the institute, called for the further popularization of statistics, and predictably bemoaned the low levels of Italian fertility.[33]

Throughout the Savorgnan period, Mussolini regularly called on ISTAT to provide him with statistical data. These data were almost exclusively demographic and the requests were at times revealing. *Il duce* repeatedly required lists of population or fertility rates for provinces and provincial capitals in descending order (and so headed by Littoria). In 1937, contemporary with the renewed demographic policy, he called for information on Italian age structure, fertility, suicides, occupation, ruralism, and agricultural population. Frequently he asked for information on other nations as well: Germany and Yugoslavia in 1934, Germany and Turkey in 1935, France, Germany and England in 1936. In January 1938, as international tension increased and it became ever more evident that Italy would eventually have to side either with Germany or Britain, Mussolini requested data on British age structure, suicides, madness, idiocy and divorces, apparently an attempt to assess the level of decadence to which that society had descended. In this same period, of course, Germany was experiencing a renewal of nuptiality and fertility (and quietly eliminating the mad and mentally ill), and ISTAT reported to Mussolini on the results of the German population policy as well (ACS SPD-ord. b.1171 f.509.560/II). In 1939 he called for information on recent Italian migration abroad and also on "mixed" marriages in Alto Adige (between German-speakers and Italian-speakers) in the context of the planned emigration of ethnic Germans (see chapter 3, pp. 138–9 above); the latter data, however, were not available. In January of 1940 he requested fertility, mortality, and nuptiality data on his soon-to-be ally, the German Reich (including Austria), and in December of that same year figures for the population over sixty of Italy, France – already defeated, an event linked to its history of fertility decline and resulting aged population – and Great

---

[33] *Annali di statistica* 6, 33 (1934), pp. 4–7; ACS SPD-ord. b.1171 f.509.560/II sf.2.

Britain (Atti C. D.l. N.1279-A, p.12; ACS SPD-ord. b.1171 f.509.560/II sff.2–4; b.1172 f.509.560/IV).

As all other state agencies, ISTAT went through the processes of Fascistization and racial "purification". Employees were instructed to wear black shirts and Fascist uniforms on special occasions, and checks were made to determine the level of PNF membership, eventually obligatory, among the staff. The racist laws led to the elimination of all Jews from the staff by January 1939.[34] A problem which must have been shared by many other state agencies caused Savorgnan to complain to the PCM in 1938 that personnel expenses were becoming more difficult to meet due to family growth (and so wage increases) among the ISTAT staff (ACS PCM 1940–3 b.2671 f.1.1.16.3.1.27000–3 sf.10).

The greatest changes at ISTAT came about as a result of World War II. Although Italy would not intervene until June 1940, Mussolini ordered suspension of the publication of all but demographic statistics on 3 September 1939, the same day that France and Great Britain declared war on Germany (and the day after Italy declared its neutrality) (ACS SPD-ord. b.1171 f.509.560/II sf.4). In addition to most of the monthly statistical bulletin, the 1941 census was also a war-related casualty. It had been scheduled for 31 December, as the Roman birthday used in 1931 and 1936 had proved to be a poor choice (L. 5 January 1939, n.61). Had it been taken, the 1941 census presumably would have served – as claimed in the *Camera* – to "ascertain and make known the way in which Mussolini's historic demographic battle . . . is rapidly leading to a stunning victory, affirming the ever greater numeric power of the Italian people" (Atti C. D.l. N.2623-A [10 December 1938]). In addition to the population of the Italian peninsula, that of Libya, the Empire, the Aegean possessions, and Albania were to be included (ACS SPD-ord. b.1172 f.509.560/IV sf.3). Italy had "conquered" Albania without resistance in April 1939 and incorporated it into the Kingdom. By September, ISTAT had sent a mission there to create population registers in preparation for this census,[35] and in 1940 an Albanian demographic and census office was created.[36] However, in mid-February 1941, days after the British had taken Cyrenaica, the PCM communicated to Savorgnan that the entire census would be postponed (ACS PCM b.2690 f.1.1.16.7.27000-108; L. 4 July 1941, n.786).

The planned demographic annexation of Albania resembled other examples discussed above in which political occupation was consoli-

---

[34] In November 1938 Savorgnan received a note from the PNF alerting him to the fact that four Jews were still employed by ISTAT (ACS SPD-ord. b.1171 f.509.560/II sf.4; b.1172 f.509.560/III sf.3).   [35] *Annali di statistica* 7, 5 (1940), p. 19.
[36] *Annali di statistica* 7, 7 (1943), p. 259.

dated by the cataloging of population data; this process accompanied Italian unification, the creation of Italian colonies and empire, and Italy's post World War I expansion. It would be repeated for the territories occupied during World War II. Subsequent to the Italian debacle in Greece, Italy did successfully occupy Western Yugoslavia. In May 1941, a new province of Lubiana (Ljubljana) was created, Fiume (Rijeka) province was expanded, and a Governatorato della Dalmazia (essentially all the territory from Fiume to Albania) was created.[37] In early May (the day after it had been made a province), Mussolini instructed Savorgnan to include Lubiana in the next statistical bulletin, to which the ISTAT president responded that it was impossible to calculate the population of the new provinces (ACS SPD-ord. b.1172 f.509.506/IV sf.1), though data from a 1931 census of the area were published in the 1 August 1941 *Demographic Bulletin*. Later in May, Mussolini ordered that a census of Lubiana and the new part of Fiume be conducted and this was done on 31 July. Just as under Crispi, the organization and collection of demographic statistics that were of special official interest were accomplished quickly at a time when the national census was on hold.[38] By March 1942 population registers were apparently functioning in all of the ex-Yugoslav territory (ACS PCM 1940–3 b.2690 f.1.1.16.7.27000–108; ISTAT AC cassetta 21 [1942]). The Fascist regime had always demonstrated great conviction in the ability to manage population. In these examples, they displayed the associated (and widespread) belief that a first step of societal organization and control was to know population quantitatively.

During the war, statistical services were partially reorganized. Nonessential statistical gathering (i.e. non-essential to the war effort) was to be eliminated, and a special commission including a representative of the armed forces was created within ISTAT to determine which these might be. In addition, a special statistical office was created for each branch of the military (R.d.-l. 1 November 1941, n.1481). Many members of the ISTAT staff were of course called to arms (32% by December 1942) and temporary employees, mostly female, were hired to replace them (ACS PCM 1940–3 b.2672 f.1.1.16.3.2.27000–9).

ISTAT continued its publication schedule, albeit reduced, until August 1943. Most subsequent statistical data would only appear after the war. Savorgnan remained ISTAT president after the fall of Fascism,

---

[37] This Governatorato consisted of the provinces of Zara (Zadar), Spalato (Split) and Cattaro (Kotor); the city of Zara had been part of Italy since 1920 (R.d.-l. 3 May 1941, n.291; R.d.-l. 18 May 1941, n.452; R.d. 7 June 1941, n.453).

[38] Crispi canceled the 1881 national census, but carried out a colonial one (see chapter 1, p. 39 above).

even making reference – in a memo penned in the brief period between Mussolini's July arrest and the Nazi occupation of Rome in September – to "these days in which Italy has regained her liberty," a little hollow-sounding given the source. This memo made its way eventually to the German embassy (and then to an RSI file on Savorgnan's behavior), perhaps causing him some difficulty (ISTAT AC ordini di servizio n. 28 [28 August 1943]; ACS RSI PCM b.125 f.219). On 12 October, after Badoglio had signed an armistice with the Americans and fled Rome, leaving it to the Germans, and after the creation of the Repubblica sociale italiana (the Mussolini puppet government headquartered in Salò – RSI), Savorgnan resigned, remarking on the transfer of the Institute and the appointment of a new *commissario* and expressing his gratitude to *il duce* (ACS PCM 1940–3 b.2678 f.1.1.16.4b.27000 sf.16).

Following a December 1943 decree, ISTAT became the Istituto nazionale di statistica (National Statistics Institute – INS) and was transferred to Venice.[39] Its *commissario* was Giuseppe Adami who had been the General Director of personnel for ISTAT (ACS PCM 1940–3 b.2669 f.1.1.16.1.8.27000–15 I/I). What information there is on the INS suggests that it published a statistical handbook and yearbook for 1943, took over collection of war statistics from the ministry, relayed statistics requested by the German *Reich*, and kept a special population registry for Italian workers going to Germany. With regard to the latter, Adami was at least planning a trip to Germany in early 1945 (ACS PCM 1940–3 b.2675 f.1.1.16.3.8, b.2694 f.1.1.16.8.27000 sff.149–149bis; RSI PCM b.83 f.XI.P.2238). In January 1944, the German authorities ordered a census of all male workers (of all categories) aged 16–60 in the *Governatorato* of Rome and *il duce* decreed that all males in this age group were obliged to engage in some form of manual or intellectual work. This census was carried out by Alberto Molinari, General Director of ISTAT since Gini's tenure, who had apparently remained in Rome (ACS PCM 1940–3 b.2690 f.1.1.16.7.27000–152). In 1944 the institute was again moved, this time to Menaggio (on Lake Como), and by early 1945 Adami had organized about half of the male employees into a *brigata nera* combat unit (ACS RSI PCM b.32 f.1.1.16.4A.27000–63). The last references I have found to the INS date from April 1945, the month in which the Nazis were defeated.

Rome was liberated in June 1944. Evidence of a reinstalled ISTAT, under Molinari, dates from August of that year (and so for a time ISTAT

---

[39] The loss of much of ISTAT's archival material may be attributable to this and subsequent moves, though some of the lost material seems unfortunately to have been discarded in the post-war period. Showing perhaps a lack of historical sensitivity, ISTAT has recently changed its name again to the Istituto Nazionale di Statistica.

and the *Repubblica sociale*'s INS coexisted). On 22 August, Molinari issued a circular to the Mayors (*sindaci*, the Fascist title of *podestà* having been dropped) of all the liberated *comuni* in which he announced:

an exceptionally important task with regard to our national resurgence ... (and) for the reconstruction of our country devastated by twenty years of Fascist rule and by war ... In order to proceed concretely with national reconstruction, we must ascertain first of all the state of things in the various sectors of our national life, because in order to "act" we must "know". First of all we must consider the demographic sector.

Specifically he referred to a planned census of the liberated zones that was executed the following month.[40]

The few details given above regarding the INS and this first act of the revived ISTAT point out the remarkable degree to which a statistical institute is considered an indispensable tool of government even in the most desperate situations, and the fact that, at least until 1944, the most important task of such an institute was – employing Molinari's causality – to know population in order that the government might act.

Fascist demographic policy and general pronatalism exerted considerable influence over official statistics gathering in interwar Italy both with regard to the sort of data gathered and the nature of its dissemination. The significantly improved status and funding of statistical work owed much to official interest in the demographic problem, and this was a two-way relationship: Italian statistics were reinvigorated because of official interest in the data it could provide and these data in turn informed policy and provided the means for its evaluation.

Specific policy interests were revealed by the ISTAT studies of large families and marital fertility. The desire to vaunt Italy's role as a leader in demographic policy and study showed itself in the 1931 population congress, while Fascist concern to keep the Italian demographic problem, the "problem of problems," in the forefront of national consciousness was expressed in the incessant publication of demographic figures in newspapers, magazines, and journals, as well as in the propaganda accompanying population censuses. The hasty 1936 census and its significant omissions suggested a contrary desire to *not* publicize the scope of Italian failure in the fight against urbanization. Statistics gathering accompanied Fascist programs of internal colonization, colonization in Africa, expansion into Albania, and eventually wartime conquests in Yugoslavia.

Official statistics generally aim to further official policy, for statistics

---

[40] ISTAT AC cassetta 21 (circ. n. 3–1944). See Commissione alleata e PCM–ISTAT 1945.

are a tool which the state uses both to know itself and to make itself known. It is an especially important tool for a regime pursuing a corporativist economy and attempting to control the demographic behavior of its subject population. The activities and publications of the statistics institute in this context are then particularly revealing of policy considerations. Just as Liberal statistics reflected Liberal demographic concerns (especially emigration) so did Fascist statistics reflect Fascist concerns (especially fertility), but with the added magnification provided by greater funding and greater scrutiny. And, again as in the Liberal period, the work of population theorists centered on those questions of greatest political relevance, yet while population theorists in the earlier period voiced opinions of all sorts – pro and anti emigration, Malthusian, populationist, etc. – those concerning themselves with similar questions in the Fascist period predictably restricted their comments to a rather narrow and politically acceptable range.

Population theory

From time to time certain scientists advance claims regarding the objective or value-free nature of their disciplines, presenting them as somehow immune from political and ideological contamination. It is not surprising then to read the following statement about demography in the Fascist period:

Modern statisticians and demographers, generally unbiased by theoretical or abstract prejudices . . . have pursued fruitful lines of research and conducted similarly worthwhile surveys which have demonstrated the importance of demographic phenomena to the nation and so have alerted policy makers to both the economic and political importance of population. (Marsigli 1933, p. 996)

This author's statement reveals the important place that demography had achieved in Fascist policy-making. It is also part of an ongoing attempt to further enhance the legitimization of demography and carve out for it an ever larger sphere of competence. Demography is special among the social sciences in its objectiveness, its freedom from "theoretical and abstract prejudices" which – we can imagine – might infect sociology or psychology. Demography gathers the quantifiable facts of population and treats them statistically, and in this it better resembles the standard of positivistic knowledge, namely the physical or natural sciences. Demography then could be counted on to provide reliable information for the enunciation of an important area of Fascist policy.

Furthermore, the author suggests that this relationship was unidirectional. Demographers and statisticians reveal the truth about population to policy-makers, but there is no hint that this truth might in turn be informed by political considerations. I have found just the reverse, namely that the choices made by demographers in the Fascist period were significantly conditioned by political considerations. For although demographers were not directly involved in drafting policy measures, their research and interpretation of demographic data were often tailored to the policy process and so reflected the influence of dominant political and ideological positions. Fascist demography – if we can call it that – was not unique in this respect, for the sort of science that is pursued is frequently a product of the sociopolitical context in which it is enunciated.[41]

The most pressing demographic problem of the interwar period was to explain the precipitous decline of fertility in Europe, and in the populationist atmosphere of Fascist Italy this problem took on special significance. In 1927, for example, shortly after Mussolini's Ascension Day speech, Corrado Gini wrote: "Lower fertility is one of the most characteristic and important aspects of the demography of the white race . . . and the explanation of its causes certainly represents the number one problem of population science today" (Gini 1927c, p. 55). The status of the fertility decline as the greatest demographic problem was based on its identification as a serious threat to society. For while Malthusian views survived – especially in England – Italian condemnation of denatalism in the interwar period was essentially unanimous. The attendant problems included a general decline of the white race (as suggested by Spengler and Korherr); a reduction of national military, economic, and political power; and disintegration of the family and family values.

Fertility was of course not the only population issue of the period, though it did tend to submerge all others, emigration for example. Furthermore, the fertility debate is the key to other aspects of population theory in the period as well. These included a distinctly Italian theory of the evolution of population, Italian reactions to optimum population theory and eugenics, and general views on population growth and economic development. As the most politically charged population question, the fertility debate also reveals much about the interaction between demography and policy, the way in which official positions and expectations influenced scientific study. In this final section I shall look at Gini's unique explanation of fertility decline by means of his cyclical theory of population; alternative explanations

---

[41] On value-free science (social and otherwise), see Proctor 1991; on science in its social context, see also Barnes and Shapin 1979.

offered by other demographers, economists, sociologists and occasional clerics or physicians; and the politically relevant discussions by some of these same players regarding other population issues.

Scientific populationism

The Italian population debate was carried out primarily in the economics journals of the period. These included Gini's *Metron* and *Genus*[42] edited in Rome, Livi's *Economia* in Florence, Mortara's *Giornale degli economisti* in Milan, and the *Rivista italiana di statistica* (which became the *Rivista italiana di scienze economiche*) published by Felice Vinci, professor of statistics at the University of Bologna. Each of these journals reflected the point of view of its editor and so a different opinion on the question of the determinants of fertility and its decline.

Gini, Livi, and Mortara were the most important Italian demographer/economist/statisticians of the interwar period. The demographic work of Mortara, a Jew who emigrated to Brazil after the racist laws of 1938, was the most insightful and modern.[43] Livi's work, too, generally stands the test of time and his demographic treatise can be read with profit today.[44] Gini is rightly remembered for his important contributions to statistics; his demographic work, on the other hand, largely based on a commitment to outdated evolutionary theory and compromised by its attachment to Nationalist ideology, is generally ignored. For these very reasons he is the most interesting figure for the present study.

Other significant voices in the population debate included several journals dealing with the social sciences in general, and in particular two publications of the Catholic University of the Sacred Heart in Milan edited by its rector, the pro-Fascist Father Agostino Gemelli.[45] Economists, demographers, physicians, and others also published monographs on relevant topics, and the period also saw several important collections which considered the population problem, as well as the published proceedings of population conferences and a number of pedagogical treatises.

[42] *Genus* was the first Italian journal dedicated exclusively to population questions.
[43] See, for example, the series of articles appearing in the *Giornale degli economisti* following publication of the 1931 census results and also Mortara's contribution to the 1931 Population Congress (Mortara 1934c). For a harsher judgement of Mortara, see Lanaro 1979, pp. 51–6.
[44] Livi 1974 (1941); in particular, his emphasis on the biological bases of demographic (and social) behavior might well be incorporated into present-day curricula and so counterbalance the occasionally misleading presentation of demographic events as mathematical phenomena.
[45] These were *Vita e pensiero* and the *Rivista internazionale di scienze sociali e discipline ausiliarie*. The latter was founded by Leo XIII. For the link between Gemelli's Catholic University and Fascism, see Gemelli 1937b and Webster 1960, pp. 153–61.

Already in the pre-World War I period, both Mortara and Gini had identified the impending threat of a falling birth rate. In 1911, Gini predicted that Italy would not be immune from fertility decline, and, considering the history of French fertility, he suggested a causal link between demographic decadence and economic stagnation (Gini 1912, pp. 83, 93). In that same year, Mortara wrote that fertility decline of the sort affecting France and Germany, generally the result of voluntary limitation for economic motives, was making headway in Italy as well. It was an evil immune to legislation and requiring a national raising of consciousness, a mission that he suggested should appear loftier to any sincere Nationalist than the encouragement of hatred between peoples (Mortara 1911).

Indeed it was the Nationalists, like Gini, who were most concerned, and isolated comments like the above multiplied in the interwar period becoming a torrent of demographic alarmism. On a national level, so went the general argument, fertility decline, because it led to population aging (a population with a higher average age) and eventually reduction, posed a threat to military, productive and political strength. If each individual is a potential worker/producer, then a declining working-age population translates into reduced national production and wealth. Militarily, population equals soldiers; World War I had made ample use of human cannon fodder and the comments of Mussolini and others attest to a general belief that population size would be a decisive factor in future wars. The combination of reduced military and economic strength would in turn lower a nation's international standing and impair its potential for imperial expansion. This standard Nationalist position was incorporated into Fascist ideology in the early years of the regime, as revealed in the development of Mussolini's populationism described above (see chapter 2, pp. 65–8 above).[46]

There existed another, subtler, economic argument regarding the negative economic effects of population decline put forward at the time which attracted a degree of international attention including that of the noted economist John Maynard Keynes (Keynes 1937). While some economists argued then (as now) that population growth led to increased unemployment, this argument was generally rejected by Italian authors, who emphasized instead the role increased population density played in stimulating innovation and increasing

---

[46] The advantages to the state of a larger population were so well and generally accepted as to hardly require citation, but see Gini 1930b, pp. 21–42; 1931, pp. 27–62; Curcio 1934; Grossi 1935; Lojacono 1934a; Marconcini 1935.

production.[47] Thus the unemployment crisis of the 1930s was due in part to fertility decline and so declining consumption. In the 1934 collection *Population and Fascism*, Guglielmo Tagliacarne, professor of statistics at the University of Milan, cited the Swiss economist L. Hersch on this "structural unemployment" or unemployment due to changes in population age structure and so the ratio between net producers and net consumers.[48]

Once the threat of population decline had been targeted as a trend to be combated, there followed the problem of identifying its immediate and underlying causes. Fewer births might be the result of changes in nuptiality, age structure, or fertility (the number of babies each woman bears). Evaluation of these immediate causes required accurate measures of fertility, and increased international concern over fertility decline in the interwar years led to the development of new and more sophisticated measures which required more and better data. Calculation of these measures (for example, the net reproduction rate) using the improved data gathered by ISTAT made it only more clear that the declining Italian birth rate was the result of women having on average fewer babies (Del Chiaro 1940; Marconcini 1935, pp. 184–90; Mortara 1935; Vinci 1939b, pp. 27–32).

This fact established, the possible causes of reduced procreation included a reduction in fecundity (a population's ability to procreate), an increase in diseases affecting conception and childbearing, or an increase in the voluntary limitation of fertility.[49] Most assumed that birth control was the dominant factor, though the most original Italian population theory of the interwar period, Gini's cyclical theory, depended on a perceived fecundity decline. Finally, the underlying causes of this change in procreational behavior were sought: moral or spiritual reasons, socio-economic ones, or, as explained below, the result of a racial biological change.

---

[47] Giovanni Fasolis countered the negative view of population growth put forward by the German economist Kuczynski and cited Gini's observation of the lack of correlation between population density and unemployment levels (Fasolis 1932); Giuseppe Tagliacarne rejected similar arguments made by the American geneticist E. M. East (Tagliacarne 1934a).

[48] Tagliacarne 1934a. Others who considered Hersch's views included Livi and Vinci, who, however, generally considered the link between unemployment and fertility decline to be exaggerated; see Livi 1933b; 1936b; Vinci 1939b, pp. 147–57; as well as Somogyi 1933b; Somogyi 1935 (reviewed in *Economia* (April 1935)).

[49] Less frequent *coitus* is also a possibility, though it received little or no discussion in the literature.

The cyclical theory of population

Gini first presented his cyclical theory in 1911 and continued to champion it through the early 1940s; after World War II he never again published on the subject.[50] It was a theory tied to certain ideological and political positions, and when these fell from favor he ceased propounding the theory. Its 1911 presentation took place at a conference held in the northern Adriatic port city of Trieste. Trieste, inhabited primarily by Italian speakers, was then still a part of the Austro-Hungarian Empire, and in what was a highly charged atmosphere of interethnic tension between Italians and Slavs, Gini asked how one might explain the evolution of peoples such that a wealthier, more intelligent race with a glorious past should be unable to expand in the face of an intellectually and economically inferior one. This was a question which, according to Gini, passionately interested both the Italians of Trieste and those like himself who lived in united Italy. Gini's theory provided a possible answer as he hypothesized that the evolution of different peoples depended fundamentally on their differing reproductive power, and the high fertility of Slavs was well known. Gini succeeded then in casting the "Slavic threat" in biological as well as political terms (Gini 1912). The passion he referred to related to the sentiments of Italian Nationalists who wanted to see Trieste and other "Italian" regions united to the kingdom. Gini himself moved in Nationalist circles and was from a town in Venetia (Motta di Livenza) not far from the Austro-Hungarian border. Clearly he was especially sensitive to irredentist sentiments in this region.

The basic tenets of Gini's cyclical theory were set out in this pre-war presentation, but the theory only received its mature enunciation nearly two decades later in lecture series presented in Brazil in 1927 and at the University of Chicago in 1929. The Chicago lectures were published in both Italian and English, and the Italian title, *The Birth, Evolution, and Death of Nations,* dramatically describes the parabolic path all "nations" followed according to Gini's theory.[51]

Gini used nation in the sense of a reproductive unit, interchangeable with race or population: "By 'nation' I mean a group of people that has its own individuality, not only politically and culturally, but also biologically" (Gini 1930b, p. 17). The biological aspect was crucial and, according to Gini, distinguished his theory from others, including that of Malthus, which only considered environmental or external factors. In

---

[50] See Gini bibliography in Castellano 1965.
[51] The English version, "The Cyclical Theory of Population," appeared in a volume entitled *Population* (Gini et al. 1930).

contrast to Malthus, Gini also posited differences in the internal factors or reproductive capacities of different peoples. Barring outside influences, a population would follow the parabolic path of birth, evolution, and death dictated by its internal factors. During the declining phase, external factors might, however, intercede, revitalizing the population and engendering a new cycle (Gini 1930b).

In one instance, which makes an interesting comparison with his 1911 comments, Gini suggested that the relatively high (for Italy) fertility of Venetia was due to the fact that the population there incorporated a notable mixing of Slavic blood. The "unredeemed" parts of Venetia, and other regions as well, had been transferred to Italy from defeated Austria-Hungary following World War I, and so the Slavic threat there instead came to constitute an element of racial reinvigoration for the now also politically Italian population. In a curious twist, Gini was attacked for these observations and accused of anti-Fascism.[52]

A central role was played in Gini's theory by the differential birth rate, namely the fact that a disproportionately large percentage of each generation descended from a smaller percentage of the previous one, and that this smaller percentage was generally from the lower social classes. Differential fertility was a hot topic in the interwar period, particularly among Anglo-American eugenicists.[53] Taking for granted that ability and intelligence were both hereditary and positively correlated with social class, the British eugenicist Francis Galton and his followers saw the combination of low fertility among the wealthy and more gifted classes and higher fertility among the poor and inferior as a serious menace to racial fitness.[54] Gini and other Italian intellectuals addressed the issue as well, but their general conclusion was that differential fertility did not cause population to suffer from either a psychological or physiological point of view.[55]

Gini viewed differential fertility instead as a natural aspect of what he called "demographic exchange." As a result of this exchange, the upper classes, unable to reproduce themselves, were replenished by a demographic "upward current" flowing from the more prolific lower classes. Gini's ideas on this subject resembled those of Vilfredo Pareto on population circulation and the circulation of elites, and Pareto's work

---

[52] See also Gini 1931, p. 252, and Gini's defence by the Senator Paolo Fortunati in Fortunati 1932.

[53] At the 1931 population conference in London, an entire session (out of five total) was devoted to differential fertility (Pitt-Rivers 1932, pp. 87–141). For another Italian treatment, see Boldrini 1931b; 1939b.

[54] On Galton and the history of eugenics in England and America, see Kevles 1986; Soloway 1990.

[55] See, for example Boldrini 1939b; Gini 1927a; 1927e; Livi 1927b; Uggè 1939.

may have provided Gini with an initial inspiration. Pareto, who died in 1923, was influential among Italian economists and sociologists during the first half of the twentieth-century, and Gini certainly read him while a university student.[56]

According to Gini, the parabolic evolution of a "nation" parallels that of an individual and passes through the stages of youth, maturity, and old age. In the first stage, the upper classes are still sufficiently virile to reproduce themselves, and the excess from the lower classes is siphoned off by emigration and war; this is the period of national expansion. At maturity, the upper classes have become less prolific and so are drawing on the "upward current" to replace themselves. The lower classes meanwhile have lost their most prolific elements. Finally, in the period of demographic decadence, the upward current intensifies but becomes insufficient as the reproductive capacity of all sectors of the nation declines. Barring outside intervention, the population will die a natural death.

Gini went on to claim that the military, economic, political and scientific fortunes of a nation follow its biological evolution. Not only for organic reasons, but also because a growing population is younger and so brings a "daring spirit" to social organization: "Thus a secret harmony is revealed to us between the numerical development, the intellectual development, the physical characteristics and the age composition of populations; initiative is also tied to favorable demographic conditions which help to favor its success" (Gini 1930b, p. 29). Within this framework, Gini pointed out that the white races, particularly in northern and western Europe, were declining, and this situation had led to demographic imbalance in Europe (especially between the northwest and east) and increasing migration. A more distant problem was that of the equilibrium between the European and non-European races.

While an aging nation can conceivably die, this rarely happens as it is normally infiltrated by individuals coming from an expanding nation that is still in its youthful stage. Political barriers may for a time resist this demographic pressure but eventually, through war and migration, the barrier will be crossed and the younger population will merge with and eventually replace the older. An alternative to foreign intervention

[56] Lyttelton 1973, p. 373 describes Gini as a student of Pareto. Mussolini had admired and been familiar with Pareto's work since his Socialist days as an exile in Switzerland and Gini's intellectual link to *il duce*'s former professor may have contributed to the official favor in which Gini was held. For Pareto on circulation of elites, see Pareto 1971, pp. 281–319; Gini cites Pareto repeatedly in Gini 1912, though not with regard to demographic exchange.

is domestic racial mixing. Unlike dogmatic racists, Gini rejected the suggestion that all racial hybrids are necessarily biologically inferior and less fecund than the racially pure. Instead, they simply display more biological variation, variation upon which natural selection might act. Occasionally, racial crossings will produce a superior population. Among those examples where favorable miscegenation was taking place were Japan (where the caste system had been abolished), Spain, and post-unification Italy.[57] Indeed, Italian unification (and so the mixing of regional populations) had created a general sense of rebirth that "is not only demographic, but political, cultural, economic and military" (Gini 1912, p. 87). According to Gini, Italian racial mixing suggested a biological foundation for the belief that a renewed Italy was entering a great and glorious new historical period (Gini 1931, p. 323).

By the time of the 1929 Chicago lectures,[58] Gini had worked out the analogy between society and the individual organism on which his theory was based in some detail. According to the doctrine he called "neo-organicism" and which entailed the search for the biological laws of society, nations were in fact organisms and obeyed the "fundamental biogenetic law" according to which ontogeny recapitulates phylogeny (Gini 1927d).

The recapitulation theory to which Gini referred had generally been applied to embryos and stated that embryonic development revealed the previous stages of the evolution of the species. It had been introduced in the early nineteenth century and then revived in the latter half of the century by Ernst Häckel who used, like Gini, the term "biogenetic law" (Bowler 1989, pp. 127, 202). Recapitulation theory was later advocated by the noted American paleontologist and zoologist (and neo-Lamarckian) Adolph Hyatt who expanded beyond embryonic development, positing the individual life cycle as the best model for evolution and racial senility as its final phase. Under the rubric of orthogenesis, related ideas regarding internally directed, non-adaptive evolution leading eventually to racial or species decadence (and extinction) were pursued by various American and European scholars, in particular the Germans Carl Nägeli and Theodor Eimer, in the decades leading up to and after the turn of the century (Bowler 1989, pp. 263–4,

---

[57] One of Gini's disciples went so far as to identify Tuscany as the locus of ideal racial mixing. See Olivieri 1934. Also on internal racial mixing see Casanova 1940 and Nannini 1938.

[58] In addition to being invited to lecture at the University of Chicago, Gini also held an honorary degree from Harvard, both measures of the international esteem in which he was held.

268–70). The period when these ideas were current corresponded with Gini's intellectual formation and the ideas of orthogenetic evolution and racial senility bear obvious parallels to his cyclical theory.

Another parallel, rejected however by Gini's colleague Savorgnan (Savorgnan 1935, pp. 120-1), was with the theory of the British sociologist Herbert Spencer whose work was influential in Italy (see chapter 1, p. 43). While Spencer explained the decline of Western European fertility in terms of an inverse correlation between fecundity and "civilization" (and so mental exertion), Gini considered fecundity decline to be a more normal stage of the evolution of races, and so it might be detected among primitive peoples as well as those of Europe. Both theories, however, attributed lower fertility to an evolutionary decline of what Gini called "genetic instinct" or fecundity, namely the physiological capacity to bear children.

Gini explicitly discussed his general ideas on evolution in the 1931 *Scientific Basis of Population Theory* (Gini 1931). While admitting some role for environmental factors in evolution (a qualified Lamarckism), he emphasized the role of internal factors and an orthogenetic evolution that basically followed the same sort of parabolic path he used in the cyclical theory. Gini cited Nägeli, Eimer and also the Italian zoologist Daniele Rosa whose *"ologenesi"* was a variation on orthogenesis (and relied on Nägeli). Rosa had first published his theory in 1909, just as Gini was finishing his degree at Bologna, a degree which included courses in biology. Clearly, the anti-Darwinian climate of the period had an important influence on Gini and informed the population theory he would propound for the next thirty-five years.[59]

Also central to Gini's theory was the analogy between human societies and living organisms. In his *Neo-organicismo* he sought to revive and revise earlier organicist doctrines which had been generally rejected. Eschewing literal parallels between human and social organs, he concentrates instead on the definition of an organism as a system normally in static equilibrium and generally able to reestablish this equilibrium when it is upset. From this observation, Gini derives several of the fundamental aspects of his cyclical theory according to which populations indeed follow the individual life cycle. Gini also draws political conclusions from his neo-organicism, as it helps to explain why long-term national interests – those of the body as a whole – should take precedence over the immediate interests of its parts (even

---

[59] Gini 1931, pp. 101–48. For *ologenesi* see Rosa 1909; Rosa 1931. Ideas nearly identical to those of Gini were expressed by the Italian anthropologist Giulio Rugiu in a volume edited by Gini; see Rugiu 1933, p. 16.

the majority of citizens). Finally, Gini notes that as a result, the doctrine of neo-organicism had been well received in Nationalist circles (Gini 1927d).

Gini frequently mixed political and scientific considerations in this way and was criticized for it at the time. Shortly after his 1930 lectures were published, the American (environmentalist) sociologist E. B. Reuter wrote a critical review of the American edition. Reuter's comments include a concise description of Gini's theory and harsher criticism than one encounters in Italian publications. It appeared, it should be recalled, in just that period when it was decided not to hold the International Population Conference in Rome, partially because of Gini's politics:

Mr. Gini's version runs to the effect that nations (races) pass through a more or less rigidly predetermined life-cycle: they have a definite birth which is followed by periods of youth, maturity, senescence, and death. This is a part of the natural (biological) (providential) plan. The origin of nations (races) is in the process of hybridization, and the selective forces operating upon the heterogeneous hybrid population. While the struggle for existence and sex selection are both factors of importance, the chief selective mechanism is immigration. This takes the ill-adapted persons to regions suited to them: it purifies the homeland at the same time that it provides other countries with the types of men pre-adapted to them. Those who emigrate are highly reproductive; and the new country is a melting-pot where these intellectually, morally, and physically heterogeneous elements are blended. In the early stages of this nation-building process the upper classes are highly reproductive, so that the still more prolific lower classes, unable to rise, go to war and emigrate and so produce a glorious period of national expansion. Then comes the period of maturity. The upper classes lose their power to reproduce. Their ranks are filled from the middle and lower classes. But these classes, because they have lost their most prolific members through war and emigration, have also declined in reproductive power. There is in consequence a population equilibrium. But fertility farther declines, and immigration is necessary to fill the gaps in the upper classes. There is thus decadence and death and replacement.

In the presence of such a position serious comment is difficult, perhaps unnecessary. The position is so untenable and vulnerable at so many points that, under other authorship and other auspices, one would dismiss it as a vagary of the human mind operating unscientifically and without a command of the facts. The position is essentially magical: a cause outside of the phenomena is posited to explain economic, social, and political reality; and the cause is outside of the facts whether it is located in biology or in Providence. To support the position, Mr. Gini marshals a great mass of historical, statistical, and biological data. Some of this is pertinent – though it contradicts as often as it supports the thesis – and much of it is simply irrelevant. If the position is a biological one, it is simply nonsense to attempt to demonstrate it by historical evidence. Furthermore, to cite historical occurrences as proof of a force that is used to explain the historic occurrences is logical circuitry reduced to the lowest possible terms. If there be a biologically predetermined racial life-cycle – and either there is or there is not – the(n) human behavior is an expression and not the cause. Hence any discussion and condemnation of family limitation or voluntary sterility is meaningless. Moreover, it cannot be harmonized with the position that a man's decision to limit the number of his offspring is a rationalization of his impotency. The latter position is fantastic.

A flood of light seems to fall upon the position if two widely separated statements of Mr. Gini are brought into juxtaposition. In his preliminary remarks he makes the statement that "I have been, and I am, a convinced supporter of the cyclical rise and fall of population, and for the past twenty years and more I have tried to collect facts and arguments in its support" (p. 4). This is an unusual scientific procedure, and to frankly admit it is truly remarkable. Twenty thousand words later is the statement that "....the hope ....the intimate feeling.... that the Italian nation is now renewing itself to write new and glorious pages in its history is not without biological foundations" (p. 114). The doctrine thus becomes understandable as an effort to put a pseudo-scientific foundation under a nationalistic complex. There is of course no question as to Mr. Gini's scientific integrity. But the position does show to what incredible lengths a man is capable of pushing a position to which he is emotionally committed. (Reuter 1931)

Vitriol of this sort aimed at Gini was not to be found in Italian publications. It would have been considered inappropriate to condemn a colleague in these terms and also professionally dangerous to criticize a figure of Gini's academic and, for a time, political importance.[60] This is not to say that Gini's theory was accepted uncritically or represented *the* Italian position on population development. On the contrary, many of the aspects of Gini's theory were subjected to criticism and in fact no other prominent demographer/economist of the interwar period supported his cyclical theory.

The most distinctive, and controversial, aspect of Gini's theory was his belief that fertility decline was an essentially biological phenomenon, caused by a diminished "genetic instinct" and so the diminished ability of the white races to conceive offspring. In response to competing birth control arguments, Gini had carried out while at ISTAT a study of firstborns. He hypothesized that if couples were in fact resorting to contraception in order to limit family size, they would only do so after having borne the desired number of children or at least not until after their firstborn. The average interval between marriage and first birth then should be unchanged in spite of fertility decline if the cause were birth control. Gini found that this interval had indeed lengthened considerably and cited this as evidence that European fecundity (ability

[60] In fact, Felice Vinci, in spite of his sharing objections to Gini's biological theory of fertility decline, criticized Reuter's harsh and disrespectful tone (Vinci 1931; 1939b, p. 91).

to procreate) was declining.[61] Until at least 1934 Gini continued to claim that fertility decline was primarily due to the "gradual decline of the natural aptitude of woman to procreate," and that explanations assigning responsibility to the spread of contraceptive practices were "inadequate" (Gini 1934f).

The fertility debate

In spite of Gini's scientific, academic, and political stature, his cyclical theory found few proponents. Among those who explicitly rejected Gini's explanation of fertility decline were Guglielmo Tagliacarne and Felice Vinci. Already in 1928, Tagliacarne questioned the theory of racial aging (and cited the well-known French demographers Arsène Dumont and Jacques Bertillon on this point). In particular, he rejected the conclusions drawn by Gini from the firstborn studies, claiming that there was indeed motivation for fertility limitation immediately after marriage and also plenty of indications that it was being widely practiced and encouraged. According to Tagliacarne, economic considerations – the need to save or pay off debts, the desire of the new wife to keep her job – explained the postponement and limitation of childbearing (Tagliacarne 1928).

A few years later, shortly after the publication of Gini's *Birth, Evolution, etc.*, Vinci penned a complete refutation of the cyclical theory. Describing Gini's theory as wildly conjectural, Vinci countered it on all points: the evolutionary selection of dominant populations from an array of racial mixtures, the role of differential fertility and social exchange, the analogy between individual and population aging, and – specifically with regard to recent fertility decline – Gini's conclusions drawn from the firstborn studies; Vinci also questioned how biological factors might explain a halving of marital fertility in Piedmont and Liguria over the previous half century, while levels in not-distant Venetia had actually increased. He cited instead Mortara's observation that fertility decline seemed to be spreading from the northwestern border with low-fertility France as evidence that its cause was voluntary and not biological. On various occasions, Vinci rejected the theory of racial decadence or the aging of the reproductive cells in the white races and he cited alternative explanations of fertility decline offered by biologists who should have been, he suggested, the most likely converts to Gini's position (Vinci 1939b, pp. 81–91; also 1930b, 1931, 1939a) Vinci

---

[61] Sanger 1927, pp. 239–41; Gini 1927c; 1930a; 1930b, p. 56. Battara conducted a similar study several years later and found even lower rates for firstborns in months ten, eleven and twelve of marriage; he, however, attributed the decline to birth control practices (Battara 1935b, p. 117).

questioned economic explanations of fertility decline as well, noting that it was a phenomenon that had affected capitalist, Fascist, and Communist regimes alike. He attributed denatalism instead to class-based materialism and the "psychology of the century" (Vinci 1939b, pp. 183–91; see also Parenti 1938).

Voluntary limitation was indeed the most frequently cited culprit with regard to interwar fertility decline.[62] Mortara had already identified birth control as the primary cause of fertility decline before World War I, and he continued to advocate this explanation, though generally did not criticize Gini directly on this point (Mortara 1908, p. 144; 1933b; 1933c; 1934a; 1934b). At the 1931 Rome Population Congress, presided over by Gini, Mortara repeated his assertion and suggested further that fertility had in part declined in response to the prior decline in mortality, an inevitable process, as continued high fertility combined with lower mortality would have led to impossibly large populations.[63]

In a Gini/ISTAT sponsored article which formed part of the same section of the conference, Stefano Somogyi, an ISTAT functionary and later professor of statistics at Palermo, rejected the causal relationship suggested by Mortara and claimed instead that fertility decline preceded mortality decline in as many countries as not.[64] Somogyi, however, did not long remain in the Gini camp. Two years later he published (in Livi's journal) an article attributing fertility decline to rising standards of living and the associated hedonistic lifestyle which argued for smaller families, as well as to the professional factor, namely that professionals had fewer children than small businessmen who had fewer children than industrial workers who had fewer than agricultural workers. The latter factor was accentuated by urbanization as cities contained fewer agricultural workers, more professionals etc. Somogyi also stated, without naming Gini, that the existence of a process of organic weakening that might explain fertility decline was absolutely to be rejected.[65]

As most believed that fertility decline was caused by voluntary

---

[62] In addition to above citations, see Galvani 1934; Gini 1934c, vol. X, pp. 59–60; Lenti 1935; Medolaghi 1934.

[63] Mortara 1934c; Mortara also claimed that the number of Italian births would almost certainly continue to decline (Mortara 1933b).

[64] Somogyi claimed that his data revealed seventeen cases in which fertility decline preceded, nineteen in which mortality decline preceded, and two cases in which they coincided. Looking over the data provided in the article I have come up instead with the following tally: three, fifteen, and one, numbers which support Mortara's hypothesis (Somogyi 1934b).

[65] Somogyi 1933a; he made similar comments regarding fertility decline in Somogyi 1934a and Somogyi 1937.

limitation – and as we shall see even Gini eventually incorporated this factor into his theory – the problem became to identify why more couples were practicing birth control and choosing ever smaller family sizes. The underlying or fundamental causes of fertility decline were generally considered to be economic, moral, or social. According to the economic argument, a rising standard of living or at least its expectation encouraged couples to limit fertility. According to the moral or social argument, a series of nineteenth-century developments (materialism, individualism, utilitarianism, egoism) had undermined family and religious values and so made fertility limitation acceptable (and desirable) to much of society, especially in the urban areas.

Catholics like Father Gemelli were quick to point out the role played by moral decadence aggravated by economic factors. The remedy, they claimed, lay in a restoration of the family and family values and general spiritual rebirth (Gemelli 1928a). Bishop Cazzani, another supporter of Fascist policy (see chapter 2, p. 76 above), claimed that the major cause of fertility decline was neither physiological, social or economic, but that it was instead a purely moral problem, the triumph of egoism and of sensuality; the selfish desire for individual wealth and pleasure had led couples to limit their family size. Cazzani singled out for attack dancing, indecent fashions for women, early romantic attachments, hedonist writers and artists, and the "deformation of the female soul."[66] Cazzani's view that the effect of moral decline on women was particularly significant in lowering fertility was not unique. Livi, for example, suggested that the rapidity of fertility decline could be ascribed to the fact that social poisons had begun to attack women as well as men (Livi 1929b).

The changing social role and status of women in relation to fertility was also considered by Giuseppe Grossi, director of the Provincial Maternal Nursery of Milan and a representative of ONMI. In *The Law and Power of Numbers* (Grossi 1935), a general treatment of demographic problems and policy, Grossi identified "social homosexuality" as a force contrary to the family and maternity and so the major cause of the declining birth rate. Social homosexuality, a product of urbanism, consisted of sexual equality and the emancipation and masculinization of women who were abandoning the home in order to engage in the same employments as men (and also sports that were considered incompat-

---

[66] Cazzani 1929; The question of fashion and fertility would subsequently be dealt with by Grillenzoni who published in Gini's *Metron* an article which claimed to detect a negative correlation between female elegance and fertility (Grillenzoni 1932).

ible with maternity).[67] The Fascist revolution and demographic policy had responded to this threat by the exaltation of the family and by impressing on the population the individual's obligation to have one. Grossi singled out as a special danger the employment of women in industry, pointing out the danger to mothers and their offspring posed by the physical requirements and toxic environments associated with industrial work.[68]

The potentially pathological effect of work on childbearing age women was an oft-repeated theme. In addition to the physical and toxic dangers of the workplace, it was feared that the simple fact of paid employment exerted a negative psychological effect on women, creating an "anti-procreational mentality" (e.g. Lorenzoni 1934; Rossi Ragazzi 1939). The Catholic proposal for a family wage was again raised, in Gemelli's journal, as a means to prevent the return of women to industrial employment in the context of economic recovery (Racca 1930). Whatever other objections there might have been to the employment of women in industry, Tagliacarne nonetheless revealed in a 1934 study that the percentage of women in industry had actually *decreased* considerably over the previous fifty years and so this seemed an unlikely explanation of fertility decline. Furthermore, he found that the fertility of women in industry did not differ markedly from that of Italian women as a whole (Tagliacarne 1934b).

Grossi's was one of a number of monographs inspired by the general concern over fertility decline. Their titles, like that of Grossi's work, give some idea of the general tone of the discussion: *Empty Cradles* (Marconcini 1935), *The Psychological and Moral Factors of Denatalism* (Battara 1935b), *Europe without Europeans* (Danzi 1934), *Fertility is Power* (Pellizzi 1930), *Denatalism. The Great Social Evil as Seen by a Physician* (Palmieri 1935). Their authors generally agreed that the immediate cause of fertility decline was voluntary limitation by married couples and sought to explain the underlying economic, social and psychological reasons for this relatively recent change in behavior. It is worth noting that this literature was not uniquely Italian, and it was in just this period that a spate of similar works appeared in Britain (Soloway 1990, p. 234).

The explanation of Pietro Battara, a student and assistant of Livi,

---

[67] Pellizzi 1930 uses this curious term as well which might better be expressed as social unisexuality; Spolverini 1938 also attributes fertility decline to the "masculinization of women."

[68] Grossi 1935, pp. 207–23; Grossi cites startling data on the very high rates of miscarriage, stillbirth, and infant mortality due to lead poisoning in print shops and other industrial poisons; ibid., pp. 164–8.

combined social and economic factors. He blamed denatalism on a bourgeois mentality which had created newly felt needs but not the economic means to satisfy them; as a result, economic considerations had entered into sexual morality and made possible the adoption of contraceptive practices (Battara 1935b, esp. pp. 15, 73–8). Danzi, whose work, like Korherr's before, boasts a preface by Mussolini himself, also cited the bourgeois spirit inherited from Liberalism as a major cause. He reserved still greater scorn for American values and practices which had infected Europe. These included materialism, industrialism, urbanism, increased female employment, and what he described as the "law of comfort", apparently the egotistical desire for individual well being and freedom from responsibility. Danzi described his work as a cry of alarm and a call to Italian blackshirts to *"creare"* (Danzi 1934).

The most extensive Italian interwar treatment of the causes and possible cures for fertility decline was probably Marconcini's *Culle vuote* (empty cradles). Marconcini taught political economy (at Turin) and finance (at the Catholic University of Milan). *Culle vuote* reveals his familiarity with a vast amount of literature on the topic and repeats many of the standard arguments. On the question of causes, he rejected bio-psychological (*à la* Gini), physiological (i.e. pathological), and statistical (a decline in the crude birth rate due to changes in nuptiality or age structure) possibilities, as well as the Spencerian suggestion that increased civilization led to decreased reproductive capacity. He attributed fertility decline instead to increased contraceptive practice, an increase brought about by "general relative impoverishment," urbanization, and women working. According to his impoverishment argument, the needs of the middle class had expanded more quickly than the means to satisfy them, contributing to general feelings of inferiority, frustration, and envy. The denatalist effects of urbanization, on the other hand, were due to the poor and crowded housing of cities, the sexual promiscuity encouraged there (both factors which discouraged the formation of "normal" families), and a general psychological crisis of urban life. Female employment reduced fertility for both physiological and psychological reasons and was linked to the problem of urbanization.

These factors constituted, however, only the first layer of causation. Marconcini followed the roots of denatalism still deeper to the rise of materialist individualism and an "anti-procreational mentality" during the nineteenth century, a development which had encouraged divorce, reduced the feeling that having a family was a social obligation, and made possible eugenic movements and the spread of contraception, abortion, and sterilization. This new mentality had affected women in particular, as manifested by the feminist calls for social and economic equality and "genetic emancipation." Among the cures, Marconcini called for a gradual reduction of female labor in industry, the creation of a family wage and the construction of public housing – all with the intention of returning women to their natural domestic environment – as well as "deurbanization," land reclamation and internal colonization, and a revival of religious values and religious education (Marconcini 1935).

In 1934, a large volume entitled *Population and Fascism* appeared (Lojacono 1934b). By that time Gini was no longer president of ISTAT and his influence seems to have waned somewhat; he is notably absent from the volume and, in spite of the inclusion of several authors friendly to him, it comes across as something of an anti-Gini manifesto.[69] Mortara and several others identified voluntary limitation as the immediate cause of fertility decline (Consiglio 1934; Medolaghi 1934; Mortara 1934a); and Filippo Virgilii, a law professor at Siena who had long concerned himself with population questions, claimed that economic imbalance was its fundamental cause.[70] Several authors including the sociologist Roberto Michels and the demographer Luigi Galvani – the latter had collaborated with Gini on constructing revised Italian life tables – specifically rejected the possibility of a physiological fertility decline (Consiglio 1934; Galvini 1934; Michels 1934, also 1925). Michels claimed that an evolutionary/biological process could not explain the rapidity of European fertility decline.

Livi made similar objections to Gini's theory, though he published his opinion on the subject somewhat later.[71] In his treatise on *The Bio-demographic factors of Social Organization*, which first appeared in 1937, Livi rejected Gini's organicism (Livi 1974 [1941], vol. I, pp. 2–19); and in his presidential address to the first meeting of the Comitato di consulenza per gli studi sulla popolazione (Advisory Committee on Population Studies) in 1938, he objected to those "pseudo-scientific" theories which attributed fertility decline to the biological decay of the white race, claiming that a process of this sort could not take place over the course of only a few years (*Economia* 1938, pp. 340–1). Finally in his 1940

---

[69] A review of this publication in *Genus* by Federici is primarily devoted to countering the suggestion that the cyclical theory implies pessimism with regard to pronatalist measures; *Genus* 1, 1–2 (June 1934), pp. 185–9.

[70] Virgilii 1934; for Virgilii's earlier demographic concerns, see Virgilii 1892; 1928.

[71] Vinci, however, mentioned Livi as a critic of Gini's demographic views in 1931; see Vinci 1939b, p. 91. Livi and Vinci seem to have been on good terms and to have constituted a something of a (Florence–Bologna) alternative to Gini's (Rome) demographic camp. Note the collaboration of the former two on the 1937 Comitato di consulenza (Vianelli 1938).

volume, *The Natural Laws of Population*, Livi specifically rejected Gini's biological hypothesis of fertility decline, and also criticized the conclusions drawn by Gini from his study of the interval between marriage and first birth. In addition to pointing out a statistical problem with this study, Livi claimed that all indications suggested that contraceptive practices had increased among newlyweds in the post-war period (Livi 1974 [1941], vol. II, pp. 344–50). Livi instead attributed fertility decline to increased voluntary limitation, a trend favored by economic well-being, industrialization, and the weakening of religious beliefs. He linked these processes to the transition from an artisan to an industrial culture in which wealth was greater but also individual vulnerability to economic fluctuations (Livi 1974 [1941], vol. II, pp. 351–4).

Still later, criticism came from Mario De Vergottini, ISTAT functionary and in the post-war period professor of statistics at Pisa. De Vergottini engaged in a heated debate with Federici (and Gini's Rome school) over the magnitude of social exchange, a debate which included his rejection of the cyclical theory.[72]

Seemingly unmoved by the criticisms of Reuter, Vinci, Livi, and others, Gini sought empirical verification for his theory. As evidence for the decay of European genetic instinct and so fertility, he cited the first-born studies discussed above. He also looked outside of Europe for evidence of population evolution and as early as 1924 identified primitive populations in general as being in a state of decline brought about not only by increased mortality but also fertility reduction caused by internal factors.[73] As president of the relatively well-endowed CISP, Gini directed studies which might confirm his hypothesis. The original directives of CISP included in fact a call for the study of recently born and aging populations. In this context, the committee conducted scientific expeditions to study the demography of small and isolated populations in Libya, Palestine, Mexico, and elsewhere. Gini himself identified the purpose of the expeditions as the resolution of the debates over the biological basis of fertility decline. A large amount of data was gathered, though much remained in its raw form. Both the CISP budget cuts (see previous section) and then the war seem to have hindered the completion of these projects. The results that were published included an article in *Genus* (organ of the CISP) by Nora Federici, a student and protégée of Gini. She concluded: "We believe moreover that the population of

---

[72] See De Vergottini 1941; 1943; and Federici's response in *Economia*, March–April 1943, p. 121.

[73] Gini 1924; in this article Gini made the (fantastic) claim that the numerical decline of the indigenous American peoples was not due to exposure to European diseases, asking why African races had not suffered a similar fate (p. 275).

Mandara is perhaps to be considered demographically more decadent due to its having arrived at a more advanced stage of biological evolution linked to the economic factor" (Federici 1942b, p. 101). Evidence for the cyclical theory derived from the CISP expeditions, however, seems to have been no more conclusive than this tentative "consideration."[74]

With regard to the apparent decline of small populations like those studied by CISP, Livi suggested an alternative explanation. Among his primary topics of research in this period was the concept of population minimum. Based in part on studies that he had conducted in the Aegean islands, Livi determined that populations numbering fewer than about 500 persons were demographically unstable, vulnerable to catastrophe, and might easily suffer from structural problems including sexual imbalance and a disadvantageous age structure. Livi specifically offered his explanation for the decline of small primitive populations as preferable to Gini's explanation based on aging germinal cells.[75]

Gini continued to advocate his cyclical theory and a biological explanation of fertility decline in spite of the almost universal opinion that this decline was due to voluntary limitation. He accomplished this in part by adapting his theory to the evidence in a way which robbed it of some of its explanatory power. Already in 1927, Gini identified the spread of neo-Malthusian practices as "an index of physiological decadence" (Gini 1931, p. 216), that is the decline of a race's genetic instinct predisposed that group to consider and pursue fertility limitation. Gini's biological decline then could be measured by the sociologist who found a rise in the acceptance and practice of birth control. This device would save Gini's theory in the face of evidence regarding the immediate causes of fertility decline, but, lacking other physiological confirmation, it placed it on a weak footing as compared to economic, social, and moral explanations for this change of behavior.

At a 1940 conference in Portugal, Gini did finally concede that a major part of fertility decline was due to contraceptive practices and discussed the relevance of economic factors as well. Nonetheless, he maintained his biological position and reemphasized his earlier argument. The profound psychological changes which had occurred in the West, including a process of "cerebralization" (a term which smacks of Spencer) and the

---

[74] In addition to Federici's article (1942b), see the *presentazione* to *Genus* 1, 1–2 (June 1934), pp. 1–2 on CISP directives; Gini 1930b, p. 73; 1934b; 1934d for explicit statements linking CISP expeditions and confirmation of the cyclical theory; and Gini 1934e; 1936a; 1936c; 1937; Federici 1942a. I have learned from personal communication with Professor Federici that much of the CISP expedition data remains unused.

[75] Livi 1938c; 1974 (1941), vol. I, pp. 111–19, 170–97. In the first of these citations Livi also pointed out that low fertility was in general incompatible with a "structural optimum."

decline of religious sentiment, had a basis in physiological evolution of an orthogenetic sort. He was now able to explain the rapid rate of fertility decline as resulting, by means of voluntary limitation, from the sudden upsetting of the fragile equilibrium which had existed between instinct and reason.[76]

In this same address, Gini regretted that the various physicians to whom he had posed the problem of determining the biological basis of the weakening of reproductive instincts had not taken up the challenge. His own research had identified a high frequency of frigidity in women as a sign of a degenerate population. He linked frigidity to under-sexuality and physiological infantilism, namely a highly positioned clitoris and under-developed pelvis (*faible déclivité du bassin*). Infantilism, moreover, had been selected for in recent generations, since according to modern aesthetic ideals men preferred – and so often chose in marriage – women with slender infantile figures.[77] Infantilism had affected modern European males as well, as their penises were generally smaller than those observed in ancient Egyptian bas-reliefs, in the Renaissance artwork of Dürer, and in modern-day Africans. Though generally unable to ask questions on this topic, CISP expeditions had discovered in one case that the women of a primitive and (still more) decadent society feared the relatively large European penises.[78]

Thirty years after the Trieste conference, Gini continued to propound his cyclical theory in spite of general skepticism among his colleagues and a scarcity of physiological evidence in its favor. How are we to explain his persistence? First, as revealed during his tenure at ISTAT, Gini was a strong-willed individual and not likely to admit error. Even those who remember him fondly concede that he was difficult and combative. Second, he seems to have been profoundly impressed with the originality of his theory from its inception. It was compatible with both the evolutionary and economic theory he encountered as a student and provided a scientific basis for his political beliefs as well. And original work is the stuff of successful academic careers: Gini's quick rise through Italian academe, presidency of ISTAT and of so many Italian and international societies, and founding of a new faculty at the university of Italy's capital city all suggest that his work in general received more encouragement than discouragement.

Nor should Gini be considered an isolated intellectual without allies

---

[76] Gini 1940; for an account of the conference, see Federici 1943–9.
[77] Gini had already mentioned the denatalist effect of recent patterns of sexual selection in his 1927 lectures (Gini 1931, pp. 212–15).
[78] Gini 1940; Gini gives no citation for his rates on the frequency of frigidity (10–80%); on infantilism he cites the Dutch gynecologist T. van de Velde.

or supporters. Within ISTAT, both Molinari and Savorgnan defended Gini's cyclical theory. Molinari did so, however, in the context of the institute's study of declining population *comuni* which pointed to the economic and social (rather than biological) causes behind an increase in the practice of birth limitation (Molinari 1932), and Savorgnan too attempted lamely to reconcile social and biological explanations of fertility decline: "we can affirm that the decline of legitimate fertility among the populations of western and central Europe . . . is primarily due to the voluntary limitation of births caused by a series of sociological factors, though we should not rule out the possible role of biological factors as well" (Savorgnan 1936, p. 164). Savorgnan gave a degree of prominence to Gini's theory in his works on the dynamics of population while at the same time claiming that the current state of demographic/economic/sociological knowledge did not allow enunciation of a general law of population, which Gini's theory certainly claimed to be.[79] More enthusiastic praise came from Grossi, who, in spite of his basically sociological explanation of fertility decline, was a convinced advocate of Gini's cyclical theory. His 1935 volume cited above begins: "The utterly Fascist theory of the Italian school – whose most authoritative representative is Corrado Gini – constitutes the inspiration for this work on population policy" (Grossi 1935, p. 1).

Constitutionalists and physicians
Gini's work was also praised by Marcello Boldrini, a constitutionalist statistician at the Catholic University of the Sacred Heart in Milan; and both constitutionalists, including Pende, and the Catholic University, represented by the medically trained Gemelli, were friendly to Gini.[80] Boldrini's primary topic of research in the period was the fecundity of "biotypes," or the relationship between fecundity and physical "constitution." Using anthropometric data gathered by the military on a group of 730 Paduan fathers, Boldrini found greater fertility (and so presumably fecundity) among *"brevilinei"* individuals (large framed, large bellied, short limbed) than among *"longilinei"* (narrow framed, small

---

[79] Savorgnan 1935; 1936; Gini had explicitly referred to his cyclical theory as the law of population; see, e.g., Gini 1924.

[80] Relationships seem to have been generally good between Gini, Pende, Gemelli, Carlo Foà and Boldrini, all of whom, for example, were on the scientific directory council of *Genus*. For more on the link between Pende and Gemelli, see Cosmacini 1984. For other pro-Gini positions, see the population work of the anthropologist Giulio Rugiu (1933) and that of Federici (1941), and also Parenti (1935), who adopted that version of Gini's theory which conceded the prevalence of contraceptive practices, but attributed this new behavior to biological causes.

bellied, long limbed).[81] Boldrini went on to note a correlation between constitution and social class, namely the prevalence of *longilinei* in the higher classes and *brevilinei* in the lower. Combined with the observation that fecundity appeared to be hereditary, he could explain to some degree the fact of differential fertility. The constitutional (physiological and psychological) characteristics that are conducive to social success were also those associated with low fecundity. Boldrini himself pointed out the possible connections between the constitutional study of fecundity and Gini's cyclical theory, though he remained uncommitted regarding the theory's validity in spite of his praise for its author. It is something of a surprise that Gini did not make greater use of Boldrini's work as here was a physiological study which proposed to explain both differential fertility and "social exchange." A point of incompatibility might have been Boldrini's dependence on the inheritability of fecundity which suggested that, all things being equal, fecundity should increase from generation to generation; Boldrini imagined, however, that this process might be complicated by sexual selection and other factors.[82]

Boldrini added a couple of interesting provisoes to his observation that those who rose up in society tended to be *longilinei*. In 1929 he wrote:

Let me be careful to point out that I am speaking of the mass of those who rise up through the ranks of society, though I am certainly aware that there are those who have achieved exceptional positions of command and would seem to completely contradict the theory. It may be that the man of genius, able to dominate both men and events, escapes all standard evaluation. (Boldrini 1929, pp. 341–2)

This was clearly a reference to the *brevilineo* Mussolini.[83] By 1936 Boldrini had refined his theory still more and identified two types of genius, the contemplative (markedly *longilineo*) and the active (markedly *brevilineo*). The great movers of history fell into these two classes; the latter included Stalin, Pilsudski, Hitler and Mussolini: "The example of the greatest modern statesman is highly expressive . . . I speak of

---

[81] Boldrini 1929; Boldrini described *brevilinei* as those individuals in whom width (or transverse measurements) dominated length (or longitudinal measurements). In *longilinei* the reverse was true; between the two stood Quetelet's "average man" (Boldrini 1931a, pp. 1–31). For further interest in the relation between constitution and biotype, see Clinica della R. Università di Bologna 1934; Ghigi 1934; Vinci 1939b, pp. 105–16 and in general on the anthropometry of the parents of large families, see Gini 1934c, vol. VII.

[82] Boldrini 1929; 1931a, esp. pp. 147–8, 199–204; for Boldrini's praise of Gini 1930b see Boldrini 1931c.

[83] Mussolini himself may not have been a great fan of anthropometry. At the age of nineteen he had been arrested (in Bern, Switzerland) and subjected to measurements which he later described as "humiliating and exasperating" (De Felice 1965, p. 31).

Mussolini whose square outline, Caesarian forehead, indomitable will and easy resourcefulness has captured the popular imagination" (Boldrini 1936, p. 15). Among the characteristics of the active man of genius Boldrini also noted an interest in statistics (Boldrini's profession), shared for example by Mussolini and Napoleon.

Constitutionalist studies made up two sections of the 1931 Rome Population Congress. On that occasion, Pende presented a paper on "Constitution and fertility" in which he found that a wide pelvis and narrow shoulders were conducive to maternity (Pende 1934a). In the same forum, Gini referred to an ongoing CISP study of the fecundity of biotypes as part of the study of large families (Gini 1934a, vol. I, pp. xxiv–xxv). The latter study revealed (at least) that in Emilia a large majority of the parents of large families were *"brevilinei"* (Vinci 1939b, pp. 105–16). Both Pende and Gini's results corroborated Boldrini's findings.

Also at the 1931 Congress, Pende suggested that there existed an inverse relationship between high fertility in women and sensuality, for which there was an endocrinological basis (Gini 1934c, vol. x, p. 226). That Pende should link low fertility to excessive sensuality while Gini and others identified a similar link to frigidity suggests that there was considerable disagreement over the relationship between sexuality and fertility or else that any deviation from "normal" was considered to exert a negative effect.

Apart from the constitutionalists, the contribution of the medical profession to population theory was generally limited to casting the standard arguments in medical terms. Carlo Foà had addressed the question of the possible biological factors of fertility decline at both the 1930 Italian Society for the Progress of Science conference and again at the 1931 Population Congress. On those occasions, he considered the link between infantilism and sterility, the pathological causes of sterility, and the likelihood of a physiological decline in fecundity. While citing both Pende and Gini approvingly on these topics, Foà concluded that economic, social, and moral factors played a much larger role in regulating fertility (Foà 1931/34).

Gemelli meanwhile – again at the Rome Congress which clearly lived up to its characterization as primarily concerned with the "important crisis of fertility" (Uggè 1931) – considered psychological and psychiatric aspects of the fertility problem. He referred to Gini and the likely link between psychological and biological factors in this context. As causes of denatalism he identified a "psychological sterility," produced by social and moral influences which had changed fundamental sexual instincts, and also "sexual neuroses": "Sexual neurotic struggle and insecurity are manifestations of the individual's inability to fit his life to the social, moral and religious aims that he sets for himself. These neuroses then become a source of conjugal unhappiness and denatalism" (Gemelli 1934b, p. 345). This more psychological approach of Gemelli to the problem was certainly not incompatible with his earlier and more general call for a religious/moral solution (Gemelli 1928a and above).

Other physicians who addressed the fertility problem included Sileno Fabbri, the director of ONMI, and the Catholic physician Vincenzo Palmieri (whose book included a preface by Gemelli). Both identified the generally described social pathology of birth control as not simply due to economic causes, but the result of a new sexual morality for which the remedy was a strong church. The medical profession was to act as a collaborator – particularly with regard to the repression of voluntary abortion – in the demographic policy of Mussolini, "the great physician."[84] Palmieri added curious observations regarding health and parity (the third, fourth, and fifth children were presumably the healthiest), the positive effects of repeated childbearing on female physiology and psychology, and the pathological effects of contraceptive practices (including coitus interruptus) especially for women.[85]

Demographers on policy

In addition to the general concentration on the fertility problem, the interests and publications of demographers in the interwar period followed the vicissitudes of Fascist population policy in other more specific ways as well. So, for example, not only did a spate of articles on fertility decline appear immediately following Mussolini's May 1927 Ascension Day speech, but at about the same time the once dominant topic of emigration was virtually abandoned. General references to pronatalist policy became fairly frequent after 1927 and predictably were almost always laudatory (though Mussolini's 1937 statement that the policy had failed to date permitted others to advance similar criticisms).

One interesting and fruitful link between the political and scientific realms derived from Mussolini's identification of "industrial urbanism" as a prime culprit in denatalism. Subsequently, Livio Livi devoted considerable attention to the interaction between economic

---

[84] Allaria 1935; Fabbri 1932c; Palmieri 1935. Both Boldrini and Grossi describe Mussolini in these terms (Grossi 1935, p. 87).

[85] Palmieri 1935; In this regard Palmieri wrote: "The organs employed in this precious function follow the general biological law according to which they become sturdier and better with use" (ibid., p. 155).

and demographic variables. In two articles from 1928–29 he estimated that the maximum possible absorption of workers in agriculture over the next fifty years would support a total Italian population of 58 million, 10 million short of his projection for 1978 (and also short of Mussolini's impossible demand for 60 million by 1950). While praising the intensification of land reclamation efforts, in part as a measure to maintain higher rural levels of fertility, Livi nonetheless claimed that industrial development, "one of the greatest conquests of human ability," would have to continue as well in order to ensure full employment.

In these articles, Livi was openly skeptical about the negative correlation between "industrial urbanism" and fertility, finding that the culprit was more urbanism than industrialism.[86] For these views, he was attacked as an opponent of the recently introduced *bonifica integrale* by Gino Arias in Mussolini's newspaper *Il Popolo d'Italia*, an accusation Livi countered in the second of the articles cited. Nor did Livi find the condemnation of urban demographic trends entirely well founded. In 1931, several years after his disagreements with Gini began (see above p. 82), Livi criticized ISTAT conclusions regarding mortality, nuptiality and fertility in *comuni* with populations over 10,000. In particular, he pointed out that urban mortality was inflated by non-residents coming to die in the cities where they could find medical care, and urban nuptiality lowered by city dwellers leaving to wed in their family homes (Livi 1931a). ISTAT apparently interpreted these observations as a criticism of their methods and in reporting the Livi article took issue with him, concluding:

all of which shows that, with regard to certain statistical problems, even those who enjoy a good reputation and have held important positions in ISTAT may be misled when basing their judgement on a first impression; in formulating a problem one must instead have at one's disposition all the necessary elements and carefully ponder whatever other factors might come into play.[87]

As these studies suggest, Livi was not inclined to attribute fertility decline to purely economic factors, preferring a broader social explanation. His "defense" of industrialization and his belief that no sector was immune from denatalism was somewhat vindicated by studies that he and Ugo Giusti carried out in the late 1930s and early 1940s revealing that while rural fertility rates were continuing to decline, those in many provincial capitals were either holding steady or even increasing and so urban and

---

[86] Livi 1928; 1929a; Livi's projection for 1978 (68 million) overshot the 1981 resident population of 56.557 million. For other discussions of the denatalist effects of urbanism see Bellero 1927; Noble 1929.   [87] *Notiziario demografico* (1 February 1932), pp. 62–5.

rural levels were equalizing.[88] And in an interesting postscript, further research on the relationship between fertility and industrialism/urbanism was carried out by Livi's son in the 1970s. Analyzing half a dozen possible socio-economic factors in the history of Italian fertility decline, he found that urbanization correlated (negatively) only weakly with fertility and that in the case of industrialization the correlation was more often than not the reverse of that expected (Livi Bacci 1977, pp. 189–215).

With regard to pronatalist policy in general and the specific Fascist measures, demographers took a variety of positions (which did not of course include outright opposition). Gini's theory at first glance appears fatalistic with regard to the possible effects of legislative measures on fertility. In its 1911 form, he described the decadent phase of national evolution as that in which the state resorted to "extreme remedies" including bachelor taxes, marital tax exemptions, and prizes for large families (Gini 1912, p. 41). And as already mentioned, he several times stated that the Roman population legislation introduced under Augustus had been ineffective.[89] Gini observed that the raising of a child was, from an economic point of view, a bad investment, and so he feared that the introduction of economic considerations into childbearing decisions by means of subsidies or prizes might in fact backfire if they brought an element of "rationalization" or economic calculation into the traditionally "instinctual" realm of fertility (Gini 1930b, p. 123; 1931, pp. 89–100; see also Ferrari 1934). On the positive side, he claimed that the cyclical theory did not imply that government intervention would always be ineffective, provided that it came early enough in the cycle of decline and that both economic and, especially, moral encouragements were part of the policy (Gini 1924, p. 227; 1931, p. 154; 1930a, p. 264). Father Gemelli seconded Gini's observation that the state could not possibly make childrearing economically attractive and so might encourage denatalism by introducing economic considerations into childrearing decisions. Nonetheless, he made the standard Catholic appeal for the creation of a family wage.[90]

---

[88] For these studies, see *Economia* 1938; Giusti 1936; 1939; 1941a; Livi 1938a; Parenti 1938; *Maternità ed infanzia* (January–February 1939), pp. 52–62; *Razza e civiltà* (23 March 1940), pp. 83–90, (May–June 1940), pp. 333–41; (25 March 1941), pp. 93–108; ACS Min. Int. Demorazza bb.15–17; See also Ministero dell'interno – Demorazza n.d. In another study Livi found that, in spite of the generally held view that increased wealth led to declining fertility, the reverse was true in the short term; see Livi 1931b and subsequent yearly articles entitled "Il bilancio demografico nell'anno 19--" in *Economia*; see also Battara 1931; 1935a; 1935b, pp. 51–60; Livi 1932b; 1933c. Vinci expressed doubts regarding Livi's method in Vinci 1939b, pp. 123–30.

[89] See chapter 2, p. 84 above; Gini 1912, pp. 55–6, 91; 1931, pp. 162–3.

[90] Gemelli 1928a; 1928b. Gemelli restated essentially these same ideas in 1937 on the occasion of the renewal of demographic policy (1937a).

Gini did not, however, have any reservations about the *legitimacy* of state intervention in the demographic sphere. Already in 1922, he had asserted that the state might legitimately regulate emigration (Jacini 1923, p. 3), and in his 1931 *Scientific Basis of Population Policy* he defended the right of the state to pursue collective interests even when these were in conflict with the rights of individuals. In spite of his misgivings regarding population legislation in general, he did hold out hope that the recently introduced Italian measures would be successful (Gini 1931, pp. 1–2, 149–64).

Stefano Somogyi took a more enthusiastic and optimistic view of Fascist pronatalism than did Gini. In both an article (in Livi's *Economia*) and a short monograph on Fascism and demographic policy he praised the general transformation of social thinking undertaken by the regime. He attributed the increasing tendency of couples to limit their fertility to individualistic, egotistical, and hedonistic values that he associated with Liberalism. A Fascist and authoritarian regime, on the other hand, would inspire a sense of collectivism and so reverse the denatalist trend. Somogyi not only defended the moral and legal basis of the existing legislation, but suggested that further measures requiring that certain categories of the population marry and bear children would also be legitimate (Somogyi 1934a, Somogyi 1937).

Concern about denatalism and a generally pronatalist attitude naturally predisposed most Italian writers on population in favor of Fascist policy.[91] In response to the observation that demographic variables did not appear to respond to the regime's efforts, they pointed out that fertility might have dropped more in the absence of government measures. Livi added that the policy was especially directed at the very young and so its effect would not be fully felt until this group reached childbearing age (Livi 1932a; 1933a).

After 1933, Italian demographers and policy makers looked with increasing interest at Nazi population policy. Though critical of its eugenic aspects, in particular forced sterilization, they did find material for emulation in the measures to increase fertility.[92] From at least 1935, Livi followed closely the German developments and in early 1937 suggested, in view of the evident successes of Nazi pronatalism, that economic measures could apparently be effective and that the German

---

[91] See, for example, Amoroso 1934; Benini 1929; Grossi 1935, pp. 69–90; Livi 1932a; Vinci 1930a; 1934; 1939b, pp. 117–21, 131–8. Benini's work represents something of an apology for his earlier Malthusianism and probably also an attempt to establish his Fascist credentials.

[92] On the reverse phenomenon, Italian influence on German policy, see Vinci 1939b, pp. 205–20; Weindling 1989, pp. 446–9.

measures might with certain modifications serve as a guide to future Italian policy. Livi did add the observation that the dramatic increase in German fertility was made possible in part by the low levels to which it had fallen prior to 1933, levels well below those of Italy; and low fertility might more easily be raised than medium or high fertility (Livi 1935; 1937a). His suggestions came just prior to the Fascist Grand Council meeting which relaunched the population policy and which resulted in emulation of various aspects of the Nazi policy (marriage loans, for example). Livi responded to these developments as well, criticizing certain aspects of the new proposals, including measures to penalize sterile couples and the suggestion that sterility be grounds for marital annulment (Livi 1937c; also 1940b).

The 1937 GCF meeting also led to the creation of the Comitato di consulenza per gli studi sulla popolazione (mentioned above) with Livi as president. Two of the Committee's first tasks were studies of international population policy and Italian fertility. As part of the policy study, Livi conducted a survey of learned German and Italian opinion regarding a series of his own policy recommendations; response was generally favorable.[93] The fertility study revealed continuing rural decline, but some recovery in provincial capitals and low fertility areas, a development Livi attributed to the renewed policy.[94]

One of the last contemporary observations regarding Fascist pronatalist policy was Boldrini's in 1942, and it speaks to what must in retrospect be seen as that policy's futility. Boldrini noted that Fascist policy had in fact increased Italian nuptiality, but that the effects on fertility were questionable, as nuptiality increase included, for example, those who married for careerist rather than procreational reasons. In addition, he pointed out that young couples in which the wife held a salaried job might well opt for economic reasons to keep the wife employed after childbirth rather than benefit from cancellation of the marriage loan (Boldrini 1942). Boldrini's remarks support to a degree Gini's longstanding warning regarding the introduction of economic considerations into childbearing decisions.

International debates and race

The Italian demographic debates of the Fascist period were of course not exclusively restricted to the fertility question, though as often as not

---

[93] Livi 1937b, 1938b; on Nazi policy, see also Allaria 1936, 1937.

[94] Giusti 1941b; Livi 1938a; Parenti 1938; Vianelli 1938; As further evidence of policy effectiveness, L. Nina noted in 1940 a decline in the number of men paying the bachelor tax (Nina 1941); conclusions drawn from Italian tax paying behavior should of course be treated cautiously.

other problems were considered in relation to it. Nor was Italian demography isolated from the work going on in other countries. As is clear from the preceding pages, the Italians both hosted and attended international conferences. And in spite of internal dissension, they did put forward a fairly unified position in relation to some of the more controversial debates of the day.

Migration, the great topic of Liberal demography, had of course lost pride of place to fertility after 1927 and what little attention was paid to it was generally in relation to birth rates. Already in 1911, Gini had identified emigration as denatalist, insofar as return migrants often brought back with them the aspirations and habits (including low reproductivity) of higher social classes.[95] And in the 1930s, Zingali too predicted that emigration lowered fertility, because of sexual imbalance, age structure changes, and the fact that migrants generally came from the lower and more prolific classes (Zingali 1934).

At a 1938 conference in Palermo, Gini discussed an American theory according to which migration did not significantly affect the demographic growth of either receiving or sending countries.[96] According to this argument, which had been used by the anti-immigration forces in the US, the respective populations adjusted their fertility up or down accordingly. Gini cited contrary examples of unchanged fertility in spite of massive emigration (especially Ireland) and countered the American claims. Regarding the European demographic contribution to the US and the evident scientific, industrial, commercial, political, and artistic superiority of Europeans as a group, Gini claimed: "Much of America's wealth is not the product of American labor and ingenuity, but is instead a gift from Europe, namely the free contribution of human capital in the form of adult emigrants" (Gini 1938, p. 344). Gini used the Palermo rostrum to address not only the generally past phenomenon of, especially Sicilian, migration to the US, but also the planned new direction for that migration, namely to Italy's colonies in Africa. He noted that although these colonies were at the time demographically small, it was not unusual for colonies to go through an "incubation period" prior to their significant growth, and he predicted that Italy's colonies would eventually serve as significant demographic outlets.[97]

Gini's address betrayed renewed interest in the question of demographic colonization as inspired by creation of the Italian Empire. In another example from May 1936, the month in which Ethiopia fell, Livi

[95] Gini 1912, pp. 102–6; migration was of course central to the birth phase of Gini's cyclical population evolution; see above and Gini 1930b, pp. 72–103.
[96] Gini 1938; Gini attributed this theory to Franklin, Walker and others.
[97] Gini 1938; Gini's defense of colonization is repeated by Federici, see Federici 1938.

renewed his discussion of the limited possibilities for the absorption of
Italy's future population in agriculture. To the previously suggested
alternative of industrial expansion he added demographic colonization
and concluded the article with reference to the necessity and justice of
the Italian conquest.[98] In an article which appeared the following year,
Mortara countered British arguments (and figures) on the economic
uselessness of colonies, an argument which he compared to the warnings of the rich to the poor on the risks and headaches of wealth
(Mortara 1937). The comments of Gini, Livi, and Mortara (together with
official comment) all asserted the demographic and economic advantages to Italy of colonial possessions.

The Italians rejected other aspects of Anglo-American demographic
thought as well, in particular "optimum" population theory and eugenics. A leading proponent of the standard version of optimum population
theory was the Englishman Henry Pratt Fairchild who presented a
paper on the topic at the 1927 Geneva Population Conference (Fairchild
1927). According to this theory, since there obviously exist states of both
underpopulation and overpopulation, there must lie in between an
optimum population size for any state. In the theory's standard form,
this optimum is that population size at which per capita income is maximized.

Gini refuted Fairchild's view at the same conference, pointing out that
optimum population size from an individual point of view might not
coincide with optimum size from the point of view of the state.[99] Gini
expanded his criticism of optimum theory in his *Scientific Basis of
Population Policy*, criticizing the individualistic and exclusively economic aspects of optimum theory, and also pointing out that the
optimum might change as society passed through different economic
stages (pastoral, agricultural, industrial, service). Moreover, a combination of population increase and declining per capita income might not
be a sign of overpopulation but simply the downside of the curve
leading to a new optimum at which well-being is increased relative to
the previous optimum (Gini 1931, pp. 18–62). Similar arguments were
made by other Italian theorists (e.g. Rugiu 1933). The optimum of
Celestino Arena, for example, professor of finance at La Sapienza
(Rome) and authority on emigration questions, was one which combined increasing per capita income and increasing total productivity
and so required a rate of return to labor increasing faster than popula-

---

[98] Livi 1936b. For earlier discussion, see Livi 1928; 1929a and above. On another occasion
Livi defended Italian population policy against the accusation that it was exclusively
imperialist in inspiration (*Economia* [September 1938]), pp. 147–8).
[99] Gini 1927e, also reprinted as Gini 1927a.

tion. It was, he claimed (as did Gini and others), just the stimulation of population pressure which engendered a more dynamic and economically/technologically progressive society.[100]

In Italy, "negative" eugenics, or a policy aimed at the discouragement of procreation and marriage by the "unfit," would of course have encountered strong opposition from the Church. The Pope specifically condemned eugenic sterilization in his 1930 *Casti connubii*, and similar objections were voiced by Father Gemelli on the occasion of the encyclical and again several years later in reaction to the Nazi program of forced sterilization. The medically trained Gemelli claimed that the Nazi program was based on insufficient scientific knowledge and the myth of racial purity. He rejected on scientific, moral, and religious grounds state efforts to limit the freedom of individuals to marry and procreate.[101] Even the suggestion, for example, that a physician-issued certificate attesting to good health (freedom, for example, from venereal disease) be a prerequisite to marriage was attacked in Catholic circles (Marconcini 1935, p. 427; Palmieri 1935, pp. 107–9).

Scientific arguments against Anglo-American and German eugenics were of course marshaled as well. Prior to the rise of Fascism, eugenics had generated a degree of interest in Italy and certain Italian intellectuals had advocated eugenics in its mainline version.[102] Gini was among the leading Italian eugenicists and eventually served as president of the Italian Society of Genetics and Eugenics.[103] However, contrary to the standard eugenic line of selective discouragement or encouragement of procreation with an eye toward improvement of the race, Gini claimed that the only insurance of qualitative progress was a larger population which would display a greater degree of variation upon which natural selection might operate (Gini 1931, pp. 101–48; 1945, pp. 108–11).

Moreover, it was argued, the state of genetic knowledge was not sufficient to allow for the selection of the eugenically best procreators. And in general, "fertility rationalization" was seen as potentially accelerating fertility decline (Boldrini 1934; 1939a; Gini 1931, pp. 89–148; Livi 1932a; Palmieri 1935, pp. 91–137; Rugiu 1933). Gini added that the time necessary to realize any degree of eugenic progress was so long that even if the eugenic ideal were realized, that ideal would by the time of

---

[100] Arena 1930; similar ideas on the positive role of increasing population density can be found in Grossi 1935, pp. 1–14; Majorana 1929.

[101] Gemelli 1931; 1934a; for additional Catholic objections see Boldrini 1934; 1939a.

[102] On eugenics in Italy, see Pogliano 1984; as well as de Grazia 1992, pp. 52–9; Wanrooij 1990, pp. 112–16; for a definition of mainline eugenics, see Kevles 1986.

[103] The society was founded in 1919; Gini became president in 1934. His eugenic interests were however of earlier vintage as witnessed by his participation in the International Conference of Eugenics in London in 1912.

its attainment be an ideal of the past, and so inappropriate to a changed environment.[104] Carlo Foà claimed that rather than improving the race, eugenic programs would lead to the creation of more "average men" by the elimination of variation (Foà 1931, p. 447).

While anti-eugenical by northern European or American standards, the Italians nonetheless retained the term for their own uses. Their eugenics, however, was a watered-down version: "By eugenics . . . we mean that science that studies all the conditions that are favorable or harmful to healthy procreation" (Perondi 1933, p. 473). Gini referred to a "renewing eugenics" as opposed to the positive or negative eugenic programs proposed elsewhere. Basically eugenics came to be used in Italy to refer to the various programs of pre- and postnatal care, of physical fitness, and of the dietary improvement of the race.[105]

In an article written on the occasion of the tenth anniversary of the Fascist seizure of power, Livi identified an Italian school in complete opposition to the Anglo-Saxon optimum school that advocated "fertility rationalization," rationalization that entailed the establishment of quantitative and qualitative criteria regarding who should or should not procreate and how much. Livi countered: "The Italian school responds to the school of birth rationalization by stating that the best insurance of population quality is precisely the genetic (procreational) activity of the healthiest classes, those from which will spring the generations of the future" (Livi 1932a, p. 415; also 1936a, b). Livi's characterization of the Italian school echoed two of the major points of Gini's *Scientific Basis*, namely opposition to optimum theory and to the rationalization of fertility. His repeated and approving citations of Gini on this occasion reveal that, in spite of internal debates, there was a degree of consensus among Italian demographers and that they did agree on a number of fundamental points (in particular the desirability of reversing fertility decline). The collectivist appeal of Fascist demographic policy (and Fascism in general) applied to the academic disciplines as well and population theorists presented a fairly unified front to the rest of the world. In this same article, Livi wrote that "the Fascist revolution has had a considerable impact on the direction of demographic studies" (Livi 1932a, p. 414), and while the effect of political developments on intellectual activity may be more subtle than on policy or an institute like ISTAT, the Italian reactions to optimum theory and eugenics – valid

---

[104] Gini reportedly expressed this view at the First Italian Congress of Genetics and Eugenics. See Palmieri 1935, p. 128.

[105] See Gini 1936b, p. 80; for another contemporary statement, see Foà 1931/34. Pogliano concludes that Italian eugenics in this period might be better described as "social hygiene." See Pogliano 1984, p. 76.

scientific objections, it should be pointed out – do provide useful examples of the influence of official pronatalism on demographic thought. The absence of any dissenting Italian voices in this case is also in keeping with the dictatorial environment created by the regime.

The introduction of racist policy, however, strained the unity of this school. Racial policy was considered an aspect of population policy, and sections of university texts, for example, dealt with the topic.[106] With regard to Italy's population experts, Mortara ,as a Jew, suffered directly from the new policy and chose to emigrate. Livi, for his part, had maintained close ties with the Italian Jewish community since his days as a university student,[107] and during the period of the racist laws he secretly kept a Jewish friend at his home. As a result of his position in the UCD, however, and as something of an expert on demographic policy, he became a member of the Demorazza *consiglio superiore* (governing council) and also published in the not very appealing *Razza e civiltà* (*Race and Civilization*). Apparently he was expected to make a pronouncement on racism and so wrote an odd response to the overseas (= American) critics of Italian racism in *Economia*. Although not of course critical of Fascist policy, the article does not include condemnation of Italian Jews.[108]

Gini, instead, was able to interpret racial policy in the context of his cyclical theory. Limited racial mixing was the mechanism for the birth of new populations in that theory, and once that mixing had been accomplished, the new population required a degree of isolation from extraneous elements in order that it might evolve. In 1941 at a conference held in Uppsala, Gini – whose frequent conference going seems not to have been hindered by wartime – identified this isolation as the "biological function of nationalism" which created geographical-political barriers to further racial mixing. He added that a racist policy might serve a similar purpose by erecting physiological barriers within a geographical territory (Gini 1945, pp. 121–2).

Gini's ideas on the topic were echoed by Nicola Pende. In his 1938 orthogenetic treatise, Pende described, as Gini had in 1930, the salutary sort of racial mixing that had been taking place in Italy since political unification and went on to implicitly endorse the racist policy for essentially biological reasons:

---

[106] See, e.g., the inclusion of racist policy in Federici's elaborate pedagogical typology of population policy in Federici 1941, pp. 122–37, 162, 290–1. On racial/demographic studies at the university level, see also Koon 1985, pp. 169–70.

[107] His degree thesis was a demographic study of the Jewish population of Rome.

[108] He does describe foreign Jews who had migrated to Italy since the rise of National Socialism as "irreducible enemies of Fascism" (and undoubtedly they had become so); Livi 1938d; this article appeared in the last issue of *Economia* edited by Livi and his (Jewish) co-director Fresco.

Moreover, we know that the mixing of different, but closely related and civilized races, as might be the case for two different ethnic groups from different parts of Italy, often produces better offspring than does the union of two individuals representing families from the same small locality . . . Furthermore, all indications are that the crossing of human groups that differ not just in color, but also in mental level and type and in centuries-old traditions (even staying within the category of European populations) can produce many generations characterized by decadence or at least mental imbalance. It seems to me then that we Italians can conclude that the principle *Italians with Italians* must prevail in order to insure and improve the pure and civilized characteristics of the offspring of Rome.[109]

Gini ultimately came to see the German–Italian war against the allies in racial terms as well. Five months after the Uppsala conference cited above, Gini was in Berlin presenting a paper on the crisis of the bourgeoisie and the tasks facing the "imminent new order," a reference to the anticipated Nazi–Fascist victory. One of these tasks, Gini predicted, would be the opening up of much larger areas for expansion of the "most vigorous races" which had formerly been restricted to the narrow confines of single states. Gini also traced the origins of the war partially to demographic factors, namely the closure of the US and British dominions to immigration which had forced expanding nations to resort to arms in order to insure the necessary demographic outlets.[110] Later that year, the tide of war began to turn and Gini's predictions became moot as German–Italian expansion in Europe and Africa was reversed.

The Nationalist Gini formulated his population theory prior to World War I, and just as that theory was well received by prominent Nationalists, so did it fit well into Fascist ideology once that movement moved toward Nationalist positions. And in spite of Gini's initial skepticism regarding pronatalist measures, he nonetheless managed to extract a degree of optimism regarding Italy and the Fascist experiment

---

[109] Pende 1938, p. 203; this argument is essentially repeated by Gedda in Gemelli's *Vita e pensiero* (Gedda 1938). After the war Pende claimed that his name had been attached to the racial manifesto against his will in order to lend the document a degree of scientific legitimacy, a claim accepted by the *Commissione di epurazione universitaria*. See Pende 1961 and De Felice 1988, pp. 279–80. His claim to have been the only university scholar to have opposed Nazi-Fascist racism (Pende 1961), however, is hard to swallow, given his various statements regarding the scientific basis of Fascist racism, his warnings against the threat of Semitic pollution in Italy, and his stated support of legislation banning marriage between Italians and Jews (Pende 1939, 1940a). De Felice 1988 does refer to Pende's being under a threat of ostracism for his opposition to the manifesto; this opposition may in part have been overcome in connection with the planning of his new orthogenetic institute in Rome (see chapter 4, p. 187 above).

[110] Gini 1942; Gini also published in the racist Nazi journal *Archiv für Rassen- und Gesellschaftsbiologie* (35 [1942], pp. 177–208), cited in Weindling 1988, pp. 112, 119.

out of his theory. For, although the Italian nation found itself on the downward trajectory of the population evolution cycle, the potential for biological rebirth presented itself thanks to the post-unification mixing of Italy's various races. Biological rebirth accompanied spiritual rebirth, and one might invoke the curious combination of Italy's political and racial "youth" – and youth was of course an important Fascist theme – together with its cultural age. Moreover, Gini's theory also provided a biological justification of Fascist Nationalism (closed borders) and ultimately racism as well. On policy measures Gini's position varied. While describing pronatalist legislation as an "extreme remedy" in 1911, he later (and repeatedly) defended his theory against the accusation of pessimism or fatalism. Finally, he would present pronatalist policy, as well as an authoritarian political regime, as natural developments of the latter half of the population cycle.[111]

Gini's political position as a Nationalist turned Fascist, his generally populationist stance on questions of emigration and fertility policy, and his determined personality all helped him attain important positions at the head of government agencies from which he could pursue his theoretical agenda. In spite of his prominent position, however, he did not succeed in dominating the demographic discourse of the period and debate continued in spite of censorship and dictatorship. To be sure, voices advocating birth control, eugenic sterilization, or liberalized emigration were not to be heard, and the Italians did present themselves as a unified school in opposition to optimum theory, neo-Malthusianism, and other aspects of, in particular, Anglo-American demographic theory. Within this school, however, there was considerable disagreement over, especially, the root causes of fertility decline.

The Italian demographic school reflected Fascist (and also Catholic) positions in a number of ways. The advantages of a large and growing population were universally accepted, and a strong church and the restoration of family values were regularly cited as solutions to the problem of denatalism. Demographers argued for the legitimacy of state encouragement of marriage and childbirth, analyzed Italy's need for demographic outlets, and found that colonization served both economic and demographic purposes. They supported pronatalist measures and studied the nature and effects of both Italian measures and those adopted elsewhere. Their work in the Fascist period emphasized those areas that were of concern to the regime, ignored those that were not and lacked dissenting voices of the sort heard before or since that might have gone counter to official position. Demography (and

---

[111] On this point see Federici 1941, pp. 164–73 and her citation to Gini.

demographers) earned prestige and power by their enlistment in the population battle, though at the price of a degree of intellectual freedom. This is not to say that valid demographic work was not done in the period. It was, along with some that strikes the reader today as silly; the inevitably political nature of science need not compromise scientific activity, though it will almost certainly help to determine the sort of science that is done.[112]

[112] See again Proctor 1991, esp. pp. 10-13, on this point.

Conclusion

As Fascism fell, so too did its demographic policy. Certain aspects disappeared entirely – the bachelor tax, pronatalist prizes and celebrations, colonization in Africa, and racist measures – while others survived into the post-war period: ONMI, the new cities, and anti-urban legislation. These holdovers, however, no longer constituted part of a larger demographic plan, and subsequently both ONMI and the anti-urban legislation were dismantled. Indeed in the area of population policy, postwar Italy distinguishes itself in Europe for a relative lack of either family or migration measures. And reluctance on the part of politicians in Republican Italy to deal with these problems is in large part a legacy of Fascism.

Demographic policy reveals the complexity of Italian Fascism. It was part of a larger plan to control Italian industry, labor, culture, society, and politics, a corporativist totalitarian program which has characterized both Fascist and Communist regimes in the twentieth century. And while Fascism in Italy was relatively benign on this score – at times absurd – compared to Nazi Germany or the Soviet Union under Stalin, this question of degree does not exempt it from the general category. The example of demographic policy confirms that Mussolini did aspire to create a totalitarian regime.

Population policy responded to Fascist aspirations in several ways. Increased (or at least stable) fertility and lower mortality would guarantee the future growth of Italy's labor, military, and colonizing potential. In contrast to the Liberal *laissez-faire* approach, the Fascists sought to manipulate these demographic variables and, in particular, the reproductive behavior of couples, bringing the state, as it were, into the bedroom. Internal and external migration policies represented a parallel attempt to manage the spatial movements of individuals and families.

The intrusion of state power into these intimate areas is a modern development characteristic of our century. Equally modern, the new relationship between the individual and the state inherent in Fascist policy translated into a new role for women who were called upon not only to bear many children but also to volunteer their services in order to insure the success of ONMI's battle against infant and maternal mortality and morbidity. This new and more public role for women placed them in the position of choosing between family and state interests and opened new avenues of passive resistance to political authority.

In some ways, the call for female participation in the Fascist program harkened back to the movement's futurist and D'Annunzian origins when a decidedly more emancipated role for women had been envisioned. This association was, however, at best ideological, for in practice Fascist population policy and women's policy revealed what was most anti-modern about the regime: an emphasis on ruralism, repression of birth control and abortion, and promotion of the female role as housewife and mother.

The fertility decline debate revealed still more anti-modernist strains as the effect (especially on women) of industrial urbanism, bourgeois and American values, and a decline of morality and the strength of the Church were all blamed for Italian denatalism; and these are the same factors that the Fascist new man, uncorrupted by Liberal decadence and hardened by the experience of world war, would combat. Fertility decline was symptomatic of the general decline of Western civilization, whether considered in the cultural/political terms of Spengler or the biological ones of Gini.

The population policy also served as a tool for the attainment of non-demographic ends. The much publicized programs of internal and African colonization and infant and maternal care put forward the image that Fascism was both providing land for the traditionally landless Italian peasants and day laborers and also looking after unfortunate mothers whether unwed or simply poor. These measures contributed to the formation of public opinion and consensus among the general population, while the policing of urban migration served the complementary purpose of quelling dissent.

Fascist demographic policy was part of the larger Fascist aim to create a new society that would be both obedient and transparent to the regime. Mussolini at an early date enlisted Italian statisticians in his cause, recognizing in statistical authority a means to pry information from a reluctant population. The information obtained served several purposes: it provided a measure of the demographic situation, revealing the areas in greatest need of attention, and also served as a rhetorical tool for alerting the Italian population to the need for collective action in the area of fertility decline. In addition, Italian statistics would announce to the world Fascist demographic, not to mention economic, successes.

The invasive nature of population statistics gathering was ideologically compatible with a regime that placed the state above all other institutions, including the family, locus of fertility decisions and the source of much demographic data. The continued resistance of the Italian family to yield up either the desired progeny or the desired information was symptomatic of Fascism's failure to get below the surface either socially or ideologically.

Faced with reluctance of this sort, Mussolini resorted to ever more drastic measures. Primary among these was racism, introduced as an integral part of the population policy. In large part racism was a product of the gradual Nazification that Italian Fascism underwent and which culminated in the creation of the *Repubblica sociale*; though for all its mimicking of the Nazi example, Fascist racism nonetheless found Italian sources and a receptive niche in the regime itself. For the introduction of official anti-Semitism was just one more attempt on the part of Mussolini to remold the Italian character and Italian society, and so fit the general logic of population policy of which it represented the culmination.

Ultimately, Fascist population policy revealed the resistance of demographic variables to political manipulation, confirming observations made in 1930 by the physiologist Carlo Foà on the demographic problem: "Faced with these grandiose phenomena which, while seemingly developing as social phenomena, nonetheless share the characteristics and fatality of natural phenomena, the position of any scholar is modest; both the scientist and the politician are forced to take on the role of spectator and annotator" (Foà 1931, p. 426). The Italian Fascist regime proved unable to manipulate demographic phenomena to the degree and in the direction desired, a warning perhaps to those who presume to make similar attempts in other political contexts.

Bibliography

Official and archival sources and abbreviations
(for abbreviations used in the text, see pp. xvi–xvii.)

Archival sources
ACS   Archivio centrale dello stato (Rome)
ISTAT AC   Istituto centrale di statistica, Archivio centrale (Rome)
MAE AS   Ministero degli affari esteri, Archivio storico (Rome)

Laws
D.l.   Decreto-legge
L.   Legge
R.d.   Regio decreto
R.d.-l.   Regio decreto-legge
T.U.   Testo unico

Parliamentary acts
Atti C. disc.   Camera dei Deputati, *Atti del parlamento italiano*
Atti C. D.l.   Camera dei Deputati, *Atti stampati per ordine della Camera*
Atti S. disc.   *Atti parlamentari della Camera dei Senatori*
Atti S. D.l.   Senato del Regno, *Atti interni*

MAIC   Ministero dell'agricoltura, industria e commercio.

Periodicals from which anonymous articles are cited
(these articles/notices do not appear in the bibliography)

Annali di statistica
Barometro economico
Bollettino dell'emigrazione
Bollettino del MAE
Bollettino del Ministero dell'interno
Bollettino mensile di statistica
Bollettino statistico dell'Africa Italiana
Bollettino ufficiale della Somalia

Bollettino ufficiale del Ministero delle corporazioni
Bonifica e colonizzazione
Conquista della terra
Corriere della Sera
Economia
Gazzetta ufficiale
Giornale degli economisti
Maternità ed infanzia
Il Messaggero
Notiziario demografico
Il Popolo d'Italia
Rassegna economica
Razza e civiltà
Rivista internazionale di scienze sociali e discipline ausiliarie

Multiyear official publications (some titles change over time;
the ISTAT series are generally continuations of DIRSTAT ones)

CPMI/CMC, *Le migrazioni interne in Italia*
ISTAT, *Annuario di statistiche demografiche*
ISTAT, *Annuario statistico*
ISTAT, *Cause di morte*
ISTAT, *Censimento generale della popolazione* (Censimento)
ISTAT, *Statistiche delle migrazioni da e per l'estero* (Migrazioni)
ISTAT, *Movimento della popolazione secondo lo stato civile* (Movimento)

Other works cited

Adamson, W. 1993 *Avant-Garde Florence. From Modernism to Fascism.*
    Cambridge (Mass.)–London, Harvard University Press.
Alessandri, C. 1928 Lavoro e maternità. *Maternità ed infanzia*, March,
    pp. 218–25.
    1929 Maternità e economia. *Maternità ed infanzia*, February, pp. 167–71.
    1930a Natalità e lavoro materno. *Maternità ed infanzia*, February, pp. 179–83.
    1930b Statistica del lavoro delle donne e dei fanciulli. *Maternità ed infanzia*,
    April, pp. 415–19.
    1931 Lavoro e natalità. *Maternità ed infanzia*, April, pp. 409–13.
    1936 Esperienze demografiche. *Maternità ed infanzia*, July, pp. 1–2.
Alfieri, E. 1930 La protezione della maternità di fronte al problema
    demografico. *Maternità ed infanzia*, February, pp. 281–99.
Alivìa, G. 1938 *La colonizzazione interna e la Sardegna*. Florence, Casa editrice
    poligrafica universitaria.
Allaria, G. 1935 *Il problema demografico italiano osservato da un pediatra*. Turin, Bona.
    1936 I prestiti per i matrimoni in Germania. *Difesa sociale*, June, pp. 479–500.
    1937 Per la validità demografica della stirpe. *Difesa sociale*, April–May,
    pp. 477–506.
Alonso, W. and Starr, P. (eds.) 1987 *The Politics of Numbers*. New York, Russell
    Sage Foundation.
Alvaro, C. 1935 *Terra nuova: Prima cronaca dell'Agro Pontino*. Rome, Istituto
    nazionale fascista di cultura.

Amoroso, L. 1934 La dinamica della popolazione. In Lojacono 1934b, pp. 19–21.

Aquarone, A. 1965 *L'organizzazione dello Stato totalitario.* Turin, Einaudi.

Arena, C. 1930 Dell'ottima popolazione. *Rivista di politica economica,* 31 January, pp. 12–27; 28 February, pp. 139–59.

Arendt, H. 1951 *The Origins of Totalitarianism.* New York, Harcourt Brace.

Azimonti, E. 1929 *La colonizzazione in Basilicata.* Rome, CPMI.

Balbo, I. 1938 Coloni in Libia. *Nuova antologia,* 1 December.

Ballestrero, M. 1979 *Dalla tutela alla parità.* Bologna, Il Mulino.

Barnes, B. and Shapin, S. (eds.) 1979 *Natural Order: Historical Studies of Scientific Culture.* Beverly Hills, Sage.

Battaglia, R. 1958 *La prima guerra d'Africa.* Turin, Einaudi.

Battara, P. 1931 Influenza delle condizioni economiche e sanitarie sull'andamento della natalità. *Economia,* November, pp. 425–36.

1935a Le curve della natalità nei paesi agricoli ed industriali. *Economia,* May, pp. 409–38.

1935b *Fattori psicologici e morali di denatalità.* Florence, Le Monnier.

Bellero, F. 1927 Problemi della piccola proprietà nel dopoguerra – l'urbanesimo. *Rivista internazionale di scienze sociali,* July–August, pp. 224–40.

Beneduce, A. 1904 Capitali sottratti all'Italia dall'emigrazione per l'estero. *Giornale degli economisti,* December.

1907–8 Della natalità e della fecondità. *Giornale degli economisti,* August–September–October 1907, February 1908.

Benini, R. 1901 *Principii di demografia.* Florence, Barbèra.

1929 Da Malthus a Mussolini. *Educazione fascista,* April, pp. 232–49.

Bergamaschi, G. 1938 La difesa della razza e l'ONMI. *Maternità ed infanzia,* July–October.

1940 L'ONMI per la difesa della razza. *Razza e civiltà,* 23 March, pp. 91–7.

Bernardini, G. 1977 The Origins and Development of Racial Anti-Semitism in Fascist Italy. *Journal of Modern History,* 49, pp. 431–53.

Blanc, G. 1930 Funzione e compiti dell'ONMI. *Maternità ed infanzia,* July, pp. 680–7.

1931 Relazione sullo sviluppo dell'attività dell'ONMI (1926–30). *Maternità ed infanzia,* December, pp. 1079–164.

Blumerù, I. 1885 Saggio di statistica demologica. *Annali di statistica,* 3, n. 13, pp. 89–184.

Bock, G. 1983 Racism and Sexism in Nazi Germany. *Signs,* Spring, pp. 400–21.

Bodio, L. 1892 Sulla emigrazione italiana e sul patronato degli emigrati. In *Atti del primo congresso geografico italiano,* vol. II, pp. 109–48.

Boidi, A. 1931 *Provvedimenti tributari demografici.* Turin, UTET.

Boldrini, M. 1927 La conferenza mondiale della popolazione a Ginevra. *Vita e pensiero,* November, pp. 648–58.

1929 Di alcuni fattori dell'aumento della popolazione. *Rivista italiana di statistica,* October, pp. 332–43.

1931a *La fertilità dei biotipi,* vol. 4 of *Pubblicazioni dell'Università cattolica del sacro cuore.* Milan, Vita e pensiero.

1931b Fertilità e intelligenza. *Rivista internazionale di scienze sociali e discipline ausiliarie,* January, pp. 3–21.

1931c Review of Gini 1930b. *Rivista internazionale di scienze sociali e discipline ausiliarie*, May–July, pp. 454–60.

1934 La fertilità delle classi povere. In Lojacono 1934b, pp. 92–5.

1936 Tipi e attitudini costituzionali e sostituzione delle aristocrazie. In *Contributi del laboratorio di statisitica*, vol. ix of *Pubblicazioni dell'Università cattolica del sacro cuore*. Milan, *Vita e pensiero*, pp. 1–64.

1939a Costituzione ed eugenica. In *Contributi del laboratorio di statisitica*, vol. xi of *Pubblicazioni dell'Università cattolica del sacro cuore*. Milan, *Vita e pensiero*, pp. 181–212.

1939b La fertilità degli individui deficienti e difettosi. In *Contributi del laboratorio di statisitica*, vol. xi of *Pubblicazioni dell'Università cattolica del sacro cuore*. Milan, *Vita e pensiero*, pp. 49–82.

1942 Sulla fertilità matrimoniale in Italia. *Rivista internazionale di scienze sociali e discipline ausiliarie*, July, pp. 214–22.

Bonarini, F. 1994 Controllo e pianificazione dei concepimenti e abortività. In M. Livi Bacci, G. Blangiardo and A. Golini (eds.), *Guide agli studi delle scienze sociali in Italia. Demografia.* Turin, Fondazione Giovanni Agnelli, pp. 307–21.

Bononi, A. 1897 La questione degli esposti e una importante riforma. *La riforma sociale*, 4, n. 7, pp. 861–71.

Bosworth, R. 1979 *Italy, the Least of the Great Powers.* Cambridge–New York, Cambridge University Press.

Bottai, G. 1933 La madre e il fanciullo nella previdenza sociale. *Difesa sociale*, December, pp. 645–7.

Bourguet, M.-N. 1988 *Déchiffrer la France: La statistique départementale à l'époque napoléonienne.* Paris, Editions des archives contemporaines.

Bowler, P. 1989 *Evolution.* Berkeley, University of California Press.

Buffa, A. 1937 Problemi della maternità e dell'infanzia. *Maternità ed infanzia*, October, pp. 1–4.

Buttafuoco, A. 1985 *Le mariuccine: Storia di un'istituto laica, l'asilo Mariuccia.* Milan, Angeli.

Cajoli, R. 1958 *La "questione" Alto Adige.* Rocca San Carciano, Capelli.

Caldwell, L. 1985 Reproducers of the Nation: Women and the Family in Fascist Policy. In D. Forgacs (ed.), *Rethinking Italian Fascism.* London, Lawrence and Wishart.

Canestrelli, S. and Fatica, M. 1978 Nicolò Castellino. In *Dizionario biografico degli italiani*, vol. xxi, Rome, Enciclopedia italiana, pp. 764–6.

Cannistraro, P. and Rosoli, G. 1979 *Emigrazione, chiesa e fascismo.* Rome, Studium.

Caravaggi, G. 1976 La lavoratrice madre. In *La donna e il diritto.* Rome, Editrice sindacale italiana, pp. 123–33.

Carelli, A. 1929 La prolificità in rapporto alle condizioni economiche. *Maternità ed infanzia*, November, pp. 1285–8.

Carpi, L. 1874 *Delle colonie e dell'emigrazione degli italiani all'estero sotto l'aspetto dell'industria, commercio, agricoltura e con trattazione d'importanti questioni sociali.* Milan, Lombarda.

Carrara, M. 1925 La questione sessuale e l'aborto. *Difesa sociale*, May–June, pp. 125–32.

Casalini, E. 1928 Il nuovo concetto demografico della bonifica e la sua applicazione nel Polesine. *Economia*, January, pp. 29–45.

Casanova, E. 1940 Le colonie allogene dell'Italia meridionale e della Sicilia. *Genus*, November–December.
Casini, P. 1941 La bonifica di Mussolinia in Sardegna. *Quaderni italiani*, 11, Rome, Irce.
Castellano, V. 1965 Corrado Gini: a Memoir. *Metron*, 31 December, pp. 2–84.
Cavaglieri, G. 1902 L'emigrazione dal Polesine (1881–1901). *La riforma sociale*, 9, n. 12, pp. 925–32, 1031–58.
Cazzani, G. 1929 Il problema demografico e la religione. *Rivista internazionale di scienze sociali e discipline ausiliarie*, February–March, pp. 99–129.
CGE 1924–5 *L'emigrazione italiana*, vol. III. Rome.
   1926 *Annuario statistico della emigrazione italiana dal 1876 al 1925*. Rome.
Chiarelli, G. 1934 La religione e la natalità. In Lojacono 1934b, pp. 102–5.
Ciocca, P. and Toniolo, G. (eds.) 1976 *L'economia italiana nel periodo fascista*. Bologna, Il Mulino.
Cipriani, L. 1937 Politica demografica in Francia e altrove. *Gerarchia*, December, pp. 836–40.
Ciuffoletti, Z. and Degl'Innocenti, M. 1978 *L'emigrazione nella storia dell'Italia*, vol. 1: *1868–1914* (Ciuffoletti), vol. 2: *1914–1975* (Degl'Innocenti). Florence, Vallecchi.
Clinica della R. Università di Bologna 1934 Contributo alla ricerca dei rapporti fra fecondità e costituzione. In Gini 1934c, vol. III, pp. 103–17.
Clough, S. 1964 *The Economic History of Italy*. New York, Columbia University Press.
Coale, A. and Watkins, S. 1986 *The Decline of Fertility in Europe*. Princeton University Press.
Colajanni, N. 1891 *Politica coloniale*. Palermo, Clausen.
   1904 *Manuale di demografia*. Naples, L. Pierro.
   1912 *Dell'emigrazione italiana*. Milan (also in *Cinquant'anni di storia italiana*, vol. III, Milan, Hoepli, 1911).
Coletti, F. 1912 *Dell'emigrazione italiana*. Milan. Also in *Cinquanti'anni di storia italiana*, vol. III. Milan, Hoepli, 1911.
Collotti, E. 1989 *Fascismo, fascismi*. Florence, Sansoni.
Commissione alleata and PCM–ISTAT 1945 *Censimenti e indagini per la ricostruzione nazionale eseguiti nel September 1944*. Rome, February.
Confederazione fascista dei lavoratori dell'agricoltura 1939 *I rurali di Mussolini nella Germania di Hitler*. Rome.
Consiglio, V. 1934 La sterilità delle classi ricche. In Lojacono 1934b, pp. 81–7.
Corsini, C. 1983 La mobilità interna della popolazione nel periodo fascista. In G. Cherubini et al. (eds.), *Storia della Società italiana*, vol. XXII: *La dittatura fascista*. Milan, Testi, pp. 163–93.
   1985 L'acculturazione mancata. Il processo formativo dell'organizzazione delle fonti demografiche nel periodo post-unitario. In SIDES, *La popolazione italiana nell'ottocento*, Bologna, Clueb.
   1989 (ed.), *Da osservazione sperimentale a spiegazione razionale. Per una storia della statistica in Italia*. Catalogue from the exhibition (Pisa, 1989), Pisa, Società italiana di statistica.
Cosmacini, G. 1984 Scienza e ideologia nella medicina del novecento: dalla scienza egemone alla scienza ancillare. In Franco della Peruta (ed.), *Storia d'Italia*, Annali 7: *Malattia e medicina*. Turin, Einaudi.

Crollalanza, A. (di) 1937 La valorizzazione dell'impero. *Conquista della terra*, April, pp. 3–10.
1939 L'attività colonizzatrice dell'ONC nell'impero. *Conquista della terra*, December 1939, pp. 3–18.
Crosby, A. 1986 *Ecological Imperialism: The Biological Expansion of Europe 900–1900*. Cambridge, Cambridge University Press.
Curcio, C. 1934 La decadenza demografica della razza bianca in rapporto alle razze di colore. In Lojacono 1934b, pp. 32–5.
Dalmazzo, F. 1923 (ed.) *Atti del Congresso nazionale per l'assistenza ai minorenni abbandonati o traviati*. Rome, 27–30 May.
1930 L'assistenza all'infanzia illegittima. *Vita e pensiero*, October, pp. 597–603.
Danzi, G. 1934 *Europa senza europei?* Rome, Edizioni Roma.
Daston, L. 1988 *Classical Probability in the Enlightenment*. Princeton University Press.
Dau Novelli, C. 1994 *Famiglia e modernizzazione in Italia tra le due guerre*. Rome, Studium.
D'Autilia, M. 1992 *L'amministrazione della statistica nell'Italia fascista. Il caso dell'agricoltura*. Rome, Gangemi.
De Bernardinis, L. 1940 Il movimento naturale della popolazione nell'ultimo quadriennio. *Razza e civiltà*, April, pp. 223–8.
De Bernardinis, L., C. Micheli, and P. Gaifami 1930 Le vere cifre della nostra nati-mortalità, neonati-mortalità e mortalità infantile. *Maternità ed infanzia*, October, pp. 986–1002.
De Felice, R. 1965 *Mussolini il rivoluzionario*. Turin, Einaudi.
1966 *Mussolini il fascista, I: La conquista del potere 1921–25*. Turin, Einaudi.
1968 *Mussolini il fascista II: L'organizzazione dello Stato fascista*. Turin, Einaudi.
1973 *Il problema dell'Alto Adige*. Bologna, Il Mulino.
1974 *Mussolini il duce I. Gli anni del consenso*. Turin, Einaudi.
1977 *Interpretations of Fascism*. Cambridge (Mass.), Harvard University Press.
1978 *D'Annunzio politico, 1918–1938*. Bari, Laterza.
1981 *Mussolini il duce II. Lo stato totalitario*. Turin, Einaudi.
1988 *Storia degli ebrei italiani sotto il fascismo*. Turin, Einaudi.
De Grand, A. 1976 Women Under Italian Fascism. *The Historical Journal*, 19, n. 4, pp. 947–68.
1995 *Fascist Italy and Nazi Germany: The "Fascist" Style of Rule*. New York, Routledge.
de Grazia, V. 1981 *The Culture of Consent. Mass Organization of Leisure in Fascist Italy*. Cambridge, Cambridge University Press.
1992 *How Fascism Ruled Women. Italy, 1922–1945*. Berkeley, University of California Press.
Del Boca, A. 1982 *Gli italiani in Africa Orientale. La caduta dell'Impero*. Bari, Laterza.
Del Chiaro, A. 1940 Indici di riproduttività della popolazione italiana. *Annali di statistica*, 7, n. 6.
D'Elia, E. 1942 Sull'andamento della mortalità italiana per le malattie della gravidanza, parto e puerperio. *Razza e civiltà*, October–December.
De Marzio, E. 1936 Il lavoro e la donna. *Maternità ed infanzia*, January–February, p. 3.

Demorazza 1942 *Correnti migratorie e urbanesimo.* Rome.
De Polzer, A. 1938 La colonizzazione nell'Impero in rapporto alle condizione demografiche ed agrarie della pianura del Veneto. *Bonifica e colonizzazione,* January, pp. 35–47.
De Stefani, A. 1921 *Decadenza demografica e decadenza economica.* Rome, La Voce.
Detragiache, D. 1980 Un aspect de la politique démographique de l'Italie fasciste: la répression de l'avortement. *Mélanges de l'école française de Rome,* 92, n. 2, pp. 691–735.
De Tuddo, A. 1940 Valore demografico della previdenza sociale: L'assicurazione nuzialità e natalità. *Rivista italiana di scienze economiche,* November, pp. 1236–9.
De Vergottini, M. 1935 Migrazioni ed esodi. In Gini 1933–7, vol. II, part 1, pp. 195–238.
    1941 Osservazioni sul differente accrescimento delle classi sociali. *Economia,* November–December, pp. 459–74.
    1943 Sul differente accrescimento delle classi sociali. *Economia,* January–February, pp. 43–8.
Di Felice, M. n.d. Bonifiche e migrazioni interne nell'Italia fascista: Mussolinia e l'archivio della società bonifiche sarde. In *Atti del congresso Fonti archivistiche e ricerca demografica.* Trieste, April 1990, seen as typescript.
Di Rienzo, P. 1965 Movimento migratorio interno a base alle iscrizioni e cancellazioni anagrafiche per trasferimento di residenza. *Annali di statistica,* 8, n. 17.
di Robilant, D. 1929 Previdenza materna in regime fascista. *Difesa sociale,* April, pp. 144–7.
    1936 Il lavoro e la donna. *Maternità ed infanzia,* April, pp. 7–10.
Di San Giuliano, A. 1905 L'emigrazione italiana negli Stati Uniti d'America. *Nuova antologia,* 1 July.
Donzelot, J. 1977 *La police des familles.* Paris, Minuit.
Dorn Brose, E. 1987 Generic Fascism Revisited: Attitudes Toward Technology in Germany and Italy, 1919–1945. *German Studies Review,* 10, n. 2 (May), pp. 273–97.
Dumont, A. 1890 *Dépopulation et civilisation.* Paris, Lecrosnier et Babé.
Dupâquier, J. and Dupâquier, M. 1985 *Histoire de la démographie.* Paris, Perrin.
Dupâquier, J. Sauvy, A. and Le Roy Ladurie, E. 1988 *Histoire de la population française,* vol. IV. Paris, PUF.
Economia 1938 Riunione del Comitato di consulenza per gli studi sulla popolazione (Florence, April). *Economia,* May, pp. 333–44.
Fabbri, S. 1932a L'assistenza per la maternità e l'infanzia in Italia. *Maternità ed infanzia,* May, pp. 431–7.
    1932b Fasci femminili ed ONMI. *Maternità ed infanzia,* June, pp. 545–50.
    1932c La politica demografica. *Maternità ed infanzia,* August, pp. 717–25.
    1934 La casa della madre e del bambino. *Maternità ed infanzia,* September, pp. 2–3.
    1936a L'esaltazione della famiglia fascista. *Maternità ed infanzia,* December, pp. 1–4.
    1936b Valori ideali e pratici dell'ONMI. *Maternità ed infanzia,* May, pp.1–5.
    1937 Il problema dei problemi. *Maternità ed infanzia,* March, pp.1–2.
Fahlbeck, F. 1903 *Der Adel Schwedens.* Jena, Fischer.
Fairchild, H. 1927 Optimum Population. In M. Sanger 1927, pp. 72–84.

Fasolis, G. 1932 Popolazione, politica demografica fascista e pubblica finanza. *Rivista di politica economica*, 31 May, pp. 536–46.

Federici, N. 1938 Le correnti migratorie e le correnti commerciali tra colonie e madre-patria. *Annali dell'Africa Coloniale*, 9 May, pp. 37–51.

1941 *La politica della popolazione*. Rome, Failli.

1942a Le più recenti spedizioni scientifiche del C.I.S.P. *Genus*, 5, n. 3–4 (December), pp. 119–32.

1942b Su talune caratteristiche bio-fisiologiche e demografiche di una popolazione primitiva (Dauada). *Genus*, 5, n. 3–4 (December), pp. 45–101.

1943–9 Congresso nazionale di scienze della popolazione. *Genus*, 6–8, pp. 405–11.

Ferrari, G. 1934 Il costo monetario dell'uomo. In Gini 1934c, vol. IX, pp. 115–75.

Foà, C. 1931 Aspetti biologici del problema demografico. In *Atti della Società italiana per il progresso delle scienze (7–15.ix.1930)*, vol. I, Rome, pp. 426–70.

1934 I fattori biologici della diminuzione delle nascite. In Gini 1934c, vol. II, pp. 9–57 (a revision of Foà 1931).

Foà, P. 1922 Per la riforma dei brefotrofi. *Difesa sociale*, 1, n. 6 (June), pp. 122–4.

Foerster, R. 1919 *The Italian Emigration of Our Times*. Cambridge (Mass.), Harvard University Press.

Forni, S. 1940 Mortalità infantile. *Razza e civiltà*, July–September, pp. 509–17.

Fortunati, P. 1932 *Polemiche statistiche*. Ferrara, Nuovi problemi.

Fossa, D. 1937 Colonizzazione demografica dell'Impero. *Bonifica e colonizzazione*, October.

Franchetti, L. 1894 La colonizzazione dell'Eritrea. *La riforma sociale*, 1, n. 2, pp. 5–24.

Frontoni, A. 1942 Bonifica umana. *Maternità ed infanzia*, May–June, pp. 72–9.

Gaifami, P. 1929 Come diminuire la mortinatalità. *Maternità ed infanzia*, November, pp. 1187–95.

1936 Il lavoro delle donne. *Maternità ed infanzia*, March, pp. 5–6.

Galvani, L. 1934 L'andamento della natalità nel settentrione e nel mezzogiorno d'Italia. In Lojacono 1934b, pp. 43–54.

Gedda, L. 1938 A proposito di razza. *Vita e pensiero*, September, pp. 403–17.

Gemelli, A. 1928a Il problema delle famiglie numerose. *Vita e pensiero*, March, pp. 131–8.

1928b Punti di vista diversi nel problema della diminuzione delle nascite. *Vita e pensiero*, November, pp. 645–52.

1931 Ancora sulla condanna della eugenetica. *Vita e pensiero*, October, pp. 603–14.

1934a La 'sterilizzazione coattiva e preventiva' nell'insegnamento degli studiosi italiani. In Lojacono 1934b, pp. 117–28.

1934b Le vedute della psicologia e della psichiatria nel problema della natalità. In Gini 1934c, vol. II, pp. 343–6.

1937a Attualità del problema demografico. *Vita e pensiero*, March, pp. 134–8.

1937b Il compito di una università cattolica ed italiana nella lotta del communismo contro cattolicesimo e fascismo. *Vita e pensiero*, January, pp. 72–3.

Geremicca, A. 1918 *Per l'avvenire della vita economica italiana*. Naples, Gianna e figli.

Ghigi, A. 1934 Costituzione e fertilità. In Gini 1934c, vol. III, pp. 63–76.

Ghirardo, D. 1989 *Building New Communities. New Deal America and Fascist Italy*. Princeton, Princeton University Press.
Gillis, J., Tilly, L., and Levine, D. (eds.) 1992 *The European Experience of Declining Fertility*. Cambridge (Mass.), Oxford, Blackwell.
Gini, C. 1909 Il diverso accrescimento delle classi sociali e la concentrazione della ricchezza. *Giornale degli economisti*, January.
1912 *I fattori demografici dell'evoluzione delle nazioni*. Turin, Bocca.
1924 Le leggi dell'evoluzione della popolazione. *Economia*, December, pp. 265–96.
1927a Alcune ricerche italiane sulla riproduttività differenziale. *Economia*, August–September, pp. 67–80.
1927b Considerazioni su l'*optimum* di densità della popolazione. *Economia*, July, pp. 1–6.
1927c La fertilità della donna in relazione al problema della popolazione. *Economia*, August–September, pp. 55–62.
1927d *Il neo-organicismo*. Catania, Studio Editoriale Moderno.
1927e Some Italian Enquiries into Differential Fertility. In Sanger 1927, pp. 157–69.
1930a Il problema demografico italiano e la politica mussoliniana della popolazione. In *Lo Stato mussoliniano e le realizzazioni del fascismo nella nazione*, Rome, Rassegna Italiana.
1930b *Nascita, evoluzione e morte delle nazioni: La teoria ciclica della popolazione e i vari sistemi di politica demografica*. Rome, Libreria del Littorio.
1931 *Le basi scientifiche della politica della popolazione*. Catania, Studio Editoriale Moderno.
1933–7 (ed.) *Trattato di statistica*. Milan, Giuffrè.
1934a Discorso inaugurale. In Gini 1934c, vol. I, pp. xvii–xxv.
1934b Premiers résultats d'une expédition italo-mexicaine parmi les populations indigènes et métisses du Mexique. *Genus*, June, pp. 147–76.
1934c (ed.) *Proceedings of the International Congress for the Scientific Study of Population Problems*. Rome, Istituto poligrafico dello Stato.
1934d Relazione della missione demografica del Comitato italiano per lo studio dei problemi della popolazione in Tripolitania. *Genus*, June, pp. 109–16.
1934e I samaritani. *Genus*, June, pp. 117–46.
1934f La intensità della diminuzione della fecondità matrimoniale secondo l'età della madre. In Gini 1934c, vol. II, pp. 71–132 (see also *Metron*, 1 March 1934, pp. 3–63).
1936a I caraimi di Polonia e Lituania. *Genus*, June, pp. 1–56.
1936b Parole inaugurali del Professore Corrado Gini lette alla Riunione della Società di eugenica dell'America Latina tenutasi a Messico il 12 ott. 1935. *Genus*, June.
1936c Relazione su l'inchiesta demografica antropologica e medico-biologica sopra i Dauada (Fezzan-Tripolitania) seguita dal Comitato italiano per lo studio dei problemi della popolazione (January–February 1935). *Genus*, June, pp. 57–75.
1937 Appunti sulle spedizioni scientifiche del Comitato italiano per lo studio dei problemi della popolazione. *Genus*, June, pp. 225–58.
1938 Emigrazione e colonie. *Rivista di politica economica*, April, pp. 341–52.

1940 *Les facteurs de la décroissance de la natalité à l'époque contemporaine*. Porto, Imprensa portuguesa.

1942 La crisi della borghesia e il compito dei regimi totalitari. *Archivio di studi corporativi*, vol. VIII, Pisa, Pacini Mariotti.

1945 *Teorie della popolazione*. Rome, Castellani.

Gini, C. et al. 1930 *Population*. Chicago, University of Chicago Press.

Giusti, U. 1936 Note di demografia italiana. *Difesa sociale*, January, pp. 3–8.

1939 Sulla natalità differenziale dei capoluoghi di provincia. *Economia*, December, pp. 383–5.

1941a L'andamento della natalità in Italia nel decennio 1931–40 e i suoi aspetti ambientali. *Economia*, March–April, pp. 107–17.

1941b Caratteristiche ambientali della natalità italiana dal 1801 al 1940. *Razza e civiltà*, 25 March, pp. 93–108.

Glass, D. 1940 *Population Policies and Movements in Europe*. Oxford, Oxford University Press.

Goglia, L. 1988 Note sul razzismo coloniale fascista. *Storia contemporanea*, n. 6, pp. 1223–66.

Gorni, M. 1974 Il problema degli "esposti" in Italia dal 1861 al 1900. In M. Gorni and L. Pellegrini (eds.), *Un problema di storia sociale: l'infanzia abbandonata in Italia nel secolo XIX*. Florence, La Nuova Italia, pp. 1–107.

Grillenzoni, C. 1932 I caratteri del fisico e del vestire come fattori demografici. *Metron*, 10, n. 3, 30 September, pp. 131–84.

Grossi, G. 1935 *Legge e potenza del numero*. Bologna, Zanichelli.

Hacking, I. 1975 *The Emergence of Probability*. Cambridge, Cambridge University Press.

Hecht, J. 1991 Il caso francese. In A. Golini (ed.), *Famiglia, figli e società in Europa*. Turin, Fondazione Giovanni Agnelli.

Höhne, H. 1970 *The Order of the Death's Head*. New York, Coward-McCann.

Horkheimer, M. 1949 Authoritarianism and the Family. In R. Anshen (ed.), *The Family. Its Function and Destiny*. New York, Harper.

Horn, D. 1994 *Social Bodies. Science, Reproduction, and Italian Modernity*. Princeton University Press.

Hughes, H. and Kolinsky, M. 1976 'Paradigmatic Fascism' and Modernization: A Critique. *Political Studies*, 34, no. 4, pp. 371–96.

Hunecke, V. 1989 *I trovatelli di Milano*. Bologna, Il Mulino.

Ipsen, C. 1990 Demography and the Fascist 'Revolution'. In E. Vilquin (ed.), *Révolution et population*. Louvain-la-Neuve, Academia, pp. 163–9.

1992a *Dictating Demography: The Problem of Population in Fascist Italy*. Ph.D. dissertation, University of California at Berkeley.

1992b The Statistics of Population in Liberal Italy. *Bollettino di demografia storica*, n. 16, pp. 7–33.

Isenburg, T. 1977 Il dibattito su Malthus e sulla popolazione nell'Italia di fine '800. *Studi storici*, 18, n. 3, pp. 41–67.

ISTAT 1936 *Decennale 1926–1936*. Rome.

1961 (Fracassi), *Dal censimento dell'Unità al censimento del centenario*. Rome.

1968 *Sommario di statistiche storiche italiane 1861–1965*. Rome.

1976 *Sommario di statistiche storiche italiane 1861–1975*. Rome.

1977 *Cinquant'anni di statistica*. Rome.

Istituto nazionale di economia agraria 1932–38 *Lo spopolamento montano in Italia*, 8 vols. Rome.

IUSSP 1985 *The IUSSP in History*. Florence.

Jacini, S. (ed.) 1923 Questionario sulla emigrazione. *Opera Bonomelli,* March.

Kevles, D. 1986 *In the Name of Eugenics*. Berkeley, University of California Press.

Keynes J. 1937 Some Economic Consequences of a Declining Population. *The Eugenics Review*, April, pp. 13–17.

Kirk, D. 1946 *Europe's Population in the Interwar Years*. Geneva, League of Nations.

Korherr, R. 1928 *Regresso delle nascite, morte dei popoli*. Rome, Libreria del Littorio.

Koon, T. 1985 *Believe, Obey, Fight. Political Socialization of Youth in Fascist Italy*. Chapel Hill, University of North Carolina Press.

Lanaro, S. 1979 *Nazione e lavoro. Saggio sulla cultura borghese 1870–1925*. Venice, Marsilio.

Larebo, H. 1994 *The Building of an Empire: Italian Policy and Practice in Ethiopia 1935–41*. Oxford, Clarendon Press.

La Rosa, G. 1923 Il regolamento generale per il servizio di assistenza agli esposti. *Difesa sociale*, 2, n. 6 (June), pp. 91–2.

Laurinisch, A. 1936 La funzione del medico nell'opera nazionale maternità ed infanzia. *Maternità ed infanzia*, August–September, pp. 111–14.

Ledeen, M. 1977 *The First Duce. D'Annunzio at Fiume*. Baltimore–London, Johns Hopkins University Press.

Lees, L. 1992 Safety in Numbers: Social Welfare Legislation and Fertility Decline in Western Europe. In Gillis, Tilly and Levine 1992, pp. 310–25.

Lesthaeghe, R. 1992 The Second Demographic Transition in Western Countries: An Interpretation. In *IUSSP Seminar on Gender and Family Change in Industrialized Countries. Rome 26–30 Jan. 1992*. (IPD Working Paper, no. 1991–2, 1992.31, Vrije Universiteit Brussel, Interuniversity Program in Demography, Brussels, Belgium.)

Leti G. 1989 Verso una Società nazionale di statistica. In Società italiana di statistica, *Statistica e società*. Pisa, pp. 9–72.

Leti G. and Gastaldi, T. 1989 Cinquanta anni di storia della SIS. In Società italiana di statistica, *Statistica e società*. Pisa, pp. 73–195.

Livi, L. 1927a Indagine sulla natalità in rapporto ai tipi di contratto agricolo dominanti ed al frazionamento della proprietà fondiaria. *Economia*, October, pp. 155–62.

1927b Sulla natalità differenziale in Italia. *Economia*, August–September, pp. 63–6.

1928 La politica per la ruralizzazione del paese in rapporto al problema demografico. *Economia*, September, pp. 209–16.

1929a Il problema della natalità in rapporto alla produzione agricola ed industriale. *Rivista di politica economica*, 28 February, pp. 124–54.

1929b Rassegna demografica. *Economia*, April, pp. 400–2.

1931a Differenze tra città e campagna in fatto di nuzialità (ed altre note). *Economia*, July, pp. 54–8.

1931b. Sulla relazione esistente tra la frequenza dei concepimenti, lo stato sanitario del popolo e la disoccupazione. *Economia*, June, pp. 725–9.

1932a La politica demografica fascista nella pratica e nella scienza. *Economia*, October, pp. 408–13.

1932b Rassegna demografica. *Economia*, February, pp. 205–10.
1933a Il bilancio demografico del 1932. *Economia*, January–February, pp. 99–106.
1933b Review of L. Hersch. *Economia*, October, pp. 254–5.
1933c Sulla connessione tra concepimenti, mortalità ed occupazione agraria negli S.U. d'America. *Economia*, July–August, pp. 57–61.
1935 I primi risultati della politica demografica nazista. *Economia*, May, pp. 498–501.
1936a Sui concetti di "popolazione ottima" e "sovrapopolamento". *Economia*, April, pp. 118–28.
1936b Ancora sul concetto di poplazione ottima e di sovrapopolamento. *Economia*, May, pp. 415–27.
1937a Considerazioni sui risultati della politica demografica nazional-socialista e sull'andamento della natalità in Italia. *Economia*, February, pp. 112–23.
1937b Un'inchiesta sugli effetti della politica demografica nazional-socialista. *Economia*, July–August, pp. 20–36.
1937c I recenti provvedimenti per l'incremento demografico. *Economia*, June, pp. 398–403.
1938a Indagine sulle recenti tendenze della natalità nell'Italia settentrionale. *Economia*, December, pp. 359–67.
1938b Uno sguardo alla legislazione straniera nel campo demografico. *Economia*, January, pp. 3–15.
1938c Sui concetti di "minimum di popolazione" e di "optimum strutturale". *Economia*, August, pp. 78–88.
1938d In tema di razzismo. Risposta ai critici d'oltre oceano. *Economia*, September–October, pp. 153–9.
1940a La geografia della natalità e la nuova carta della Direzione generale della demografia e la razza. *Razza e civiltà*, May–June, pp. 333–41.
1940b Sui risultati della politica demografica in Italia. *Economia*, January, pp. 9–15.
1974 (1941) *Trattato di demografia*. Padova, Cedam.
Livi Bacci, M. 1961 *L'immigrazione e l'assimilazione degli italiani negli stati uniti*. Milan, Giuffrè.
1977 *A History of Italian Fertility During the Last Two Centuries*. Princeton, Princeton University Press.
1991 *Population and Nutrition: An Essay on European Demographic History*. Cambridge, Cambridge University Press.
1992 *A Concise History of World Population*. Cambridge (Mass.)–Oxford, Blackwell.
Livi Bacci, M. and Santini, A. 1969 *Tavole di fecondità della donna italiana secondo le generazioni di appartenenza*. Florence, Dipartimento statistico-matematico Università degli studi di Firenze.
Loffredo, F. 1938 Politica demografica e lavoro femminile. *Difesa sociale*, October, pp. 994–7.
Lojacono, L. 1934a Il numero è potenza. In Lojacono 1934b, pp. 3–15.
1934b (ed.) *Popolazione e fascismo*. Rome, L'Economia Italiana.
Lorenzoni, A. 1934 L'impiego delle donne nell'industria e sue conseguenze. In Lojacono 1934b, pp. 69–73.
Loria, A. 1882 *La legge di popolazione e il sistema sociale*. Siena, Lazzeri.

1897 La vecchia e la nuova fase della teoria della popolazione. *Rivista italiana di sociologia*, July.
1909 *Malthus*. Bologna–Modena, Formìggini.
1912 *La dernière évolution de la théorie de l'évolution*. Paris, Girard et Brière.
Loschiavo, G. 1936 Il commissariato per le migrazioni e la colonizzazione interna e gli uffici di collocamento. *Diritto del lavoro*, n. 12.
Lyttelton, A. 1973 *The Seizure of Power: Fascism in Italy 1919–1929*. London, Weidenfeld and Nicolson.
McDougall, M. 1983 Protecting Infants: The French Campaign for Maternity Leaves, 1890–1913. *French Historical Studies*, Spring, pp. 79–105.
McEvedy, C. and Jones, R. 1978 *Atlas of World Population History*. New York, Penguin Books.
McKeown, T. 1976 *The Modern Rise of Population*. London, Edward Arnold.
McLaren, A. 1983 *Sexuality and the Social Order: The Debate Over the Fertility of Women and Workers in France, 1770–1920*. New York, Holmes and Meier.
MAE 1928 *Censimento degli italiani all'estero 1927*. Rome.
1934 *Raccolta delle circolari e istruzioni ministeriali riservate*, vols. I–II: 1863–1933. Rome.
Majorana, S. 1929 Aspetti del problema demografico. *Rivista internazionale di scienze sociali e discipline ausiliarie*, April, pp. 57–62.
Manzotti, F. 1962 *La polemica sull'emigrazione nell'Italia unita fino alla prima guerra mondiale*. Milan, Società editrice Dante Aligheri.
Marconcini, F. 1935 *Culle vuote*. Como, Cavalleri.
Mariani, R. 1976 *Fascismo e città "nuove"*. Milan, Feltrinelli.
Marsigli, A. 1933 Il problema demografico nelle dottrine politiche ed economiche italiane. *Rivista di politica economica*, 30 June, pp. 714–37; 31 July–31 August, pp. 844–60; 30 September–30 October, pp. 974–1001.
Martinelli, R. and Nuti, L. 1981 *Le città di strapaese: La politica di "fondazione" nel ventennio*. Milan, Angeli.
Mason, T. 1987 Moderno, modernità, modernizzazione: un montaggio. *Movimento operaio e socialista*, 10, n. 1–2 (January–August), pp. 45–61.
Medolaghi, P. 1934 Natalità e mortalità in Italia. In Lojacono 1934b, pp. 38–42.
Messedaglia, A. 1858 *Della teoria della popolazione principalmente sotto l'aspetto del metodo*. Verona, Vincentini e Franchini.
1879 La statistica, i suoi metodi e la sua competenza. *Archivio di statistica*, 4, f. 2.
Michaelis, M. 1989 Fascism, Totalitarianism and the Holocaust: Reflections on Current Interpretations of National Socialist Anti-Semitism. *European History Quarterly*, 19, pp. 85–103.
Micheli, C. 1930a I medici condotti e il problema della madre nell'ONMI. *Maternità ed infanzia*, June, pp. 574–81.
1930b *Nati-mortalità*. Rome.
Michels, R. 1925 Appunti sull'aspetto morfologico del problema della nazione. *Giornale degli economisti*, March, pp. 157–63.
1934 Le classi medie e la natalità. In Lojacono 1934b, pp. 88–91.
Millon, H. 1978 Some New Towns in Italy in the 1930s. In H. Millon and L. Nochlin (eds.), *Art and Architecture in the Service of Politics*. Cambridge (Mass.), MIT Press, pp. 326–41.
Ministero dell'interno – Demorazza n.d. *Carta della natalità*, Rome.
Mitchell, B. 1981 *European Historical Statistics*. New York, Facts on File.

Modigliano, E. 1923 Provvedimenti governativi nel campo dell'igiene e assistenza sociale. *Difesa sociale*, 2, 3 (February), pp. 42–5.

Molinari, A. 1932 Un'indagine sulle motivazioni della diminuzione delle nascite. *Metron*, 15 September, pp. 349–92.

1937 *La struttura della popolazione rurale italiana e le nuove figure agricole rilevate nell'VIII° censimento*. Rome, Istituto poligrafico dello stato.

Montanari, M. 1994 *The Culture of Food*. Cambridge (Mass.)–Oxford, Blackwell.

Montemartini, G. 1907 Il fenomeno migratorio e l'intervento dello Stato. *Giornale degli economisti*, January.

Moretto, S. 1991 Le statistiche italiane dello stato civile dal 1862 al 1930. *Bollettino di demografia storica*, n. 14, pp. 51–65.

Mortara, G. 1908 *Le popolazioni delle grandi città italiane*. Turin, UTET.

1911 L'incubo dello spopolamento e l'Italia. *Rivista d'Italia*, November.

1921 *Prospettive economiche*. Città di Castello, Società editrice Leonardo da Vinci.

1933a Review of F. Savorgnan, "La statistica delle nascite legittime secondo l'ordine di generazione." *Giornale degli economisti*, October, pp. 736–45.

1933b Nuovi dati sulla natalità in Italia. *Giornale degli economisti*, November, pp. 823–35.

1933c Sui metodi per lo studio della fecondità dei matrimoni. *Giornale degli economisti*, December, pp. 890–7.

1934a La fecondità dei matrimoni in Italia nel 1930 e nel 1905 In Lojacono 1934b, pp. 36–7.

1934b Nuovi dati sulla natalità in Italia. *Giornale degli economisti*, February, pp. 736–45.

1934c Relazione tra la diminuzione della natalità e la diminuzione della mortalità. In Gini 1934c, vol. VII, pp. 235–52.

1935 La capacità di riproduzione della popolazione italiana. *Giornale degli economisti*, April, pp. 338–40.

1937 Sull'inutilità economica delle colonie. *Giornale degli economisti*, March, pp. 173–7.

Mosse, G. 1979 Towards a General Theory of Fascism. In G. Mosse (ed.), *International Fascism*. London–Beverly Hills, Sage, pp. 1–41 (also in G. Mosse, *Masses and Man*. New York, Fertig, 1980, pp. 159–96).

1985 *Nationalism and Sexuality*. Madison, University of Wisconsin Press.

Mussolini, B. 1934 *Scritti e discorsi di Benito Mussolini*. Milan, Hoepli, 1934.

1951–63 *Opera omnia*, 35 vols. Florence, La Fenice (cited as Mussolini).

Myrdal, A. 1945 *The Swedish Experiment in Democratic Family and Population Policy*. London, Kegan Paul, Trench, Trubner.

Myrdal, A. and Myrdal, G. 1934 *Kris i befolkningsfragen*. Stockholm.

Nannini, S. 1935 Migrazione e colonizzazione. *La Conquista della terra*, December, pp. 88–98.

1937 Migrazione e colonizzazione. *La Conquista della terra*, October, pp. 137–42.

1938 Migrazioni interne e razza. *Difesa sociale*, August, pp. 715–17.

Nazzaro, P. 1972 L'*Immigration quota act* del 1921, la crisi del sistema liberale e l'avvento del fascismo. In Istituto di studi americani (Università degli studi di Firenze), *Gli italiani negli Stati Uniti*, Florence.

Nina, L. 1941 Politica demografica fascista. *Razza e civiltà*, April, pp. 261–91.

Nitti, F. 1888 *L'emigrazione ed i suoi avversari*. Turin, Roux.

1894 *La popolazione ed il sistema sociale*. Turin, Roux.

Nobile, A. 1974 Politica migratoria e vicende dell'emigrazione durante il fascismo. *Il Ponte*, November–December, pp. 1322–41.

1987 Testi italiani di demografia: evoluzione dei contenuti. In E. Sonnino et al. (eds.), *Demografia: Scienza, insegnamento, professione*. Milan, Angeli.

1989 Per una storia dell'insegnamento della demografia nelle università italiane dalle origini al 1961. In Corsini 1989.

1990a La colonizzazione demografica della Libia: progetti e realizzazioni. *Bollettino di demografia storica*, n. 12, pp. 173–88.

1990b La politique démographique du gouvernement fasciste dans le contexte européen. *Materiali di studi e ricerche*, n. 40 (December), Dipartimento di scienze demografiche, Università degli studi di Roma.

1990c Gli studi demografici sulle colonie italiane: fonti e problemi. *Materiali di studi e ricerche*, n. 42 (December), Dipartimento di scienze demografiche, Università degli studi di Roma.

Noble, F. 1929 Urbanesimo e natalità. *Economia*, January, pp. 21–31.

Nolte, E. 1965 *Three Faces of Fascism*. London, Weidenfeld and Nicolson.

1979 Reply to Allardyce. *American Historical Review*, April, pp. 391–5.

Olivieri, G. 1934 Gli effetti eugenici degl'incroci etnici sulla genialità umana. *Genus*, April, pp. 467–9.

Orano, P. 1938 Bonifica della razza, *Maternità ed infanzia*, November–December, pp. 329–39.

Pacilio, V. 1941–42 Le nascite legittime in Italia secondo l'ordine di generazione. *Razza e civiltà*, October 1941–February 1942, pp. 713–35.

Palmieri, V. 1935 *Denatalità. La grande insidia sociale vista da un medico*. Milan, Società palmeritana editrice medica.

Pantano, E. 1925 *Per la colonizzazione interna*. Rome.

Papini, I. 1933–34 La seconda conquista della terra in Tripolitania. *La Conquista della terra*, October–November 1933, January 1934, pp. 23–30, 33–41, 29–38.

Parenti, G. 1935 *Lezioni di demografia (anno accademico 1934–35)*.

1938 Nuovi studi sul problema della natalità. *Economia*, December, pp. 413–20.

Pareto, V. 1964 (1896) *Cours d'économie politique*. Geneva, Droz.

1971 (1906) *Manual of Political Economy*. New York, Kelley.

Passerini, L. 1984 *Torino operaia e fascismo*. Bari, Laterza.

Patriarca, S. 1989 *L'impresa statistica nell'Italia ottocentesca*. In Corsini 1989.

1996 *Numbers and Nationhood: Writing Statistics in Nineteenth-Century Italy*. Cambridge, Cambridge University Press.

Payne, S. 1980 *Fascism. Comparison and Definition*. Madison, University of Wisconsin Press.

Pellegrini, R. 1925 Sugli aborti procurati quale fattore di limitazione di natalità in Germania. *Difesa sociale*, December, pp. 319–20.

Pellizzi, G. 1930 *Fecondità è potenza*. Milan. Libreria d'Italia.

Pende, N. 1923 Per la creazione in Italia di istituti di biologia e psicologia dell'individuo e della razza. *Difesa sociale*, 2, n. 4 April, pp. 53–5.

1933 *Bonifica umana nazionale*. Bologna, Capelli.

1934a Costituzione e fecondità. In Gini 1934c, vol. III, pp. 77–102.

1934b Eugenica e politica demografica. In Lojacono 1934b, pp. 113–16.

1938 *La scienza dell'ortogenesi*. Bergamo, Istituto italiano d'arti grafiche.

1939 I principi scientifici del razzismo. In E. Poletti (ed.), *Razzismo. Autarchia della stirpe*. Bergamo, Tavecchi.

1940a La politica fascista della razza. *Annali di medicina navale e coloniale*, ff. vii–viii.

1940b La scienza dell'ortogenesi. *Difesa sociale*, March, pp. 257–62.

1961 *Documenti contro l'accusa di antisemitismo*. Rome, Saet.

Perondi, G. 1929 La nati-mortalità in Italia e i limiti d'azione della levatrice. *Maternità ed infanzia*, June, pp. 643–50.

1933 Origine, storia e scopi dell'eugenica. *Difesa sociale*, 12, n. 9 (September), pp. 473–9.

Pietra, G. 1936 La politica fascista della popolazione. *Maternità ed infanzia*, August–September, pp. 107–10.

Pitt-Rivers, G. (ed.) 1932 *Problems of Population*. London, Allen and Unwin.

Pius XI 1939 (1931) Casti connubii. In *Five Great Encyclicals*, New York, Paulist Press.

PNF 1938 *Il Gran Consiglio del Fascismo nei primi quindici anni dell'era fascista*. Bologna, Il Resto del Carlino.

Pogliano, C. 1984 Scienze e stirpe: eugenica in Italia (1912–1939). *Passato e presente*, n. 5.

1985 L'enigma demologico. Natalità, popolazione, socialismo. *Schema*, 7, n. 1.

Pomata, G. 1980 Madri illegittime tra '800 e '900. *Quaderni storici*, 44, pp. 497–542.

Porter, T. 1986 *The Rise of Statistical Thinking*. Princeton, Princeton University Press.

Pravato, L. 1990 Evoluzione dei censimenti demografici italiani nel periodo che va dal 1861 al 1931. *Bollettino di demografia storica*, n. 10, pp. 59–79.

Preti D. 1984 La lotta antitubercolare nell'Italia Fascista. In F. Della Peruta (ed.), *Storia d'Italia Annali 7: malattia e medicina*. Turin, Einaudi.

1987 *La modernizzazione corporativa (1922–1940)*. Milan, Angeli.

Proctor, R. 1988 *Racial Hygiene: Medicine Under the Nazis*. Cambridge (Mass.), Harvard University Press.

1991 *Value-Free Science? Purity and Power in Modern Knowledge*. Cambridge (Mass.), Harvard University Press.

Prost, A. 1988 Catholic Conservatives, Population and the Family in Twentieth Century France. In *Population and Resources in Western Intellectual Traditions*, supplement to *Population and Development Review*, vol. 14, pp. 147–64.

Racca, A. 1930 Il lavoro salariato della donna-madre. *Vita e pensiero*, October, pp. 661–7.

Rafaelli, G. 1926 Un grande problema sociale: La protezione dell'infanzia. *Vita e pensiero*, November, pp. 676–87.

Rameri, L. 1898 Tavola di sopravvivenza. *Giornale degli economisti*, February.

Raseri, L. 1894 L'assistenza ai fanciulli esposti o abbandonati dai genitori in Italia e all'estero. *La riforma sociale*, 1, n. 2, pp. 950–66.

Ravicini, S. 1930 Per la difesa della natalità italiana. *Difesa sociale*, March, pp. 81–8.

Razza, L. 1933 Le migrazioni interne e la colonizzazione. In L. Federzoni (ed.), *I problemi attuali dell'agricoltura italiana*. Bologna, Zanichelli.

Razzell, P. 1974 "An Interpretation of the Modern Rise of Population" – a Critique. *Population Studies*, March, pp. 5–17.

Reuter, E. 1931 Population. *American Journal of Sociology*, January, pp. 647–8.

Rochat, G. 1973 *Il colonialismo italiano*. Turin, Loescher.

Rochat, G. and Massobrio, G. 1978 *Breve storia dell'esercito italiano dal 1861 al 1943*. Turin, Einaudi.

Romanelli, R. 1980 La nuova Italia e la misurazione dei fatti sociali. Una premessa. *Quaderni storici*, 45 (December).

Rosa, D. 1909 Saggio di una nuova spiegazione dell'origine e della distribuzione geografica della specie - Ipotesi dell'ologenesi. *Bollettino dei Musei di zoologia di Torino*, xiv.

1931 *L'ologenèse*. Paris, Félix Alcan.

Rossi Ragazzi, B. 1939 Le conseguenze sociali del lavoro femminile in relazione alla recente legislazione fascista. *Rivista italiana di scienze economiche*, July, pp. 881–92.

Rugiu, G. 1933 Teoria della popolazione e politica demografica. In Gini 1933–7, vol. ii, part 2, no. 6.

Ruinas, S. 1939 *Viaggio per le città di Mussolini*. Milan, Bompiani.

Salvemini, G. 1963 *Opere III: Scritti di politica estera*, vol. i. Milan, Feltrinelli.

1974 *Opere VI: Scritti sul fascismo*, 3 vols. Milan, Feltrinelli.

Salvia, E. 1922 Necessità di protezione legislativa dell'infanzia in Italia. *Difesa sociale*, 1, n. 6 (June), pp. 120–2.

Sanger, M. (ed.) 1927 *Proceedings of the World Population Conference*. London, Edward Arnold.

Sangiorgi, G. 1937 Un problema da evitare. In Centro di studi coloniale – Istituto coloniale fascista, *Atti del terzo congresso di studi coloniali*, vol. ii. Florence.

Santarelli, E. 1976 Il fascismo e le ideologie antifemministe. *Problemi del socialismo*, n. 4, pp. 75–106.

Saraceno, C. 1979–80 La famiglia operaia sotto il fascismo. *Annali della Fondazione Giangiacomo Feltrinelli*, 20, pp. 189–230.

1992 Constructing Families, Shaping Women's Lives: The Making of Italian Families Between Market Economies and State Interventions. In Gillis, Tilly, and Levine 1992, pp. 251–69.

Savorgnan, F. 1935 Movimento naturale della popolazione. In Gini 1933–7, vol. ii, part 1, n. 3.

1936 *Corso di demografia*. Pisa, Nistri-Lischi.

Scarzanella, E. 1977 L'emigrazione veneta nel periodo fascista. *Studi storici*, April–June.

Schneider, J. and Schneider, P. 1984 Demographic Transitions in a Sicilian Rural Town. *Journal of Family History*, Autumn, pp. 245–72.

Segré, C. 1978 *L'Italia in Libia*. Milan, Feltrinelli.

Seton-Watson, C. 1967 *Italy from Liberalism to Fascism: 1870–1925*. London, Methuen and Co.

Siniscalchi, A. 1943 Aspetti demografico-sociali della colonizzazione agraria libica. *Conquista della terra*, March, pp. 7–13.

Solmi A. 1934 Il matrimonio e la famiglia in rapporto alla natalitá. In Lojacano 1934b, pp. 106–7.

Soloway, R. 1990 *Demography and Degeneration*. Chapel Hill, University of North Carolina Press.

Somogyi, Istvan 1933a Sui fattori biologici della natalità. *Economia*, April, pp. 259–81.

1933b Variazioni strutturali della popolazione e disoccupazione. *Economia*, November, pp. 324–62.

Somogyi, Stefano 1934a La concezione fascista della politica demografica. *Economia*, February, pp. 119–34.

1934b Sull'ammontare e sul movimento della popolazione attraverso il tempo. In Gini 1934c, vol. VII, pp. 253–85.

1935 Existe-t-il un lien entre la dénatalité et le chômage? *Revue internationale du travail*, February.

1937 *Fascismo e politica demografica*. Rome, L'Economia Italiana.

Sori, E. 1979 *L'emigrazione italiana dall'Unità alla seconda guerra mondiale*. Bologna, Il Mulino.

Spallanzani, A. 1934 I reati di infanticidio e procurato aborto secondo le statistiche giudiziarie italiane. In Gini 1934c, vol. VII, pp. 180–97.

Spencer, H. 1972 *On Social Evolution*. Chicago, Chicago University Press.

Spengler, J. 1979 (1938) *France Faces Depopulation*. Durham, Duke University Press.

Spengler, O. 1926–28 *The Decline of the West*. New York, Knopf.

Spolverini, L. 1938 Vita moderna e problema demografico. *Difesa sociale*, May, pp. 457–64.

Sternhell, Z. 1972 *Maurice Barrès et le nationalisme français*. Paris, Armand Colin.

1978 *La droite révolutionnaire 1885–1914: Les origines françaises du fascisme*. Paris, Editions du Seuil.

1984 *Nè destra, nè sinistra. La nascita dell'ideologia fascista*. Naples, Akropolis.

1994 *The Birth of Fascist Ideology. From Cultural Rebellion to Political Revolution*. Princeton, Princeton University Press.

Stigler, S. 1986 *The History of Statistics*. Cambridge (Mass.), Harvard University Press.

Tagliacarne, G. 1925 Infanticidio, abbandono d'infante e procurato aborto nella vita sociale, studiati sulle nostre statistiche della criminalità. *Giornale degli economisti*, August, pp. 401–42, October, pp. 547–65.

1928 La diminuzione delle nascite è dovuta a cause biologiche? *La cultura moderna*, November, pp. 545–9.

1934a Gli insegnamenti demografici della crisi. In Lojacono 1934b, pp. 58–61.

1934b L'occupazione delle donne nelle fabbriche e negli uffici durante gli ultimi cinquant'anni e la diminuzione delle nascite. *Giornale degli economisti*, December, pp. 927–39.

Teitelbaum, M. and Winter, J. 1985 *The Fear of Population Decline*. New York, Academic Press.

Toscano, M. 1967 *Storia diplomatica della questione dell'Alto Adige*. Bari, Laterza.

1986 Gli ebrei in Italia e la politica antisemita del fascismo. In N. Caracciolo (ed.), *Gli ebrei e l'Italia durante la guerra 1940–45*, Rome, Bonacci.

Tosi, E. 1928 La famiglia numerosa. *Rivista diocesana milanese*, 19, pp. 52–61.

Tranfaglia, N. 1989 *Labirinto italiano. Il fascismo, l'antifascismo, gli storici*. Scandicci, La Nuova Italia.

Treves, A. 1976 *Le migrazioni interne nell'Italia fascista* Turin, Einaudi.

Triolo, N. 1989 *The Angelmakers: Pronatalism and the Normalization of Midwives in Sicily*. Doctoral dissertation, University of California at Berkeley.
Uggè, A. 1931 Il congresso internazionale per lo studio dei problemi della popolazione. *Vita e pensiero*, November, pp. 635–9.
1939 Effetti sulla popolazione di un paese del diverso accrescimento delle sue classi. In *Contributi del laboratorio di statisitica*, vol. xi of *Pubblicazioni dell'Università cattolica del sacro cuore*. Milan, *Vita e pensiero*, pp. 155–80.
Vacchini, A. 1941 *La popolazione italiana*. Milan, Giuffrè.
Valagussa, F. 1928a L'azione dell'ONMI nella difesa del bambino lattante. *Maternità ed infanzia*, October, pp. 812–23.
1928b Intendiamoci. *Maternità ed infanzia*, February, pp. 120–7.
1930 I compiti assistenziali dell'ONMI. *Maternità ed infanzia*, March, pp. 273–80.
Valeri, N. 1962 *La lotta politica in Italia*. Florence, Felice Le Monnier.
Vecchi, B. 1963 *Navi bianche*. Milan, Gastaldi.
Viana, M. 1921 *Le bonifiche in Italia*. Bari, Laterza.
Vianelli, S. 1938 Il problema della natalità. *Rivista italiana di scienze economiche*, December, pp. 999–1012.
Villari, L. 1909 L'emigrazione negli Stati Uniti d'America. *Nuova antologia*, 16 September.
Vinci, F. 1930a L'aumento delle nascite. *Rivista italiana di statistica*, October–December, pp. 353–60.
1930b Recenti analisi sul declino delle nascite. *Rivista italiana di statistica*, April–June, pp. 130–4.
1931 Le nascite e la biologia. *Rivista italiana di statistica*, January–March, pp. 25–9.
1934 Economia e demografia. *Rivista italiana di statistica*, April, pp. 257–63.
1936 Censimenti fascisti. *Rivista italiana di scienze economiche*, May, pp. 371–9.
1939a Fascismo e communismo nella lotta demografica. *Rivista italiana di scienze economiche*, February, pp. 140–6.
1939b *Problemi demografici*. Bologna, Zanichelli (articles from 1927–39).
Virgilii, F. 1892 Il problema della popolazione – critica dei sistemi. *Giornale degli economisti*, 1 March, pp. 240–74.
1928 *Le leggi fasciste*. *Emigrazione*. Rome, Libreria del Littorio.
1934 Il regresso delle nascite nella storia della civiltà. In Lojacono 1934b, pp. 22–6.
Vitali, O. 1974 Le migrazioni interne in Italia: una sintesi storico-statistica. *Affari sociali internazionali*, n. 1–2, pp. 3–26.
Vöchting, F. 1940 La colonizzazione italiana in Libia. *Bonifica e colonizzazione*, January–February–March, pp. 10–37, 96–111, 179–210.
Volpe, G. 1937 Bonifica e colonizzazione. *Bonifica e colonizzazzione*, January, pp. 3–11.
Wanrooij, B. 1990 *Storia del pudore*. Venice, Marsilio.
Weber, E. 1964 *Varieties of Fascism*. New York, Van Nostrand.
Webster, R. 1960 *The Cross and the Fasces*. Stanford, Stanford University Press.
Weindling, P. 1988 Fascism and Population in Comparative European Perspective. In *Population and Resources in Western Intellectual Traditions*, supplement to *Population and Development Review*, vol. 14, pp. 102–21.
1989 *Health, Race and German Politics Between National Unification and Nazism, 1870–1945*. Cambridge, Cambridge University Press.

Winter, J. 1988a Socialism, Social Democracy and Population Questions in Western Europe: 1850–1950. In *Population and Resources in Western Intellectual Traditions*, supplement to *Population and Development Review*, vol. 14, pp. 122–46.

1988b Some Paradoxes of the First World War. In R. Wall and J. Winter (eds.), *The Upheaval of War. Family, Work and Welfare in Europe, 1914–1918.* Cambridge, Cambridge University Press, pp. 9–42.

1992 War, Family, and Fertility in Twentieth-Century Europe. In Gillis, Tilly, and Levine 1992, pp. 291–309.

Woolf, S. 1989 Statistics and the Modern State. *Comparative Studies in Society and History*, 31, n. 3 (June), pp. 588–604.

Zingali G. 1934 L'emigrazione e la natalità. In Lojacono 1934b, pp. 108–10.

Index

Cambridge Studies in Population, Economy and Society in Past Time

Titles available in paperback are marked with an asterisk